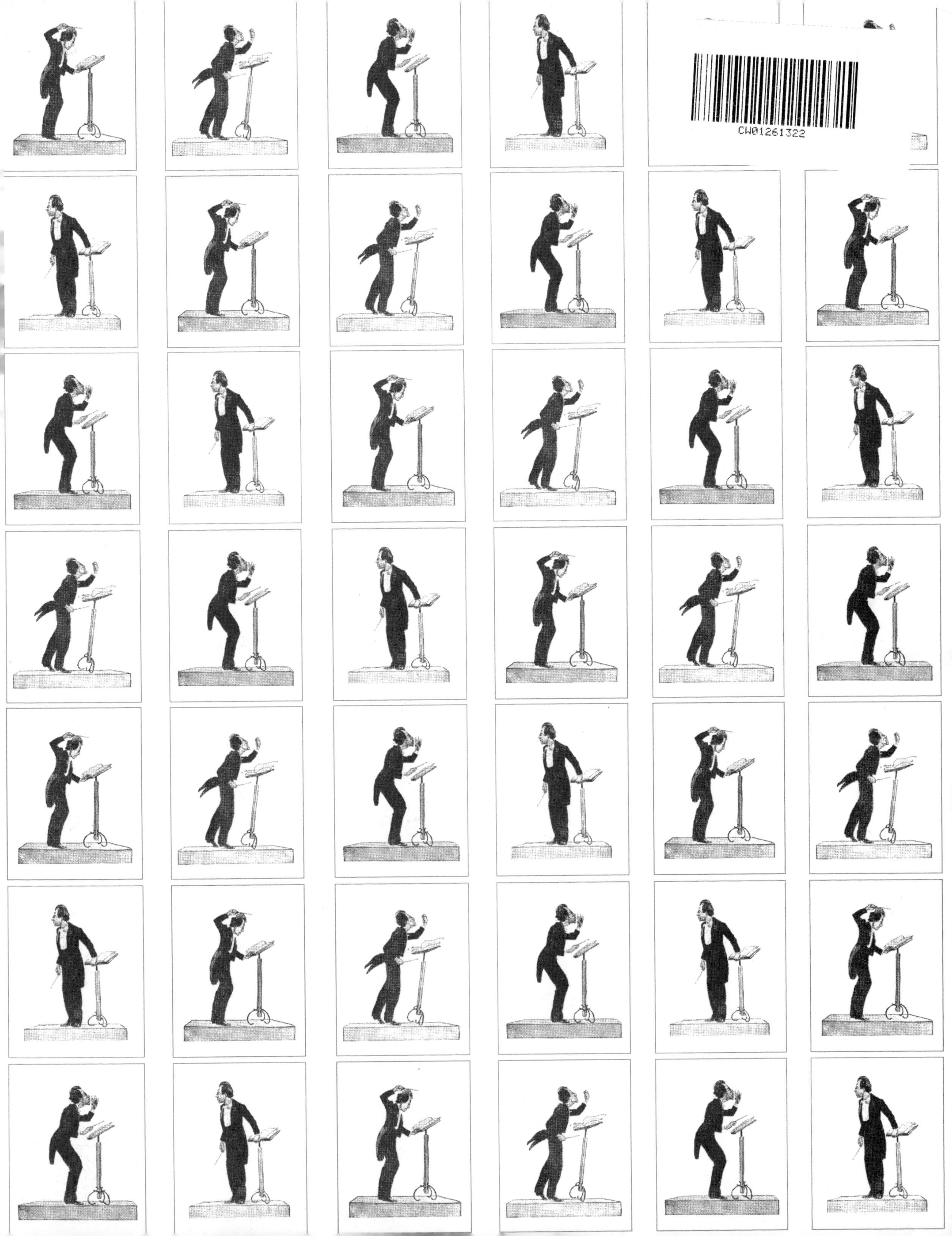

MAHLER's CONCERTS

I dedicate this book to my beloved companion and wife,

Eva Bruun Hansen,

who for thirty years has supported me during my many research travels,

and has been the motivating force behind the birth of this book.

MAHLER's CONCERTS

Knud Martner

KAPLAN FOUNDATION

The Overlook Press

Contents

	Introduction by Gilbert Kaplan	*i*
	Preface	*iii*
	Acknowledgements	*ix*
	Mahler, the Interpreter: A Summary	*xi*
	Abbreviations	*xix*
1	Childhood and Youth in Iglau (1860-1875)	1
2	Student in Vienna (1875-1880)	9
3	The First Steps: The Young Conductor (1880-1883)	25
	Laibach	29
	Olmütz	33
4	On the Road: Years of Maturing (1883-1888)	35
	Kassel	39
	Prague	49
	Leipzig	57
5	Budapest: The Royal Hungarian Opera (1888-1891)	65
6	Hamburg and Altona: The Combined Stadttheater (1891-1897)	75
	Subscription Concerts (1894-1895)	99
7	Vienna I: The Imperial-Royal Court Opera (1897-1901)	127
	Vienna Philharmonic Orchestra (1898-1901)	131
8	Vienna II: The Imperial-Royal Court Opera (1901-1907)	165
9	New York: The Metropolitan Opera (1908-1909)	223
10	The 1908 – 1909 Season	231
11	The New York Philharmonic Society's 68th Season (1909-1910)	241
12	The New York Philharmonic Society's 69th Season (1910-1911)	279
13	The New York Philharmonic Society (February 24 - April 2, 1911)	311
Appendix I	Additional Concerts (February 24 - April 2, 1911)	311
Appendix II	Composers Index	317
Appendix III	Mahler's Repertoire	341
Appendix IV	Mahler's Concert Itinerary	351
Appendix V	Mahler's Soloists	361
Appendix VI	Mahler at the Opera: the Complete Stage Repertoire	365
Appendix VII	General Index	373

Introduction

Now recognized as one of history's greatest composers, during his lifetime (1860-1911) Gustav Mahler was better known as a conductor – perhaps the foremost of his generation. He began with opera and gradually added the concert hall to his repertoire. Finally, late in life, he focused exclusively on the concert hall.

Mahler's Concerts provides the first detailed history of Mahler on the podium with a wealth of fresh material unearthed by Knud Martner, a leading Mahler scholar. This book traces Mahler's conducting career from his earliest days with provincial orchestras through his positions in Budapest, Hamburg and Vienna, to his final appointment as music director of the New York Philharmonic.

In addition to offering a chronological listing of more than 300 concerts, various indexes provide devotees with the opportunity to track down concerts in any city, with any composer, work or soloist. Fascinating tables also rank which composers and works were Mahler's favorites, while introductions for each chapter of Mahler's conducting life provide a rich context for his musical activities. A special feature of this book is its reproductions of some 250 rare programs, playbills and advertisements covering the concerts Mahler conducted.

For more than 25 years, the Kaplan Foundation's program devoted to the works and life of Gustav Mahler has produced a wide range of publications, facsimiles, exhibitions, symposia and historical recordings. We are pleased to continue that tradition with *Mahler's Concerts*.

Gilbert Kaplan, Chairman
Kaplan Foundation

Preface

"It was my lifelong desire to have my own concert orchestra. I am glad to be able to enjoy this for once in my life." [1] Thus wrote 49-year-old Gustav Mahler on January 1, 1910, two months after he launched his first season as artistic director and conductor of the New York Philharmonic. It is indeed one of the great ironies in the history of music that one of the most formative interpreters of symphonic performance had to spend the greater part of his life as a *Kapellmeister* in various opera houses and theaters, rather than lead a symphony orchestra.

Due to special circumstances, which will be discussed later, Mahler began his professional career as a theater conductor at the age of 20, and for many years he was rarely given the opportunity to conduct symphonic music, not to mention full-length symphony concerts. It was only from November 1909 that Mahler was able to dedicate himself exclusively to the concert repertoire. Before that, he had twice directed two series of subscription concerts: first in Hamburg (for the 1894–1895 season) and later in Vienna (for three seasons, 1898–1901).

*

In a first attempt to clear up confusion in the relevant literature on Mahler, old and new, regarding *where* and *when* Mahler appeared in concert, and exactly *what* he performed, I presented a small volume, *Gustav Mahler im Konzertsaal. Eine Dokumentation seiner Konzerttätigkeit 1870–1911* (Private print, Copenhagen, 1985), containing a total of 304 concert entries. (The reader is kindly asked to accept my liberal use of the term "concert," which, besides the ordinary use of the word, also encompasses isolated performances of orchestral pieces, chamber music works, *Lieder*, etc.)

In the years following this publication I became involved in other projects on Mahler, requiring renewed and detailed research into his life and work, which resulted in a number of new discoveries regarding his concert activities, offering valuable new insight into relevant aspects of 19th century musical life.

In light of this, I welcomed Gilbert Kaplan's proposal that the Kaplan Foundation, an organization engaged in Mahler research since 1985, publish a new and revised edition in English.

The new edition differs in substantial ways from its German predecessor. In the first place, the number of concert entries is increased by 41, for a total of 345. I have added a concert in Vienna (concert 12a), a concert in Wlaschim (concert 12b), and the two Vienna Philharmonic Concerts of March 1901 (concerts 141a & 141b), which Mahler was forced to cancel owing to an acute sickness. The same goes for the remaining concerts of the 1910–1911 season in New York (from February 24, 1911) which Mahler was prevented from conducting for similar reasons (see Appendix I). In both cases the programs accord with Mahler's original intentions with only minor modifications.

In the course of his career, Mahler frequently assisted in mixed concerts, undertaking a limited part of a program. Unlike the first edition, which only documented the works for which Mahler was responsible, this new edition reproduces—with few exceptions—the complete programs, i.e., works performed by other artists or led by different conductors. To distinguish them from Mahler's contributions, they are printed in smaller type.

Further innovations are the inclusion of (more or less objective) notes and comments, and also references to press reviews, although only to those available in easily accessible publications.

Also new is Appendix VI: "Mahler at the Opera"; a survey of his stage repertoire from 1880–1910 which, although comprising dry facts and figures, rounds off, I hope, the picture of Mahler "the interpreter", illustrating especially the vast difference between Mahler's stage obligations and his concert activities.

* * *

The concerts are arranged in chronological order, numbered in succession, and divided into thirteen parts according to the stages in Mahler's career as a theater *Kapellmeister*. The Vienna years are split into two parts, the dividing line determined by Mahler's resignation from the Vienna Philharmonic Orchestra in 1901. Likewise - although for different reasons - the New York period is divided into two parts (including the last five weeks of the 1910–1911 season). Biographical summaries of Mahler's life frame the various parts and should make it easier for the reader to follow his life and especially the circumstances surrounding his conducting career.

The entry for each concert is laid out in the following order and contains, when it is available, the following information:

(1) *When and Where*
   (a) Date and time
   (b) Place and hall (with seating capacity). The names of the halls are presented in the original languages and English translations are given in the General Index, with the exception of Russian or Slavonic languages.
   (c) The nature, purpose or occasion of the concert

(2) *Contents of the Programs*

   Please note that the contents of the programs are not exact transcriptions of the original printed sources (handbill, program or newspaper advertisement), which do not always correspond to the music actually performed, or the sequence of items. In the vast majority of cases the original source has been cross-checked with reviews and revised accordingly, including the insertion of reported encores. Discrepancies are discussed in the notes.

   Music titles are often inadequately described in the original sources and to secure an instant and precise identification of a composition, the necessary details (key and opus number) are added. In some cases this has unfortunately not been possible.

   All titles are presented in the original language, again, with the exception of Russian or Slavonic languages for which English or German translations have been used. Genres are given in English.

   A dot (•) after a composition indicates Mahler's last performance of the work.

(3) *Soloist(s)* are listed according to their order of appearance in the concert.

(4) *Conductor(s)* and/or *pianist(s)/accompanist(s):* If no conductor or pianist is named it is understood that Mahler performed.

(5) *Orchestra(s);* with number of players.

(6) *Chorus(es):* with number of singers, and the name of the permanent conductor.

(7) *Source(s):* This refers to either the handbill, program, or newspaper advertisement, or all three. If none has been located, the concert is reconstructed from other sources, e.g. previews and/or reviews.

(8) *Notes:* These register the date and time of general rehearsals (which in those days were usually open to the public), world premieres or first performances. They also discuss discrepancies between the published program and the music actually performed.

(9) *Review:* References are primarily given to Henry-Louis de La Grange's detailed and indispensable four-volume Mahler biography (HLG I–IV), and to Zoltan Roman's two excellent studies, *Mahler and Hungary* and *Mahler's American Years* (Roman and ZR II).

*

INDEXES

Indexes are provided to facilitate the search for particular information and details:

(1) *Works performed*
   (a) An alphabetical "Composers Index," covering all works performed, with the exception of complete operas, single opera acts, plays or poems; all of which are registered in the "General Index." All numbers refer to the concert numbers. An asterisk (*) attached to a number indicates a performance that Mahler was not involved in, i.e. he did not perform.
   (b) From the above index is extracted a survey of Mahler's "Repertoire" according to categories, with the number of performances of every work in each category.

(2) *General Index*
   This does not include composers and their works (see Composers Index), except those mentioned in the biographical commentaries and in the notes. Also excluded are the composers and their works in Appendix VI, "Mahler at the Opera."

   Capitalized NAMES indicate artists who appeared under Mahler's direction. They are also listed in Appendix V, "Mahler's Soloists", according to their profession (pianists, violinists, cellists, and vocalists).

I am, of course, conscious of certain shortcomings of this new edition, e.g. missing programs (concerts 1, 12b, 79 and 204), as well as a number of unidentified titles, etc. Nevertheless, I am sure that this represents the nearest we can come to a definitive survey of Mahler's concert activities. And yet there might be a few minor gaps to fill. In this respect, the recollections on Mahler by Theodor Fischer, a childhood friend of the composer, are of concern. In his article, published in 1931, Fischer alludes to two concerts at least, which—judging from certain remarks—apparently took place in Vienna between 1877 and 1880. The particular passage in his article reads:

"So far as I can recall he [Mahler] gave piano lessons and acted frequently as piano accompanist in solo concerts at the Bösendorfer Saal [in Vienna]. I myself went to various of these concerts; at one of them Mahler trod on the train of the advancing singer's dress, earning an enraged glance. At another concert with a Polish violinist, he forgot himself in the accompaniment thinking of God alone knows what until the virtuoso had to stamp out the beat with his foot to awaken Mahler from his self-engrossment." [2]

Aside for a few minor slips of his memory, on the whole, Theodor Fischer's recollections ring true. However, my scrutiny of the Viennese newspapers from this period (including Mahler's later, infrequent stays in Vienna up until May 1883) has so far not produced the slightest documentation to support his memories of these recitals.

Knud Martner
Copenhagen, October 2009

Notes

[1] Letter to Guido Adler, New York, January 1, 1910: "... gerade die Leitung eines Konzertorchesters war lebenslang mein Wunsch. Ich bin froh, dies einmal in meinem Leben zu genießen ..." (from GMB 430/MSL 408).
[2] "Soweit ich mich erinnern kann, gab damals Mahler in Wien auch Klavierunterricht und fungierte häufig als Klavierbegleiter bei den Solistenkonzerten im Bösendorfer Saal. Ich selbst war bei einigen dieser Konzerte anwesend; bei dem einen trat Mahler der voranschreitenden Sängerin auf die Schleppe ihres Kleides, was ihm wütende Blicke eintrug; bei dem anderen Konzerte eines polnischen Violinvirtuosen, mag Mahler während der Klavierbegleitung an Gott weiß was gedacht haben; erst das Aufstampfen

des Virtuosen, der mit dem Fuße den Takt zu schlagen begann, weckte Mahler aus seiner Versunkenheit." ("Aus Gustav Mahlers Jugendzeit", *Deutsche Heim at,* Vol. 7, Iglau, 1931, p. 267; translated into English by Norman Lebrecht and published in his book *Mahler Remembered*; Faber and Faber, London, 1987, p. 25).

Acknowledgements

I owe a debt of deep gratitude to many persons and institutions for their help in preparing this book. In particular, I am indebted to Donald Mitchell (London) for invaluable help and advice and similarly to Henry-Louis de la Grange (Paris), both dear friends and Mahler colleagues for many decades.

For their illuminating and valuable information, and critical comments, I would like to thank the following individuals:

My thoughts go first to those who are no longer amongst us, devoted Mahlerians and research pioneers of the 20th century: Robert R. Becqué (Hoek v. Holland), Herta and Kurt Blaukopf (Vienna), Helmut Brenner (Düsseldorf), Jonathan C. Carr (1942–2008), Jack Diether (1920–1987), composer-conductor Berthold Goldschmidt (1903–1996), the indefatigable secretary of the International Mahler Society in Vienna, Emmy Hauswirth (Vienna), composer Tage Nielsen (Copenhagen), Peter Riethus (Vienna), Hans Joachim Schaefer (Kassel), Eleonore Vondenhoff (1903–1994), and her husband, conductor Bruno Vondenhoff.

Further: Christine and Paul Banks (London), Inna Barssova (Moscow), Otto Biba (Vienna), Peter Franklin (Oxford), Peter Fülöp (Budapest, now Canada), Bernt M. Hage (Vienna), Mathias Hansen (Berlin), Niels & Inger Bruun Hansen (Aarhus), Renate Stark-Voit (Vienna), Renate and Kurt Hofmann (Lübeck), Primoz Kuret (Ljubljana), Norman Lebrecht (London), Jitka Ludvová (Prague), Herman J. Nieman (The Hague), Zoltan Roman (Canada), Jiri Rychetsky (Humpolec), Hans Skaarup (Copenhagen) and Mary Wagner (University of Michigan).

I would like to thank the following institutions, many of which have provided reproductions of programs: Archiv der Gesellschaft der Musikfreunde (Vienna), Internationale Gustav Mahler Gesellschaft (Vienna), Wiener Männergesangverein (Vienna), Hamburg Stadtbibliothek, Kassel Stadtarchiv, Lübeck Stadtarchiv, Hannoversch-Münden Stadtarchiv, Wiener Stadt- und Landesbibliothek, the archives of the New York Philharmonic Orchestra, Carnegie Hall, and Brooklyn Academy of Music, the Metropolitan Opera Archives, the Amsterdam Concertgebouw Orchestra, and the Berlin Philharmonic Orchestra.

Finally, my great gratitude goes to Gilbert Kaplan and the staff of the Kaplan Foundation (Gail Ross and Marcela Silva) and Monica Parks for their invaluable help, patience and support in preparing this book.

Knud Martner
Copenhagen, October 2009

Gustav Mahler: The Interpreter
A Summary

On February 21, 1911, the 50-year-old Gustav Mahler mounted the podium in New York's Carnegie Hall to conduct what was, alas, his final concert. Probably nobody, including Mahler himself, was aware of the fact that 25 years earlier, on exactly the same date, he had made his debut as a symphony conductor (concert 28). However, from what we know of Mahler, he never cared much for his own red-letter days; otherwise he might have chosen a more appropriate program to celebrate his silver jubilee concert.

Mahler's public debut as a performer had taken place, at the age of 10, as a pianist. A decade later, and with only a dozen public appearances as a solo pianist or accompanist to his credit, Mahler decided to make a career as a professional performing artist. Publicly he had so far appeared solely for charitable purposes, and his sudden decision to become a professional was hardly borne out of an urge to interpret other composers' music, but was rather a necessary evil—in short, a means to earn a living and provide the wherewithal so he could compose. And perhaps he also wanted to prove to his parents that his costly education at the Conservatory had not been a complete waste of time and money.

Considering his three years of study at the Conservatory (1875–1878) — piano was his principal subject for the first two years and in the last year he turned to composition — it might seem surprising that Mahler did not make a career as a virtuoso pianist or as an accompanist. Instead he chose to take up a job as a theater *Kapellmeister*, despite the fact that he had not received any formal conducting training. The Vienna Conservatory did not yet include conducting as an obligatory subject. However, students in the third-year composition class received some informal instruction in conducting, and they were also occasionally invited to conduct the Conservatory's orchestra. Indeed, the records of the Conservatory reveal that a few of Mahler's classmates appeared on the podium at the Conservatory's internal and public soirées, and some of them even appeared with their own compositions.

Although Mahler's name does not appear in the Conservatory's official records in this capacity, it is unlikely that he had not been given the same opportunity, at least at rehearsals. It is perhaps significant that it was Mahler's piano professor, Julius Epstein who, in 1880, urged his former pupil to accept his first conducting assignment. Epstein would hardly have done so if he had not had an inkling of his pupil's talents and abilities. Or did he merely consider it a matter of fact that his young protégé would be able to face an orchestra, owing to the musical training the Conservatory had equipped him with? Was that all that was needed, all that was expected from an aspiring *Kapellmeister*? The art of conducting was, after all, not considered an art in its own right; it was thought that it could only be learned from experience, and perhaps from instruction from experienced conductors. Books on the subject were non-existent. Conductors were not "made" but rather made themselves.

If one wants to know what was expected from a conductor it is illuminating to read Mahler's earliest surviving contract from Kassel (1883) and to take into consideration the report of the one-week trial, which Mahler had to go through before he was finally accepted and engaged.

The contract is undoubtedly a standard formula. He was not only expected to make the necessary changes in the scores to accommodate the needs of the theater, but he was also expected to compose incidental music to plays, farces, etc. — and all on short notice. The balance of his responsibilities was considered a matter of daily practice and experience. In the last quarter of the 19th century an aspiring conductor faced three fundamental demands (which of course are still valid). First, that he could sight-read a score, implying also that he was acquainted "inside-out" with all the instruments of the orchestra. Second, that he could master any score at the piano, and transpose voices and instruments at sight. Last but not least, that he could beat time.

Although Mahler's first conducting assignment can be seen as a means to escape momentary financial needs, he instantaneously became aware of his conducting potential and immediately decided to proceed in this occupation. In view of Mahler's later fame as a symphonic composer, one might perhaps find it surprising that he did not from the very beginning choose the concert platform, but instead the pit of an opera house.

By 1880 Mahler had not yet shown any interest in the symphonic genre but was still occupied with various opera projects (i.e. *Rübezahl*), and of course *Das klagende Lied* for soloists, chorus, and orchestra. It was only eight years later that he turned his full attention to the symphonic genre. In addition, whereas it was comparatively easy to become a theater *Kapellmeister*, the chances or possibility of making a career, not to mention a living, as a full-time conductor of symphony concerts were in fact reserved for the very few. The reason is obvious.

At the time Mahler entered the musical scene no orchestra existed in Austria or Germany that based its existence solely on giving symphonic concerts. Every orchestra was attached to an opera house or a theater, either a *Stadt-Theater* (Municipal Theater) or a *Hoftheater* (Court Theater). Until the end of the 19th century only the Court theaters arranged symphonic or philharmonic concerts, and as a rule only a limited number, from six to ten concerts each season. The theater's principal *Kapellmeister* was normally in charge of all the concerts, and guest conductors were almost unheard of, but from time to time composers were invited to present their own works.

The only exception was the famous Leipzig Gewandhaus Orchestra, founded by Felix Mendelssohn, which gave approximately 22 concerts each season. The Gewandhaus Orchestra also performed at the Leipzig *Stadt-Theater*, but it chose its own conductor for these 22 concerts. It was a permanent post. Carl Reinecke was the orchestra's conductor from 1860 and was followed by Arthur Nikisch in 1895. The orchestra frequently invited contemporary composers to conduct their own works. It is surprising that Mahler was never invited. In July 1888, Mahler tried in vain to get his First symphony performed, but not until November 1, 1906 did the Gewandhaus perform one of his symphonies; the Second was conducted by Nikisch.

Another exception was Mahler's former director in Prague, the enterprising Angelo Neumann, who in November 1887 initiated a series of four philharmonic concerts, for each season, at his theater. His example was followed a decade later by other theater directors in German speaking countries. In March 1894, when Mahler renewed his contract with Bernhard Pollini at the Hamburg *Stadt-Theater*, he made it a condition that four symphonic concerts were to be included and Pollini surprisingly accepted Mahler's demands (letter 371, MFL, p. 273.) The concerts never materialized. In the meantime, Mahler took over eight philharmonic concerts in Hamburg, after the death of Hans von Bülow, and as a consequence he did not press his demands with Pollini.

The orchestral situation underwent a radical change during the last two decades of the 19th century with the foundation of a number of independent and full-time symphony orchestras. Among the most important were the Berlin Philharmonic Orchestra (1882), the Amsterdam Concertgebouworkest (1883), the Kaim Orchestra in Munich (1893), the Winderstein Symphony Orchestra in Leipzig (1896), and the Vienna Konzert-Verein (1901). Common to them all was that they were privately financed, and in each case the chosen conductor was in charge of all the concerts, but occasionally guest conductors, mostly contemporary composers, were invited, from which Mahler benefited.

Table I below covers Mahler's entire concert career (1870–1911) and is divided into seven periods. His 324 appearances are subdivided into four parts (A–D) according to the following categories: Conductor of (A) full-length concerts, (B) partial concerts, (C) choral works, and (D) pianist or accompanist in *Lied* & chamber music recitals.

Period (1) covers his childhood in Iglau and student years in Vienna, (2) comprises the years in Bad Hall, Laibach, Olmütz and Kassel, and (3) the years in Prague via Leipzig to Budapest. The fourth period concerns his years in Hamburg. For reasons discussed below the decade in Vienna (1897–1907) is divided into two periods (5 & 6). Finally, his American years are covered in column 7, which also include his rare European assignments during these years.

Table I

Mahler's Involvement	1 1870-1880	2 1880-1885	3 1885-1891	4 1891-1897	5 1898-1901	6 1901-1907	7 1908-1911	Total
A – Conductor of complete concert				19	33	38	112	202
B – Conductor of partial concert		6	14	23	8	24	5	80
C – Conductor of choral concert		2		12	3			17
D – Piano acc.	13	6	4			1	1	25
Total	13	14	18	54	44	63	118	324
Works by Mahler	3 25 %	0	3 17 %	8 15 %	8 18 %	51 81 %	39 33 %	112 35 %

Please note that in a number of concerts Mahler appeared both as conductor and piano accompanist. In such cases his role as *conductor* has been given preference, and registered under A or B, respectively. The table's bottom line registers the number of concerts that included compositions by Mahler and their percentage of concerts.

The year 1901 was a watershed for Mahler, earning him serious recognition as a composer and a drastic change of his personal circumstances after he met the 22-year-old Alma Maria Schindler, on November 7. They were engaged only a month later and married on March 9, 1902.

The year had in fact begun very promisingly with the world premiere of *Das klagende Lied*, of which a repeat performance was scheduled to take place a few weeks later (see concert 140, note 2). However, on February 24, Mahler fell severely ill and underwent a serious operation, which was followed by a long sick leave. Because of this illness he resigned as conductor of the Vienna Philharmonic Orchestra, in early April, and he simultaneously reduced his conducting schedule at the Court Opera considerably.

At 41, Mahler did not yet share Richard Strauss's international success as a conductor. In four seasons as conductor of the Vienna Philharmonic Orchestra, he gave just 5 concerts abroad, excluding a commercially-arranged Paris tour (concerts nos. 129-132). There may have been other invitations that he was obliged to decline due to pressure of work in Vienna.

The turning point of Mahler's career as a symphonic conductor was the great success of his 3rd Symphony in Krefeld, in 1902 (concert no. 150). Suddenly, he could pick and choose amongst numerous invitations from orchestras at home and abroad, but owing to his obligations at the Vienna Court Opera he probably turned down many opportunities.

During his last six seasons in Vienna (1901-1902 to 1906-1907) Mahler conducted 53 concerts outside Vienna or an average of 9 concerts each season. In other words, he conducted no more than what he conducted during his first four seasons in Vienna.

Table II

Mahler's concerts at home and abroad (1901-1907)

Season	Vienna	Austria [1]	Abroad	Total	incl. symphonic works by Mahler abroad [2]
1901-02	2	0	6	6	6 performances of 3 works
1902-03	1	0	4	4	4 performances of 3 works
1903-04	0	0	9	9	9 performances of 3 works
1904-05	5	1	9	10	10 performances of 4 works
1905-06	1	1	6	7	9 performances of 3 works
1906-07	1	5	12	17	10 performances of 4 works
Total	10	7	46	53	48 performances of 7 works

[1] The Austro-Hungarian Empire (apart from Vienna).
[2] Symphonies Nos. 1-6, and *Das klagende Lied,* but not the *Lieder* at the four concerts in Vienna and Graz (1905), and Berlin (1907).

Mahler was invited to conduct primarily in his capacity as composer-conductor, leaving the remainder of the program to the local conductor; only in the last season did he begin to include other composers' works in his programs.

Mahler's frequent absences from Vienna, to conduct concerts abroad has often been mentioned in the literature, especially during his last seasons. This caused many venomous attacks on him from local, mostly anti-Semitic papers and magazines who blamed him for neglecting his duties towards the Opera in order to promote his own works. The question is: was it only spiteful gossip spread by disappointed and frustrated singers whom Mahler had denied opportunities for guest appearances abroad, or had the critics any proof to support these allegations? Table III below shows that there was some foundation for criticizing Mahler for his absences but it seems disproportionate and very petty.

In terms of numbers of concerts and days abroad there is indeed a sharp dividing line between Mahler's first four seasons at the Opera and the following six seasons, not only in the number of appearances at the Opera but also in the number of days he was out of town. Whereas from 1897 to 1901 he appeared 352 times in the Opera's pit, this number was reduced in the last six seasons to "only" 272 times. Proportionally the number of his days away from Vienna increased considerably:

Table III

Mahler's absences from Vienna on concert tours:

1897-1901	1901-02	1902-03	1903-04	1904-05	1905-06	1906-07	Total
15 days	45 days	20 days	27 days	35 days	29 days	65 days	236 days

The data is reconstructed from Mahler's letters, newspaper notices, and railway time-tables. Clearly, Mahler did not fritter away his time on tours; on the contrary, he meticulously planned nearly every minute. He developed the following routine: he left Vienna 3-4 days prior to a concert by night train, upon his arrival the following morning or afternoon he immediately started the 3 or 4 scheduled rehearsals, culminating in the concert. It was expected that the local conductor prepared the orchestra in advance, especially when one of Mahler's own works was programmed. After a concert, he immediately returned to Vienna by night train, or departed early the following morning. There are several examples of Mahler conducting at the Vienna Opera, having returned to the city that same day (concert no. 187, note 2).

Mahler deviated from this practice only once: on his tour in January 1907 to Berlin, Frankfurt, and Linz (concerts nos. 192-194). Quite extraordinarily, Mahler left for Berlin eight days before the concert, and after his last concert in Linz, a matinee, Mahler did not return to Vienna, but inexplicably remained in Linz in order to attend an unimportant operetta at the local theater. He stayed overnight in a hotel even though Linz was only a few hours ride from Vienna. It was during that tour that the Viennese press launched a massive attack on Mahler for his "long absences," which he read about in the papers and mentions in letters to his wife.

Like everybody else at the Court Opera, Mahler was obliged to apply for leave in the intendant's office. It appears he considered it only a matter of form since most of his letters of application are dated just a few days before his planned departure. He often noted that he would hear new operas and singers during his travels; and he engaged several singers for guest appearances at the Court Opera.

"Cancel" was not in Mahler's vocabulary. Owing to illness, he was forced to cancel three scheduled concerts in Vienna (1901), and of course, the remaining concerts in New York in the spring of 1911. He had also cancelled his participation in a concert in Olmütz (1883), and another one in Prague (1885), both as pianist. Then, in the spring of 1910, he unexpectedly cancelled a concert in Rome (May 5, 1910) owing to the indolent orchestra, (concert no. 270, note 1). On two occasions he cancelled performances of single works in order to catch an early train back to Vienna (concerts nos. 184 & 187).

Mahler and his Agents

In May 1885, Mahler's 5 year contract with the theatrical agent, Gustav Lewy expired, and was not renewed, nor did he enter into a new contract with another agent. It appears that from now on Mahler took his career in his own hands and negotiated directly with theater directors and orchestras. Independently from Lewy, he already secured engagements in Prague and Leipzig (both 1885), and later in Hamburg.

In the spring of 1904 he was approached by Norbert Salter, in Strasbourg, concerning a festival scheduled for May 1905 (concerts nos. 176-178). Salter, like Mahler, was educated at the Vienna Music Conservatory, but as a cellist. He was engaged by the Royal Hungarian Opera in Budapest and in 1894-1895 by the *Stadt-Theater* in Hamburg during Mahler's tenures in both cities. At the turn of the century he settled in Strasbourg as cellist at the *Stadt-Theater* orchestra and opened a theatrical and music agency which later moved to Berlin. The meeting between Mahler and Salter was the beginning of a collaboration lasting until 1910, although not exclusive. Mahler continued to receive offers from several other impresarios and orchestras, and sometimes asked Salter to help sort them out.

Approximately 35 of Mahler's letters to Salter have survived, as well as another 26 to the impresario Emil Gutmann. These letters give us a picture of Mahler as a concert organizer. Unfortunately, and surprisingly, the vast majority of these business letters are undated.

From these letters, we learn that Mahler demanded a fee of 1,000 to 1,200 German marks (in Austria and Germany), 1,000 florins (gulden) "abroad" and in Russia 1,000 rubles for each concert. It appears, from his letters to Alma, that he covered his own travel expenses. We may assume that only his expenses were covered for the charitable concerts (nos. 187, 189-190), and regarding the two *Lieder* concerts in Vienna in 1905 (nos. 173-174) he declined his fee in order to support Schoenberg's and Zemlinsky's "Society of Creating Musicians" (probably also concert no. 169).

The increased demand for Mahler's works and conducting caused him to voluntarily inform the tax authorities about his extra income from royalty payments and conducting fees in September 1906 (letter to Alma from September 7, 1906).

Between 1901 and 1907 Mahler conducted 53 concerts. If we average his fee to 1,000 florins per concert (after tax), Mahler's concert income came to 53,000 florins or 106,000 Austrian crowns (plus royalties when he conducted his own works). By way of comparison, Mahler's salary as director of the Viennese Court Opera was 12,000 florins.

Mahler financially profited from his symphonic works, but it was also characteristic of him to sacrifice the greater part of his fee to secure a flawless performance of his spiritual children. On several occasions Mahler hired additional musicians to augment certain sections of the orchestra, particularly for an important woodwind solo or to enhance fortissimo levels.

This was of course not necessary when he conducted orchestras like the Concertgebouw in Amsterdam, or the Berlin Philharmonic, but in the smaller provincial cities in Germany and Austria he could not always rely on finding competent musicians. The first instance was at the important performance of *Titan* in Weimar, in 1894 (concert no. 64) when he asked for extra basses. Later, in Brünn (concert no. 188), he brought three reliable musicians from the Vienna Philharmonic Orchestra, and for his concert in Linz in January 1907 (concert no. 194) he asked 20 musicians from Vienna to reinforce the local orchestra. They didn't go for free. Mahler covered their travel expenses, hotel accommodations and fees.

Abbreviations

AMM	Mahler, Alma, *Gustav Mahler: Memories and Letters*, eds. Donald Mitchell and Knud Martner, London: Abacus, 1990.
DM II	Mitchell, Donald, *Gustav Mahler. Volume II: The Wunderhorn Years*, Berkeley/Los Angeles: University of California, 1975.
GMB	Blaukopf, Herta (ed.), *Gustav Mahler: Briefe*, Vienna/Hamburg: Zsolnay, 1996.
HLG I	La Grange, Henry-Louis de, *Mahler, Vol. 1*, New York: Doubleday, 1973.
HLG II	La Grange, Henry-Louis de, *Gustav Mahler. Vienna: The Years of Challenge (1897-1904), Vol. 2*, New York: Oxford, 1995.
HLG III	La Grange, Henry-Louis de, *Gustav Mahler. Vienna: Triumph and Disillusion (1904-1907), Vol. 3*, New York: Oxford, 1999.
HLG IV	La Grange, Henry-Louis de, *Gustav Mahler. A New Life Cut Short (1907-1911), Vol. 4*, New York: Oxford, 2008.
KB^2	Blaukopf, Kurt (ed.), *Mahler: His Life, Work and World*, with contributions by Zoltan Roman, New York: Thames and Hudson, 1992.
MFL	McClatchie, Stephen (ed. and transl.) *The Mahler Family Letters*, New York: Oxford, 2006.
MSL	Martner, Knud (ed.), *Selected Letters of Gustav Mahler*, Eithne Wilkins (trans.), Ernst Kaiser and Bill Hopkins, New York: Farrar-Straus-Giroux, 1979.
NBL	Bauer-Lechner, Natalie, *Gustav Mahler in den Erinnerungen von Natalie Bauer-Lechner*, ed. Herbert Killian, notes and commentary Knud Martner, Hamburg: Karl Dieter Wagner, 1984.
Pfohl	Pfohl, Ferdinand, *Gustav Mahler: Eindrücke und Erinnerungen aus den Hamburger Jahren*, ed. Knud Martner, Hamburg: Karl Dieter Wagner, 1973.
Reilly	Reilly, Edward R., *Gustav Mahler and Guido Adler: Records of a Friendship*, Cambridge: Cambridge University Press, 1982.

Roman   Roman, Zoltan, *Gustav Mahler and Hungary (Studies in Central and Eastern European Music, 5),* Budapest: Akademiai Kiado, 1991.

ZR II   Roman, Zoltan, *Gustav Mahler's American Years: 1907 – 1911. A Documentary History,* New York: Pendragon Press, 1989.

PART I
CHILDHOOD AND YOUTH IN IGLAU
1860–1875

In 1857, Bernhard Mahler (1827-1889), a 30-year-old Jewish traveling tradesman married Maria Hermann (1837-1889), ten years his junior. They settled in the small village of Kalischt in Bohemia, where Bernhard became partner of a modest family-owned distillery, and in addition, opened a small tavern in the house where his family lived. Within the first year Maria gave birth to a boy named Isidor, who was killed in an accident the following year.

On July 7, 1860, Maria Mahler gave birth to a second child, Gustav. Three months later the family moved to a nearby town, Iglau (Jihlava) in Moravia, which had approximately 20,000 inhabitants, most of them German-speaking and Roman Catholic. The Mahler family soon joined the Jewish community which numbered approximately 1,100.

In Iglau, Bernhard reestablished his distillery and opened a tavern. Slowly but steadily his business prospered, as did his family, which within the following two decades was increased by 12 children (three girls and nine boys). Six boys died in infancy. Maria Mahler was almost constantly pregnant until 42-years-old and she probably had several abortions. Her third child, Ernst, born two years after Gustav, died at the age of 13 on April 13, 1875.

Gustav Mahler's extraordinary musicality was discovered at an early age. He was six years old when local musicians started to give him piano lessons which led to his public debut in 1870 at the age of ten (concert no. 1).

Mahler began primary school at 6-years-old and four years later he entered the German Gymnasium. He was the only child from the family to attend. By summer 1871, the three-room flat was crowded with seven children, and Maria Mahler was again pregnant. This is probably the reason why Gustav was sent to Prague in October to study at the German Gymnasium. Only five months later, in February 1872, after a disastrously bad semester, and following the death of two of his brothers in December, his father brought him back to Iglau.

In the summer of 1875, Gustav spent a few weeks on holiday at an estate outside Iglau. The estate manager, Gustav Schwarz, became aware of the young man's astounding talent, and strongly advised him to study piano at the Vienna Conservatory. His father initially opposed the idea but finally relented, with the condition that Gustav complete his studies at the Gymnasium in Iglau as an extern pupil.

| Iglau | 1870–1872 | Concerts Nos. 1–3 |

1. October 13, 1870, Soirée.
IGLAU - Stadttheater [1,350 seats] [1]

Non Subscription Evening

- Program not known -

SOURCE According to the review in the Iglau newspaper *Der Vermittler* (October 16, 1870, the only source for the event) the ten-year-old Mahler performed one or more unidentified piano piece(s). Besides his contribution(s) the evening consisted of two unidentified plays, *Die Virtuosen* and *Tosti*, the latter described as a "comic scene."
NOTE [1] The Municipal Theater, which that season was directed by Gottfried Denemy.
REVIEW HLG I, 23; KB[2] 148.

2. January 15, 1871, Soirée.
IGLAU - Festsaal des Gymnasiums

In Celebration of Franz Grillparzer's 80th Birthday

The evening's program consisted of 13 entries and ranged from oratory to choruses and transcriptions for piano four-hands, all performed by the students. Though Mahler is not specifically named, we may assume that he was among the performers of the following works for piano four-hands:

(1)	Beethoven	Overture to *Egmont*, Op. 84
(7)	Haydn	Andante, from an unspecified symphony
(11)	Haydn	Symphony in G major (3rd movement)

SOURCE *Jahresbericht des Gymnasiums* (Iglau, 1871, p. 29).

3. November 11, 1872, Soirée.
IGLAU - Festsaal des Gymnasiums

Concert in Commemoration of Friedrich Schiller's Birthday [1]

(1)	Beethoven	Overture to *Die Geschöpfe des Prometheus*, Op. 43
		- *Prologue* spoken by one of the students -
(2)	Meyerbeer	Fantasy (unspecified), for Orchestra
(3)	Hummel	"Festmarsch," (Festival March) [2]
(4)	Donizetti	Potpourri from *Lucia di Lammermoor* for 2 Pianos 8-hands
(5)	Three compositions for Boy's Choir:	
	Dürrner	"Sturmbeschwörung"
	Méhul	"Gebet," (Prayer)
	Engelsberg	"So weit"
(6)	Liszt	Paraphrase on the "Wedding March" from Mendelssohn's *Ein Sommernachtstraum*, for Piano ● [3]

SOLOISTS (4 & 5) Pupils from the *Gymnasium*; (6) Mahler.
ORCHESTRA (1, 2, 3) The Iglau *Stadtkapelle,* cond. H. Fischer.

SOURCE Program reconstructed from the review in the Iglau newspaper *Der Vermittler* of November 12, 1872. Except for the first three items the precise sequence cannot be deduced from the review.

NOTES [1] Schiller's birthday (November 10, 1759) was annually commemorated at the Iglau *Gymnasium*. According to the review an audience of about 800 attended the concert. The evening also included a recital of five unidentified poems by Schiller and a dialogue from his play *Wallensteins Tod* ("The Death of Wallenstein").

[2] Johann E. Hummel was a very industrious composer of marches but no "Festival March" has been found in his catalog. One of the following may have been performed: *Kronprinz Rudolf-Marsch*, Op. 300, *Für unser Vaterland*, Op. 334, or *Erzherzog Leopold Salvator*, Op. 530.

[3] In addition to the "Wedding March," this work also comprises a paraphrase on the *Elfentanz* ("Dance of the Elves"). It must be assumed that Mahler played the entire composition, which has a duration of about ten minutes.

REVIEW HLG I, 25-26.

4. **April 20, 1873, 7 p.m.**
   IGLAU - Stadttheater [1,350 seats]

In Celebration of the Marriage between Archduchess Gisela [daughter of Emperor Franz Joseph I of Austria] and Prince Leopold [son of Prince Regent Luitpold] of Bavaria

(1)	Westmeyer	*Kaiser-Ouverture* [1]
(2)	Fiby	"Österreich, mein Vaterland," Op. 3, for Men's Chorus
(3)	Jansa	Double Rondo, Op. 33, for 2 Violins and Piano
(4)	Suppé	"Das letzte Lied," Lied
(5)	Suppé	"O du mein Österreich," arr. for Brass Band & solo *Flügelhorn* [2]
(6)	Eckert	"Schifferlied," for Men's Chorus
(7)	Thalberg	Fantasy on Bellini's *Norma*, for Piano [3]
(8)	Wagner	"Festmarsch," (Festival March) [4]

SOLOISTS (3) R. Schraml, and his brother (not named), acc. by Mr. Dworzak; (4) L. Mikon [5], acc. by Mr. Dworzak; (5) *Feldwebel* [Sergeant] Truka, *Flügelhorn* solo; (7) Mahler.

ORCHESTRA (1, 5, 8) The combined *k.k. Militärkapelle* and *Stadtkapelle* in Iglau, including (in item 8) a number of local dilettantes, conducted by J. Schwadbik.

CHORUS (2 & 6) The Iglau *Männergesang-Verein* (Men's Choral Society), conducted by H. Fischer.

SOURCE Program reconstructed from the review in the newspaper *Mährischer Grenzbote*, Iglau, April 24, 1873.

NOTES [1] The composer provided two endings for this overture: one for orchestra alone, and another, an "apotheosis" on the Austrian national hymn, for orchestra with men's chorus and solo trombone. Judging from the review it was the former that was performed.

[2] Originally a *Lied* for tenor solo, mixed choir, and piano. The arrangement played on the present occasion was probably the March, Op. 117, by Gustav Kunze, based on the well-known *Lied* by Suppé.
[3] The *Flügelhorn* (bugle horn), used normally only in military bands, was introduced into the symphony orchestra about two decades later by Mahler in the 1st movement of his Third Symphony, completed in 1896.
[3] Thalberg left two sets of Fantasies on Bellini's *Norma*: (1) *Grande fantaisie et variations* Op. 12, originally for 2 pianos, later arranged for one piano, and (2) *Fantasie sur Themes de l'opera "Norma" de Bellini* Op. 57, 4 for one piano. Mahler probably played Op. 12, (duration: 15 minutes).
[4] Not specified, but in light of the occasion, it was likely the "Bridal Chorus" from *Lohengrin*, arranged for military band.
[5] Leopold Mikon made his living as a cobbler, and locally was a much sought-after amateur bass singer. He was also a member of the Iglau Town Council (1885–1887).
REVIEW HLG I, 26; KB[2] 148.

5. May 17, 1873, Soirée.
IGLAU - Kleiner Fest-Saal des Hotel Czap

In Celebration of the 21st Anniversary of the Iglau Männergesang-Verein [1]

(extract of program):

(7)   Thalberg   Fantasy on Bellini's *Norma*, for Piano • [2]

SOURCE The review in the Iglau newspaper *Mährischer Grenzbote*, May 18, 1873, according to which the program was very mixed, consisting of several choruses and quartets (not all identified), some declamations and speeches, and a transcription of Suppé's *Dichter und Bauer* Overture for piano 4-hands, performed by two ladies.
NOTES [1] The "Men's Choral Society" was founded on May 16, 1852. Alterations of the society's regulations were carried out twice: on August 22, 1863, and on May 18, 1872. The chorus numbered 71 active male singers and a women's choir of 42 active members. Both choruses participated in this celebration.
[2] See concert no. 4, note 3.

PART II
STUDENT IN VIENNA
1875–1880

On September 10, 1875, the 15-year-old Mahler, along with 254 other new students, enrolled at the Music Conservatory in Vienna. (Curiously enough, another resident of Iglau, ten-year-old pianist Marie Koziol, was enrolled as well). For the term in question, the Conservatory registered a total of 648 students, between 9 and 28 years old.

From the outset, Mahler chose the piano as his principal subject, and was admitted into Professor Julius Epstein's first-year piano class. Limited to seven students, Mahler was not only the youngest, but also the only male. He opted to study composition as his secondary subject with Professor Franz Krenn (ten pupils). However, at the beginning of his third and last term (1877–78), Mahler suddenly reversed the priority of his two areas of study, with composition becoming his principal subject. To all appearances, this decision seems to have been reached immediately after concert no. 10, perhaps as a result of it.

During the first two years at the Conservatory Mahler continued his studies at the Iglau *Gymnasium* as an external pupil, finally receiving his graduation certificate — only after retaking the examination — in September 1877. He then immediately began to attend various lectures at Vienna University and continued this practice, rather infrequently, until the spring of 1880, but not surprisingly, without ever attaining a university degree.

It is undisputed that Mahler won four first prizes during his three years at the Conservatory, two honors each in piano and composition. On paper, regarded out of context, this might appear to be an impressive achievement, but compared with the results achieved by his fellow students, it can scarcely be considered absolutely outstanding. In fact, he did not distinguish himself from his comrades by his achievements. Rather, a careful study of the surviving documents leaves one with the impression that he was a somewhat passive, retiring student, who did not make himself conspicuous either as a pianist or as a composer. In light of the activity that he displayed *outside* the Conservatory, his strange reticence appears all the more puzzling and contradictory.

Two examples will illustrate this:

Each term, about 15 internal soirées, and also a few public concerts, were arranged at the Conservatory. The students were expected to take part in the former voluntarily, at least occasionally. With the knowledge of Mahler's later career as a performing artist, it is surprising to note that he only took advantage of this opportunity once (concert no. 10).

And as a composer *in spe* it is perhaps even more inexplicable that the young Mahler — unlike most of his fellow composition students — never bothered to present any of his own works at the student soirées. At the examination (*Concurs*) at the conclusion of each term, he was obliged to appear, either in his capacity as a pianist or as a composer, or as both: such was the case in concert no. 11.

It is unclear why Mahler, who had started his studies with wild enthusiasm, suddenly became so indifferent. There are strong indications that during the first months of 1876 he had a discouraging, unforgivable experience, which even made him abandon the Conservatory, although only for a short while. The unhappy incident probably concerns his Violin Sonata, which he had handed in for performance at one of the internal soirées, but which the Conservatory's jury rejected after hearing. In her *Recollections of Gustav Mahler,* Natalie Bauer-Lechner refers to the incident but, apparently out of ignorance, she misses the real point (London 1980, pp. 81–82).

Nevertheless, in July 1878 Mahler, one of 50 students, graduated on time from the Conservatory with a Diploma, a distinction he shared with 32 other fellow students. Nine of them were awarded the coveted "Silver Medal" of the Conservatory, an exceptional honor, for which Mahler apparently did not qualify (although in his letter of application to the Kassel Theater he claims the contrary; GMB 18).

6. **June 23, 1876, 3 p.m.**
   VIENNA - Kleiner Saal des Conservatoriums (598 seats) [1]

   Annual Concurs [Exam] for First-Year Piano Students [2]

   (extract of program)

       Schubert   Piano Sonata, A minor (1st movement) [3]

   SOURCE "Bericht über das Conservatorium und die Schauspielschule der Gesellschaft der Musikfreunde in Wien. Für das Schuljahr 1875–1876." (Vienna, 1876, p. 83) and a notice in the newspaper *Neue Freie Presse* on June 25, 1876, p. 6.
   NOTES [1] Since January 6, 1870, the Conservatory was housed on the second floor, in the right wing of the "Musikvereingebäude." The small hall is known as the "Brahms–Saal" since 1937.
   [2] According to the *Bericht über das Conservatorium* only students with a 1st or 2nd grade were accepted at the annual *Concurs* [i.e. exam]. Of the 16 students recorded in the 1876 report, only five attained a 1st grade, and four, including Mahler, were granted it unanimously.
   [3] A set subject. It is unknown which of Schubert's three piano sonatas in the key of A minor Mahler performed: Deutsch 537 (1st movement duration: ca. 6 minutes), D 784 (ca. 10'), or D 845 (ca. 10').

7. **July 31, 1876, Soirée.**
   IGLAU - Großer Fest-Saal des Hotel Czap [600 seats]

   Concert of the "Städtische Musikkapelle"

(1)	Kittl	Concert Overture, D major, Op. 22
(2)	Mahler	Sonata for Violin and Piano [1]
(3)	Beethoven	Trio for Piano, Violin, and Cello (unspecified) •
(4)	Ernst	Violin Concerto (unspecified), with Piano Acc. • [2]
(5)	Liszt	*Gnomenreigen*, for Piano •
(6)	Anon.	Quartets (unspecified) for Men's Chorus
(7)	Vieuxtemps	Tarantella, Op. 22, No. 5, for Violin and Piano • [3]
(8)	Schubert	"Wanderer" Fantasy, Op. 15, C major, D 760, for Piano

   SOLOISTS (2, 4, 7) R. Schraml and Mahler; (3) Mahler, R. Schraml, and Professor N. Eichler; (5 & 8) Mahler; (6) The Iglau *Männergesang-Verein*.
   ORCHESTRA (1) The Iglau *Städtische Kapelle*, cond. H. Fischer.
   SOURCE The preview in the *Mährischer Grenzbote* (July 30, 1876) reads: "The program of tomorrow's concert at the Hotel Czap, given by the two prize-winning Iglau fellow townsmen, Mahler and Schraml, consists of the following eight pieces...etc." The concert seems not to have been reviewed.
   NOTES [1] Probably the world premiere, certainly the first recorded public performance. The sonata must be considered lost, and as consequence the key and the number of movements remain unknown.
   [2] Probably his *Concerto Pathétique* in F-sharp minor, Op. 23 (pub. 1851).
   [3] At his final exam at the Conservatory, on June 28, 1876, Richard Schraml had performed the same piece (perhaps with Mahler at the piano), and gained a first prize for his interpretation.

CONCERT

des Conservatoristen

Gustav Mahler,

unter gefälliger Mitwirkung

der Herren

Aug. Siebert, und Aug. Grünberg,

Mitglieder des k. k. Hofopernorchesters,

und des Herrn

Rudolf Kržýžanowski,

Dienstag den 12. September 1876

im

Saale des Hotel Czap.

Das Reinerträgniss wird zur Anschaffung von Lehrmittelgegenständen am hiesigen k. k. Gymnasium gewidmet.

PROGRAMM:

1. **Kržýžanowski Rudolf.** Quartett für Piano und 2 Violinen und Viola.
2. **Vieuxtemps H.** Concert D mol für Violine 1. Satz (Herr Siebert.)
3. **Schubert Franz.** Wanderer-Fantasie für Piano, (Herr Mahler.)
4. **Mahler Gustav.** Sonate für Violin und Piano. (Herr Siebert, Herr Mahler.)
5. **Mahler Gustav.** Quartett für Piano, 2 Violinen und Viola.
6. **Chopin Frédèrik.** Ballade für Piano (Herr Mahler.)
7. **Alard D.** Concert für 2 Violinen mit Clavierbegleitung. (Herr Siebert, Herr Grünberg.)

Anfang um halb 8 Abends.

Preise der Plätze:

Cerclesitz 1 fl., Parterresitz 60 kr., Entrée 40 kr.
Gallerie 20 kr.

Die Karten sind zu haben in der Buchhandlung des Hrn. CARL LEHMANN und am Abende des Concertes an der Cassa.

8. September 12, 1876, 7, 30 p.m.
IGLAU - Großer Fest-Saal des Hotel Czap [600 seats]

Benefit Concert organized by Gustav Mahler, Student at the Conservatory [in Vienna], with kind assistance of August Siebert and Eugen Grünberg, both members of the Court Opera Orchestra [in Vienna], and Rudolf Krzyzanowski. The net income will be donated to the local Imperial and Royal Gymnasium to provide teaching materials.

(1)	Krzyzanowski	Quartet for Piano, 2 Violins, and Viola (1st mvmt.) • [1]
(2)	Vieuxtemps	Violin Concerto No. 4, D minor, Op. 31 (1st mvmt.) • [2]
(3)	Schubert	"Wanderer" Fantasy, Op. 15, C major, D 760 for Piano •
(4)	Mahler	Sonata for Violin and Piano •
(5)	Mahler	Quartet for Piano, 2 Violins, and Viola • [1]
(6)	Chopin	Ballade, for Piano • [3]
(7)	Alárd	Concerto for 2 Violins, with Piano Acc. • [4]

SOLOISTS (1 & 5) A. Siebert, E. Grünberg, R. Krzyzanowski, and Mahler, see note 5 below; (2 & 4) A. Siebert; (3 & 6) Mahler; (7) E. Grünberg & A. Siebert.
PIANO ACC. Mahler was probably the pianist for the entire concert, see note 5.
SOURCE Handbill; see illustration on opposite page.
NOTES [1] Divergences between the wording of the handbill and the only review (*Mährischer Grenzbote,* September 17, 1876) raise the important question as to whether we are dealing with two *quartets* or two *quintets.*
The reviewer states that only the *1st movement* of Krzyzanowski's work was given, which there is no reason to question. However, it is strange and bewildering that he refers to both *quartets* as *quintets,* especially because the handbill unambiguously announces them as *quartets*, specifies the *four* instruments required, and names only four musicians, which all seems to preclude a printing error. However, the reviewer also points out that Mahler's work recently had gained the first prize at the Vienna Conservatory.
Indeed, at his exam on July 1, 1876, Mahler was unanimously awarded first prize for an unspecified *quintet,* and only for its *1st movement* (probably all he completed, because students normally only composed a single movement for the exams). All prize-winning works were entitled to be performed at the final concert at the Conservatory, though as a rule only in the presence of the composer, and with his participation. Unfortunately, Mahler had to travel home right after his exam in order to take the Iglau *Gymnasium*'s annual exam. For that reason his *quintet* movement was not performed at either of the two final concerts at the Conservatory, which took place on July 12 and 15. Consequently, details regarding its instrumentation cannot be gleaned from the Conservatory's annual *Bericht*.
This leaves us with two alternatives: (a) the reviewer either confused the "Conservatory Quintet" with a newly composed "Iglau Quartet," i.e. there are *two* different compositions, or (b) the Quintet was transformed into a Quartet, i.e. there was only *one* composition, offered in *two* different guises.

In this connection it is interesting that the *Bericht* records a performance of the *1st movement* of a Piano *Quintet* in C minor by Krzyzanowski, given at the Vienna Conservatory on December 22, 1875, with the composer at the piano and, among others, Eugen Grünberg as the violist.
One is indeed tempted to assume that the two recorded "Conservatory Quintets" were the works performed in Iglau. However, for the apparent lack of a cellist, both compositions of course would have had to be adapted for the rather unusual combination of a piano, two violins, and viola. This might perhaps also explain why only the *first movement* of Krzyzanowski's work was performed. With regard to Mahler's composition, we do not know whether it was a *complete* quintet/quartet, or only an excerpt, say the *1st mo vement* that was presented. Both his and Krzyzanowski's compositions must be considered lost.

[2] At his final exam at the Conservatory, on June 28, 1876, August Siebert had performed the same piece (perhaps with Mahler at the piano?), and was awarded a first prize and, in addition, the much-coveted "Silver Medal." Two years later Siebert joined the Vienna Court Opera Orchestra, where he was still active during Mahler's tenure as artistic director of the Opera (1897–1907).

[3] The precise identity cannot be deduced from the surviving documents. However, of Chopin's four Ballades (Op. 23, 38, 47, and 52) only the first, in G minor, was part of the students repertoire at the Vienna Conservatory during this period.

[4] The French composer Alárd published three "Symphony Concertantes" for two violins and orchestra: in G major, Op. 31; D major, Op. 33; and A major, Op. 34b. It has not yet been resolved which was performed on this occasion.

[5] Neither the handbill nor the review specifies the performers of nos. 1 & 5, nor the piano accompanist of nos. 2 & 7. Among the four named musicians Mahler alone studied piano as principal subject; on the other hand, he did not master any string instrument at all — in contrast with his three comrades, who were all violinists who also studied piano as subsidiary subject. However, if Krzyzanowski played the piano in his own composition, then who played the viola? It may be significant that the reviewer in connection with Mahler's solo appearances (nos. 3 and 6) describes him as the "unermüdliche Konzertgeber" ("the untiring concert-giver"). The remark primarily refers to Mahler's role as the concert's organizer. However, it could also indicate that Mahler was considerably more active as *pianist* than the handbill suggests. It is indeed most likely that Mahler was *the* pianist *throughout* the concert, whereas Krzyzanowski, presumably, only participated as violist in the two quartets. (We cannot rule out the possibility that the latter also accompanied the two concertos, i.e. nos. 2 & 7).

REVIEW KB[2] 151; HLG I, 37–38.

9. **June 21, 1877, 3 p.m.**
   VIENNA - Kleiner Saal des Conservatoriums [598 seats]

   Annual Concurs [Exam] for the Second-Year Piano Students

   (extract of program)

   Schumann   Humoreske, B-flat major, Op. 20, for Piano (excerpt)[1]

Schluß-Produktionen

der mit

allen Concurspreisen gekrönten Abiturienten des Schuljahres 1877/78

unter der Leitung des Directors Herrn

Josef Hellmesberger.

I. Produktion: Donnerstag, den 11. Juli 1878.

1. **Chopin**: Concert für Clavier, F-moll (Finale). — Herr Robert Fischhof.
2. **Mozart**: Arie aus „Don Juan." Für Posaune. — Herr Ferdinand Schubert.
3. **Bach-Saint-Saëns**: Arie und Chor für Clavier. — Frln. Asta Liebetrau.
4. **Rud. Krzyzanowsky**: Sextett für 2 Violinen, 2 Violen, 2 Violoncelle (Adagio). — Die Herren: Fried. Skalitzky, Stefan Wahl, Joh. Kreuzinger, Hanns Winter, Alex. Fimpel und Eduard Rosenblum.
5. **C. M. Weber**: Rondo für Clarinett. — Herr Carl Kappeller.
6. **Gustav Mahler**: Clavier-Quintett (Scherzo). Clavier: der Componist und die Herren: Fried. Skalitzky, Stefan Wahl, Joh. Kreuzinger und Ed. Rosenblum.
7. **Godefroid**: Danse des sylphes für Harfe. — Frln. Angelika Gstl.
8. **Weber-Liszt**: Polonaise für Clavier, E-dur. — Frln. Amalia Neuß.

| Vienna | 1877–1878 | Concerts Nos. 9–11 |

SOURCE *Bericht über das Conservatorium und die Schauspielschule ... etc.* (Vienna 1877, p. 71) and a notice in the newspaper *Die Presse* from June 23, 1877, p. 10.
NOTE [1] Mahler was awarded a first prize for his interpretation of this set subject, although not unanimously. The duration of the complete piece is ca. 20 minutes.

10. **October 20, 1877, Soirée.**
VIENNA - Kleiner Saal des Conservatoriums [598 seats]

Second Internal Student Concert [1]

(1)	Hummel	Piano Septet, D minor, Op. 74 (1st movement)
(2)	Schulhoff	*Le Zephir*, for Harp
(3)	Zamara	Variations on Gounod's "Au Printemps," for Harp
(4)	Mozart	Aria (unspecified) from *Le nozze di Figaro*, K. 492
(5)	Chopin	Nocturne, Op. 27, No. 2
(6)	Chopin	Étude, Op. 10, No. 4
(7)	Verdi	Aria (unspecified)] from *Un ballo in maschera*
(8)	Scharwenka	Piano Concerto No. 1, B-flat minor, Op. 32, (1st mvmt) • [2]
(9)	Mendelssohn	"Ich hör' ein Vöglein," *Lied*
(10)	Mendelssohn	"Venetianisches Gondellied," *Lied*, Op. 57, No. 5
(11)	Chopin	Piano Concerto No. 1, E minor, Op. 11, (1st movement)
(12)	Brahms	"Liebestreu," *Lied*, Op. 3, No. 1
(13)	Kirchner	"Es wäre so," *Lied*
(14)	Gounod	Meditation on Bach's C major Prelude, arr. for Violin, Cello, and Organ

SOLOISTS (1) A. Margulies, H. Benkö, C. Brosch, A. Fimpel, E. Schreiber, C. Stix, W. Weber; (2 & 3) P. Günz; (4) E. Lamm; (5 & 6) F. Zottmann; (7) H. Harmsen; (8) Mahler; (9 & 10) S. Weltlinger; (11) B. Schönberger; (12 & 13) E. Kohn; (14) H. Wessely, A. Fimpel, F. Weber.
ORCHESTRA (4, 7, 8, 10) The Conservatory's Orchestra, cond. J. Hellmesberger.
SOURCE *Bericht über das Conservatorium ... etc.* (Vienna 1877, p. 46).
NOTES [1] The student soirées were not open for the public and therefore were never reviewed. This was Mahler's first and only appearance in these soirées.
[2] First performance of the movement in Vienna, the marking of which reads *Allegro patetico*. It takes about 12 minutes to play. This very taxing work was dedicated to Franz Liszt, who seems to never have played it. The world premiere, with the composer as soloist, had taken place in Berlin on April 14, 1875. Bearing in mind that the full score and the piano reduction were published in April 1877, one realizes that Mahler had only a few months to learn the difficult solo part. One wonders whether he may have overestimated his pianistic skills and failed at the concert. It is thought provoking that at about this time he abandoned the piano as his principal subject in favor of composition.

11. **July 11, 1878, 3 p.m.**
VIENNA - Großer Saal des Conservatoriums [2,063 seats]

First Concert [of two] by the First-Prize-Winning Students at the Annual "Concurs"

(1)	Chopin	Piano Concerto No. 2, F minor, Op. 21 (Finale)
(2)	Mozart	Aria (unspecified) from *Don Giovanni*, arr. for Trombone
(3)	Bach	Aria and Chorus, arr. C. Saint-Saëns for Piano
(4)	Krzyzanowski	Sextet for Strings (Adagio)

Zur
FESTLICHEN FEIER
des
25. Jahrestages der Vermählung
Ihrer kaiserl. und königl. Majestäten
des
Kaisers und der Kaiserin von Oesterreich
findet
Donnerstag den 24. April 1879
im
STADT-THEATER
ein
FEST-CONCERT
unter gefälliger Mitwirkung der
Frau **Luiga Giordani**, der Herren **Gustav Mahler**, **Leopold Mikon** und
J. Žižka, des **Iglauer Männergesang-Vereines** und des **Damenchores** und
der **Stadt-Kapelle** statt.

PROGRAMM:

1. **Prolog** von Leopold Prohaska. Volkshymne.
2. **C. M. v. Weber**, Ouverture zur Oper: „Euryanthe" für Orchester.
3. a) **Mendelssohn-Bartholdy F.** „Morgengebet." Chor für Sopran, Alt, Tenor und Bass.
4. b) **Abt Franz**, „Sonntagsmorgen." Chor für Sopran, Alt, Tenor und Bass.
5. **Liszt Franz**, „Rhapsodie hongroise" für Pianoforte.
6. **Kücken Franz**, „Gut' Nacht fahr' wohl treues Herz." Lied mit Pianoforte-Begleitung.
7. **Ferd. Laub**, Polonaise für Violine mit Pianoforte-Begleitung.
8. **Vogl F. A.**, „Rudolf von Habsburg" Ballade für eine Bassstimme mit Orchesterbegleitung.
9. a) **Schumann Rob.**, Humoreske. b) **Schubert Franz**, Sonate A moll für Pianoforte.
10. **Rossini G.**, Aria dell' Opera: „Il Barbiere di Siviglia."
11. **Steiber Ernst**, „Festhymne." Männerchor mit Pianoforte-Begleitung.

Concert-Flügel aus dem Claviersalon des Herrn Bělohlavek.

PREISE DER PLÄTZE:

Logen à 5 fl. Theaterlogen à 3 fl. Logensitz in der ersten Reihe 1 fl. 50 kr. Logensitz in den beiden andern Reihen 1 fl. Sperrsitz ins Parterre 1 fl. Nummerirter Parterresitz 60 kr. Nummerirter Sitz auf der 1. Gallerie 50 kr. Parterre-Entrée 40 kr. 1. Gallerie 25 kr. 2. Gallerie 15 kr.

ANFANG 8 UHR.

Druck von J. Rippl & Sohn in Iglau.

| Vienna–Iglau | 1878–1879 | Concerts Nos. 11–12 |

(5)	Weber	Rondo (unspecified), for Clarinet and Piano
(6)	**Mahler**	**Piano Quintet (Scherzo)** ● [1]
(7)	Godefroid	*Danse des Sylphes*, for Harp
(8)	Weber-Liszt	Polonaise, E major, Op. 21 & 72, arr. for Piano and Orch. [2]

SOLOISTS (1) R. Fischhof; (2) F. Schubert; (3) A. Liebetrau; (4) F. Skallitzky, S. Wahl, J. Kreuzinger, H. Winter, A. Fimpel, E. Rosenblum; (5) C. Kappeller; (6) Mahler, F. Skallitzky, S. Wahl [3], J. Kreuzinger [3], E. Rosenblum [3]; (7) A. Göstl; (8) A. Neuss.

SOURCE *Bericht über das Conservatorium... etc.* (Wien 1878, p. 59); see illustration on previous page.

NOTES [1] World premiere. At his final exam (*Concurs*) in composition, on July 2, 1878, Mahler's set subject was to compose a *Scherzo* for a Piano Quintet, which earned him a first prize, though not unanimously. His manuscript is considered lost.

[2] Liszt combined the opening *Largo* from Weber's Op. 21 with Weber's *Polacca brillante*, Op. 72, and orchestrated both for piano and orchestra.

[3] A few years later Stefan Wahl and Johann Kreuzinger both joined the Vienna Court Opera Orchestra, and were still active during Mahler's tenure as the Opera's director. On August 25, 1898, the cellist Eduard Rosenblum [later Rosé] married Emma, Mahler's youngest sister.

REVIEW HLG I, 53.

12. April 24, 1879, 8 p.m.
IGLAU - Stadttheater [1,350 seats]

Festive Concert in Celebration of the Silver Wedding of the Imperial and Royal Majesties, the Emperor [Franz Josef I] and the Empress [Elisabeth] of Austria

The concert opened with a prologue spoken by Leopold Prohaska, followed by the Austrian National Hymn [J. Haydn's "Gott erhalte Franz der Kaiser"].

(1)	Weber	Overture to *Euryanthe*
(2)	Mendelssohn	"Morgengebet," for Mixed Chorus
(3)	Abt	"Sonntagsmorgen," Op. 192, No. 1, for Mixed Chorus
(4)	**Liszt**	**Hungarian Rhapsody** (unspecified), **for Piano** ●
(5)	Kücken	"Gut' Nacht, fahr' wohl," *Lied*, Op. 52, No. 1 [1]
(6)	Laub	Polonaise, Op. 8, for Violin and Piano [2]
(7)	Vogl	"Rudolf von Habsburg," *Lied*, for Bass and Orchestra
(8)	**Schumann**	**Humoreske, B-flat major, Op. 20, for Piano (excerpt)** ● [3]
(9)	**Schubert**	**Piano Sonata, A minor** ● [4]
(10)	Rossini	Aria (unspecified) from *Il barbiere di Siviglia*
(11)	Stoiber	"Festhymne," for Men's Chorus and Piano [1 & 5]

SOLOISTS (4, 8, 9) Mahler; (5 & 10) L. Giordani; (6) J. Ziška; (7) L. Mikon.
PIANO ACC. (5, 6, 10, and 11) probably Mahler, see note 1 below.
ORCHESTRA The Iglau *Stadtkapelle*, cond. H. Fischer.
CHORUS The Iglau *Männergesang-Verein* and a Ladies' chorus, cond. H. Fischer.
SOURCE Handbill; see illustration on opposite page.
NOTES [1] Although neither the handbill nor the review identifies the name of the piano accompanist, it may have been Mahler.
[2] Replaced H. Vieuxtemps' *Rêverie*, Op. 22, No. 3, according to a preview.

COTTAGE-CASINO IN WÄHRING.

I. CONCERT

am 22. November 1879.

L. v. Beethoven.	Sonate für Violine und Clavier (A dur) Herr Concertmeister **Grün** und Herr Professor **Leschetizky.**
Mozart.	Arie aus „Figaro's Hochzeit", Frau Ida **Gassebner.**
Godefroid.	La danse des Silphes für Harfe, Fräulein **Therese Zamara.**
Verdi.	Arie aus „Maskenball", Herr **Georges Schütte-Harmsen.**
Schumann.	Variationen für zwei Claviere, Frau **Varette Stepanoff** und Herr Professor **Leschetizky.**
Kärnthner Lieder.	Frau Ida **Gassebner.**
Chopin.	Nocturne
Bach.	Gigue } Frau **Varette Stepanoff.**
Leschetizky.	Valse chromatique
Schumann.	Frühlingsnacht
Sucher.	Liebesglück } Herr **Georges Schütte-Harmsen.**

Begleitung der Lieder: Herr **Gustav Mahler.**

Claviere: Bösendorfer.

Anfang 9 Uhr.

[3] Probably an excerpt only, as was the case in concert no. 9.
[4] No doubt the same sonata as in concert no. 6 and probably the 1st movement only.
[5] Probably Stoiber's "Des Liedes Sendung," Hymn Op. 62.
REVIEW HLG I, 55.

12a. November 22, 1879, 9 p.m. [△]
VIENNA – The Casino of the "Cottage-Verein" in Währing [1]

First Concert

(1)	Beethoven	Sonata for Violin and Piano in A major [2]
(2)	Mozart	Aria (unspecified) from *Le nozze di Figaro*
(3)	Godefroid	*Danse des Sylphes*, for Harp
(4)	Verdi	Aria (unspecified) from *Un ballo in maschera*
(5)	Schumann	Variation for two Pianos [3]
(6)	Anonymous	Songs from Kärnten [Carinthia, Austria]
(7)	Chopin	Nocturne (unspecified), for Piano
(8)	Bach	Gigue, for Piano
(9)	Leschetizky	Valse chromatique, for Piano
(10)	Schumann	"Frühlingsnacht" *Lied*, Op. 39, No. 12
(11)	Sucher	"Liebesglück," *Lied*

SOLOISTS (1) J.M. Grün and T. Leschetizky; (2 & 6) I. Gassebner, acc. by Mahler; (3) T. Zamara; (4, 10 & 11) G. Schütte–Harmsen, acc. by Mahler; (5) V. Stepanoff and T. Leschetizky; (7–9) V. Stepanoff.
SOURCE Handbill from *Im Cottage von Währing/Döbling*, Vol. III, by Heidi Brunnbauer, Edition Weinviertel, Austria, 2009, p. 97; see illustration on opposite page.
NOTES [1] The Cottage Association in the northern district of Vienna was founded in 1873. Mahler rented a room in a villa, Karl–Ludwig Straße 24, in the autumn of 1879.
[2] Beethoven composed three Violin Sonatas in A major: Op. 12, No. 2; Op. 30, No. 1 and Op. 47, "Kreutzer."
[3] Probably Schumann's "Andante und Variationen," Op. 46.

12b. August 18, 1881 [△ & 1]
WLASCHIM – Restaurant "Karl IV"

Benefit concert for the Czech National Theater in Prague [1]

- Program not known -

SOURCE Jihlava exhibition catalog, "In Gustav Mahler's Footsteps in Bohemia and Moravia" by Milan Palák (Jihlava, 2003, unpaginated, p. 68).
NOTE [1] A month before Mahler left for Laibach he visited his cousin Gustav Frank in Wlaschim. During this visit he participated in an impromptu benefit concert, the details are unknown, but we may assume that Mahler played piano pieces.
[2] The theater was inaugurated on June 11, 1881 but burned down on August 12. It was reopened on November 18, 1883 after a national subscription provided funding.

[△] These concerts were discovered at press time and therefore have been incorporated as 12a and 12b.

PART III
THE FIRST STEPS: THE YOUNG CONDUCTOR
BAD HALL — LAIBACH — OLMÜTZ
1880–1883

In the spring of 1880, after two years of futile studies at the University, and several more or less abortive attempts as a composer, the 19-year-old Mahler realized that the time had come to turn over a new leaf. His poor financial circumstances probably played a major factor in his decision to abandon student life, and to seek regular work with a fixed monthly salary.

We do not have access to Mahler's thoughts concerning his future and prospects, but in view of his musical training, especially as a pianist, he clearly had a number of choices. The most obvious one — a career as a virtuoso pianist — he had already renounced in the autumn of 1877. In all likelihood Mahler, at that time, abandoned the piano as *his* instrument once and for all, although he occasionally did appear in chamber music and song recitals. It appears that the stage was his only alternative, and the vast Empires of Austro-Hungary and Germany were literally covered with large and small theaters with varied repertoires, including operas. Thus there was a steady demand for able pianists to coach soloists and choirs.

In fact, in April 1880 Mahler had been on the look-out for a job as a choirmaster, but was evidently dissuaded by his former fellow student, the tenor Franz Schaumann, who wrote to Guido Adler, another friend of Mahler's: "I would advise against such a post, simply because of his [Mahler's] competence; for he would certainly be disillusioned in the first weeks." (Reilly, p. 83.) It seems that Adler had been acting on Mahler's behalf.

Despite this "warning," on May 12, 1880, Mahler signed a *non-specific* five-year contract with the theater agent, Gustav Lewy, who instantly — despite the fact that Mahler had not received any formal training as a conductor — secured him a post as *Kapellmeister* at the small provincial spa of Bad Hall. It was an inconspicuous post; a small summer theater (178 seats) with an orchestra of about 20 musicians and a repertoire comprising operettas, plays and farces. The bathing season in Bad Hall ran from May 15 until September 30, 1880. The months Mahler spent at Bad Hall are the least documented of all his engagements. Only a few documents and 8 theater programs have survived. Among them, a performance on June 16, 1880, of a farce which was preceded by a concert recital. Mrs. *N.* Petzer-Löscher (a soprano from Prague) sang Leonora's aria, "Tacea la notte placida" from *Il trovatore,* "Casta diva" from Bellini's *Norma*, and finally a selection of unspecified *Lieder* by Schubert, all accompanied by Mahler at the piano.

Mahler apparently soon became aware of his gifts and aptitude for conducting an orchestra. After only one month at Bad Hall, his mind was already made up, and he implored Lewy to find him a new post for the forthcoming winter season, preferably in Germany. Most significantly, this time he did not request just *any* job but specifically, and very confidently, a post as *Kapellmeister*. Of course, this specific demand made it more problematic and difficult for Lewy to obtain Mahler new employments, not least in view of his protégé's limited conducting experience. On the other hand, Mahler firmly turned down an urgent invitation to take up the post as *Kapellmeister* in his hometown, at the *Stadttheater* in Iglau. He seems to have done so out of consideration for his family. One can imagine that Mahler, inwardly, was aware of his inexperience, and had no intention of disgracing his family by exhibiting his shortcomings. Abroad, however, in a foreign city, unknown to everybody, that mattered less. Out there he could test himself and learn the craft and art of conducting.

In view of this, and at such a short notice, Lewy was unable to find a new post for Mahler, who after the few months at Bad Hall, had no other option but to return to Vienna. There, at the end of October 1880, he completed the score of *Das klagende Lied,* his first major work, which had occupied him for the preceding two years.

A whole year passed before Mahler got a new job, but when he did it suited his demands and wishes; as a first *Kapellmeister* at the Landschaftliches Theater in Laibach (Ljubljana, Slovenia), from September 24, 1881, to April 2, 1882. Before leaving Iglau for Laibach, Mahler submitted the score of *Das klagende Lied* for the coveted "Beethoven-Prize" in Vienna (deadline: September 30). Three months later he learned that the jury had selected another composer's work. This severe rebuff was probably the reason that for several years he "buried" all his dreams of Mahler-the-*Composer*, and instead devoted all his energy to furthering the career of Mahler-the-*Conductor.*

Viertes Concert

der

philharmon. Gesellschaft in Laibach

unter der Leitung ihres Musik-Directors Herrn

Anton Nedvěd

und freundlicher Mitwirkung des Herrn

Gustav Mahler,

Kapellmeister des landschaftl. Theaters in Laibach,

Sonntag, den 5. März 1882

im landschaftlichen Redoutensaale.

Anfang um halb 5 Uhr nachmittags.

PROGRAMM.

1.) **J. O. Grimm:** **Suite** in Canonform für Streichorchester:
   a) *Allegro con brio;*
   b) *Andante lento;*
   c) *Tempo di Menuetto;*
   d) *Allegro risoluto.*

2.) **F. Mendelssohn-Bartholdy:** **Capriccio brillant,** op. 22, H-moll, für das Pianoforte mit Begleitung eines Streichquartettes; Herr *G. Mahler.*

3. a) **J. Brahms:** **Liebestreue,** } Lieder mit Pianofortebegl.,
   b) **A. Dorn:** **Schneeglöckchen,** } ges. v. Frl. *Carol. Witschl.*

4.) **L. Boccherini:** **Menuett** für Streichorchester.

5. a) **R. Schumann:** **Waldscenen,** a) *Jagdlied,*
                                    b) *Vogel als Prophet,* } Herr
   b) **F. Chopin:** **Polonaise,** op. 53. As-dur.   } *G. Mahler.*

6.) **Ant. Dvořák:** **Serenade,** E-dur, für Streichorchester:
   a) *Moderato;*
   b) *Tempo di Valse;*
   c) *Scherzo;*
   d) *Larghetto;*
   e) *Finale.*

Der Saal wird um halb 4 Uhr geöffnet.

Der Eintritt ist nur den Vereinsmitgliedern gegen Abgabe der auf Namen lautenden Eintrittskarten gestattet. — Da nach § 16 der Statuten Familien das Recht zum Eintritte für drei in gemeinschaftlicher Haushaltung lebende nicht selbständige Angehörige zusteht, so wolle für jedes weitere, an den statutenmässigen musikalischen Aufführungen theilnehmende Familienmitglied eine separate Eintrittskarte beim Herrn Vereinskassier Carl **Karinger** gegen Entrichtung des statutenmässigen Jahresbeitrages von 1 fl. gelöst werden.

Anmeldungen zum Eintritte in die philharm. Gesellschaft werden in der Handlung des Herrn **Carl Karinger**, Rathhausplatz, entgegengenommen.

> **LAIBACH**
> **Landschaftliches Theater**
> Season 1881–1882

13. **September 24, 1881, 7 p.m.**
LAIBACH - Landschaftliches Theater [1,000 seats]

Festive Inauguration of the New Season

      Beethoven   Overture to *Egmont*, Op. 84

[followed by a complete performance of Eduard Bauernfeld's play *Bürgerlich und Romantisch*]

SOURCE Review in the *Laibacher Zeitung*, September 25, 1881.
REVIEW HLG I, 83-84.

14. **February 4, 1882, 7 p.m.**
LAIBACH - Landschaftliches Theater [1,000 seats]

Concert inserted into Ferdinand Raimund's play Der Verschwender *(Act 2)*

(1)	Rossini	"Sombre fôret, désert triste," from *Guillaume Tell*
(2)	Meyerbeer	"Ah! Mon fils!" from *Le Prophète*
(3)	Verdi	"Celeste Aida," from *Aida*
(4)	Mozart	"Deh, vieni alla finestra," from *Don Giovanni*

SOLOISTS (1) C. Fischer; (2) L. Bruck; (3) F. Erl; (4) A. Luzzato.
SOURCE Reconstructed from a review in the *Laibacher Zeitung*.
NOTE All four arias were sung in German.

15. **March 5, 1882, 4:30 p.m.**
LAIBACH - Landschaftlicher Redoutensaal [800 seats]

Fourth Subscription Concert of the Philharmonic Society

(1)	Grimm	Suite, C major, Op. 10, for String Orchestra
(2)	Mendelssohn	*Capriccio brillant*, B minor, Op. 22, for Piano & Orchestra, "acc. by a string quartet" [sic] • [1]
(3)	Brahms	"Liebestreu," *Lied*, Op. 3, No. 1 [2]
(4)	Dorn	"Schneeglöckchen," *Lied*, Op. 85 [2]
(5)	Boccherini	String Quintet, E major, Op. 11, No. 5 (Minuet), arr. for String Orchestra
(6)	Schumann	*Waldszenen*, Op. 82, Nos. 7 & 8, for Piano • (7) "Vogel als Prophet," (8) "Jagdlied"
(7)	Chopin	Polonaise No. 6, A-flat major, Op. 53
(8)	Fuchs	Serenade No. 3, E minor, Op. 21, for String Orchestra [3]

SOLOISTS (2, 6–7) Mahler; (3–4) C. Witschl.
ORCHESTRA (1–2, 5, 8) The Strings of the Laibach Philharmonic Society, cond. A. Nedved.
SOURCE Concert poster, see illustration on opposite page, and the review in the *Laibacher Zeitung*.

Landschaftliches Theater in Laibach.

Direktion: Alexander Mondheim-Schreiner.

Gerader Tag.

Sonntag den 2. April 1882.

Zum Vortheile des hies. Chorpersonals.

Aussergewöhnliche

Künstler-Akademie

unter gefälliger Mitwirkung der hiesigen Opern- und Schauspiel-Mitglieder, sowie der Hrn. Concertmeister H. Gerstner und Capellmeister J. Mahler und der Regimentscapelle des k. k. 26. Lin.-Inf.-Reg. unter persönlicher Leitung des Hrn. Capellmeisters Czerny.

Erste Abtheilung:

1. Adolf Müller: Ouverture zu Mädchen von der Spule, vorgetragen von der k. k. Regimentscapelle.
2. v. Hölzl: Hab in der Brust ein Vögelein, Lied.
3. In den Augen liegt das Herz, Lied. } gesungen von Herrn Erl.
4. v. Mozart: Recit. und Arie aus der Oper Don Juan, gesungen von Fräulein Fischer.
5. v. Truhn: Herr Schmied, Lied für Bak. gesungen von Herrn Unger.

Zweite Abtheilung:

6. Richard v. Wagner: Erstes Finale aus der Oper Lohengrin, vorgetragen von der k. k. Regimentscapelle.

Eine Vorlesung bei der Hausmeisterin.

Posse in einem Akt nach dem Französischen von Alexander Bergen. — (Regie: Herr Linori.)

Personen:

Dritte Abtheilung:

7. Ch. v. Gounod: Meditation über Sebastian Bach's erstes Präludium, vorgetragen von der k. k. Regimentscapelle.
8. H. Vieuxtemps: Ballade und Polonaise, für Violin und Clavierbegleitung, vorgetragen von den Herren H. Gerstner und G. Mahler.
9. v. Suppé: Vergissmeinnicht, Lied, gesungen von Herrn Amenth.
10. v. Meyerbeer: Bettler-Arie aus der Oper der Prosel, gesungen von Fräulein Bruck.
11. v. Mattai: Es is nicht wahr, Lied, gesungen von Herrn Luzzatto.

Zu dieser Vorstellung macht die ergebenste Einladung — Das Chorpersonale.

Preise der Plätze: Eine Loge im Parterre und 1. Range sammt Entrée 5 fl. — Eine Loge im 2. Range sammt Entrée 4 fl. — Fauteuil 80 kr. — Sperrsitz im Parterre 70 kr. — Gallerie-Sperrsitz 50 kr. — Parterre oder Logen-Entrée 50 kr. — Gallerie 20 kr. — Garnisonsbillet und für Studierende 30 kr.

Kassa-Eröffnung halb 7 Uhr. — Anfang 7 Uhr.

| Laibach | 1882 | Concerts Nos. 15–16 |

NOTES [1] The *Capriccio brillant* (duration: ca. 11 minutes) is originally scored for a standard symphony orchestra, but also appeared in different transcriptions, including one for piano and string orchestra, which no doubt was the one played at this concert.
[2] Neither handbill nor review identifies the piano accompanist of nos. 3–4. It seems most likely that is was Mahler, because in a board meeting of the Philharmonic Society on March 25, it was decided, extraordinarily, to pay Mahler 20 florins for his assistance, which was a substantial sum in those days.
[3] Replaced the announced Serenade, Op. 22, by Antonín Dvořák.
REVIEW KB[2], 162; HLG I, 85.

16. **April 2, 1882, 7 p.m.**
   LAIBACH - Landschaftliches Theater [1,000 seats]

For the Benefit of the Theater's Chorus. An Exceptional Artist's Academy.

                                    Part I
(1)	Müller	Overture to *Das Mädchen von der Spule*
(2)	Hölzl	"Hab' ich in der Brust ein Vöglein," *Lied*
(3)	Hölzl	"In den Augen liegt das Herz," *Lied*
(4)	Mozart	Recitative and Aria (unspecified) from *Don Giovanni* for Soprano with Piano Acc.
(5)	Truhn	"Herr Schmied, beschlagt mir mein Rößlein," *Lied*, Op. 66, No. 4

                                    Part II
| (6) | Wagner | Finale I (unspecified), from *Lohengrin*, arr. for Military Band |
| (7) | Bergen | *Eine Vorlesung bei der Hausmeisterin*, Farce in 1 Act |

                                    Part III
(8)	Gounod	Meditation on Bach's C-major Prelude, arr. for Military Band
(9)	Vieuxtemps	*Ballade et Polonaise de Concert*, Op. 38, for Violin & Piano •
(10)	Suppé	"Das Vergißmeinnicht," *Lied*
(11)	Meyerbeer	"Ah! Mon fils" from *Le Prophète*, with Piano Acc.[1]
(12)	Mattei	"Es ist nicht wahr" ("Non è ver'"), Op. 20, No. 1, Romance

SOLOISTS (2 & 3) F. Erl; (4) C. Fischer; (5) E. Unger; (7) actors from the theater; (9) H. Gerstner & Mahler; (10) A. Amenth; (11) L. Bruck; (12) A. Luzzato.
PIANO ACC. (items 2–5 & 10–12) Neither the handbill nor the review identifies the accompanist, but considering the concert's purpose, and the fact that the singers were soloists at the theater, Mahler appears to be the most likely candidate.
ORCHESTRA (1, 6, 8) The "Regimentscapelle des k.k. 26. Linien Infanterie Regiment," cond. *Kapellmeister* N. Czerny.
SOURCE Concert poster; see illustration on opposite page.
NOTE [1] Sung in German: "O mein Sohn."
REVIEW HLG I, 86.

> **OLMÜTZ**
> **Königliches Städtisches Theater**
> **Season 1882–1883**

From the outset of the 1882–83 season Gustav Lewy failed to obtain Mahler a new engagement. However, in the beginning of January 1883, Lewy unexpectedly received an urgent inquiry from the *Königliches Theater* in Olmütz (today Olomouc, Moravia, in the Czech Republic), which was looking for a replacement for the first conductor, who had suddenly resigned. The offer was only for the remaining months of the season, i.e. until March 18, but Mahler immediately accepted the conditions. The theater was of moderate size (1,000 seats) and with an orchestra consisting of 30 players.

During the 65 days that Mahler's stay at Olmütz lasted, he conducted ten different works, of which six were new to him. They were, in addition to works by Auber, Méhul, and Meyerbeer, also Bizet's *Carmen* and Verdi's *Un ballo in maschera.*

In other respects, during this period, Olmütz had little to offer musically. The only concerts were a performance of Beethoven's Ninth Symphony with the local *Musikverein* (Music Society) and a recital by the famous Viennese string quartet, named after the leader, Josef Hellmesberger, director at the Vienna Music Conservatory.

17. February 24, 1883, 8:30 p.m.
OLMÜTZ - Deutsches Casino [300 seats]

Entertainment in the Olmütz "Damen-Verein" [1]

(extracts of program)

(1)	Schubert	Two *Lieder* (unspecified)
(2)	Schumann	"Die beiden Grenadiere," *Lied*, Op. 49, No. 1
(3)	Verdi	"È strano! ... Sempre libera," from *La traviata* [2]

SOLOISTS (1) M. Mayer; (2) H. Fuchs; (3) L. Milles; acc. at the piano by Mahler.
SOURCE Program reconstructed from the review in the Olmütz newspaper *Mährischer Tageblatt*.
NOTES [1] The "Ladies' Society," a charitable organization, held a number of meetings during the winter season. Various artists, actors, and musicians were requested to entertain in order to attract an audience.
[2] Sung in German: "Es ist seltsam ... Er ist es."

Musikalisch-deklamatorische
AKADEMIE

unter gefälliger Mitwirkung der Damen:

Frl. Mila Ott von Ottenfeld, Frau Warhanek, Frau Schwarz, Fr. Bělohlavek, Fr. Trampisch, Frl. Fischer,

und der Herren:

Kapellmeister Gustav Mahler, Mikon, Vorreiter und Bruckmüller.

Programm:

1. Beethoven. „Sonate", (Kreutzer gewidmet), Frl. Mila v. Ott, Hr. Gust. Mahler.
2. Haslinger. „Ein schöner Tod." Lied Hr. Mikon.
3. Wienawski. „Faust-Fantasie." Frl. Mila v Ott.
4. a) Chopin — Impromptu) Hr. Mahler.
   b) Chopin — Ballade)
5. Deklamation. „Das begrabene Lied" Gedicht v. Rud. Baumbach. Hr. Vorreiter.

Ein Kaffeekränzchen.

Musikalischer Schwank in 1 Akt von Kunze.

PERSONEN:

Frau Landstrassenbauinspektor Schmid — Fr. Trampisch
Frau Landgerichtsreferendarius Müller — Fr. Schwarz
Frau Colonialhandlungsbesitzer Fischer — Fr. Bělohlavek
Frau Vicebürgermeister Lehmann — Frl. Mila Ott
Frl. Lina Mayer — Fr. Warhanek
Dienstmädchen im Hause Schmid — Frl. Fischer

Zeit 1840.

Den Conzertflügel hat Herr Bělohlavek bereitwilligst zur Verfügung gestellt

PART IV
ON THE ROAD: YEARS OF MATURING
VIENNA – KASSEL – PRAGUE (I) – LEIPZIG – PRAGUE (II)
1883–1888

After leaving Olmütz rather abruptly on March 18, 1883 (a press notice indicates that he had promised to assist in a charity concert the following day), Mahler returned to Vienna, where Gustav Lewy had obtained employment for him as chorus coach to an Italian opera *Stagione,* visiting the Carl-Theater, from March 30 until May 4.

Shortly afterward, Lewy received an inquiry from the Royal Theater in Kassel, which advertised for a new *Musik und Chordirector* (choirmaster). This was a subordinate post, but it was in Germany, and at a more prestigious theater than any of Mahler's previous engagements. Perhaps Mahler realized that he needed more fundamental conducting training and he may well have hoped for quick advancement. He immediately considered the inquiry. However, contrary to Mahler's earlier experience, the authorities in Kassel, in particular the theater's Intendant, Adolf von und zu Gilsa, was not content with written assurances of the applicant's musical proficiency, but demanded a personal interview as well as tangible proof of his ability. Therefore, at the end of May, Mahler had to go through a week's trial which he passed successfully.

The initial outcome was a 3 year contract (beginning on October 1, 1883 through June 30, 1886). Later, it was arranged at Mahler's request that he begin as early as the start of the new season, August 1883.

If Mahler had hoped that Lewy would find him a temporary post for the summer he was disappointed. Instead, he paid his first visit to the Bayreuth Festival during July — and was duly overwhelmed by a performance of Wagner's *Parsifal.*

Before leaving Iglau for Kassel, Mahler assisted in a charity concert, which was not only to be his last public appearance in his hometown, but also his last as a solo pianist.

18. **August 11, 1883, 7:30 p.m.**
IGLAU - Stadttheater [1,350 seats]

For the Benefit of the Austrian Branch of the Red Cross [1]

(1)	Beethoven	Violin Sonata No. 9, A major, Op. 47, "Kreutzer" •
(2)	Haslinger	"Ein schöner Tod," *Lied* •
(3)	Wieniawski	Fantaisie Brillante on motifs from Gounod's opera *Faust*, Op. 20, for Violin & Piano •
(4)	Chopin	Impromptu, for Piano • [2]
(5)	Chopin	Polonaise No. 6, A-flat major, Op. 53, for Piano • [3]
(6)	Baumbach	*Das begrabene Lied*, Poem
		- Intermission -
(7)	Kuntze	"Ein Kaffeekränzchen," Op. 231, with Piano Acc. • [4]

SOLOISTS (1 & 3) M. von Ott, acc. by Mahler; (2) L. Mikon, acc. by Mahler (?); (4 & 5) Mahler; (6) I. Vorreiter [5]; (7) Mrs. Trampisch, Mrs. Schwarz, Mrs. Bělohlávek, Mrs. Warhanek and Miss Fischer (all dilettantes, and members of the Iglau community), and finally M. von Ott, acc. at the piano by Mahler.
One handbill announces Hans Bruckmüller [6] as a performer. However, according to his own account he only turned pages for Mahler in items nos. 1 and 7.
SOURCE Two different handbills; see illustrations on opposite and following pages.

EINLADUNG

zu der **Samstag den 11. August**

im

hiesigen Stadt-Theater

stattfindenden

musikalisch-deklamatorischen

AKADEMIE,

unter gefälliger Mitwirkung der

Violin-Virtuosin Frl. Mila Ott, Edle v. Ottenfeld und des Clavier-Virtuosen Herrn Kapellmeister G. Mahler.

PROGRAMM:

1. Beethoven. Sonate. (Kreutzer gewidmet.) Vorgetragen von Frl. Mila von Ott und Herrn Gustav Mahler.
2. „Ein schöner Tod." Lied für eine Bassstimme von C. Haslinger. Vorgetragen vom Hrn. Mikorn.
3. Wienawski. „Faust-Fantasie" Vorgetragen vom Frl. Mila von Ott.
4. a) Impromptu von Chopin, b) Polonaise grande von Chopin. Vorgetragen vom Hrn. Gustav Mahler.
5. Deklamation.
6. „Kaffeekränzchen". Operette in 1 Akt von Kuntze. Personen: Fr. Landstrassen-baninspektor Schmidt. Fr. Landgerichtsreferendarius Müller. Fr. Colonial-Handlungsbesitzerin Fischer. Fr. Vice-Bürgermeister Lehmann und Fräulein Lina Mayer.

Der Reinertrag wird zum Theile den auf Ischia durch Erdbeben Verunglückten und der österr. Gesellschaft vom „rothen Kreuze" gewidmet.

Mit Rücksicht auf den wohlthätigen Zweck ladet zu zahlreichem Besuch ein

der Vereinsausschuss
des Zweig-Vereines Iglau des patr. Frauen-Hilfsvereines für Mähren.

PREISE DER PLÄTZE:

Loge 4 fl., Sitz in der Fremdenloge 1 fl., Galleriesitz 80 kr. Sperrsitz 60 kr., Parterre 30 kr., I. Gallerie 40 kr., II. Gallerie 20 kr.
Vormerkungen für Logen und Sitzplätze werden aus Gefälligkeit bei Herrn **Körber**, (Hauptplatz) bis Freitag den 10. August Abends übernommen.

Cassa-Eröffnung 6 Uhr.   Anfang 7½ Uhr.

| Iglau | 1883 | Concert No. 18 |

NOTES [1] Proceeds from the concert benefited the Austrian branch of the Red Cross and victims of the recent earthquake on the Italian island of Ischia (Juy 28, 1883).

[2] The precise selection cannot be deduced from the surviving documents. Chopin composed four Impromptus: Opp. 29, 36, 51, and 66.

[3] The handbill announces a "Ballade" by Chopin, which according to the review, was replaced by the Polonaise.

[4] In his memoirs, Hans Bruckmüller (see note 5 below) calls "Ein Kaffeekränzchen" ("The Coffee Party") a *Singspiel,* i.e. a play with singing, whereas the handbills announce it as a *Musikalischer Schwank* ("a musical farce") in one act or as an operatta. However, the work appears originally to have been a quintet for soprano, contralto (with an optional tenor), and three baritones, with piano accompaniment, Kuntze's Op. 231. In this form it was published by the music publishing house C.F. Leuckart of Leipzig. For the present occasion it was apparently dramatized for the stage and set in 1840.

As stated in both handbills, violin virtuoso Mila von Ott (Camilla Ottilie, Edle von Ottenfeld, born 1858 at Dubrovnik/Ragusa, Croatia) also assisted in the *Schwank/Singspiel/operetta* as singer-actress. In July 1875 she graduated from the Vienna Conservatory with the "Silver Medal," two months before Mahler enrolled. During the following years she appeared in several recitals in Vienna and elsewhere, including the present one in Iglau. It was probably at that time that she and Mahler first met. The relationship lasted for many years, though only from a distance (see Mahler's only known letter to her, dating from April 25, 1897, GMB 238/MSL 226). Her musical career stopped when she married.

[5] Ignaz Vorreiter was a bookbinder by profession, but he was also a respected amateur actor, and from 1875 to 1887 he was also member of the Iglau Town Council.

[6] Born October 30, 1862, in Iglau, where his father, Ernst Bruckmüller, ran a hotel. In his youth Hans took lessons from local musicians in piano, organ, cello, and voice. Later, as a law student in Vienna, he became a pupil of Anton Bruckner (organ & harmony), and of Franz Suppé (orchestration & composition). After earning a doctoral degree, he settled in Brünn (Brno), where in time he became director of an insurance office. In his spare time Hans Bruckmüller continued his musical activities on an amateur basis, composing songs, piano pieces, ballets and farces etc., some of which were performed and even published. In December 1932 he published a small article on Mahler, "Aus Gustav Mahlers Jugendzeit," mainly concerning the concert in question ("Igel-Land," a supplement of the *Mährischer Grenzbote*. An extract of this is reprinted in N. Lebrecht's book, *Mahler Remembered*, London, 1987, pp. 32–33). Bruckmüller's last meeting with Mahler apparently took place in connection with the latter's concert in Brünn, on November 11, 1906 (concert no. 188).

REVIEW HLG I, 107.

> **KASSEL (I)**
> **Königliche Schauspiele**
> **Season 1883–1884**

Soon after his arrival, Mahler had to recognize the fact that his new post was a subordinate one, offering him few artistic challenges and absolutely no prospect of an early promotion. His main tasks were to rehearse the chorus, conduct operettas, farces, and incidental music. Beyond that, he was also assigned a number of operas, which were carefully defined by his superiors. His situation was discouraging. Moreover, it seems that Mahler had difficulties in coping with the iron Prussian discipline prevailing the theater, which, governed by numerous strict rules and paragraphs, were relentlessly carried out to the letter. (Later however, soon after leaving Kassel permanently, in a letter to von Gilsa, Mahler admitted with appreciation that he had learned from this hard school.)

Conflicts with his superiors, especially with Wilhelm Treiber, the principal *Kapellmeister,* whom Mahler disliked, were inevitable and broke out soon. An unrequited love for soprano Johanne Richter (born in Berlin, August 18, 1859), a soloist at the theater, only added insult to injury; on the other hand, it led to the composition of the song cycle *Lieder eines fahrenden Gesellen,* begun at the end of 1884, and later revised and orchestrated.

The theater's strict rules prevented Mahler from taking an active part in Kassel's musical life outside its premises, except for one occasion (concert no. 21). However, he received permission to take charge of the choral society at the nearby town of Münden, or Hannoversch-Münden (see concert no. 23).

Each season the Royal Orchestra organized six philharmonic concerts, all conducted by Wilhelm Treiber, and assisted by several outstanding artists, including pianist Hans von Bülow, who also visited Kassel in his capacity as conductor of the famous Meiningen Court Orchestra (January 24 & 25, 1884). Bülow's way of conducting was no doubt Mahler's greatest artistic experience during his years in Kassel. The impression remained indelibly stamped on his memory, and he took Bülow's art for a model.

However, in his usual brusque way, the famous pianist-conductor turned down Mahler's urgent and passionate petition to take him in as an apprentice; Bülow was even so tactless as to hand Mahler's letter over to his superior.

All performances at the Theater are with the Royal Orchestra

19. **January 19, 1884, 7 p.m.**
KASSEL - Das Königliche Theater [1,177 seats]

    Schumann   *Julius Caesar*, Overture, Op. 128 • [1]

[followed by a complete performance of Shakespeare's play of the same name]

SOURCE Newspaper advertisement.
NOTE [1] It has not been proved that Mahler was in charge of this performance. However, with reference to Mahler's *Dienst-Instruction* ["Employment Instruction"], articles 3 & 16, it can reasonably be concluded that he was. His conducting of Goldmark's overture *Sakuntala* (concert no. 24), which is confirmed by a review, seems to support this conclusion (K. Martner, "Mahler's Activities in Kassel from a New Perspective," in *News about Mahler Research*, No. 21, Vienna, 1989).

Zum Besten des Krankenpflege-Instituts „Kaiserin Augusta-Stiftung"
des vaterländischen Frauenvereins:

Matinée

Sonntag den 23. März, Vormittags 11 Uhr,

im Hanusch'schen Saal,

unter gefälliger Mitwirkung der Königl. Schauspielerin, Frau **Lewinsky-Precheisen**, der Königl. Sängerin, Fräulein **J. Sieber**, der Pianistin, Fräulein **Hofmann**, des Königl. Musikdirectors, Herrn **Mahler**, des Herrn **Th. Wagner**, des Königl. Kammermusikers, Herrn **Dilcher**, sowie der Schülerinnen der Gesangsschule der Frau **N. Zottmayr**.

PROGRAMM.

1. **Wildenbruch.** Prolog, gesprochen von Frau Lewinsky.
2. **Beethoven.** Sonate C-moll, op. 30, für Pianoforte und Violine . . Herren Mahler u. Dilcher.
3. **Mozart.** Arie aus »Figaro's Hochzeit« (»Neue Freuden, neue Schmerzen«) . . . . Frl. Sieber.
4. a) **M. Calm.** »Des Seemann's Braut«,
   b) **A. v. Droste-Hülshoff.** »Die junge Mutter«,
   c) **R. Hamerling.** »Liebe im Schnee«,
   Declamation . . . . Frau Lewinsky.
5. **Mendelssohn.** Arie aus »Paulus« (»Gott sei mir gnädig«)
   Herr Th. Wagner.
6. **Spohr.** Concert Nr. 10, für Violine . Herr Dilcher.
7. a) **Schubert.** »Liebesbotschaft«, } Frl. Sieber.
   b) **Brahms.** »Liebestreu«,
8. a) **Schulz-Delitz.** »Ave Maria«, } Frauenchöre,
   b) **Urban.** »Frühlingslied«,
   gesungen von Schülerinnen der Frau N. Zottmayr.

Billets zu nummerirten Plätzen à 2 Mk., zu unnummerirten à 1 Mk. sind in den Kunst- und Musikalienhandlungen der Herren **Paul Voigt**, **Otto Kuprion**, vormals **Augustin** und **Ernst Hühn** und an der Kasse zu haben.

Das Concert-Pianino ist aus der Fabrik des Herrn **Scheel**, Hoflieferanten Sr. Kaiserl. u. Königl. Hoheit des Kronprinzen.

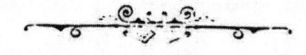

20. March 11, 1884, 7 p.m.
KASSEL - Das Königliche Theater [1,177 seats]

    Schumann   *Die Braut von Messina*, Overture, Op. 100 ● [1]

[followed by a complete performance of Schiller's play by the same name]

SOURCE Newspaper advertisement.
[1] See note to concert no. 19.

21. March 23, 1884, 11 a.m.
KASSEL - Hanusch-Saal [1,000 seats]

For the Benefit of the Empress Auguste Foundation, the Institute of the Patriotic Woman's Society

(1)	Wildenbruch	A spoken prologue
(2)	Beethoven	Violin Sonata No. 7, C minor, Op. 30, No. 2 ●
(3)	Mozart	"Non so più cosa son," from *Le nozze di Figaro* [1]
(4)	Calm	"Des Seeman's Braut," Poem
(5)	Droste-Hülshoff	"Die junge Mutter," Poem
(6)	Hamerling	"Liebe im Schnee," Poem
(7)	Mendelssohn	"Gott sei mir gnädig," from *Paulus,* Oratorio, Op. 36
(8)	Spohr	Violin Concerto No. 10, A minor, Op. 62, with Piano Acc. ●
(9)	Schubert	"Liebesbotschaft," *Lied*, D 957, No. 1
(10)	Brahms	"Liebestreu," *Lied*, Op. 3, No. 1
(11)	Schulz-Delitz	"Ave Maria," for Women's Chorus
(12)	Urban	"Frühlingslied," for Women's Chorus

SOLOISTS (1, 4–6) O. Lewinsky-Precheisen; (2 & 8) H. Dilcher & Mahler; (3, 9–10) J. Sieber; (7) Th. Wagner; (11–12) Children from Mrs. Zottmann's Singing School.
PIANO ACC. Neither preview nor handbill mentions the accompanist of items 3 and 7–10, and the concert was apparently not reviewed. Therefore it remains a qualified guess that it was Mahler. In this connection it is perhaps of significance that both singers, Sieber and Wagner, were soloists at the Royal Theater. It is true that another pianist assisted, a Miss Hofmann; however, as a teacher at Mrs. Zottmann's Singing School, she was probably only responsible for accompanying the two final choruses.
SOURCE Handbill; see illustration on opposite page.
NOTE [1] Sung in German: "Neue Freuden, neue Schmerzen."

Freitag, den 13. Februar 1885,
im Saale **Hôtel Nickel,**
Abends 7 Uhr.

Concert des Chorvereins

unter gefl. Mitwirkung der Königl. Opernsängerin Fräulein **Richter** und der Königl. Opernsänger Herren **Greeff** und **Simon,** sowie zahlreicher Mitglieder der Königl. Capelle und unter Leitung des Königl. Musikdirectors Herrn **Mahler,** sämmtlich aus **Cassel.**

Die Jahreszeiten.

Cantate in 4 Theilen für Soli, Chor und Orchester nach Thomsons „Seasons", comp. von Jos. Haydn im Jahre 1802.

1. Theil: Der Frühling.
2. „ Der Sommer.
3. „ Der Herbst.
4. „ Der Winter.

Eintrittskarten à ℳ 1,25 und Schülerbillets à 50 ₰, (letztere jedoch nur im Vorverkauf), sowie Textbücher sind in der Buchhandlung des Herrn **Hans Augustin,** und an der Abendcasse zu haben. Das Eintrittsgeld an der Abendcasse ist ℳ 1,50 pro Person.

> **KASSEL (II)**
> Königliche Schauspiele
> Season 1884–1885

22. **October 18, 1884, 7 p.m.**
    KASSEL - Das Königliche Theater [1,177 seats]

        Mozart   *Maurerische Trauermusik,* K. 477 • [1]

    SOURCE Newspaper advertisement.
    NOTE [1] It cannot be established definitely that Mahler conducted this performance, see note to concert no. 19. The piece functioned as an *entr' act* before the 2nd act of Heinrich Kleist's play *Friedrich, Prinz von Homburg.* Repeat performances of the play, including Mozart's composition, were given on October 28 & November 15, 1884, and for the last time on January 2, 1885.

23. **February 13, 1885, Soirée.**
    MÜNDEN - Festsaal des Hotel Nickel (or Zur Krone) [500 seats] [1]

        Haydn   *Die Jahreszeiten,* Oratorio •

    SOLOISTS J. Richter (*Hanne*), H. Simon [2] (*Lukas*), P. Greeff (*Simon*).
    ORCHESTRA Members of the Royal Theater in Kassel.
    CHORUS "Der Chorverein zu Münden"
    SOURCE An advertisement in the *Mündensche Nachrichten,* February 12, 1885, and reviews in the same newspaper (February 19) and the Kassel newspaper *Hessische Morgenzeitung* (February 15); see illustration on opposite page.
    NOTES [1] In October 1884, Mahler was appointed conductor of an amateur chorus (about 100 members) in the nearby town of Münden. According to the review in the newspaper *Mündensche Nachrichten* the concert was "überfüllt" (packed). The same newspaper published a "review" in the form of a poem in 8 verses which had first been presented as a toast during the banquet following the concert.
    [2] The tenor Hugo Simon, a regular chorus member at the Royal Theater in Kassel, replaced the scheduled but indisposed Fritz Heuckeshoven, a soloist at the theater. Hugo Simon and his wife, Lina, later joined Mahler as members of the Hamburg *Stadttheater.*

24. **February 19, 1885, 7 p.m.**
    KASSEL - Das Königliche Theater [1,177 seats]

        Goldmark   *Sakuntala,* Concert Overture, Op. 13 •

    [followed by a complete performance of Grillparzer's play *Der Traum ein Leben*] [1]

    SOURCE The review in the *Casseler Allgemeine Zeitung,* February 21, 1885.
    NOTE [1] The play was repeated twice, on February 26, and March 11, 1885, but it is impossible to prove whether Goldmark's *Overture* was also performed, as repeat performances of plays were almost never reviewed.

25. June 29, 1885, 6 p.m. [1]
KASSEL - Die "Musik Festhalle" [2,500 seats] [2]

First Concert at the First Great Music Festival in Kassel [3]

      Mendelssohn   *Paulus,* Oratorio, Op. 36 •

SOLOISTS R. Papier-Paumgartner [4], H. Gudehus, P. Bulß.
ORCHESTRA An *ad hoc* orchestra consisting of players from the *Hofkapellen* [Royal Orchestras] from Weimar, Meiningen, and Braunschweig, as well as the band of the 83rd Infantry Regiment in Kassel (cond. A. Müller), a total of 80 players.
CHORUS An *ad hoc* chorus (430 singers) made up of the Casseler Oratorien Verein (cond. A. Brede, 217 members), the Mündener Chorverein (cond. Mahler, 97 members), the *Früh'scher Gesang-Verein* from Nordhausen (cond. A. Früh, 31 members), and the Marburg Akademischer Gesang-Verein (cond. O. Freiberg, 85 members).
SOURCE Handbill.
NOTES [1] The general rehearsal took place at 9 a.m. the same day.
[2] In fact, a military drill hall; it was rebuilt and electric lights were installed for the event, which was an extraordinary novelty in those days.
[3] The arrangement of the Festival (June 29–July 1) was a joint enterprise between the City Council of Kassel and the Society of Tradesmen, with the primary purpose of attracting more tourists, and also an attempt to compete with the annual "Niederrheinische Musikfeste" (Lower-Rhine Music Festivals) at Düsseldorf.
A Festival Committee was set up at the end of February 1885, and at its inaugural meeting, on March 1, Mahler was appointed "musical director." This caused quite a stir and met with some opposition, especially from anti-Semitic circles. It was pointed out that *Kapellmeister* Treiber, Mahler's superior, had directed a successful performance of *Paulus* with almost the same forces in July 1883, so it would be natural for him again to be in charge. Intendant von Gilsa of the Royal Theater, who had been named honorary President of the Festival Committee at its inaugural meeting, voiced this opinion and tried to persuade Mahler to resign. Whether he offered Mahler some form of compensation is not known, but the young conductor was adamant. Thereafter von Gilsa did everything to sabotage the Festival, first by withdrawing as president of the Committee, then by preventing the Festival from taking place at the Royal Theater, and, finally, by refusing to let the Royal Orchestra assist at the concerts. Considering the precarious situation, one can only admire the Festival Committee for its stanch support of Mahler.
Mahler himself gives cause for a puzzle regarding the program. In a letter from March 26, 1885, to Prof. Julius Epstein in Vienna, Mahler proudly claims that Beethoven's Ninth Symphony is included in his Festival conducting schedule (GMB 34/MSL 31). This is rather strange in that none of the numerous newspaper articles on the Festival at any point, either before or after that date, refer to a performance of Beethoven's symphony. One wonders whether Mahler tried (and kept trying) to outmaneuver Mendelssohn in favor of Beethoven. He would no doubt have preferred to conduct the Ninth which would have brought him considerably more honor and prestige. (He finally got that opportunity only a year later, see concert no. 28).

[4] Soprano Marie Langsdorf became indisposed in the last minute, and her minor part was sung by Rosa Papier-Paumgartner.

REVIEW HLG I, 128-129; H. J. Schaefer, *Gustav Mahler in Kassel* (Kassel 1982, pp. 41–43), and 2nd ed., *Gustav Mahler. Jahre der Entscheidung in Kassel 1883–1885* (Kassel, 1990, pp. 66–69).

* * *

Exit Kassel

Mahler had already plainly revealed his strong desire and inevitable decision to leave Kassel at the expiration of his contract in June 1886 by having his subsequent appointment with the Leipzig *Stadttheater* announced in the Kassel newspapers 18 months in advance (in January 1885).

We are not certain how Mahler managed to get appointed at Leipzig, but we can assume that he had applied for the post himself. It may be relevant that several singers from Kassel had appeared as guests at the Leipzig Opera during the preceding season. It is also worth mentioning that the actress-singer Amelie Heusner, a member of the Kassel Theater since August 1884, was engaged to Arthur Nikisch, principal *Kapellmeister* at Leipzig (they married in July 1885).

Mahler's desperate state of mind during the early months of 1885 is apparent in his request, made in early April, to be released prematurely from his contract by the close of the season. This was not only an unusual step, but also an ill-considered one, since he faced the prospect of a year's unemployment. Only after repeated requests did the Kassel director realize the pointlessness in holding on to a reluctant collaborator, and finally recommended his release to the "headquarters" in Berlin, which complied with Mahler's wishes and annulled his contract by April 27, 1885.

Mahler's appointment in Prague was announced on June 7, in the Kassel newspapers, only three weeks after Angelo Neumann had been appointed new director of the Prague Theater.

PRAGUE
Königlich Deutsches Landestheater
Season 1885–1886

Mahler's luck changed for the better in the beginning of June 1885. Angelo Neumann, the recently appointed director of the German Royal Theater, brought his long-standing friend and collaborator, the famous Wagner-conductor Anton Seidl to Prague. Seidl was only available in August, as he could not get released from his contract with the Bremen *Stadttheater*, which opened its new season on September 1, 1885. (Seidl eventually broke his contract and moved to New York).

It was not easy to find a competent, unemployed conductor at that time of year. Neumann must have recalled Mahler, who had applied to him in vain for a job about six months earlier, when Neumann was still director of the Bremen *Stadttheater*. Neumann, presumably lacking alternatives, gambled and gave young Mahler a chance. It paid off. Mahler fully redeemed his proud promises, and lived up to Neumann's best hopes. In a single season Mahler not only revealed himself to be a conductor to reckon with, but he also regained his confidence and self-respect.

In those years Prague did not yet have a permanent symphony orchestra. Occasional orchestral concerts were scheduled between other performances arranged by the German Theater (concerts nos. 27 & 28).

26. **October 10, 1885, 7:30 p.m.**
PRAGUE - Grand Hotel's "Wintergarten" [1,800 seats] [1]

For the Benefit of the Journalist Section of the "Concordia Society" [2]

(1)	Litolff	Overture to *Maximilian Robespierre*, Op. 55
(2)	Rubinstein	"Wanderers Nachtlied," Duet, Op. 48
	Brahms	"Die Boten der Liebe," Duet, Op. 61, No. 4
	Mendelssohn	"Gruß" & "Herbstlied," Duets, Op. 63, Nos. 3–4
(3)	Tosti	"Chanson d'amour," *Lied*
	Eckert	"Schweizer Echo-Lied," *Lied*, Op. 21
	Meyer-Helmund	"Der Schwur," *Lied*, Op. 8, No. 4 [encore]
(4)	Esser	"Grüner Frühling," *Lied*
	Hinrichs	"Die Prinzessin," *Lied*, Op. 1, No. 3
	Schumann	"Er ist's," *Lied*, Op. 79, No. 24 [encore]
(5)	Wallnöfer	"Dort unter'm Lindenbaum," *Lied*, Op. 3, No. 1
	Wallnöfer	"Woher die Liebe," *Lied*, Op. 24, No. 2
	Rubinstein	"Es blinkt der Tau," *Lied*, Op. 72, No. 1
	Gounod	"Au Printemps" ("Frühlingslied"), *Lied*
(6)	Schumann	"Spanisches Liederspiel," Op. 74 (excerpts) • [3]
		- Intermission -
(7)	Strauß	"Deutsche Grüsse," Waltz, Op. 101
	Nessler	Fantasy on Motives from *Der Trompeter von Säckingen*
	Westmeyer	*Das Engellied*, arr. for Military Band
	Schubert	Incidental Music from *Rosamunde*, Op. 26, D 797

SOLOISTS (2) M. Rochelle & L. Hilgermann; (3) B. Frank; (4) S. Le Pirk; (5) A. Wallnöfer; (6) M. Rochelle, L. Hilgermann, A. Wallnöfer, F. Ehrl.
PIANO ACC. (2–5) L. Slansky; (6) Mahler.
ORCHESTRA (1 & 7) The band of the 102nd Infantry Regiment's, cond. F. Lehár, Sr.
SOURCE Program reconstructed from previews in the newspapers *Bohemia* and *Prager Tagblatt*, from October 8, and reviews in both from October 13.

Königl. deutsches Landestheater.

Abonnement aufgehoben.

RICHARD WAGNER-FEIER I.

☞ Samstag den 13. Februar 1886. ☜

(Todestag.)

Große Musik-Aufführung.

Orchester-Aufstellung auf der Bühne.

Das Orchester ist auf 85 Mann verstärkt durch die Mitwirkung hervorragender Künstler, Kunstfreunde und Schüler des Conservatoriums.

I. Abtheilung.

1. **Prolog** zum „13. Februar" von Eduard Pietzcker, gesprochen von Johanna Buska.
2. **Duett** „Götterdämmerung" (Brünnhilde und Siegfried) . . Richard Wagner. Brünnhilde — Marie Rochelle. Siegfried — Adolf Wallnöfer. Das Orchester des königl. deutschen Landestheaters. Dirigent: Ludwig Slansky.
3. **Verwandlungsmusik**, große Chor- und Schlußscene des 1. Actes „Parsifal" . . . . Richard Wagner. Chorpart: Deutscher Männergesangverein. Gesangverein Sct. Veit. Chordirigent: Musikdirector Friedrich Heßler. Das Orchester des königl. deutschen Landes-Theaters. Dirigent: Gustav Mahler.

II. Abtheilung.

Neunte Symphonie

für Soli, Chor u. großes Orchester Ludwig van Beethoven.

Chorpart: Deutscher Männergesangverein.
Gesangverein Sct. Veit.

Chordirigent: Musikdirector Friedrich Heßler.

Das Orchester des königl. deutschen Landes-Theaters.

Dirigent: Dr. Carl Muck.

Die Soli gesungen von Betty Frank, Laura Hilgermann, Adolf Wallnöfer, Johannes Elmblad.

Der Chor besteht aus 200 Mitwirkenden (100 Damen und 100 Herren).

Zum Benefice-Antheil des Orchesters des königl. deutschen Landestheaters.

Zwischen der ersten und zweiten Abtheilung findet eine längere Pause statt.

Anfang um 7 Uhr. Ende um halb 10 Uhr.

NOTES The concert was advertised as a "Bierkonzert;" the audience was seated and served refreshments at small tables, which reduced the hall's seating capacity by 500. The original program underwent some changes owing to the indisposition of soprano Katharina Rosen and bass Joseph Beck. The former was replaced by Betty Frank.
[1] Today the "Wintergarten" is the breakfast room of a student hostel, situated at 38, Opletalova.
[2] The "Concordia Verein," the German-Austrian Society of Authors and Writers.
[3] A collection of ten *Lieder*, duets, and quartets with piano accompaniment. According to the reviews, three titles, nos. 4, 6, and 10, were omitted. This was the first performance in Prague. The work was repeated at a concert at the Royal Theater on December 8, 1885, with the same singers. Mahler had promised again to assist, but for unknown reasons, and at short notice, he turned over the piano accompaniment to Friedrich Rehbock, the theater's chorus director.

27. February 13, 1886, 7 p.m.
PRAGUE - Königlich Deutsches Landestheater [1,800 seats]

Partly in Commemoration of the Third Anniversary of Richard Wagner's Death and partly for the benefit of the Theater Orchestra

(1)	Pietzchar	"Zum 13 Februar," Spoken Prologue
(2)	Wagner	"Zu neuen Thaten," Duet, from *Götterdämmerung*
(3)	Wagner	Transformation Music & Grail Scene, from *Parsifal*
		- Intermission -
(4)	Beethoven	Symphony No. 9, D minor, Op. 125

SOLOISTS (1) J. Buska; (2) M. Rochelle & A. Wallnöfer; (4) B. Frank, L. Hilgermann, A. Wallnöfer, J. Elmblad.
CONDUCTORS (2) L. Slansky; (3) Mahler; (4) K. Muck[1]
ORCHESTRA Orchestra of the Royal Theater, augmented with "well-known artists, amateur musicians, and students from the Conservatory," a total of 85 players.
CHORUS (3 & 4) "Deutscher Männergesangverein" and "Gesangverein Sanct Veit," a total of 200 singers, cond. F. Hessler. The review in *Bohemia* (February 16) named seven soloists from the Theater who spontaneously joined the chorus.
SOURCE Newspaper advertisement; see illustration on opposite page.
NOTE [1] Director Neumann engaged Karl Muck, then *Kapellmeister* at Graz, to replace Mahler from the beginning of the following season. The concert's success called for a second hearing (see below) which Muck was prevented from conducting. During the two weeks prior to Muck's arrival (on February 10), Mahler had rehearsed the orchestra in Beethoven's Ninth daily.
REVIEW HLG I, 140.

Königl. Deutsches Landestheater.

Sonntag, den 21. Februar 1886
um 12 Uhr Mittags

zum Besten des deutschen Schulpfennig-Vereines.

Grosse Musik-Aufführung.

Orchester-Aufstellung auf der Bühne.

Das Orchester ist auf **85 Mann** verstärkt durch die Mitwirkung hervorragender Künstler, Kunst-Freunde und Schüler des Conservatoriums.

I. Abtheilung.

1. Duett: Götterdämmerung
(Brünnhilde und Siegfried)
Richard Wagner.

Brünnhilde – Marie Rochelle.   Siegfried – Adolf Wallnöfer.
Das Orchester des königl. deutschen Landestheaters.   Dirigent: LUDWIG SLANSKY.

2. Verwandlungsmusik, grosse Chor- und Schlussscene des I. Actes

Parsifal
Richard Wagner.

Chorpart: Deutscher Männer-Gesangverein, Gesangverein Sct. Veit.
Chordirigent: Musikdirector FRIEDRICH HESSLER
Das Orchester des königl. deutschen Landestheaters.   Dirigent: GUSTAV MAHLER

II. Abtheilung.

NEUNTE SYMPHONIE
für Soli, Chor und grosses Orchester
Ludwig van Beethoven.

Chorpart: Deutscher Männergesang-Verein, Gesangverein Sct. Veit.
Chordirigent: Musikdirector FRIEDRICH HESSLER.
Das Orchester des königl. deutschen Landestheaters.   Dirigent: Gustav Mahler.
Die Soli gesungen von Betty Frank, Laura Hilgermann, Adolf Wallnöfer, Johannes Elmblad.

Der Chor besteht aus 200 Mitwirkenden (100 Damen und 100 Herren.)

Zwischen der 1. und 2. Abtheilung findet eine längere Pause statt.

Anfang 12 Uhr.   Ende halb 3 Uhr.

Preise der Plätze

Königl. Deutsches Landestheater.

Montag, den 22. Februar 1886.   59. Abonnements-Vorstellung (3. Serie weiss.)

FAUST und MARGARETHE.

Romantische Oper in 4 Aufzügen von J. Barbier und M. Carré. Musik von Ch. Gounod.

28. **February 21, 1886, 12 a.m.**
PRAGUE - Königlich Deutsches Landestheater [1,800 seats]

For the Benefit of the German "Schulpfennig-Verein"

- Above program repeated -

SOLOISTS, ORCHESTRA AND CHORUSES: the same forces as above concert.
CONDUCTORS (1) L. Slansky; (2 & 3) Mahler.
SOURCE Newspaper advertisement; see illustration on opposite page.
NOTE According to the reviews Mahler conducted both compositions from memory, which apparently was an unusual sight in those days, because on March 8, the *Prager Abendblatt*, reviewing the preceding afternoon's performance of a farce, *Posse*, notes: "Mr. [Gustav] Löwe prepared for us the most amusing of surprises with his burlesque imitation of Maler [sic], conducting an 'overture,' without a conductor's stand, without a score, and without — a baton." To set the record straight, Mahler always conducted with a baton.
REVIEW HLG I, 140-141.

29. **April 18, 1886, 12 p.m.**
PRAGUE - Grand Hotel's "Wintergarten" [1,800 seats]

In Aid of the (newly founded) Society of Needy German Law Students

(1)	Mozart	Symphony No. 40, G minor, K. 550
(2)	Meyerbeer	"Donnez, donnez, pour une pauvre âme," from *Le Prophète* [1]
	Grieg	"Ich liebe dich," *Lied*, Op. 5, No. 3 •
	Heinefetter	"Im wunderschönen Monat Mai," *Lied*, Op. 18, No. 4 •
	Schumann	"Frühlingsnacht," *Lied*, Op. 39, No. 12 •
	Rubinstein	"Gelb rollt mir zu Füßen," *Lied*, Op. 34, No. 9
(3)	Boccherini	String Quintet, E major, Op. 13, No. 5 (Minuet only), arr. for String Orchestra •
(4)	Bruckner	Symphony No. 3, D minor (Scherzo) • [2]
(5)	Winter	"Allmächtige Sonne" from *Das unterbrochene Opferfest*
	Mahler	Three *Lieder* with Piano Acc. [3]
		"Frühlingsmorgen"
		"Lied der fahrenden Gesellen" [sic] [4]
		"Hans und Grethe"
(6)	Haydn	"Und Gott sprach ... Gleich öffnet sich der Erde Schoß," from *Die Schöpfung*, Oratorio
	Schubert	"An Schwager Kronos," *Lied*, D 369 •
	Anon.	Three Swedish Folk Songs [5]
(7)	Raff	Violin Concerto No. 2, A minor, Op. 206 •
	Brahms/Joachim	Three Hungarian Dances, arr. for Violin and Piano •
(8)	Wagner	*Kaisermarsch*, B-flat major

SOLOISTS (2) M. Renard; (5) B. Frank [replacing at short notice the indisposed Katharina Rosen]; (6) J. Elmblad; (7) C. Halir.
CONDUCTOR (1, 3–4, 7a), & PIANO ACC. (2, 5–6,7b) Mahler.
ORCHESTRA The augmented orchestra of the German Royal Theater.

| Prague | 1886 | Concerts Nos. 29–30 |

SOURCE Program reconstructed from the reviews in *Bohemia*, the *Prager Zwischenacts-zeitung*, and the *Prager Tagblatt*, all from April 20, 1886. According to the latter, the "genius" Mahler conducted everything by heart "and with admirable skill."
NOTES [1] Sung in German.
[2] In December 1876, Mahler attended the world premiere of the symphony in Vienna (the 2nd version). He was commissioned to make a reduction for piano 4-hands which was published in Vienna in January 1880. In light of this major task it is surprising that Mahler never conducted the symphony in its entirety.
[3] World premieres of all three songs. According to all the reviews, "Hans und Grethe" (originally "Maitanz im Grünen," composed 1880) was encored.
[4] Probably the second song, "Ging heut' morgen übers Feld."
[5] The only title identified in the reviews is given in German, i.e. "Der Schweinehirt" (in Swedish, "Pehr svinaherde," in English, "Pehr, the Swine Shepherd"). The Swedish-born Johannes Elmblad sang these folk songs in his native language, as he did in the recital he gave with Betty Frank two weeks later, on May 5, which included another well known Swedish folksong, "Ack, Wärmeland, du sköna."
REVIEW HLG I, 143; Jitka Ludvová, *Gustav Mahler und Prag* (Prague 1996, pp. 53–54).

30. **May 7, 1886, 7 p.m.**
    PRAGUE - Deutsches Interim Theater [3,000 seats][1]

    For the Benefit of Max Löwenfeld[2]

    (1) Flotow   "So war es denn erreicht...Seid meiner Wonne,"
                              Recitative and Aria from *Alessandro Stradella*, Act 2 [3]
    (2) Loewe   "Kleiner Haushalt," *Lied*, Op. 71
    (3) Two *Lieder* with Piano acc.:
        a) Mendelssohn   "Wenn sich zwei Herzen scheiden", Op. 99, No. 5 •
        b) Suppé   "Das Vergißmeinnicht" •
    (4) Geibel   "Wie es geht," Poem
    (5) Schumann   "Ballade vom Haideknaben," Recitative with Piano Acc.,
                              Op. 122, No. 1 •
    (6) Two *Lieder* with Piano acc.:
        a) Meyer-Helmund "Der Schwur," *Lied*, Op. 8, No. 4 •
        b) Taubert   "Der Vogel im Walde," *Lied*, Op. 158 •

SOLOISTS (1) L. Hilgermann; (2 & 6) B. Frank; (3) J. Beck; (4) A. Scholz; (5) F. Bognar.
PIANO ACC. (1–3, 5–6) Mahler.
SOURCE Newspaper advertisement. The order is not necessarily correct.
NOTE [1] "The German Interim Theater," situated at the Karolinenthal, Palacky Street (today, Hudebni divadlo v Karlin), was a vaudeville (variety) theater.
[2] The actor Max Löwenfeld was a regular member of the German Royal Theater. This concert was held in commemoration of his 100th stage appearance. The recital formed the first part of the evening's program; the second part consisted of three one-act plays and farces. Mr. Löwenfeld generously donated the profits of the evening (150 guilders) to the German Theater Society in Prague.
[3] According to a review in the *Prager Tagblatt* from May 9, 1886, Laura Hilgermann sang the aria in Italian although the opera was originally composed in German.

LEIPZIG (I)
Die Vereinigte Stadttheater
Seasons 1886–1888

By July 15, 1886, Mahler had to leave Prague to fulfill his six-year contract with the Leipzig *Stadttheater,* dating from January 1885.

In fact, he made the move somewhat reluctantly. He had done well in Prague and feared that he might be outshone in Leipzig by the principal conductor there, Arthur Nikisch, five years his senior and already a prominent figure. Indeed, as early as November 1885 Mahler had sought to be released from his Leipzig contract, but had been turned down by the theater's director, Max Staegemann.

As it turned out, fairly soon Mahler had more work in Leipzig—and chances to shine—than he had bargained for. Nikisch became ill in February 1887 and was absent for almost three months. During that time Mahler conducted nearly every night and acquitted himself with success.

The *Stadttheater's* orchestra was also obliged to play at the famous *Gewandhaus* Concerts (22 concerts each season), although neither the theater's director nor its conductors had any influence on the works performed. The composer-conductor Carl Reinecke (1824-1910) had been in charge of the orchestra since 1860 and conducted all the concerts, though composers were occasionally invited to perform their own works. During Mahler's two Leipzig seasons, the most prominent of these guest conductors were Max Bruch, Anton Rubinstein, Pyotr Ilyich Tchaikovsky, and a 23-year-old Richard Strauss.

The latter appeared on October 13, 1887, conducting his Second Symphony in F minor. There could well be a connection between this event and the fact that Mahler, who met Strauss at the time, suddenly embarked on a symphony of his own roughly three months later.

The *Stadttheater's* tight schedule (probably contractual clauses also) prevented Mahler and Nikisch from taking part in Leipzig's musical life outside the theater. On the other hand, both were offered a few opportunities to perform symphonic works inside it.

Season 1886–1887

31. March 19, 1887, 8 p.m.
   LEIPZIG – Altes Gewandhaus [900 seats]

   Fourth Concert of the Leipzig "Liszt-Verein" [The Liszt Society]

(1)	Cherubini	String Quartet, No. 3, D minor
(2)	Beethoven	32 Variations, C minor, for Piano
(3)	Bach	Prelude & Fugue, No. 16, G minor, BWV 861, for Piano
(4)	Liszt	*Valse mélancolique*
(5)	Bülow	*Lacerta*, Impromptu, Op. 27, for Piano
(6)	Liszt	*Gnomenreigen,* for Piano

   (7) Five *Lieder* with Piano Acc.:
   - a) Volkmann — "Die Bekehrte," Op. 54
   - b) Alyabyev — "The Nightingale"
   - c) Jensen — "Frühlingslied"
   - d) Bach — "Willst du dein Herz mir schenken," BWV 518
   - e) Schubert — "Der Neugierige" from *Die schöne Müllerin*, D 795, No. 6

Soirée
zum Besten der
Hilfscasse der Leipziger Journalisten u. Schriftsteller
in Verbindung mit einer
Uhland-Feier
Sonnabend, den 30. April, Abends 8 Uhr
im Saale d. alt. Gewandhauses.

PROGRAMM.

Gesangverein „Phönix". Zwei Männerchöre:
    a. „Schäfers Sonntagslied" (Das ist der Tag des Herrn), von Uhland, comp. von C. Kreutzer.
    b. „Frühlingsglaube", von Uhland, comp. von Rud. Tschirch.

Herr Professor **Rich. Gosche**. Fest-Rede auf Uhland.

Frau Kammersängerin **Moran-Olden**. Zwei Lieder:
    a. „Du fragst mich täglich, liebst Du mich? von Erick Meyer Hellmund.
    b. „Luftschloss", von C. Reinecke.

Herr Piano-Virtuos **Feruccio Busoni**. Zwei Stücke für Pianoforte:
    a. Toccata und Orgelfuge in Dmoll — Bach — Tausig.
    b. Fantasie über „Lucrezia Borgia" — Liszt.

Herr Kammer-Virtuos **Alwin Schröder**. Zwei Stücke für Cello:
    a. Nocturne von Glinka.
    b. Warum von Popper.

Frau **Charles-Hirsch**. Aria di Bravoura del Opera: Linda di Chamounit — Donizetti.

Herr **Ernst v. Wildenbruch**. Erster Act aus „Der Fürst von Verona", Drama von Ernst v. Wildenbruch.

Herr **Otto Schelper**. Drei Lieder:
    a. „Heinrich der Vogler", von C. Löwe.
    b. „Einen Brief soll ich schreiben", von C. Hauer.
    c. „Wanderlied", von R. Schumann.

Frau **Olga Lewinsky**. „Des Sängers Fluch", Ballade von Uhland.

Fräulein **Ottilie Andes**. Drei Lieder:
    a. „Des Goldschmieds Töchterlein", Ballade von Uhland, comp. von Carl Löwe.
    b. „Ueberselig", von Eckert.
    c. „Mädchen mit dem rothen Mündchen", von J. Gall.

Gesangverein „**Phönix**". Männerchor: „Frühlingsnacht", von C. L. Fischer.

Die Begleitung der Solo-Gesänge hat Herr Capellmeister **Mahler** gütigst übernommen.

Billets sind in den Buch- und Kunsthandlungen der Herren Vogel, Del Vecchio und Klein zum Preise von 3 u. 2 Mark zu haben, und für die Studirenden an der Universität und am Conservatorium zu ermässigten Preisen bei Herrn Castellan Vieweg bez. im Bureau des Conservatoriums.

Der Vorstand und das Comité.
Pantenius, Tischler, Reissner, Soyaux, Schumann, Pfeil, Dr. Simon, Werner.

| Leipzig | 1887 | Concert No. 31–33 |

SOLOISTS (1) Henri Petri String Quartet; (2-6) E. Grosscurth, piano; (7a-e) C. Charles-Hirsch, acc. by Mahler (piano).
SOURCE Reconstructed from a newspaper review in the *Leipziger Zeitung*, March 21, 1887 (p. 910). The order is not necessarily correct.

32. March 22, 1887, 6:30 p.m.
LEIPZIG - Das Neue Stadttheater [2,000 seats]

In Celebration of the Emperor's [Wilhelm I] 90th Birthday

    Wagner   *Huldigungsmarsch*, E-flat major •

[followed by a complete stage performance of Wagner's *Lohengrin*, cond. by Mahler]

SOURCE Newspaper advertisement.

33. April 30, 1887, 8 p.m.
LEIPZIG - Altes Gewandhaus [900 seats]

For the Benefit of the Relief Fund of the Leipzig Journalists and Authors, combined with a Celebration of [the poet Ludwig] Uhland's Centenary

(1)	Kreutzer	*Schäfers Sonntagslied*, Op. 23, for Men's Chorus
(2)	Tschirch	*Frühlingsglaube*, for Men's Chorus
(3)	Ceremonial address in honor of Ludwig Uhland	
(4)	Meyer-Helmund	"Du fragst mich täglich," *Lied*, Op. 5, No. 5 •
(5)	Reinecke	"Luftschloß," *Lied*, Op. 185 •
(6)	Bach–Tausig	Toccata and Fugue, D minor, BWV 565, arr. for Piano
(7)	Liszt	Fantasy on Donizetti's *Lucrezia Borgia*, for Piano
(8)	Glinka	Nocturne, for Cello and Piano •
(9)	Popper	*Warum*, Op. 3, No. 2, for Cello and Piano •
(10)	Donizetti	"O luce di quest' anima," from *Linda di Chamounix* [1]
(11)	Wildenbruch	*Der Fürst von Verona*, Act 1 [Play]
(12)	Loewe	"Heinrich der Vogler," *Lied*, Op. 56, No. 1 •
(13)	Hauer	"Einen Brief soll ich schreiben," *Lied*, Op. 32 •
(14)	Schumann	"Wanderlied," *Lied*, Op. 35, No. 3 •
(15)	Schumann	"Der Contrabandiste," *Lied*, Op. 74, No. 10 [encore] •
(16)	Uhland	"Des Sängers Fluch," Poem
(17)	Loewe	"Des Goldschmieds Töchterlein," *Lied*, Op. 8, No. 1 •
(18)	Eckert	"Überselig," *Lied*, Op. 29, No. 5 •
(19)	Gall	"Mädchen mit dem rothen Mündchen," *Lied* •
(20)	Fischer	"Frühlingsnacht," Op. 17, No. 3, for Men's Chorus

SOLOISTS (3) spoken by R. Gosche; (4 & 5) P. Andriessen; (6 & 7) F. Busoni; (8 & 9) A. Schröder, cello; (10) C. Charles-Hirsch; (11) read by the author; (12–15) O. Schelper; (16) read by O. Lewinsky; (17–19) O. Andes.
PIANO ACC. (4, 5, 10, 12–14, 17–19) Mahler, who probably also acc. items 8 & 9.
CHORUS (1 & 20) Gesangverein "Phönix."
SOURCE Newspaper advertisement; see illustration on opposite page.
NOTE [1] Sung in German.
[2] The announced but indisposed F. Moran-Olden was replaced by P. Andriessen, both members of the Leipzig *Stadttheater*.

LEIPZIG (II)
Season 1887–1888

In December 1886 Leipzig marked the centenary of Carl Maria von Weber's birth with a cycle of his operas conducted by Mahler and Nikisch. In this connection, Mahler got to know Weber's grandson, Alexander Carl von Weber, an army captain, and his wife Marion Mathilde. Together with the director, Staegemann, the couple persuaded Mahler to "complete" Weber's unfinished opera *Die drei Pintos.* The world premiere in Leipzig, on January 20, 1888, under Mahler's direction, was a great success, and the opera was soon being presented all over Germany.

Mahler's work on the opera had a highly significant aftereffect. His creative urge, in hibernation for a few years, was suddenly reawakened. During the first months of 1888, in an almost feverish excitement, he sketched and completed the score of a Symphonic Poem or a Symphony in Five Movements. For years afterward Mahler alternately used both designations, finally settling on the term "Symphony," his first, in fact, in 1896. By that time, though, the score had gone through many revisions and had become very different (concert no. 84).

It was hardly Weber's music itself which caused this sudden creative outburst in 1888, but rather the procedure which Mahler had employed to complete the opera. In a flash he realized the potential of this same method to create a work of his own. Hence he selected and refashioned some of his older scores, using their themes and motifs, welding them all into a new composition. The symphony is truly a "recycled" work, although it also contains many new and strikingly original ideas.

Since the material Mahler used is (partly) derived from pieces he had composed in his Kassel years, including the *Lieder eines fahrenden Gesellen* (1884–85) and the incidental music to Scheffel's *Der Trompeter von Säkkingen* (1884), one can claim, with some justification, that the symphony has its origin in Kassel. On the other hand, it is incontrovertible that the initial idea of embarking on the symphony was born in Leipzig and brought to fruition there, in the early months of 1888.

34. **November 30, 1887, 7:30 p.m.**
LEIPZIG - Das Neue Stadttheater [2,000 seats]

All-Wagner Program:

(1) Symphony in C major
(2) Four *Lieder* with Piano Acc.:
   a) "Der Engel"
   b) "Träume"
   c) "Dors mon enfant" ["Schlummerlied"] [1]
   d) "Mignonne" ["Die Rose"] [1]
(3) *Eine Faust*-Ouverture
(4) The Final Scenes from Acts 1 and 3 of *Parsifal*

SOLOIST (2) F. Moran-Olden, acc. by A. Nikisch.
CONDUCTORS (1 & 3) A. Nikisch; (4) Mahler.
CHORUSES The "Riedel-Verein" and the "Leipzig Lehrergesangverein."
SOURCE Newspaper advertisement.
NOTE [1] Sung in German.
REVIEW HLG I, 171.

> **EXIT LEIPZIG – PRAGUE REVISITED**
> August–September 1888

Mahler's worst enemy was very probably his own ego. He could often be intolerant, arrogant, and officious to the point of paranoia, constantly putting himself at odds with his superiors and colleagues. All of that contributed to his premature departure from Leipzig, where he was committed until the close of the 1891–92 season. Nonetheless, in early May 1888 he suddenly asked for an instant release, which the director, Max Staegemann, at first ignored but to which he finally complied. But why was Mahler so anxious to get away from Leipzig?

Ostensibly because during a rehearsal he had had a row with the singer and stage director, Albert Goldberg, who appears to have shouted at Mahler: "You have conducted here for the last time today!" (GMB 57/MSL 66). As this happened in the presence of other employees, Mahler sought his release on the grounds that he had been publicly humiliated. However, there was something far more hazardous at the bottom of this.

In fact, Mahler faced a dilemma quite unconnected with the quarrel. It appears from an unpublished letter that he had secretly agreed with Angelo Neumann to rehearse and conduct the premiere of Weber's *Die drei Pintos* in Prague, in August. This was a clear breach of his Leipzig contract, and Mahler was of course aware of it, as well as of the fatal consequences for his career if he was exposed. Staegemann had heard rumors of the Prague deal which Mahler naturally denied. On the other hand, he had to bring matters to a head before Staegemann went on holiday in early June. The Goldberg incident most conveniently provided Mahler with the excuse he sought and he persisted stubbornly, blowing the trifling affair out of proportion, and finally having his way.

Though Mahler's agreement with Prague is not known in detail, he undoubtedly hoped for permanent employment—and, of course, only as the principal conductor. However, this was out of the question because the director, Neumann, already had Karl Muck in that post and had recently extended his contract for an additional three years.

During August 1888, Mahler rehearsed and conducted five performances of *Die drei Pintos*, his last ever. In early September he was again involved in a heated argument, this time with Neumann, over a relatively trivial matter, causing Neumann to fire him—the only time in his life.

Between July and early September, Mahler tried in vain to arrange performances of his "Symphonic Poem" in Leipzig, Dresden, and Munich. Simultaneously, he sketched and completed a new symphonic score which five years later would form the opening movement of his Second Symphony (completed in Hamburg, 1893–94).

Now, at 28, Mahler was once more at a crossroads, but on a much sounder basis than at any time earlier or later in his life. He was in every way a free and independent man. The sale of *Die drei Pintos* (10,000 Marks in cash) and future royalties from its performances made him financially secure, at least for a year or two. Indeed, this would have been the ideal moment to turn his attention, once again, exclusively to Mahler-*the Composer*.

If that prospect ever crossed his mind, Mahler refrained from seizing the opportunity, because he suddenly was offered a new post in Budapest as Artistic Director of the Opera, one which he could not resist.

PART V
BUDAPEST
A Magyar Királyi Operaház ("The Royal Hungarian Opera")
Seasons 1888–1891

It was in the middle of September 1888, while staying with his family in Iglau, that the Royal Hungarian Opera in Budapest invited Mahler to immediately take on its artistic directorship. In early October Mahler accepted and signed a ten-year contract. However, he did so with some anxiety, mostly owing to his inexperience in the business of running an opera house.

The center of musical life in Budapest was the Opera House, the orchestra of which gave six Philharmonic Concerts each season, all conducted by Sandór Erkel, the Opera's second *Kapellmeister*. It was undoubtedly an opportune act, when Erkel invited Mahler to conduct the world premiere of his "Symphonic Poem" (concert no. 36). (Erkel tried in vain to be released from his contract.)

As artistic director of the Opera, Mahler occasionally seized the opportunity to conduct some of the masterworks from the symphonic repertoire, including Beethoven's Fifth Symphony (concert no. 39), and Mozart's Symphony No. 40 (concert no. 43).

However, during his first season in Budapest Mahler concentrated his energies mostly on the administration of the Opera, and in preparing the Hungarian premieres of Wagner's *Das Rheingold* and *Die Walküre* (both in Hungarian translations) in January 1889.

Season 1889–1890

35. **November 13, 1889, 7:30 p.m.**
BUDAPEST - The Small Hall of the "Vigadó" [500 seats][1]

Second Subscription Concert of the Krancsevics String Quartet[2]

(1)	Cherubini	String Quartet No. 3, D minor
(2)	Mahler	*Lieder* with Piano Acc.:[3]
		a) "Frühlingsmorgen"
		b) "Erinnerung"
		c) "Scheiden und Meiden"
(3)	Loewe	*Lieder* with Piano Acc.:
		a) "Der Fischer," Op. 43, No. 1 •
		b) "Kleiner Haushalt," Op. 71 •
(4)	Mozart	String Quartet No. 21, D major, K. 575

SOLOIST (2 & 3) B. Bianchi, acc. by Mahler.
SOURCE Program reconstructed from the preview in *Pester Lloyd*, November 12, 1889 and the same paper's review on November 14, 1889 (DM II, 155–56).
NOTES [1] The "Vigadó" (in German "Redoutengebäude," literally "fancy-dress hall") was built between 1859 and 1865 in a Roman–Moorish style.
[2] Formed by members of the Royal Opera Orchestra, and named after the orchestra's concertmaster, Dragomir Krancsevics.
[3] World premieres of 2b & c.
REVIEW HLG I, 202; Roman I, 77–78.

Hangversenybérlet II. szám.

Budapest, szerdán 1889. november hó 20-án esti 7½ órakor
a magyar királyi operaház zenekarából alakult filharmoniai társulat

BRAGA HERMIN
asszony, csász. és kir. kamaraénekesnő és

MAHLER GUSZTÁV
úr, a magyar kir. operaház művészeti igazgatója szives közreműködésével

ERKEL SÁNDOR
karnagy vezénylete alatt

FILHARMONIAI HANGVERSENYT
rendez

A FŐVÁROSI VIGADÓ NAGY TERMÉBEN.

MŰSOR:

1. *Cherubini.* »Abencerage«, nyitány.
2. *Mahler.* »Symphoniai költemény« két részben.
   I. rész: 1. Bevezetés és Allegro commodo. 2. Andante. 3. Scherzo.
   II. rész: 4. A la pompes funebres; attacca. 5. Molto appassionato.
   Kézirat, *első előadás* a szerző vezénylete alatt.
3. *Mozart.* Magándal »Figaro lakodalmából«. (Cherubin dallama.) *Braga Hermin* asszony.
4. *Bach-Abert.* »Präludium, choral és fuga«.

Jegyek kaphatók: **Rózsavölgyi és társa** cs. és kir. udv. zeneműkereskedésében, Kristóftér 3., valamint a hangverseny napján az esteli pénztárnál.

Előadás alatt az ajtók zárva maradnak.

III-ik filharmoniai hangverseny 1889. decz. 4-én

| Budapest | 1889 | Concerts Nos. 36–37 |

36. **November 20, 1889, 7:30 p.m.** [1]
BUDAPEST - The Large Hall of the "Vigadó" [1,000 seats]

Second Philharmonic Subscription Concert

(1) Cherubini — *Les Abencérages,* Overture
(2) Mahler — Symphonic Poem in 2 Parts ● [2]
    Part I: 1. Introduction and Allegro commodo. 2. Andante. 3. Scherzo.
    Part II: 4. A la pompes funèbres, *attacca* 5. Molto appassionato
(3) Mozart — "Voi, che sapete," from *Le nozze di Figaro*
(4) Thomas — "Connais-tu le pays?" from *Mignon* [encore]
(5) Bach — Prelude, Fugue and Chorale, arr. for Orchestra by J.J. Abert

SOLOIST (3 & 4) H. Braga.
CONDUCTORS (1, 3–5) S. Erkel; (2) Mahler.
ORCHESTRA The Budapest Philharmonic Orchestra.
SOURCE Handbill; see illustration on opposite page.
NOTES [1] The general rehearsal took place the preceding day at 11 a. m.
[2] World premiere of the original though revised score. At the third reworking, in 1893, the symphony was titled "Titan," concert no. 55. Between June 1894 and March 1896 Mahler revised the score once more, discarding the *Andante* (2nd movement, titled "Blumine") and all the other titles, concerts nos. 64 & 84.
REVIEW HLG I, 204–206; DM II, 151–154 (including facsimile of review in the *Pester Lloyd*, November 21, 1889); Roman I, 78–83.

37. **December 11, 1889, 7 p.m.**
BUDAPEST - Népszinház (The Hungarian Folk Theater) [2,400 seats]

For the Benefit for the Pension Fund of the Hungarian Journalists' Society

[extract of program]

(1) Arditi — *Forosetta,* Tarantella, for Soprano and Orchestra ●
(2) Anon. — Two Hungarian Folk Songs, with Piano Acc. [encores] [1]
    a) "Lehullott a rezgö nyárfa levele" ●
    b) "Ritka búza, ritka rozs" ●
(3) Schubert — "Der Wanderer," *Lied*, D 649 [1]
(4) Anon. — "Schilflied," *Lied* [encore] ● [1]
(5) Massenet — Duet (unspecified), from *Le Roi de Lahore*

SOLOISTS (1 & 2) B. Bianchi. (3 & 4) D. Ney. (5) P. Rossini & F. Broulik.
Mahler: (1 & 5) conductor; (2–4) piano acc.
ORCHESTRA The Royal Hungarian Opera Orchestra.
SOURCE Program reconstructed from the review in the *Pester Lloyd*. The review reports that Mahler smashed a lamp with his baton during the last item.
NOTE [1] Nos. 2–4 were sung in Hungarian. No. 4, "Schilflied" (literally, "Song on Reeds"), was probably one from the well-known cycle of five poems by the German poet Nikolaus Lenau (1802–1850), which inspired many composers (e.g. Mendelssohn and, a decade later, the young Alma Maria Schindler, Mahler's wife-to-be).
REVIEW HLG I, 208.

38. **January 3, 1890, 7 p.m.**
BUDAPEST - The Royal Hungarian Opera House [1,100 seats]

Charity Concert for the Employees of the burned-down German Theater [1]

[extract of program]

      Beethoven   *Leonore* Overture No. 3, Op. 72b

SOURCE Newspaper review.
NOTE [1] In Budapest, on December 20, 1889. The theater was never reopened.
REVIEW HLG I, 208; Roman I, 88.

39. **February 24, 1890, 7 p.m.**
BUDAPEST - The Royal Hungarian Opera House [1,100 seats]

For the Benefit of the Society of the Polyclinic

[extract of program]

      Beethoven   Symphony No. 5, C minor, Op. 67

ORCHESTRA The Budapest Philharmonic Orchestra (i.e. the Opera Orchestra).
SOURCE Newspaper review.
REVIEW Roman I, 89.

40. **March 12, 1890, 7 p.m.**
BUDAPEST - The Kasino

For the Benefit of the Society "Children's Friend"

[extract of program]

(1) Schumann   "Frühlingsnacht," *Lied*, Op. 39, No. 12 •
(2) Schubert   "Aufenthalt," *Lied*, D 957, No. 5 •
(3) Brahms   "Wiegenlied," *Lied*, Op. 49, No. 4 •

SOLOIST L. Hilgermann, acc. by Mahler.
SOURCE Program reconstructed from the review in the *Pester Lloyd*.

41. **April 16, 1890, 7:30 p.m.** [1]
BUDAPEST - The Royal Hungarian Opera House [1,100 seats]

For the Benefit of the Hungarian Actors' Society

[extract of program]

(1) Donizetti   "Oh, mio Fernando," from *La favorita* • [2]
(2) Weber   "So weih' ich mich," from *Euryanthe*
(3) Massenet   Salomé's Aria (unspecified), from *Hérodiade* • [2]
(4) Halévy   "Rachel, quand du Seigneur," from *La Juive* [2]

SOLOISTS (1) L. Hilgermann; (2) D. Ney; (3) I. Vasquez-Molina; (4) H. Prévost.
SOURCE The review in *Pester Lloyd*.
NOTES [1] It has not been unequivocally proved that Mahler conducted this concert.
[2] Sung in German, "Gott erleuchte meinen Sinn."

| Budapest | 1890 | Concerts Nos. 42–43 |

Season 1890–1891

42. **October 29, 1890, 7:30 p.m.**
BUDAPEST - The Royal Hungarian Opera House [1,100 seats]

Gala Evening to Celebrate the Centenary of the Foundation of the Hungarian Dramatic Art

1st Part

(1)	Huber	Festival March, for Orchestra
(2)	A Spoken Prologue	
(3)	Liszt	*Festklänge,* Symphonic Poem
(4)	Mihalovich	Overture to *Toldi's Liebe* ● [1]
(5)	Mihalovich	"Royal Hymn," for Chorus and Orch. ● [1]

2nd Part

(6)	Erkel, F.	Festival Overture
(7)	Szabó	Dramatic Symphony
(8)	Berlioz	*Ráckóci March*

CONDUCTORS (1, 6–8) S. Erkel; (3–5) Mahler.
SOURCE Various previews and reviews.
NOTE [1] World premieres. According to the review in the *Pester Lloyd,* Mahler conducted both works from memory.
REVIEW Roman I, 108.

43. **December 5, 1890, 7 p.m.**
BUDAPEST - The Royal Hungarian Opera House [1,100 seats]

For the Benefit of the National Theater's Pension Fund, the Journalists' Society and the Charity Society "Children's Friends" [1]

(1)	Weber	Overture to *Oberon*
(2)	Mozart	Symphony No. 40, G minor, K. 550
(3)	Thomas	"Je suis Titania" (Polonaise), from *Mignon* [2]
(4)	Wagner	Prelude to Act 1 of *Die Meistersinger von Nürnberg*

[followed by a complete stage performance of Rudolf Raimann's operetta *Szimán basa*, cond. by the composer]

SOLOIST (3) L. Lehmann.
SOURCE Handbill.
NOTES [1] The concert's patroness was Countess Emanuel Andrássy.
[2] Sung in German: "Titania ist herabgestiegen."
REVIEW HLG I, 220.

***

Budapest	1890

Budapest Epilogue

In February 1889 Mahler's father died; eight months later, in October, his mother died. Mahler assumed responsibility of his younger sisters and brothers: Alois (aged 22), Justine (21), Otto (16), and Emma (14). Alois was already semi-independent, and Otto had been studying at the Vienna Conservatory since September 1888. Now the two sisters also moved to Vienna and were installed in a flat with Otto, and Mahler's friend, Friedrich Löhr, whose wife, Uda, looked after them.

Although Mahler did achieve wonders at the Budapest Opera, including the Hungarian premieres of Wagner's *Das Rheingold* and *Die Walküre*, and a new production of Mozart's *Don Giovanni*, things did not go smoothly. He was under constant attack from various quarters, anti-Semitic as well as nationalist. Therefore, in early 1890, when he learned about the impending retirement of the intendant, Ferenc Beniczky (who had always been well disposed toward him), and that he would probably be replaced by Count Géza Zichy (a particularly fierce nationalist), Mahler realized the time had come to seek a new engagement.

From the early autumn of 1890, he secretly negotiated with director Bernhard Pollini of the Hamburg *Stadttheater,* who badly needed a first-rate *Kapellmeister*. Pollini had in fact signed up Wilhelm Kienzl for that post for the 1890–91 season, but according to all contemporary reviews he proved so incompetent that by mid-January 1891 he was forced to leave Hamburg.

Almost simultaneously, Mahler and Pollini reached an accord and signed—in deep secrecy—an interim three-year contract. The precise date of the contract is not known, but there is a strong presumption that it was January 15, 1891.

The next problem Mahler faced was to engineer a quick release from his Budapest commitments without openly violating his contract, which would have cost him dearly. On February 2, Count Zichy took office, and he made no secret of his desire to get rid of Mahler. Hence it was easy to "provoke" him, and Mahler soon proved well able to exploit this "weakness."

On March 14, 1891, the "game" was settled to Mahler's advantage. When he left the Hungarian capital ten days later, it was not only with an indemnity of 25,000 florins in cash—the price he had demanded for the annulment of his ten-year contract—but also with his honor intact.

Mahler arrived in Hamburg on March 26 following a short visit to Vienna.

> **PART VI**
> **HAMBURG AND ALTONA**
> **The Combined *Stadttheater***
> **Seasons 1891–1897**

Hamburg was more than a mere stepping stone in Mahler's career. It can fairly be said that during his six years in the Elbe metropolis, a booming, cosmopolitan "Free and Hanseatic" city-state that felt itself not one whit inferior to Berlin or Vienna, the peripatetic conductor-composer at last came of age. He not only extended his repertoire in an opera house that was one of Germany's finest – and best-funded; he also became far more active in the concert hall besides completing (in his "spare time") his huge Second and Third symphonies.

Although Mahler had always proved to be a "workaholic," even back in those lowly jobs in Laibach and Olmütz when he had had precious little to work *with*, the load he took on in Hamburg was truly immense. Spurred and sometimes whipped on by Pollini, a tough businessman and hard taskmaster, he led all-in-all no less than 740 performances of works that spanned the opera and operetta repertoire – from Wagner's *Tristan und Isolde* to Humperdinck's *Hänsel und Gretel*, from the German premiere of Tchaikovsky's *Eugene Onegin* to Millöcker's *Der Bettelstudent*. Several associate conductors came and went, most unable to stand the pace. One died, apparently from exhaustion. The indefatigable Mahler, though, flanked his opera duties with dozens of choral and symphony concerts – around 40 in Hamburg alone, as well as others as far a field as Moscow and Budapest. In London he even led an afternoon concert of Wagner excerpts before racing off to conduct the whole of *Die Walküre* at the Covent Garden opera house the same evening.

Mahler did not regard his concert work as an added burden – quite the contrary. In a letter to the Hamburg critic Ferdinand Pfohl, he stressed that the job of opera Kapellmeister became "in the long run insupportable, almost deadly. In the interests of self-preservation and self-respect, I have to conduct concerts, to regenerate myself in the concert hall." Since Mahler regularly received accolades for his achievements on the operatic "treadmill," even from the caustic Hans von Bülow who had spurned him years before in Kassel, surely, one would think, the concerts he gave to "regenerate" himself would have achieved still greater success. In fact they did not – at least not consistently. A subscription series of concerts Mahler put together in Hamburg (only a part of his overall concert work) actually ran up a big deficit and he was not booked for the following season. What went wrong?

Although audiences regularly cheered the fire and drama Mahler brought to symphonic works, influential critics were often hostile – complaining about tempi and dynamics they felt were exaggerated and about the conductor's *Retuschen*, i.e. his partial reorchestration of scores by masters like Bach and Beethoven. Mahler found strong - or at least cogent - arguments for his "retouching," noting that much of the concert repertoire had been composed for performance in the acoustic of halls far smaller than those common at the end of the 19th century. As for his alleged "exaggeration," stories are legion of Mahler demanding (and often extracting) from his benighted players more shattering fortissimos and breathless pianissimos than they initially felt able to give. It is also plain that he was no "slave to the bar line," making liberal use of rubato and adopting the most flexible of tempi. Critics who admired this approach in the opera house by no means always felt it appropriate when applied from the concert podium.

On the other hand there were clearly many listeners who felt that in his ability to breathe life into music old and new, whatever the venue, Mahler was simply unique. Bruno Walter called him the "greatest performing musician" he had ever met; Otto Klemperer judged him "a thousand times greater than Toscanini." In other words – throughout his career Mahler's conducting polarized opinion at least as much as his compositions did.

Thanks above all to his official duties, Mahler had to pack virtually all his creative work into his summer holidays – setting a pattern during those Hamburg years that he retained for the rest of his life. Between 1893 and 1896 he rented rooms for himself and his sisters at an inn by the Attersee, the largest lake in the Austrian Alps; and it was there – in an isolated *Komponierhäuschen* (composing hut) by the water's edge – that he completed his Second symphony, the "Resurrection" and set down the whole of his pantheistic Third. Mahler had, in fact, long been brooding over the "Resurrection" but had failed to make much progress, partly no doubt for lack of time but probably also because von Bülow had fiercely rejected the first movement, *Todtenfeier* funeral march that Mahler had completed in Prague. At any rate, it was only at von Bülow's funeral in Hamburg in March 1894 that Mahler had what he called a "lightning flash" of inspiration for the choral finale, enabling him to go on and finish the work at his Attersee refuge a few months later. When he gave the premiere of the whole piece in Berlin in December 1895, the audience reacted with wild enthusiasm and most critics, typically, with at best disdain.

Also at the Attersee inn during three of those four summers was Natalie Bauer-Lechner, a musician who felt close to Mahler and wanted to get closer still. It is thanks to her published *Recollections* that we have one of the most vivid and detailed pictures of Mahler as man and artist. But by 1896 Natalie had a serious rival for Mahler's affections – the passionate, dramatic soprano Anna von Mildenburg who had joined the Hamburg opera in the previous autumn. Mahler might even have married Anna had it not been for his sisters, who were living with him in Hamburg and wholly dependent on him. Besides, by the end of 1896 he was busy pulling every possible string to haul in the biggest prize in music in the Habsburg Empire – the directorship of the Court Opera in Vienna. In principle, at 36, he seemed too young even to be considered for the job – and besides, he was a Jew. Mahler could do nothing about his youth but he could, and did, deal with the other "obstacle." On February 23, 1897 he was baptized a Catholic and a few months later he joined the opera, soon becoming the director. True to form, he presented a mammoth program for his last concert in Hamburg as director (although he did return much later as a guest conductor) – Beethoven's *Eroica* symphony followed by a complete performance of *Fidelio*.

Hamburger Stadt-Theater.

(Director **B. Pollini**.)

Heute, Mittwoch, den 27. Mai 1891.

259. Abonnements-Vorstellung.   38. Mittwochs-Vorstellung.

Benefiz für Herrn und Frau Lissmann.

Der Wasserträger.

Oper in 3 Acten. Musik von Cherubini.

Regie: Herr Fr. Bittong.

Dirigent: Herr Capellmeister **Gustav Mahler**.

Graf Armand, Parlaments-Präsident	Hr. Cronberger
Constanze, seine Gemahlin	Fr. Brandt
Micheli, Savoyard, Wasserträger	Hr. Lißmann
Anton, sein Enkel	Hr. Landau
Marzelline, seine Schwester	Fr. Lißmann
Semos, ein reicher Pächter in Gonesse	Hr. Lohfeldt
Angelina, seine Tochter, Anton's Braut	Fr. Wolff
Hauptmann der italienischen Truppen	Hr. Lorent
Lieutenant	Hr. Wiegand
Sergeant } in Mazarin's Solde	Hr. Meyer
Korporal	Hr. Weidmann
Ein Mädchen	Frl. Merelli
Erster } Soldat	Hr. Retiz
Zweiter	Hr. Jansen

Italienische Soldaten, Einwohner, Mädchen, Kinder in Gonesse.

Hierauf:

Unter Leitung des Capellmeisters Herrn **Gustav Mahler**.

Ouverture „Leonore III."

von L. van Beethoven.

Zum Schluß:

Gesangsvorträge.

1. a) „Wenn der Frühling auf die Berge steigt" von Robert Franz,
   b) „Frühlingsglaube" von Schubert, gesungen von Frl. **Polna**.
2. a) „Die Lotosblume" von R. Schumann,
   b) „Widmung" von R. Schumann. gesungen von Fr. **Heink**.
3. „Hochzeitslied" von C. Löwe, gesungen von Hrn. Lißmann.
4. a) „Der kleine Sandträger" v. Aug. Bungert (Aus den Handwerkerliedern von Carmen Sylva).
   b) „Wiegenlied" von W. Taubert, gesungen von Frau Lißmann.
5. Auswahl aus Opus 34, 74, 101 und 138 von Robert Schumann.
   a) „Ich bin geliebt", gesungen von Frau Heink, Frau Lißmann und den Herren Alvary und Lißmann.
   b) „Liebesgarten", gesungen von Frau Lißmann und Herrn Alvary.
   c) „Mit Myrthen und Rosen", gesungen von Herrn Alvary.
   d) „Es ist verrathen", gesungen von Frau Lißmann, Frau Heink und den Herren Alvary und Lißmann.

Klavierbegleitung: Herr Capellmeister **Gustav Mahler**.

Der Concertflügel ist aus der Pianofabrik von Steinway & Sons, neue Rosenstraße 20—24, St. Pauli.

Kassenöffnung 6 Uhr.   **Anfang 7 Uhr.**

Ende nach 10 Uhr.

Große Preise: 1. Rang, Parquet und Parquetloge M. 6. 2. Rang-Mittelloge und 1. Parterre M. 4. 2. Rang-Seitenloge und Sitz-Parterre M. 3. 3. Rang-Mittelloge M. 2.70. 3. Rang-Seitenloge M. 2.10. Steh-Parterre M. 1.50. Gallerie-Sitzplatz M. 1.20. Gallerie 75 ₰.

Donnerstag, den 28. Mai. Zu ermäßigten Preisen. „Nathan der Weise".

Freitag, den 29. Mai. **X**. und letzte Vorstellung im „Wagner-Cyclus". „Götterdämmerung".

44. **May 27, 1891, 7 p.m.**
HAMBURG - Stadttheater [2,000 seats]

Annual Benefit for Marie and Friedrich Lißmann [1]

(After a complete stage performance of Cherubini's opera *Les deux journées*, cond. by Mahler, the evening closed with the following concert)

(1)	Beethoven	*Leonore* Overture No. 3, Op. 72b
(2)	Franz	"Wenn der Frühling auf die Berge," *Lied*, Op. 42, No. 6 •
(3)	Schubert	"Frühlingsglaube," *Lied*, D 686b •
(4)	Schumann	"Die Lotusblume," *Lied*, Op. 25, No. 7 •
(5)	Schumann	"Widmung," *Lied*, Op. 25, No. 1 •
(6)	Loewe	"Hochzeitslied," *Lied*, Op. 20, No. 1 •
(7)	Bungert	"Der Sandträger," *Lied*, Op. 49, No. 12 •
(8)	Taubert	"Wiegenlied," *Lied*, Op. 27, No. 5 •
(9)	Schumann	"Ich bin geliebt," Quartet, Op. 74, No. 9 •
(10)	Schumann	"Liebesgarten," Duet, Op. 34, No. 1 •
(11)	Schumann	"Mit Myrthen und Rosen," *Lied*, Op. 24, No. 9 •
(12)	Schumann	"Es ist verrathen," Quartet, Op. 74, No. 5 •

SOLOISTS (2 & 3) O. Polna; (4 & 5) E. Schumann-Heink; (6) F. Lißmann; (7 & 8) M. Lißmann; (9 & 12) M. Lißmann, E. Schumann-Heink, M. Alvary, F. Lißmann; (10) M. Lißmann, M. Alvary; (11) M. Alvary; all accompanied on the piano by Mahler, who also conducted the first item.
SOURCE Newspaper advertisement; see illustration on opposite page.
NOTE [1] Mr. and Mrs. Lißmann were soloists at the *Stadttheater*.
REVIEW HLG I, 236.

Season 1891–1892

45. **November 27, 1891, 7:30 p.m.** [1]
LÜBECK - The Colosseum [1,000 seats]

Grand Instrumental & Vocal Concert

(1)	Haydn	Symphony No. 101, D major, "Clock"
(2)	Mozart	"Deh vieni, non tardar," from *Le nozze di Figaro*, K. 492 [2]
(3)	Beethoven	Introduction to Act 2 and "Gott, welch Dunkel hier ... In des Lebens Frühlingstagen," from *Fidelio*
(4)	Beethoven	*Leonore* Overture No. 3, Op. 72b
(5)	Wagner	Overture to *Tannhäuser*
(6)	Wagner	"Winterstürme wichen dem Wonnemond" and Final Duet, from *Die Walküre* [3]
(7)	Wagner	Prelude to Act 1 of *Die Meistersinger von Nürnberg*

SOLOISTS (2 & 6) M. Wolf-Kauer; (3 & 6) G. Seidel.
ORCHESTRA The Hamburg *Stadttheater* Orchestra (86 players).
SOURCE Newspaper advertisement; see illustration on following page.

COLOSSEUM.

Freitag den 27. November 1891 Abends 7½ Uhr:

Grosses Instrumental- u. Vocal-Concert,

ausgeführt

von dem aus 86 Musikern bestehenden Orchester des

Hamburger Stadt-Theaters,

unter Leitung des Herrn

Capellmeisters Director **Gustav Mahler**,

sowie von dem

Tenoristen Herrn **Dr. Gustav Seidel**

und der

Sopranistin Frau **Marie Wolff-Kauer**.

Vortragsfolge:

I. Abtheilung.

1. **Jos. Haydn.** Symphonie in D-dur (Breitkopf & Härtel Nr. 4).
2. **W. A. Mozart.** Arie: „Endlich naht sich die Stunde" aus „Figaro's Hochzeit".
   Frau **Marie Wolff-Kauer**.
3. **L. v. Beethoven.** Einleitung zum II. Act und Arie des Florestan aus „Fidelio"
   Herr **Dr. Gustav Seidel**.
4. **L. v. Beethoven.** Ouverture Nr. 3 zu „Leonore".

II. Abtheilung.

5. **R. Wagner.** Ouverture zu „Tannhäuser".
6. **R. Wagner.** Liebeslied und Schlussduett aus dem I. Act „Walküre".
   Frau **Marie Wolff-Kauer** und Herr **Dr. Gustav Seidel**.
7. **R. Wagner.** Vorspiel zu „Die Meistersinger von Nürnberg".

Bei Beginn einer Musiknummer werden die Saalthüren geschlossen, und ist während der Dauer derselben der Eintritt nicht gestattet.

Eintrittskarten: nummerirter Platz 3 ℳ, nichtnummerirter Platz 2 ℳ, Stehplatz 1 ℳ in der Kunst- und Musikalienhandlung von **F. W. Kaibel**.

| Lübeck – Hamburg | 1891–1892 | Concerts Nos. 45–49 |

NOTES [1] The Hamburg Senate had by law designated this day to be the annual "Day of "Buß- und Bettag" ("Prayer and Repentance") on which public entertainment was forbidden. Usually the *Stadttheater* was allowed to perform sacred works, but this year the director, Pollini, chose to arrange performances by his artists in various cities in northern Germany, including this one, in Lübeck.
[2] Sung in German: "Endlich naht sich die Stunde."
[3] The "Final Duet" (with Siegmund & Sieglinde) probably began with "Du bist der Lenz" and continued through the end of the act.
REVIEW HLG I, 243.

46. February 29, 1892, 7 p.m.
47. March 3, 1892, 7 p.m.
HAMBURG - Stadttheater [2,000 seats]

In Celebration of Rossini's Centenary

      Rossini   *Stabat Mater*, for Soloists, Chorus, and Orch. ● [1]

[followed by a complete stage performance of Rossini's *Guillaume Tell*, cond. by Mahler]

SOLOISTS K. Klafsky, E. Schumann-Heink, W. Cronberger and H. Wiegand.
SOURCE Newspaper advertisement.
NOTE [1] According to the review in the Hamburg *Correspondent*, March 1, 1892, three movements were omitted: the 2nd (an aria), the 3rd (a duet), and oddly, the *Finale*.

48. March 14, 1892, 7 p.m.
HAMBURG - Stadttheater [2,000 seats]

Annual Benefit for Mahler

      Beethoven   Symphony No. 3, E-flat major, Op. 55, "Eroica" [1]

[followed by a complete stage performance of Beethoven's *Fidelio*, cond. by Mahler]

SOURCE Newspaper advertisement.
NOTE [1] Mahler's first performance of this work.
REVIEW HLG I, 251.

49. April 15, 1892, 7 p.m.
HAMBURG - Stadttheater [2,000 seats]

Good Friday Concert [1]

    (1)   Mozart   *Requiem*, D minor, K. 626
                                  - Intermission -
    (2)   Bruckner   *Te Deum*, for Soloists, Chorus, and Orch. [2]

SOLOISTS (1) M. Lißmann, E. Schumann-Heink, W. Cronberger, F. Lißmann.
(2) K. Bettaque, E. Heink, L. Landau, H. Wiegand.
SOURCE Newspaper advertisement.

THE BUGLE BRAND.

M. B. FOSTER & SONS
LIMITED (Established 1829),
ALE AND BEER MERCHANTS,
Offices—27 & 29, BROOK STREET, BOND STREET, W.
Stores—242 & 244, MARYLEBONE ROAD, N.W.
BASS' ALE & GUINNESS' STOUT.
The above Bottling supplied to this Theatre.

ST. JAMES'S HALL.

Sir AUGUSTUS HARRIS'S
GRAND
VOCAL, ORCHESTRAL & CHORAL
WAGNERIAN CONCERT
WEDNESDAY, JUNE 29th, 1892,
Commencing at THREE o'clock.

Artistes:

Madame MELBA AND Madame EMMA EAMES,
Mlle. GIULIA RAVOGLI AND Mlle. TELEKI.
Frau ENDE-ANDRIESSEN AND Fraulein HEINK
Fraulein TRAUBMANN AND Fraulein KOLLAR,
Fraulein RALPH AND Fraulein UPLEGER,
Fraulein SIMON AND Fraulein FROEHLICH,
Fraulein MEISSLINGER.

Herr MAX ALVARY AND Mons. VAN DYCK,
Mons. MONTARIOL AND Herr JULIUS LIEBAN.
Mons. MAUREL AND Mons. PLANÇON
Signor ABRAMOFF

Solo Violinists:
Mons. TIVADAR NACHEZ AND Mlle. PANTEO.

The ORCHESTRAS of the ITALIAN and GERMAN OPERAS.

Conductors:
Signor MANCINELLI AND Signor BEVIGNANI
Mons LÉON JEHIN AND Herr MAHLER.

PROGRAMME.

Part I.—WAGNER.

MARCH, ... "Tannhäuser,"
    ORCHESTRA and CHORUS.
LIEBESGESANG, ... "Die Walküre," (Act I.)
    Herr ALVARY.
VORSPIEL and LIEBESTOD, .. "Tristan und Isolde."
    Frau ENDE-ANDRIESSEN.
LIEDER, ...
    Fräulein HEINK.
SOLO—Violin, ... "Albumblatt,"
    Mlle. PANTEO.
WALKÜRENRITT.
    Frl. KOLLAR, Frl. TRAUBMANN, Frl. RALPH,
Frl. UPLEGER, Frl. HEINK, Frl. SIMON, Frl. FROEHLICH,
    Frl. MEISSLINGER.
GESANG DES WALTHER, .. "Tannhäuser," (Act II.)
    Herr JULIUS LIEBAN.
DUO, (Elsa and Ortruda) .. .. .. "Lohengrin,"
    Mme. MELBA and Mlle. GIULIA RAVOGLI.

Part II.—WAGNER.

OVERTURE, ... "Tannhäuser,"
SCHIEMEDELIEDER, .. "Siegfried," (Act I.)
    Mons. VAN DYCK.
ROMANCE, ... "Tannhäuser," (Act III.)
    Mons. MAUREL.
ARIA, ... "Lohengrin,
    Mme. EMMA EAMES.
VORSPIEL and ARIA— Elizabeth, "Tannhäuser," (Act II)
    Mlle. TELEKI.
SOLO—Violin, .. "Preislied," (Die Meistersinger)
    Mons. TIVADAR NACHEZ.
ARIA, ... "Flying Dutchman," (Act II,
    Mons. PLANÇON.
PRAYER from .. .. "Lohengrin," (Act I.)
    Mmes. MELBA, GIULIA RAVOGLI,
Mons. MONTARIOL, Mons. MAUREL and Signor ABRAMOFF

Conductors: Sig. MANCINELLI, Sig. BEVIGNANI,
Mons. LEON JEHIN, and Herr MAHLER.

Sofa Stalls, 10/6. Reserved Seats, 7/6. Balcony, Unreserved, 5/-
Area and Orchestra, 2/6. Admission, 1/-
Tickets at the Box-Office, Covent Garden Theatre; the usual Agents
and BASIL TREE'S OFFICE, St. James's Hall, Piccadilly, W.

NOTES [1] While the law did not allow opera performances on Good Friday, the Hamburg Senate did license performances of sacred works.
[2] First performance in Hamburg.
REVIEW HLG I, 253.

50. June 29, 1892, 3 p.m.
LONDON - The Main Hall of St. James's Hall [2,127 seats]

Third Operatic Concert, Part I [1]

All-Wagner Program:

    (1)   Prelude and "Liebestod," from *Tristan und Isolde*
    (2)   "Träume," *Lied*, with Orchestra
    (3)   "Walkürenritt," from *Die Walküre* [2]
    (4)   Duet from Act 2 (unspecified) for Elsa and Ortrud, from *Lohengrin* [3]

SOLOISTS (1) P. Andriessen; (2) E. Schumann-Heink; (3) S. Kollár, S. Traubmann, P. Ralph, E. Uplegger, E. Schumann-Heink, L. Simon, M. Fröhlich, L. Meisslinger; (4) L. Meisslinger & E. Eames.
ORCHESTRA The orchestra of the Hamburg *Stadttheater*, reinforced by musicians from London.
SOURCE The program is pieced together from various previews and especially the review in *The Sunday Times* from July 3, 1892. The order is not necessarily correct. See the broadsheet on the opposite page.
NOTES Since the duration of the program is less than one hour, it is possible that additional works were performed.
Between June 8 and July 22, 1892, the ensembles of the Hamburg *Stadttheater* presented a "German Season" at The Royal Opera House, Covent Garden, and at the Drury Lane Theater. Mahler conducted 18 performances of the following works: Wagner's *Das Rheingold* (2 performances), *Die Walküre* (2), *Siegfried* (4), *Götterdämmerung* (2), *Tristan und Isolde* (4), *Tannhäuser* (2), and finally, Beethoven's *Fidelio* (2). Two additional performances of Nessler's *Der Trompeter von Säckingen* were, as usual, conducted by Leo Feld, the 2nd *Kapellmeister* in Hamburg.
[1] The second half of the concert was comprised of extracts from French and Italian operas. Immediately after the first part of the concert, Mahler, his soloists, and the orchestra hastened to Covent Garden for a 7:30 p.m. performance of Wagner's *Die Walküre*.
[2] The original version for 8 soloists and Orchestra from Act 3, Scene 1.
[3] Probably begun with Elsa's "Wer ruft? Wie schauerlich und klagend…" from Act 2, Scene 2. Emma Eames was not part of the German Opera troupe.

Montag, 12. December, Abends 7½ Uhr präc., **Convent-Garten:**

V. Abonnement-Concert

(In Vertretung des Herrn Dr. **Hans von Bülow**, mit gütiger Bewilligung des Herrn Hofrath **B. Pollini**)
unter Leitung des Herrn

Capellmeister Gustav Mahler.

Solist: Herr Professor **Carl Halir.**

PROGRAMM:

1. **Mendelssohn:** Ouvertüre Sommernachtstraum.
2. **Lalo:** Violin-Concert (Symphonie espagnole).
3. **Wagner:** Siegfried Idyll.
4. **Violinsolo.**
5. **Beethoven:** V. Sinfonie, C-moll.

Billets à 2, 4, 5 M. i. d. Musikalienhandlung v. **J. A. Böhme** u. a. d. Casse.

Sonntag, 11. December, Mittags 12½ Uhr:

Hauptprobe.

Billets à 1 M. 50 ₰ bei **J. A. Böhme** u. a. d. Casse.

| Hamburg | 1892–1893 | Concerts Nos. 51–52 |

Season 1892–1893

51. December 12, 1892, 7:30 p.m.
HAMBURG - Convent Garten [3,000 seats]

Fifth Subscription Concert [1]

    (1) Mendelssohn   Overture to *Ein Sommernachtstraum*, Op. 21
    (2) Lalo   *Symphonie espagnole,* D minor, Op. 21
    (3) Wagner   *Siegfried Idyll*
    (4) Paganini   Violin Concerto No. 1, D major, Op. 6, 1st movement •
    (5) Beethoven   Symphony No. 5, C minor, Op. 67

SOLOIST (2 & 4) C. Halir.
ORCHESTRA The Orchestra of the Hamburg "Subscription Concerts."
SOURCE Newspaper advertisement; see illustration on opposite page.
NOTE [1] For reasons of health, Hans von Bülow, the Subscription Concerts' permanent conductor, invited Mahler to replace him. Mahler reluctantly accepted, because on the same evening two of his new orchestral songs from *Des Knaben Wunderhorn* were premiered in Berlin, concert no. 55, note 2.
REVIEW HLG I, 262–263.

52. March 19, 1893, 1 p.m.
HAMBURG - Stadttheater [2,000 seats]

Gala Performance for the Benefit of the Schröder Pension Fund [1]

    Haydn   Symphony No. 99, E-flat major •

[followed by a complete stage performance of Gluck's *Orfeo ed Euridice*, Act 1, and an aria from Ignaz Holzbauer's opera *Günther von Schwarzburg*, cond. by Robert Erben]

SOURCE Program reconstructed from reviews in the local press. The event was by invitation only.
NOTE [1] Founded in 1793 by Friedrich Ludwig Schröder, former director of the Hamburg *Stadttheater,* to support pensioned members of the theater.
REVIEW HLG I, 267.

Stadt-Theater.

(Direction: B. Pollini.)

Freitag, den 31. März 1893.

191. Abonnem.-Vorstellung.   26. Freitags-Vorstellung.

Mit Bewilligung des Hohen Senats.

Zum ersten Male:

Messe in D

von

Anton Bruckner

für Soli, Chor, Orchester und Orgel.

Die Soli gesungen von Frau Lißmann, Frau Heink und den Herren Seidel und Lißmann.

Dirigent: Herr Kapellmeister Gustav Mahler.

Kyrie eleison!
Gloria in excelsis Deo.
Credo in unum Deum.
Sanctus Dominus Deus Sabaoth.
Benedictus qui venit in nomine Domini.
Agnus Dei.

Hierauf:

TE DEUM

von

Anton Bruckner

für Soli, Chor, Orchester und Orgel.

Die Soli gesungen von Fräul. Bettaque, Frau Heink und den Herren Landau und Wiegand.

Dirigent: Herr Kapellmeister Gustav Mahler.

Nach der Messe findet eine Pause von 10 Minuten statt.

| Hamburg | 1893 | Concerts Nos. 53–55 |

53. March 31, 1893, 7 p.m.
HAMBURG - Stadttheater [2,000 seats]

Good Friday Concert

    (1)   Bruckner   Mass No. 1, D minor, for Soloists, Chorus and Orch. ● [1]

    - Intermission -

    (2)   Bruckner   *Te Deum*, for Soloists, Chorus and Orch.

SOLOISTS (1) M. Lißmann, E. Schumann-Heink, G. Seidel, F. Lißmann; (2) K. Bettaque, E. Schumann-Heink, L. Landau, H. Wiegand.
SOURCE Newspaper advertisement; see illustration on opposite page.
NOTE [1] First performance outside of Austria and also the first concert performance unaffiliated to church services. The world premiere had taken place in Linz, on November 20, 1864; the 2nd performance was in Vienna, on February 10, 1867, both in connection with church services.
REVIEW HLG I, 267–268.

54. April 15, 1893, 7 p.m.
HAMBURG - Stadttheater [2,000 seats]

Annual Benefit for Mahler [1]

    Beethoven   Symphony No. 5, C minor, Op. 67

[followed by a complete stage performance of Beethoven's *Fidelio*, cond. by Mahler]

SOURCE Newspaper advertisement.
NOTE [1] It was on this occasion that Hans von Bülow, who had snubbed Mahler eight years earlier (p. 39), publicly acknowledged Mahler-*the-Conductor* with a laurel wreath dedicated "to the Pygmalion of the Hamburg Theater." (It has erroneously been assumed that the dedication was printed on the ribbon of the wreath. Bülow had in fact scribbled these words on his calling card which is now in the collection of the Brahms-Institut in Lübeck.)
REVIEW HLG I, 268.

Season 1893–1894

---

55. October 27, 1893, 7:30 p.m.
HAMBURG - Concerthaus Hamburg (Gebrüder Ludwig) [2,000 seats]

First Popular Concert in Philharmonic Style

    (1)   Beethoven   Overture to *Egmont*, Op. 84
    (2)   Marschner   "An jenem Tag," from *Hans Heiling*
    (3)   Adam   Aria (unspecified), from *La Poupée de Nuremberg* [1]
    (4)   Mendelssohn   *Die Hebriden* (*Fingal's Cave*), Overture, Op. 26

Concerthaus Hamburg (Gebr. Ludwig).

Freitag, den 27. October 1893, Abends 👉 7½ Uhr.

Erstes populäres Concert
(im philharmonischen Styl)

unter Leitung des Herrn Capellmeisters

Gustav Mahler

(mit gütiger Bewilligung des Herrn Hofrath **Pollini**) unter Mitwirkung der

Kgl. Kammersängerin Frau **Clementine Schuch-Prosska** aus Dresden,

Kgl. Kammersängers Herrn **Paul Bulss** aus Berlin.

Programm:

Ouverture zu Egmont von Beethoven,
Arie a. d. Nürnberger Puppe von Adam.
Balladen und Humoresken aus »Des Knaben Wunderhorn« von Mahler,
Ouverture »Hebriden« (Fingalshöhle) Mendelssohn,
Arie aus »Hans Heiling« von Marschner,
»Titan«. Eine Tondichtung in Symphonieform von Mahler.

Abonnement für 6 Concerte Saal ℳ. 7.—, Loge ℳ. 12.—, Balcon ℳ. 15.—, numerirte Plätze ℳ. 2.— und ℳ. 3.—, nichtnumerirte ℳ. 1.— bei Herrn **Max Leichssenring**, Neuerwall 46.

| Hamburg | 1893 | Concerts Nos. 55–56 |

  (5) Mahler   "Humoresken" (songs) from *Des Knaben Wunderhorn*
             with Orch.:
             a) "Das himmlische Leben" [2]
             b) "Verlor'ne Müh' "
             c) "Wer hat dies Liedlein erdacht?" [2]

  (6) Mahler   "Gesänge" (songs) from *Des Knaben Wunderhorn* with
             Orch.:
             a) "Der Schildwache Nachtlied (eine Scene aus dem
              Lagerleben der Landsknechte)" [3]
             b) "Trost im Unglück, (aus dem Leben der
              Landsknechte)" [2 & 4]
             c) "Rheinlegendchen" [encore] [2]
             - Intermission -

  (7) Mahler   *Titan*, eine Tondichtung in Symphonieform [5]

SOLOISTS (2 & 6) P. Bulß; (3 & 5) C. Schuch-Prosska.
ORCHESTRA The reinforced "Laube'sche Capelle."
SOURCE Newspaper advertisement; see illustration on opposite page.
NOTES [1] Sung in German.
[2] World premiere. Nos. 5b and 6a had previously been premiered in Berlin on December 12, 1892, by Amalie Joachim and the Berlin Philharmonic Orchestra, conducted by Rafael Maszkowski. Regarding no. 5a, this performance appears to be the only one in Mahler's lifetime of the song as an independent orchestral *Lied*. Six years later (1899), when Mahler embarked on his Fourth Symphony, he incorporated this *Lied* as its *Finale*, also using it as the thematic basis for the entire work.
[3] "A scene from the soldier's camp."
[4] "From the life of the Lansquenets."
[5] World premiere of the recently revised score of the "Tone Poem in Symphonic Form," premiered four years earlier in Budapest (concert no. 36). For this occasion Mahler titled it "*Titan*" after a novel by Jean Paul, and also added subtitles and programmatic descriptions to the individual movements.
REVIEW HLG I, 281–83; DM II, 238–41; Pfohl, 64–67.

56. November 10, 1893, 6:30 p.m.
HAMBURG - Stadttheater [2,000 seats]

On the Occasion of the 25th Anniversary of the Society "Kunst und Wissenschaft" [1]

    Weber   *Jubel*–Overture, Op. 59 •

  [followed by a complete stage performance of Beethoven's *Fidelio*, cond. by Mahler]

SOURCE The review in the Hamburg *Correspondent*.
NOTE [1] i.e. "Art and Science."

CURHAUS ZU WIESBADEN.

Cyklus von 12 Concerten unter Mitwirkung hervorragender Künstler.

Freitag, den 17. November 1893, Abends 7½ Uhr:

III. CONCERT.

Mitwirkende:

Herr PAUL BULSS,

Königl. Sächs. Kammersänger und Hofopernsänger aus Berlin

und das

verstärkte städtische Cur-Orchester

unter Leitung des

Concertmeisters Herrn **Franz Nowak**.

Pianoforte-Begleitung: Herr Benno Voigt.

PROGRAMM.

1. **Ouverture** zu Collin's Trauerspiel „Coriolan" . . BEETHOVEN.
2. **Drei Gesänge** mit Orchester . . . . GUSTAV MAHLER.
   (unter Leitung des Componisten).
   - a) Der Schildwache Nachtlied (eine Scene aus dem Lagerleben).
   - b) Trost im Unglück.
   - c) Rheinlegendchen.

   Herr BULSS.
3. **Gavotte** aus der 6. Orchester-Suite in C-dur . . FRZ. LACHNER.
4. **Prolog** aus „Die Bajazzi" . . . . LEONCAVALLO.

   Herr BULSS.
5. **Vorspiel** zum 5. Akt aus „König Manfred" . . REINECKE.
6. **Vier Lieder** mit Pianoforte:
   - a) Frühlingsgruss . . . . FRZ. SCHUBERT.
   - b) Bergfahrt . . . . HERM. HUTTER.
   - c) Ganz leise ⎱ . . . . REINHOLD BECKER.
   - d) Erwartung ⎰

   Herr BULSS.
7. **Ländliche Hochzeit**, Symphonie in Es-dur . . GOLDMARK.
   - I. Hochzeitsmarsch (Variationen).
   - II. Brautlied (Intermezzo).
   - III. Serenade (Scherzo).
   - IV. Im Garten (Andante).
   - V. Tanz (Finale).

☞ Bei Beginn des Concertes werden die Eingangsthüren des grossen Saales geschlossen und nur in den Zwischenpausen der einzelnen Nummern geöffnet.   Der Curdirector: F. Hey'l.

☞ Nach Schluss des Concertes fährt vom **Theaterplatz** ab ein **Dampf-Strassenbahnzug** nach **Biebrich** und ein **Pferdebahnwagen** bis Station **Emilienstrasse**.

| Wiesbaden–Hamburg | 1893 | Concerts Nos. 57–58 |

57. November 17, 1893, 7:30 p.m. [1]
WIESBADEN - Kurhaus [1,200 seats]

Third Subscription Concert

- (1) Beethoven — Overture to *Coriolan*, Op. 62
- (2) Mahler — Three "Gesänge" (songs) from *Des Knaben Wunderhorn* with Orch.:
    - a) "Der Schildwache Nachtlied (eine Scene aus dem Lagerleben der Landsknechte)" [2]
    - b) "Trost im Unglück"
    - c) "Rheinlegendchen"
- (3) Lachner — *Gavotte*, from Suite No. 6, C major, Op. 150, for String Orch.
- (4) Leoncavallo — "Si può? ... Un nido di memoire" (Prologue), from *Pagliacci*
- (5) Reinecke — Prelude to Act 5 of *König Manfred*
- (6) Four *Lieder* with Piano Acc.:
    - a) Schubert — "Frühlingsgruß," (unspecified)
    - b) Hutter — "Bergfahrt"
    - c) Becker — "Ganz leise," Op. 61, No. 5
    - d) Becker — "Erwärtung," Op. 61, No. 4
- (7) Goldmark — Symphony No. 1, E-flat major, Op. 26, "Ländliche Hochzeit"

SOLOIST (2, 4, 6) P. Bulss, acc. in no. 6 by B. Voigt.
CONDUCTORS (1, 3–5, 7) F. Nowak; (2) Mahler.
ORCHESTRA The reinforced Wiesbaden *Cur-Orchester*.
SOURCE Handbill; see illustration on opposite page and a review in the newspaper *Rheinischer Kurier* from November 18.
NOTE [1] Mahler's first ever out-of-town engagement as composer-conductor. No doubt this was initiated at the request of Paul Bulss (concert no. 55), whom Mahler had first met at Kassel (concert no. 26), and later Bulss had also appeared as a guest under Mahler in Leipzig, and most recently at the *Stadttheater* in Hamburg.
[2] "A scene from the soldier's camp."
REVIEW HLG I, 284.

58. November 18, 1893, 7 p.m.
HAMBURG - Stadttheater [2,000 seats]

In Memory of Pyotr Tchaikovsky [1]

- (1) Tchaikovsky — "Letter Scene," from *Eugene Onegin*
- (2) Tchaikovsky — *Romeo and Juliet*, Fantasy-Overture

[followed by complete stage performances of Tchaikovsky's *Iolanta*, cond. by Mahler, and Leoncavallo's *Pagliacci*, cond. by O. Lohse]

SOLOISTS (1) K. Bettaque (Tatyana) and H. Felden (Nurse Filippyevna).
SOURCE Newspaper advertisement.
NOTE [1] Tchaikovsky died on November 6, 1893. Two months earlier, on September 7, he had been on a quick visit to Hamburg and, after attending a performance of his *Iolanta* conducted by Mahler, he spent the rest of the evening with Mahler and Bernhard Pollini at the latter's villa.

✳ Concerthaus — Conventgarten. ✳

Montag den 26. Februar 1894, Abends 7½ Uhr pünktlich

IX. ABONNEMENT-CONCERT

GEDENKFEIER FÜR
HANS VON BÜLOW

Dirigent:
Kapellmeister Herr Gustav Mahler
(Mit gütiger Bewilligung des Herrn Hofrath Pollini).

Unter Mitwirkung eines Chores von Damen und Herren, unter Leitung des Herrn **Julius Spengel**.

Orgel: Herr **Carl Armbrust**.

PROGRAMM.

1. Praeludium für Orgel u. Choral: „Wenn ich einmal soll scheiden". . . . . . . *J. S. Bach.*
2. Gedenkrede.
3. Zwei Chöre aus: „Ein deutsches Requiem" *J. Brahms.*
   I. „Selig sind, die da Leid tragen".
   II. „Denn alles Fleisch ist wie Gras".

4. Sinfonie No. 3, Es-dur (Eroica) (1804) . *L. v. Beethoven.*
   Allegro con brio. — Marcia funebre (Adagio assai). — Scherzo (Allegro vivace), — Finale (Allegro molto).

X. (letztes) Abonnement-Concert: Montag den 12. März 1894.
Dirigent: *Eugen d'Albert.*
Solisten: Frau **Teresa d'Albert-Carreño** und Frl. **Katharina Rösing** (Gesang).

| Altona - Hamburg | 1893–1894 | Concerts Nos. 59–61 |

59. November 22, 1893, 5 p.m.
ALTONA - Stadttheater [1,050 seats]

On the Occasion of the Day of Prayer and Repentance

(1) Haydn *Die Schöpfung*, Oratorio
- Intermission -
(2) Mendelssohn "O rest in the Lord," from *Elijah*, Oratorio, Op. 70 [1]
(3) Mendelssohn "Gott sei mir gnädig," from *Paulus*, Oratorio, Op. 36

SOLOISTS (1) J. von Artner (Eva & Gabriel), L. Landau (Uriel), F. Lißmann (Raphael & Adam); (2) E. Schumann-Heink; (3) W. Vilmar.
CONDUCTORS (1) Mahler; (2 & 3) O. Lohse.
SOURCE Newspaper advertisement.
NOTE [1] Sung in German: "Sei stille dem Herrn."

60. February 26, 1894, 7 p.m.
HAMBURG - Convent Garten [3,000 seats]

Ninth Subscription Concert. In Memory of Hans von Bülow [1]

(1) Bach a) Prelude, on Hassler's "Herzlich thut mich verlangen," A minor, BWV 727, for Organ
b) "Wenn ich einmal soll scheiden," from *Matthäus-Passion*, BWV 244, No. 72, for Chorus and Orchestra
(2) Commemorative address by Hermann Behn.
(3) Brahms Two choruses from *Ein deutsches Requiem*, Op. 45
a) "Selig sind, die da Leid tragen"
b) "Denn alles Fleisch es ist wie Gras"
- Intermission -
(4) Beethoven Symphony No. 3, E-flat major, Op. 55, *Eroica*

PERFORMERS (1a) C. Armbrust, organ; (2) H. Behn; (4) Mahler, conductor.
ORCHESTRA The Orchestra of the "Subscription Concerts."
CHORUS (1b, 3) The "Cäcilien-Verein," cond. J. Spengel.
SOURCE Handbill and newspaper advertisement; see illustrations on opposite and following pages.
NOTE [1] Conductor-pianist Hans von Bülow had died in Cairo on February 12, 1894.
REVIEW HLG I, 293-294.

61. March 3, 1894, 7 p.m.
HAMBURG - Stadttheater [2,000 seats]

Annual Benefit for Mahler

Beethoven Symphony No. 7, A major, Op. 92 [1]

[followed by a complete stage performance of Beethoven's *Fidelio*, cond. by Mahler]

SOURCE Newspaper advertisement.
NOTE [1] Mahler's first performance of this work.
REVIEW HLG I, 297-298.

Gedenkfeier für Hans von Bülow.

Montag, den 26. Februar, Abends 7½ Uhr, grosser Saal Convent-Garten:

IX. Abonnement-Concert.

Dirigent: **Herr Capellmeister Gustav Mahler.**

(Mit gütiger Bewilligung des Herrn Hofrath Pollini.)

Unter Mitwirkung eines **Chores von Damen und Herren** unter Leitung des **Herrn Julius Spengel.**

Programm.

Bach: Choral a.d. Matthäus-Passion »Wenn ich nun mal muss scheiden«, für Chor u. Orchester.
Gedächtnissrede.
Beethoven: Ouverture »Leonore«, Nr. 3.

Beethoven: Eroica-Sinfonie.
Brahms: Zwei Chöre mit Orchester aus »Ein deutsches Requiem«.

Billets à 5, 4 u. 2 M. i. d. Musikalienhandlung von **Joh. Aug. Böhme**, Neuerwall 35, und an der Casse.

Sonntag, den 25. Februar, Mittags 12½ Uhr

Oeffentliche Hauptprobe

Billets à M. 1.50.

62. **March 23, 1894, 7 p.m.**
HAMBURG - Stadttheater [2,000 seats]

Good Friday Concert

(1)	Haydn	*Die Schöpfung*, Oratorio
		- Intermission -
(2)	Mendelssohn	"O rest in the Lord," from *Elijah*, Oratorio, Op. 70 [1]
(3)	Mendelssohn	"Gott, sei mir gnädig," from *Paulus*, Oratorio, Op. 36
(4)	Mendelssohn	"Hear ye, Israel," from *Elijah*, Oratorio, Op. 70 [1]

SOLOISTS (1) J. von Artner (Eva & Gabriel), L. Landau (Uriel), I. Waldmann (Raphael), W. Vilmar (Adam). (2) E. Schumann-Heink, (3) W. Vilmar, (4) K. Bettaque.
CONDUCTORS (1) Mahler; (2–4) O. Lohse.
SOURCE Newspaper advertisement.
NOTE [1] Sung in German: (2) "Sei stille dem Herrn," and (4) "Höre Israel."

63. **March 29, 1894, ca. 12 p.m.**
HAMBURG - The Loggia of the Stadttheater

On the Occasion of the Funeral of Hans von Bülow [1]

	Wagner	"Siegfried's Tod," Funeral March, from *Götterdämmerung*

SOURCE Various articles in the local press.
NOTE [1] Immediately after attending the funeral service in the "Große Michaelis Kirche," Mahler hurried to the *Stadttheater*, where the orchestra had assembled in the room adjoining the loggia. When the cortege passed, the march sounded through the open doors. It was at the funeral service that Mahler was inspired to employ Klopstock's psalm "Auferstehung" ("Resurrection") for the *Finale* of his Second Symphony. The psalm was set to a melody by Karl Heinrich Graun (1701–1759).

64. **June 3, 1894, 5 p.m.**
WEIMAR - Großherzogliches Hof-Theater [1] [1,000 seats]

Second Concert at the 30th Festival of the "Allgemeiner Deutscher Musikverein"

(1)	Liszt	"Weimars Volkslied," for Men's Chorus and Winds
(2)	Rubinstein	Cello Concerto, A minor, Op. 65
(3)	Wagner	5 *Wesendonck-Lieder*, for Soprano and Orch.
(4)	Bülow	*Des Sängers Fluch*, Symphonic Ballad, Op. 16
(5)	Stavenhagen	Piano Concerto, B minor, Op. 4
(6)	Wagner	"Starke Scheite schichtet," from *Götterdämmerung*
		- Intermission -
(7)	Mahler	*Titan,* Symphonie in zwei Abtheilungen und fünf Sätzen [2]
		Part I: Abtheilung: "Aus den Tagen der Jugend"
		Frühling und kein Ende, Blumine, Mit vollen Segeln.
		Part II: Abtheilung: "Commedia humana"
		Todtenmarsch in Callot's Manier, Dell Inferno al Paradiso.

Tonkünstler-Versammlung zu Weimar.

Dritte Aufführung.

Mit höchster Genehmigung von der Generalintendanz des Grossherzoglichen Hoftheaters für die Tonkünstlerversammlung des „Allgemeinen Deutschen Musikvereins" veranstaltet.

Sonntag den 3. Juni, Nachmittags 5 Uhr,
im Grossherzoglichen Hoftheater:

Grosses Concert

für Orchester, Chor und Soli. Dirigent: Herr Hofkapellmeister Dr. Eduard Lassen.

---

1. **Franz Liszt: Weimars Volkslied** für Chor und Harmoniemusik.
   Der Hoftheaterchor verstärkt durch Mitglieder des Chorvereins, der Singakademie und andere Musikfreunde.

2. **Anton Rubinstein: Concert** für Violoncello und Orchester. A moll. (Op. 65.)
   I. Allegro moderato. — II. Moderato con moto, Andante con moto. — III. Allegro con fuoco, Allegro non troppo.
   Herr Professor Julius Klengel (Leipzig).

3. **Richard Wagner: Fünf Lieder** für eine Sopranstimme und Orchester.
   a) Der Engel. Instrumentirt von Richard Wagner.
   b) Stehe still!
   c) Im Treibhaus. } Instrumentirt von Felix Mottl.
   d) Schmerzen.
   e) Träume.
   Frau Rosa Sucher, Kgl. Kammersängerin (Berlin).

4. **Hans von Bülow: Des Sängers Fluch.** Ballade für Orchester.

5. **Bernhard Stavenhagen: Concert** für Pianoforte und Orchester.
   I. Sehr energisch und lebhaft. — II. Langsam. — III. Erstes Zeitmass.
   Herr Hofpianist Bernhard Stavenhagen (Weimar).

6. **Richard Wagner: Schlussgesang der Brünnhild** aus der »Götterdämmerung.«
   Frau Rosa Sucher (Berlin).

Zwischen 6. und 7. findet eine Pause von 20 Minuten statt.

7. **Gustav Mahler: Titan.** Symphonie in zwei Abtheilungen und fünf Sätzen.
   I. Abtheilung: »Aus den Tagen der Jugend.«
   Frühling und kein Ende. — Blumine. — Mit vollen Segeln.
   II. Abtheilung: Commedia humana.
   Todtenmarsch in Callot's Manier. — Dell Inferno al Paradiso.
   Unter Direction des Componisten.

8. **Richard Wagner: Kaisermarsch** für grosses Orchester und Chor.
   Der Hoftheaterchor verstärkt durch Mitglieder des Chorvereins, der Singakademie und andere Musikfreunde.

Orchester: Die Grossherzogliche Hofkapelle verstärkt durch Mitglieder der Meininger Hofkapelle.

Concertflügel: *C. Bechstein* (Berlin).

| Weimar | 1894 | Concert No. 64 |

(8) Wagner *Kaisermarsch* (version for Orch. and Chorus)

SOLOISTS (2) J. Klengel, (3 & 6) R. Sucher, (5) B. Stavenhagen.
CONDUCTORS (1–6, 8) Eduard Lassen; (7) Mahler.
ORCHESTRA & CHORUS The Weimar Court Opera Orchestra, reinforced with members of the Meiningen *Hofkapelle*; the Weimar Court Opera Chorus, reinforced with singers from the Weimar *Chorverein*, the *Singakademie,* and a number of "musical friends."
SOURCE Program (Weimar, 1894, pp. 43–44); see illustration on opposite page.
NOTES [1] The Grand Ducal Court Theater. Originally the Festival was scheduled to take place in Nuremberg.
[2] "*Titan,* Symphony in two parts and five movements." One notices the significant re-titling of the "Tone Poem in Symphonic Form" performed seven months earlier (concert no. 55). Also of note: the program booklet omits the descriptive programs, but retains the titles of the individual movements, which are identical with those in the autograph score kept at Yale University, New Haven (Osborn Collection). This was apparently done without Mahler's approval, because on the day of the concert a new program was printed on a separate paper and distributed, which—with some modifications—is identical with the Hamburg program (concert no. 55). Unfortunately, a copy of this additional "Weimar program" has not been located. Of additional interest, this was the second and last time Mahler presented his symphony as *Titan*. At the next performance (Berlin 1896, concert no. 84) Mahler renounced all titles and programmatic descriptions, and he discarded the second movement, "Blumine."
REVIEW HLG I, 299–301.

1894/1895.

RÜCKBLICK
auf die
Acht Abonnement-Concerte.

Dirigent: Kapellmeister **Gustav Mahler**.

I. Concert: Montag, den 22. October 1894.
1. Symphonie G-moll .... *Mozart.*
2. a) „Soll sich der Mond nicht heller scheinen"
   b) „Jungfräulein, soll ich mit Euch geh'n"
   c) „Schwesterlein"
   d) „So will ich frisch und fröhlich sein"
   e) „Feinsliebchen, du sollst" .... } *Brahms* — Neue deutsche Volkslieder zum 1. Mal.
3. Concertstück für Klavier und Orchester .... *Weber.*
4. a) „Wo gehst du hin, du Stolze?"
   b) „Es reit' ein Herr und auch sein Knecht"
   c) „Mein Mädel hat einen Rosenmund"
   d) „Ach Moder, ich well en Ding han" (Kölnisch). } *Brahms* — Neue deutsche Volkslieder zum 1. Mal.
5. Spanische Rhapsodie, Bearbeitung für Klavier und Orchester ... *Busoni-Liszt.*
6. Symphonie No. 7, A-dur, op. 92 *Beethoven.*

Solisten: *Amalie Joachim (Gesang), Ferruccio B. Busoni (Klavier).*

II. Concert: Montag, den 5. November 1894.
1. Ouverture „Le Carneval Romain" *Berlioz.*
2. Symphonie Espagnole für Violine und Orchester, op. 21 . *Lalo.*
3. Siegfried-Idyll .... *Wagner.*
4. Muiñeira, thème montagnard varié für Violine mit Begleitung des Orchesters .... *Sarasate.*
5. Symphonie C-dur .... *Schubert.*

Solist: *Pablo de Sarasate (Violine).*

III. Concert: Montag, den 19. November 1894.
1. Ouverture: „Coriolan", op. 62 *Beethoven.*
2. Altitalienische Arien:
   a) „Per la gloria" .... *Buononcini.*
   b) La Zingarella .... *Paesiello.*
   c) Le Violette .... *Scarlatti.*
3. Concert für Klavier mit Orchester, D-moll, op. 70 .... *Rubinstein.*
4. Lieder:
   a) „Ouvre tes yeux bleus" .. *Massenet.*
   b) Pastorale .... *Bizet.*
5. Symphonie F-dur, op. 90, No. 3 *Brahms.*

Solisten: *Maria Antonietta Palloni (Gesang), Fannie Bloomfield-Zeisler (Klavier).*

IV. Concert: Montag, den 3. December 1894.
1. Eine Faustouverture für grosses Orchester .... *Wagner.*
2. Dem Gedächtniss Anton Rubinstein's, gedichtet von Dr. Julius Rodenberg, gesprochen von Herrn Carl Leisner, mit gütiger Erlaubniss des Hofrath Herrn B. Pollini.
3. I. Satz aus der Ocean-Symphonie, (C-dur) op. 42 ....
4. Lieder:
   a) Der Traum
   b) Der Asra
   c) Neue Liebe } *Rubinstein.*
5. Balletmusik a. d. Oper: „Der Dämon"
6. Symphonie No. 6, F-dur, op. 68 (Pastorale) .... *Beethoven.*

Solist: *Raimund von Zur-Mühlen (Gesang).*

V. Concert: Montag, den 21. Januar 1895.
1. Ouverture „Die Hebriden" .. *Mendelssohn.*
2. Concert für die Violine mit Begleitung des Orchesters, C-dur, op. 30 .... *Moszkowski.*
3. Ouverture zu: „Leonore", No. 3, C-dur .... *Beethoven.*
4. Elégie et Rondo für Violine mit Begleitung des Orchesters, op. 48 .... *Sauret.*
5. Symphonie B-dur, op. 38 ... *Schumann.*

Solist: *Emile Sauret (Violine).*

VI. Concert: Montag, den 4. Februar 1895.
1. Symphonie fantastique, op. 14 *Berlioz.*
2. Concert für Klavier mit Begleitung d. Orchesters, A-moll, op. 16 .... *Grieg.*
3. Vorspiel zu: „Guntram" (zum 1. Mal) .... *Rich. Strauss.*
4. Soli:
   a) Rondo G-dur, op. 51, No. 2 *Beethoven.*
   b) Impromptu, op. 142, No. 3 *Schubert.*
   c) Rhapsodie No. 6 .... *Liszt.*
5. Vorspiel zu: „Tristan u. Isolde" *Wagner.*

Solist: *Teresa d'Albert-Carreño (Klavier).*

VII. Concert: Montag, den 18. Februar 1895.
1. Symphonie No. 4, Es-dur (Romantische) .... *Bruckner.*
2. Terzette:
   a) „Hebe deine Augen auf" *Mendelssohn.*
   b) Belooning .... *Rennes.*
   c) Volkslied .... *Brahms.*
3. Concert für Klavier mit Begleitung des Orchesters No. 1, D-moll, op. 15 .... *Brahms.*
4. Terzette:
   a) Zwei Madrigalen ...... *Fabricius.*
   b) Kerstnacht (holländ. Volkslied) .... *Rennes.*
5. Vorspiel zu den Meistersingern von Nürnberg .... *Wagner.*

Solisten: *Die holländischen Sängerinnen Jeannette de Jong, Anna Corver, Marie Synders. Robert Freund (Klavier).*

VIII. Concert: Montag, den 11. März 1895.
1. Ouverture: „Zur Namensfeier" (C-dur) op. 115 .... *Beethoven.*
2. Neunte Symphonie D-moll, mit Schlusschor über Schiller's Ode „An die Freude", op. 125 *Beethoven.*

Solisten: *Josefine von Artner (Sopran), Anna Bünz (Alt), Nicola Doerter (Tenor), Hermann Gausche (Bass).*

Es waren in obigen Concerten vertreten: **Beethoven** 7 mal, **Brahms**, **Rubinstein**, **Wagner** je 4 mal, **Berlioz**, **Liszt**, **Mendelssohn**, **Schubert** je 2 mal, **Bizet**, **Bruckner**, **Buononcini**, **Fabricius**, **Grieg**, **Lalo**, **Massenet**, **Moszkowski**, **Mozart**, **Paesiello**, **Rennes**, **Sarasate**, **Sauret**, **Scarlatti**, **Schumann**, **Rich. Strauss**, **Weber** je 1 mal.

Montag, d. 22. October, Abends 7½ Uhr präc., grosser Saal Convent-Garten:

1. Abonnements-Concert.

Dirigent: Herr Capellm. **Gustav Mahler.**

Solisten: Frau **Amalie Joachim.** Herr Hofpianist **Ferruccio Busoni.**

Programm:
1. **Mozart:** Sinfonie, G-moll.
2. **Brahms:** Neue deutsche Volkslieder. (Z. e. M.)
   a. „Soll sich der Mond nicht heller scheinen."
   b. „Jungfräulein, soll ich mit Euch geh'n".
   c. „Schwesterlein".
   d. „So will ich frisch und fröhlich".
   e. „Feinsliebchen".
3. **Weber:** Concertstück f. Clavier m. Orchester.
4. **Brahms:** Neue deutsche Volkslieder. (Z. e. M.)
   a. „Wo gehst Du hin?"
   b. „Es reit ein Herr".
   c. „Mein Mädel hat ein Rosenmund".
   d. „Ach Moder". (Kölnisch.)
5. **Liszt:** Spanische Rhapsodie. Clavier m. Orchester.
6. **Beethoven:** 7. Sinfonie, A-dur.

Numerirte Billets à 4 u. 5 M., nicht numerirte à 2 M., in d. Musikalienhandlung von **Joh. Aug. Böhme**, Neuerwall 35 und Abends an der Casse.
Abonnements auf 8 Concerte à 24 und 32 M.
Concert-Direction Herm. **Wolff**.
☞ Eine öffentliche Hauptprobe findet **nicht** statt. ☜
Eingang auch Kaiser Wilhelmstrasse, Casse nur Neust. Fuhlentwiete.

65

Montag, den 5. November, Abends 7½ Uhr, Casseöffnung 7 Uhr, im grossen Saale des Convent-Gartens:

II. Abonnements-Concert.

Dirigent: Herr Capellm. **Gustav Mahler.**

Solist: Herr **Pablo de Sarasate.**

Programm:
1. **Berlioz:** Le Carneval romain. Ouverture caractérisque f. Orchester.
2. **Lalo:** Rhapsodie espagnole f. Violine m. Orchester. Herr **Sarasate**.
3. **Wagner:** Siegfried-Idyll f. Orchester.
4. Violinsolo: Herr **Sarasate**.
5. **Schubert:** Symphonie C-dur f. Orchester.

Numerirte Billets à 5 und 4 M., nicht numerirte à 2 M., in der Musikalienhandlung von **Joh. Aug. Böhme**, Neuerwall 35, und an der Casse.
Concert-Direction Hermann Wolff.

66

65, 66, 67, 70, 71, 72, 73 & 76

Season 1894–1895

On March 30, 1894, the day after von Bülow's funeral, Mahler reported to his sister Justine that he had just been appointed von Bülow's successor as conductor of the 8 annual "Abonnement-Konzerte" ("Subscription Concerts") in Hamburg, run by the Berlin impresario Hermann Wolff. Because of Mahler's contractual obligations with Pollini, Wolff had to pay Pollini a compensation of 500 Marks for each concert, which probably explains why the usual public rehearsals were abandoned. The concerts took place fortnightly, on Monday evenings.

65. **October 22, 1894, 7:30 p.m.** [1]
HAMBURG - Convent Garten [3,000 seats]

First Subscription Concert

(1)	Mozart	Symphony No. 40, G minor, K. 550
(2)	Brahms	[9] *Neue Deutsche Volkslieder*, with Piano Acc. ● [2]
(3)	Weber–Liszt	*Konzertstück,* F minor, Op. 79, for Piano & Orch.
(4)	Liszt–Busoni	*Rhapsodie espagnole*, for Piano & Orch. ●
		- Intermission -
(5)	Beethoven	Symphony No. 7, A major, Op. 92

SOLOISTS (2) A. Joachim, acc. by Mahler; (3 & 4) F. Busoni.
SOURCE Handbill and newspaper advertisement; see illustrations on opposite page.
NOTES [1] The general rehearsal (closed) took place the preceding day at 10 a.m.
[2] World premiere. A selection from the 49 "[New] German Folk Songs," published in seven volumes (Berlin, June 1894): "Soll sich der Mond," "Jungfräulein, soll ich," "Schwesterlein," "So will ich frisch und frölich," "Feinsliebchen," "Wo gehst du hin, du Stolze?" "Es reit ein Herr," "Mein Mädel hat einen Rosenmund," "Och Moder, ich well en Ding han."
REVIEW HLG I, 315.

66. **November 5, 1894, 7:30 p.m.**
HAMBURG - Convent Garten [3,000 seats]

Second Subscription Concert

(1)	Berlioz	*Le carnaval romain,* Overture, Op. 9
(2)	Lalo	*Symphonie espagnole*, D minor, Op. 21 ●
(3)	Wagner	*Siegfried Idyll*
(4)	Sarasate	*Muñeira, Thème varié (Montagnarde)*, Op. 32, for Violin & Orch. ●
		- Intermission -
(5)	Schubert	Symphony No. 9 (8), C major, D 944, "The Great"

SOLOIST (2 & 4) P. de Sarasate.
SOURCE Handbill and newspaper advertisement; see illustrations on opposite page.
REVIEW HLG I, 315.

Montag, den 19. November, Abends 7½ Uhr,
im grossen Saale des Convent-Garten:

III. Abonnements-Concert.

Dirigent: Capellmeister **Gustav Mahler.**

Solisten: Frl. **Maria Antonietta Palloni** (Gesang).
Fr. **Fannie Bloomfield-Zeisler** (Clavier).

Programm:

1. **Beethoven:** Ouverture »Coriolan« für Orchester.
2. Altitalienische Arien.
    a) **Buononcini:** »Per la gloria« (1672—1764).
    b) **Paisiello:** »La Zingarella« (1741—1816).
    c) **Scarlatti:** »Le Violette« (1650—1725).
3. **Rubinstein:** Clavierconcert D-moll, op. 70, mit Orchester.
4. Lieder.
    a) **Massenet:** »Ouvre tes yeux bleus«.
    b) **Bizet:** Pastorale.
5. **Brahms:** Symphonie F-dur f. Orchester. op. 90.

Billets à **5, 4,** und **3** M., nicht num à **2** M., in der Musikalienhandlung von **Joh. Aug. Böhme, Neuerwall 35,** und Abends an der Casse.

✳ Concerthaus — Conventgarten. ✳

Montag den 19. November 1894, Abends 7½ Uhr pünktlich

III. ABONNEMENT-CONCERT

Dirigent:
Kapellmeister **Gustav Mahler.**

Solisten: Fräulein **Maria Antonietta Palloni** (Gesang)
Frau **Fannie Bloomfield-Zeisler** (Klavier).

PROGRAMM.

1. Ouverture: „Coriolan", op. 62 (1807) . . *L. v. Beethoven.*
2. Altitalienische Arien:
    a) „Per la gloria" . . . . *Buononcini* (1672— ?).
    b) La Zingarella . . . . *Paesiello* (1741—1816).
    c) Le Violette . . . . *Scarlatti* (1659—1725).
3. Concert für Klavier mit Orchester, D-moll, op. 70 . . . . *A. Rubinstein.*
    Moderato. — Moderato assai. — Allegro assai.
4. Lieder:
    a) „Ouvre tes yeux bleus" . . . . . *J. Massenet.*
    b) Pastorale . . . . *G. Bizet.*

---

5. Symphonie F-dur, op. 90, No. 3 . . . *J. Brahms.*
    Allegro con brio. — Andante. — Poco Allegretto. — Allegro.

Concertflügel: Bechstein.

IV. Abonnement-Concert: Montag den 3. Dezember 1894.
Dirigent: Kapellmeister **Gustav Mahler.**
Solistin: Frau Professor Selma Nicklas-Kempner aus Wien (Gesang).

| Hamburg | 1894 | Concert No. 67 |

67. November 19, 1894, 7:30 p.m.
HAMBURG - Convent Garten [3,000 seats]

Third Subscription Concert

- (1) Beethoven — Overture to *Coriolan*, Op. 62
- (2) Three Songs with Piano Acc.:
    - a) Buononcini — "Per la gloria d'adorarvi," from *Griselda* •
    - b) Paisiello — "Chi vuol la zingarella" •
    - c) Scarlatti, A. — "Le violette" •
- (3) Schubert — *Andante con moto* (2nd mvmt.), from Death and the Maiden String Quartet, No. 14, D 810, arr. for String Orch. by Mahler • [1]
- (4) Rubinstein — Piano Concerto No. 4, D minor, Op. 70 •
- (5) Scarlatti, D. — Piano Sonata, D minor, "Pastorale" [encore]
- (6) Four Songs with Piano Acc.:
    - a) Massenet — "Ouvre tes yeux bleus" •
    - b) Bizet — "Pastorale" •
    - c) d'Albert — "Das Mädchen und der Schmetterling," Op. 3 [encore] •
    - d) Schubert — "Heidenröslein," D 257 [encore] •
- (7) Bizet — Menuetto, from *L'Arlésienne* Suite [No. 1] [2]
- - Intermission -
- (8) Brahms — Symphony No. 3, F major, Op. 90

SOLOISTS (2 & 6) M. A. Palloni, acc. by Mahler; (4 & 5) F. Bloomfield-Zeisler.
SOURCE Handbill and newspaper advertisement; see illustrations on opposite page.
NOTES [1] World premiere. Although neither the handbill nor the newspaper advertisement announce the piece, which seems to be a last minute inclusion, the performance is confirmed by several reviews. Mahler apparently had intended to perform the complete quartet, since he reworked the entire score, which has survived and was published by Josef Weinberger (London, 1984), ed. Donald Mitchell and David Matthews.
[2] Apparently also a last minute inclusion. However, the present writer has not been able to confirm the performance, but relies on information given by HLG I, 890, note 52.
REVIEW HLG I, 315–316.

Montag, den 3. December, Abends 7½ Uhr, grosser Saal Convent-Garten:

IV. Abonnements-Concert.
(Gedenkfeier für Anton Rubinstein)
(† 20. November in Peterhof)

Dirigent: Herr Capellmeister **Gustav Mahler.**

Solist: Herr **Raimund von zur Mühlen aus Berlin** (Tenor).

Herr **Carl Leisner**, Mitglied des hiesigen Stadttheaters, hat es (mit gütiger Bewilligung des Herrn Hofrath Pollini) freundlichst übernommen, einen, von Dr. **Julius Rodenberg** verfassten poetischen Nachruf auf **Anton Rubinstein**, zu sprechen.

Programm:

1. **Rich. Wagner:** Eine Faust-Ouverture f. Orchester.
2. **Nachruf.**
3. **Anton Rubinstein:** »Ocean-Symphonie« I. Satz f. Orchester.
4. **Anton Rubinstein:** Lieder.
   a. Der Traum. b. Asra. c. Neue Liebe.
5. **Anton Rubinstein:** Balletmusik aus »Dämon« f. Orchester.
6. **L. van Beethoven: Pastoral-Symphonie.**
   1. Erwachen heiterer Empfindungen bei der Ankunft auf dem Lande. 2. Scene am Bach. 3. Lustiges Zusammensein der Landleute. 4. Gewitter, Sturm. 5. Hirtengesang, frohe und dankbare Gefühle nach dem Sturme.

Numerirte Billets à 5, 4, 3 ℳ., nicht num. à 2 ℳ., in der Musikalienhandlung von **Joh. Aug. Böhme, Neuerwall 35,** und an der Casse.

| Altona - Hamburg | 1894 | Concerts Nos. 68–70 |

68. **November 21, 1894, 7 p.m.**
ALTONA - Stadttheater [1,050 seats]

On the Occasion of the Day of Prayer and Repentance (Extraordinary Concert)

- (1) Haydn — *Die Schöpfung*, Oratorio
  - Intermission -
- (2) Mendelssohn — "O rest in the Lord," from *Elijah*, Oratorio, Op. 70 [1]
- (3) Mendelssohn — "Gott sei mir gnädig," from *Paulus*, Oratorio, Op. 36

SOLOISTS (1) J. von Artner (Eva & Gabriel), W. Birrenkoven (Uriel), W. Vilmar (Adam), I. Waldmann (Raphael). (2) E. Schumann-Heink. (3) W. Vilmar.
SOURCE Program.
NOTE [1] Sung in German: "Sei stille dem Herrn."

69. **November 24, 1894, 7 p.m.**
HAMBURG - Stadttheater [2,000 seats]

[Preceded by a complete stage performance of Humperdinck's *Hänsel und Gretel*, cond. by Mahler]

- (1) Fauré — *Hymne à Apollon*, Op. 63bis, for Men's Chorus, acc. by 1 flute, 2 clarinets, and 1 harp ● [1]

[followed by a complete stage performance of Mozart's *Bastien und Bastienne*, cond. by Bruno Schlesinger (Walter)]

- (3) Wilhelm II — "Sang an Aegir," for Chorus and Orch. ● [2]

SOURCE Newspaper advertisement and various reviews.
NOTES [1] The Hamburg *Correspondent* (November 24, 1894) reports that "The text of the *Hymn* and the music were discovered at the excavation last year at Delphi by a French expedition, and stems from the year 278 B.C. The text deals with the rescue of Delphi from the siege by the Gauls."
[2] Encored by public demand. The music, a setting of a poem by Count Philipp zu Eulenburg, was composed by the German *Kaiser,* and orchestrated by Professor Albert Becker. It was published in November 1894 in a dozen different arrangements.

70. **December 3, 1894, 7:30 p.m.**
HAMBURG - Convent Garten [3,000 seats]

Fourth Subscription Concert: In Memoriam Anton Rubinstein [1]

- (1) Wagner — *Eine Faust-Ouverture*
- (2) Rubinstein — Symphony No. 2, C major, Op. 42, "Ocean", 1st mvmt. ●
- (3) Rubinstein — Four *Lieder* with Piano Acc.:
  - a) "Der Traum," Op. 8, No. 1 ●
  - b) "Der Asra," Op. 32, No. 6 ●
  - c) "Neue Liebe," Op. 57, No. 3 ●
  - d) "Es blinkt der Tau," Op. 72, No. 1 [encore] ●

Zum Besten des Bülow-Denkmals.
Montag, den 21. Januar, Abends 7½ Uhr, Convent-Garten:

V. Abonnement-Concert.

Dirigent: Herr Capellmeister Gustav Mahler.

Solist: Herr **Emil Sauret** (Violine.)

PROGRAMM.

1. Mendelssohn: Ouverture „Fingalshöhle".
2. Moszkowski: Concert für Violine mit Orchester.
3. Beethoven: Ouverture „Leonore" No. 3, C dur.
4. Sauret: Elegie u. Rondo für Violine mit Orchester.
5. R. Schumann: Symphonie No. 1, B-dur, f. Orchester.

Numerirte Billets à 5, 4, 3 ℳ., nicht numerirte à 2 ℳ. in der Musikalienhandlung von **J. A. Böhme**, Neuerwall 35, und an der Casse.

☛ Abonnements auf den zweiten Cyclus der Abonnement-Concerte (4 Concerte) à 12 und 16 ℳ.

Concert-Direction Hermann Wolff.

✴ **Concerthaus — Conventgarten.** ✴

Montag den 21. Januar 1895, Abends 7½ Uhr pünktlich

V. ABONNEMENT-CONCERT

Dirigent:
Kapellmeister **Gustav Mahler.**

Solist: **Emile Sauret** (Violine).

PROGRAMM.

1. Ouverture „Die Hebriden", op. 26 . . *F. Mendelssohn.*
2. Concert für die Violine mit Begleitung des Orchesters, C-dur, op. 30 . . . *M. Moszkowski.*
   Allegro commodo. — Andante. — Vivace.
3. Ouverture zu: „Leonore", No. 3, C-dur *L. v. Beethoven.*
4. Elégie et Rondo für Violine mit Begleitung des Orchesters, op. 48 . . . *E. Sauret.*
5. Symphonie B-dur, op. 38 . . . . . *R. Schumann.*
   Andante. — Larghetto. — Scherzo. — Allegro.

VI. Abonnement-Concert: Montag den 4. Februar 1895.
Dirigent: Kapellmeister **Gustav Mahler.**
Solistin: Frau **Teresa d'Albert-Carreño.**

Berlioz: Symphonie fantastique. — Klavier-Concert. — **Rich. Strauss:** Vorspiel zu: „Guntram" (zum 1. Mal). — Klavier-Soli. — **Wagner:** Vorspiel zu: „Tristan und Isolde".

(4)	Rubinstein	Ballet Music (Two Dances), from *the Demon*
		- Intermission -
(5)	Beethoven	Symphony No. 6, F major, Op. 68, "Pastoral" [2]

SOLOIST (3) R. Von zur-Mühlen, acc. by Mahler. According to the preview in the program booklet of concert no. 67, Selma Nicklas-Kempner had initially been scheduled to be the soloist.
SOURCE Handbill and newspaper advertisement; see illustration on previous page.
NOTES [1] Anton Rubinstein had died on November 20, 1894.
[2] Mahler's first performance of the symphony.
REVIEW HLG I, 316-317.

71. **January 21, 1895, 7:30 p.m.**
HAMBURG - Convent Garten [3,000 seats]

Fifth Subscription Concert: For the Benefit of the Bülow Monument [1]

(1)	Mendelssohn	*Die Hebriden* (*Fingal's Cave*), Overture, Op. 26
(2)	Moszkowski	Violin Concerto, C major, Op. 30 •
(3)	Beethoven	*Leonore* Overture No. 3, Op. 72b
(4)	Sauret	Elegie and Rondo, Op. 38, for Violin and Orch. •
		- Intermission -
(5)	Schumann	Symphony No. 1, B-flat major, Op. 38, "Spring"

SOLOIST (2 & 4) E. Sauret.
SOURCE Handbill and newspaper advertisement; see illustrations on opposite page.
NOTE [1] Together with friends and admirers of the late Hans von Bülow, the Berlin impresario Hermann Wolff had initiated fundraising for a bust of the famous interpreter, concert no. 92.
REVIEW HLG I, 322.

72. **February 4, 1895, 7:30 p.m.**
HAMBURG - Covent Garten [3,000 seats]

Sixth Subscription Concert: For the Benefit of the Bülow Monument

(1)	Berlioz	*Symphonie fantastique*, Op. 14
		- Intermission -
(2)	Grieg	Piano Concerto, A minor, Op. 16
(3)	Strauss	Prelude to Act 1 of *Guntram*, Op. 25
(4)	Beethoven	Rondo, G major, Op. 51, No. 2, for Piano
	Schubert	Impromptu, A-flat major, Op. 143, No. 2, D 935, for Piano [1]
	Liszt	Hungarian Rhapsody No. 6, D-flat major, for Piano
(5)	Wagner	Prelude to Act 1 of *Tristan und Isolde*

※ **Concerthaus — Conventgarten.** ※

Montag den 4. Februar 1895, Abends 7½ Uhr pünktlich

VI. ABONNEMENT-CONCERT

Dirigent:

Kapellmeister **Gustav Mahler.**

Solistin: Frau **Teresa d'Albert-Carreño** (Klavier).

PROGRAMM.

1. Symphonie fantastique, op. 14 . . . . *H. Berlioz.*
   Rêveries, Passions. — Un bal. Valse. — Scène aux champs. — Marche au supplice. — Songe d'une nuit de sabbat.

2. Concert für Klavier mit Begleitung des Orchesters, A-moll, op. 16 . . . . . *Ed. Grieg.*
   Allegro molto moderato. — Adagio. — Allegro moderato molto e marcato quasi Presto.

3. Vorspiel zu: „Guntram" (zum 1. Mal). . *Rich. Strauss.*

4. Soli:
   a) Rondo G-dur, op. 51, No. 2 . . . *L. v. Beethoven.*
   b) Impromptu, op. 142, No. 3 . . . . *F. Schubert.*
   c) Rhapsodie No. 6 . . . . *F. Liszt.*

5. Vorspiel zu: „Tristan und Isolde" . . . *R. Wagner.*

Concertflügel: Bechstein.

VII. Abonnement-Concert: Montag den 18. Februar 1895.

Dirigent: Kapellmeister **Gustav Mahler.**

Solisten: Die holländischen Sängerinnen:
Jeannette de Jong, Anna Corver, Marie Snyders.
Robert Freund (Klavier).

Haydn: Symphonie D-dur. — Terzette. — Klavierconcert. — Terzette. —
Mendelssohn: Symphonie A-moll.

Zum Besten des Bülow-Denkmal in Hamburg.
Montag, den 18. Februar, Abends 7½ Uhr, Convent-Garten:

VII. Abonnement-Concert

Dirigent: Herr **Capellmeister Gustav Mahler.**

Solisten:
Das holländische Damen-Terzett: Frl. **de Jong** (Sopran)
Frl. **Corver** (Mezzo-Sopran), Frl. **Snyders** (Alt),
Herr **Rob. Freund** (Clavier).

PROGRAMM.

1. **A. Bruckner:** Symphonie No. 4, Es-dur. (Romantische) f. Orchester.
2. Terzette:
   Mendelssohn: Hebe deine Augen auf.
   Rennes: Belooning.
   Brahms: Volkslied.
3. **Brahms:** Concert f. Clavier m. Orchester, D-moll, op. 15.
4. Terzett:
   Fabricius: Zwei Madrigale.
   Rennes: Kerstnacht.
5. **Wagner:** Vorspiel zu ›Die Meistersinger von Nürnberg‹, f. Orchester.

Numerirte Billets à 5, 4, 3 ℳ, nicht numerirte à 2 ℳ in der Musikalienhandlung von
J. A. Böhme, Neuerwall 35, und Abends an der Casse.

Concert-Direction Herm. Wolff.

SOLOIST (2 & 4) M. T. Carreño.
SOURCE Handbill and newspaper advertisement; see illustration on opposite page.
NOTE [1] The program announces the Impromptu, Op. 143, No. 3, in B-flat major, but all reviews agree that it was the A-flat major Impromptu that was performed.
REVIEW HLG I, 322.

73. **February 18, 1895, 7:30 p.m.**
HAMBURG - Convent Garten [3,000 seats]

Seventh Subscription Concert: For the Benefit of the Bülow Monument

(1)	Bruckner	Symphony No. 4, E-flat major, "Romantic" [1]

- Intermission -

(2)	Three terzettos for women's voices a capella:	
	Mendelssohn	"Hebe deine Augen auf," from *Elijah*, Oratorio, Op. 70
	Rennes	"Belooning," Op. 10
	Brahms	"Da unten im Tale" [encore] [2]
	Grimm	"Ich fahr' dahin" [encore]
(3)	Brahms	Piano Concerto No. 1, D minor, Op. 15 ●
(4)	Three terzettos for women's voices a capella:	
	Fabricius	"Jetzt, o Frühling"
	Fabricius	"Durch die stille Sommernacht"
	Rennes	"Kerstnacht," Op. 10
(5)	Wagner	Prelude to Act 1 of *Die Meistersinger von Nürnberg*

SOLOISTS (2 & 4) The Dutch Trio: J. de Jong, A. Corver, M. Snijders; (3) R. Freund.
SOURCE Handbill and newspaper advertisement; see illustration on opposite page.
NOTES [1] Mahler's first performance of this work, and only the second in Hamburg.
[2] According to Emil Krause's review in the Hamburg *Fremdenblatt*, this arrangement was especially made for and dedicated to the Dutch Trio, by the composer. It apparently remains unpublished and the whereabouts of the manuscript is unknown.
REVIEW HLG I, 322–323.

74. **March 1, 1895, 7 p.m.**
HAMBURG - Stadttheater [2,000 seats]

Annual Benefit for Mahler

Beethoven	Symphony No. 6, F major, Op. 68, "Pastoral"

[followed by a complete stage performance of Beethoven's *Fidelio*, cond. by Mahler]

SOURCE Newspaper advertisement.
REVIEW HLG I, 317.

✱ Philharmonie. ✱

Montag, den 4. März 1895, Abends 7½ Uhr **sehr präcise.**

IX. Philharmonisches Concert.

Dirigent:
Hofkapellmeister **Rich. Strauss.**

Solist: Josef Hofmann (Klavier).

PROGRAMM.

1. Ouverture: „Die Hebriden," op. 26 . . *F. Mendelssohn.*
2. Concert für Klavier mit Begleitung des Orchesters No. 4, C-moll, op. 44 . . *C. Saint-Saëns.*
   Allegro moderato ed Andante. — Allegro vivace, Andante ed Allegro finale.
3. 3 Sätze a. d. Symphonie No. 2 (z. 1. Mal) *G. Mahler.*
   I. Allegro maëstoso.
   II. Andante con moto.
   III. (Scherzo) Allegro commodo.
   } Diese 3 Sätze bilden den 1. Theil der Symphonie.
   (Unter Leitung des Componisten).
4. Klavier-Soli:
   a) Nocturne, C-moll . . . . *F. Chopin.*
   b) Rhapsodie No. 6 . . . . *F. Liszt.*
5. Ouverture zu: „Oberon" . . . . . . *C. M. v. Weber.*

Concertflügel: **BECHSTEIN.**

X. (letztes) Philharmonisches Concert: Montag, 18. März 1895.
Dirigent: Hofkapellmeister **Rich. Strauss.**
Unter Mitwirkung des Philharmonischen Chors **(S. Ochs).**

Rich. Strauss: Vorspiel zum II. Act, Friedenserzählung, Vorspiel zum I. Act, Schluss des III. Act aus der Oper: „Guntram". — **Beethoven:** IX. Symphonie (mit Chor).

☞ **Zum Besten des Bülow-Denkmal in Hamburg.** ☜
Montag, den 11. März, Abends 7½ Uhr, Convent-Garten:

VIII. (letztes) Abonnement-Concert

Dirigent: Herr **Capellmeister Gustav Mahler**
unter gütiger Mitwirkung der **„Bach-Gesellschaft"**
(Director: Herr Musikdirector Ad. Mehrkens)

PROGRAMM.

L. van Beethoven:
1. Ouvertüre „Zur Namensfeier" für Orchester.
2. Neueste Symphonie für Soli, Chor und Orchester
(mit Schlusschor über Schiller's Ode „An die Freude").

Numerirte Billets à 5, 4, 3 M., nicht numerirte à 2 M. in der Musikalienhandlung von **J. A. Böhme**, Neuerwall 35, und Abends an der Casse.

☞ **Hauptprobe** ☜
Sonntag, den 10. März, Mittags 12½ Uhr.
Billets à 1 M.

Concert-Direction Herm. Wolff.

75. **March 4, 1895, 7:30 p.m.**
BERLIN - Philharmonie [2,500 seats]

Ninth Philharmonic Subscription Concert

(1)	Mendelssohn	*Die Hebriden* (*Fingal's Cave*), Overture, Op. 26
(2)	Saint-Saëns	Piano Concerto No. 4, C minor, Op. 44
(3)	Mahler	Symphony No. 2, C minor, "Resurrection" (*1st, 2nd, and 3rd movements*) [1]
(4)	Chopin	Nocturne, Op. 48, No. 1
(5)	Liszt	Hungarian Rhapsody No. 6, D-flat major
(6)	Weber	Overture to *Oberon*

SOLOIST (2, 4 & 5) J. Hofmann.
CONDUCTORS (1 & 2, 6) Richard Strauss; (3) Mahler.
ORCHESTRA The Berlin Philharmonic Orchestra; Richard Strauss had taken over the leadership from the late Hans von Bülow. At the close of the season he was replaced by Arthur Nikisch who held the post until his death in 1922.
SOURCE Handbill; see illustration on opposite page.
NOTE [1] World premiere. For the first complete performance of the symphony, see concert no. 83.
REVIEW HLG I, 319–321.

76. **March 11, 1895, 7:30 p.m.**
HAMBURG - Convent Garten [3,000 seats]

Eighth Subscription Concert: For the Benefit of the Bülow Monument

(1)	Beethoven	*Zur Namensfeier*, Overture, Op. 115
		- Intermission -
(2)	Beethoven	Symphony No. 9, D minor, Op. 125

SOLOISTS (2) J. von Artner, A. Bünz, N. Doerter, H. Gausche.
CHORUS The Hamburg "Bach-Gesellschaft," cond. A. Mehrkens.
SOURCE Handbill and newspaper advertisement; see illustration on opposite page. The text at the bottom of the handbill informs that "The New Subscription Concerts (8) will be continued next winter." However, much to Mahler's annoyance, Hermann Wolff cancelled the concerts and instead arranged a series of concerts with the Berlin Philharmonic Orchestra under Felix Weingartner.
REVIEW HLG I, 323.

77. **March 17, 1895, 7 p.m.**
78. **March 26, 1895, 7 p.m.**
HAMBURG - Stadttheater [2,000 seats]

Beethoven	Symphony No. 6, F major, Op. 68, "Pastoral"

[followed by a complete stage performance of Beethoven's *Fidelio*, cond. by Mahler]

SOURCE Newspaper advertisement.

Gratis.

Concert-Direction
HERMANN WOLFF.

Freitag, den 13. December 1895
Abends 8 Uhr:

IM SAAL DER PHILHARMONIE

Aufführung

der

SYMPHONIE IN C-MOLL

für Soli, Chor und Orchester

von

Gustav Mahler

unter Leitung des Componisten.

MITWIRKENDE:

Fräulein **Josefine von Artner** (Sopran), ⎫
Fräulein **Hedwig Felden** (Alt), ⎬ vom Stadttheater in Hamburg.
Der **Stern'sche Gesangverein** (Director: Prof. F. Gernsheim).
Das **Philharmonische Orchester** (120 Künstler).

Vor Beginn der Symphonie werden die Saalthüren geschlossen.

Im Verlaufe der Symphonie findet keine längere Pause statt.

Eintritts-Karten: Saal 3 und 2 Mk., Stehplatz 1 Mk., Loge 4 Mk.
sind in der Königlichen Hofmusikhandlung von ED. BOTE & G. BOCK, Leipziger Strasse 37,
und Abends an der Kasse zu haben.

Auszug der vollständigen Symphonie für 2 Klaviere vierhändig (in Partitur beider Stimmen) von **Hermann Behn**
zum Preise von Mk. 6 vorräthig bei Ed. Bote & G. Bock, Leipzigerstr. 37, und bei **Raabe & Plothow**,
Potsdamerstr. 7a. Ebendaselbst separat zu haben: „Urlicht" Altsolo mit Klavierbegleitung zum Preise von M. 1.

Umstehend das Programm!

79. **March 31, 1895, 1 p.m.**
HAMBURG - Stadttheater [2,000 seats] [1]

Annual Benefit for Josephine von Artner

[The matinee began with a complete stage performance of Humperdinck's *Hänsel und Gretel*, cond. by Mahler, followed by an unspecified recital of *Lieder* by Behn [2], Schumann, Schubert, and Loewe.]

SOLOISTS J. von Artner, E. Schumann-Heink, W. Birrenkoven, and B. Hoffmann, accompanied at the piano by Mahler.
NOTES [1] No handbill or review has been located. A preview in the Hamburg *Correspondent* specifies the composers and the performers only.
[2] The *Lieder* by Behn could be some of the five titles suggested by Mahler in his letter of February 2, 1895, to Hermann Behn, see *Gustav Mahler. Unknown Letters*, ed. by H. Blaukopf (London, 1986, p. 23).

80. **April 2, 1895, 7:30 p.m.**
HAMBURG - Stadttheater [2,000 seats] [1]

Concert Arranged by the "Society of Art and Science in Hamburg" to Celebrate the 80th Anniversary of Fürst [Otto] von Bismarck

> Beethoven   Overture to *Egmont*, Op. 84

[followed by a complete stage performance of Kleist's play *Die Hermannsschlacht*, and concluded with Wagner's *Kaisermarsch*, cond. C. Pohlig]

SOURCE Newspaper preview.
NOTE [1] By invitation only.

81. **April 12, 1895, 7 p.m.**
HAMBURG - Stadttheater [2,000 seats]

Good Friday Concert

> (1) Haydn   *Die Schöpfung*, Oratorio
>   - Intermission -
> (2) Mozart   *Requiem*, D minor, K. 626

SOLOISTS (1) T. Saak (Eva), J. von Artner (Gabriel), W. Grüning (Uriel), W. Vilmar (Adam), I. Waldmann (Raphael); (2) S. Traubmann, E. Schumann-Heink, F. Weidmann, B. Hoffmann.
CHORUS The Chorus of the *Stadttheater*, reinforced by soloists [S. Kornfeld, G. Neumann, H. Felden, C. Rodemund, J. Grosser, and W. Hesch], all regular members of the theater.
SOURCE Newspaper advertisement.
REVIEW HLG I, 317.

PROGRAMM

Symphonie Cmoll, für Soli, Chor und Orchester . . . . . . G. Mahler.

    I. **Allegro maestoso.**

    II. **Andante con moto.**

    III. **Scherzo.**

    IV. **Alt Solo** („Urlicht" aus des Knaben Wunderhorn).

O Röschen roth!
Der Mensch liegt in grösster Noth!
Der Mensch liegt in grösster Pein!
Je lieber möcht' ich im Himmel sein!

Da kam ich auf einen breiten Weg.
Da kam ein Engelein
Und wollt' mich abweisen.
Ach nein! ich liess mich nicht abweisen!
Ich bin von Gott,
Und will wieder zu Gott.
Der liebe Gott wird mir ein Lichtchen geben,
Wird leuchten mir
Bis in das ewig' selig' Leben!

    V. **Einleitung und Allegro energico** (mit Chor, Sopran- und Alt Solo).

Text der Schluss-Gesänge.

Aufersteh'n, ja aufersteh'n wirst du
Mein Staub nach kurzer Ruh'!
Unsterblich' Leben
Wird, der dich rief, dir geben!

Wieder aufzublüh'n wirst du gesä't!
Der Herr der Ernte geht
Und sammelt Garben
Uns ein, die starben!

O glaube, Herz: Es geht dir nichts verloren;
Dein ist, was du gesehnt, geliebt, gestritten!
O glaube: Du wardst nicht umsonst geboren,
Hast nicht umsonst gelebt, gelitten!

Was entstanden ist, das muss vergeh'n —
Vergangen, aufersteh'n!
Hör' auf zu beben!
Bereite dich zu leben!

O Schmerz, du Alldurchdringer!
Dir bin ich entrungen!
O Tod, du Allbezwinger!
Nun bist du bezwungen!

Mit Flügeln, die ich mir errungen
In heissem Liebesstreben,
Werd' ich entschweben
Zum Licht, zu dem kein Aug' gedrungen:
Sterben werd' ich, um zu leben!

Aufersteh'n, ja aufersteh'n wirst du
Mein Herz in einem Nu!
Was du geschlagen,
Zu Gott wird es dich tragen!

Freitag, den 13. Dezbr., Abds. 8 Uhr in der Philharmonie:
Sinfonie C-moll für Soli, Chor und Orchester
von **Gustav Mahler.**
Dirigent: der **Componist.**
Mitw.: Frl. **v. Artner** (Sop.). Frl. **Felden** (Alt), der
Stern'sche Gesangverein (Dir.: Prof. **Gernsheim**), das
Philharmon. Orchester (120 Künstler).
Kart.: Saal 3 u. 2 Mk., Stehpl. 1 Mk., Loge 4 Mk. b. Bote u. Bock (9—6).

| Altona—Berlin | 1895–1896 | Concerts Nos. 82–84 |

Season 1895–1896

82. **November 20, 1895**, 7 p.m.
   ALTONA - Stadttheater [1,050 seats]

   On the Occasion of the Day of Prayer and Repentance

   (1)   Haydn   *Die Schöpfung*, Oratorio
                          - Intermission -
   (2)   An unspecified recital of *Lieder* and arias with piano acc.

   SOLOISTS (1) J. von Artner (Eva & Gabriel), W. Birrenkoven (Uriel), W. Vilmar (Adam), I. Waldmann (Raphael); (2) The same soloists, acc. at the piano by Carl Pohlig.
   SOURCE Newspaper advertisement.

83. **December 13, 1895**, 8 p.m.
   BERLIN - Philharmonie [2,500 seats]

   [First] Orchestral Concert by Gustav Mahler [1]

         Mahler   Symphony No. 2, C minor, "Resurrection" [2]

   SOLOISTS J. von Artner & H. Felden [3] ("Urlicht").
   ORCHESTRA The Berlin Philharmonic Orchestra.
   CHORUS The "Stern'scher Gesangverein", cond. F. Gernsheim, and the "Sängerbund des Lehrervereins."
   SOURCE Handbill and newspaper advertisement; see illustrations on opposite and previous pages.
   NOTES [1] Mahler arranged this and the following concerts privately, with financial support from his Hamburg friends, the businessman Wilhelm Berkhan and the composer and lawyer Hermann Behn. The latter had also made a reduction for two pianos, four hands, and paid for its publication, which appeared in commission in December 1895 by music publisher Friedrich Hofmeister in Leipzig.
   [2] World premiere of the *complete* symphony (see concert no. 75 for incomplete performance).
   [3] Replaced the originally scheduled Marie Ritter-Götze.
   REVIEW HLG I, 342–347; F. Pfohl, 72–75.

84. **March 16, 1896**, 7:30 p.m.
   BERLIN - Philharmonie [2,500 seats]

   Second Orchestral Concert by Gustav Mahler [1]

   All-Mahler Program:

   (1)   "Todtenfeier" [2]
   (2)   *Lieder eines fahrenden Gesellen,* with Orch. [3]
                          - Intermission -
   (3)   Symphony No. 1, D major [4]

Hamburger Stadt-Theater.

(Direction: **B. Pollini.**)

Donnerstag, den 2. April: **Geschlossen.**
Freitag, den 3. April 1896.

☞ Vom Abonnement ausgeschlossen. ☜

☞ **Anfang 7 Uhr.** ☜

Mit Bewilligung des Hohen Senats.

Requiem von **W. A. Mozart** für Soli, Chor und Orchester. Die Soli gesungen von Frl. v. Artner, Fr. Schumann-Heink u. d. Hrn. Gießwein u. Hoffmann. Hierauf: 1. „**Vater unser**" von **Krebs**, 2. Arie aus „**Samson**" von **Händel** („O hör' mein Flehen!") Fr. Schumann-Heink. 3. **Arie aus „Elias"** von **Mendelssohn** („So Ihr mich von ganzem Herzen suchet".) Herr Birrenkoven. 4. Arie aus „**Messias**" von **Händel** („Ich weiß, daß mein Erlöser lebt!"), Frl. v. Mildenburg. 5. **Engel-Terzett** aus „**Elias**" v. **Mendelssohn**, Frl. v Artner, Frl. v. Mildenburg und Fr. Schumann-Heink. 6. **Schluß-Chor** aus „**Matthäus-Passion**" v. Bach.

Dirigent: Herr Kapellmeister **Gustav Mahler**.

Preise der Plätze zu dieser Vorstellung:
1. Rang, Parquet und Parquetloge M. 3.—. 2. Rang-Mittelloge und 1. Parterre M. 2.50. 2. Rang-Seitenloge und Sitz-Parterre M. 2.—. 3. Rang-Mittelloge M. 1.50. 3. Rang-Seitenloge M. 1.20. Gallerie-Sitzplatz M. 1.—. **Anfang 7 Uhr.**

SOLOIST (2) A. Sistermans.
ORCHESTRA The Berlin Philharmonic Orchestra.
SOURCE Handbill.
NOTES [1] See concert no. 83, note 1.
[2] The first movement of the Symphony No. 2, C minor, "Resurrection." The title "Todtenfeier" ("Funeral Rite") was probably first attached to the movement in November 1891, when Mahler offered the score to music publisher B. Schott's Söhne in Mainz, who eventually rejected it.
[3] World premiere, except perhaps for the second song, concert no. 29.
[4] World premiere of the recently *revised* score of the "Symphonic Poem," previously performed in Budapest (1889), Hamburg (1893), and Weimar (1894) (concerts nos. 36, 55, and 64). The original 2nd movement, in 1893 named "Blumine," was discarded, as were all titles, subtitles, and descriptive programs. The orchestration had been enlarged (i.e. quadruple woodwinds).
REVIEW HLG I, 350, 356–357.

85. April 2, 1896, 7 p.m.
HAMBURG - Stadttheater [2,000 seats]

Good Friday Concert

(1)	Mozart	*Requiem*, D minor, K. 626
		- Intermission -
(2)	Krebs	*Vater unser* ("Lord's Prayer"), Op. 198, for Voice & Orch.
(3)	Handel	"O hör' mein Flehen," from *Samson*, Oratorio [1]
(4)	Mendelssohn	"If with all your hearts," from *Elijah*, Oratorio, Op. 70 [1]
(5)	Handel	"I know that my Redeemer liveth," from *Messiah*, Oratorio, Part 3 [1]
(6)	Mendelssohn	"Lift thine eyes," Terzetto, from *Elijah*, Oratorio, Op. 70 [1]
(7)	Bach	"Wir setzen uns," Final Chorus, from *Matthäus-Passion*, BWV 244, No. 78 for Chorus and Orchestra

SOLOISTS (1) J. von Artner, E. Schumann-Heink, M. Gießwein, B. Hoffmann; (2) E. Schumann-Heink; (3 & 4) W. Birrenkoven; (5) A. von Mildenburg; (6) A. von Mildenburg, J. von Artner, E. Schumann-Heink.
SOURCE Newspaper advertisement; see illustration on opposite page.
NOTE [1] Sung in German: (4) "So Ihr mich von ganzen Herzen suchet," (5) "Ich weiß, daß mein Erlöser lebt," (6) "Hebe deine Augen auf."

86. April 13, 1896, 7 p.m.
87. April 25, 1896, 7 p.m.
HAMBURG - Stadttheater [2,000 seats]

Annual Benefit for Bertha Foerster-Lauterer [1]

(1)	Foerster	Symphony No. 3, D major, Op. 36, "Das Leben" [2]

Stadt-Theater.

Heute, Montag, den 13. April 1896.
214. Abonnem.-Vorstellg.   32. Montags-Vorstellg.

Anfang 7 Uhr.

Zum Benefiz
für **Frau Bertha Förster-Lauterer.**
Symphonie III (D-dur)
von Jos. B. Förster
Dirigent: Hr. Capellmeister Gustav Mahler.

Hierauf:

Mignon.

Oper mit Tanz in 3 Acten, mit Benutzung des Goethe'schen Romans „Wilhelm Meister's Lehrjahre" von Michel Carré und J. Barbier.
Deutsch von Ferdinand Gumbert.
Musik von Ambroise Thomas.
Regie: Herr Franz Bittong.
Dirigent: Herr Capellmeister Carl Pohlig.

Wilhelm Meister	Hr. Birrenkoven
Friedrich	Hr. Weidmann
Philine	Fr. Wolff-Kauer
Laërtes	Hr. Auspitz
Lothario	Hr. Bilmar
Mignon	Fr. Förster-Lauterer
Antonio	Hr. Bartels
Jarno	Hr. Lorent
Zafari	Hr. Meyer
Der Fürst v. Tiefenbach	Hr. Bann
Der Baron v. Rosenberg	Hr. Kirchberg
Die Baronin	Fr. Kirchberg
Der Souffleur	Hr. Thormeyer
Ein Diener des Barons	Hr. Jansen

Zigeuner. Schauspieler. Herren und Damen.
Bürger. Bauern. Bäuerinnen.

Im 1. Akt: **Zigeunertanz,** ausgeführt von Frl. Genée, Frl. Mende, Hrn. Oehlschläger und den Damen vom Corps de Ballet.

Zum Schluß: **Concert**

I. a. Jos. B. Förster: „Aubade", b. Ferd. Pfohl: „Satanella", Frl. v. Artner. II. a. R. Schumann: „Intermezzo", b. R. Schumann „Ich wand're nicht", Hr. Gießwein. III. Franz Schubert: „Die Allmacht", Fr. Schumann-Heink. IV. a. J. Brahms: „Mainacht", b. R. Schumann: „Wanderlied", Hr. Hoffmann. V. a. Rudolf Philipp: „Herzallerliebster Schatz", b. Rudolf Philipp: „O Welt, du bist so wunderschön", Fr. Förster-Lauterer.

Clavier-Begleitung:
Herr Capellmeister Carl Pohlig.
Concertflügel von Steinway & Sons, Newyork-Hamburg.

Richtige Programme werden nur im Theater verkauft.
Große Preise.
Kassenöffnung 6½ Uhr.   Anfang 7 Uhr.
Ende 10½ Uhr.

| Hamburg–Altona | 1896 | Concerts Nos. 86–88 |

[followed by a complete stage performance of Thomas' *Mignon*, cond. by C. Pohlig, who also acc. the following *Lied*-recital at the piano]:

(2)	Foerster	"Aubade"
	Pfohl	"Satanella," Op. 6, No. 3
(3)	Schumann	"Intermezzo," Op. 39, No. 2
	Schumann	"Ich wand're nicht," Op. 51, No. 3
(4)	Schubert	"Die Allmacht," D 852
(5)	Brahms	"Die Mainacht," Op. 43, No. 2
	Schumann	"Wanderlied," Op. 35, No. 3
(6)	Philipp	"Herzallerliebster Schatz"
	Philipp	"O Welt, du bist so wunderschön," Op. 31

SOLOISTS (2) J. von Artner; (3) M. Gießwein; (4) E. Schumann-Heink; (5) B. Hoffmann; (6) B. Foerster-Lauterer.
SOURCE Newspaper advertisement; see illustration on opposite page.
NOTES [1] Wife of the composer Josef Bohuslav Foerster, and from September 1893 a regular member of the Hamburg *Stadttheater*. On Mahler's invitation she joined the Vienna Court Opera in 1901.
[2] World premiere.
REVIEW HLG I, 361.

Season 1896–1897

88. **November 18, 1896, 7 p.m.**
ALTONA - Stadttheater [1,050 seats]

On the Occasion of the Day of Prayer and Repentance

        Haydn   *Die Schöpfung*, Oratorio •

[followed by a *Lied*-recital with W. Sichel as accompanist]

SOLOISTS J. von Artner (Eva & Gabriel), W. Grüning (Uriel), W. Vilmar (Adam), and M. Lorent (Raphael).
SOURCE Newspaper review.
REVIEW HLG I, 385–386.

LISZT-VEREIN.

Unter dem Protektorate Sr. Kgl. Hoheit des Grossherzogs Alexander von Sachsen.

V. Konzert

Montag, den 14. Dezember 1896, abends 7½ Uhr,

Alberthalle.

Mitwirkende:

Herr Hofopernsänger **Karl Lang** aus Schwerin, Herr **Wassilj Sapellnikoff**, Pianist aus Petersburg, die vereinigten Kapellen des Herrn Kapellmeister Winderstein und des 134. Regiments.
Dirigent: Herr Kapellmeister **Gustav Mahler** aus Hamburg.

PROGRAMM.

Gustav Mahler, Symphonie, Nr. 2 C moll.
 I. Maestoso. II. Andante con moto.
10 Minuten Pause.
Robert Schumann, Konzert für Pianoforte und Orchester, Op. 54, A moll.
 I. Allegro affetuoso. II. Andante grazioso. III. Allegro vivace.
Hugo Wolf, 6 Lieder mit Pianofortebegleitung.
Franz Liszt, Sonate H moll für Pianoforte allein (An Robert Schumann).
Beethoven, Ouverture zu „Coriolan".

Klavierbegleitung: Herr **Emil Wagner**.

Konzertflügel: **Blüthner**.

Erläuterungen und Texte zum Programm umstehend.

Das 6. Konzert findet Ende Januar statt.

89. December 14, 1896, 7:30 p.m.
LEIPZIG - Albert Halle des "Kristallpalastes" [3,000 seats]

Fifth Concert of the [Leipzig] "Liszt-Verein"

(1)	Mahler	Symphony No. 2, C minor, (1st & 2nd movements) [1]
(2)	Wolf	Six *Lieder* with piano acc.:
		a) "Verborgenheit"
		b) "Der Tambour"
		c) "Der Freund"
		d) "Das Ständchen"
		e) "Heimweh"
		f) "Der Genesene an die Hoffnung"
(3)	Schumann	Piano Concerto, A minor, Op. 54
(4)	Liszt	Piano Sonata, B minor
(5)	Liszt	Hungarian Rhapsody (unspecified) [encore]
(6)	Chopin	Berceuse, Op. 57 [encore]
(7)	Beethoven	Overture to *Coriolan*, Op. 62

SOLOISTS (2) C. Lang, acc. by E. Wagner (3–6) V. Sapelnikov.
ORCHESTRA The Orchestra of the "Liszt-Verein" (Liszt Society), identical with the "Winderstein" Symphony Orchestra, which was founded 1896 by the conductor Hans Winderstein. On the present occasion the orchestra was reinforced by players from the band of the 143rd Military Regiment.
SOURCE Program reconstructed from various reviews and the handbill; see illustration on opposite page.
NOTE [1] First performance in Leipzig. Ten years later, on November 1, 1906, a complete performance was given in Leipzig, conducted by Arthur Nikisch.
REVIEW HLG I, 387–389.

90. January 30, 1897, 7 p.m.
91. February 1, 1897, 7 p.m.
HAMBURG - Stadttheater [2,000 seats]

In Celebration of Franz Schubert's Centenary

[The evening was opened with a complete stage performance of Schubert's *Der vierjährige Posten*, D.190, cond. by R. Krzyzanowski, followed by G. Burckhard's *Franz Schubert*, a play with musical accompaniment, and concluded with the following concert]:

(1) Symphony No. 8 (7), B minor, D 759, "Unfinished"
   Ten *Lieder* with Piano Acc.:
(2) "Am Meer," No. 12, D 957 •
(3) "Du bist die Ruh," D 776 •
(4) "Suleika," Op. 14, No. 1, D 720 •
(5) "Gretchen am Spinnrade," Op. 2, D 118 •
(6) "Der Wanderer," D 649 •

(7) "An die Musik," D 547 •
(8) "Das Echo," D 868 •
(9) "Trockne Blumen," No. 18, D 795 •
(10) "Wandrers Nachtlied," No. 2, D 768 •
(11) "Horch! Horch! die Lerch!" D 889 •
(12) Overture to *Rosamunde* (*Die Zauberharfe*, D 644)

SOLOISTS (2 & 3) L. Demuth; (4 & 5) A. von Mildenburg; (6–8) E. Schumann-Heink; (9–11) W. Birrenkoven; all acc. at the piano by Mahler.
CONDUCTOR (1 & 12) Mahler.
SOURCE Newspaper advertisement.
REVIEW HLG I, 395.

92. February 12, 1897, 12 p.m.
HAMBURG - The Foyer of the Stadttheater

On the Occasion of the Unveiling of the Bust of Hans von Bülow

Wagner   "Siegfried's Tod," Funeral March, from
                         Götterdämmerung

SOURCE Reviews in the local press.
The ceremony was by invitation only. The unveiling of the marble bust of Bülow by sculptor Hermann Haase, took place at the foyer of the theater with a speech by the lawyer Hermann Behn. After his address, Mahler conducted the Wagner march.

93. March 15 (3), 1897, 9 p.m. [1]
MOSCOW - The Assembly Hall of the Nobles (Blagorodnoye Sobranie) [3,000 seats]

Eighth Subscription Concert of the Imperial Russian Philharmonic Society

(1) Beethoven   Symphony No. 5, C minor, Op. 67
(2) Wagner   *Siegfried Idyll*
(3) Gounod   "Je veux vivre," from *Romeo et Juliette*
(4) Simon   Piano Concerto, A-flat major, Op. 19 •
(5) Wagner   Overture to *Rienzi*

SOLOISTS (3) M. Antonova; (4) V. Staub.
ORCHESTRA The Orchestra of the Imperial Russian Philharmonic Society.
SOURCE Program reconstructed from various reviews.
NOTE [1] The date in brackets refers to the Russian calendar.
REVIEW HLG I, 402.

| Munich–Budapest | 1897 | Concerts Nos. 94–95 |

94. March 24, 1897, 7:30 p.m.
MUNICH - Großer Saal des Kaim-Konzertgebäudes [3,500 seats] [1]

Tenth (and last) Kaim Subscription Concert [2]

(1)	Beethoven	Symphony No. 5, C minor, Op. 67
(2)	Berlioz	*Symphonie fantastique*, Op. 14 (2nd & 3rd movements)
(3)	Six *Lieder* with Piano Acc.: [3]	
	a) Schumann	title not established
	b) Schubert	"Wohin," from *Die schöne Müllerin*, No. 2, D 795
	c) Brahms	title not established
	d) Reinecke	title not established
	e) Fielitz	title not established
	f) Umlauf	title not established
	g) Sommer	"Wiegenlied," Op. 41, No. 1
(4)	Wagner	Prelude to Act 1 of to *Die Meistersinger von Nürnberg*

SOLOIST (3) K. Polscher, acc. at the piano by Mahler.
ORCHESTRA The Munich *Kaim* Orchestra.
SOURCE Newspaper advertisement and various reviews.
NOTES [1] The general rehearsal took place in the morning of the same day.
[2] According to previews the original program was comprised of the *complete* Berlioz symphony, Beethoven's Overture to *Coriolan*, and the Wagner prelude. However, due to insufficient rehearsal time, and Kaim's refusal to engage extra players for the Berlioz, Mahler only performed two movements of the Berlioz symphony, and added Beethoven's Fifth.
In a letter to his sister Justine, Mahler also intended to include the 2nd movement (*Blumenstück*) from his Third Symphony, but dropped the idea because the score and parts did not arrive in due time from Justine.
[3] The originally announced but indisposed contralto Charlotte Huhn was replaced by mezzo-soprano Klara Polscher. According to one review, the announced *Lieder* by Reinecke, Fielitz, and Umlauf were not performed.
REVIEW HLG I, 404–405.

95. March 31, 1897, 7:30 p.m.
BUDAPEST - The Large Hall of the "Vigadó" [1,000 seats]

Benefit for the Relief Fund of the Budapest Journalists' Society

(Extraordinary Philharmonic Concert)

(1)	Wagner	Overture to *Rienzi*
(2)	Wagner	"Dich teure Halle," from *Tannhäuser*
(3)	Mahler	"Was mir die Blumen auf der Wiese erzählen," from the Symphony No. 3 ("Blumenstück") [1]
		- Intermission -
(4)	Weber	*Aufforderung zum Tanze*, rondo brillant, Op. 65, orch. F. Weingartner [2]
(5)	Beethoven	"Abscheulicher ... Komm Hoffnung," from *Fidelio*
(6)	Beethoven	Symphony No. 5, C minor, Op. 67

Donnerstag, den 15. April: **Geschlossen.**
Freitag, den 16. April 1897.
Vom Abonnement ausgeschlossen.
Anfang 7 Uhr.
Mit Bewilligung des Hohen Senats.

1. **Requiem** von **W. A. Mozart** für Soli, Chor und Orchester. Die Soli gesungen von Frl. v. Artner, Fr. Schumann-Heink und den Herren Gießwein und Demuth.
2. **Tedeum** von **Anton Bruckner** für Soli, Chor, Orchester und Orgel. Die Soli gesungen von Frl. v. Mildenburg, Fr. Schumann-Heink und den Herren Birrenkoven und Wittekopf.
3. **„Vater unser"** von **Krebs**, gesungen von Fr. Schumann-Heink.
4. **„Largo"** von **Händel** für Violinen, Violen, Harfen und Orgel arrangirt von J. Hellmesberger.

Preise der Plätze zu dieser Vorstellung:
1. Rang, Parquet und Parquetloge M. 3.—. 2. Rang-Mittelloge und 1. Parterre M. 2.50. 2. Rang-Seitenloge und Sitz-Parterre M. 2.—. 3. Rang-Mittelloge M. 1.50. 3. Rang-Seitenloge M. 1.20. Gallerie-Sitzplatz u. Stehpart. M. 1.—. Gallerie-Stehpl. 50 ₰.

Sonnabend, den 17. April: **Geschlossen.**

Große Preise. Anfang 7 Uhr.
Sonnab., 24. April. 224. Ab.-Vorst. 31. Sonnab.-Vorst.
Abschieds-Benefiz für Herrn Kapellmeister Gustav Mahler.
Symphonie No. 3 Es-dur (Eroica)
von **L. van Beethoven.**
Hierauf: **Fidelio**,
Gr. Oper in 2 Akten von L. van Beethoven.
Leonore: Frl. v. Mildenburg; Florestan: Hr. Birrenkoven; Rocco: Hr. Wittekopf; Pizarro: Hr. Dörwald; Marzelline: Frl. v. Artner; Jacquino: Hr. Weidmann; Fernando: Hr. Vilmar.

SOLOIST (2 & 5) S. Sedlmair.
ORCHESTRA The Budapest Philharmonic Orchestra.
SOURCE Handbill.
NOTES When the concert was first advertised on March 27, 1897, the program also included Liszt's Symphonic Poem, *Mazeppa*, and Wagner's Prelude to Act 1 of *Die Meistersinger* (replaced by the Overture to *Rienzi*).
[1] "What the Flowers on the Meadow Tell Me" had been premiered five months earlier in Leipzig by Arthur Nikisch and also performed by Weingartner in Hamburg and Berlin, concert 150, no. 1.
[2] Weingartner's orchestration of Weber's *Invitation to the Dance* in D flat major, Op. 65, for piano, published in April 1896, retains the original key, contrary to Berlioz's more well-known but transposed version, which Mahler never included in his repertoire.
REVIEW HLG I, 406–407; Roman I, 172–173.

96. April 16, 1897, 7 p.m.
HAMBURG - Stadttheater [2,000 seats]

Good Friday Concert

(1)	Mozart	*Requiem*, D minor, K. 626 •
		- Intermission -
(2)	Bruckner	*Te Deum*, for Soloists, Chorus, and Orch. •
(3)	Krebs	*Vater unser* ("Lord's Prayer"), Op. 198, for Voice & Orch. •
(4)	Handel	*Largo* ("Ombra mai fu"), arr. for String Orchestra and Organ by Josef Hellmesberger Sr. •

SOLOISTS (1) J. von Artner, E. Schumann-Heink, M. Gießwein, and L. Demuth; (2) A. von Mildenburg, E. Schumann-Heink, W. Birrenkoven, and R. Wittekopf; (3) E. Schumann-Heink.
SOURCE Newspaper advertisement; see illustration on opposite page.
REVIEW HLG I, 409.

97. April 24, 1897, 7 p.m.
HAMBURG - Stadttheater [2,000 seats]

Annual Benefit for Mahler [1]

Beethoven — Symphony No. 3, E-flat major, Op. 55, "Eroica"

[followed by a complete stage performance of Beethoven's *Fidelio*, cond. by Mahler]

SOURCE Newspaper advertisement; see illustration on opposite page.
NOTE [1] The evening also marked Mahler's farewell to Hamburg. The following morning he left for Vienna, and only eight years later did he again visit the city as guest conductor (concert no. 175).
REVIEW HLG I, 409–410.

PART VII
VIENNA (I)
Kapellmeister and Artistic Director of the Imperial-Royal Court Opera
1897–1901

Within a year of taking over as director of the Court Opera, Mahler also became conductor of the Vienna Philharmonic Orchestra, thus holding simultaneously the two top music posts in the Habsburg Empire. It is worth stressing that the jobs did not simply fall into his lap thanks to the perspicacity of high-minded officials who recognized his genius. In both cases Mahler worked behind the scenes – some might even say with subterfuge – to get where he wanted to be. In the case of the opera he contrived to oust the aged director Wilhelm Jahn (pragmatically noting that if he had not replaced the old man, who was going blind, then someone else would have done so). As for the Philharmonic, whose players were and still are drawn solely from the ranks of the opera orchestra, exactly how he came to take over remains something of a mystery. Documents released only in the 1980s show that in May 1898 the veteran Hans Richter, popular alike with players and public, was re-elected conductor at the Philharmonic's annual meeting. But just three months later Mahler turned up to chair the orchestra's organizing committee, a post that was actually Richter's, and soon afterwards Richter stepped down as conductor complaining of pain in his arm (although he headed orchestras elsewhere for years after that). Mahler was then acknowledged as Richter's successor with a show of hands.

Natalie Bauer-Lechner claims that Mahler had actually hesitated when "invited" to head the Philharmonic – one sign that her recollections, compelling though they are, cannot always be taken on trust. Mahler was hugely ambitious, not because he was interested in the prestige of this job or simply because he yearned to make music with the very best the world had to offer. Not that the "best" ever satisfied him for long. In Vienna, he praised his players at the start for their musicianship and vitality, but privately he was soon complaining that at close range he had uncovered a mass of faults that had to be eradicated – by terror if necessary. He scheduled far more rehearsals than either Jahn or Richter had done, even of works the players thought they knew well; he would pick on individuals he felt were slovenly or incompetent and scold them in front of their colleagues; and he used some instrumentalists as "spies" (usually quickly uncovered) to pass on to him private backstage chit-chat. Where he felt players could be adequately improved neither through threats nor exhortation, he summarily replaced them. Small wonder that after Mahler's first Philharmonic season, the orchestra voted (by a narrow majority) to ask Richter to return. "Honest Hans" thanked the players for their "flattering request" – but said no.

In the event, Mahler led the Philharmonic for only three seasons, during which he conducted close to eighty works and took the orchestra on its first foreign tour – an ill-fated trip to Paris in 1900 that brought mixed reviews and financial disaster. As to his choice of repertoire, around a third of the pieces he conducted were by Beethoven; but there were also novelties by composers like Franck, Goetz, Kienzl and Perosi as well as pieces such as Berlioz's *Symphonie fantastique* (of 1830) that to many Viennese ears still sounded outlandishly modern. Of his own compositions he gave the Vienna premieres of his First and Second symphonies and, in 1901, the world premiere of that Klagende Lied cantata that had failed to win him the coveted Beethoven prize in the Habsburg capital two decades before. Overall his concert work polarized opinion just as it had in Hamburg. Almost inevitably, Mahler was attacked in anti-Semitic circles simply

because of his Jewish background (and despite his conversion in Hamburg). But even fairer and more balanced critics took issue with his continued Retuschen and, sometimes, with what they felt to be an over-emphasis of detail at the expense of structure in his interpretations. Mahler's fans, of course, would have none of this. For them an implacable idealist was at last revealing the true essence of works too long obscured by slovenly performing tradition, much as a restorer of genius could clean up the faded paintings of old masters. Perhaps Max Graf, a thoughtful critic, came close to the truth when he commented that Mahler was at his remarkable best in music of extremes, whether of passion or serenity: "It is at these frontiers that his talent explodes most brilliantly."

Intense and wide-ranging as it was Mahler's concert work during this era might almost be described as a sideshow to his opera duties. In the four years between his arrival in Vienna and his break with the Philharmonic in 1901, he conducted some 370 opera performances including nearly thirty premieres. He was at least as merciless with aged and/or incompetent singers as he was with unsatisfactory instrumentalists, throwing out cases he felt were hopeless and playing dictator as well as wet nurse to worthy ones. Audiences were not let off lightly either. Mahler made war on the claque (fans noisily backing their favorite singers), insisted that the lights be turned down before performances began and ordered that latecomers be barred entry. On top of all that, he sifted dozens of scores for possible stage presentation, sought to placate obstreperous contemporary composers (like Ruggero Leoncavallo) who felt he was not giving them their due – and all the while struggled with nit-picking Imperial bureaucrats.

Not surprisingly, after completing his Third Symphony in Steinbach in 1896, Mahler did little composing for three years. In 1897 he was fighting for and then taking up the Vienna opera post; in the summer of 1898 he was convalescing after an operation for hemorrhoids – and in the summer after that he found it desperately hard to get started on his Fourth Symphony, then ran out of time. He only managed to complete the work during the summer of 1900. By then he had suffered another serious blow to his health, badly hemorrhaging after conducting – on the same February day – Bruckner's massive Fifth Symphony in the afternoon and Mozart's *Die Zauberflöte* in the evening. The 21-year-old Alma Schindler, daughter of Austria's most famous landscape painter, attended the concert and wrote afterwards that Mahler had looked "like Lucifer" with "a face as white as chalk, eyes like burning coals." A year later she and Mahler were married.

PHILHARMONISCHE CONCERTE.

Sonntag den 6. November 1898,

Mittags präcise ½1 Uhr,

im grossen Saale der Gesellschaft der Musikfreunde:

1ˢᵗᵉˢ Abonnement-Concert

veranstaltet von den

Mitgliedern des k. k. Hof-Opernorchesters

unter der Leitung des Herrn

Gustav Mahler.

PROGRAMM:

L. v. Beethoven.....Ouverture zu: „Coriolan".

W. A. Mozart......Symphonie in G-moll (Köch. 550).
- 1. Allegro molto.
- 2. Andante.
- 3. Menuetto — Allegro.
- 4. Finale — Allegro assai.

L. v. Beethoven.....Symphonie in Es-dur, Nr. 3 (Eroica).
- 1. Allegro con brio.
- 2. Marcia funebre — Adagio assai.
- 3. Scherzo — Allegro vivace.
- 4. Finale — Allegro molto.

Streich-Instrumente: **Gabriel Lemböck's Nachfolger Carl Haudeck.**

Programme unentgeltlich.

Das **2. Philharmonische Concert** findet am **20. November** statt.

Buchdruckerei Wien, I. Dorotheergasse 7.

Season 1897–1898

98. March 3, 1898, 7:30 p.m.
PRAGUE - Neues Deutsches Theater [1,900 seats] [1]

Fourth Philharmonic Concert

For the Benefit of the Orchestra and Chorus' Pension Fund

(1)	Mahler	Symphony No. 1, D major [2]
		- Intermission -
(2)	Beethoven	"An die Hoffnung," *Lied,* Op. 94
(3)	Berlioz	From *La Damnation de Faust*: Menuet des follets & Ballet des sylphes
(4)	Three *Lieder* with piano acc.:	
	Hermann	"Drei Wanderer," Op. 5, No. 3
	Schumann	"Mit Myrthen und Rosen," Op. 24, No. 9
	Schubert	"Sei mir gegrüßt," D 305
(5)	Beethoven	*Leonore* Overture No. 3, Op. 72b

SOLOIST (2 & 4) K. Scheidemantel, acc. at the piano by F. Schalk.
CONDUCTORS (1) Mahler; (3 & 5) Franz Schalk.
ORCHESTRA The Theater Orchestra, reinforced by 25 players from the Czech National Theater, a total of 90 players.
SOURCE Newspaper advertisement; see illustration on following page.
NOTES [1] The New German Regional Theater (1888), today the National Theater.
[2] First performance in Prague. It is interesting that a decade earlier, on July 22, 1888, the *Bohemia* reported that "Gustav Mahler's Symphonie will be performed next season [i.e.1888–1889] at Prague, conducted by the composer."
REVIEW HLG II, 99.

Season 1898–1899

All concerts in Vienna are with the Philharmonic Orchestra.

99. November 6, 1898, 12:30 p.m.
VIENNA - Großer Saal des Musikvereins [2,063 seats]

First Philharmonic Subscription Concert

(1)	Beethoven	Overture to *Coriolan*, Op. 62
(2)	Mozart	Symphony No. 40, G minor, K. 550
		- Intermission -
(3)	Beethoven	Symphony No. 3, E-flat major, Op. 55, "Eroica"

SOURCE Handbill; see illustration on opposite page.
REVIEW HLG II, 121–124.

Neues deutsches Theater.

Donnerstag, den 3. März 1898. Mit aufg. Abonn.
Anfang 7½ Uhr.
Zum Besten des Orchester- und Chor Pensionsfondes.

Viertes (letztes)
Philharmonisches Concert
unter persönlicher Leitung von
Gustav Mahler.
k. u. k. Director des k. k. Hofoperntheaters in Wien
und unter Mitwirkung des
Königl. Sächsischen Kammersängers
Karl Scheidemantel.

Programm:
I. Abtheilung:
Symphonie Nr. 1 für großes Orchester
von **Gustav Mahler.**
(Erste Aufführung.)
I. Langsam. — Gemächlich. II. Kräftig bewegt.
III. Feierlich und gemessen. IV. Stürmisch bewegt.
Das Orchester des Königl. deutschen Landestheaters.
Dirigent: Gustav Mahler.

II. Abtheilung:
1. „An die Hoffnung" von Ludwig van Beethoven.
Karl Scheidemantel.
2. Zwei Orchestersätze aus „Fausts Verdammung" von Hector Berlioz.
   a) Irrlichter-Menuett.
   b) Sylphentanz.
3. Lieder:
   a) „Drei Wanderer" von Heinrich Hermann.
   b) „Mit Myrthen und Rosen" von Robert Schumann.
   c) „Sei mir gegrüsst" von Franz Schubert.
   Karl Scheidemantel.
4. Leonoren - Ouverture Nr. 3 von Ludwig van Beethoven.
Das Orchester des Königl. deutschen Landestheaters
(verstärkt auf 90 Musiker.)
(Orchesteraufstellung auf der Bühne.)
Dirigent: Franz Schalk.
Der Concertflügel „Bösendorfer" ist aus der Niederlage des k. und k. Hof- und Kammerlieferanten
Vincenz Micko.
Zwischen der 1. und 2. Abteilung findet eine
Pause von 10 Minuten statt.
Anfang 7½ Uhr. Ende gegen 9½ Uhr.

Freitag, den 4. März 1898.
(129. Abonnements-Vorstellung.) (1. Serie.)
ANDREA.
Komödie in 6 Abtheilungen von B. Sardou.

PHILHARMONISCHE CONCERTE.

Sonntag den 20. November 1898,
Mittags präcise ½1 Uhr,
im grossen Saale der Gesellschaft der Musikfreunde:

2tes Abonnement-Concert
veranstaltet von den
Mitgliedern des k. k. Hof-Opernorchesters
unter der Leitung des Herrn
Gustav Mahler.

PROGRAMM:

C. M. v. Weber .... Ouverture zu: „Oberon".
F. Schubert ...... Symphonie in H-moll.
(Die zwei vorhandenen Sätze.)
1. Allegro moderato.
2. Andante con moto.
H. Berlioz .... Episode aus dem Leben eines Künstlers,
Symphonie phantastique.
1. Träumereien — Leidenschaften.
2. Ein Ball.
3. Im Freien.
4. Der Gang zum Hochgericht.
5. Traum vom Hexensabbath.

Streich-Instrumente: Gabriel Lemböck's Nachfolger Carl Haudeck.

Programme unentgeltlich.

Das **3. Philharmonische Concert** findet am
4. December statt.

Buchdruckerei Wien, I. Dorotheergasse 7.

PHILHARMONISCHE CONCERTE.

Sonntag den 4. December 1898,
Mittags präcise ½1 Uhr,
im grossen Saale der Gesellschaft der Musikfreunde:

3tes Abonnement-Concert
veranstaltet von den
Mitgliedern des k. k. Hof-Opernorchesters
unter der Leitung des Herrn
Gustav Mahler.

PROGRAMM:

J. Brahms .... Symphonie in Dur, Nr. 2.
1. Allegro non troppo.
2. Adagio non troppo.
3. Allegretto grazioso quasi Andantino.
4. Allegro con spirito
A. Dvořák .... „Heldenlied", symphonische Dichtung.
(Manuscript, I. Aufführung.)
J. Haydn ...... Variationen über die Volkshymne für Streichorchester.
F. Mendelssohn .... Ouverture zu: „Ein Sommernachtstraum".

Streich-Instrumente: Gabriel Lemböck's Nachfolger Carl Haudeck.

Programme unentgeltlich.

Das **4. Philharmonische Concert** findet am
18. December statt.

Buchdruckerei Wien, I. Dorotheergasse 7.

| Vienna | 1898 | Concerts Nos. 100–102 |

100. November 20, 1898, 12:30 p.m.
VIENNA - Großer Saal des Musikvereins [2,063 seats]

Second Philharmonic Subscription Concert

    (1) Weber   Overture to *Oberon*
    (2) Schubert   Symphony No. 8 (7), B minor, D 759, "Unfinished"
                          - Intermission -
    (3) Berlioz   *Symphonie fantastique*, Op. 14

SOURCE Handbill; see illustration on opposite page.
REVIEW HLG II, 124–125.

101. December 4, 1898, 12:30 p.m.
VIENNA - Großer Saal des Musikvereins [2,063 seats]

Third Philharmonic Subscription Concert

    (1) Brahms   Symphony No. 2, D major, Op. 73 •
                          - Intermission -
    (2) Dvořák   *Heldenlied,* Symphonic Poem, Op. 111 • [1]
    (3) Mendelssohn Overture to *Ein Sommernachtstraum*, Op. 21
    (4) Haydn   "Poco adagio, cantabile" (Theme and Variations on the Emperor's Hymn) from String Quartet in C major, Op. 76, No. 3, arr. for String Orchestra • [2]

SOURCE Handbill; see illustration on opposite page.
NOTES [1] *Hero's Song* (comp. 1897, published 1899); world premiere.
[2] 2nd movement only. According to various reviews this movement concluded the concert. Two days earlier, the Austrian Emperor Franz Joseph had celebrated the 50th anniversary of his accession to the throne.
REVIEW HLG II, 126.

102. December 18, 1898, 12:30 p.m.
VIENNA - Großer Saal des Musikvereins [2,063 seats]

Fourth Philharmonic Subscription Concert

    (1) Bizet   *Roma,* Suite de Concert No. 3
    (2) Wagner   *Siegfried Idyll*
                          - Intermission -
    (3) Beethoven   Symphony No. 8, F major, Op. 93 •

SOURCE Handbill; see illustration on following page.
REVIEW HLG II, 127.

Philharmonische Concerte.

Sonntag den 18. December 1898, mittags präcise ½1 Uhr
im
grossen Saale der Gesellschaft der Musikfreunde:

IV. Abonnement-Concert

veranstaltet von den

Mitgliedern des k. k. Hof-Opernorchesters

unter der Leitung des Herrn

Gustav Mahler.

Programm:

G. Bizet . . . . . Roma, Suite Nr. 3.
    1. Andante tranquillo.
    2. Allegretto vivace.
    3. Andante molto.
    4. Allegro vivacissimo (Carneval).
    (I. Aufführung in den Philharmonischen Concerten.)

R. Wagner . . . Siegfried-Idyll.

L. v. Beethoven . Symphonie in F-dur, Nr. 8.
    1. Allegro vivace e con brio.
    2. Allegro scherzando.
    3. Tempo di Menuetto.
    4. Allegro vivace.

Streich-Instrumente: Gabriel Lemböcks Nachfolger Carl Haudeck.

Programme unentgeltlich.

Das 5. Philharmonische Concert findet am **15. Jänner 1899** statt.

PHILHARMONISCHE CONCERTE.

Sonntag, den 15. Jänner 1899

Mittags präcise ½1 Uhr

im grossen Saale der Gesellschaft der Musikfreunde

V. Abonnement-Concert

veranstaltet von den

Mitgliedern des k. k. Hof-Opernorchesters

unter Leitung des Herrn

GUSTAV MAHLER

k. und k. Hofopern-Director.

PROGRAMM:

L. v. BEETHOVEN . . . . . Streichquartett in F-moll, op. 95.
ROBERT SCHUMANN . Symphonie Nr. 1, B-dur, op. 38.
P. J. TSCHAIKOWSKY. »1812.« »Ouverture solenelle«, für grosses Orchester, op. 49.

Das VI. Abonnement-Concert findet am 29. Jänner 1899 statt.

Bösendorfer Concertflügel

benützten in diesen Concerten: Eugen d'Albert, Marie Baumayer, Dr. Johannes Brahms, Dr. Hans von Bülow, B. F. Busoni, Teresa Carreno, Fanny Davies, Illona Eibenschütz, Annette Essipoff, Art. Friedheim, Alfred Grünfeld, Josef Hofmann, Sofie Menter, Adele a. d. Ohe, Max Pauer, Wladimir de Pachmann, Hugo Reinhold, Anton Rubinstein, Moriz Rosenthal, Camillo Saint-Saëns, Emil Sauer, F. X. Scharwenka, Ed. Schütt, Bernhard Stavenhagen etc.

| Vienna–Liege | 1899 | Concerts Nos. 103–105 |

103. January 15, 1899, 12:30 p.m.
VIENNA - Großer Saal des Musikvereins [2,063 seats]

Fifth Philharmonic Subscription Concert

    (1) Beethoven — String Quartet No. 11, F minor, Op. 95, "Serioso," arr. for String Orchestra by Mahler ● [1]
    - Intermission -
    (2) Schumann — Symphony No. 1, B-flat major, Op. 38, "Spring"
    (3) Tchaikovsky — *1812 Overture*, Op. 49

SOURCE Two handbills; see illustration on opposite page.
NOTE [1] World premiere, and the only performance in Mahler's lifetime.
REVIEW HLG II, 136–138; NBL, 127–129.

104. January 22, 1899, 3:30 p.m.
LIEGE - Salle des Fêtes du Conservatoire Royal de Musique [1,700 seats]

Third "Noveaux-Concert"

    (1) Mahler — Symphony No. 2, C minor, "Resurrection" [1]
    - Intermission -
    (2) Weber–Liszt — *Konzertstück*, F minor, Op. 79, for Piano and Orch. [2]
    (3) Saint-Saëns — *Danse macabre*, Op. 40
    (4) Liszt — Piano Concerto No. 2, A major

SOLOISTS (1) M. Lignière and Mme. N. Caro-Lucas; (2 & 4) F. Busoni.
CONDUCTORS (1) Mahler; (2–4) S. Dupuis.
ORCHESTRA L'Orchestra Philharmonique.
CHORUS Société Royale La Légia and "d'un groupe des Dames-amateurs," cond. Sylvain Dupuis.
SOURCE Handbill.
NOTES [1] Second performance in Liege; the first one, on March 6, 1898, was conducted by Sylvain Dupuis.
[2] According to previews two days before the concert, the 2nd part originally included Beethoven's Piano Concerto No. 3, three piano pieces by Chopin, and the "Turkish March" from Beethoven's incidental music to *Die Ruinen von Athen*, Op. 113.
REVIEW HLG II, 141–143.

105. January 29, 1899, 12:30 p.m.
VIENNA - Großer Saal des Musikvereins [2,063 seats]

Sixth Philharmonic Subscription Concert

    (1) Liszt — *Festklänge*, Symphonic Poem ●
    (2) Mendelssohn — *Die Hebriden (Fingal's Cave)*, Overture, Op. 26
    (3) Rameau — *Rigaudon*, Ballet from the Opera *Dardanus*
    (4) Goetz — Symphony, F major, Op. 9 ●

SOURCE Handbill; see illustration on following page.
REVIEW HLG II, 143–144.

PHILHARMONISCHE CONCERTE.

Sonntag den 29. Jänner 1899,
Mittags präcise ½1 Uhr,
im grossen Saale der Gesellschaft der Musikfreunde:

6tes Abonnement-Concert
veranstaltet von den
Mitgliedern des k. k. Hof-Opernorchesters
unter der Leitung des Herrn
Gustav Mahler.

PROGRAMM:

F. Liszt .... Festklänge.
(I. Aufführung in den Philharmonischen Concerten.)
F. Mendelssohn ..Ouverture zu: „Die Fingalshöhle" (Hebriden).
J. Ph. Rameau ..Rigaudon aus: „Dardanus".
(I Aufführung in Wien.)
H. Goetz .... Symphonie in F-dur.
1. Allegro moderato.
2. Intermezzo — Allegretto.
3. Adagio ma non troppo lento.
4. Finale — Allegro con fuoco.
(I. Aufführung in Wien.)

Streich-Instrumente: Gabriel Lemböck's Nachfolger Carl Handeck.

Programme unentgeltlich.

Das **7. Philharmonische Concert** findet am **26. Februar** statt.

Buchdruckerei Wien, I. Dorotheergasse 7.

Dieses Programm ist unentgeltlich.

PROGRAMM
zu dem am
Sonntag, den 19. Februar 1899
um halb 1 Uhr Mittags im grossen Musikvereins-Saale
stattfindenden

Novitäten-Concerte
zu Gunsten des
Pensions- und Unterstützungsfondes der Gesellschaft der Autoren, Componisten und Musikverleger in Wien.

Orchester: Das k. k. Hofopernorchester.

I. Ouverture zur Oper „Der Bärenhäuter".
Dichtung und Musik von Siegfried Wagner.

a) Charakteristik des Bärenhäuters: Hans Kraft. Voll muntern Trotzes zieht er in die Welt, keck den herausfordernd, der ihm etwas anhaben möchte. (Hornruf.)
b) Seinen Ruf erwiedert Einer, auf den Hans Kraft nicht gefasst war: der leibhaftige Teufel selbst. (Monsieur Pferdefuss —.) Zunächst schwirrt's in der Luft. — Hans lauscht: er ruft nochmals; die Erscheinung wird deutlicher; schwächer erklingt der Hornruf und dreist schlängelt sich der Teufel an Hans heran.
c) Da hält das „Ewig-Weibliche" schützend die Hand über den Harmlosen. Es folgt das Thema der Frauengestalt. (Luise.) Wonniges Entzücken des beglückten Hans.
d) aus dem ihn nur zu bald der frech sich einschleichende Teufel stört. (Holzbläser-Fugato, Durchführungstheil.) Ein Kampf entspinnt sich zwischen Hans Kraft und dem Teufel. Hans droht zu erliegen, da greift als Schutzengel das Mädchen mit ein. Der Teufel, immer wüthender und drohender sich geberdend, wird schliesslich durch die Kraft der Liebe besiegt.
e) Hans, von Dank und Freude erfüllt, geht geläutert und gestählt aus dem Kampfe hervor.

Dirigent: **Der Componist.**

II. Maurische Rhapsodie.
Dichtung von Gustav Humperdinck, Musik von Engelbert Humperdinck.

1. Tarifa.
(Elegie bei Sonnenuntergang.)

Hier, wo Europas sonnig Felsenhaupt
Des Atlas schneebeglänzten Kuppen winkt,
Hier, wo im Säulenthor des Hercules
Der beiden Meere Fluthen sich vermählen;
Hier denkst du, Wanderer, der fernen Zeit,
Da Sidons Schiffe reich vorüberzogen,
Denkst jenes Tags, da blutig, schreckenvoll
Der Halbmond dem unwill'gen Meer entstieg.

Längst ist verschollen des Erob'rers Ruf —
Hin sank der letzten Gotenherrscher Macht —
Wie dort der Sonnenball vom Himmel schwindet,
Mit letztem Purpurglanz die Welt bestrahlend.

Wie ist's so still, so öd und einsam rings!
Nur dass von grauer Felswand leise noch
Und wehmuthsvoll ein Hirtenlied ertönt.
Die ew'ge Menschenklage mahnt dich hier.
Die Trauer um vergang'ne Herrlichkeit.
O Geiserich! Tarik! ihr Siegesstolzen!
Du im Verzweiflungskampf, Held Roderich
Vorbei — vorbei — vorbei!

CONCERTE
des Concertbureaus der k. u. k. Hof-Musikalienhandlung
ALBERT GUTMANN
in Wien.

SAISON 1898/99.

Künstler-Vereinigungen:

Böhmisches Streich-Quartett.	Prill-Quartett.
Hellmesberger-Quartett.	Joachim-Quartett.
Fitzner-Quartett.	Kaim-Orchester.

Dirigenten:

Felix Mottl. Bernhard Stavenhagen. Felix Weingartner.

Clavier:

Eugen d'Albert.	Frédéric Lamond.
Ferruccio Busoni.	Sophie Menter.
Fanny Davies.	Max Pauer.
Ernst v. Dohnányi.	Eduard Risler.
Mark Hamburg.	Emil Sauer.

Gesang:

Lillian Blauvelt.	Camilla Landi.
Paul Bulss.	Jean Lassalle.
Ben Davies.	Raimund v. Zur Mühlen.
Rose Ettinger.	Anton Sistermans.
Nina Faliero.	Julia Uzielli.
Lula Gmeiner.	Erika Wedekind.
Eugen Gura.	Dr. Ludwig Wüllner.

Violine:

Bronislaw Hubermann.	Alexander Petschnikoff.
Franz Ondricek.	Pablo de Sarasate.
Rudolf Kemény.	Eugène Ysaye.

Violoncell:

Hugo Becker.	David Popper.

PHILHARMONISCHE CONCERTE.

Sonntag, den 26. Februar 1899
Mittags präcise ½1 Uhr
im grossen Saale der Gesellschaft der Musikfreunde

VII. Abonnement-Concert
veranstaltet von den
Mitgliedern des k. k. Hof-Opernorchesters
unter Leitung des Herrn
GUSTAV MAHLER
k. und k. Hofopern-Director.

PROGRAMM:

ANTON BRUCKNER . Sechste Symphonie A-Dur.
L. v. BEETHOVEN . . Ouverture zu »Egmont«, op. 84.
L. v. BEETHOVEN . . Lieder des Klärchen aus »Egmont« von Goethe mit Orchesterbegleitung.
Gesungen von Fräulein **Maroella Pregi**.
FRANZ SCHUBERT . . Ouverture zur »Zauberharfe«

Das VIII. Abonnement-Concert findet am 19. März 1899 statt.

Bösendorfer Concertflügel
benützten in diesen Concerten: Eugen d'Albert, Marie Baumayer, Dr. Johannes Brahms, Dr. Hans von Bülow, B. F. Busoni, Teresa Carreno, Fanny Davies, Illona Eibenschütz, Annette Essipoff, Art. Friedheim, Alfred Grünfeld, Josef Hofmann, Sofie Menter, Adele a. d. Ohe, Max Pauer, Wladimir de Pachmann, Hugo Reinhold, Anton Rubinstein, Moriz Rosenthal, Camillo Saint-Saëns, Emil Sauer, F. X. Scharwenka, Ed. Schütt, Bernhard Stavenhagen etc.

| Vienna | 1899 | Concerts Nos. 106–108 |

106. February 10, 1899, 7 p.m.
VIENNA - Das Hof-Operntheater [2,500 seats]

      Haydn   Symphony No. 104, D major, "London"

SOURCE Poster.
NOTE The symphony functioned as an "overture" to Haydn's opera *Lo speziale (Der Apotheker)*, and was repeated on February 11, 16, 21, and 24, and again on March 10 and 17 – all conducted by Mahler. The opera was cancelled on February 16 owing to an indisposed singer. According to a notice in the *Neue Freie Presse* (February 7), Mahler originally intended to play a different Haydn symphony at each repeat performance of the opera.

107. February 19, 1899, 12:30 p.m. [1]
VIENNA - Großer Saal des Musikvereins [2,063 seats]

For the Benefit of the Pension and Relief Fund of the "Gesellschaft der Autoren, Componisten und Musikverleger in Wien" [2]

   (1)   Wagner, Siegfried   Overture to *Der Bärenhäuter*
   (2)   Humperdinck   *Maurische Rhapsodie*, Orchestral Suite
   (3)   Kienzl   Two Symphonic Entr'acts from *Don Quixote*
   (4)   Strauss   Preludes to Acts 1 and 2 of *Guntram*, Op. 25 [3]

CONDUCTORS (1) S. Wagner; (2) E. Humperdinck; (3) W. Kienzl; (4) Mahler.
ORCHESTRA Members of the Vienna Court Opera Orchestra.
SOURCE Handbill; see illustration on opposite page.
NOTES [1] The general rehearsal, by invitation only, took place at 3 p.m. the preceding day.
[2] The "Society of Authors, Composers and Music Publishers in Vienna" was founded in December 1897 with music publisher Josef Weinberger as chairman. It was immediately joined by Mahler who however left it on December 31, 1903. The purpose of the Society was to protect the rights of the parties involved.
[3] Mahler had invited Strauss to conduct but he declined due to a lack of time.
REVIEW HLG II, 144.

108. February 26, 1899, 12:30 p.m.
VIENNA - Großer Saal des Musikvereins [2,063 seats]

Seventh Philharmonic Subscription Concert

   (1)   Bruckner   Symphony No. 6, A major ● [1]
                                          - Intermission -
   (2)   Beethoven   Incidental Music to Goethe's *Egmont*, Op. 84:
                                            a) Overture
                                            b) "Die Trommel gerühret," *Lied,* with Orch. ●
                                            c) "Freudvoll und Leidvoll," *Lied,* with Orch. ●
   (3)   Schubert   Overture to *Die Zauberharfe,* D 644 ● [2]

SOLOIST M. Pregi.
SOURCE Program and handbill; see illustration on opposite page.

137

Frankfurter Opernhaus.

Mittwoch, den 8. März 1899.

Sechstes (letztes)
Abonnement-Concert

Dirigent: Herr Kapellmeister Dr. Rottenberg.

Erster Theil.

1. Ouverture zu „Coriolan" . . . Beethoven
2. Symphonie No. 1 (D-dur) . . . Gustav Mahler
   Unter Leitung des Componisten.
   (Zum ersten Male.)
   - I. Satz: Langsam, Allegro commodo.
   - II. Satz: Scherzo.
   - III. Satz: Andante (à la Marcia) funebre — grotesce.
   - Attacca. IV. Satz: Allegro furioso.

Zweiter Theil.

3. Arie „Auf starkem Fittige schwinget sich"
   aus dem Oratorium „Die Schöpfung" . Josef Haydn
   Gesungen von Fräulein Hedwig Schacko.
4. Symphonie No. 8 (F-dur) . . . Beethoven
   - Allegro vivace e con brio.
   - Allegretto scherzando.
   - Tempo di Menuetto.
   - Allegro vivace.

Nach dem 1. Theil 15 Minuten Pause.

Concertbureau Alexander Rosé
Wien, I. Kärntnerring 11.

Unter dem höchsten Protectorate Ihrer k. u. k. Hoheit der durchlauchtigsten Frau Erzherzogin **Maria Josepha** zu Gunsten der **Heilanstalt Alland**

Montag den 13. März 1899 und
Dienstag den 14. März 1899
Abends halb 8 Uhr

im

Grossen Musikvereins-Saale

Zwei Aufführungen

von

„La Risurrezione di Lazzaro"

Oratorium in zwei Theilen von

Don Lorenzo Perosi.

Dirigent:

Gustav Mahler.

Solisten:

Storico [Evangelist] (Tenor)	Guido Vaccari.
Cristo (Bariton)	Silla Carobbi.
Marta (Sopran)	Amelia Fusco.
Maria (Mezzo-Sopran)	Lotte Barensfeld.
Servo (Bass)	Emil Vaupèl.

Das k. k. Hofopern-Orchester.
Grosser Chor.
(300 Herren und Damen.)

K. k. Hoftheater-Druckerei, Wien, I., Wollzeile 17.

| Frankfurt am Main–Vienna | 1899 | Concerts Nos. 108–112 |

NOTES [1] World premiere of complete symphony. However, Mahler had made several cuts in the score and also retouched the orchestration. Previously, only the 2nd and the 3rd movements had been performed on February 11, 1883, by the Vienna Philharmonic Orchestra, conducted by Wilhelm Jahn.
[2] Today widely—but incorrectly—identified as the Overture to *Rosamunde*.
REVIEW HLG II, 144–145.

109. **March 8, 1899, 7 p.m.**
FRANKFURT am MAIN - Das Neue Opernhaus [1,900 seats][1]

Sixth Subscription Concert

(1)	Beethoven	Overture to *Coriolan*, Op. 62
(2)	Mahler	Symphony No. 1, D major [2]
		- Intermission -
(3)	Haydn	"Auf starkem Fittiche," from *Die Schöpfung*, Part 2
(4)	Beethoven	Symphony No. 8, F major, Op. 93

SOLOIST (3) H. Schacko.
CONDUCTORS (1, 3 & 4) L. Rottenberg; (2) Mahler.
ORCHESTRA The Orchestra of the Opera House.
SOURCE Handbill; see illustration on opposite page.
NOTES [1] The "New Opera House," was opened on October 20, 1880, and is now known as "Die alte Oper" ("The Old Opera"), and was rebuilt exclusively for concerts.
[2] First performance in Frankfurt am Main.
REVIEW HLG II, 145–146.

110. **March 13, 1899, 7:30 p.m.**
111. **March 14, 1899, 7:30 p.m.**
VIENNA - Großer Saal des Musikvereins [2,063 seats]

For the Benefit of the Sanatorium "Alland"

Perosi	*La risurrezione di Lazzaro*, Oratorio for Soloists, Chorus and Orch. ● [1]

SOLOISTS A. Fusco (Martha), L. v. Barensfeld (Maria), G. Vaccari (the Evangelist), S. Carobbi (Jesus Christ), E. Vaupél (a Servant).
ORCHESTRA The Imperial and Royal Court Opera Orchestra.
CHORUS An *ad hoc* chorus consisting of 300 singers.
SOURCE Handbill; see illustration on opposite page.
NOTE [1] First performance in Vienna. The composer had conducted the world premiere in Venice on July 26, 1898.
REVIEW HLG II, 146.

112. **March 19, 1899, 12:30 p.m.**
VIENNA - Großer Saal des Musikvereins [2,063 seats]

Eighth Philharmonic Subscription Concert

All-Beethoven Program

PHILHARMONISCHE CONCERTE.

Sonntag den 19. März 1899,
Mittags präcise ½1 Uhr,
im grossen Saale der Gesellschaft der Musikfreunde:

Achtes und letztes

Abonnement-Concert

veranstaltet von den

Mitgliedern des k. k. Hof-Opernorchesters
unter der Leitung des Herrn

Gustav Mahler.

PROGRAMM:

L. v. Beethoven...Ouverture zu „Fidelio".
L. v. Beethoven...Concert Nr. 5, Es-dur, für Pianoforte mit Begleitung des Orchesters. — Vorgetragen von Herrn **Feruccio B. Busoni**.
L. v. Beethoven...Symphonie in A-dur, Nr. 7.
    1. Poco sostenuto — Vivace
    2. Allegretto.
    3. Presto.
    4. Allegro con brio.

Clavier: **Bösendorfer**.
Streich-Instrumente: **Gabriel Lemböck's Nachfolger Carl Haudeck**.

Programme unentgeltlich.

Sonntag den 9. April 1899, Mittags präcise ½1 Uhr:

CONCERT

zu Gunsten des Vereines „Nicolai", Krankenkassa der Mitglieder des k. k. Hof-Opernorchesters
veranstaltet von den

Philharmonikern

unter der Leitung des Herrn **GUSTAV MAHLER**, k. u. k. Hof-Operndirector,
und unter gefälliger Mitwirkung
der Damen: Fräulein **Marcella Pregi**, Frau **Lotte Barensfeld** und des
Singvereines der Gesellschaft der Musikfreunde.

PROGRAMM:

Gustav Mahler........Symphonie Nr. 2, C-moll, für Soli, Chor, Orchester und Orgel.
(I. Aufführung in Wien.)

Der Kartenverkauf findet ausschliesslich in der Musikalienhandlung **Emil Berté & Cie** I. Kärnthnerring 6 statt. Der allgemeine Verkauf beginnt **Mittwoch den 29. d. M.**

Buchdruckerei Wien I. Dorotheergasse 7.

Grosser Musikvereins-Saal.

Verein „Nicolai"

Krankenkassa der Mitglieder des k. k. Hof-Opernorchesters.
13. Vereinsjahr.

Sonntag den 9. April 1899, Mittags ½1 Uhr:

CONCERT

veranstaltet von den

PHILHARMONIKERN

unter der Leitung des Herrn

Gustav Mahler,

k. u. k. Hof-Operndirector,

und gefälliger Mitwirkung der Damen: Fräulein **Marcella Pregi**,
Lotte v. Barensfeld und des **Singvereines** der Gesellschaft
der Musikfreunde.

PROGRAMM:

Gustav Mahler: Symphonie Nr. 2, C-moll, für Soli, Chor, Orchester und Orgel.

1. Satz: Allegro maëstoso. (Mit durchaus ernstem und feierlichem Ausdruck.)
2. Satz: Andante con moto.
3. Satz: Scherzo. (In ruhig fliessender Bewegung.)
4. Satz: „Urlicht" aus „Des Knaben Wunderhorn". —
    Altsolo, gesungen von Fräulein **Pregi**.
5. Satz: Finale.
(I. Aufführung in Wien.)

Streich-Instrumente: **Gabriel Lemböck's Nachfolger Carl Haudeck**.

Programme unentgeltlich.

Buchdruckerei Wien I. Dorotheergasse 7.

| Vienna–Prague | 1899 | Concerts Nos. 112–114 |

    (1) Overture to *Fidelio*, Op. 72
    (2) Piano Concerto No. 5, E-flat major, Op. 73, "Emperor"
         - Intermission -
    (3) Symphony No. 7, A major, Op. 92

SOLOIST F. Busoni.
SOURCE Program and handbill; see illustration on opposite page.
REVIEW HLG II, 146–148.

113. **April 9, 1899, 12:30 p.m.** [1]
VIENNA - Großer Saal des Musikvereins [2,063 seats]

"Nicolai Concert." For the Benefit of the Health Insurance for the Members of the Imperial and Royal Court Opera Orchestra

      Mahler   Symphony No. 2, C minor, "Resurrection" [2]

SOLOISTS L. v. Barensfeld and M. Pregi (in "Urlicht").
ORCHESTRA The Court Opera Orchestra, a total of 130 players.
CHORUS The "Singverein der Gesellschaft der Musikfreunde."
SOURCE Handbill; see illustration on opposite page.
NOTES [1] The public general rehearsal took place on April 7 at 2:30 p.m.
[2] First complete performance in Vienna. Previously only the 2nd movement had been performed on March 3, 1898, by the Munich Kaim Orchestra under Ferdinand Löwe. At the present concert the 4th movement, *Urlicht*, was encored. The 25-year-old Arnold Schoenberg attended the performance but was not particularly impressed by the symphony, which he found faulty in several respects. Therefore a year later he refused to attend the Viennese premiere of Mahler's *First* symphony (concert 135), exclaiming, according to Alma Mahler (then Schindler), "How can Mahler do anything with the *First* when he had already failed to do anything with the *Second?*" (AMM, pp. 78 & 374).
In her memories Alma Mahler wrongly attributes this incident to the Viennese premiere of Mahler's *Fourth* in January 1902 (concert no. 144) as opposed to the *First* in November 1900 – which does not make sense. At the time of the concert in question Alma Schindler was on holiday in Italy.
REVIEW HLG II, 148–155.

114. **June 4, 1899, 7 p.m.**
PRAGUE - Neues Deutsches Theater [1,900 seats]

Conclusion of the Richard Wagner Festival

    (1) Wagner   Prelude to Act 1, and Finale of Act 3, from *Parsifal*
    (2) Wagner   Good Friday Spell, from *Parsifal*
    (3) Wagner   Transformation Music, and Finale of Act 1, from *Parsifal*
         - Intermission -
    (4) Beethoven   Symphony No. 9, D minor, Op. 125

SOLOISTS (1 & 3) W. Elsner (Parsifal), H. Gärtner (Gurnemanz), E. Hunold (Amfortas), A. Haydter (Titurel); (4) M. Ruzek, M. Claus, E. Guszalewicz, M. Dawison.

PHILHARMONISCHE CONCERTE.

Sonntag den 5. November 1899,
Mittags präcise ½1 Uhr,

im grossen Saale der Gesellschaft der Musikfreunde:

1stes Abonnement-Concert

veranstaltet von den

Mitgliedern des k. k. Hof-Opernorchesters

unter der Leitung des Herrn

Gustav Mahler,

k. u. k. Hof-Operndirector.

PROGRAMM:

C. M. v. Weber .... Ouverture zu „Euryanthe".

W. A. Mozart ...... Symphonie in C (mit der Schlussfuge).
1. Allegro vivace.
2. Andante cantabile.
3. Menuetto — Allegretto.
4. Finale — Allegro molto.

L. v. Beethoven .... Symphonie in C-moll, Nr. 5.
1. Allegro con brio.
2. Andante con moto.
3. Scherzo — Allegro.
4. Finale — Allegro.

Streich-Instrumente: Gabriel Lemböck's Nachfolger Carl Haudeck.

Programme unentgeltlich.

Das ausserordentliche philharmonische Concert findet am 8. November, Abends ½8 Uhr, statt.

Verlag der Philharmonischen Concert-Unternehmung. — Buchdruckerei: I. Dorotheergasse 7.

PHILHARMONISCHE CONCERTE.

Sonntag den 19. November 1899,
Mittags präcise ½1 Uhr,

im grossen Saale der Gesellschaft der Musikfreunde:

2tes Abonnement-Concert

veranstaltet von den

Mitgliedern des k. k. Hof-Opernorchesters

unter der Leitung des Herrn

Gustav Mahler,

k. u. k. Hof-Operndirector.

PROGRAMM:

Richard Strauss ... „Aus Italien", sinfonische Fantasie (G-dur) für grosses Orchester.
I. Auf der Campagna (Andante).
II. In Rom's Ruinen (Allegro molto con brio).
 Fantastische Bilder entschwundener Herrlichkeit, Gefühle der Wehmut und des Schmerzes inmitten sonnigster Gegenwart.
III. Am Strande von Sorrent (Andantino).
IV. Neapolitanisches Volksleben [Finale] (Allegro molto).
(I. Aufführung in den Philharmonischen Concerten.)

L. v. Beethoven .. Symphonie Nr. 2. D-dur.
1. Adagio molto — Allegro con brio.
2. Larghetto.
3. Scherzo — Allegro.
4. Finale — Allegro molto.

Streich-Instrumente: Gabriel Lemböck's Nachfolger Carl Haudeck.

Programme unentgeltlich.

Das 3. Philharmonische Concert findet am 3. December statt.

Verlag der Philharmonischen Concert-Unternehmung. — Buchdruckerei: I. Dorotheergasse 7.

| Prague–Vienna | 1899 | Concerts Nos. 114–118 |

CONDUCTORS (1) L. Slansky, (2) J. Manas, (3) D. Markus, (4) Mahler.
ORCHESTRA The Orchestra of the New German Theater.
CHORUS Members of the "Deutscher Singverein," the "Deutscher Männergesangverein," and the "Sängerverein Tauwitz." The choruses were prepared by Friedrich Heßler (concerts 27 & 28).
SOURCE Handbill.
REVIEW HLG II, 172–174.

Season 1899–1900

115. **August 27, 1899, 7 p.m.**
VIENNA - Das Hof-Operntheater [2,500 seats]

In Celebration of the 150th Anniversary of Johann Wolfgang von Goethe

      Beethoven   Overture to "Egmont" op. 84

[followed by a complete stage performance of Mozart's *Die Zauberflöte*, cond. by Mahler]

SOURCE Poster.

116. **November 5, 1899, 12:30 p.m.**
117. **November 8, 1899, 7:30 p.m.** [1]
VIENNA - Großer Saal des Musikvereins [2,063 seats]

First Philharmonic Subscription Concert

    (1)   Weber   Overture to *Euryanthe*
    (2)   Mozart   Symphony No. 41, C major, K. 551, "Jupiter"
                        - Intermission -
    (3)   Beethoven Symphony No. 5, C minor, Op. 67

SOURCE Handbill; see illustration on opposite page.
NOTE [1] In order to give a larger audience the chance to hear the program, it was decided to repeat the Sunday concerts on Wednesday evenings, but the idea proved to be unsuccessful and was abandoned after the first concert.
REVIEW HLG II, 202–205.

118. **November 19, 1899, 12:30 p.m.**
VIENNA - Großer Saal des Musikvereins [2,063 seats]

Second Philharmonic Subscription Concert

    (1)   Strauss   *Aus Italien*, Symphonic Fantasy, G major, Op. 16 •
                        - Intermission -
    (2)   Beethoven Symphony No. 2, D major, Op. 36

SOURCE Handbill; see illustration on opposite page.
REVIEW HLG II, 205–207.

PHILHARMONISCHE CONCERTE.

Sonntag den 3. December 1899,
Mittags präcise ½1 Uhr,

im grossen Saale der Gesellschaft der Musikfreunde:

3tes Abonnement-Concert

veranstaltet von den

Mitgliedern des k. k. Hof-Opernorchesters

unter der Leitung des Herrn

Gustav Mahler,
k. u. k. Hof-Operndirector.

PROGRAMM:

J. Brahms........Symphonie in F-dur, Nr. 3.
- I. Allegro con brio.
- II. Andante.
- III. Poco Allegretto.
- IV. Allegro.

A. Dvořák........„Die Waldtaube" Symphonische Dichtung für grosses Orchester (Neu).
- I. Andante, Marcia Funebre. *Wehklagend folgt die junge Frau dem Sarge ihres verstorbenen Gatten.*
- II. Allegro, später Andante. *Ein fröhlicher, schmucker Bursche begegnet der schönen Wittwe, tröstet und überredet sie, ihren Kummer zu vergessen und ihm zum Manne zu nehmen.*
- III. Molto vivace, später Allegretto grazioso. *Sie erfüllt den Wunsch des Freiers; fröhliche Hochzeit.*
- IV. Andante. *Aus den Zweigen der frisch grünenden Eiche, die das Grab ihres — durch sie vergifteten — ersten Gatten beschattet, ertönt das klagende Gurren der Waldtaube. Die wehklagenden Laute dringen zum Herzen des verbrecherischen Weibes, das, von Gewissensbissen gepeinigt, dem Wahnsinn verfällt und in den Wellen den Tod findet.*
- V. Andante Tempo I, später Piu lento. *(Epilog).*

L. v. Beethoven..Ouverture: „Die Weihe des Hauses".

Streich-Instrumente: Gabriel Lemböck's Nachfolger Carl Haudeck.

Programme unentgeltlich.

Das 4. Abonnement-Concert findet am **17. December** statt.

Verlag der Philharmonischen Concert-Unternehmung. — Buchdruckerei: I. Dorotheergasse 7.

PHILHARMONISCHE CONCERTE.

Sonntag den 17. December 1899,
Mittags präcise ½1 Uhr,

im grossen Saale der Gesellschaft der Musikfreunde:

4tes Abonnement-Concert

veranstaltet von den

Mitgliedern des k. k. Hof-Opernorchesters

unter der Leitung des Herrn

Gustav Mahler,
k. u. k. Hof-Operndirector.

PROGRAMM:

L. Spohr..........Ouverture zur Oper „Jessonda".

J. Brahms........Violin-Concert, vorgetragen von Frau **Marie Soldat-Roeger**.

L. v. Beethoven....Symphonie in F-dur, Nr. 6 (Pastorale).
1. Erwachen heiterer Empfindungen bei der Ankunft auf dem Lande (Allegro ma non troppo).
2. Scene am Bache (Andante molto moto).
3. Lustiges Zusammensein der Landleute (Allegro) — Gewitter, Sturm (Allegro) — Frohe und dankbare Gefühle nach dem Sturme (Allegretto).

Streich-Instrumente: Gabriel Lemböck's Nachfolger Carl Haudeck.

Programme unentgeltlich.

Das V. philharm. Abonnement-Concert findet am **14. Jänner 1900** statt.

Verlag der Philharmonischen Concert-Unternehmung. — Buchdruckerei: I. Dorotheergasse 7.

| Vienna | 1899–1900 | Concerts Nos. 119–121 |

119. **December 3, 1899, 12:30 p.m.**
VIENNA - Großer Saal des Musikvereins [2,063 seats]

Third Philharmonic Subscription Concert

    (1)   Brahms   Symphony No. 3, F major, Op. 90
                               - Intermission -
    (2)   Dvořák   *Die Waldtaube*, Symphonic Poem, Op. 110 ● [1]
    (3)   Beethoven   *Die Weihe des Hauses,* Overture, Op. 124

SOURCE Handbill; see illustration on opposite page.
NOTE [1] *The Wild Dove* (comp. 1896; publ. 1899); first performance in Vienna.
REVIEW HLG II, 207–208.

120. **December 17, 1899, 12:30 p.m.**
VIENNA - Großer Saal des Musikvereins [2,063 seats]

Fourth Philharmonic Subscription Concert

    (1)   Spohr   Overture to *Jessonda*, Op. 63 ●
    (2)   Brahms   Violin Concerto, D major, Op. 77
                                   - Intermission -
    (3)   Beethoven   Symphony No. 6, F major, Op. 68, "Pastoral"

SOLOIST (2) M. Soldat-Roeger.
SOURCE Handbill; see illustration on opposite page.
REVIEW HLG II, 209–210.

121. **January 14, 1900, 12:30 p.m.**
VIENNA - Großer Saal des Musikvereins [2,063 seats]

Fifth Philharmonic Subscription Concert

    (1)   Schumann   Symphony No. 4, D minor, Op. 120
    (2)   Mahler   From *Lieder eines fahrenden Gesellen*:
                                No. 2: "Ging heut' morgen übers Feld"
                                No. 4: "Die zwei blauen Augen"
    (3)   Mahler   Three "Gesänge" (songs) from *Des Knaben Wunderhorn:*
                                "Das irdische Leben" [1]
                                "Wo die schönen Trompeten blasen" [1]
                                "Wer hat dies Liedlein erdacht?"
    (4)   Berlioz   *Le carnaval romain,* Overture, Op. 9

SOLOIST (2 & 3) S. Kurz, substituting the indisposed M. Michalek.
SOURCE Handbill; see illustration on following page.
NOTE [1] World premiere.
REVIEW HLG II, 230.

121

PHILHARMONISCHE CONCERTE.

Sonntag den 14. Jänner 1900, Mittags präcise ½1 Uhr,
im grossen Saale der Gesellschaft der Musikfreunde:

5tes Abonnement-Concert

veranstaltet von den

Mitgliedern des k. k. Hof-Opernorchesters

unter der Leitung des Herrn

Gustav Mahler,
k. u. k. Hofopern-Director.

PROGRAMM:

R. Schumann: Symphonie in D-moll, Nr. 4.
    Ziemlich langsam, Lebhaft — Romanze. Ziemlich langsam — Scherzo, Lebhaft — Langsam, Lebhaft.

G. Mahler: Gesänge für eine Singstimme mit Orchesterbegleitung, vorgetragen von Fräulein **Selma Kurz**, k. k. Hof-Opernsängerin.
  a) Nr. 2 aus dem Cyclus „Lieder eines fahrenden Gesellen": „Gieng heut Morgens über's Feld"
  b) Nr. 4   dto.   „Die zwei blauen Augen"
  c) aus „Des Knaben Wunderhorn": „Das irdische Leben"
  d)   dto.   „Wo die schönen Trompeten blasen"
  e)   dto.   „Wer hat dies Liedlein erdacht".
    (1. Aufführung in den Philharmonischen Concerten.)
    (Texte auf der Rückseite.)

H. Berlioz: Ouverture: „Carneval romain".

Streich-Instrumente: **Gabriel Lemböck's Nachfolger Carl Haudeck.**

Programme unentgeltlich.

Das **VI. Abonnement-Concert** findet am **28. Jänner** statt.

122

PHILHARMONISCHE CONCERTE.

Sonntag den 28. Jänner 1900,
Mittags präcise ½1 Uhr,
im grossen Saale der Gesellschaft der Musikfreunde:

6tes Abonnement-Concert

veranstaltet von den

Mitgliedern des k. k. Hof-Opernorchesters

unter der Leitung des Herrn

Gustav Mahler,
k. u. k. Hofopern-Director.

PROGRAMM:

A. Bruckner . . . . . . Symphonie (romantische) in Es-dur, Nr. 4.
  1. Ruhig bewegt.
  2. Andante.
  3. Bewegt.
  4. Mässig bewegt

F. Mendelssohn . . Ouverture zu: „Meeresstille und glückliche Fahrt".
    Text auf der Rückseite.

R. Wagner . . . . Kaisermarsch.

Streich-Instrumente: **Gabriel Lemböck's Nachfolger Carl Haudeck.**

Programme unentgeltlich.

Sonntag den 18. Februar 1900, Mittags ½1 Uhr

CONCERT

zu Gunsten des Vereines „Nicolai", Krankenkassa der Mitglieder des k. k. Hof-Opernorchesters:

L. v. Beethoven: Neunte Symphonie.

Das **VII. Philharmonische Concert** findet am **18. März** statt.

Verlag der Philharmonischen Concert-Unternehmung. — Buchdruckerei: I. Dorotheergasse 7.

123 & 124

GROSSER MUSIKVEREINS-SAAL.

Verein „Nicolai"
Krankenkassa der Mitglieder des k. k. Hof-Opernorchesters.
14. Vereinsjahr.

Sonntag den 18. Februar 1900, Mittags präcise ½1 Uhr:

CONCERT

veranstaltet von den

PHILHARMONIKERN

unter der Leitung des Herrn

GUSTAV MAHLER,
k. u. k. Hofopern-Director.

und gefälliger Mitwirkung der Damen:
Fräulein **Marie Katzmayr**, Concertsängerin, Fräulein **Leonore Rellée**, k. k. Hof-Opernsängerin;
der Herren: **Franz Pacal**, k. k. Hof-Opernsänger, **Wilhelm Hesch**, k. k. Hof-Opernsänger,
der **Wiener Singakademie** und des „**Schubertbund**".

PROGRAMM:

L. v. Beethoven . . . . Symphonie Nr. 9, D-moll
    für Soli, Chor und Orchester.
  1. Allegro ma non troppo, un poco maestoso.
  2. Molto vivace.
  3. Adagio molto e cantabile.
  4. Presto.   (Text auf der Rückseite.)

Streich-Instrumente: **Gabriel Lemböck's Nachfolger Carl Haudeck.**

Programme unentgeltlich.

Donnerstag den 22. Februar 1900, Abends präcise ½8 Uhr, im grossen Musikvereins-Saale:

Ausserordentliches Nicolai-Concert

veranstaltet von den

Philharmonikern

unter der Leitung des Herrn **Gustav Mahler**, k. k. Hofopern-Director,
und gefälliger Mitwirkung der Damen:
Fräulein **Marie Katzmayr**, Concertsängerin, Fräulein **Leonore Rellée**, k. k. Hof-Opernsängerin; der Herren:
Franz Pacal, k. k. Hof-Opernsänger, **Wilhelm Hesch**, k. k. Hof-Opernsänger, der **Wiener Singakademie**
und des „**Schubertbund**".

PROGRAMM:

L. v. Beethoven . . . . Ouverture „Die Weihe des Hauses".
L. v. Beethoven . . . . Symphonie Nr. 9, D-moll. für Soli, Chor und Orchester.

Der Kartenverkauf findet ausschliesslich in der Musikalienhandlung Emil Berté & Comp., I., Kärnthnerring 6, statt.

| Vienna | 1900 | Concerts Nos. 122–125 |

**122. January 28, 1900, 12:30 p.m.
VIENNA - Großer Saal des Musikvereins** [2,063 seats]

Sixth Philharmonic Subscription Concert

    (1)   Bruckner   Symphony No. 4, E-flat major, "Romantic" [1]
                                    - Intermission -
    (2)   Mendelssohn   *Meeresstille und glückliche Fahrt*, Overture, Op. 27 •
    (3)   Wagner   *Kaisermarsch*

SOURCE Handbill; see illustration on opposite page.
NOTE [1] Mahler had made many cuts in the score and retouched the orchestration. A reconstruction of Mahler's edition was recorded by Gennadi Rozhdestvensky and the USSR Ministry Symphony Orchestra (on Melodyia C 1022411004, Moscow, 1985).
REVIEW HLG II, 231–232.

**123. February 18, 1900, 12:30 p.m.
124. February 22, 1900, 7:30 p.m.
VIENNA - Großer Saal des Musikvereins** [2,063 seats]

Annual "Nicolai" Concert

    (1)   Beethoven   *Die Weihe des Hauses,* Overture, Op. 124
    (2)   Beethoven   Symphony No. 9, D minor, Op. 125 [1]

SOLOISTS (2) M. Katzmayr, L. Rellée, F. Pacal, W. Hesch.
CHORUS Members of the Vienna "Singakademie," and the male chorus "Schubertbund."
SOURCE Program and handbill; see illustrations on opposite and following pages.
NOTE [1] Mahler had effected some editing of the *Ninth,* and was violently attacked by the press for this "sacrilege." He therefore decided to give an extraordinary repeat performance of the symphony, for which he wrote an explanation of his motives. His "defense" was distributed gratis at the second performance (see pp. 148–149) in which the overture was not included.
REVIEW HLG II, 232–238.

**125. March 18, 1900, 12:30 p.m.
VIENNA - Großer Saal des Musikvereins** [2,063 seats]

Seventh Philharmonic Subscription Concert

    (1)   Haydn   Symphony No. 103, E-flat major, "Drum Roll"
    (2)   Weber–Liszt   *Konzertstück,* F minor, Op. 79, for Piano and Orch.
                                      - Intermission -
    (3)   Liszt   "Mephisto Waltz," for Orchestra
    (4)   Goldmark   *Im Frühling,* Overture, Op. 36

SOLOIST (2) F. Busoni.
SOURCE Program and handbill; see illustration on following page.
REVIEW HLG II, 239.

Da in Folge gewisser öffentlich gefallener Aeusserungen bei einem Theil des Publikums die Meinung entstehen könnte, als wären seitens des Dirigenten der heutigen Aufführung an den Werken Beethoven's, und insbesondere an der Neunten Symphonie, willkürliche Umgestaltungen in irgend welchen Einzelnheiten vorgenommen worden, so scheint es geboten, mit einer aufklärenden Bemerkung über diesen Punkt nicht zurückzuhalten.

Beethoven hatte durch sein in völlige Taubheit ausgeartetes Gehörleiden den unerlässlichen innigen Contact mit der Realität, mit der physisch tönenden Welt gerade in jener Epoche seines Schaffens verloren, in welcher ihn die gewaltigste Steigerung seiner Conceptionen zur Auffindung neuer Ausdrucksmittel und zu einer bis dahin ungeahnten Drastik in der Behandlung des Orchesters hindrängte. Ebenso bekannt wie diese Thatsache, ist die andere, dass die Beschaffenheit der damaligen Blechinstrumente gewisse zur Bildung der Melodie nöthige Tonfolgen schlechterdings ausschloss. Gerade dieser Mangel hat mit der Zeit eine Vervollkommnung jener Instrumente herbeigeführt, welche nunmehr nicht zu möglichst vollendeter Ausführung der Werke Beethoven's auszunützen, geradezu als Frevel erschiene.

Richard Wagner, der sein ganzes Leben hindurch in Wort und That leidenschaftlich bemüht war, den Vortrag Beethoven'scher Werke einer nachgerade unerträglich gewordenen Verwahrlosung zu entreissen, hat in seinem Aufsatze „Zum Vortrag der Neunten Symphonie Beethoven's" (Ges. Schriften, Bd. 9) jenen Weg zu einer den Intentionen ihres Schöpfers möglichst entsprechenden Ausführung dieser Symphonie gewiesen, auf dem ihm alle neueren Dirigenten gefolgt sind. Auch der Leiter des heutigen Concertes hat dies in vollster, aus eigenem Durchleben des Werkes gewonnener und gefestigter Ueberzeugung gethan, ohne im Wesentlichen über die von Wagner angedeuteten Grenzen hinauszugehen.

Von einer Uminstrumentirung, Aenderung, oder gar „Verbesserung" des Beethoven'schen Werkes kann natürlich absolut nicht die Rede sein. Die längst geübte Vervielfachung der Streichinstrumente hat — und zwar ebenfalls schon seit Langem — auch eine Vermehrung der Bläser zur Folge gehabt, die ausschliesslich der Klangverstärkung dienen sollen, **keineswegs aber eine neue orchestrale Rolle zugetheilt erhielten.** In diesem, wie in jedem Punkte, der die Interpretation des Werkes im Ganzen wie im Einzelnen betrifft, kann an der Hand der Partitur (und zwar je mehr in's Detail eingehend, desto zwingender) der Nachweis geführt werden, dass es dem Dirigenten überall nur darum zu thun war, fern von Willkür und Absichtlichkeit, aber auch von keiner „Tradition" beirrt, den Willen Beethoven's bis in's scheinbar Geringfügigste nachzufühlen und in der Ausführung auch nicht das Kleinste von dem, was der Meister gewollt hat, zu opfern, oder in einem verwirrenden Tongewühle untergehen zu lassen.

Wien, im Februar 1900.

Gustav Mahler.

Mahler on his retouchings of Beethoven

As a consequence of certain published statements it is possible that some members of the public might be led to conclude that the works of Beethoven, and in particular the Ninth Symphony, had been subjected to arbitrary alterations in matters of detail. It seems appropriate, therefore, to make an explanatory statement.

By the time his deafness became total, Beethoven had lost the intimate contact with reality, with the world of physical sound, which is indispensable to a composer. This happened at the very period in his creative life when the increasing power of his conceptions impelled him to seek new means of expression and a previously unheard-of forcefulness in the treatment of the orchestra. This is well known, as is the fact that the construction of the brass instruments of the period rendered unplayable certain sequences of notes which were necessary to complete the melodic line. It was this same deficiency which ultimately occasioned the improvement of these instruments; and to fail to take advantage of this, in order to achieve perfection in the performance of Beethoven's works, would be perverse.

Richard Wagner, who endeavored all his life, in word and deed, to rescue Beethoven's works in performance from an intolerable state of decadence and neglect, has shown in his essay "On the Performance of the Ninth Symphony of Beethoven" (*Works*, Vol. 9) the way to achieve a performance of this symphony which is as close as possible to the intentions of its creator. All recent conductors have followed Wagner's lead; the director of today's concert has done the same, out of a firm conviction acquired and fortified through his own experience of the work, and without essentially going beyond the bounds set by Wagner.

There can of course be no question of re-scoring, altering, or 'emending' Beethoven's work. The long customary augmentation of the strings has long ago brought in its train an increase in the number of wind instruments, which are there purely to reinforce the sound, and *have not in any way been allotted a new orchestral role*. In this matter, as in every point concerning the interpretation of the work as a whole or in detail, it can be shown by reference to the score (the more detailed the better), that the conductor, far from imposing his own arbitrary intentions on the work – but also without allowing himself to be led astray by any 'tradition' – has been concerned to identify himself completely with Beethoven's wishes, down to the most apparently insignificant detail, and to avoid sacrificing in performance, or allowing to be submerged in a confusion of sound, the least particle of the Master's intentions.

Vienna, in February 1900.   Gustav Mahler

Mahler: A Documentary Study, by Kurt Blaukopf, Oxford University Press, 1976, pp. 221-222

PHILHARMONISCHE CONCERTE.

Sonntag, den 18. März 1900

Mittags präcise ½1 Uhr

im grossen Saale der Gesellschaft der Musikfreunde

VII. Abonnement-Concert

veranstaltet von den

Mitgliedern des k. k. Hof-Opernorchesters

unter Leitung des Herrn

GUSTAV MAHLER

k. u. k. Hofopern-Director.

PROGRAMM:

JOSEF HAYDN .... Symphonie, Es-dur, Nr. 1 (Br. & H.)
CARL MARIA v. WEBER Concertstück in F-moll für Clavier und Orchester, vorgetragen von Herrn Ferruccio Busoni.
FRANZ LISZT .... »Mephisto-Walzer.«
CARL GOLDMARK .... Ouverture »Im Frühling«.

Das VIII. Abonnement-Concert findet am 1. April 1900 statt.

Bösendorfer Concertflügel

benützten in diesen Concerten: Eugen d'Albert, Marie Baumayer, Dr. Johannes Brahms, Dr. Hans von Bülow, B. F. Busoni, Teresa Carreno, Fanny Davies, Ilona Eibenschütz, Annette Essipoff, Art. Friedheim, Alfred Grünfeld, Josef Hofmann, Sofie Menter, Adele a. d. Ohe, Max Pauer, Wladimir de Pachmann, Hugo Reinhold, Anton Rubinstein, Moriz Rosenthal, Camillo Saint-Saëns, Emil Sauer, F. X. Scharwenka, Ed. Schütt, Bernhard Stavenhagen etc.

PHILHARMONISCHE CONCERTE.

Sonntag den 1. April 1900,

Mittags präcise ½1 Uhr,

im grossen Saale der Gesellschaft der Musikfreunde:

Achtes und letztes

Abonnement-Concert

veranstaltet von den

Mitgliedern des k. k. Hof-Opernorchesters

unter der Leitung des Herrn

Gustav Mahler,

k. u. k. Hofopern-Director.

PROGRAMM:

F. Schubert ...... Symphonie in C-dur.
    1. Andante — Allegro ma non troppo.
    2. Andante con moto.
    3. Scherzo — Allegro vivace.
    4. Finale — Allegro vivace.

J. Brahms ...... Variationen über ein Thema von J. Haydn.
    Choral des St. Antonius.
    Var. 1. Poco piu animato.
        2. Piu vivace.
        3. Con moto.
        4. Andante con moto.
        5. Vivace.
        6. Vivace.
        7. Grazioso.
        8. Presto non troppo.
    Finale — Andante.

L. v. Beethoven .. Ouverture zu: „Leonore" Nr. 3.

Streich-Instrumente: Gabriel Lembőck's Nachfolger Carl Handeck.

Programme unentgeltlich.

Verlag der Philharmonischen Concert-Unternehmung in Wien.
Buchdruckerei: L. Dorotheergasse 7.

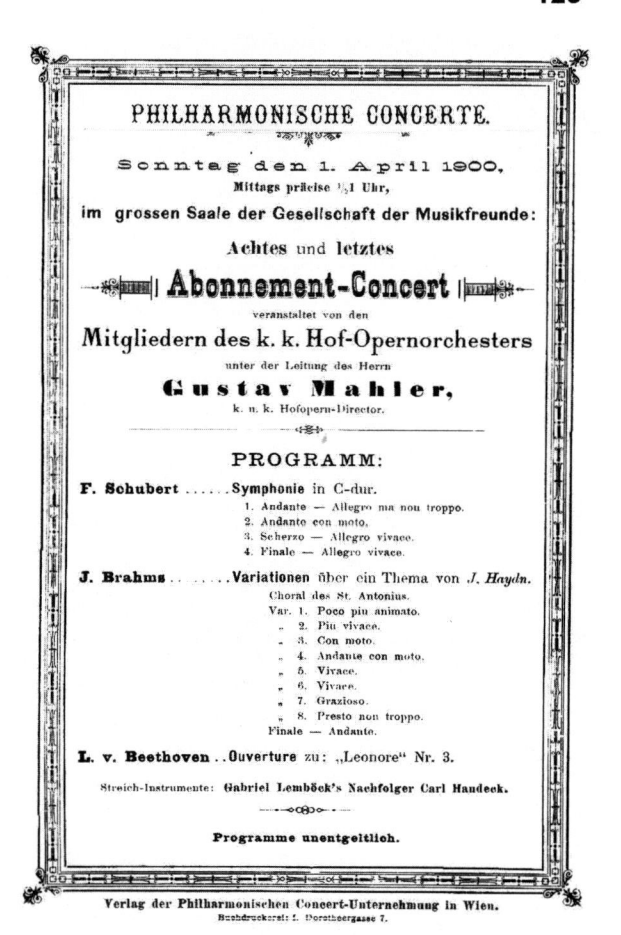

Théâtre Municipal du Châtelet

LUNDI 18 JUIN 1900, à 2 heures 1/2

SOUS LE HAUT PATRONAGE DE

Madame la Princesse de METTERNICH SÁNDOR

1er Concert Philharmonique

DONNÉ PAR LA

Société Philharmonique DE VIENNE

(WIENER PHILHARMONIKER)

Dont tous les Artistes sont Membres de l'Opéra I. et R. de la Cour

SOUS LA DIRECTION DE

M. Gustav MAHLER

Directeur de l'Opéra I. et R. de la Cour

PROGRAMME

Première Partie

1. Ouverture des Maîtres Chanteurs de Nuremberg .... R. WAGNER.
2. Symphonie en sol mineur ...... W. A. MOZART.
3. Ouverture de Léonore (N° 3) .. L. V. BEETHOVEN.

Deuxième Partie

4. Ouverture d'Obéron .... C. M. WEBER.
5. Symphonie en ut mineur (N° 5). L. V. BEETHOVEN.

| Vienna–Paris | 1900 | Concerts Nos. 126–128 |

126. April 1, 1900, 12:30 p.m.
VIENNA - Großer Saal des Musikvereins [2,063 seats]

Eighth Philharmonic Subscription Concert

- (1) Schubert — Symphony No. 9 (8), C major, D 944, "The Great"
- *Intermission*
- (2) Brahms — Variations on a Theme by Joseph Haydn, Op. 56a •
- (3) Beethoven — *Leonore* Overture No. 3, Op. 72b

SOURCE Handbill; see illustration on opposite page.
REVIEW HLG II, 239–242.

127. April 23, 1900
VIENNA - Augustinerkirche [The Church of St. Augustine]

On the Occasion of Wilhelm Jahn's Funeral [1]

Beethoven — Symphony No. 7, A major, Op. 92 (2nd movement)

ORCHESTRA Members of the Court Opera Orchestra.
SOURCE A notice in the Viennese newspaper *Neue Freie* Presse from April 24, 1900, p. 6. Two days earlier (April 22, p. 6) the same paper reports that Mahler intends to conduct Wagner's Funeral March from *Götterdämmerung*, and in addition, deliver a speech at Jahn's grave on behalf of the Court Opera.
NOTE [1] Jahn (born 1834) was Mahler's predecessor as artistic director of the Vienna Court Opera (1881–1897). He died on April 21, 1900.

128. June 18, 1900, 2:30 p.m.
PARIS - Théâtre du Châtelet [2,500 seats]

1er Concert Philharmonique de Vienne [1]

- (1) Wagner — Prelude to Act 1 of *Die Meistersinger von Nürnberg*
- (2) Mozart — Symphony No. 40, G minor, K. 550
- (3) Weber — Overture to *Oberon*
- *Intermission*
- (4) Beethoven — *Leonore* Overture No. 3, Op. 72b
- (5) Beethoven — Symphony No. 5, C minor op. 67

ORCHESTRA The Vienna Philharmonic Orchestra.
SOURCE Handbill; see illustration on opposite page.
NOTE [1] On the occasion of the World Fair in Paris the Vienna Philharmonic made its first concert tour abroad. Besides giving three concerts of its own, the orchestra also participated in two additional concerts, arranged by the Vienna "Männergesang-Verein" (Men's Choral Society).
REVIEW HLG II, 258–261.

Salle des Fêtes du Trocadéro

MERCREDI 20 JUIN 1900, à 2 h. 3/4

SOUS LE HAUT PATRONAGE DE

Madame la Princesse de METTERNICH SÁNDOR

2me Concert Philharmonique

DONNÉ PAR LA

Société Philharmonique
DE VIENNE

(WIENER PHILHARMONIKER)

Dont tous les Artistes sont Membres de l'Opéra I. et R. de la Cour

SOUS LA DIRECTION DE

M. Gustav MAHLER

Directeur de l'Opéra I. et R. de la Cour

PROGRAMME

PREMIÈRE PARTIE

1. **Ouverture d'Egmont** .... L. V. BEETHOVEN.

2. **Romance**, pour violon et orchestre .... L. V. BEETHOVEN.
   Solo : M. ARNOLD ROSÉ, premier violon de l'Opéra I. et R.

3. **Prélude et mort d'Iseult** (Tristan et Iseult) .... R. WAGNER.

DEUXIÈME PARTIE

4. **Symphonie fantastique** .... H. BERLIOZ.

Salle des Fêtes du Trocadéro

JEUDI 21 JUIN 1900, à 2 h. 3/4

SOUS LE HAUT PATRONAGE DE

Madame la Princesse de METTERNICH SÁNDOR

3me Concert Philharmonique

DONNÉ PAR LA

Société Philharmonique
DE VIENNE

(WIENER PHILHARMONIKER)

Dont tous les Artistes sont Membres de l'Opéra I. et R. de la Cour

SOUS LA DIRECTION DE

M. Gustav MAHLER

Directeur de l'Opéra I. et R. de la Cour

PROGRAMME

PREMIÈRE PARTIE

1. **Symphonie en mi majeur.**
   (Héroïque n° 3) .... L. V. BEETHOVEN.

DEUXIÈME PARTIE

2. **Symphonie incomplète**, si mineur .... F. SCHUBERT.
   a) *Première partie.*
   b) *Andante.*
   Scherzo de la symphonie romantique (4°) .... A. BRUCKNER.
   Ouverture « Au Printemps » ... C. GOLDMARK.

3. **Ouverture du "Tannhauser"** . R. WAGNER.

| Paris | 1900 | Concerts Nos. 129–131 |

129. June 19, 1900, 2:30 p.m.
PARIS - Théâtre Municipal du Châtelet [2,500 seats]

1er Grand Choral Concert of the Vienna "Männergesang-Verein"

- (1) Herbeck — "Werners Gruß aus Welschland," *Lied*, Op. 8, for Men's Chorus
- (2) Brahms — "Wiegenlied," *Lied,* Op. 49, No. 4
- (3) Schubert — "Der Gondelfahrer," D 809, for Men's Chorus
- (4) Schumann — "Ritornelle," Op. 65, for Men's Chorus with Piano Acc.
- (5) Kremser — Two *Altniederländische Volkslieder*
- (6) Wagner — "In fernem Land," from *Lohengrin,* with Orch. Acc.
- (7) Kremser — "An die Madonna," Op. 134, for Tenor Solo and Men's Chorus
- (8) Wagner — "Das Liebesmahl der Apostel," for Men's Chorus and Orchestra
- (9) Weber — Overture to *Der Freischütz*

SOLOIST (6 & 7) H. Winkelmann.
CONDUCTORS (1–8) R. v. Perger; (9) Mahler.
SOURCE Handbill.
REVIEW HLG II, 262.

130. June 20, 1900, 2:45 p.m.
PARIS - Palais du Trocadero (Grande Salle de Fêtes) [4,500 seats]

2me Concert Philharmonique de Vienne

- (1) Beethoven — Overture to *Egmont*, Op. 84
- (2) Wagner — Prelude and "Liebestod," from *Tristan und Isolde*
- (3) Beethoven — Romance No. 1, F major, Op. 50, for Violin and Orchestra ●

- Intermission -

- (4) Berlioz — *Symphonie fantastique*, Op. 14

SOLOIST (3) A. Rosé.
SOURCE Handbill; see illustration on opposite page.
REVIEW HLG II, 264.

131. June 21, 1900, 2:45 p.m.
PARIS - Palais du Trocadero (Grande Salle de Fêtes) [4,500 seats]

3me Concert Philharmonique de Vienne

- (1) Beethoven — Symphony No. 3, E-flat major, Op. 55, "Eroica"
- (2) Schubert — Symphony No. 8 (7), B minor, D 759, "Unfinished"
- (3) Bruckner — Symphony No. 4, E-flat major (Scherzo)
- (4) Goldmark — *Im Frühling,* Concert Overture, Op. 36
- (5) Wagner — Overture to *Tannhäuser*

SOURCE Handbill; see illustration on opposite page.
REVIEW HLG II, 264.

Wiener Männergesang-Verein
(Société Chorale de Vienne)

57ème année | 668ème audition publique

Grand Concert

donné au

Palais du Trocadero à Paris

(Grande Salle de Fêtes)

le Vendredi 22 Juin 1900, à 2h 3/4

sous le haut patronage de

Madame la Princesse de Metternich-Sándor

au profit de la

Société de Charité Maternelle

et de la

Société de Bienfaisance Austro-Hongroise de Paris.

Sous la direction des chefs de chœurs de la Société, M. M. **Edouard Kremser** (chef de chœurs honoraire de la Société) et **Richard de Perger** (directeur du Conservatoire de Vienne) et avec le concours de M. **Gustave Mahler**, directeur de l'Opéra Impérial et Royal de Vienne, et de l'**Orchestre Philharmonique de Vienne** (membres de l'Orchestre de l'Opéra Impérial et Royal).

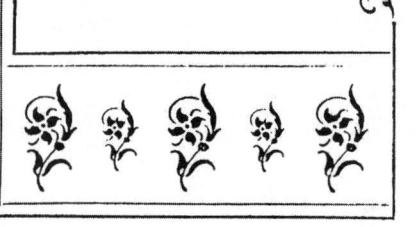

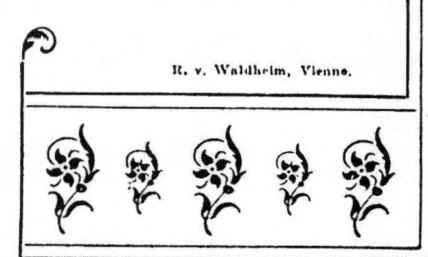

R. v. Waldheim, Vienne.

| Paris–Munich | 1900 | Concerts Nos. 132–133 |

132. **June 22, 1900, 2:45 p.m.**
PARIS - Palais du Trocadero (Grande Salle de Fêtes) [4,500 seats]

Grand Concert Choral of the Vienna "Männergesang-Verein" [1]

   (1) Herbeck   "Zum Walde," for Men's Chorus Acc. by Four French horns
   (2) Storch   "Nachtzauber," for A-Cappella Men's Chorus
   (3) Grieg   "Landkjennung" ("Land Sighting"), Op. 31, for Baritone, Men's Chorus & Orchestra
   (4) Spohr   Violin Concerto No. 9, D minor, Op. 55 (Adagio)
   (5) Schubert   "Sehnsucht," D 656, for Five-Part A-Cappella Chorus
   (6) Anonymous   *Braun Maidelein,* arr. for Chorus by Hugo Jüngst
   (7) Wagner   "Pilgrims' Chorus," from *Tannhäuser*
                    - Intermission -
   (8) **Wagner**   Prelude and "Liebestod," from *Tristan und Isolde* [2]
   (9) Abt   "Mir träumte von einem Königskind," for A-Cappella Chorus
 (10) Schumann   "Ritornelle," Op. 65, for Men's Chorus, with Piano Acc.
 (11) Goldmark   "Frühlingsnetz," Op. 15, for Men's Chorus, Acc. by Piano & Four French horns
 (12) Kremser   "Dankgebet," for Men's Chorus, Acc. by Organ and Orch.

SOLOIST (3) C. Musch, member of the chorus; (4) C. Prill.
CONDUCTORS (8) Mahler; all the other pieces under E. Kremser and R. v. Perger.
SOURCE Program; see illustration on opposite page.
NOTES [1] Due to the indisposition of the tenor H. Winkelmann, the originally announced program underwent a few modifications.
[2] Wagner's Overture to *Der fliegende Holländer,* originally announced, was replaced "à la demande génerale" ("by general request") by the *Tristan* excerpts.

Season 1900–1901

133. **October 20, 1900, 7:30 p.m.**
MUNICH - Großer Saal des Kaim-Konzertgebäudes [3,500 seats]

First Concert of the "Hugo Wolf-Verein"

   (1) Berlioz   *Rob Roy*, Overture
   (2) Strauss   "Hymnus," *Lied*, Op. 33, No. 3, Acc. by Orch.
                   - Intermission -
   (3) **Mahler**   Symphony No. 2, C minor, "Resurrection" [1]

SOLOISTS (2) E. Feinhals; (3) A. Denis-Stavenhagen and E. Feinhals. [2]
CONDUCTORS (1 & 2) S. v. Hausegger; (3) Mahler.
ORCHESTRA The "Kaim" Orchestra, reinforced by 18 musicians from the Munich Hof-Orchester (Royal Orchestra), 14 of which were wind players.
CHORUS The "Porges'cher Choral Society" and the "Lehrergesangverein."
ORGAN (3) A. Hempel.
SOURCE Various newspaper reviews.
NOTES [1] First performance in Munich. Conductor Bernhard Stavenhagen, who had prepared the performance, repeated the symphony on Nov. 1 (not on the 8th, as one sometimes reads), with soloists Agnes Denis-Stavenhagen and Hertha Ritter.
[2] Replaced the originally announced but indisposed Hertha Ritter.
REVIEW HLG II, 300–307.

PHILHARMONISCHE CONCERTE.

Sonntag, den 4. November 1900,
Mittags präcise ½1 Uhr,
im grossen Saale der Gesellschaft der Musikfreunde:

1tes Abonnement-Concert

veranstaltet von den
Mitgliedern des k. k. Hof-Opernorchesters
unter der Leitung des Herrn
GUSTAV MAHLER,
k. u. k. Hofopern-Director.

PROGRAMM:

H. Berlioz .... Ouverture zu: „Rob-Roy".
(I. Aufführung in den Philharmonischen Concerten.)

R. Wagner .... Eine Faust-Ouverture.

L. v. Beethoven .. Symphonie Nr. 3 (Eroica).
    1. Allegro con brio.
    2. Marcia funebre — Adagio assai.
    3. Scherzo — Allegro vivace.
    4. Finale - Allegro molto.

Streich-Instrumente: Gabriel Lemböck's Nachfolger Carl Haudeck.

Programme unentgeltlich.

Das 2. Philharmonische Abonnement-Concert findet am 18. November 1900 statt.

Verlag der Philharmonischen Concert-Unternehmung in Wien.
Buchdruckerei: Wien, I., Dorotheergasse 7.

PHILHARMONISCHE CONCERTE.

Sonntag, den 18. November 1900,
Mittags präcise ½1 Uhr,
im grossen Saale der Gesellschaft der Musikfreunde:

2tes Abonnement-Concert

veranstaltet von den
Mitgliedern des k. k. Hof-Opernorchesters
unter der Leitung des Herrn
GUSTAV MAHLER,
k. u. k. Hofopern-Director.

PROGRAMM:

L. v. Beethoven ..... Ouverture zu: „Prometheus".

R. Schumann .... Ouverture zu: „Manfred".

G. Mahler .... Symphonie Nr. 1, D-dur.
    Einleitung — Allegro commodo.
    Scherzo.
    Feierlich und gemessen.
    Stürmisch bewegt.
(I. Aufführung in den Philharmonischen Concerten.)

Streich-Instrumente: Gabriel Lemböck's Nachfolger Carl Haudeck.

Programme unentgeltlich.

Das 3. Philharmonische Abonnement-Concert findet am 2. December 1900 statt.

Verlag der Philharmonischen Concert-Unternehmung in Wien.
Buchdruckerei: Wien, I., Dorotheergasse 7.

PHILHARMONISCHE CONCERTE.

Sonntag, den 2. December 1900
Mittags präcise ½1 Uhr
im grossen Saale der Gesellschaft der Musikfreunde

III. Abonnement-Concert

veranstaltet von den
Mitgliedern des k. k. Hof-Opernorchesters
unter Leitung des Herrn
GUSTAV MAHLER
k. u. k. Hofopern-Director.

PROGRAMM:

JOH. SEB. BACH .... Concert D-moll, für Clavier und Streich-Instrumente.
    Clavier: Herr **Carl Friedberg**.

L. v. BEETHOVEN .. Ouverture Nr. 2 zur Oper: »Leonore«.

CÉSAR FRANCK .... Symphonische Variationen für Clavier und Orchester.

FRIEDR. SMETANA . Vorspiel zur Festoper: »Libuša«.

FRIEDR. SMETANA . »Moldau«, Symphonische Dichtung.
    (Nr. 2 aus dem Cyclus »Mein Vaterland«.)

Das IV. Abonnement-Concert findet am 16. December 1900 statt.

Bösendorfer Concertflügel

benützten in diesen Concerten: Eugen d'Albert, Marie Baumayer, Dr. Johannes Brahms, Dr. Hans von Bülow, B. F. Busoni, Teresa Carreno, Fanny Davies, Illona Eibenschütz, Annette Essipoff, Art. Friedheim, Alfred Grünfeld, Josef Hofmann, Sofie Menter, Adele a. d. Ohe, Max Pauer, Wladimir de Pachmann, Hugo Reinhold, Anton Rubinstein, Moriz Rosenthal, Camillo Saint-Saëns, Emil Sauer, F. X. Scharwenka, Ed. Schütt, Bernhard Stavenhagen etc.

| Vienna | 1900 | Concerts Nos. 134–136 |

134. **November 4, 1900, 12:30 p.m.**
VIENNA - Großer Saal des Musikvereins [2,063 seats]

First Philharmonic Subscription Concert

- (1) Berlioz — *Rob Roy*, Overture •
- (2) Wagner — *Eine Faust-Ouvertüre*
- *- Intermission -*
- (3) Beethoven — Symphony No. 3, E-flat major, Op. 55, "Eroica"

SOURCE Handbill; see illustration on opposite page.
REVIEW HLG II, 313–314.

135. **November 18, 1900, 12:30 p.m.**
VIENNA - Großer Saal des Musikvereins [2,063 seats]

Second Philharmonic Subscription Concert

- (1) Beethoven — Overture to *Die Geschöpfe des Prometheus*, Op. 43
- (2) Schumann — Overture to *Manfred*, Op. 115
- *- Intermission -*
- (3) Mahler — Symphony No. 1, D major [1]

SOURCE Handbill; see illustration on opposite page.
NOTE [1] First performance in Vienna. The concert was attended by Alma Maria Schindler (aged 21), Mahler's future wife, who had played through the symphony at the piano before the concert, but left the hall with mixed feelings ("stimulating, but no less upsetting," she noted in her diary).
REVIEW HLG II, 307–312.

136. **December 2, 1900, 12:30 p.m.**
VIENNA - Großer Saal des Musikvereins [2,063 seats]

Third Philharmonic Subscription Concert

- (1) Bach–Busoni — Piano Concerto No. 1, D minor, BWV 1052 •
- (2) Beethoven — *Leonore* Overture No. 3, Op. 72b
- *- Intermission -*
- (3) Franck — Symphonic Variations, for Piano and Orchestra •
- (4) Smetana — Overture to *Libuše* •
- (5) Smetana — "Die Moldau," ("Vlatava") from *Má vlast*, Symphonic Poem

SOLOIST (1 & 3) C. Friedberg.
SOURCE Program; see illustration on opposite page.
REVIEW HLG II, 314–315.

137

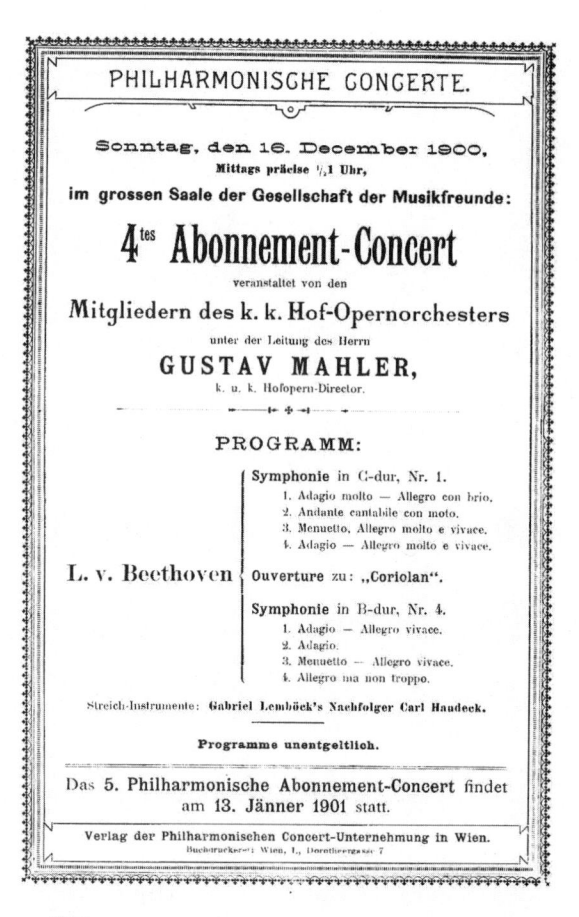

PHILHARMONISCHE CONCERTE.

Sonntag, den 16. December 1900,
Mittags präcise ½1 Uhr,
im grossen Saale der Gesellschaft der Musikfreunde:

4tes Abonnement-Concert

veranstaltet von den

Mitgliedern des k. k. Hof-Opernorchesters

unter der Leitung des Herrn

GUSTAV MAHLER,
k. u. k. Hofopern-Director.

PROGRAMM:

L. v. Beethoven
- Symphonie in C-dur, Nr. 1.
  1. Adagio molto — Allegro con brio.
  2. Andante cantabile con moto.
  3. Menuetto, Allegro molto e vivace.
  4. Adagio — Allegro molto e vivace.
- Ouverture zu: „Coriolan".
- Symphonie in B-dur, Nr. 4.
  1. Adagio — Allegro vivace.
  2. Adagio.
  3. Menuetto — Allegro vivace.
  4. Allegro ma non troppo.

Streich-Instrumente: Gabriel Lemböck's Nachfolger Carl Haudeck.

Programme unentgeltlich.

Das 5. Philharmonische Abonnement-Concert findet am 13. Jänner 1901 statt.

Verlag der Philharmonischen Concert-Unternehmung in Wien.
Buchdruckerei Wien, I., Dorotheergasse 7.

138

PHILHARMONISCHE CONCERTE.

Sonntag, den 13. Jänner 1901,
Mittags präcise ½1 Uhr,
im grossen Saale der Gesellschaft der Musikfreunde:

5tes Abonnement-Concert

veranstaltet von den

Mitgliedern des k. k. Hof-Opernorchesters

unter der Leitung des Herrn

GUSTAV MAHLER,
k. u. k. Hofopern-Director.

PROGRAMM:

F. Mendelssohn .. Symphonie in A-moll, Nr. 3.
Die einzelnen Sätze dieser Symphonie müssen gleich aufeinander folgen und nicht durch die sonst gewöhnlichen längeren Unterbrechungen von einander getrennt werden.
  1. Andante con moto — Allegro un poco agitato.
  2. Vivace non troppo.
  3. Adagio.
  4. Allegro vivacissimo.

P. Tschaïkowsky .. „Manfred" Symphonie in vier Bildern nach dem dramatischen Gedicht von Byron.
  1. Lento lugubre.
  2. Vivace con spirito.
  3. Andante con moto.
  4. Allegro con fuoco.
(I. Aufführung in den Philharmonischen Concerten.)

Streich-Instrumente: Gabriel Lemböck's Nachfolger Carl Haudeck.

Programme unentgeltlich.

Sonntag, den 27. Jänner 1901, Mittags präcise ½1 Uhr:

CONCERT

zu Gunsten des Vereines „Nicolai", Krankencassa der Mitglieder des k. k. Hof-Opernorchesters:

L. v. Beethoven: Neunte Symphonie.

Das 6. Philharmonische Abonnement-Concert findet am 24. Februar 1901 statt.

Verlag der Philharmonischen Concert-Unternehmung in Wien.
Buchdruckerei Wien, I., Dorotheergasse 7.

139

GROSSER MUSIKVEREINS-SAAL.

Verein „Nicolai"
Krankenkassa der Mitglieder des k. k. Hof-Opernorchesters.
15. Vereinsjahr.

Sonntag, den 27. Jänner 1901, Mittags präcise ½1 Uhr:

CONCERT

veranstaltet von den

PHILHARMONIKERN

unter der Leitung des Herrn

GUSTAV MAHLER,
k. u. k. Hofopern-Director,

und gefälliger Mitwirkung der Damen: Frau **Elise Elizza**, k. k. Hof-Opernsängerin,
Fräulein **Charlotte Kusmitsch**, k. k. Hof-Opernsängerin;
der Herren: **Franz Naval**, k. k. Hof-Opern- und herzogl. sächs. Kammersänger,
Moritz Frauscher, k. k. Hof-Opernsänger, der **Wiener Singakademie** und des
„**Schubertbund**".

PROGRAMM:

L. v. Beethoven: Symphonie Nr. 9, D-moll
für Soli, Chor und Orchester.
  1. Allegro ma non troppo, un poco maestoso.
  2. Molto vivace.
  3. Adagio molto e cantabile.
  4. Presto.

(Text auf der Rückseite.)

Streich-Instrumente: Gabriel Lemböck's Nachfolger Carl Haudeck.

1901. **Programme unentgeltlich.** 1901.

| Vienna | 1900–1901 | Concerts Nos. 137–139 |

137. **December 16, 1900, 12:30 p.m.**
VIENNA - Großer Saal des Musikvereins [2,063 seats]

Fourth Philharmonic Subscription Concert

All-Beethoven Program [to commemorate his 130th birthday]

- (1) Symphony No. 1, C major, Op. 21 •
- (2) Overture to *Coriolan*, Op. 62
  - Intermission -
- (3) Symphony No. 4, B-flat major, Op. 60

SOURCE Handbill; see illustration on opposite page.
REVIEW HLG II, 315–316.

138. **January 13, 1901, 12:30 p.m.**
VIENNA - Großer Saal des Musikvereins [2,063 seats]

Fifth Philharmonic Subscription Concert [1]

- (1) Mendelssohn — Symphony No. 3, A minor, Op. 56, "Scottish" •
  - Intermission -
- (2) Tchaikovsky — *Manfred*, Symphony in Four Pictures, Op. 58

SOURCE Program and handbill; see illustration on opposite page.
NOTE [1] When first announced, the program also included Weber's Overture to *Turandot*, which was then postponed to concert no. 141.
REVIEW HLG II, 323–324.

139. **January 27, 1901, 12:30 p.m.** [1]
VIENNA - Großer Saal des Musikvereins [2,063 seats]

Annual "Nicolai" Concert

Beethoven — Symphony No. 9, D minor, Op. 125

SOLOISTS E. Elizza, K. Kußmitsch, F. Pacal, M. Frauscher.
CHORUS The "Sing-Akademie" of the "Gesellschaft der Musikfreunde," and the men's chorus "Schubert-Bund."
SOURCE Program and handbill; see illustration on opposite page.
NOTE [1] At the general rehearsal on January 25 (at 3 p.m.), the solo quartet consisted of E. Elizza, L. Radó-Hilgermann, H. Winkelmann and W. Hesch, who had also been announced when the concert was first advertised on January 10. It remains a mystery why Mahler suddenly replaced three of the soloists.
REVIEW HLG II, 324–325.

GROSSER MUSIKVEREINSSAAL.

Sonntag, 17. Februar, halb 1 Uhr Mittags:

Ausserordentliches Concert der Wiener Singakademie.

Zur ersten Aufführung gelangt:

Das klagende Lied

für Soli, gemischten Chor und grosses Orchester

von

Gustav Mahler

unter persönlicher Leitung des Componisten.

Mitwirkende:

Frau **Elise Elizza**, k. k. Hofopernsängerin.
Fräulein **Anna v. Mildenburg**, k. k. Hofopernsängerin.
Fräulein **Edith Walker**, k. k. Hofopernsängerin.
Herr **Fritz Schrödter**, k. u. k. Kammer- und Hofopernsänger.
Das k. k. **Hofopernorchester**, verstärkt durch einen Bläserchor.
Die Mitglieder der „**Wiener Singakademie**" und des „**Schubertbund**".

Das Concert wird eingeleitet mit:

R. Wagner, Eine „Faust"-Ouvertüre.

Sitze à fl. 5, 4, 3, 2 und 1.50, Entrées à fl. 1.

Alexander Rosé, Concertbureau, I., Kärntnerring Nr. 11.

| Vienna | 1901 | Concerts Nos. 140–141 |

140. February 17, 1901, 12:30 p.m. [1]
VIENNA - Großer Saal des Musikvereins [2,063 seats]

Extraordinary Concert of the "Singakademie"

 (1) Wagner *Eine Faust-Ouverture*
 (2) Mahler *Das klagende Lied,* for Soloists, Chorus, and Orch. [2]

SOLOISTS E. Elizza, A. v. Mildenburg, E. Walker, F. Schrödter [3].
ORCHESTRA The Court Opera Orchestra, reinforced by extra wind players.
CHORUS Members of the "Wiener Singakademie," and the "Schubert-Bund," 500 singers in all.
SOURCE Newspaper advertisement; see illustration on opposite page.
NOTES [1] The general rehearsal took place the preceding day at 3 p.m.
[2] World premiere. A scheduled repeat performance of the cantata on March 15 was eventually cancelled owing to Mahler's sudden, serious illness. Interestingly, the announced program included premieres of some of Mahler's "Humoresken und Balladen" from *Des Knaben Wunderhorn* (titles not specified), and the 2nd movement ("Blumenstück") from his Third Symphony.
[3] Mahler apparently had some difficulties in casting the work. On January 20, when the concert was first advertised, the soloists were E. Elizza, K. Kußmitsch, L. Hilgermann and A. Preuss. According to a newspaper notice on February 2, Preuss had been replaced by Schrödter, and a week later Mildenburg and Walker were announced as replacing Kußmitsch and Hilgermann. Though Mahler's score calls for only *one* soprano, he employed *two* for the premiere. According to one review, the two thematic corresponding "songs of lament," "Ach Spielmann, lieber Spielmann mein!" (in the 1st part) and "Ach Bruder, lieber Bruder mein" (in the 2nd part), were sung by Elizza and Mildenburg respectively, owing to the latter's more steely and dramatic voice.
REVIEW HLG II, 326–331.

141. February 24, 1901, 12:30 p.m.
VIENNA - Großer Saal des Musikvereins [2,063 seats]

Sixth Philharmonic Subscription Concert [1]

 (1) Weber Overture to *Turandot*, Op. 37 •
 (2) Dvořák Serenade, D minor, Op. 44, for Wind Instruments •
    - Intermission -
 (3) Bruckner Symphony No. 5, B-flat major • [2]

SOURCE Program and handbill; see illustration on following page.
NOTES [1] Mahler's last Philharmonic Concert. The same evening he conducted Mozart's *Die Zauberflöte* at the Court Opera. During the following night he became very ill, and after a serious operation he convalesced for two weeks in Abbazia. Mahler therefore cancelled the two remaining Philharmonic concerts (see below), and withdrew his candidacy as conductor of the Philharmonic Orchestra for the next season after his return to Vienna in early April. At a board meeting on May 28 the Philharmonic elected Josef Hellmesberger Jr. to be Mahler's successor.

PHILHARMONISCHE CONCERTE.

Sonntag, den 24. Februar 1901,

Mittags präcise ½1 Uhr,

im grossen Saale der Gesellschaft der Musikfreunde:

6tes Abonnement-Concert

veranstaltet von den

Mitgliedern des k. k. Hof-Opernorchesters

unter der Leitung des Herrn

GUSTAV MAHLER,

k. u. k. Hofopern-Director.

PROGRAMM:

C. M. v. Weber ..Ouverture zu: „Turandot".
    (I. Aufführung in den Philharmonischen Concerten.)

A. Dvořák ....Serenade für Blasinstrumente.
    1. Moderato quasi Marcia.
    2. Menuetto.
    3. Andante con moto.
    4. Finale, Allegro molto.
    (I. Aufführung in den Philharmonischen Concerten.)

A. Bruckner .....Symphonie Nr. 5 (B-dur).
    1. Adagio, Allegro.
    2. Adagio.
    3. Scherzo, Molto vivace.
    4. Finale, Adagio, Allegro moderato.
    (I. Aufführung in den Philharmonischen Concerten.)

Streich-Instrumente: **Gabriel Lemböck's Nachfolger Carl Haudeck.**

Programme unentgeltlich.

Das 7. Philharmonische Abonnement-Concert findet am 10. März 1901 statt.

Verlag der Philharmonischen Concert-Unternehmung in Wien.
Buchdruckerei: Wien, I., Dorotheergasse 7.

| Vienna | 1901 | Concerts Nos. 141–141a & b |

[2] The third performance in Vienna. Mahler had made several heavy cuts in the score and also retouched the orchestration.
REVIEW HLG II, 331–334.

* * *

The Season's Two Remaining Philharmonic Concerts

Several press notices and previews prove that the programs of the following two concerts, with one exception, accord with Mahler's original intentions. It is interesting that they contain three works that were new to his repertoire: Dvořák's overture *In der Natur*, Tchaikovsky's Sixth Symphony, and a Sinfonia by Bach which eventually was replaced by a Haydn symphony (concert no. 141b). The two guest conductors were both *Kapellmeister* at the Vienna Court Opera.

141a. March 10, 1901, 12:30 p.m.
VIENNA - Großer Saal des Musikvereins [2,063 seats]

Seventh Philharmonic Subscription Concert

(1) Dvořák — *In der Natur*, Concert Overture, Op. 91 [1]
(2) Beethoven — Piano Concerto No. 4, G major, Op. 58
(3) Beethoven — Symphony No. 8, F major, Op. 93

SOLOIST (2) I. Eibenschütz.
CONDUCTOR Josef Hellmesberger Jr.
NOTE [1] *In Nature's Realm*. Later performed by Mahler in New York, (concert no. 243).

141b. March 24, 1901, 12:30 p.m.
VIENNA - Großer Saal des Musikvereins [2,063 seats]

Eighth Philharmonic Subscription Concert

(1) Haydn — Symphony No. 88, G major [1]
(2) Tchaikovsky — Symphony No. 6, B minor, Op. 74, "Pathétique" [2]
(3) Beethoven — *Leonore* Overture No. 1, Op. 138

CONDUCTOR Franz Schalk.
NOTES [1] Replaced the originally announced Sinfonia in F major (BWV 1071) by J. S. Bach, which is the composer's own arrangement of his First *Brandenburg Concerto*.
[2] At the time Mahler programmed the symphony he had almost certainly never heard an actual performance of it, nor could he have previously studied the score very thoroughly. This is the conclusion one arrives at in light of his spontaneous reaction to the symphony after attending a performance of it in Vienna on April 17, 1901, with the Berlin Philharmonic Orchestra under Arthur Nikisch. In her *Recollections*, Natalie Bauer-Lechner remembers that Mahler "called it a shallow, superficial, distressingly homophonic work—no better than salon music" (N. Bauer-Lechner, *Recollections of Gustav Mahler,* London, 1980, p. 166). A decade later special circumstances forced Mahler to perform the symphony at six concerts in New York.

* * *

PART VIII
VIENNA (II)
1901–1907

Resigning his Philharmonic post in April, 1901 did not mean Mahler conducted less in the concert hall: quite the opposite. Over the next six years he more than made up for his reduced concert activity in Vienna with a stream of engagements in cities far and wide – from Rome to St. Petersburg, from Lemberg (now Lvov in the Ukraine) to Trieste, from Helsinki to Prague. The time he spent traveling – and rehearsing with many different, sometimes recalcitrant orchestras – inevitably brought charges from his foes that he was neglecting his Vienna duties. There was precious little substance to these complaints, however, as his outstanding opera record shows.

Although the concert repertoire Mahler chose was fairly wide (much of his beloved Beethoven, of course, as well as regular smatterings of Wagner along with Tchaikovsky and Rachmaninoff, Schumann and Liszt), he especially used these tours to present his own symphonies. He did so not only in the hope (by no means always fulfilled) that his work would draw keen applause, but also to learn how it could be improved. After creating his pieces in the seclusion of his summer Häuschen and hearing them for the most part on the piano alone, he badly needed to find out how they sounded in the concert hall. Once he had done so, he set to work as soon as he could revising the orchestration – and went on revising it whenever a new hearing told him further change was desirable. That endless pursuit of the "perfect" instrumentation apart, Mahler also sought to establish a style in the interpretation of his works (tempi, dynamics and so on) that could serve as a model for other conductors. In this, however, he did not really succeed; witness the strikingly varied approaches adopted by maestros like Klemperer, Walter and Oskar Fried who knew Mahler and observed him at work in rehearsal and concert.

It was thus always with a new orchestra in a new city that Mahler gave the premieres of his hugely complex and demanding symphonies; the Third in Krefeld (in June 1902), the Fourth in Munich (November 1901), the Fifth in Cologne (October 1904) and the Sixth in Essen (May 1906). By far his happiest times on the concert trail, though, were spent in Amsterdam where he found a responsive public, a magnificent instrument in the Concertgebouw Orchestra and a vital ally in the conductor Willem Mengelberg, who throughout his subsequent long career did all he could to promote Mahler's work. It was in Amsterdam in 1904 that Mahler actually gave a concert consisting simply of his fourth symphony played twice over – an experiment that went down well there but that would hardly have done so elsewhere!

Mengelberg apart, Mahler enjoyed particularly effective support from his composer-conductor colleague (and rival) Richard Strauss. It was Strauss who in the 1890s had helped put Mahler's First and Second Symphonies on the map; and it was Strauss who used his influence as chairman of the prestigious Allgemeiner Deutscher Musikverein (General German Music Association) to ensure that the Third Symphony was premiered in Krefeld – to acclaim, as it turned out, from public and critics alike. Naturally this aid was not wholly selfless; especially not after Mahler won his influential post in Vienna. Already famed for his exotic (shocking to delicate ears) orchestral tone poems, Strauss was developing as an opera composer and knew how useful to him the director of the Court Opera could be - in the event things did not work out quite as Strauss surely hoped. Mahler did conduct the Vienna premiere of *Feuersnot*, Strauss's second opera, in 1902, but when he later sought to schedule *Salome*, Strauss's third, the lurid piece was rejected by the censors as "unfit for our Court stage." Mahler was incensed. He by

no means approved of all his colleague's works (although, whatever his reservations, he gave quite a lot of the orchestral pieces in the concert hall). He did regard *Salome* as a real masterpiece and its rejection was one factor that prompted him to give up his Vienna post for good.

For all his battles with bureaucrats and his intense concert activity "on the road," Mahler was simultaneously achieving great things in what became known as the Vienna Opera's "golden age." Thanks to his close partnership with the brilliant artist and stage designer Alfred Roller, he was able to present a series of productions – from Wagner's *Tristan* and Beethoven's *Fidelio* to five of Mozart's mature operas - that for musical excellence and dramatic veracity have rarely been approached anywhere and have probably never been excelled. In sum, Mahler was at the height of his career. Moreover, he was now married to the lovely Alma Schindler and had two daughters – Maria ("Putzi") in 1902 and Anna ("Gucki") two years later. The summer holidays were spent mainly at a villa at Maiernigg on the Wörthersee in Carinthia. There – or rather in the solitary Häuschen in the woods nearby where he had completed his Fourth Symphony back in 1900 – Mahler was able to compose his symphonies Five to Eight.

By the end of 1907, though, Mahler had resigned his directorship and left for America. His decision has often been ascribed to the intensity of anti-Semitic attacks on him, but such attacks were anything but new and Mahler had plenty of powerful allies had he wanted to stay. In fact he was weary of the sheer grind of running the opera, and of artistic disappointments of which the *Salome* affair was just one. Besides, he wanted more time to compose, and when Heinrich Conried, director of the New York Metropolitan Opera House, offered him far more money for doing less work, Mahler decided – after some rumination – to accept. By the winter, too, he had other reasons to look for a new start elsewhere, with hopefully less stress and fewer bureaucratic chores. His beloved little Putzi had died of scarlet fever and diphtheria in Maiernigg in July and shortly afterwards he was diagnosed with a heart problem – not, in itself, a very serious one but enough for doctors to insist (or try to) that he take things easier in the future.

On December 9th, 1907, Mahler and Alma took the train from Vienna en route for Cherbourg and a liner to New York. Around 200 friends and fans – including the avant-garde triumvirate Schoenberg, Berg and Webern – gathered to see them off. For his farewell concert on November 24th Mahler had conducted his "Resurrection" Symphony – the work with which he had introduced himself as a composer to Vienna eight years before and which had not been given there again since.

Neues Königl. Operntheater (Kroll).
III. Gr. Sinf.-Abonnements-Concert des
Berliner Tonkünstler-Orch. (ca. 100 Musiker).
Dir.: **Richard Strauss** und **Gustav Mahler.**
Sol.: Frl. **Tila Plaichinger.**
Sonntag, den 15., Mitt. 12 Uhr: Oeffentliche Hauptprobe (1 Mk.).
Montag, den 16., Abds. 8 Uhr: Aufführung (5, 3, 2, 1 Mk.).

PHILHARMONISCHE CONCERTE.

Sonntag, den 12. Jänner 1902

mittags präcise ½1 Uhr

im grossen Saale der Gesellschaft der Musikfreunde

V. Abonnement-Concert

veranstaltet von den

Mitgliedern des k. k. Hof-Opernorchesters

unter der Leitung des Herrn

JOSEPH HELLMESBERGER

k. u. k. I. Hof-Capellmeister

PROGRAMM:

L. v. BEETHOVEN . . . . Ouverture zu »König Stephan«, op. 117.

GUSTAV MAHLER . . . . Symphonie in G-dur Nr. 4 (neu), unter der Leitung des Componisten. (Erste Aufführung in den philharmonischen Concerten.)
Gesang: Frl. M. Michalek, k. k. Hofopernsängerin.

Das Nicolai-Concert findet am 26. Jänner 1902 statt.

Bösendorfer Concertflügel

benützten in diesen Concerten: Eugen d'Albert, Maria Baumayer, Dr. Johannes Brahms, Dr. Hans von Bülow, B. F. Busoni, Teresa Carreno, Fanny Davies, Illona Eibenschütz, Annette Essipoff, Art. Friedheim, Alfred Grünfeld, Josef Hofmann, Sofie Menter, Adele a. d. Ohe, Max Pauer, Wladimir de Pachmann, Hugo Reinhold, Anton Rubinstein, Moriz Rosenthal, Camillo Saint-Saëns, Emil Sauer, F. X. Scharwenka, Ed. Schütt, Bernhard Stavenhagen etc.

| Munich–Berlin | 1901 | Concerts Nos. 142–143 |

Season 1901–1902

142. **November 25, 1901, 7:30 p.m.**
MUNICH - Großer Saal des Kaim-Konzertgebäudes [3,500 seats]

Fifth Subscription Concert of The Kaim Orchestra

   (1) Mozart   Symphony in G major [1]
   (2) Weingartner   "Die Wallfahrt nach Kevlar," Ballad, Op. 12, for Contralto and Orch.
                         - Intermission -
   (3) Mahler   Symphony No. 4, G major [2]
   (4) Four *Lieder* with piano acc.:
        Brahms   "Immer leiser wird mein Schlummer," Op. 105, No. 2
        Schumann   "Waldesgespräch," Op. 39, No. 3
        Reisenauer   "Der wunde Ritter," Op. 13, No. 3
        Cornelius   "Wiegenlied," Op. 1, No. 3
   (5) Beethoven   Overture to *Egmont*, Op. 84

SOLOISTS (2 & 4) T. Behr, acc. in no. 4 by F. Weingartner; (3) M. Michalek.
CONDUCTORS (1, 2, 5) F. Weingartner; (3) Mahler.
ORCHESTRA The Kaim Orchestra.
SOURCE Program reconstructed from various newspapers and music magazines.
NOTES [1] Not identified. According to one review Mozart was 13 years old when he composed the symphony (i.e. about 1769–1770), which suggests that it was either No. 10 (K. 74) or No. 12 (K. 110).
[2] World premiere. On a subsequent tour with the orchestra, Weingartner gave four repeat performances of the symphony in Nuremberg (November 26), Darmstadt (27), Frankfurt am Main (28), Karlsruhe (29, the 4th movement only, because Weingartner was indisposed), and finally in Stuttgart (30).
REVIEW HLG II, 392–404.

143. **December 16, 1901, 8 p.m.** [1]
BERLIN - Neues Königliches Operntheater (Kroll Oper) [1,600 seats]

Third Subscription Concert: "Novitäten-Konzert" [Concert of Novelties]

   (1) Liszt   *Les Préludes*, Symphonic Poem
   (2) Mahler   Symphony No. 4, G major [2]
   (3) Rösch   Three *Lieder* with Orchestra:
                         "Bekenntnis"
                         "Wie wundersam"
                         "Lied vom Winde"
   (4) Strauss   "Liebesszene" ("Love Scene"), from *Feuersnot*, Op. 50

SOLOIST (2 & 3) T. Plaichinger, replacing the originally scheduled E. Destinn.
CONDUCTORS (1, 3 & 4) R. Strauss; (2) Mahler.
ORCHESTRA The Berlin *Tonkünstler* Orchestra (only recently founded and directed by Strauss, for the distinct purpose to perform contemporary music), (100 players).
SOURCE Newspaper reviews; see illustration on opposite page.
NOTES [1] The general rehearsal took place the preceding day at noon.
[2] First performance in Berlin, which Strauss was to conduct, but after the first rehearsal Mahler persuaded him to hand the baton over to him.
REVIEW HLG II, 410–413.

28. December 1901 Nr. 13414

Wiener Singakademie.

III. (ausserordentliches) Concert

Montag 20. Januar, Abends halb 8 Uhr,
im grossen Musikvereins-Saale.

Zur **zweiten** Aufführung gelangt:

Das klagende Lied

für Soli, gemischten Chor und grosses Orchester von

Gustav Mahler

unter **persönlicher** Leitung des Componisten.

Preise der Plätze:

Parterre 1.—10. Reihe	} fl. 5.—	Logensitze VI—X, 2. Reihe	} fl. 3.—
Logensitze I—V, 1. Reihe		Divansitze	
Parterre 11.—20. Reihe	} fl. 4.—	I. Galerie, 1. Reihe	
Logensitze I—V, 2. Reihe		I. Galerie, 2. u. 3. Reihe, Seite	} fl. 2.—
Logensitze VI—X, 1. Reihe		I. Galerie, 2.—7. Reihe, Mitte	
Parterre 21.—30. Reihe	} fl. 3.—	Orgelgalerie und II. Galerie	fl. 1.50
Logensitze I—V, 3. Reihe		Entrée	fl. 1.—

Vorbezugsrechte der Gesellschaft der Musikfreunde **bis 4. Januar.**

Der Kartenverkauf beginnt **am 7. Januar** bei

Alexander Rosé, Concertbureau, I., Kärntnerring Nr. 11,
Cassastunden an Wochentagen von 9—1 und 3—7 Uhr.

Concertbureau
ALEXANDER ROSÉ
I., Kärntnerring II.

WIENER SINGAKADEMIE
44. Vereinsjahr.
Ausgezeichnet mit der goldenen Medaille für Wissenschaft und Kunst.

Montag den 20. Jänner 1902, abends halb 8 Uhr

im Grossen Musikvereins-Saale

III. (AUSSERORDENTLICHES) CONCERT.

o o o o

Zur **zweiten** Aufführung gelangen unter persönlicher Leitung
des Componisten:

1. GUSTAV MAHLER: **Das klagende Lied**
   für Soli, gemischten Chor und
   grosses Orchester.

   Mitwirkende:
   Soli: Frau Elise Elizza, k. k. Hof-Opernsängerin.
   Frl. Anna v. Mildenburg, k. u. k. Kammer- u. Hof-Opernsängerin.
   Frl. Edith Walker, k. k. Hof-Opernsängerin.
   Frl. Hermine Kittel, k. k. Hof-Opernsängerin.
   Herr Erik Schmedes, k. u. k. Kammer- und Hof-Opernsänger.
   Das k. k. Hof-Opernorchester, verstärkt durch einen Bläserchor.
   Die Mitglieder der Wiener Singakademie.

2. GUSTAV MAHLER: Symphonie G-dur, Nr. 4.
   1. Satz: Heiter. — Bedächtig.
   2. Satz: Scherzo.
   3. Satz: Poco Adagio.
   4. Satz: Rondo (Sopran-Solo).
   Sopran-Solo: Frl. Rita Michalek, k. k. Hof-Opernsängerin.

o o o o

Texte umstehend.

Programm: Preis 20 Heller.

| Vienna | 1902 | Concerts Nos. 144–145 |

144. January 12, 1902, 12:30 p.m.
   VIENNA - Großer Saal des Musikvereins [2,063 seats]

   Fifth Philharmonic Subscription Concert

   (1) Beethoven   Overture to *König Stephan*, Op. 117
   (2) Mahler   Symphony No. 4, G major [1]

   SOLOIST M. Michalek.
   CONDUCTORS (1) J. Hellmesberger Jr.; (2) Mahler.
   SOURCE Program and handbill; see illustration on previous page.
   NOTE [1] First performance in Vienna.
   REVIEW HLG II, 471–476.

145. January 20, 1902, 7:30 p.m.
   VIENNA - Großer Saal des Musikvereins [2,063 seats]

   Third (Extraordinary) Concert of the "Singakademie"

   All-Mahler Program

   (1) *Das klagende Lied,* for Soloists, Chorus, and Orch.
       - Intermission -
   (2) Symphony No. 4, G major [1]

   SOLOISTS (1) E. Elizza, A. v. Mildenburg, E. Walker, H. Kittel and E. Schmedes [2]; (2) M. Michalek.
   ORCHESTRA Members of the Court Opera Orchestra.
   CHORUS The Vienna "Singakademie."
   SOURCE Handbill and newspaper advertisement; see illustrations on opposite page.
   NOTES [1] According to a notice in the *Neues Wiener Tagblatt*, December 29, 1901, Mahler's original intention was, once more, to include a number of his "Gesänge" (songs) from *Des Knaben Wunderhorn* for voice and orchestra (concert no. 140). When the concert was officially advertised, on January 10, 1902, the songs had been replaced by Mahler's *First* Symphony. However, four days later the concert was re-advertised and surprisingly, a repeat performance of Mahler's *Fourth* symphony was announced. This sudden—and in a sense provocative—decision might be seen in light of the extremely negative reviews of his new symphony, which had appeared the day after the Viennese premiere.
   [2] The score calls for only one soprano and one contralto. For the distribution between the two sopranos see the note to concert no. 140. For the present performance Mahler inexplicably employed two contraltos, Walker and Kittel.
   REVIEW HLG II, 472–476.

| St. Petersburg | 1902 | Concerts Nos. 146–148 |

146. March 18 [5], **1902, 9 p.m.**[1]
ST. PETERSBURG - The Large Hall of the Nobles [2,000 seats]

Subscription Concert of the Imperial Russian Philharmonic Society

(1)	Beethoven	Symphony No. 3, E-flat major, Op. 55, "Eroica"
		- Intermission -
(2)	Mozart	Symphony No. 40, G minor, K. 550
(3)	Rossini	"Una voce poco fa," from *Il barbiere di Siviglia*
(4)	Delibes	"Où va la jeune Hindoue," from Act 2 of *Lakmé*
(5)	Chopin	Piano Concerto No. 1, E minor, Op. 11
(6)	Chopin	Polonaise No. 6, A-flat major, Op. 53 [encore]
(7)	Wagner	Prelude and "Liebestod," from *Tristan und Isolde*[2]

SOLOISTS (3 & 4) O. Boronat; (5 & 6) E. Schelling.
CONDUCTORS (1 & 2, 7) Mahler; (3–5) N. Kroichevsky.
ORCHESTRA The Orchestra of the Mariinsky Theater (102 players).
SOURCE Handbill.
NOTE [1] The date in brackets refers to the Russian calendar.
[2] Replaced the originally announced Beethoven Overture to *Coriolan*.
REVIEW HLG II, 491–493.

147. March 22 [9], **1902, 9 p.m.**
ST. PETERSBURG - The Large Hall of the Nobles [2,000 seats]

Subscription Concert of the Imperial Russian Philharmonic Society

(1)	Tchaikovsky	*Manfred*, Symphony in Four Pictures, Op. 58 •
		- Intermission -
(2)	Beethoven	Overture to *Egmont*, Op. 84
(3)	Sauer	Piano Concerto No. 1, E minor •
(4)	Chopin	Waltz (unspec.) [encore]
(5)	Sauer	Étude (unspec.) [encore]
(6)	Wagner	*Eine Faust-Ouverture*

SOLOIST E. Sauer.
ORCHESTRA The Orchestra of the Mariinsky Theater (102 players).
SOURCE Handbill.
REVIEW HLG II, 493.

148. March 27 [14], **1902, 9 p.m.**
ST. PETERSBURG - The Large Hall of the Nobles [2,000 seats]

Subscription Concert of the Imperial Russian Philharmonic Society

(1)	Haydn	Symphony No. 103, E-flat major, "Drum Roll" •[1]
(2)	Weber	Overture to *Der Freischütz*
(3)	Wagner	"Siegfried's Tod," Funeral March, from *Götterdämmerung*[2]
(4)	Tchaikovsky	Violin Concerto, D major, Op. 35
(5)	Saint-Saëns	Havanaise, Op. 83, for Violin and Piano [encore]
(6)	Cui	Cavatine, Op. 25, for Violin and Piano [encore]
(7)	Wagner	Prelude to Act 1 of *Die Meistersinger von Nürnberg*

Kurhaus zu Wiesbaden.

Cyclus von 12 Konzerten unter Mitwirkung hervorrag. Künstler.

Freitag, den 23. Januar 1903, Abends 7½ Uhr:

VIII. KONZERT.

Leitung: Herr **Gustav Mahler**, Direktor des Kaiserl. Königl. Hofoperntheaters in Wien.

Solisten:
Herr **Eugen d'Albert** (Klavier),
Frl. **Grace Fobes**, Konzertsängerin aus Wiesbaden (Koloratur)

Orchester: **Verstärktes Kur-Orchester.**

Pianoforte-Begleitung: Herr **Victor Biart** aus Wiesbaden.

PROGRAMM.

1. Zum ersten Male: Vierte Symphonie; G-dur . G. Mahler.
2. Konzert in Es-dur für Klavier mit Orchester Liszt.
    Herr d'Albert.
3. Le carneval romain, Ouverture caractéristique Berlioz.
4. Lieder mit Klavier:
    a) Serenata . . . . Moszkowski.
    b) „Murmelndes Lüftchen" . . . A. Jensen.
    c) La calandrina (mit Variationen von Pauline Viardot-Garcia) . . . Jomelli (1750).
    Fräulein Fobes.
5. Fantasie f. Klavier über Motive a. Moniuszko's
    Oper „Halka" . . . . . C. Tausig.
    Herr d'Albert.

Eintrittspreise:
I. nummerirter Platz: 5 Mk.; II. nummerirter Platz 4 Mk.;
Gallerie vom Portal rechts: 2 Mk. 50 Pf.; Gallerie links: 2 Mk.
Karten-Verkauf an der Tageskasse im Hauptportal.
Bei Beginn des Konzertes werden die Eingangsthüren des Saales und der Gallerien geschlossen und nur in den Zwischenpausen der einzelnen Nummern geöffnet.

Städtische Kur-Verwaltung.

| St. Petersburg–Vienna | 1902 | Concerts Nos. 148–149 |

SOLOIST (4–6) A. Petchnikov, acc. in nos. 5 & 6 by G. Dulov.
ORCHESTRA The Orchestra of the Mariinsky Theater (102 players).
SOURCE Handbill.
NOTES [1] Replaced the originally announced Bruckner Fourth Symphony.
[2] Replaced the previously announced Beethoven Overture to *Coriolan*.
REVIEW HLG II, 493–494.

149. **April 14, 1902, Evening**
VIENNA - The Building of the "Secession"

For the Opening of the Secession's Fourteenth Exhibition[1]

      Beethoven   "Seid umschlungen, Millionen!," Chorus from the Symphony No. 9, arr. for 6 Trombones by Mahler ● [2]

PERFORMERS Probably members of the Court Opera Orchestra.
NOTES [1] The "Secession's" 14th exhibition had Beethoven as its subject, and Max Klinger's famous statue of the naked composer sitting in a chair was the main attraction. According to contemporary accounts, the event—by invitation only—took place in the evening of the 14th, the day before the private view. Mahler and the musicians were standing on the staircase in the vestibule.
[2] World premiere, and the only known performance. At first a complete performance of the *Ninth* had been considered, but a disagreement between Mahler and the Vienna Philharmonic made this impossible. Instead, Mahler arranged a passage from the *Finale's* chorus for six trombones. His autograph score has never has been located, and therefore some doubts exist regarding the exact passage chosen and its precise extent.
Certainly Alma Mahler remembered the excerpt to be the chorus "Ihr stürzt nieder Millionen" (cf. bars 631ff of the *Finale*), but this passage alone (marked *piano*) does not match her subsequent description of the impact that the performance actually made on her: "He [Mahler] conducted the chorus ... [and] *it rang out* as *starkly as granite*" [my italics] (see Alma Mahler, *Gustav Mahler. Memories and Letters;* ed. by D. Mitchell and K. Martner, London 1990, pp. 37 & 367).
In general, there is no reason to question Alma Mahler's memory, but from a musical point of view, Mahler's arrangement must have been introduced by the preceding 36 bars, i.e. the passage beginning with the chorus "Seid umschlungen, Millionen! Diesen Kuß der ganzen Welt!" (*Andante maestoso*, marked *forte fortissimo,* cf. bars 595f). Unlike the chorus quoted by Alma Mahler, this one would at least have produced her described intensity and impression. It should be noted, too, that one of the 'Beethoven' frescoes by Gustav Klimt was titled "Diesen Kuss der ganzen Welt!"
The performance probably did not last more than 3–5 minutes, which included a suitable ending for the chosen passages that Mahler may have added.

Tonkünstler-Versammlung zu Krefeld.

IV. Konzert

Montag, den 9. Juni, Abends 8 Uhr,
in der Stadthalle.

Programm:

Symphonie No. 3

in 2 Abtheilungen

für grosses Orchester, Alt-Solo, Frauen- und Knabenchor

von

Gustav Mahler.

Unter Leitung des Komponisten.

I. Abtheilung.

No. 1. Einleitung und I. Satz.

II. Abtheilung.

No. 2. Tempo di Menuetto.
No. 3. Rondo.
No. 4. Altsolo.
attacca No. 5. Frauen- und Knabenchor mit Alt-Solo.
attacca No. 6. Adagio.

Nach der I. Abtheilung findet eine Pause statt.

Alt-Solo: Frau **L. Geller-Wolter.**

150. June 9, 1902, 8 p.m.
KREFELD - Großer Saal der Stadthalle [1,600 seats]

Fourth Concert at the Thirty-Eighth Festival of the "Allgemeiner Deutscher Musikverein"

      Mahler   Symphony No. 3, D minor [1]

SOLOIST L. Geller-Wolter.
ORCHESTRA The combined orchestras of the Krefeld "Städtische Kapelle" and the Cologne "Gürzenich" Orchestra, a total of 112 players.
CHORUS Women's voices of the Krefeld "Oratorien-Verein" and the boys chorus of the church "St. Anna."
SOURCE Handbill; see illustration on opposite page.
NOTE [1] World premiere of the complete symphony. Separate performances of the 2nd, 3rd and 6th movements had previously been given by Arthur Nikisch (*no. 2:* Berlin, November 9, 1896, and Leipzig, January 21, 1897); by Felix Weingartner (*no. 2:* Hamburg, December 7, 1896, and *nos. 2, 3 & 6:* Berlin, March 9, 1897); by Mahler (*no. 2,* see concert no. 95), and finally by Josef Großmann (*no. 2:* Frankfurt, March 2, 1898).
An intermission followed the opening movement at the premiere.
REVIEW HLG II, 529–532.

Season 1902–1903

151. January 23, 1903, 7:30 p.m.
WIESBADEN - Das Kurhaus [1,200 seats]

Eighth Subscription Concert

  (1) Mahler   Symphony No. 4, G major [1]
                    - Intermission -
  (2) Liszt   Piano Concerto No. 1, E-flat major •
  (3) Three *Lieder* with Piano Acc.: [2]
         Moszkowski   "Serenata," Op. 15, No. 1
         Jensen   "Murmelndes Lüftchen," Op. 21, No. 4
         Jomelli   "La calandrina," with Variations by Pauline Viardot-Garcia
  (4) Tausig   Fantaisie de Concert on Moniuszko's *Halka*, for Piano, Op. 2
  (5) Berlioz   *Le carnaval romain,* Overture, Op. 9 [3]

SOLOISTS (1 & 3) G. Fobes, acc. in no. 3 by L. Lüstner (2 & 4) E. d'Albert.
ORCHESTRA The augmented "Kurhaus" Orchestra.
SOURCE Newspaper advertisement; see illustration on previous page.
NOTES [1] First performance in Wiesbaden.
[2] The announced accompanist, Victor Biart, was replaced by Louis Lüstner.
[3] According to the reviews Berlioz's Overture closed the concert.
REVIEW HLG II, 557.

Symphoniekonzert

Montag den 15. Juni, Abends 7 Uhr

im Münster

(Hauptprobe Montag 15. Juni, Vormitt. 8 Uhr).

---

1. Das Sonnenlied
    nach Worten des « Sôlarliodh », von
    Max Bamberger, für Chorgesang,
    Einzelstimmen, Orchester und Orgel
    op. 26 No. I, III und IV . *Friedrich E. Koch.*

    Sopran: Frau *Val. Riggenbach-Hegar*, Basel.
    Mezzosopran: Fräulein *Frieda Hegar*, Zürich.
    Alt: Fräulein *Anna Hindermann*, Basel.
    Tenor: Herr *Richard Fischer*, Frankfurt a. M.
    Bariton: Herr *Paul Boepple*, Basel.
    Orgel: Herr *Karl Straube*.

2. Ew'ges Licht, Dichtung von Friedrich
    Rückert, für Tenorsolo mit Orchester
    op. 7 Manuscript . *Hans Schilling-Ziemssen.*

    Herr *Richard Fischer*, Frankfurt a. M.

---

3. Symphonie in C-moll No. 2 . *Gustav Mahler.*

    I. Allegro maestoso. II. Andante con moto.
    III. In ruhig fliessender Bewegung. IV. „Urlicht"
    für Altsolo (aus „des Knaben Wunderhorn")
    sehr feierlich, aber schlicht. V. Allegro energico — der Rufer in der Wüste — der grosse
    Appell.

    Sopransolo: Frau *Maria Knüpfer-Egli.*
    Altsolo: Fräulein *Hermine Kittel.*

    Chor: Der Basler Gesangverein.

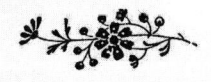

| Lemberg–Vienna | 1903 | Concerts Nos. 152–154 |

152. April 2, 1903, 7:30 p.m.
LEMBERG - The Philharmonie [2,000 seats]

Philharmonic Subscription Concert

    (1) Beethoven   *Leonore* Overture No. 3, Op. 72b
    (2) Mahler   Symphony No. 1, D major [1]
    (3) Berlioz   *Le carnaval romain*, Overture, Op. 9
    (4) Wagner   Overture to *Tannhäuser*

ORCHESTRA The Lemberg Philharmonic Orchestra.
SOURCE Program reconstructed from the review in *Die Musik*.
NOTES [1] First performance in Lemberg (then capital of the Austrian province of Galizia), today known as Lviv in Ukraine.
REVIEW HLG II, 602–603.

153. April 4, 1903, 7:30 p.m.
LEMBERG - The Philharmonie [2,000 seats]

Philharmonic Subscription Concert

    (1) Mahler   Symphony No. 1, D major [1]
                 - Intermission -
    (2) Beethoven   Symphony No. 7, A major, Op. 92
    (3) Wagner   Prelude to Act 1 of *Tristan und Isolde*
    (4) Wagner   Prelude to Act 1 of *Die Meistersinger von Nürnberg*

NOTE [1] According to a notice in the Vienna newspaper *Neue Freie Presse* from January 20, 1903, Mahler had originally scheduled his *Fourth* Symphony. However, in a letter to his wife from Lemberg (April 3, 1903) Mahler writes: "The Symphony [No. 1] yesterday, made a great impression. There was a general desire for a second hearing, and so I am giving it again at tomorrow's concert" (AMM, 227). In fact, the orchestra was so delighted with the symphony that it was included in its tour in October of the same year to the Baltic countries and performed in Riga, along with other works, and conducted by its permanent conductor, L. Czelanski.

154. April 28, 1903, 7:30 p.m.
VIENNA - Das Hof-Operntheater [2,500 seats]

Théâtre paré in Honor of the King [Georg I] of Saxony [1]

    (1) Verdi   Prelude to *Aida*, Act 1 & all of Act 2 [2]
                 - Intermission -
    (2) Nicolai   Overture to *Die lustigen Weiber von Windsor* •
    (3) Nedbal   *Der faule Hans (Lazy Hans)*, Ballet, Act 1 & 2 [2]

CONDUCTORS (1 & 2) Mahler; (3) O. Nedbal.
SOURCE The review in the *Wiener Zeitung*, April 29, 1903, p. 13.

PROGRAMMA.

1. Symphonie No. 3 . . . Gustav Mahler.

(Eerste uitvoering.)

1ste Afdeeling.

No. 1. Inleiding en 1ste deel.

— PAUZE. —

2de Afdeeling.

No. 2. Tempo di Menuetto.
" 3. Scherzando.
" 4. Alt-Solo (woorden van Nietzsche).
" 5. Vrouwen- en Jongenskoor met Alt-Solo (woorden uit "Des Knaben Wunderhorn".)
" 6. Slot: Adagio.

Medewerkenden:

Mejuffrouw Hermine Kittel.

K. K. Hofopera-Zangeres uit Weenen.

Vrouwenkoor: Het Dameskoor der Zangvereeniging van de Afdeeling Amsterdam der Maatschappij tot Bevordering der Toonkunst.

Een Jongenskoor, van de Vereeniging tot Verbetering van den Volkszang.

Het versterkte Concertgebouw-Orkest.

Het geheel onder leiding van den Componist.

BUITENGEWOON ABONNEMENTS-CONCERT
Donderdag 22 en Vrijdag 23 October 1903,
onder leiding van den Heer Gustav Mahler.

PROGRAMMA.

1. Ouverture van de Opera "Oberon" . . . . . C. M. von Weber.
(1786 – 1826)

2. Eine kleine Nachtmusik, Serenade voor Strijkorkest . . . . W. A. Mozart.
(1756 – 1791)

a. Allegro.
b. Romance: Andante.
c. Menuetto: Allegretto. Trio. Menuetto da capo.
d. Rondo: Allegro.

3. Ouverture van de Opera "Tannhäuser" . . . . . R. Wagner.
(1813 – 1883)

No. 1, 2 en 3 onder leiding van den Heer Willem Mengelberg.

— PAUZE. —

4. Symphonie No. 1 (D gr. t.) . . . . Gustav Mahler.
(geb. 1860)

a. Langzaam. Allegro.
b. Krachtig, opgewekt.
c. Plechtig.
d. Stormachtig bewogen.

(Eerste uitvoering in Nederland.)

Onder leiding van den Componist.

| Vienna–Basel–Amsterdam | 1903 | Concerts Nos. 154–157 |

NOTES [1] At this gala performance, King Georg II presented Mahler with the Saxony order of "Albrecht," 2nd Class. Commenting on the audience, the *Neue Freie Presse* (April 29, p. 7) reports: "Frau Director *Mahler* was especially observed, gazing down [from her box] on her husband in the pit with conspicuous pride."
[2] Complete stage performances of new productions.

155. June 15, 1903, 7 p.m.[1]
BASEL - Münster

Sixth Concert at the Thirty-Ninth Festival of the "Allgemeiner Deutscher Musikverein"

(1)	Koch	"Das Sonnenlied," Op. 26, for Soloists, Chorus and Orch.
(2)	Schilling-Ziemssen	"Ew'ges Licht," Op. 7, for Tenor and Orch.
		- Intermission -
(3)	Mahler	Symphony No. 2, C minor, "Resurrection"

SOLOISTS (1) V. Riggenbach-Hegar, F. Hegar, A. Hindermann, R. Fischer, P. Boepple; (2) R. Fischer; (3) M. Knüpfer-Egli and H. Kittel[2].
CONDUCTORS (1 & 2) H. Suter; (3) Mahler.
ORCHESTRA The orchestra of the "Allgemeine Musikalische Gesellschaft" in Basel, reinforced with players from Lausanne und Meiningen; a total of 110 players.
CHORUS The "Basler Gesangverein" and "Der Liedertafel"
ORGAN (1) K. Straube; (3) A. Glaus.
SOURCE Handbill; see illustration on previous page.
NOTES [1] The general rehearsal took place at 8 a.m. the same day.
[2] Hermine Kittel replaced the originally announced Ernestine Schumann-Heink.
REVIEW HLG II, 610–614.

Season 1903–1904

156. October 22, 1903, 8 p.m.
157. October 23, 1903, 8 p.m.
AMSTERDAM - The Concertgebouw [1,800 seats]

Non-Subscription Concert

      Mahler   Symphony No. 3, D minor[1]

SOLOIST H. Kittel[2]
ORCHESTRA The Concertgebouw Orchestra.
CHORUS The Amsterdam choruses "Bevordering der Toonkunst" ["Society for the Encouragement of Music"] and "Verbetering van den Volkszang" ["Society for Improvement of Folk Singing"], and an unspecified boys' chorus.
SOURCE Program and handbill; see illustration on opposite page.
NOTES [1] First performance in Amsterdam. An intermission followed the 1st movement.
[2] The originally announced soloist, Adrienne v. Kraus-Osborne, was indisposed and was first replaced by Pauline de Haan-Manifarges. When she too fell ill Hermine Kittel of the Vienna Court Opera was engaged.
REVIEW HLG II, 644–646.

Abonnements-Konzerte des Bach-Vereins zu Heidelberg 1903/04.

Montag, den 1. Februar 1904, abends pünktlich 7½ Uhr
im grossen Saale der Stadthalle

Fünftes Konzert

(bei offenem Orchester)

unter gütiger Leitung des Herrn **Gustav Mahler**, k. k. Hofoperndirektors aus Wien:

Gustav Mahler, dritte Symphonie.

Erste Abteilung:
1. Satz. Kräftig. Entschieden.

Pause von 10 Minuten.

Zweite Abteilung:
2. Tempo di Menuetto. 3. Comodo. Scherzando. Ohne Hast. 4. Sehr langsam. Misterioso.
(Altsolo nach Worten von Friedrich Nietzsche):

Eins!	Fünf!	Neun!
Oh Mensch! Gieb Acht!	„Die Welt ist tief,	„Weh spricht: Vergeh!
Zwei!	Sechs!	Zehn!
Was spricht die tiefe Mitternacht?	„Und tiefer als der Tag gedacht.	„Doch alle Lust will Ewigkeit —,
Drei!	Sieben!	Elf!
„Ich schlief, ich schlief —,	„Tief ist ihr Weh —,	„— will tiefe, tiefe Ewigkeit!"
Vier!	Acht!	Zwölf!
„Aus tiefem Traum bin ich erwacht: —	„Lust — tiefer noch als Herzeleid:	(„Also sprach Zarathustra.")

5. Lustig im Tempo und keck im Ausdruck.
(Frauenchor, Altsolo und Knabenchor):

Es sungen drei Engel einen süssen Gesang,	Ach! sollt' ich nicht weinen, du gütiger Gott,	Die himmlische Freud ist eine selige Stadt,
Mit Freuden es im Himmel klang;	Ich hab übertreten der zehen Gebot,	Die himmlische Freud, die kein End mehr hat;
Sie jauchzten fröhlich auch dabei,	Ich gehe und weine ja bitterlich;	Die himmlische Freude war Petro bereit
Dass Petrus sey von Sünden frey,	Ach komm, erbarme dich über mich,	Durch Jesum und allen zur Seeligkeit,
Von Sünden frey.	Ach über mich!	Zur Seeligkeit.
Und als der Herr Jesus zu Tische sass,	„Hast du denn übertreten die zehen Gebot,	(Aus „Des Knaben Wunderhorn".)
Mit seinen zwölf Jüngern das Abendmahl ass,	So fall auf die Knie und bete zu Gott,	
So sprach der Herr Jesus: „Was stehest du hier,	Und bete zu Gott nur allezeit,	
Wenn ich dich ansehe, so weinest du mir,	So wirst du erlangen die himmlische Freud."	
So weinest du mir."		

6. Langsam. Ruhevoll. Empfunden.

Orchester: Das Heidelberger **städtische Orchester** und das Mannheimer **Hoftheaterorchester** (60 Streichinstrumente, 44 Blas- und Schlaginstrumente, 2 Harfen, ferner einige Schlag- und Blasinstrumente hinter der Scene).

Altsolo: Fräulein **B. Kofler**, Hofopernsängerin aus Mannheim.

Frauenchor des **Bachvereins**.

Knabenchor vom **Grossh. Gymnasium Heidelberg**.

Preise der Plätze: Balkon (Mitte) I. und II. Reihe Mk. 6.—, III.—V. Reihe Mk. 5.—, (Seite) Mk. 4.—. Sperrsitz (Saal) Mk. 4.—. Saal (unnummeriert) I. Abteilung Mk. 3.—, II. Abteilung (unter dem Balkon, Mitte) Mk. 2.50, III. Abteilung (unter dem Balkon, Seite) Mk. 2.—; obere Galerie Mk. 1.50. Studentenkarten (für Saal und Stehplatz auf dem Balkon) Mk. 1.50.

Eintrittskarten für **alle** Plätze in der Hof-Musikalienhandlung des Herrn Eugen Pfeiffer, Ludwigsplatz; Karten für **unnummerierte** Plätze (Saal und obere Galerie) in den Musikalien- und Buchhandlungen der Herren Karl Hochstein, F. W. Rochow und Alois Kunst; Studentenkarten bei Herrn F. W. Rochow (Winter'sche Univ.-Buchhandlung).

===== **An der Kasse erhöhte Preise.** =====

Freitag, den 19. Februar: **Hugo Wolf-Liederabend** von Dr. Ludwig Wüllner. Montag, den 29. Februar: VI. Abonnements-Konzert unter Mitwirkung des **Bachvereins** und **akademischen Gesangvereins**, der Frau Kammersängerin **Agnes Stavenhagen** aus München, des Fräulein Mathilde Haas, Kammersängerin aus Mainz, der Konzertsänger Herren **George Walter** aus Düsseldorf und Adam Wunderlich aus Nürnberg: Ludwig van Beethoven, Messe in C-dur; Johann Sebastian Bach, Kantate: Ich bin ein guter Hirte; Johann Sebastian Bach, Magnificat (5stimmig).

158. October 25, 1903, 8 p.m.
AMSTERDAM - The Concertgebouw [1,800 seats]

(1)	Mahler	Symphony No. 1, D major [1]
		- Intermission -
(2)	Weber	Overture to *Oberon*
(3)	Mozart	Serenade, G major, "Eine kleine Nachtmusik," K. 525
(4)	Wagner	Overture to *Tannhäuser*

CONDUCTORS (1) Mahler; (2–4) W. Mengelberg.
SOURCE Handbill; see illustration on previous page. According to the reviews, the order of the program printed on the handbill was reversed, i.e. Mahler's symphony opened the concert.
NOTE [1] First performance in Amsterdam.
REVIEW HLG II, 646.

159. December 2, 1903, 7 p.m. [1]
FRANKFURT am MAIN - Das Neue Opernhaus [1,900 seats]

Third Subscription Concert: Commemorating the Centenary of Hector Berlioz

      Mahler   Symphony No. 3, D minor [2]

SOLOIST C. Weber.
ORCHESTRA Orchestra and Chorus of the Opera.
SOURCE Handbill.
NOTE [1] The general rehearsal took place the same morning.
[2] First complete performance in Frankfurt am Main. Previously the 2nd movement had been conducted by Josef Großmann on March 2, 1898.
REVIEW HLG II, 649.

160. February 1, 1904, 7:30 p.m. [1]
HEIDELBERG - Großer Saal der Stadthalle [2,000 seats]

Fifth Subscription Concert of the "Bach-Verein"

      Mahler   Symphony No. 3, D minor [2]

SOLOIST B. Kofler.
ORCHESTRA The combined Heidelberg "Städtisches Orchester" (Municipal Orchestra) and the Mannheim Court Opera Orchestra, a total of 60 string instruments, 44 wind and percussion instruments, and two harps, plus some percussion and wind instruments behind the stage.
CHORUS Women's voices of the "Bach-Verein," and a boys' chorus from the Großherzogliches Gymnasium at Heidelberg
SOURCE Handbill; see illustration on opposite page.
NOTES [1] The general rehearsal took place at 12:15 p.m. on the same day.
[2] First performance in Heidelberg. The choruses were hidden from the audience by a big, white screen of canvas.
REVIEW HLG II, 665–666.

Städtische Abonnements-Konzerte Mainz.

Mittwoch den 23. März 1904

X. Symphonie-Konzert

im Stadttheater

unter Leitung des städtischen Kapellmeisters Emil Steinbach
und unter freundl. Mitwirkung des Hrn. **Gustav Mahler**, K. K. Hofoperndirektor in Wien.

Solisten: Frl. **Stephanie Becker**, Herr **Joseph Hofmann**.

PROGRAMM.

1. **Symphonie in G-dur,** No. 4 .... Gust. Mahler
   I. Heiter, bedächtig. II. In gemächlicher Bewegung. III. Ruhevoll.
   IV. Sehr behaglich; Sopran-Solo: „Wir geniessen die himmlischen
   Freuden". (Aus „Des Knaben Wunderhorn".)
   Zum ersten Male unter persönlicher Leitung des Komponisten.
   ===== Pause von 10 Minuten. =====

2. **Konzert in D-moll,** op. 70 für Pianoforte mit Orchester .... Rubinstein
   Moderato assai — Allegro. Andante — Allegro.

3. **Liedervorträge:** Mondnacht .... Schumann
   Auf Flügeln des Gesanges .... Mendelssohn
   Die Forelle .... Schubert

4. **Klaviervorträge:** Nocturno (Des-dur) ⎫
   Etude (Ges-dur) ⎬ .... Chopin
   Scherzo (H-moll) ⎭

5. **Ouverture zu „Leonore"** (No. 3) .... Beethoven

Konzertflügel Bechstein aus der Niederlage von Gebr. Schulz.

Mittwoch den 6. April 1904, bei aufgehobenem Abonnement:

SYMPHONIE-KONZERT zum Besten des Orchester-Pensionsfonds.
SOLISTEN: Herr Prof. Dr. Joseph Joachim, Herr Hans Rodius.
PROGRAMM: Symphonie in C-moll (No. 1) von Brahms. Violinkonzert in A-dur von Mozart. Ouverture zu „Euryanthe" von Weber. Romanze in F-dur für Violine von Beethoven. Das Hexenlied von Wildenbruch-Schillings.

Die verehrlichen Abonnenten der Symphonie-Konzerte haben das Vorrecht auf ihre Plätze bis **Samstag den 2. April 1904**, nachmittags 1 Uhr zu ermässigten Preisen und zwar:

Fremdenloge	Mk. 4.—	Num. Parterre und I. Reihe	
Balkon	„ 3.50	der II. Rangloge	Mk. 2.—
I. Rangloge und Sperrsitz	„ 3.—	II. u III. Reihe d. II. Rangloge	„ 1.50
Stehplatz im Sperrsitz	„ 2.40	Rondel	„ —.80

Eine Liste zum Einzeichnen wird den Abonnenten vorgelegt werden, auch nimmt die **Stadtkasse**, Stadionerhofstrasse 2, Bestellungen von Plätzen entgegen.

Während der einzelnen Musikstücke bleiben die inneren Eingangstüren geschlossen.

161. **February 2, 1904, 7:30 p.m.**
MANNHEIM - Musensaal des Rosengarten [1,400 seats]

Sixth Musical Academy

- Above program repeated by the same forces -

NOTE The same day, Mahler wrote to his wife that repeat performances of his *Third,* in both Mannheim and Heidelberg, were considered for the "near future," and a performance of his *Second* was agreed upon for the following year. None of the plans materialized, see *Gustav Mahler: Letters to his Wife* (London, 2004, p. 149).

162. **February 25, 1904, 7:30 p.m.** [1]
PRAGUE - Neues Deutsches Theater [1,900 seats]

Fourth Philharmonic Subscription Concert

      Mahler   Symphony No. 3, D minor [2]

SOLOIST O. Fellwock.
ORCHESTRA The New German Theater's orchestra; a total of 110 players.
CHORUS The Theater's women's choir, augmented by 9 soloists and an unspecified children's chorus consisting of 40 voices. [3]
SOURCE Handbill.
NOTE [1] Mahler arrived in Prague at 7 a.m. the same morning. The general rehearsal was held at 10 a.m. for critics only.
[2] First performance in Prague. *Kapellmeister* Leo Blech had prepared the orchestra in advance of Mahler's arrival. Forty years later (1944) he conducted it in Stockholm, of which an almost complete recording is preserved.
[3] Soprano Betty Frank, Mahler's sweetheart from his 1885-1886 season, founded a "singing school" in the early 1890's which included a children's choir. It was probably this choir which participated in the concert.
REVIEW HLG II, 667–669.

163. **March 23, 1904, 7 p.m.**
MAINZ - Großer Saal des Musikvereins Liedertafel [1,200 seats]

Tenth Subscription Concert

(1)	Mahler	Symphony No. 4, G Major [1]
		- Intermission -
(2)	Rubinstein	Piano Concerto No. 4, D minor, Op. 70
(3)	Chopin	Nocturne, Op. 27, No. 2
(4)	Chopin	Étude, Op. 10, No. 2
(5)	Chopin	Scherzo, No. 1, Op. 20
(6)	Three *Lieder* with Piano Acc.:	
	Schubert	"Die Forelle," D 550
	Schumann	"Die Mondnacht," Op. 39, No. 5
	Mendelssohn	"Auf Flügeln des Gesanges," Op. 34, No. 2
(7)	Beethoven	*Leonore* Overture No. 3, Op. 72b

Concert-Gesellschaft in Köln.

Dienstag, 18. Okt. 1904, abends punkt 7 Uhr:

I. Gürzenich-Konzert

unter Leitung des städtischen Kapellmeisters Herrn Generalmusikdirektor **Fritz Steinbach.**

1. Fünfte Sinfonie . . . . . . **Gustav Mahler.**
   Uraufführung unter Leitung des Komponisten.
2. a) Ständchen für Frauenchor und Altsolo,
   b) Drei Lieder . . . . . **F. Schubert.**
   Frau **Lula Mysz-Gmeiner.**
3. Ouverture zu Leonore Nr. 3 . . . . **L. van Beethoven.**

Konzertflügel: **Rud. Ibach Sohn.**

Der Abonnementspreis für die 12 Gürzenichkonzerte beträgt: Saalplatz **60 Mk.**, Galerieplatz **36 Mk.**, Platz in den Generalproben **24 Mk.** Einzelsaalkarten zu **7 Mk.** und Galeriekarten zu **4 Mk.** bei **J. F. Weber**, Köln, Schildergasse 6 und an der Kasse.

Die Generalprobe
ist mit Solisten **Montag 7 Uhr** im Gürzenich. Abonnement für numerierten Sitz **24 Mk.**, Einzelkarte **3 Mk.** bei **J. F. Weber** und an der Kasse.

Concert-Gesellschaft in Köln.

Palmsonntag, 27. März 1904, abends 7 Uhr,

XI. Gürzenich-Konzert,

unter Leitung des Hofkapellmeisters Herrn **Gustav Mahler.**
Sinfonie III. für grosses Orchester, Altsolo, Frauen-
und Knabenchor, zum 1. Mal . . . . **Gustav Mahler.**
Altsolo: Frau **Marie Hertzer-Deppe.**
Die Generalprobe ist **Samstag 7 Uhr** im Gürzenich.

Karfreitag, 1. April 1904, abends 6 Uhr,

XII. Gürzenich-Konzert,

unter Leitung des städtischen Kapellmeisters Herrn Generalmusikdirektor **Fritz Steinbach.**
Die grosse Passions-Musik nach dem
Evangelisten Matthaeus für Soli, Doppel-
chor, Knabenchor, Doppelorchester und
Orgel . . . . **Joh. Seb. Bach.**
Frau **Hedy Brügelmann**, Frl. **M. Philippi**,
Herr **Ludw. Hess**, Herr Prof. **J. Messchaert**,
Herr **L. Bauer**; Violinsolo: Herr **Bram Eldering.**
Orgel: Herr Professor **F. W. Franke.**
Die Generalprobe ist **Gründonnerstag 6 Uhr** im Gürzenich.

Saalkarten zu diesen Konzerten zu **6 Mk.**, **Galeriekarten** 1—190 zu **3 Mk.**, 191—338 zu **2 Mk.**, Eintrittskarten für die Generalproben zu **2 Mk.** bei **J. F. Weber**, Schildergasse 6 (11—1 vorm., 3—4 nachm.) und an der Kasse.

SOLOISTS (1 & 6) S. Becker, acc. in no. 6 by E. Steinbach; (2–5) J. Hofmann.
CONDUCTORS (1) Mahler; (2 & 7) E. Steinbach.
ORCHESTRA The Mainz "Städtische Musikkapelle."
SOURCE Handbill and various newspapers reviews; see illustration on opposite page.
NOTE [1] First performance in Mainz.
REVIEW HLG II, 671.

164. **March 27, 1904, 7 p.m.**
COLOGNE - Großer Saal des Gürzenich [1,500 seats]

Eleventh Gürzenich Subscription Concert

      Mahler   Symphony No. 3, D minor [1]

SOLOIST M. Hertzer-Deppe.
ORCHESTRA AND CHORUS The Gürzenich Orchestra and Chorus.
SOURCE Newspaper advertisement; see illustration on opposite page.
NOTE [1] First performance in Cologne. An earlier scheduled performance under Mahler, on November 19, 1902, came to nothing owing to the sudden death of conductor Franz Wüllner (September 9, 1902), who had invited Mahler; MSL, p. 434.
REVIEW HLG II, 672.

Season 1904–1905

165. **October 18, 1904, 7 p.m.** [1]
COLOGNE - Großer Saal des Gürzenich [1,500 seats]

First Gürzenich Subscription Concert

(1)	Mahler	Symphony No. 5 [2]
		- Intermission -
(2)	Schubert	"Ständchen," D 921, for Contralto, Chorus, and Orch.
(3)	Schubert	Three *Lieder* with Piano Acc.:
		"Bei Dir allein, D 866, No. 2
		"Nacht und Träume," D 827
		"Das Lied im Grünen," D 917
(4)	Beethoven	*Leonore* Overture No. 3, Op. 72b

SOLOIST (2 & 3) L. Mysz-Gmeiner, acc. in no. 3 by F. Steinbach.
CONDUCTORS (1) Mahler; (2 & 4) F. Steinbach.
ORCHESTRA AND CHORUS The Gürzenich Orchestra and Chorus.
SOURCE Newspaper advertisement; see illustration on opposite page.
NOTE [1] The general rehearsal took place the preceding day at 7 p.m.
[2] World premiere.
REVIEW HLG III, 27-32.

PROGRAMMA
VAN HET
BUITENGEWOON CONCERT
TE GEVEN DOOR DEN HEER
GUSTAV MAHLER
MET MEDEWERKING VAN
MEVROUW OLDENBOOM-LUTKEMANN
EN VAN
HET CONCERTGEBOUW-ORKEST.

ZONDAG 23 OCTOBER 1904 — 8 UUR.

1. Symphonie No. 4 (G-dur) . . Gustav Mahler.
   IN 4 DEELEN.
   I. Heiter, bedächtig.
   II. Scherzo. In gemächlicher Bewegung. (Todtentanz).
   III. Adagio.
   IV. Sopran-Solo (Das himmlische Leben").

   DE SOPRAAN-SOLO VOOR TE DRAGEN DOOR MEVROUW
   ALIDA OLDENBOOM-LUTKEMANN.

   (EERSTE UITVOERING.)

   — PAUZE —

2. Herhaling van de Symphonie No. 4 (G-dur) . . . Gustav Mahler.

166

PROGRAMMA
VAN HET
BUITENGEW. ABONNEMENTS-CONCERT
ONDER LEIDING VAN DEN HEER
GUSTAV MAHLER.

WOENSDAG 26 EN DONDERDAG 27 OCTOBER 1904 — 8 UUR.

Symphonie No. 2 (C kl. t.) . . Gustav Mahler.
  I. Allegro maëstoso.
  II. Andante.
  III. Scherzo.
  IV. „Urlicht" Alt Solo (tekst z. o. z.).
  V. Finale.

CHOR, SOPRAN U. ALT-SOLO (tekst z. o. z.).

N. B. Op verzoek van den Componist wordt geene analyse der Symphonie gegeven.

167 & 168

Vereinigung schaffender Tonkünstler in Wien.

Mittwoch den 23. November 1904, abends halb 8 Uhr
im Großen Musikvereinssaale

I. Orchesterkonzert.

Mitwirkend:

Direktor Gustav **Mahler** (Ehrenpräsident).
Kapellmeister Alexander v. **Zemlinszky** (ordentliches Mitglied).
Hermann **Bischoff** (auswärtiges Mitglied).
K. k. Hofopernsänger Friedrich **Weidemann**.
Das Orchester des Wiener Konzertvereines.

Programm:

1. Siegmund v. Hausegger: Dionysische Phantasie.
   Dirigent: Alexander v. Zemlinszky.
2. Hermann Bischoff: Drei Gesänge mit Orchester.
   a) Das Trinklied.
   b) Der Schlaf.
   c) Bewegte See.
   K. k. Hofopernsänger Friedrich Weidemann. — Dirigent: Der Komponist.
3. Richard Strauss: Symphonia domestica. Dirigent: Gustav Mahler.

I. Kammermusik- und Liederabend	II. Orchesterkonzert	II. Kammermusik- u. Liederabend
20. Dezember 1904, halb 8 Uhr abends im Saale Bösendorfer.	25. Jänner 1905, halb 8 Uhr abends im Großen Musikvereinssaale.	20. Jänner 1905, halb 8 Uhr abends im Saale Bösendorfer.
1. Gerhard v. Keussler: Gesänge.	1. Alexander v. Zemlinszky: Die Seejungfrau. Phantasie für Orchester.	Ein Liederabend mit Orchester 29. Jänner 1905, halb 8 Uhr abends im Kleinen Musikvereinssaale.
2. Hans Pfitzner: Klaviertrio F dur.	2. Oskar C. Posa: Fünf Gedichte von Detlev v. Liliencron für Bariton mit Orchester.	Zur Aufführung gelangen ausschließlich Lieder von Gustav Mahler.
3. Rudolf St. Hoffmann: Gesänge.	3. Arnold Schönberg: Pelleas und Melisande, symphonische Dichtung.	III. Kammermusik- u. Liederabend 20. Februar 1905, halb 8 Uhr abends im Saale Bösendorfer.
4. Kurt Schindler: Gesänge.		III. Orchesterkonzert 11. März 1905, halb 8 Uhr abends im Großen Musikvereinssaale.

Programme à 20 Heller.

169

166. October 23, 1904, 8 p.m.
   AMSTERDAM - The Concertgebouw [1,800 seats]

Extraordinary Concert

    (1)   Mahler   Symphony No. 4, G major [1]
                - Intermission -
    (2)   Mahler   Symphony No. 4, G major

SOLOIST A. Oldenboom-Lütkemann.
ORCHESTRA The Concertgebouw Orchestra.
SOURCE Handbill; see illustration on opposite page.
NOTE [1] First performance in Amsterdam. The idea of giving the symphony twice seems to have been a sudden impulse of Mengelberg's. Alma Mahler is mistaken however, in claiming that Mengelberg conducted the repeat performance (AMM, p. 73). He was present at all of Mahler's rehearsals, making comments and instructions and entering them into his personal copy of the score. Mengelberg's live recording of the symphony, made 35 years later and based on his annotated score, is probably the closest we can come to Mahler's own reading.
REVIEW HLG III, 38-40.

167. October 26, 1904, 8 p.m.
168. October 27, 1904, 8 p.m.
   AMSTERDAM - The Concertgebouw [1,800 seats]

Extraordinary Subscription Concert

    Mahler   Symphony No. 2, C minor, "Resurrection" [1]

SOLOISTS A. Oldenboom-Lütkemann and M. Stapelfeldt.
ORCHESTRA The Concertgebouw Orchestra.
CHORUS The Amsterdam choruses "Bevordering der Toonkunst" and "Verbetering van den Volkszang."
SOURCE Handbill; see illustration on opposite page.
NOTE [1] First performance in Amsterdam.
REVIEW HLG III, 41-42.

169. November 23, 1904, 7:30 p.m.
   VIENNA - Großer Saal des Musikvereins [2,063 seats]

First Orchestral Concert of the "Vereinigung Schaffender Tonkünstler in Wien" [1]

    (1)   Hausegger   *Dionysische Phantasie*, Symphonic Poem for Orchestra
    (2)   Bischoff   Three *Lieder* with Orchestra:
                          "Das Trinklied," Op. 8, No. 3
                          "Der Schlaf"
                          "Bewegte See," Op. 12, No. 5
                          - Intermission -
    (3)   Strauss   *Symphonia Domestica*, Op. 53 ●[2]

SOLOIST (2) A. Moser, replacing the original announced F. Weidemann.
CONDUCTORS (1) A. Zemlinsky; (2) H. Bischoff; (3) Mahler.

Gesellschaft der Musikfreunde in Wien

unter dem Protektorate Sr. k. u. k. Hoheit des hochwürdigst-durchlauchtigsten Herrn **Erzherzogs Eugen.**

Mittwoch, den 14. Dezember 1904,

abends halb 8 Uhr:

Erstes außerordentliches

Gesellschafts-Konzert

Zur Aufführung gelangt:

III. Sinfonie von Gustav Mahler

für großes Orchester, Altsolo, Frauen- und Knabenchor

unter persönlicher Leitung des Komponisten.

I. Aufführung in Wien.

Mitwirkende:

Frl. **Hermine Kittel,** k. k. Hof-Opernsängerin (Alt-Solo).
Der **Singverein.**
Ein **Knabenchor.**
Das **k. k. Hof-Opernorchester.**

Dieses Programm 20 Heller. **Texte auf der Rückseite.**

Donnerstag, den 15. Jänner 1905, mittags halb 1 Uhr:

Zweites ordentliches Gesellschafts-Konzert.

Zur Aufführung gelangt:

J. S. Bach . . . **Magnificat** für Soli, Chor, Orchester und Orgel.
Rich. Strauss . . „**Taillefer**", Ballade für Soli, Chor und Orchester.

(Neu, I. Aufführung.)

Karten zu 6, 5, 4, 3 und 2 Kronen

sind an Wochentagen in der Gesellschaftskanzlei von 9—1 und von 3—5 Uhr zu haben.

ORCHESTRA The orchestra of the Vienna "Konzertverein."
SOURCE Handbill; see illustration on previous page.
NOTES [1] Literally "The Society of Creating Musicians in Vienna," i.e. Composers, was founded in March 1904 by Alexander Zemlinsky and Arnold Schoenberg. Mahler was offered and accepted the title of Honorary President. However, the society was dissolved as early as the spring of 1905, for economic reasons.
[2] First performance in Vienna. Strauss had been invited to conduct his own work but had declined due to lack of time. A repeat performance was planned for March 11, 1904, to be conducted by Strauss, but was cancelled.
REVIEW HLG III, 58-59.

170. November 28, 1904, 7:30 p.m.
LEIPZIG - Festsaal des Zoologischen Gartens [2,000 seats]

Fourth Philharmonic Concert. First Modern Evening

      Mahler   Symphony No. 3, D minor [1]

SOLOIST M. Hertzer-Deppe.
ORCHESTRA The Leipzig Winderstein Orchestra, reinforced with private artists and the entire band of the 107th Military Regiment (cond. Colonel Giltsch).
CHORUS Women's voices of the Leipzig "Singakademie" and a boys' choir.
SOURCE Newspaper review.
NOTE [1] First complete performance in Leipzig. The 2nd movement had been given previously by Arthur Nikisch, on January 21, 1897.
REVIEW HLG III, 63-66.

171. December 14, 1904, 7:30 p.m.
172. December 22, 1904, 7:30 p.m. [1]
VIENNA - Großer Saal des Musikvereins [2,063 seats]

Extraordinary Concert of the "Gesellschaft der Musikfreunde"

      Mahler   Symphony No. 3, D minor [2]

SOLOIST H. Kittel.
ORCHESTRA The Court Opera Orchestra, 120 players.
CHORUS Women's voices of the "Singverein der Gesellschaft der Musikfreunde" (200 singers), and a boys chorus from the "Löwenberg'sches Konvikt," (60 singers).
SOURCE Handbill; see illustration on opposite page.
NOTE [1] The general rehearsal took place on December 12 at 3:30 p.m. and was, on Mahler's invitation, attended by Arnold Schoenberg who afterwards wrote a passionate letter to Mahler, expressing the strong impression that the music had made on him (see AMM, p. 256).
[2] First performance in Vienna. The great success of the premiere called for the second performance on December 22nd. When it was first announced in the newspapers on December 16, this second performance was originally scheduled to begin at 4:40 p.m. This was probably a printing error.
REVIEW HLG III, 68-76.

Vereinigung schaffender Tonkünstler in Wien.

Sonntag den 29. Jänner 1905, abends halb 8 Uhr
im Kleinen Musikvereinssaale

Ein Lieder-Abend mit Orchester.

Mitwirkend:

K. u. k. Kammersänger Fritz **Schrödter**.
K. k. Hofopernsänger Anton **Moser**.
K. k. Hofopernsänger Friedrich **Weidemann**.
Mitglieder des k. k. Hofopernorchesters.

Dirigent: Der Komponist.

Programm:

Gesänge von **Gustav Mahler**
für eine Singstimme *ex* Orchester.

Des Knaben Wunderhorn.

1. a) Lied des Verfolgten im Turm.
   b) Des Antonius von Padua Fischpredigt.
   c) Trost im Unglück.
   d) Rheinlegendchen. — Herr Anton Moser.
2. a) Der Schildwache Nachtlied.
   b) Der Tamboursg'sell (Manuskript). — Herr Friedrich Weidemann.
   c) Revelge (Manuskript). — Herr Fritz Schrödter.

= Pause. =

Rückert.

3. Kindertotenlieder, ein Cyclus.
   a) Nun will die Sonn' so hell aufgehn.
   b) Nun seh' ich wohl, warum so dunkle Flammen.
   c) Wenn dein Mütterlein tritt zur Tür herein.
   d) Oft denk' ich, sie sind nur ausgegangen.
   e) In diesem Wetter, in diesem Braus. — Herr **Friedrich Weidemann**.
4. a) Ich atmet' einen linden Duft.
   b) Blicke mir nicht in die Lieder. — Herr **Anton Moser**.
   c) Ich bin der Welt abhanden gekommen.
   d) Um Mitternacht. — Herr **Friedrich Weidemann**.

Manuskript.

III. Kammermusik- und Liederabend
20. Februar 1905, halb 8 Uhr abends
im Saale Bösendorfer.

1. **Max Reger**: Streichquartett D moll.
2. **Theodor Streicher**: Gesänge.
3. **Bruno Walter**: Klavierquintett Fis moll.

III. Orchesterkonzert
11. März 1905, halb 8 Uhr abends
im großen Musikvereinssaale.

1. **Josef V. v. Wöss**: Sonate D dur für Orchester.
2. **Hans Pfitzner**: Gesänge mit Orchester.
3. **Franz Dubitzky**: a) Nachts, b) Märchen, c) Herbst (Monodie) für Orchester.
4. **Richard Strauss**: Friedenserzählung und Schlußszene aus »Guntram«.

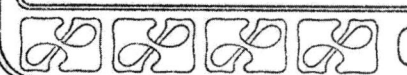

Programme à 20 Heller.

173. **January 29, 1905, 7:30 p.m.** [1]
VIENNA - Kleiner Saal des Musikvereins [598 seats]

Second Orchestral Concert of the "Vereinigung Schaffender Tonkünstler"

All-Mahler Program: "Lieder und Gesänge" with Orchestra:

- (1) "Lied des Verfolgten im Turm" * [2]
  "Des Antonius von Padua Fischpredigt" *
  "Trost im Unglück"
  "Rheinlegendchen"
- (2) "Der Schildwache Nachtlied"
  "Der Tamboursg'sell" *
- (3) "Revelge" *
  - Intermission -
- (4) [5] *Kindertotenlieder* *
- (5) "Ich atmet' einen linden Duft" *
  "Blicke mir nicht in die Lieder" *
- (6) "Ich bin der Welt abhanden gekommen" *
  "Um Mitternacht" *

SOLOISTS (1, 5) A. Moser; (2, 4, 6) F. Weidemann; (3) F. Schrödter.
ORCHESTRA Members of the Vienna Court Opera Orchestra.
SOURCE Handbill; see illustration on opposite page.
NOTE [1] The general rehearsal took place the previous day at 3:00 p.m. When first advertised on January 8, both Erik Schmedes and Marie Gutheil-Schoder were also announced as soloists. In December 1904, the latter had already committed herself to an evening devoted to celebrate the centenary of the publication of the *Knaben Wunderhorn* collection. The performance was postponed several times but was finally held on January 29. She sang two of Mahler's early *Wunderhorn* songs.
[2] An asterisk * designates the world premiere.
REVIEW HLG III, 107-108.

174. **February 3, 1905, 7:30 p.m.**
VIENNA - Kleiner Saal des Musikvereins [598 seats]

Extra Concert of the "Vereinigung Schaffender Tonkünstler" [1]

All-Mahler Program: "Lieder und Gesänge" with Orchestra:

- (1) "Der Schildwache Nachtlied"
- (2) "Lied des Verfolgten im Turm"
  "Des Antonius von Padua Fischpredigt"
  "Trost im Unglück" •
  "Rheinlegendchen"
- (3) "Der Tamboursg'sell"
- (4) "Verlor'ne Müh'" •
  "Lob des hohen Verstandes" • [2]
  "Dort oben am Berg" ["Wer hat dies Liedlein erdacht"] •
- (5) "Revelge"
  - Intermission -

Vereinigung Schaffender Tonkünstler

Freitag den 3. Februar 1905, Beginn halb 8 Uhr abends:

Mahler-Abend
(Wiederholung).

Mitwirkende: Die Herren Kammersänger Schrödter, Hofopernsänger Weidemann und Moser.

Dirigent: **Mahler.**

Orchester: Die Mitglieder des Hofopernorchesters.

Karten zu K. 10, 6, 4, 3 und 2 bei Karl Kehlendorfer, I., Krugerstrasse 5.

Philharmonische Gesellschaft zu Hamburg.

Montag, den 13. März 1905,
abends 7½ Uhr pünktlich,

grosser Saal, Convent-Garten:

Vierzehntes (536tes)

KONZERT.
(Siebentes Konzert der Serie B)

Dirigenten:

Gustav Mahler, Hofopern-Direktor aus Wien,

Max Fiedler.

PROGRAMM

1. **Gustav Mahler:** Fünfte Symphonie (Z. 1. Mal, unter Leitung des Komponisten.)
   I Abteilung:
   Nr. 1 Trauermarsch. (In gemessenem Schritt. Streng. Wie ein Kondukt.)
   Nr. 2 Stürmisch bewegt. Mit grösster Vehemenz.
   II Abteilung.
   Nr. 3 Scherzo. (Kräftig, nicht zu schnell.)
   III Abteilung:
   Nr 4 Adagietto (Sehr langsam)
   attacca Nr. 5 Rondo Finale.

2. **L. van Beethoven:** Achte Symphonie, F-dur, op. 93.
   I. Allegro vivace e con brio.
   II. Allegretto scherzando.
   III. Tempo di Menuetto.
   IV. Allegro vivace.

Zu diesem Konzert haben nur die Karten der Serie B Gültigkeit.

Während der Vorträge bleiben die Saaltüren geschlossen.

Fünfzehntes Konzert: Montag, den 27. März 1905.
(Achtes Konzert der Serie A)
Solisten:
Maikki Järnefelt (Gesang), Guilhermina Suggia (Violoncell).
PROGRAMM
1. **Mozart:** Symphonie, g-moll 2. **Sibelius:** »Des Fährmanns Bräute«, Ballade für Sopran und Orchester. 3. Konzert für Violoncell 4. Lieder.
5. **Strauss:** Ein Heldenleben.

Druck von Poetz & v. Ohren, Stadthausbrücke 12.

(6) [5] *Kindertotenlieder*
"Ich bin der Welt abhanden gekommen"
(7) "Blicke mir nicht in die Lieder"
"Ich atmet' einen linden Duft"
(8) "Um Mitternacht"

SOLOISTS (1, 3, 6, 8) F. Weidemann; (2, 7) A. Moser; (4) M. Gutheil-Schoder; (5) F. Schrödter.
ORCHESTRA Members of the Vienna Court Opera Orchestra.
SOURCE Newspaper advertisement; see illustration on opposite page.
NOTE [1] The great success of the preceding concert called for a second hearing, expanded with three new songs (no. 4), and in a different order.
[2] World premiere.

175. March 13, 1905, 7:30 p.m. [1]
HAMBURG - Convent Garten [3,000 seats]

Fourteenth Subscription Concert of the Philharmonic Society

(1) Mahler   Symphony No. 5 [2]
                  - Intermission -
(2) Beethoven   Symphony No. 8, F major, Op. 93

CONDUCTORS (1) Mahler; (2) M. Fiedler.
ORCHESTRA The Hamburg Philharmonic Orchestra.
SOURCE Handbill; see illustration on opposite page.
NOTES [1] The general rehearsal took place in the morning of the previous day.
[2] First performance in Hamburg.
REVIEW HLG III, 139-143.

176. May 21, 1905, 6 p.m. [1]
STRASSBURG – Sängerhaus (Palais de Fêtes) [1,500 seats]

Second Concert at The First Elsatian-Lotharingian Music Festival

(1) Mahler   Symphony No. 5 [2]
                  - Intermission -
(2) Brahms   Rhapsody, Op. 53, for Contralto, Men's Chorus, and Orch.
(3) Mozart   Violin Concerto No. 4, G major, K. 216
(4) Strauss   *Symphonia Domestica*, Op. 53

SOLOISTS (2) A. von Kraus-Osborne; (3) H. Marteau.
CONDUCTORS (1) Mahler; (2) E. Münch; (3 & 4) R. Strauss.
ORCHESTRA The "Städtisches Orchester" (City Orchestra), reinforced by local and visiting musicians, a total of 108 players.
CHORUS An *ad hoc* chorus pieced together from various local choruses.
SOURCE Program and newspaper advertisement; see illustration on following page. Several originally advertised soloists were replaced.
NOTE [1] The general rehearsal took place the same morning.
[2] First performance in Strassburg (a German city from 1871 to 1918).
REVIEW HLG III, 201-210.

Unter dem Protektorate Sr. Durchlaucht des kaiserl. Statthalters in Elsass-Lothringen, Fürsten zu Hohenlohe-Langenburg.

Erstes els.-lothr. Musikfest

Strassburg i. E., den 20., 21., 22. Mai 1905
im Sängerhause.

Unter Leitung der Festdirigenten: HHrn. Gustave **Charpentier**, Paris; Gustav **Mahler**, Direktor der k. u. k. Hofoper, Wien; Prof. Franz **Stockhausen**, Strassburg i. E.; Hofkapellmeister Dr. Richard **Strauss**, Berlin; sowie unter gefl. Mitwirkung von:

Frau Maikki **Järnefelt**, Helsingfors (Sopran); Frau Adrienne **von Kraus-Osborne**, Leipzig (Alt); Hrn. **Commène**, Paris (Tenor); Hrn. **Otto Marak**, Prag (Tenor); Hrn. **Paul Daraux**, Paris (Bass); Hrn. Dr. Felix **von Kraus**, Leipzig (Bass); Hrn. Gérard **Zalsmann**, Amsterdam (Bariton); Hrn. Ferrucio **Busoni**, Florenz (Klavier); Hrn. Henri **Marteau**, Reims (Violine).

Festorchester: Das Strassburger städtische Orchester, verstärkt durch hiesige und auswärtige Kräfte bis auf 108 Mitglieder.
1. Konzertmeister: Herr Alex. Kosmann, Amsterdam.

Festchor: Zusammengesetzt aus Mitgliedern hiesiger Chorvereine.

PROGRAMM:

20. Mai:
1. Ouverture „Oberon" . . . . . C. M. v. Weber
2. „Les béatitudes", Oratorium für Soli, Chor u. Orchester (4 Teile) C. Frank
   20 Minuten Pause.
3. Gesangsvortrag.
4. „Impressions d'Italie", Symph. Dichtung G. Charpentier
5. „Meistersinger", Schluss-Szene, III. Akt (Festwiese) . . . . R. Wagner

Dirigenten: HHrn. Charpentier, Stockhausen, Dr. Strauss.
Gesang: Frau Järnefelt, Frau v. Kraus-Osborne, HHrn. Commène, Marak, Daraux, Dr. v. Kraus, Zelsmann.

21. Mai:
1. Fünfte Symphonie . . . . . G. Mahler
   20 Minuten Pause.
2. Violinkonzert G-dur . . . . . Mozart
3. Sinfonia domestica op. 53 . . R. Strauss

Dirigenten: HHrn. Mahler, Dr. Strauss.
Violine: Marteau.

Änderung des Programms vorbehalten.

22. Mai:
Beethoven.
1. Ouverture „Coriolan"
2. Klavierkonzert G-dur op. 58
3. Lieder-Zyklus „An die ferne Geliebte"
   20 Minuten Pause.
4. Neunte Symphonie für Orchester, Chor und Vokalquartett;

Dirigent: Herr Mahler;
Gesang: Frau Järnefelt, Frau v. Kraus-Osborne, Marak, Dr. v. Kraus;
Klavier: Busoni, Klavierbegleitung: Mahler.

Beginn der Konzerte 7 Uhr abends — Dauer ungefähr 3 Stunden.

Allgemeiner Deutscher Musikverein
Tonkünstlerfest in Graz.

Donnerstag, den 1. Juni, abends 6 Uhr
(Hauptprobe vormittags 10 Uhr)
Im Stephaniensaal

Erstes Orchesterkonzert.

Roderich v. Mojsisovics: Romantische Fantasie für die Orgel (op. 9), III. (letzter) Satz.
Herr Otto Burkert.

Guido Peters: Aus der Sinfonie No. 2, E-moll.
I. Satz. Frei rezitatorisch; mit Leidenschaft und großem Ausdruck; heroisch.
IV. (letzter) Satz. Möglichst rasch; feurig; trotzig; bachantisch.

Pause.

Gustav Mahler: Gesänge für eine Singstimme mit Orchester.

I.
1. Der Schildwache Nachtlied.
2. Das irdische Leben.
3. Der Tamboursg'sell.
4. Ich bin der Welt abhanden gekommen.

Herr Friedrich Weidemann.

II.
1. Lied des Gefangenen im Turm.
2. Wo die schönen Trompeten blasen.
3. Des Antonius von Padua Fischpredigt.

Herr Anton Moser.

COMITATO PER LE GRANDI ESECUZIONI MUSICALI IN TRIESTE.

Venerdì 1. Dicembre 1905, alle ore 8 pom.
avrà luogo al
POLITEAMA ROSSETTI
il
I. Grande Concerto Sinfonico
sostenuto dalla
Orchestrale Triestina (90 esecutori)
sotto la direzione del Maestro
GUSTAVO MAHLER
direttore dell'Opera di Vienna.

PROGRAMMA:

I. **BEETHOVEN** — Ouverture „Coriolano".

II. **MOZART** — Sinfonia („Giove") in do maggiore.
   I. Allegro vivace - II. Andante cantabile
   III. Minuetto - IV. Finale.

III. **MAHLER** — V Sinfonia in do diesis minore.
   I. Marcia funebre - II. Presto - III. Scherzo
   IV. Adagietto - V. Rondò finale.
   (eseguita a Trieste per la prima volta)

Durante l'esecuzione dei singoli brani, le porte del teatro resteranno chiuse.

PREZZI SERALI:

Palchi piano . . . . . Cor. 40.—	Posti in gradinata I. fila . Cor. 2.—
„ I. Ordine . . . . . „ 25.—	„ I. Galleria I. fila . „ 2.—
Poltroncine	Ingresso alla platea ed alle
Scanni in platea . . . . „ 3.—	gradinate . . . . . „ 1.—

Ingresso al loggione Cor. 1.—

177. May 22, 1905, 7:30 p.m.
STRASSBURG – Sängerhaus (Palais de Fêtes) [1,500 seats]

Third Concert at the First Elsatian-Lotharingian Music Festival

All-Beethoven Program

(1) Overture to *Coriolan*, Op. 62
(2) Piano Concerto No. 4, G major, Op. 58 •
(3) *An die ferne Geliebte*, Op. 98, *Lied*-cycle with Piano Acc.
    - Intermission -
(4) Symphony No. 9, D minor, Op. 125

SOLOISTS (2) F. Busoni; (3) L. Hess, acc. by E. Knock; (4) J. Dietz, A. v. Kraus-Osborne, L. Hess, F. v. Kraus.
ORCHESTRA & CHORUS See preceding concert.
SOURCE Newspaper advertisement; see illustration on opposite page.
REVIEW HLG III, 202-205.

178. June 1, 1905, 6 p.m. [1]
GRAZ - Stephanie-Saal [697 seats]

First Orchestral Concert at the Forty-First Music Festival of the "Allgemeiner Deutscher Musikverein"

(1)	Mojsisovics	Romantische Fantasie, Op. 9, for Organ (3rd movement)
(2)	Peters	Symphony No. 2, E minor (1st & 4th movement)
		- Intermission -
(3)	Mahler	*Lieder* and "Gesänge" with Orchestra:
		"Der Schildwache Nachtlied"
		"Das irdische Leben"
		"Der Tamboursg'sell" •
		"Ich bin der Welt abhanden gekommen"
(4)	Mahler	"Lied des Verfolgten im Turm" • [2]
		"Des Antonius von Padua Fischpredigt"
(5)	Mahler	"Revelge" •
(6)	Mahler	"Um Mitternacht"
(7)	Mahler	*Kindertotenlieder*
		- Intermission -
(8)	Ertel	*Der Mensch*, Symphonic Poem, Op. 9

SOLOISTS (1) O. Burkert; (3 & 7) F. Weidemann; (4) A. Moser; (5) F. Schrödter; (6) E. Schmedes; (8) A. Kofler, organ.
CONDUCTORS (2 & 8) F. Löwe; (3–7) Mahler
ORCHESTRA The Graz Opera Orchestra, supplemented with members of the Vienna Court Opera Orchestra, the Vienna "Konzertverein" Orchestra, and professors from the "Steiermärkischer Musikverein" (i.e. the Conservatory).
SOURCE Handbill; see illustration on opposite page.
NOTES [1] The general rehearsal took place at 10 a.m. the same day.
[2] Anton Moser had originally also included "Wo die schönen Trompeten blasen" but omitted it.
REVIEW HLG III, 219-223.

Gesellschaft der Musikfreunde in Wien

unter dem Protektorate Sr. k. u. k. Hoheit des hochwürdigst-durchlauchtigsten Herrn **Erzherzog Eugen**.

Donnerstag, den 7. Dezember 1905, abends halb 8 Uhr:

Erstes ausserordentliches
Gesellschafts-Konzert.

Zur Aufführung gelangt:

J. S. BACH:
Motette
„Singet dem Herrn ein neues Lied"
(149. Psalm), achtstimmig a capella.

II. Aufführung in den Gesellschafts-Konzerten.

GUSTAV MAHLER.
V. SINFONIE.

1. a) Trauermarsch — b) Stürmisch bewegt. 2. Scherzo. 3. a) Adagietto — b) Rondo Finale.

Unter der Leitung des Komponisten. *I. Aufführung in Wien.*

MITWIRKENDE:
Der **Singverein**. Das **k. k. Hof-Opernorchester**.

Dieses Programm 20 Heller.   Text auf der nächsten Seite.

Sonntag, den 21. Jänner 1906, mittags halb 1 Uhr:

Zweites ordentliches Gesellschafts-Konzert.

Zur Aufführung gelangen folgende **a capella-Chöre**:

Palestrina: Kyrie, Gloria und Credo aus der Messe: „Assumpta est Maria" (sechsstimmig).
    I. Aufführung in den Gesellschafts-Konzerten.
Cherubini: Et incarnatus und Crucifixus (Achtstimmiger Doppelchor).
    I. Aufführung in den Gesellschafts-Konzerten.
Mozart: Offertorium de Venerabili (achtstimmig).
Brahms: Motette „Schaff in mir Gott" (fünfstimmig).   *I. Aufführung in den Gesellschafts-Konzerten.*
Max Reger: „Schweigen" (sechsstimmig). NEU, I. Aufführung in Wien.
Rich. Strauss: „Der Abend" (sechzehnstimmig). NEU, I. Aufführung in Wien.

Karten zu 6, 5, 4, 3.50, 3 und 2 Kronen
sind an Wochentagen in der Gesellschaftskanzlei von 9—1 Uhr und von 3—5 Uhr zu haben.

Mittwoch, den 20. Dezember 1905, abends 7½ Uhr pünktlich:

Sechstes
Abonnement-Konzert

veranstaltet vom

Breslauer Orchester-Verein
unter Leitung
des

Herrn **Gustav Mahler** aus Wien
und des
Herrn **Dr. Georg Dohrn**.

1. **Fünfte Sinfonie** . . . . *Gustav Mahler.*
 zum ersten Male unter Leitung des Komponisten.

   I. 1. Trauermarsch.
       In gemessenem Schritt. Streng. Wie ein Kondukt.
     2. Stürmisch bewegt. Mit größter Vehemenz.
  II. 3. Scherzo.
       Kräftig. Nicht zu schnell.
 III. 4. Adagietto.
      Rondo—Finale.

2. **Ouverture zu „Leonore" Nr. 3 op. 72** . . *L. van Beethoven.*

Die Saiten-Instrumente sind zum Teil von Herrn Hof-Instrumentenfabrikant
Ernst Liebich zur Verfügung gestellt.

Den bisherigen Abonnenten werden ihre Plätze für den zweiten Zyklus bis Freitag, den 29. Dezember 1905 inklusive reserviert, und die entsprechenden Billetts gegen Rückgabe der Billetthefte des I. Zyklus in der Musikalien-Handlung von Julius Hainauer verabfolgt. Über die bis Freitag, den 29. Dezember 6 Uhr nicht abgeholten Billetts wird anderweitig verfügt, zunächst zugunsten der eingetragenen Vereinsmitglieder, sofern dieselben vorher an genannter Billettstelle ihre Wünsche geäußert haben.

Das
siebente Abonnement-Konzert
findet
Mittwoch, den 10. Januar 1906
unter Mitwirkung der
Königl. sächs. Kammersängerin Frau **Marie Wittich** aus Dresden
statt.

Es ist den geehrten Damen nicht gestattet, im Konzertsaale mit Hüten zu erscheinen.

Die geehrten Damen und Herren, welche das Konzert vor Schluss zu verlassen beabsichtigen, werden höflichst ersucht, die Pause vor der letzten Nummer benutzen zu wollen. Während der Musik bleiben die Türen geschlossen.

| Triest–Vienna–Breslau | 1905 | Concerts Nos. 179–181 |

Season 1905–1906

179. December 1, 1905, 8 p.m.
TRIEST - Teatro Politeama Rossetti [1] [3,000 seats]

First "Grande Concerto Sinfonica"

    (1)   Beethoven   Overture to *Coriolan*, Op. 62
    (2)   Mozart   Symphony No. 41, C major, K. 551, "Jupiter"
    - Intermission -
    (3)   Mahler   Symphony No. 5 [2]

ORCHESTRA The orchestra of "Teatro communale Giuseppe Verdi" (the Trieste "Orchesterverein").
SOURCE Poster; see illustration on previous page.
NOTE [1] Today, Teatro Stabile.
[2] First performance in Trieste.
REVIEW HLG III, 271-272.

180. December 7, 1905, 7:30 p.m.
VIENNA - Großer Saal des Musikvereins [2,063 seats]

First Extraordinary Concert of the "Gesellschaft der Musikfreunde in Wien"

    (1)   Bach   *Singet dem Herrn ein neues Lied*, Motet No. 1, BWV 225
    (2)   Mahler   Symphony No. 5 [1]

CONDUCTORS (1) F. Schalk; (2) Mahler.
ORCHESTRA The Court Opera Orchestra.
CHORUS "Singverein der Gesellschaft der Musikfreunde in Wien."
SOURCE Handbill; see illustration on opposite page.
NOTE [1] First performance in Vienna.
REVIEW HLG III, 272-279.

181. December 20, 1905, 7:30 p.m.
BRESLAU - Konzerthaus [1,500 seats]

Sixth Philharmonic Subscription Concert

    (1)   Mahler   Symphony No. 5 [1]
    (2)   Beethoven   *Leonore* Overture No. 3, Op. 72b

CONDUCTORS (1) Mahler; (2) G. Dohrn.
ORCHESTRA The Breslau Philharmonic Orchestra.
SOURCE Handbill; see illustration on opposite page.
NOTE [1] First performance in Breslau.
REVIEW HLG III, 281-282.

KONINKLIJKE SCHOUWBURG VAN ANTWERPEN

3de JAAR   1905-1906

MAATSCHAPPIJ
DER
NIEUWE CONCERTEN

MAANDAG, 5 MAART 1906
TEN 8 1/2 URE 'S AVONDS

VIERDE ABONNEMENTSCONCERT

ONDER LEIDING VAN DEN HEER

GUSTAV MAHLER

BESTUURDER van het KEIZERLIJK OPERA van WEENEN

MET DE MEDEWERKING VAN DEN HEER

EUGEN D'ALBERT

PIANIST

PROGRAMMA

1. Synfonie N° 5 . . . . GUSTAV MAHLER
   A) *Treurmarsch.*
   B) *Allegro furioso.*
   C) *Scherzo.*
   D) *Adagietto.*
   E) *Rondo, finale.*

2. Wanderer-Fantasie . . . . . SCHUBERT-LISZT
   H. EUGEN D'ALBERT.

3. A) Nocturne in H (op. 62, n° 1) . . F. CHOPIN
   B) Scherzo (op. 16) . . . . . EUG. D'ALBERT
   H. EUGEN D'ALBERT.

4. Der Freischütz, Openingstuk . . . C. M. VON WEBER

KLAVIER BECHSTEIN

De deuren der zaal zullen gesloten blijven gedurende de uitvoering.

182

PROGRAMMA
VAN HET
BUITENGEW. ABONNEMENTS-CONCERT

ONDER LEIDING VAN DEN HEER

GUSTAV MAHLER.

DONDERDAG 8 MAART 1906 -- 8 UUR

GUSTAV MAHLER.
(GEB. 7 JULI 1860.)

1. GESÄNGE MIT ORCHESTER:
   A. DER SCHILDWACHE NACHTLIED.
   B. DES ANTONIUS VON PADUA FISCHPREDIGT.
   C. ICH BIN DER WELT ABHANDEN GEKOMMEN.

2. KINDERTOTENLIEDER.
   DE NOS. 1 EN 2 VOOR TE DRAGEN DOOR DEN HEER FRIEDRICH WEIDEMANN UIT WEENEN.

— PAUZE. —

3. SYMPHONIE No. 5.
   1. { A. Trauermarsch: In gemessenem Schritt.
       { B. Stürmisch bewegt.
   2. Scherzo: Kräftig, nicht zu schnell.
   3. { A. Adagietto: Sehr langsam.
       { B. Rondo-Finale: Allegro giocoso.

183

| Antwerp–Amsterdam | 1906 | Concerts Nos. 182–183 |

182. March 5, 1906, 8:30 p.m.
ANTWERP (Anvers) **- Théatre Royal** [1,000 seats]

Fourth Subscription Concert

    (1)   Mahler   Symphony No. 5 [1]
                                - Intermission -
    (2)   Schubert–Liszt   Fantasy, C major, "Wanderer," D 760, Op. 15, arr. for Piano & Orch.
    (3)   Chopin   Nocturne, Op. 62, No. 1, for Piano
    (4)   d'Albert   Scherzo, Op. 16, No. 2, for Piano
    (5)   Weber   Overture to *Der Freischütz*

SOLOIST (2–4) E. d'Albert.
CONDUCTORS (1, 2 & 5) Mahler
ORCHESTRA The Orchestra of the Royal Theater.
SOURCE Handbill; see illustration on opposite page.
NOTE [1] First performance in Antwerp.
REVIEW HLG III, 319-320.

183. March 8, 1906, 8 p.m.
AMSTERDAM - The Concertgebouw [1,800 seats]

Extraordinary Subscription Concert

All-Mahler Program [1]

    (1)   Symphony No. 5 [2]
          - Intermission -
    (2)   *Kindertotenlieder*
    (3)   "Ich bin der Welt abhanden gekommen"

SOLOIST (2 & 3) G. Zalsman [3]
ORCHESTRA The Concertgebouw Orchestra.
SOURCE Handbill; see illustration on opposite page.
NOTE [1] First performance of all three works in Amsterdam.
[2] In the following weeks Mengelberg went on a tour with the orchestra and repeated the *Fifth* in Rotterdam (on March 12), The Hague (14), Arnhem (19), Haarlem (20), and twice in Amsterdam (21 & 22).
[3] Replaced the originally announced but indisposed Friedrich Weidemann (Court Opera in Vienna). At such short notice the Dutch baritone Gerard Zalsman could not learn the complete program as scheduled, so two announced songs from *Des Knaben Wunderhorn* ("Der Schildwache Nachtlied" & "Des Antonius von Padua Fischpredigt") were omitted. A new handbill was not printed.
REVIEW HLG III, 323-325.

42. Tonkünstler-Fest
zu Essen.

Sonntag, den 27. Mai,
abends 5½ Uhr im grossen Saale des Stadtgartens

Mahler-Konzert

VI. Symphonie von Gustav Mahler
unter Leitung des Komponisten,

110 Musiker. Die Celestas sind aus der Fabrik von Mustel & Co., Paris.

Karten zu Mk. 5,—, 3,— und 2,— sind zu haben bei **Thaden & Schmemann**, Essen, Viehoferstrasse 14 und abends an der Kasse.

Vormittags 11 Uhr:

Haupt-Probe.

Karten zu Mk. 2,—, Schülerkarten zu Mk. 1,—.

184. March 10, 1906, 8 p.m.
   AMSTERDAM - Concertgebouw [1,800 seats]

The "Maatschappij tot bevordering der toonkunst" [1]

   (1) Schillings — "Dem Verklärten," Hymnic Rhapsody, Op. 21, for Baritone, Chorus, and Orch.
   (2) Mahler — *Das klagende Lied,* for Soloists, Chorus, and Orch. ●[2]
   (3) Strauss — "Taillefer," Op. 52, for Three Soloists, Chorus, and Orch.

SOLOISTS (1 & 3) R. Breitenfeld; (2 & 3) L. Coenen, D. Mahlendorf, M. Philippi & A. Jungblut.
CONDUCTORS (1 & 3) W. Mengelberg; (2) Mahler. (The Dutch conductor Martin S. Heukeroth oversaw the off-stage orchestra).
ORCHESTRA The Concertgebouw Orchestra.
CHORUS The Amsterdam "Toonkunst" Chorus.
SOURCE Handbill; see illustration on following page.
NOTE [1] The Society to Promote the Art of Music.
[2] First performance in Amsterdam. Mahler's repeat performance scheduled for the next day was conducted by Mengelberg, because Mahler—already before arriving in Amsterdam—had decided to withdraw. However, it seems that Mahler was unable to provide a suitable and convincing explanation, so he asked his secretary at the Vienna Court Opera to forward a "fake" telegram, summoning him back to Vienna on official matters (telegram at the "Haus-, Hof- und Staatsarchiv" in Vienna).
REVIEW HLG III, 325-326.

185. May 27, 1906, 5:30 p.m.
   ESSEN - Großer Saal des Städtischen Saalbaus [1,800 seats]

Fourth Concert at the Forty-Second Music Festival of the "Allgemeiner Deutscher Musikverein"

   (1) Mozart — *Maurerische Trauermusik,* K. 477 [1]
   - Intermission -
   (2) Mahler — Symphony No. 6, A minor [2]

CONDUCTORS (1) R. Strauss; (2) Mahler.
ORCHESTRA The combined municipal orchestras of Essen and Utrecht.
SOURCE Newspaper advertisement; see illustration on opposite page.
NOTE [1] Owing to the sudden death of the Essen *Burgomeister,* on the eve of the concert, Richard Strauss asked Mahler to open the concert with "some funeral overture or other" in honor of the deceased, a request Mahler apparently declined (AMM, p. 100).
[2] World premiere. The general rehearsal took place at 11 a.m. the same day. On May 1, Mahler had conducted a sight-reading of the work with the Vienna Philharmonic Orchestra. At some point during the rehearsals in Essen, he decided to reverse the order of the two middle movements (the *Scherzo* originally was the 2nd movement, the *Andante,* the 3rd). A notice attached to the recently published study score informs the audience about the change.
REVIEW HLG III, 412-418.

MAATSCHAPPIJ TOT BEVORDERING DER TOONKUNST,
AFDEELING AMSTERDAM.

Directeur: WILLEM MENGELBERG.

HET CONCERTGEBOUW.

ZATERDAG 10 MAART 1906, 's AVONDS 8 UUR

UITVOERING VAN

DEM VERKLÄRTEN,

Hymnische Rhapsodie,

voor Koor, Bariton-Solo en Orkest naar Woorden van

FR. SCHILLER.

VAN

MAX SCHILLING,

Op. 21.

DAS KLAGENDE LIED,

voor Sopraan-, Alt- en Tenor-Solo, Koor en Orkest

VAN

GUSTAV MAHLER.

TAILLEFER,

Ballade van LUDWIG UHLAND,

voor Soli, Koor en Orkest

VAN

RICHARD STRAUSS,

Op 52.

184

Konzert-Bureau Emil Gutmann.

Donnerstag, 8. November abends präzise 7½ Uhr

in der Tonhalle

Grosses Wohltätigkeits-Konzert.

Mitwirkende:

Hofoperndirektor

Gustav Mahler

aus Wien,

Tilly Koenen, Konzertsängerin,
Ernst von Dohnányi, Klaviervirtuose, das verstärkte **Kaim-Orchester** unter Leitung von **Gustav Mahler**.

PROGRAMM:

1. **Gustav Mahler**: Sechste Symphonie (Neu, 1. Aufführung in München).
2. **Schubert-Liszt**: „Wanderer-Fantasie" für Klavier u. Orchester. Klavier: **Ernst von Dohnányi**.
3. a) **Richard Strauss**: Hymnus; b) **Felix Weingartner**: Frühlingsgespenste (Neu); c) **Hugo Wolf**: „Er ist's", Gesänge mit Orchesterbegleitung. **Tilly Koenen**.
4. **Richard Wagner**: „Meistersinger-Vorspiel".

Das Rein-Erträgnis fliesst zu gleichen Teilen dem Oesterreich.-Ungar. Hilfsverein und den Armen Münchens zu.

Billette à M. 10.—, 8.—, 6.—, 5.—, 4.—, 3.— und 1.—.

Die Kartenausgabe erfolgt ausschliesslich in der **Hofbuchhandlung Karl Schüler** (A. Ackermanns Nachf.), Maximilianstr 2. (Kassastunden an Wochentagen v. 9—1 Uhr vorm. u. 3—6 Uhr nachm.) (1.22)

| Breslau–Munich | 1906 | Concerts Nos. 186–187 |

Season 1906–1907

186. October 24, 1906, 7:30 p.m.
BRESLAU - Konzerthaus [1,500 seats]

First Philharmonic Subscription Concert

All-Mahler Program [1]

(1) Symphony No. 3, D minor
- Intermission -
(2) Four *Lieder* and "Gesänge" with Orchestra:
"Der Schildwache Nachtlied" •
"Des Antonius von Padua Fischpredigt" •
"Das irdische Leben" •
"Ich bin der Welt abhanden gekommen"

SOLOISTS (1) T. Daeglau; (2) F. Weidemann.
ORCHESTRA The Breslau Philharmonic Orchestra, reinforced with three players (trumpet, horn and trombone) from the Vienna Court Opera's Orchestra.
CHORUS Women's voices of the Breslau "Singakademie" and a boys chorus from the "Magdalenen Gymnasium."
SOURCE Various newspaper reviews.
NOTE [1] First performance of all five works in Breslau. At two subsequent concerts, on January 22 & 23, 1907, the four songs were repeated, (with F. Weidemann again as soloist), cond. by Georg Dohrn, the orchestra's permanent conductor.
REVIEW HLG III, 525-526.

187. November 8, 1906, 7:30 p.m.
MUNICH - Tonhalle [3,500 seats]

For the Benefit of the "Austro-Hungarian Relief Fund" and the "Poor in Munich"

(1) Mahler   Symphony No. 6, A minor [1]
- Intermission -
(2) Wagner   Prelude to Act 1 of *Die Meistersinger von Nürnberg*
(3) Three *Lieder* with Orchestra:
Strauss   "Hymnus," Op. 33, No. 3
Weingartner   "Frühlingsgespenster," Op. 19, No. 4 •
Wolf   "Er ist's"
(4) Liszt   Piano Concerto No. 1, E-flat major [2]

SOLOIST (3) T. Koenen; (4) E. v. Dohnányi.
CONDUCTORS (1–3) Mahler; (4) B. Stavenhagen.
ORCHESTRA The augmented *Kaim* Orchestra.
SOURCE Program and newspaper advertisement; see illustration on opposite page.
NOTES [1] First performance in Munich. As was the case in Essen (concert no. 185), the order of the two middle movements was again *Andante, Scherzo*.
[2] Replaced the originally announced *Wanderer* Fantasy by Schubert–Liszt (see ill. p. 204). A separate piece of paper, enclosed in the program booklet, informs the audience that Mahler could not conduct the Liszt concerto because he had been

Brünner Philharmoniker.
(5. Vereinsjahr.)

Sonntag den 11. November 1906,
genau ½8 abends
im großen Festsaale des Deutschen Hauses

I. diesjähriges Konzert
der Brünner Philharmoniker

unter gefälliger Mitwirkung des Herrn
GUSTAV MAHLER,
k. u. k. Hofopern-Direktor in Wien.
des Herrn Professor
Arnold Rosé,
k. u. k. Kammervirtuosen und des Dirigenten Herrn
August Veit
sowie der k. k. Hofopernmitglieder: Solohornist Karl Stiegler, Solotrompeter Adolf Wunderer, Soloposaunist Franz Dreyer, Solobassist Otto Stix, Soloklarinettist Powolny und Solopaukist Knauer.

Vortrags-Ordnung:

1. Gustav Mahler: I. Symphonie in D-dur. (Erste Aufführung.) Für großes Orchester.
2. Hugo Wolf: Italienische Serenade. (Erste Aufführung.) Für kleines Orchester.
   Englischhorn-Solo . Herr Hugo Prochaska.
   Cello-Solo . . . . Herr Franz Mraczek.
3. Carl Maria von Weber: Ouverture zu „Euryanthe".

---

8   Nr. 333   16. Jahrg.

Stadt-Theater.

Heute Montag den 3. Dezember 1906.
Anfang 7 Uhr.

Musikerpensionsvereins-Konzert
(zur Feier des 40jährigen Bestandes)

Gustav Mahler
3. Sinfonie in D-moll
unter Leitung des Komponisten.

Mitwirkende:
Das verstärkte Theater-Orchester (94 Mitglieder), Damenchor des Singvereines und des Stadttheaters, Alt-Solo: Fräulein Bella Paalen, Knabenchor der Franz Josef-Bürgerschule.
1. Abteilung Nr. 1: Kräftig, entschieden. 2. Abteilung Nr. 2: Tempo di Munietto sehr mäßig. Nr. 3: Comodo scherzando. Nr. 4: Sehr langsam, misterioso. Nr. 5: Lustig im Tempo und keck im Ausdruck. Nr. 6: Langsam, ruhevoll, empfunden.
Gesangstexte für Nr. 4 und Nr. 5 siehe Einlage.
Zwischen den einzelnen Abteilungen finden keine Pausen statt.
Blockkarten ungiltig. Abonnement aufgehoben. Sämtliche Ermäßigungen ungiltig.

Kasse-Eröffnung ½7 Uhr.   Anfang 7 Uhr.   Ende 9 Uhr.

Morgen Dienstag: Gastspiel der Frau Pepi Glöckner-Kramer vom deutschen Volkstheater in Wien: „Die Welt ohne Männer".

summoned to Vienna. He was replaced by Bernhard Stavenhagen, who had not only prepared the concert, but on November 14 also led a repeat performance of the Sixth Symphony in Munich. Mahler, back in Vienna on the 9th, conducted an opera that evening, and departed together with his wife for Brünn the following morning.
REVIEW HLG III, 522-524.

188. **November 11, 1906, 7:30 p.m.**
BRÜNN - Festsaal des Deutschen Hauses [1,600 seats]

First Philharmonic Subscription Concert

(1)	Mahler	Symphony No. 1, D major [1]
		- Intermission -
(2)	Wolf	*Italienische Serenade*, arr. for small Orchestra by Max Reger
(3)	Weber	Overture to *Euryanthe*

CONDUCTORS (1) Mahler; (2 & 3) A. Veit.
ORCHESTRA The Brünn Philharmonic Orchestra, reinforced with 8 players from the Vienna Court Opera's Orchestra.
SOURCE Handbill; see illustration on opposite page.
NOTE [1] Alma Mahler, who had not heard the symphony since 1900 (concert no. 135), recalls this first performance in Brünn: "I had noticed that in the *Finale* [Mahler] had passed over the first appearance of the climax and chose its second appearance as the highlight. For me, the first remained the essential one, and on this occasion he restored the earlier interpretation by emphasizing it strongly, recognizing that this passage was indeed the more important." (AMM, p.106). In his footnote Donald Mitchell comments: "I assume that Alma Mahler must be referring here to the two big D major climaxes in the finale—cf. Figs. 34 and 56 in the score."
REVIEW HLG III, 528-529.

189. **December 3, 1906, 7 p.m.**
190. **December 23, 1906, 3 p.m.**
GRAZ - Stadttheater [1,200 seats]

For the Benefit of the Orchestra's Pension Fund in Celebration of its 40th Anniversary

    Mahler   Symphony No. 3, D minor [1]

SOLOIST B. Paalen.
ORCHESTRA The augmented orchestra of the *Stadttheater*, including 3 musicians from the Vienna Court Opera; a total of 94 players.
CHORUS The women's voices from the Graz "Singverein," the Theater's chorus, and a boys' choir from the "Franz Josef-Bürgerschule"; a total of 300 singers.
SOURCE Newspaper review; see illustration on opposite page.
NOTE [1] Originally only one performance was scheduled, but the great success called spontaneously for the repeat performance on the 23rd.
REVIEW HLG III, 531-533.

WIENER KONZERT-VEREIN.

FREITAG, DEN 4. JÄNNER 1907

PÜNKTLICH ½8 UHR ABENDS

AUSSERORDENTLICHES KONZERT

(NOVITÄTEN-KONZERT)
IM
GROSSEN MUSIKVEREINS-SAALE.

PROGRAMM:

GUSTAV MAHLER:
Sechste Sinfonie (Tragische).

Allegro energico, ma non troppo.
Andante moderato.
Scherzo.
Finale (Allegro moderato).

Unter Leitung des Komponisten.

Viertes Sinfonie-Konzert im Mittwoch-Zyklus
am 16. Jänner 1907, pünktlich ½8 Uhr abends.

PROGRAMM:

C. W. Gluck	Ouvertüre zu: »Alceste« (mit dem Schlusse von Felix Weingartner).
L. van Beethoven	Vierte Sinfonie.
Edgar Istel	Eine Singspiel-Ouvertüre. (I. Aufführung in Wien.)
P. Tschaïkowsky	»Romeo und Julie«, Phantasie.

Das **vierte** Sinfonie-Konzert im Dienstag-Zyklus findet am 22. Jänner 1907, pünktlich ½8 Uhr abends, statt.

=== Dieses Programm unentgeltlich. ===

Stern & Steiner, Wien.

| Vienna | 1907 | Concert No. 191 |

191. **January 4, 1907, 7:30 p.m.**[1]
VIENNA - Großer Saal des Musikvereins [2,063 seats]

Extraordinary Concert (Novelty Concert)

      Mahler   Symphony No. 6, A minor, "Tragic" ●[2]

ORCHESTRA The Orchestra of the Vienna "Konzert-Verein."
SOURCE Handbill; see illustration on opposite page.
NOTES [1] The general rehearsal took place the preceding day at 7:30 p.m.
[2] First performance in Vienna. The symphony appears here for the first time with the subtitle "Tragische" ("Tragic"), presumably with Mahler's approval.
In the history of the *Sixth* there has been, and still is, much confusion regarding the order of the two middle movements. Prior to the World premiere (concert no. 185), Mahler had reversed the original order (*Scherzo–Andante*) and retained it at his second performance (concert no. 187). Between these two concerts he had supervised the Berlin premiere, on October 8, 1906, led by Oscar Fried, at which the *Andante* again was placed second.
The crucial question is whether or not, at this fourth performance (unfortunately his last of this work), Mahler returned to the original sequence? And, if so, should we regard this as his final decision? The handbill announces, unambiguously, the *Andante* as the second movement, but the Critical Edition of the score (1963) places it third, and the editor maintains that Mahler performed it this way for this concert in Vienna.
The symphony's somber mood and its technical demands never added to the work's popularity, and hence it was rarely performed. However, for a half century it was normal practice to use the *Andante–Scherzo* order, Willem Mengelberg in Amsterdam being the only exception. His first performance, on September 14, 1916, placed the *Andante* as the 2nd movement, but four years later he apparently became unsettled by an awareness of two different editions of the score and asked Alma Mahler for advice. She answered in favor of the *Scherzo–Andante* order, but unfortunately without any amplifying explanations.
With reference to Alma Mahler, and (it seems) a single newspaper review of the 1907 performance, the late Professor Erwin Ratz, editor of the Critical Edition, considered it to be firmly established that the *Scherzo* preceded the *Andante*.
In matters concerning Mahler's music (and his life), however, his widow was never the most reliable witness, and as far as the review is concerned, matters appear to be not that simple. Professor Donald Mitchell (London), who has scrutinized all available Viennese reviews, writes in a private communication that the majority of the critics did not report any reversal, and that he believed that the two critics who mention a reversal probably only attended the general rehearsal on January 3, at which Mahler perhaps might have tried out his original concept.
It is worth mentioning that two months after the Vienna premiere, on March 4 and 11, Hans Winderstein in Leipzig conducted the last complete performances of the symphony in Mahler's lifetime, again with the *Andante* placed second. If in fact the ever painstaking composer had had second thoughts about the order of the two movements he undoubtedly would have communicated his wishes to Mr. Winderstein, either directly or through his publisher. But that appears not to have been the case.

PHILHARMONIE.

Montag, den 14. Januar 1907, Abends 7½ Uhr pünktlich:

Sechstes
Philharmonisches Concert

◩

PROGRAMM.

Gustav Mahler: Symphonie No. 3, d-moll

unter persönlicher Leitung des Komponisten

unter Mitwirkung von

Fräulein Maria Seret,

des Prof. Anna Schultzen-Asten-Chores

(Dir.: Margarete Herrmann)

——————— und der Knaben ———————

des Nikolai-Marien-Kirchen-Chores

(Dir.: Professor Th. Krause).

Eintrittskarten sind in der Hofmusikalienhdlg. von Bote & Bock, Leipziger Strasse 37, bei Wertheim, Leipziger Strasse, sowie Abends an der Kasse zu haben.

Finally, in the last months of 1906 Mahler corresponded with Mengelberg concerning a performance there of the *Sixth* on January 24, 1907, which eventually was cancelled. It seems rather strange that in his letters Mahler does not mention a reversal of the two middle movements, a fact which once again might explain why Mengelberg, a dozen years later, had to ask Alma Mahler for advice and guidance. For further reading, see "The Correct Movement Order in Mahler's Sixth Symphony," Gilbert Kaplan, editor; Kaplan Foundation, 2004 and an article in "News about Mahler Research," by Reinhold Kubik and Gilbert Kaplan (No. 57, Spring 2008).
REVIEW HLG III, 534-543.

192. January 14, 1907, 7:30 p.m. [1]
BERLIN - Philharmonie [2,500 seats]

Sixth Philharmonic Subscription Concert

       Mahler   Symphony No. 3, D minor ● [2]

SOLOIST M. Seret.
ORCHESTRA The Berlin Philharmonic Orchestra.
CHORUS The Anna-Schultzen-Asten Chorus, cond. M. Hermann, and the Boys' Choir from the Nikolai-Marien-Kirche, cond. Th. Krause.
SOURCE Program and handbill; see illustration on opposite page.
NOTES [1] The general rehearsal took place at noon the preceding day.
[2] First complete performance in Berlin. Previously the 2nd movement had been given its world premiere in Berlin, on November 9, 1896, under Arthur Nikisch, and on March 9, 1897, Felix Weingartner had conducted the world premieres of the 3rd and 6th movements in a concert which also included the 2nd movement.
REVIEW HLG III, 567-569.

193. January 18, 1907, 7 p.m. [1]
FRANKFURT am MAIN - Großer Saal des Saalbau [2,000 seats]

The Seventh Friday Concert of the Museums-Gesellschaft

    (1)   Beethoven   Overture to *Coriolan*, Op. 62
    (2)   Mahler   Symphony No. 4, G major [2]
                           - Intermission -
    (3)   Schumann   Symphony No. 1, B-flat major, Op. 38, "Spring"

SOLOIST (2) E. Gentner-Fischer.
ORCHESTRA The orchestra of the Frankfurt *Stadttheater*.
SOURCE Various newspaper reviews.
NOTES [1] The general rehearsal took place the same morning.
[2] Second performance in Frankfurt am Main; see concert no. 142, note 2.
REVIEW HLG III, 572.

Verein für Kunst
Leitung: Herwarth Walden

Gustav Mahler

XII. Abend des III. Jahres
Donnerstag / den 14. Februar 1907
im Künstlerhaus / Bellevuestraße 3

Gesang: **Johannes Messchaert**
Klavier: **Gustav Mahler**

Concertflügel: Steinway & Sons / Niederlage Oskar Agthe, Wilhelmstr. 11

Verlag B. Schotts Söhne / Mainz
Gustav Mahler
Lieder und Gesänge für eine Singstimme und Klavier
Frühlingsmorgen / Erinnerung / Hans und Grete / Serenade aus Don Juan / Phantasie aus Don Juan / Neun Lieder aus des Knaben Wunderhorn

Folgende Abende sind für das 3. Jahr des Vereins für Kunst noch festgesetzt:

Else Lasker-Schüler
Vorlesung eigener Dichtungen
Donnerstag, den 21. Februar, Salon Cassirer*

Richard Strauss
Gesang: Pauline Strauß de Ahna
Klavier: Richard Strauß
Sonnabend, den 9. März, Mozartsaal*

Paul Leppin
Vorlesung eigener Dichtungen
Donnerstag, den 14. März, Salon Cassirer*

Hermann Bahr
Vorlesung eigener Dichtungen
Donnerstag, den 21. März, Salon Cassirer*

Anfang aller Abende 8 Uhr
*Ausserordentliche Mitglieder haben freien Zutritt
Alle Abende des „V. f. K." sind öffentlich
Eintrittskarten bei Wertheim u. im Salon Cassirer

Die ausserordentliche Mitgliedschaft im Verein für Kunst wird erworben durch Zahlung eines Jahresbeitrags von Mk. 15,—. Sie berechtigt zum unentgeltlichen Besuch von zehn Kunstabenden auf Plätzen, deren Kassenpreis Mk. 3 beträgt. Für alle Sonderabende zahlen die Mitglieder nur die Hälfte des Eintrittspreises. Das Mitgliedsjahr läuft vom 1. April zum 1. April. Erfolgt bis zum 1. Januar des laufenden Jahres keine Kündigung, so gilt die Mitgliedschaft als auf ein Jahr verlängert. Die Mitgliedschaft gewährt folgende Ermässigungen: Salon Cassirer: Dauerkarte Mk. 1,— (statt Mk. 5,—) Sezession: Dauerkarte Mk. 2,— (statt Mk. 3,—) Mitgliedskarten sind an den oben angegebenen Stellen erhältlich. Sie werden auf den Namen ausgestellt und sind nicht übertragbar.

Aus des Knaben Wunderhorn
Um schimme Kinder artig zu machen
Ablösung im Sommer
Nicht wiedersehen
Starke Einbildungskraft
Selbstgefühl

Friedrich Rückert
Kindertotenlieder
Nun will die Sonne so hell aufgehen
Nun seh ich wohl, warum so dunkle Flammen
Wenn dein Mütterlein
Oft denk ich, sie sind nur ausgegangen
In diesem Wetter

> Diese fünf Gesänge sind als ein einheitliches, untrennbares Ganze gedacht und es muß daher bei ihrer Aufführung die Continuität (auch durch Hintanhaltung von Störungen, wie z. B. Beifallsbezeugungen am Ende einer Nummer) aufrecht erhalten werden

Lieder eines fahrenden Gesellen
Wenn mein Schatz
Gieng heut Morgen
Ich hab ein glühend Messer
Die zwei blauen Augen

Friedrich Rückert
Blicke mir
Ich atmet' einen linden Duft
Um Mitternacht
Ich bin der Welt abhanden gekommen

194. January 20, 1907, 3:30 p.m.
LINZ - Landschaftliches Theater [1,200 seats]

    (1)   Beethoven   *Leonore* Overture No. 3, Op. 72b [1]
    (2)   Mahler   Three *Lieder und Gesänge* with Piano Acc.:
                                "Um Mitternacht"
                                  "Erinnerung"
                                  "Aus! Aus!"
                                  - Intermission -
    (3)   Mahler   Symphony No. 1, D major [2]

SOLOIST (2) G. Kaitan, acc. by L. Materna.
CONDUCTORS (1 & 2) L. Materna; (3) Mahler.
ORCHESTRA The orchestra of the *Landschaftliches Theater*, augmented by 20 players from the Vienna Court Opera's Orchestra, and some local musicians; a total of 70 players.
SOURCE Newspaper advertisement.
NOTES [1] Originally Mahler was to have conducted the whole concert, but a delay of his train from Frankfurt left him insufficient rehearsal time.
[2] First performance in Linz.
REVIEW HLG III, 572-574.

195. February 14, 1907, 8 p.m.
BERLIN - Künstlerhaus [1]

12th Evening of the "Verein für Kunst"

All-Mahler Program: Eighteen *Lieder und Gesänge* with Piano Acc.

    (1)   Um schlimme Kinder artig zu machen •
    (2)   Ablösung im Sommer •
    (3)   Nicht Wiedersehen •
    (4)   Selbstgefühl •
    (5)   Starke Einbildungskraft •
    (6)   *[5] Kindertotenlieder*
            - Intermission -
    (7)   *[4] Lieder eines fahrenden Gesellen*
    (8)   Blicke mir nicht in die Lieder •
    (9)   Ich atmet' einen linden Duft •
    (10)   Um Mitternacht •
    (11)   Ich bin der Welt abhanden gekommen •

SOLOIST J. Messchaert, acc. by Mahler (his last appearance in Berlin).
SOURCE Handbill; see illustration on opposite page.
NOTE [1] The House of Artists, Bellevuestraße 3.
REVIEW HLG III, 603-605.

Giovedì 4 Aprile 1907

alle ore 8.15 pom.

avrà luogo al

TEATRO COMUNALE
GIUSEPPE VERDI

il

Secondo Grande
Concerto Sinfonico

sostenuto dalla

Orchestra del Teatro Comunale Giuseppe Verdi

sotto la direzione del maestro

GUSTAVO MAHLER

Direttore dell'Opera di Vienna

PROGRAMMA

1. WAGNER. - Preludio dell'opera "I Maestri Cantori"
2. BEETHOVEN. - V.a Sinfonia in Do min.
   I. Allegro con brio - II. Andante con moto - III. Allegro - IV. Allegro
3. MAHLER. - La Sinfonia in Re maggiore
   I. Lento trascinato - II. Scherzo agitato con terza Trio, molto contrasto - III. Solenne, misurato - IV. Tempestosamente mosso

---

PREZZI SERALI:

MODIANO - TRIESTE

| Rome–Triest | 1907 | Concerts Nos. 196–198 |

196. March 25, 1907, 4 p.m. [1]
ROME - Augusteo [4,000 seats]

(1)	Beethoven	Symphony No. 3, E-flat major, Op. 55, "Eroica"
		- Intermission -
(2)	Wagner	Prelude and "Liebestod," from *Tristan und Isolde*
(3)	Wagner	Prelude to Act 1 of *Die Meistersinger von Nürnberg*

ORCHESTRA Regia Accademia di Santa Cecilia.
SOURCE Program reconstructed from various newspaper reviews.
NOTE [1] The programs of the two concerts in Rome were subject to several changes because Mahler had lost the suitcase with his personal orchestral materials on the journey from Vienna.
REVIEW HLG III, 631-632.

197. April 1, 1907, 4 p.m.
ROME - Augusteo [4,000 seats]

(1)	Weber	Overture to *Der Freischütz*
(2)	Mahler	Symphony No. 5 (Adagietto) [1]
(3)	Tchaikovsky	*Romeo and Juliet,* Fantasy–Overture
		- Intermission -
(4)	Beethoven	Symphony No. 7, A major, Op 92

ORCHESTRA Regia Accademia di Santa Cecilia.
SOURCE Program reconstructed from various newspaper reviews.
NOTE [1] First performance in Rome. Originally Mahler had intended to include the symphony's final *Rondo*. The *Adagietto* replaced the announced "Danse des sylphes" from Berlioz's *La Damnation de Faust*.
REVIEW HLG III, 632-634.

198. April 4, 1907, 8:15 p.m.
TRIEST - Teatro Communale Giuseppe Verdi [1,800 seats]

"Secondo Grande Concerto Sinfonico"

(1)	Wagner	Prelude to Act 1 of *Die Meistersinger von Nürnberg*
(2)	Beethoven	Symphony No. 5, C minor, Op. 67
		- Intermission -
(3)	Mahler	Symphony No. 1, D major [1]

ORCHESTRA The Theater Orchestra.
SOURCE Poster; see illustration on opposite page.
NOTE [1] First performance in Trieste.
REVIEW HLG III, 634-635.

| Wiesbaden–St. Petersburg | 1907 | Concerts Nos. 199–200 |

Season 1907–1908

199. October 9, 1907, 7 p.m.
WIESBADEN - Großer Saal des Neuen Kurhauses [1,600 seats]

The Sixth Festival Concert [1]

- (1) Beethoven — Symphony No. 5, C minor, Op. 67
  - Intermission -
- (2) Beethoven — Overture to *Coriolan*, Op. 62
- (3) Wagner — Prelude and "Liebestod," from *Tristan und Isolde*
- (4) Wagner — Prelude to Act 1 of *Die Meistersinger von Nürnberg*

ORCHESTRA The Munich *Kaim* Orchestra, augmented with players from the Wiesbaden *Kur-Orchester,* a total of 90 players.
SOURCE Program reconstructed from various newspaper reviews.
NOTE [1] A series of festival concerts had been arranged in connection with the May 8, 1907 opening of the *Neues Kurhaus* ("New Casino") with a large concert hall.
REVIEW HLG III, 727-728.

200. October 26 [13], **1907, 8:15 p.m.** [1]
ST. PETERSBURG - Grand Hall of the Imperial Music Conservatory
[1,750 seats]

First Subscription Concert (Direction: K. M. Schröder)

- (1) Berlioz — *Le carnaval romain*, Overture, Op. 9
- (2) Beethoven — Symphony No. 7, A major, Op. 92
  - Intermission -
- (3) Beethoven — "Ah! perfido!" Scene and Aria, Op. 65
- (4) Three *Lieder* with Orchestra:
  - Strauss — "Hymnus," Op. 33, No. 3
  - Fiedler — "Die Musikantin," Op. 5
  - Wolf — "Er ist's"
- (5) Wagner — Prelude to Act 1 of *Die Meistersinger von Nürnberg*

SOLOIST (3 & 4) T. Koenen.
ORCHESTRA The Orchestra of the Mariinsky Theater.
SOURCE Program reconstructed from various reviews.
NOTE [1] The date in brackets refers to the Russian calendar.
REVIEW HLG III, 745-750.

Gustav Mahler

Konsert

i Universitetets Solennitetssal

Fredagen den 1 November 1907 kl. ½ 8 e. m.

I stället för Beethovens sinfoni N:o 3 spelas sinfonin N:o 5, c-moll.

Allegro con brio. Andante con moto. Scherzo. Allegro.

2. *Beethoven:* Uvertyr till „Coriolan."

3. *Wagner:* Vorspiel und Isoldens Liebestod ur „Tristan und Isolde."

4. *Wagner:* Uvertyr till „Die Meistersinger."

Medverkande: FILHARMONISKA ORKESTERN.

Wasastjerna 85

Helsingfors 1907. Hufvudstadsbladets Nya Tryckeri.

EDVARD FAZER'S KONSERTBYRÅ

№ 216

1907 1907

Большой залъ Консерваторіи.

ВОСЕМЬ СИМФОНИЧЕСКИХЪ КОНЦЕРТОВЪ
(ШРЕДЕРА)

Въ Субботу, 27-го Октября,

Второй Концертъ

ПРИ УЧАСТІИ:

РАУЛЯ ПЮНЬО
(изъ Парижа)

и большого симфоническаго оркестра
ИМПЕРАТОРСКОЙ Русской Оперы
подъ управленіемъ

ГУСТАВА МАЛЕРЪ
(изъ Вѣны).

Начало въ 8¼ часовъ вечера.

Весь чистый сборъ поступаетъ въ пользу Общества вспомоществованія недостаточн. учащимся въ СПБ. Консерваторіи.

| Helsinki–St. Petersburg–Vienna | 1907 | Concerts Nos. 201–203 |

201. November 1, 1907, 7:30 p.m.
HELSINKI - Universitets Solennitetssal (University Assembly Hall)

    (1) Beethoven   Symphony No. 5, C minor, Op. 67 [1]
                         - Intermission -
    (2) Beethoven   Overture to *Coriolan*, Op. 62
    (3) Wagner   Prelude and "Liebestod," from *Tristan und Isolde*
    (4) Wagner   Prelude to Act 1 of *Die Meistersinger von Nürnberg*

ORCHESTRA The Helsinki Philharmonic Orchestra.
SOURCE Handbill; see illustration on opposite page.
NOTE [1] Replaced Beethoven's *Eroica* Symphony which was originally announced.
REVIEW HLG III, 755-757.

202. November 9 [October 27], 1907, 8:15 p.m.
ST. PETERSBURG - Grand Hall of the Imperial Music Conservatory
[1,750 seats]

Second Subscription Concert (Direction: K. M. Schröder)

    (1) Mahler   Symphony No. 5 ● [1]
                         - Intermission -
    (2) Rachmaninoff   Piano Concerto No. 2, C minor, Op. 18
    (3) Mozart   Piano Concerto in E-flat major (2 movements only) [2]
    (4) Beethoven   Overture to *Coriolan*, Op. 62
    (5) Wagner   Prelude and "Liebestod," from *Tristan und Isolde*
    (6) Wagner   Prelude to Act 1 of *Die Meistersinger von Nürnberg*

SOLOIST (2 & 3) R. Pugno.
CONDUCTORS (1, 4–6) Mahler; (2 & 3) M. Vladimirov.
ORCHESTRA The Orchestra of the Mariinsky Theater.
SOURCE Handbill; see illustration on opposite page.
NOTES [1] First performance in St. Petersburg and Mahler's last performance of the symphony.
[2] Concerto not identified. Could be either K.271, 449, or 482.
REVIEW HLG III, 762-767.

203. November 24, 1907, 12:30 p.m. [1]
VIENNA - Großer Saal des Musikvereins [2,063 seats]

First Extraordinary Concert of the "Gesellschaft der Musikfreunde in Wien"

    Mahler   Symphony No. 2, C minor, "Resurrection"

SOLOISTS E. Elizza, G. Förstel, H. Kittel [in *Urlicht*] and B. Paalen.[2]
ORCHESTRA The Court Opera Orchestra.
CHORUS The "Singverein der Gesellschaft der Musikfreunde in Wien."
ORGAN R. Dittrich.

21. November 1907 — Seite 19

Gesellschaft der Musikfreunde in Wien.

Sonntag den 24. November 1907, mittags halb 1 Uhr
im grossen Musikvereinssaale:

I. ausserordentl. Gesellschaftskonzert.

Zur Aufführung gelangt:

Gustav Mahler
Zweite Symphonie (C-moll).

Unter Leitung des Komponisten.

Mitwirkend:

Frau **Elise Elizza**, k. k. Hof-Opernsängerin.
Frl. **Hermine Kittel**, k. k. Hof-Opernsängerin.
Frl. **Anna v. Mildenburg**, k. und k. Kammersängerin.
Frl. **Bella Paalen**, k. k. Hof-Opernsängerin.
Herr **Rudolf Dittrich**, k. k. Hof-Organist.
Der Singverein der Gesellschaft der Musikfreunde.
Das k. k. Hof-Opernorchester.

Preise der Plätze: 20, 16, 12, 10, 8, 6, 4 und 3 Kronen.

Samstag den 23. November, abends ½8 Uhr:
=== Oeffentliche Generalprobe. ===
Sitze à 10, 8, 6, 4, 3 und Entrees à 1.50 K. an der Konzertkasse der Gesellschaft der Musikfreunde, I., Canovagasse 4.

Das Reinerträgnis des Konzertes fliesst dem Orgelfonds der Gesellschaft der Musikfreunde zu.

GESELLSCHAFT DER MUSIKFREUNDE IN WIEN

Sonntag, den 24. November 1907, mittags halb 1 Uhr
=== im großen Musikvereins-Saale ===

I. AUSSERORDENTL. GESELLSCHAFTS-KONZERT.

ooooo

Zur Aufführung gelangt:

GUSTAV MAHLER
ZWEITE SINFONIE (C-MOLL)
=== für Soli, Chor, Orchester und Orgel. ===

1. Satz: ALLEGRO MAESTOSO. (Mit durchaus ernstem und feierlichem Ausdruck.)
2. Satz: ANDANTE CON MOTO.
3. Satz: SCHERZO. (In ruhig fließender Bewegung.)
4. Satz: „URLICHT" aus: „Des Knaben Wunderhorn".
5. Satz: FINALE.

MITWIRKENDE:

Frau ELISE ELIZZA, k. k. Hof-Opernsängerin.
Fräulein GERTRUD FÖRSTEL, k. k. Hof-Opernsängerin.
Fräulein HERMINE KITTEL, k. k. Hof-Opernsängerin.
Fräulein BELLA PAALEN, k. k. Hof-Opernsängerin.
Herr RUDOLF DITTRICH, k. k. Hoforganist.
Der SINGVEREIN DER GESELLSCHAFT DER MUSIKFREUNDE.
Das K. K. HOF-OPERNORCHESTER.

DIRIGENT: DER KOMPONIST.

Preis dieses Programmes 20 Heller.

Buchdruckerei: Wien, I., Dorotheergasse 7.

SOURCE Handbill and newspaper advertisement; see illustrations on opposite page.

NOTES [1] The public general rehearsal took place the preceding day at 7:30 p.m. The concert marked Mahler's final farewell to Vienna, interestingly featuring the same work in which he had introduced himself to Vienna as a composer (concert no. 113). In the intervening eight years the *Second* had not been performed in Vienna.

The performance was first mentioned in a notice in the *Neue Freie Presse* (Vienna) on August 20, 1907, p. 9. Mahler initially declined the invitation to conduct his *Second* due to a previous commitment to premiere his *Seventh* with the Vienna Tonkünstlerorchester, as well as a concert tour through Germany that autumn. Franz Schalk was scheduled to conduct the *Second*. However, new developments at the Opera made Mahler cancel his plans and conduct this farewell concert.

[2] The 5th movement calls for two soloists only; a soprano and a contralto. It is not clear why Mahler employed the additional singers. Also, Anna von Mildenburg was originally scheduled to sing but cancelled.

REVIEW HLG III, 770-773.

* * *

204.   **December 18, 1907, Soirée.**
S.S. Kaiserin Auguste Victoria (German Steamship)

For the Benefit of the Seamen's Pension Fund

- Program not known -

SOLOISTS A. Burgstaller, M. Holtzmann-Weymouth (Paris), and K. M. Sharn (Omaha, Nebraska), acc. at the piano by Mahler.

SOURCE An article in the New York based German newspaper *Montags-Zeitung*, [Monday's Newspaper], December 22, 1907.

NOTE Three years later, Mahler took part in a similar concert on his voyage to New York, concert 273. That program has been preserved and gives us an impression of this concert's scope and content. Although no records survive, one can easily imagine the philanthropic Mahler would have participated in similar charitable events. Benefit concerts were traditionally arranged on each of his five voyages to and from New York between the spring of 1908 and the spring of 1910.

* * *

PART IX
NEW YORK
The Metropolitan Opera
1908–1909

When Mahler sailed for New York in December 1907, he was not by any means going into exile. All in all his four American seasons up to the spring of 1911 lasted not quite twenty months, and in that relatively brief span he earned a salary that at home he could barely have dreamed of. The rest of the time he spent in Europe, mainly composing and conducting his own works. That arguably over-strained him but that is what he had always wanted to do. To that extent the hopes and expectations were fulfilled that he had had when he signed his Met contract with Conried. Moreover, although Mahler's career in the "New World" surely had its troughs, especially towards the end, it is wrong to judge it a failure - as many have tended to do. At the start, by and large, he scored one triumph after another. His debut performance at the Met of *Tristan und Isolde* on New Year's Day 1908 was almost universally acclaimed and his *Don Giovanni* three weeks later was a still greater success, drawing plaudits even from the few who had mildly criticized his Wagner.

Throughout this first New York season Mahler gave no orchestral concerts (apart from conducting a single overture at a benefit evening for Conried in March) - but that did not mean he had no ambition to do so. Even before arriving in town he had received an invitation he welcomed to make several appearances with the New York Symphony, a rival orchestra to the New York Philharmonic. Three such concerts did in fact take place at Carnegie Hall in the winter of 1908, and included the American premiere of the "Resurrection" Symphony. But Mahler found the orchestra incompetent and he also fell foul of its conductor, Walter Damrosch, who had originally invited Mahler and who now found himself unfavorably compared in the press to the guest maestro. Moreover, initially unbeknownst to Damrosch, Mahler had in the meantime accepted the proposal of a committee of rich New York ladies to form an orchestra second to none in America – if not the world. For the New York Symphony that clearly implied tougher, perhaps ruinous competition.

What had first been proposed by the ladies as the foundation of a wholly new orchestra finally emerged as a revamped version of the New York Philharmonic. It gave its first its first two concerts in March and April 1909 to somewhat mixed reviews – hardly a surprise since Mahler had been granted few rehearsals and was anyway using the occasions to weed out inadequate players before the start of the first full season in the autumn. Some critics did chide him for his partial re-orchestration of Beethoven's "Choral" Symphony, just as their counterparts in Europe had done. But most were far from hostile, and meanwhile Mahler was continuing to draw accolades for his achievements in the opera house - especially for a *Nozze di Figaro* that was widely regarded as incomparable.

That second season at the Met was, however, to be Mahler's last there (although he did return briefly in 1910 as a guest to give the American premiere of Tchaikovsky's *Pique Dame*). With his Philharmonic work now gathering pace, Mahler had no intention of committing himself to a heavy opera schedule too. It was, after all, not least to escape such a double burden that he had left Vienna. Besides, a new management structure had emerged at the Met and from the winter of 1908 Arturo Toscanini, another superb conductor, had been engaged to work alongside Mahler. At first it had seemed that Toscanini might be responsible mainly for the Italian repertoire and his colleague for the

German one; but the temperamental newcomer who had turned La Scala Milan into one of the world's greatest opera houses, and who adored Wagner, was not disposed to accept such a restriction for long. Eventually, a serious clash between two such gifted and determined maestros looked certain. Indeed, there had already been warning signs as early as the summer of 1908, when the Met tentatively suggested that Toscanini conduct a few performances of *Tristan und Isolde* at the start of the coming season. Mahler firmly rejected the idea.

When that unwelcome proposal arrived from the Met, Mahler was hard at work composing again – no longer near the Maiernigg villa that he and Alma had given up in the wake of Putzi's death, but in a new Häuschen high up in the Dolomites near the town of Toblach. For a time Mahler feared that, having abandoned on medical advice the strenuous hiking he adored, he might lack the inspiration for creative work. But in fact the months near Toblach yielded most of the song-symphony *Das Lied von der Erde*, certainly one of his finest pieces and considered by many to be his masterpiece. Composing apart, during that seven-month stay in Europe in 1908, Mahler gave just five concerts – most notably the world premiere in Prague of his Seventh Symphony. A year later he was back in Europe again, giving more concerts and setting down his Ninth Symphony. Growing marital problems aside, Mahler seemed to have grounds for elation. He had very largely freed himself of the opera, he was about to embark on a season with "his own orchestra," and he was finding time to compose. On the whole, it looked as though his ambitions were being fulfilled at last.

* * *

Metropolitan Opera House.

Lessee CONRIED METROPOLITAN OPERA CO.

TUESDAY EVENING, MARCH 24, 1908,
at 8 o'clock.

SPECIAL PERFORMANCE.

PUCCINI'S OPERA

LA BOHÊME
(IN ITALIAN.)
(Act III.)

MIMI	MMES. ABOTT
MUSETTA	DEREYNE
RODOLFO	MM. BONCI
MARCELLO	STRACCIARI
CONDUCTOR	MR. RODOLFO FERRARI

SCENE.—The Barrière d'Enfer. Paris.

PUCCINI'S OPERA

MADAMA BUTTERFLY
(IN ITALIAN.)
(Act I.)

CIO-CIO-SAN	MISS FARRAR
B. F. PINKERTON	MR. MARTIN
CONDUCTOR	MR. RODOLFO FERRARI

SCENE.—A Japanese House, Terrace and Garden in Nagasaki.

VERDI'S OPERA

IL TROVATORE
(IN ITALIAN.)
(Act IV.—Scene 1.)

LEONORA	MME. EMMA EAMES
MANRICO	MR. CARUSO
CONDUCTOR	MR. RODOLFO FERRARI

SCENE.—Exterior of the Aliaferia Palace.

GOUNOD'S OPERA

FAUST
(IN FRENCH.)
(Act II.)

MARGUERITE	MMES. FARRAR
MARTHE	GIRERD
FAUST	MM. CARUSO
MEPHISTOPHELES	PLANÇON
CONDUCTOR	MR. S. BOVY

SCENE.—Marguerite's Garden.

Overture, Leonore No. 3, Beethoven

CONDUCTOR	MR. GUSTAV MAHLER

PROGRAMME—CONTINUED.

RICHARD WAGNER'S OPERA

Die Meistersinger von Nürnberg
(IN GERMAN.)
(Act III.)

EVA	MMES. RAPPOLD
MAGDALENE	HOMER
WALTHER VON STOLZING	MM. DIPPEL
HANS SACHS	VAN ROOY
BECKMESSER	GORITZ
POGNER	BLASS
KOTHNER	MÜHLMANN
VOGELGESANG	BAYER
ZORN — MASTER	DELWARY
MOSER — SINGERS	QUESNEL
EISSLINGER	RICKER
NACHTIGALL	DUFRICHE
ORTEL	FRIEDBERG
FOLTZ	GUNTHER
SCHWARTZ	WATEROUS
DAVID	REISS
CONDUCTOR	MR. ALFRED HERTZ

SCENE 1.—Hans Sachs' Workshop.
SCENE 2.—A Meadow outside the Walls of Nuremberg.

LEONCAVALLO'S OPERA

PAGLIACCI
(IN ITALIAN.)
(Act I.)

NEDDA	MME. DEREYNE
CANIO	MM. CARUSO
TONIO	SCOTTI
PEPPE	REISS
SILVIO	SARTO
CONDUCTOR	MR. RODOLFO FERRARI

SCENE.—Outskirts of a Village in Calabria.

STAGE DIRECTORS	MR. EUGÈNE DUFRICHE
	MR. ANTON SCHERTEL
TECHNICAL DIRECTOR	MR. E. CASTEL-BERT

CHIEFS OF DEPARTMENTS.

E. CASTEL-BERT	Technical Director
EDWARD SIEDLE	Inspector of Stage
FRANK RIGO	Stage Manager
ROMEO FRANCIOLI	Masters of Ballet
GIUSEPPE BONFIGLIO	
PIETRO NEPOTI	Chorus Master
JAMES FOX	Scenic Artist
FRED HOSLI	Master Machinist
W. E. WARREN	Master Carpenter
MME. LOUISE MUSEUS	Costumer
WILLIAM PUNZEL	Wig Maker
F. G. GAUS	Electrician
W. G. SCATTERGOOD	Engineer
ANDREW BOYD	Superintendent of Building

Weber Pianos used exclusively.

Patrons would oblige the management by reporting any incivility on the part of the employees.

TELEPHONE BOOTHS in the Foyer of the Grand Tier for the convenience of the patrons.

Correct Librettos for sale in the Lobby.

Kurhaus zu Wiesbaden.

Freitag, den 8. Mai 1908, abends 8 Uhr im grossen Saale:

GROSSES KONZERT

ausgeführt von dem **städtischen Kurorchester** unter Leitung von

Gustav Mahler.

Programm: 1. Zum ersten Male: **Erste Symphonie**, Mahler. 2. Die Fingalshöhle, Konzert-Ouverture, Mendelssohn.
3. Ouverture Leonore, Nr. 3, Beethoven.

Ende gegen 10 Uhr.   Hohe Preise.   Ende gegen 10 Uhr.

Die Damen werden ergebenst ersucht, **ohne Hüte** erscheinen zu wollen.

Städtische Kurverwaltung.

Season 1907–1908

205. **March 24, 1908, 8 p.m.**[1]
NEW YORK - The Metropolitan Opera House [3,045 seats]

Annual Benefit Evening for Heinrich Conried

- (1) Puccini — *La Bohème*, Act 3 [2]
- (2) Puccini — *Madama Butterfly*, Act 1
- (3) Verdi — *Il trovatore*, Act 4, Scene 1
- (4) Gounod — *Faust*, Act 2
- (5) Beethoven — *Leonore* Overture No. 3, Op. 72b
- (6) Wagner — *Die Meistersinger von Nürnberg*, Act 3
- (7) Leoncavallo — *Pagliacci*, Act 1

CONDUCTORS (1–3, 7) R. Ferrari; (4) S. Bovy; (5) Mahler; (6) A. Hertz.
ORCHESTRA The Metropolitan Opera Orchestra.
SOURCE Handbill; see illustration on opposite page.
NOTES [1] Mahler arrived late from Philadelphia where he had conducted Wagner's *Siegfried* at a matinee the same day.
[2] The six opera extracts (1–4, 6–7) were complete staged performances.
REVIEW HLG IV, 157-158.

206. **May 8, 1908, 8 p.m.**
WIESBADEN - Großer Saal des Neuen Kurhauses [1,600 seats]

Grosses Konzert (Grand Concert)

- (1) Mahler — Symphony No. 1, D major [1]
- *- Intermission -*
- (2) Mendelssohn — *Die Hebriden* (*Fingal's Cave*), Overture, Op. 26
- (3) Beethoven — *Leonore* Overture No. 3, Op. 72b

ORCHESTRA The Wiesbaden *Kurhaus* Orchestra.
SOURCE Newspaper advertisement; see illustration on opposite page.
NOTE [1] First performance in Wiesbaden. (According to the advertisement, the audience, i.e. ladies were requested not to wear big hats.)
REVIEW HLG IV, 164-166.

JUBILEJNÍ VÝSTAVA 1908.
KONCERTNÍ SÍŇ

V sobotu dne 23. května o 7. hod. večer.

I. FILHARMONICKÝ KONCERT
výstavního orchestru.

DIRIGENT:
GUSTAV MAHLER.

POŘAD:

1. L. van Beethoven: Symfonie č. 7, A-dur, op. 92.
   a) Poco sostenuto. Vivace.
   b) Allegretto.
   c) Presto.
   d) Allegro con brio.

2. L. van Beethoven: Ouvertura ke Collinově tragedii „Koriolan", op. 62.
3. B. Smetana: Ouvertura k op. „Prodaná nevěsta".
4. R. Wagner: Předehra a Smrt z lásky z „Tristana a Isoldy".
5. „   „   Předehra k „Norimberským mistrům pěvcům".

Cena tohoto programu 10 h

V. Kotrba v Praze.

24. Program zahajovacího filharmonického koncertu pražské jubilejní výstavy, řízeného Gustavem Mahlerem

---

Verein Hamburgischer Musikfreunde.
Montag, den 9. November, abends 8 Uhr,
Musikhalle, gr. Saal (Holstenplatz):
VEREINS-KONZERT
Dirigent: **Gustav Mahler.**
Programm: 1. Beethoven: 7. Symphonie A-dur 2. Beethoven: Ouverture zu „Coriolan". 3. Tschaikowsky: Romeo und Julia Ouverture-Fantasie. 4. Wagner: Vorspiel zu Meistersinger.
Der Zutritt ist nur Vereinsmitgliedern und von diesen Eingeführten gestattet. Anmeldungen neuer Mitglieder werden bei dem Vorstand und bei Joh. Aug. Böhme entgegengenommen.
Oeffentliche Hauptprobe
Sonntag, den 8. November, mittags 12½ Uhr,
Musikhalle, gr. Saal (Holstenplatz).
Eintrittskarten zu ℳ 2.— (numeriert), ℳ 1.50 (nicht numeriert) inkl. Garderobe.

| Prague | 1908 | Concert No. 207 |

207. **May 23, 1908, 7 p.m.**
PRAGUE - The Concert Pavilion of the Exhibition Site [1,500 seats] [1]

First Philharmonic Concert in Celebration of the Chamber of Commerce and Industry's Jubilee Exhibition [2]

    (1)   Beethoven   Symphony No. 7, A major, Op. 92
                              - Intermission -
    (2)   Beethoven   Overture to *Coriolan*, Op. 62
    (3)   Smetana   Overture to *The Bartered Bride*
    (4)   Wagner   Prelude and "Liebestod," from *Tristan und Isolde*
    (5)   Wagner   Prelude to Act 1 of *Die Meistersinger von Nürnberg*

ORCHESTRA The "Exhibition Orchestra" (i.e. The Czech Philharmonic Orchestra, enhanced with 16 players from the German Theater, a total of 76 musicians).
SOURCE Handbill; see illustration on opposite page.
NOTES [1] The "Pavilion" was situated within the large exhibition site of the "Královská Obora" (i.e. The Royal Game; today the "Stromovka" Park).
[2] And to celebrate the 60th anniversary of the reign of Emperor Franz Joseph I.
REVIEW HLG IV, 177-181.

JUBILEJNÍ VÝSTAVA V PRAZE R. 1908.
KONCERTNÍ SÍŇ

V sobotu dne 19. září o 7. hod. večer.

X. (POSLEDNÍ)
FILHARMONICKÝ KONCERT

GUSTAV MAHLER:
Symfonie č. 7. (E-moll.)

První provedení vůbec.

Řídí skladatel.

I. Úvod a první věta.

II. Hudba noci. (Andante sempre sostenuto.)

III. Scherzo.

IV. Hudba noci. (Andante amoroso).

V. Rondo — Finale.

PART X
Season 1908–1909

208. September 19, 1908, 7 p.m.[1]
PRAGUE - The Concert Pavilion of the Exhibition Site [1,500 seats]

Tenth (and last) Philharmonic Concert of the Jubilee Exhibition

    Mahler   Symphony No. 7, B minor [2]

ORCHESTRA The Ausstellungs-Orchester (Exhibition Orchestra), i.e. The Czech Philharmonic Orchestra, reinforced by approximately 40 musicians from the Königliches Deutsches Landes-Theater (Royal German Theater), a total of 100 players.
SOURCE Handbill; see illustration on opposite page.
NOTES [1] The general rehearsal took place at 11 a.m. the preceding day.
[2] World premiere.
REVIEW HLG IV, 233-246.

209. October 27, 1908, 7:30 p.m.
MUNICH - Königliche Odeon [1,800 seats]

On the Occasion of The Munich Exhibition of 1908: Series "Master Conductors"

(1) Mahler   Symphony No. 7, B minor [1]
- Intermission -
(2) Wagner   Prelude and "Liebestod," from *Tristan und Isolde*
(3) Beethoven *Leonore* Overture No. 3, Op. 72b

ORCHESTRA The Munich *Tonkünstler* Orchestra, i.e. the former *Kaim* Orchestra.
SOURCE Handbill.
NOTE [1] First performance in Munich.
REVIEW HLG IV, 264-269.

210. November 9, 1908, 8 p.m.
HAMBURG - Großer Saal der Musikhalle [1,000 seats]

Concert of the Society of Music Friends in Hamburg

(1) Beethoven Symphony No. 7, A major, Op. 92
- Intermission -
(2) Beethoven Overture to *Coriolan*, Op. 62
(3) Tchaikovsky *Romeo and Juliet*, Fantasy-Overture
(4) Wagner   Prelude to Act 1 of *Die Meistersinger von Nürnberg*

ORCHESTRA The Hamburg Philharmonic Orchestra.
SOURCE Newspaper advertisement; see illustration on previous page.
REVIEW HLG IV, 285-287.

CARNEGIE HALL

The Symphony Society of New York

(Maintaining the only Orchestra in New York City which meets daily for the cultivation and study of symphonic music.)

Fifth Subscription Concert
Sunday Afternoon, November 29, 1908
at 3 o'clock

Herr Gustav Mahler
CONDUCTOR

(by invitation of Mr. Damrosch)

PROGRAM

1. SYMPHONY in B-flat, *Schumann*

   I. Andante un poco maestoso;
      Allegro molto vivace
   II. Larghetto
   III. Scherzo: Molto vivace
   IV. Finale: Allegro animato e grazioso

Program continued on second page following.

PROGRAM—Continued

2. OVERTURE, "Coriolan," . *Beethoven*

3. OVERTURE, "The Bartered Bride," *Smetana*

4. PRELUDE to "Die Meistersinger," *Wagner*

Tuesday Evening, December 8th, at 8.15
Second MAHLER Concert

Mason & Hamlin Piano Used

For explanatory notes see the Symphony Society Bulletin which is distributed at these concerts.

For special announcements see second page following

CARNEGIE HALL

The Symphony Society of New York

(Maintaining the only Orchestra in New York City which meets daily for the cultivation and study of symphonic music.)

Third Subscription Concert
Tuesday Evening, December 8, 1908
At 8.15

Herr Gustav Mahler
CONDUCTOR

(by invitation of Mr. Damrosch)

No. 1. SYMPHONY No. 2, . . *Mahler*
for Orchestra, Soprano and Alto Solos and Chorus.

(First performance in America)

1. Allegro maestoso

2. Andante moderato

Program continued on second page following.

PROGRAM—Continued

3. In a calmly flowing tempo

   (*No intermission*)

4. "The Light Eternal," very solemnly but simply

   (*No intermission*)

5. Finale

Orchestra of hundred and fifteen.
Chorus of two hundred voices from the Oratorio Society's Chorus.

Soloists:
Miss LAURA L. COMBS, . . Alto
Miss GERTRUDE STEIN-BAILEY, Soprano

Mason & Hamlin Piano Used

Sunday, December 13th
Third MAHLER Concert

For explanatory notes see Symphony Society Bulletin which is distributed at these Concerts.

For special announcements see second page following

| New York | 1908 | Concerts Nos. 211–212 |

The New York Metropolitan Opera
Season 1908–1909

211. **November 29, 1908, 3 p.m.**
NEW YORK - Carnegie Hall [2,800 seats]

    (1)   Schumann   Symphony No.1, B-flat major, Op. 38, "Spring" •
                          - Intermission -
    (2)   Beethoven   Overture to *Coriolan*, Op. 62
    (3)   Smetana   Overture to *The Bartered Bride*
    (4)   Wagner   Prelude to Act 1 of *Die Meistersinger von Nürnberg*

ORCHESTRA The New York Symphony.
SOURCE Program; see illustration on opposite page.
REVIEW HLG IV, 297-299.

212. **December 8, 1908, 8:15 p.m.**
NEW YORK - Carnegie Hall [2,800 seats]

        Mahler   Symphony No. 2, C minor, "Resurrection" [1]

SOLOISTS L. Combs and G. Stein-Bailey.
ORCHESTRA The enlarged New York Symphony (115 players).
CHORUS The New York "Oratorio Society" (200 singers, cond. Frank Damrosch).
SOURCE Program; see illustration on opposite page.
NOTE [1] American premiere. According to the review in the New York *Tribune*, the performance lasted 1 hour and 25 minutes, including two intermissions of five minutes each.
REVIEW HLG IV, 304-306.

CARNEGIE HALL

The Symphony Society of New York

(Maintaining the only Orchestra in New York City which meets daily for the cultivation and study of symphonic music.)

Sixth Subscription Concert
Sunday Afternoon, December 13, 1908
at 3 o'clock

Herr Gustav Mahler
CONDUCTOR

(by invitation of Mr. Damrosch)

PROGRAM

1. Overture, Faust - - *Wagner*
2. Overture, Oberon - - *Weber*

Program continued on second page following.

PROGRAM—Continued

3. Symphony No. 5 - *Beethoven*
   1. Allegro con brio
   2. Andante con moto
   3. Allegro (Scherzo)
   4. Allegro. Presto

Mason & Hamlin Piano Used

SUNDAY AFTERNOON, DECEMBER 27th
Holiday Program
WALTER DAMROSCH, Conductor

January 3rd and 5th First production in America of Edward Elgar's new Symphony, the first symphonic work from his pen. Soloist, Miss Geraldine Farrar of the Metropolitan Opera House.

For explanatory notes see Symphony Society Bulletin which is distributed at these concerts.

For special announcements see second page following

Metropolitan Opera House.
METROPOLITAN OPERA CO., LESSEE.
TELEPHONE BRYANT 1146.

GRAND OPERA
SEASON 1908-1909

GIULIO GATTI-CASAZZA
GENERAL MANAGER.

ANDREAS DIPPEL
ADMINISTRATIVE MANAGER.

SUNDAY EVENING, JANUARY 10, 1909
at 8.15 o'clock

GRAND SUNDAY CONCERT
FOR THE BENEFIT OF THE
EARTHQUAKE SUFFERERS
IN ITALY AND SICILY.

PROGRAM

1. —LES PRÉLUDES . . . . LISZT
   "Is our life anything else but a series of preludes to the unknown song in which Death sounds the first and solemn note?"
   METROPOLITAN OPERA HOUSE ORCHESTRA
   CONDUCTOR . . . . ALFRED HERTZ

2. —DUO from *Les Contes d' Hoffman* . . . . OFFENBACH
   MARY RANZENBERG AND MARIANNE FLAHAUT
   CONDUCTOR . . . . FRANCESCO SPETRINO

CONTINUED ON NEXT PAGE.

PROGRAMME—CONTINUED.

3. —QUARTETTE from Act III. *La Bohème* . . PUCCINI
   BERNICE DI PASQUALI, ISABELLE L'HUILLIER;
   ALESSANDRO BONCI, PASQUALE AMATO
   CONDUCTOR . . . . FRANCESCO SPETRINO

4. —DUO from Act I. *Die Walküre* . . . . . WAGNER
   OLIVE FREMSTAD AND Burgstaller
   CONDUCTOR . . . . ALFRED HERTZ

5. —DUO, "Le Crucifix" . . . . FAURE
   FÉLICIE KASCHOWSKA AND JEAN NOTÉ
   CONDUCTOR . . . . FRANCESCO SPETRINO

6. —SEXTETTE from *Lucia di Lammermoor* . DONIZETTI
   MARCELLA SEMBRICH, MARIE MATTFELD;
   ENRICO CARUSO, GIUSEPPE CAMPANARI,
   GIULIO ROSSI, ANGELO BADÀ
   CONDUCTOR . . . . FRANCESCO SPETRINO

7. —TRAUERMARSCH from *Götterdämmerung*. . WAGNER
   METROPOLITAN OPERA HOUSE ORCHESTRA
   CONDUCTOR . . . . . . ARTURO TOSCANINI

INTERMISSION

8. —OVERTURE, Leonora No. III . . . . . BEETHOVEN
   METROPOLITAN OPERA HOUSE ORCHESTRA
   CONDUCTOR . . . . GUSTAV MAHLER

9. —MISERERE from *Il Trovatore* . . . . . . VERDI
   Scoppa, ENRICO CARUSO AND CHORUS
   CONDUCTOR . . . . FRANCESCO SPETRINO

CONTINUED ON NEXT PAGE.

213. December 13, 1908, 8:15 p.m.
NEW YORK - Carnegie Hall [2,800 seats]

(1)	Wagner	*Eine Faust-Ouverture*
(2)	Weber	Overture to *Oberon* [1]
		- Intermission -
(3)	Beethoven	Symphony No. 5, C minor, Op. 67 [2]

ORCHESTRA The New York Symphony Orchestra.
SOURCE Program; see illustration on opposite page.
NOTE [1] Replaced the originally announced *Till Eulenspiegel* by Strauss.
[2] According to the December 14, 1908, *New York Tribune*, Beethoven's Seventh Symphony had initially been scheduled but was replaced by the Fifth, "probably because Mr. Mahler fancied that since Miss [Isadora] Duncan has taken to dancing the A major symphony, or rather dancing to its music, more respect could be shown to the composer by the production of a work which has not yet been enlisted in the service of Terpsichore."
REVIEW HLG IV, 312-313.

214. January 10, 1909, 8 p.m.
NEW YORK - The Metropolitan Opera House [3,045 seats]

For the Benefit of the Victims from the Earthquake at Messina [1]

(Extract of program)

(1)	Beethoven	*Leonore* Overture No. 3, Op. 72b
(2)	Mozart	"La ci darem la mano," from *Don Giovanni*

SOLOISTS (2) G. Farrar & A. Scotti.
ORCHESTRA The Metropolitan Opera Orchestra.
SOURCE Handbill and various newspapers reviews; see illustration on opposite page.
NOTE [1] On the Italian island of Sicily, on December 28, 1908.
REVIEW HLG IV, 345.

215. February 6, 1909, 8 p.m.
NEW YORK - The Metropolitan Opera House [3,045 seats]

Farewell Performance for Marcella Sembrich

(1)	Donizetti	*Don Pasquale*, Act 1 [1]
(2)	Rossini	*Il barbieri di Siviglia*, Act 2 [1]
(3)	Verdi	*La traviata*, Act 1 [1]
(4)	Mozart	March from *Le nozze di Figaro*

CONDUCTORS (4) Mahler.
ORCHESTRA The Metropolitan Opera Orchestra.
SOURCE Handbill and various newspapers reviews; see illustration on following page.
NOTE [1] A complete stage performance.
REVIEW HLG IV, 343.

Metropolitan Opera House.

METROPOLITAN OPERA CO., LESSEE.
TELEPHONE BRYANT 1146.

GRAND OPERA
SEASON 1908-1909

GIULIO GATTI-CASAZZA
GENERAL MANAGER.

ANDREAS DIPPEL
ADMINISTRATIVE MANAGER.

SATURDAY EVENING, FEBRUARY 6, 1909,
at 8 o'clock

Farewell Appearance in Opera and 25th Anniversary of

MARCELLA SEMBRICH

PROGRAM

DON PASQUALE

OPERA-COMIQUE IN THREE ACTS.
MUSIC by DONIZETTI
Book by M. A.
(IN ITALIAN)
(ACT I.)

NORINA . . . . MARCELLA SEMBRICH

DOTTORE MALATESTA . . . . . . ANTONIO SCOTTI

SCENE.—The Apartment of Norina.

CONTINUED ON NEXT PAGE.

CARNEGIE HALL
Wednesday Evening, March 31, 1909
At 8.15 o'clock

Gustav Mahler

AND

New York Philharmonic Society
OF ONE HUNDRED

Management: HENRY WOLFSOHN

I.

Overture "Manfred" - *Schumann*

II.

Symphony No. 7, A major, Op. 92
Beethoven
Poco sostenuto—Vivace
Allegretto
Presto—presto meno assai
Allegro con brio

III.

a. Siegfried Idyll
b. Overture "Tannhauser"
Wagner

CARNEGIE HALL
Tuesday Evening, April 6, 1909
At 8.15 o'clock

Gustav Mahler

AND

New York Philharmonic Society
OF ONE HUNDRED

SOLOISTS:
MRS. RIDER-KELSEY, Soprano
MISS JANET SPENCER, Contralto
MR. DANIEL BEDDOE, Tenor
MR. HERBERT WATROUS, Basso

Bach Choir of Montclair, two hundred and fifty voices.
MR. FRANK TAFT, Director

Management: HENRY WOLFSOHN

Program

I.

OVERTURE "Egmont" - *Beethoven*

Program continued on second page following.

PROGRAM—Continued

II.

SYMPHONY No. 9, D. minor   *Beethoven*

Allegro ma non troppo, un poco maestoso molto vivace—
Adagio molto e cantabile

Presto—Allegro assai

Recitative—Allegro assai

For special announcements see second page following

| New York | 1909 | Concerts Nos. 216–217 |

216. **March 31, 1909, 8:15 p.m.**
NEW YORK - Carnegie Hall [2,800 seats]

First "Festival Concert" [1]

- (1) Schumann — Overture to *Manfred*, Op. 115
- (2) Beethoven — Symphony No. 7, A major, Op. 92
  - Intermission -
- (3) Wagner — *Siegfried Idyll*
- (4) Wagner — Overture to *Tannhäuser*

ORCHESTRA The New York Philharmonic Orchestra (a total of 100 players, including reinforcements).
SOURCE Program; see illustration on opposite page.
NOTE [1] To acquaint Mahler with "his" new orchestra (the Philharmonic) and vice versa, two "Festival" concerts were arranged (by impresario Henry Wolfsohn). It was understood that Mahler would judge the orchestra's standard himself, and assess the capabilities of each individual player. For each concert Mahler was only granted 2–3 days for rehearsals.
REVIEW HLG IV, 384-390; ZR II, 233–235.

217. **April 6, 1909, 8:15 p.m.**
NEW YORK - Carnegie Hall [2,800 seats]

Second "Festival Concert"

- (1) Beethoven — Overture to *Egmont*, Op. 84
- (2) Beethoven — Symphony No. 9, D minor, Op. 125

SOLOISTS (2) C. Rider-Kelsey, J. Spencer, D. Beddoe, H. Watrous.
ORCHESTRA The New York Philharmonic Orchestra.
CHORUS The "Bach Choir of Montclair" (250 voices, cond. C. Dickinson).
SOURCE Program; see illustration on opposite page.
REVIEW HLG IV, 390-394; ZR II, 234–235.

* * *

PROGRAMMA

VAN HET

EERSTE ABONNEMENTS-CONCERT

ONDER LEIDING VAN DE HEEREN

GUSTAV MAHLER en WILLEM MENGELBERG.

ZATERDAG 2 OCTOBER 1909 — 8 UUR.

1. Symphonie No. 7 .... Gustav Mahler.
(Geb. 1860)
   A. Einleitung: Langsam. Erster Satz: Allegro con fuoco.
   B. Nachtmusik: Allegro moderato.
   C. Scherzo: Schattenhaft.
   D. Nachtmusik: Andante amoroso.
   E. Rondo finale: Allegro.

   (Eerste uitvoering in Nederland.)

— PAUZE —

2. Symphonie No. 1 (C gr. t.) .... L. v. Beethoven.
(1770—1827)
   A. Adagio molto. Allegro con brio.
   B. Andante cantabile con moto.
   C. Menuetto: Allegro molto e vivace. Trio: Menuetto da capo.
   D. Adagio. Allegro molto e vivace.

218

PROGRAMMA

VAN HET

ABONNEMENTS-CONCERT

ONDER LEIDING VAN DEN HEER

GUSTAV MAHLER.

DONDERDAG 7 OCTOBER 1909 — 8 UUR:

1. Voorspel van de Opera „Die Meistersinger von Nürnberg" .... R. Wagner.
(1813—1883)

2. Symphonie No. 7 .... Gustav Mahler.
(Geb. 1860)
   A. Einleitung: Langsam. Erster Satz: Allegro con fuoco.
   B. Nachtmusik: Allegro moderato.
   C. Scherzo: Schattenhaft.
   D. Nachtmusik: Andante amoroso.
   E. Rondo finale: Allegro.

220

| The Hague–Amsterdam | 1909 | Concerts Nos. 218–220 |

Part XI
Season 1909–1910

218. October 2, 1909, 8 p.m.
THE HAGUE - Gebouw van Kunst en Wetenschappen [2,600 seats]

First Subscription Concert

(1) Mahler   Symphony No. 7, B minor [1]
- Intermission -
(2) Beethoven   Symphony No. 1, C major, Op. 21

ORCHESTRA The Amsterdam Concertgebouw Orchestra.
CONDUCTORS (1) Mahler; (2) W. Mengelberg.
SOURCE Handbill; see illustration on opposite page.
NOTE [1] First performance in Holland.
REVIEW HLG IV, 536-538.

219. October 3, 1909, 2:30 p.m.
AMSTERDAM - Concertgebouw [1,800 seats]

Subscription Concert

- Above concert repeated -

SOURCE Handbill.
REVIEW HLG IV, 538-544.

220. October 7, 1909, 8 p.m.
AMSTERDAM - Concertgebouw [1,800 seats]

Subscription Concert

(1) Wagner   Prelude to Act 1 of *Die Meistersinger von Nürnberg*
(2) Mahler   Symphony No. 7, B minor •

ORCHESTRA The Concertgebouw Orchestra.
SOURCE Handbill; see illustration on opposite page.
REVIEW HLG IV, 538-544.

* * *

The New York Philharmonic Society's
Sixty-Eighth Season
1909–1910

For his first season Mahler drew up 24 programs which were divided into four cycles. All concerts were given at Carnegie Hall, which seated an audience of 2,800.

(a) 8 pairs of *Regular Subscription Concerts,* on Thursday evenings (repeated in the afternoon of the following day) approximately every third week.
(b) 6 *Historical Concerts,* on Wednesday evenings.
(c) 5 *Beethoven Concerts,* on Friday afternoons.
(d) 5 *Sunday Afternoon Concerts,* at popular prices (tickets $ .50–$1.00).

Eventually the *Beethoven Cycle* and the *Sunday Afternoon Cycle* were expanded by one extra concert each. Five additional concerts were given at the "The Academy of Music" in Brooklyn, and a benefit concert for the orchestra's Pension Fund was organized at the end of the season as well as a benefit concert for the Bryson Day Nursery.

The orchestra's first-ever out-of-town tour resulted in one concert each in Boston, New Haven, Providence, and Springfield, in addition to two visits to Philadelphia. The final total of concerts in Mahler's first season amounted to 47 concerts.

*

At the close of this season Mahler also bade his final farewell to the opera stage with the American premiere of Tchaikovsky's *Pique Dame* at The Metropolitan Opera, which took place on March 5, 9, 17, and 21, 1910.

*

CARNEGIE HALL

THE PHILHARMONIC SOCIETY
OF NEW YORK

1909—Sixty-eighth Season—1910

Conductor: GUSTAV MAHLER

First Evening Concert
  Thursday, November 4th, 1909
  At 8.15 o'clock

First Afternoon Concert
  Friday, November 5th, 1909
  At 2.30 o'clock

OF THE

FIRST SERIES

PROGRAM

1. *Beethoven*, Overture, Op. 124, "Consecration of the House"

2. *Beethoven*, Symphony No. 3, Op. 55, "Eroica"
   - I. Allegro con brio, E-flat major 3-4
   - II. Marcia Funebre, Adagio assai, C minor, 2-4
   - III. Scherzo, Allegro vivace, E-flat major, 3-4
   - IV. Finale, Allegro Molto, E-flat, 2-4

Program continued on second page following

PROGRAM—Continued.

3. *Strauss*, "Till Eulenspiegel's Merry Pranks"

4. *Liszt*, A Symphonic Poem (After Victor Hugo's "Mazeppa")

For special announcements see second page following

THE PHILHARMONIC SOCIETY
OF NEW YORK

GUSTAV MAHLER
CONDUCTOR

TO-MORROW EVENING
Wednesday, November 10th, at 8.15

The First of a

Series of Historical Concerts
Arranged in Chronological Order
Beginning with
SEVENTEENTH CENTURY COMPOSERS

At this Concert
MR. MAHLER will play the Bach Klavier in the Compositions of Bach and Handel

SOLOISTS
MR. THEODORE SPIERING, Violin
MME. RIDER-KELSEY, Soprano
ARTHUR S. HYDE, Organist

Special Announcement
First Concert of the BEETHOVEN CYCLE
Friday Afternoon, November 19th, at 2.30

The SUNDAY AFTERNOON Series of Concerts
Begins November 21st, at 3

| New York | 1909 | Concerts Nos. 221–223 |

221. **November 4, 1909, 8:15 p.m.**
222. **November 5, 1909, 2:30 p.m.**
NEW YORK - Carnegie Hall [2,800 seats]

First Regular Subscription Concert

(1)	Beethoven	*Die Weihe des Hauses*, Overture, Op. 124 •
(2)	Beethoven	Symphony No. 3, E-flat major, Op. 55, "Eroica"
(3)	Strauss	*Till Eulenspiegels lustige Streiche*, Op. 28
(4)	Liszt	*Mazeppa*, Symphonic Poem

SOURCE Program; see illustration on opposite page.
REVIEW HLG IV, 561-566.

223. **November 10, 1909, 8:15 p.m.**
NEW YORK - Carnegie Hall [2,800 seats]

First Historical Concert [1]

(1)	Bach–Mahler	Suite for Orchestra [2]
(2)	Handel	"Quanto dolci, quanto care," from *Flavio, Re di Longobardi*
(3)	Bach	Violin Concerto No. 2, E major, BWV 1042 •
(4)	Rameau	*Rigaudon*, Ballet from the Opera *Dardanus*
(5)	Grétry	"C'est ici le beau Céphale ... Naissantes fleurs," from *Céphale et Procris* •
(6)	Haydn	Symphony No. 104, D major, "London" •

SOLOISTS (2 & 5) C. Rider-Kelsey; (3) T. Spiering.
SOURCE Program; see illustration on opposite page.
NOTES [1] Mahler's original program draft included Handel's Concerto Grosso in B minor, Op. 6, No. 12, Bach's Overtures or Suites No. 2 in B minor, and No. 3 in D major, Rameau's Rigaudon, Gluck's Overture to *Iphigenie en Aulide,* and finally some unspecified songs (Roman, p. 271).
[2] World premiere. A later program booklet (concert no. 274) notes that "Mr. Mahler has compiled the present work from [Bach's] second and third Suites, and added to the contrast of keys thus obtained other effects by making some changes in the orchestration. He has also written out the *continuo,* which he plays upon a pianoforte with its action modified so as to produce a tone like that of the old harpsichord, but louder." In December of the same year Mahler sold his arrangement to the New York publisher G. Schirmer, who published the score and the parts in March 1910.
REVIEW HLG IV, 567-568.

CARNEGIE HALL

THE PHILHARMONIC SOCIETY
OF NEW YORK

1909—Sixty-eighth Season—1910

GUSTAV MAHLER - - Conductor

Friday Afternoon, November 19, 1909
At 2.30

FIRST CONCERT

OF THE

BEETHOVEN CYCLE

PROGRAM

SYMPHONY No. 2, D Major, Op. 36

1. Adagio molto, D Major, 3-4 time
   and Allegro con brio, D Major, 4-4 time
2. Larghetto, A Major, 3-8 time
3. Scherzo and Trio, Allegro, D Major, 3-4 time
4. Finale; Allegro molto, D Major, alla-breva

Program continued on second page following

CARNEGIE HALL

THE PHILHARMONIC SOCIETY
OF NEW YORK

1909—Sixty-eighth Season—1910

GUSTAV MAHLER - - Conductor

Sunday Afternoon, November 21, 1909
At 3

Soloist:
CHARLES GILIBERT

PROGRAM

SYMPHONY No. 3, "Eroica," Op. 55   Beethoven
  I. Allegro con brio, E-flat Major, 3-4
  II. Marcia Funebre, Adagio Assai, C Minor, 2-4
  III. Scherzo, Allegro Vivace, E-flat major, 3-4
  IV. Finale; Allegro Molto, E-flat, 2-4

a. RECITATIVE and LARGO, "Xerxes"   Handel
b. ARIA, "La Jolie Fille de Perth"   Bizet
c. LEGENDE, "Le Jongleur de Notre Dame"
                                     Massenet
    Mr. GILLIBERT

FUNERAL MARCH, "Die Goetterdæmmerung"
                                     Wagner

PRELUDE, "Die Meistersinger"   Wagner

CARNEGIE HALL

THE PHILHARMONIC SOCIETY
OF NEW YORK

1909—Sixty-eighth Season—1910

GUSTAV MAHLER - - Conductor

Second Thursday Evening Concert
NOVEMBER 25, at 8.15 o'clock
Second Friday Afternoon Concert
NOVEMBER 26, at 2.30 o'clock

OF THE

FIRST SERIES

Soloist: **MME. TERESA CARRENO**

PROGRAM

1. BRAHMS—Symphony No. 3, F Major, Op. 90
    I. Allegro con brio, F Major, 6-4 time
    II. Andante, C Major, 4-4 time
    III. Poco Allegretto, C Minor, 3-8 time
    IV. Allegro, F Minor, 2-2 time

Program continued on second page following

PROGRAM—Continued.

2. BACH—Suite for Orchestra
    I. Overture, B Minor
    II. Rondeau, B minor; Badiniere, B Minor
    III. Air, D Major

Mr. MAHLER will play the Bach Klavier in this composition

Mr. ARTHUR S. HYDE, Organist

3. WEBER—Concertstueck, in F Minor, for Pianoforte

4. DUKAS—"L'Apprenti Sorcier"

THE BACH KLAVIER is furnished by the courtesy of Steinway & Sons

MME. CARRENO PLAYS THE EVERETT PIANO

For special announcements see second page following

| New York | 1909 | Concerts Nos. 224–227 |

224. **November 19, 1909, 3 p.m.**
NEW YORK - Carnegie Hall [2,800 seats]

First Beethoven Concert [1]

- (1) Symphony No. 2, D major, Op. 36 •
- (2) *Leonore* Overture No. 3, Op. 72b
  - Intermission -
- (3) Overture to *Fidelio*, Op. 72 •
- (4) *Leonore* Overture No. 1, Op. 138 •
- (5) *Leonore* Overture No. 2, Op. 72a •

SOURCE Program; see illustration on opposite page.
NOTE [1] According to the reviews the order listed in the program booklet was changed.
REVIEW HLG IV, 570-572.

225. **November 21, 1909, 3 p.m.**
NEW YORK - Carnegie Hall [2,800 seats]

First Sunday Afternoon Concert [1]

- (1) Beethoven — Symphony No. 3, E-flat major, Op. 55, "Eroica"
- (2) Handel — "Ombra mai fu," from *Xerxes* •
- (3) Bizet — "Quand la flamme," from *La Jolie fille de Perth* •
- (4) Massenet — "Légende," from *Le jongleur de Notre-Dame* •
- (5) Wagner — "Siegfried's Tod," Funeral March, from *Götterdämmerung*
- (6) Wagner — Prelude to Act 1 of *Die Meistersinger von Nürnberg*

SOLOIST (2–4) C. Gilibert.
SOURCE Program; see illustration on opposite page.
NOTE [1] Mahler's original program draft included Beethoven's *Leonore* Overture No. 3, and *Eroica* Symphony, and Wagner's *Tristan* Prelude and *Meistersinger* Prelude (Roman, p. 269).
REVIEW HLG IV, 572-573.

226. **November 25, 1909, 8:15 p.m.**
227. **November 26, 1909, 2:30 p.m.**
NEW YORK - Carnegie Hall [2,800 seats]

Second Regular Subscription Concert [1]

- (1) Brahms — Symphony No. 3, F major, Op. 90
- (2) Bach–Mahler — Suite for Orchestra
- (3) Weber — *Konzertstück*, F minor, Op. 79, for Piano and Orch. •
- (4) Dukas — *L'Apprenti sorcier*, Scherzo after Goethe's Ballad •

SOLOIST (3) M. T. Carreño.
SOURCE Program; see illustration on opposite page.
NOTE [1] Mahler's original program draft included Goldmark's overture *Sakuntala* instead of the Bach–Mahler Suite.
REVIEW HLG IV, 574-575.

The Philharmonic Society
of New York

1909... SIXTY-EIGHTH SEASON ...1910

Gustav Mahler ... Conductor

FRIDAY, DECEMBER 3,
AT 8.15 P. M.

...AT THE...
Academy of Music, Brooklyn

RICHARD ARNOLD,
Administrative Manager

FELIX F. LEIFELS,
Business Manager

Programme

BEETHOVEN. . . . . Symphony No. 5, C Minor

BEETHOVEN. Overture, . . . "Leonore" No. 3

MENDELSSOHN. . . . . . . Violin Concerto

WAGNER. Prelude, ... "Die Meistersinger"

SOLOIST
MAUD POWELL
VIOLIN

PRINTED BY STYLES & CASH
NEW YORK.

CARNEGIE HALL

THE PHILHARMONIC SOCIETY
OF NEW YORK

1909—Sixty-eighth Season—1910

GUSTAV MAHLER - - Conductor

Wednesday, December 8, at 8.15 o'clock
SECOND HISTORICAL CONCERT

Soloist: BELLA ALTEN, Soprano

Program

1. MOZART—Symphony, C major "Jupiter"

    I. Allegro vivace, C major, 4-4 time;

    II. Andante cantabile, F major, 3-4 time;

    III. Minuet: Allegretto, C major, 3-4 and Trio;

    IV. Finale, Allegro molto, C major, 2-2 time.

Program continued on second page following

PROGRAM— Continued.

2. a. HAYDN—Aria from "The Creation," "On Mighty Pens"

    b. MOZART—Aria of Susanne, from "Le Nozze Di Figaro"

3. BEETHOVEN—Symphony No. 5, C minor

    I. Allegro con brio, C minor, 2-4 time;

    II. Andante con moto, A-flat major, 3-8 time;

    III. Allegro, C minor, Trio C major, 3-4 time;
    Finale, Allegro, C major, 4-4 time.

For special announcements see second page following

228. December 3, 1909, 8:15 p.m.
BROOKLYN - The Academy of Music [2,086 seats]

(1)	Beethoven	Symphony No. 5, C minor, Op. 67
(2)	Beethoven	*Leonore* Overture No. 3, Op. 72b
(3)	Mendelssohn	Violin Concerto, E minor, Op. 64
(4)	Wagner	Prelude to Act 1 of *Die Meistersinger von Nürnberg*

SOLOIST (3) M. Powell.
SOURCE Program; see illustration on opposite page.
REVIEW HLG IV, 575-580.

229. December 8, 1909, 8:15 p.m.
NEW YORK - Carnegie Hall [2,800 seats]

Second Historical Concert [1]

(1)	Mozart	Symphony No. 41, C major, "Jupiter," K. 551 •
(2)	Haydn	"Auf starkem Fittiche," from *Die Schöpfung* •
(3)	Mozart	"Deh vieni, non tardar," from *Le nozze di Figaro* [2]
(4)	Beethoven	Symphony No. 5, C minor, Op. 67

SOLOIST (2 & 3) B. Alten.
SOURCE Program; see illustration on opposite page.
NOTES [1] Mahler's original program draft included a Haydn symphony in D minor (perhaps No. 80?), Mozart's Serenade "Notturno" (possibly K. 239), and Beethoven's Fifth Symphony.
[2] Sung in German, "Endlich naht sich die Stunde."
REVIEW HLG IV, 577-580.

230. December 12, 1909, 3 p.m.
NEW YORK - Carnegie Hall [2,800 seats]

Second Sunday Afternoon Concert [1]

(1)	Beethoven	Symphony No. 5, C minor, Op. 67
(2)	Liszt	Piano Concerto No. 2, A major •
(3)	Strauss	*Till Eulenspiegels lustige Streiche*, Op. 28
(4)	Dvořák	Scherzo capriccioso, Op. 66 •

SOLOIST (2) Y. Mero.
SOURCE Program; see illustration on following page.
NOTE [1] Mahler's original program draft did not include the Liszt Concerto, but Franck's Symphonic Variations, and the Bach–Mahler Suite was considered as an alternative to Beethoven's Fifth Symphony (Roman, p. 270).
REVIEW HLG IV, 586.

CARNEGIE HALL

THE PHILHARMONIC SOCIETY
OF NEW YORK

1909—Sixty-eighth Season—1910

GUSTAV MAHLER - - Conductor

December 12, at 3 o'clock
Second Sunday Afternoon Concert

Soloist: YOLANDA MERO, Piano

PROGRAM

1. BEETHOVEN—Symphony No. 5, C minor

    I. Allegro con brio, C minor, 2-4 time;

    II. Andante con moto, A-flat major, 3-8 time;

    III. Allegro, C minor, Trio C major, 3-4 time;
    Finale, Allegro, C major, 4-4 time.

Program continued on second page following

CARNEGIE HALL

THE PHILHARMONIC SOCIETY
OF NEW YORK

1909—Sixty-eighth Season—1910

GUSTAV MAHLER - - Conductor

Thursday Evening, December 16, at 8.15
—AND—
Friday Afternoon, December 17, at 2.30

Third Concerts of the
FIRST SERIES

PROGRAM

SCHUBERT—Symphony in B minor (Unfinished)

BEETHOVEN—Overture, "Coriolan"

MAHLER—Symphony No. 1, in D major

CARNEGIE HALL

THE PHILHARMONIC SOCIETY
OF NEW YORK

1909—Sixty-eighth Season—1910

GUSTAV MAHLER - - Conductor

Wednesday Evening, December 29
At 8.15 o'clock

—THIRD CONCERT OF THE—
Historical Cycle

Soloist: MAUD POWELL, Violin

Program

SCHUBERT—Symphony in B minor (Unfinished)

    I. Allegro moderato, B minor, 3-4 time

    II. Andante con moto, E major, 3-8 time

Program continued on second page following

CARNEGIE HALL

THE PHILHARMONIC SOCIETY
OF NEW YORK

1909—Sixty-eighth Season—1910

GUSTAV MAHLER - - Conductor

Friday Afternoon, December 31, 1909
At 2.30 o'clock

SECOND BEETHOVEN CONCERT

Soloist - - - MAUD POWELL

PROGRAM

1. a. Overture, "Egmont"
   b. Overture, "Coriolan"

2. Concerto for Violin

Program continued on second page following

231. December 16, 1909, 8:15 p.m.
232. December 17, 1909, 2:30 p.m.
NEW YORK - Carnegie Hall [2,800 seats]

Third Regular Subscription Concert

(1) Schubert — Symphony No. 8 (7), B minor, D 759, "Unfinished" [1]
(2) Beethoven — Overture to *Coriolan*, Op. 62 [2]
(3) Mahler — Symphony No. 1, D major • [3]

SOURCE Program; see illustration on opposite page.
NOTES [1] The preview in the program booklet of December 12 promises Mozart's *Jupiter* Symphony.
[2] Not included in Mahler's original program draft, which lists "Moldau" from Smetana's *Má vlast*.
[3] American premiere and Mahler's last performances of this symphony.
REVIEW HLG IV, 586-594.

233. December 29, 1909, 8:15 p.m.
NEW YORK - Carnegie Hall [2,800 seats]

Third Historical Concert

(1) Schubert — Symphony No. 8 (7), B minor, D 759, "Unfinished"
(2) Mendelssohn — Violin Concerto, E minor, Op. 64
(3) Schumann — Symphony No. 4, D minor, Op. 120

SOLOIST (2) M. Powell.
SOURCE Program; see illustration on opposite page.
REVIEW HLG IV, 598-599.

234. December 31, 1909, 2:30 p.m.
NEW YORK - Carnegie Hall [2,800 seats]

Second Beethoven Concert

(1) Overture to *Egmont*, Op. 84
(2) Overture to *Coriolan*, Op. 62
(3) Violin Concerto, D major, Op. 61
(4) Symphony No. 4, B-flat major, Op. 60 •

SOLOIST (3) M. Powell.
SOURCE Program; see illustration on opposite page.
REVIEW HLG IV, 600-601; ZR II, 322.

CARNEGIE HALL

THE PHILHARMONIC SOCIETY

OF NEW YORK

1909—Sixty-eighth Season—1910

GUSTAV MAHLER - - Conductor

Thursday Evening, January 6, at 8.15
—AND—
Friday Afternoon, January 7, at 2.30

FOURTH CONCERTS
OF THE FIRST SERIES

Soloist: BUSONI - - - Piano
(His first appearance this season)

PROGRAM

BERLIOZ—Symphony, "Fantastic"

I. Largo, C minor, 4-4 time; Allegro agitato e appassionato assai, C major, 4-4 time.
II. Allegro non troppo, A major, 3-8.
III. Adagio, F major, 6-8 time.
IV. Allegretto non troppo, G minor and B-flat major, 4-4.
V. Larghetto, C major, 4-4 and allegro, E-flat major, C major and C minor and C major, 6-8.

Program continued on second page following

235 & 236

Saturday, January 8th, 1910
at 8:15 P. M.

SECOND CONCERT

OF THE

New York Philharmonic Society

AT THE

ACADEMY OF MUSIC
BROOKLYN

Gustav Mahler
CONDUCTOR

SOLOIST

BUSONI
PIANO

237

CARNEGIE HALL

THE PHILHARMONIC SOCIETY

OF NEW YORK

1909—Sixty-eighth Season—1910

GUSTAV MAHLER - - Conductor

Friday Afternoon, January 14, 1910
At 2.30 o'clock

THIRD
BEETHOVEN MATINEE

PROGRAM

SYMPHONY No. 6, "Pastoral"

I. Allegro ma non troppo, F major, 2-4;
II. Andante molto moto, B-flat major, 12-8;
III. Allegro, F major, 3-4 and A tempo allegro 2-4;
IV. Allegro, F minor, 4-4;
V. Allegretto, F major, 6-8.

Program continued on second page following

238

THE BULLETIN OF THE BROOKLYN INSTITUTE OF ARTS AND SCIENCES

BROOKLYN CONSERVATORY OF MUSIC
FRANKLIN AVENUE AND LEFFERTS PLACE
PHONE 3753-J PROSPECT

GRAHAM REED	Voice Culture	ADOLF WHITELAW	Violin
LLOYD RAND	Voice Culture	CLARENCE EDDY	Organ
MME. M. DEYO	Piano	AUGUST WALTHER	Harmony
IRWIN HASSELL	Piano	HANS KRONOLD	'Cello
EUGENE BERNSTEIN	Piano	HENRY GAINES HAWN	Dramatic Art

Sight Singing, Orchestral Instruments, Mandolin and Guitar
28 Instructors. Over 460 Students. ADOLF WHITELAW, Director
INSTRUMENTAL TUITION, FROM $15 FOR 20 LESSONS. VOCAL TUITION, FROM $20 FOR 20 LESSONS. Send for New Catalogue and Free Concert Tickets

BROOKLYN ACADEMY OF MUSIC

Five Concerts by the

PHILHARMONIC SOCIETY OF NEW YORK

December 3   January 8   January 28   February 11
March 18, at 8.15 P. M.

CONDUCTOR

Mr. GUSTAV MAHLER

and the

Entire Philharmonic Orchestra

Soloists:

MAUD POWELL   DR. WUELLNER
TILLY KOENEN   FERRUCCIO BUSONI

Subscriptions now open at the Brooklyn Academy of Music

228, 237, 244, 249 & 263

235. **January 6, 1910, 8:15 p.m.**
236. **January 7, 1910, 2:30 p.m.**
NEW YORK - Carnegie Hall [2,800 seats]

Fourth Regular Subscription Concert

(1) Berlioz — *Symphonie fantastique*, Op. 14
(2) Beethoven — Piano Concerto No. 5, E-flat major, Op. 73, "Emperor" [1]
(3) Wagner — Prelude to Act 1 of *Die Meistersinger von Nürnberg*

SOLOIST (2) F. Busoni.
SOURCE Program; see illustration on opposite page.
NOTE [1] Replaced the originally announced Schubert–Liszt "Wanderer" Fantasy.
REVIEW HLG IV, 631-636.

237. **January 8, 1910, 8:15 p.m.**
BROOKLYN - The Academy of Music [2,086 seats]

(1) Bach–Mahler — Suite for Orchestra
(2) Beethoven — Piano Concerto No. 5, E-flat major, Op. 73, "Emperor" [1]
(3) Wagner — Prelude and "Liebestod," from *Tristan und Isolde*
(4) Strauss — *Till Eulenspiegels lustige Streiche*, Op. 28

SOLOIST (2) F. Busoni.
SOURCE Program; see illustration on opposite page.
NOTE [1] One critic mistakenly reports that Beethoven's Concerto was replaced by Schubert–Liszt's "Wanderer" Fantasy for Piano and Orchestra although it was announced in the program booklet.
REVIEW HLG IV, 638.

238. **January 14, 1910, 3:30 p.m.**
NEW YORK - Carnegie Hall [2,800 seats]

Third Beethoven Concert

(1) Symphony No. 6, F major, Op. 68, "Pastoral"
 - Intermission -
(2) Symphony No. 5, C minor, Op. 67

SOURCE Program; see illustration on opposite page.
REVIEW HLG IV, 639-642; ZR II, 327–328.

CARNEGIE HALL

THE PHILHARMONIC SOCIETY
OF NEW YORK

1909—Sixty-eighth Season—1910

GUSTAV MAHLER - - Conductor

Sunday Afternoon, January 16, 1910
At 3 o'clock

Soloist: RACHMANINOFF, Piano

PROGRAM

BACH—Suite for Orchestra, by general request
(Mr. Mahler plays the Bach Klavier in this Suite.)

RACHMANINOFF—Piano Concerto No. 3

Program continued on second page following

The Philharmonic Society
of New York

1909... SIXTY-EIGHTH SEASON ...1910

Gustav Mahler ... Conductor

MONDAY, JANUARY 17
AT 8:15 P. M.

First Concert
AT THE
Academy of Music
PHILADELPHIA

Programme

BEETHOVEN . . . . . Symphony No. 5, C minor

SMETANA. Overture . . . "The Bartered Bride"

STRAUSS . . . . "Till Eulenspiegel"

WAGNER. Prelude . . . . "Der Meistersinger"

PRINTED BY STYLES & CASH
NEW YORK

CARNEGIE HALL

THE PHILHARMONIC SOCIETY
OF NEW YORK

1909—Sixty-eighth Season—1910

GUSTAV MAHLER - - - Conductor

Thursday Evening, January 20, at 8.15
—AND—
Friday Afternoon, January 21, at 2.30

**FIFTH CONCERTS
OF THE FIRST SERIES**

PROGRAM

TSCHAIKOWSKY—Symphony No. 6, B minor, "Pathetique"

I. Introduction, Adagio, B minor, 4-4; Allegro non troppo, B minor, 4-4;

II. Allegro con grazia, D major, 5-4;

III. Allegro molto vivace, G major, 4-4, and 12-8;

IV. Finale, Adagio lamentoso, B minor, 3-4.

Program continued on second page following

239. January 16, 1910, 3 p.m.
NEW YORK - Carnegie Hall [2,800 seats]

Third Sunday Afternoon Concert

    (1) Bach–Mahler   Suite for Orchestra
    (2) Rachmaninoff   Piano Concerto No. 3, D minor, Op. 30 ● [1]
    (3) Wagner   Prelude and "Liebestod," from *Tristan und Isolde*
    (4) Smetana   Overture to *The Bartered Bride*

SOLOIST (2) S. Rachmaninoff.
SOURCE Program; see illustration on opposite page.
NOTE [1] The world premiere of the concerto, with the composer as soloist, had taken place in New York on November 28, 1909 (and repeated on the 30th), with the New York Symphony Orchestra conducted by Walter Damrosch.
REVIEW HLG IV, 642-644; ZR II, 329–330.

240. January 17, 1910, 8:15 p.m.
PHILADELPHIA - The Academy of Music [2,900 seats]

    (1) Beethoven   Symphony No. 5, C minor, Op. 67
    (2) Smetana   Overture to *The Bartered Bride*
    (3) Strauss   *Till Eulenspiegels lustige Streiche*, Op. 28
    (4) Wagner   Prelude to Act 1 of *Die Meistersinger von Nürnberg*

SOURCE Program; see illustration on opposite page.
REVIEW HLG IV, 645-647; ZR II, 330–331.

241. January 20, 1910, 8:15 p.m.
242. January 21, 1910, 2:30 p.m.
NEW YORK - Carnegie Hall [2,800 seats]

Fifth Regular Subscription Concert [1]

    (1) Tchaikovsky   Symphony No. 6, B minor, Op. 74, "Pathétique"
    (2) Wagner   Prelude and "Liebestod," from *Tristan und Isolde*
    (3) Smetana   Overture to *The Bartered Bride*

SOURCE Program; see illustration on opposite page.
NOTE [1] Mahler's original program draft included Mozart's Symphony No. 40, Schumann's Overture to *Manfred*, and Berlioz's *Symphonie fantastique*.
REVIEW HLG IV, 648-651; ZR II, 332–333.

CARNEGIE HALL

THE PHILHARMONIC SOCIETY
OF NEW YORK

1909—Sixty-eighth Season—1910

GUSTAV MAHLER - - Conductor

Wednesday Evening, January 26, 1910
At 8.15 o'clock

FOURTH HISTORICAL CONCERT

Soloist, **Dr. LUDWIG WÜLLNER**, Baritone

Program

BRAHMS—Symphony No. 3, F major, Op. 90

    I. Allegro con brio, F major, 6-4 time;

    II. Andante, C major, 4-4;

    III. Poco Allegretto, C minor, 3-8;

    IV. Allegro, F minor, 2-2.

Program continued on second page following

PROGRAM—Continued.

SONGS—

MAHLER—Five Children's Death-Songs

    Note.—On the fly-leaf of the score of these "Children's Death-Songs" appears a note, which, translated, reads as follows: "The five songs are conceived as a unit, an indivisible whole, and their continuity at a performance should be preserved by the prohibition of interruptions of any kind; applause, for instance, at the end of a number."

DVOŘÁK—Overture, "In Nature"

SONGS—

WEINGARTNER—"Erdriese"

WEINGARTNER—"Letzter Tanz"

H. WOLF—"Anakreon's Grab"

H. WOLF—"Der Rattenfänger"

SMETANA—Overture, "The Bartered Bride"

The **Steinway** is the official **Piano** used by the Philharmonic Society.

For special announcements see second page following

The Philharmonic Society of New York

1909 - SIXTY-EIGHTH SEASON - 1910

GUSTAV MAHLER
CONDUCTOR

FRIDAY, JANUARY 28th, at 8.15 P. M.
THIRD CONCERT
AT THE
ACADEMY OF MUSIC, BROOKLYN

Soloist: Dr. **LUDWIG WUELLNER**, Baritone

PROGRAMME

Beethoven, Overture—"Egmont"

a. Kinder Totenlieder   -   -   Gustav Mahler

b. Erdriese }
    Letzter Tanz }   -   -   Felix Weingartner

c. Anakreons Grab }
    Der Rattenfaenger }   -   -   Hugo Wolf

Dr. LUDWIG WUELLNER

Berlioz, SYMPHONY "FANTASTIC"

Tickets now on Sale at the Academy of Music, Brooklyn

The Steinway is the official Piano used by the Philharmonic Society

---

CARNEGIE HALL

THE PHILHARMONIC SOCIETY
OF NEW YORK

1909—Sixty-eighth Season—1910

GUSTAV MAHLER - - Conductor

January 30th, at 3 o'clock.
Extra Sunday Afternoon Concert.

Soloist—**JOSEF WEISS**—Piano.

PROGRAM

GRIEG, March from "Sigurd Jorsalfar."

BEETHOVEN, Overture—"Coriolan."

SCHUMANN, Piano Concerto in A minor.

Program continued on second page following

243. January 26, 1910, 8:15 p.m.
NEW YORK - Carnegie Hall [2,800 seats]

Fourth Historical Concert

    (1) Brahms — Symphony No. 3, F major, Op. 90
    (2) Mahler — *[5] Kindertotenlieder* [1]
    (3) Dvořák — *In der Natur*, Concert Overture, Op. 91
    (4) Four *Lieder* with Orchestra:
        Weingartner — "Erdriese," Op. 39, No. 3
        Weingartner — "Letzter Tanz," Op. 36, No. 2
        Wolf — "Anakreons Grab"
        Wolf — "Der Rattenfänger"
    (5) Smetana — Overture to *The Bartered Bride*

SOLOIST (2 & 4) L. Wüllner.
SOURCE Program; see illustration on opposite page.
NOTE [1] American premiere.
REVIEW HLG IV, 652-654; ZR II, 333–334.

244. January 28, 1910, 8:15 p.m.
BROOKLYN - The Academy of Music [2,086 seats]

    (1) Beethoven — Overture to *Egmont*, Op. 84
    (2) Mahler — *[5] Kindertotenlieder* •
    (3) Dvořák — *In der Natur*, Concert Overture, Op. 91 •
    (4) Four *Lieder* with Orchestra:
        Weingartner — "Erdriese," Op. 39, No. 3 •
        Weingartner — "Letzter Tanz," Op. 36, No. 2 •
        Wolf — "Anakreons Grab" •
        Wolf — "Der Rattenfänger" •
    (5) Berlioz — *Symphonie fantastique*, Op. 14

SOLOIST (2 & 3) L. Wüllner.
SOURCE Program; see illustration on opposite page.
REVIEW HLG IV, 655.

245. January 30, 1910, 3 p.m.
NEW YORK - Carnegie Hall [2,800 seats]

Extra Sunday Afternoon Concert [1]

    (1) Grieg — Triumphal March, from *Sigurd Jorsalfar*, Op. 56 •
    (2) Beethoven — Overture to *Coriolan*, Op. 62
    (3) Schumann — Piano Concerto, A minor, Op. 54 •
    (4) Berlioz — *Symphonie fantastique*, Op. 14

SOLOIST (3) P. Gallico.
SOURCE Program; see illustration on opposite page.

Concert

for the benefit of the

Bryson Day Nursery

by the

Philharmonic Society

of New York

Mr. Gustav Mahler, Conductor
Mr. Riccardo Martin :: Soloist

New Theatre
Tuesday Afternoon, February First
At 2:45 P. M.

Programme

Part One

SCHUBERT—Symphony in B minor (unfinished)

RAMEAU—Gavotte

Songs: (a) Dormi Pure . . . . S. SCUDREI

(b) Caro Mio Bene . . G. GIORDANI

(c) Als die alte Mutter . . DVOŘÁK

MR. RICCARDO MARTIN

Part Two

BEETHOVEN—Overture, "Leonore" No. 3

WAGNER—Prize Song, "Die Meistersinger"
MR. RICCARDO MARTIN

WAGNER—Prelude, "Die Meistersinger"

CARNEGIE HALL

THE PHILHARMONIC SOCIETY
OF NEW YORK

1909—Sixty-eighth Season—1910

GUSTAV MAHLER - - Conductor

Thursday Evening, February 3, at 8.15
—AND—
Friday Afternoon, February 4, at 2.30

Soloist, TILLY KOENEN, Contralto

Program

SYMPHONY No. 4, D minor, Op. 120
Schumann
I. Ziemlich langsam, D minor, 2-4 time, leading to Lebhaft, D minor, 2-4;

II. Romanze, Ziemlich langsam, D minor, 3-4;

III. Scherzo, Lebhaft, D minor, 3-4;

IV. Langsam, D minor, 4-4, leading into Lebhaft, D major, 4-4.

Program continued on second page following

PROGRAM—Continued.

SCENA and ARIA, "Ah Perfido"   *Beethoven*

FANTASIA for Orchestra, "Don Juan"   *Strauss*

a. "Hymnus"   .   .   .   *Strauss*

b. "The Tambourine Player"
Max Fiedler

c. "Springtime"   .   .   *Hugo Wolf*

OVERTURE "Tannhäuser"   .   .   *Wagner*

The Steinway is the Official Piano used by the Philharmonic Society.

For special announcements see second page following

NOTES [1] According to Alma Mahler's memories (AMM, pp. 164–165) the purpose of this extraordinary concert was to present the unknown Hungarian born pianist and composer Joseph Weiss (1864–1945), whom Mahler had met privately and admired. However, during the general rehearsal on Sunday morning, Mahler and Weiss quarreled on tempi markings and the latter left the rehearsal and cancelled the concert. The same afternoon Yolanda Mero was engaged, but the following morning she fell ill, and only at noon did Paolo Gallico agree to replace her, although he was not given a rehearsal.
REVIEW HLG IV, 655-659; ZR II, 336.

246. February 1, 1910, 2:45 p.m.
NEW YORK - The New Theater [2,300 seats]

For the Benefit of the Bryson Day Nursery

(1)	Schubert	Symphony No. 8 (7), B minor, D 759, "Unfinished"
(2)	Rameau	Gavotte, for Orchestra •
(3)	Three *Lieder* with Orchestra:	
	(a) Scuderi	"Dormi pure" •
	(b) Giordani	"Caro mio ben" •
	(c) Dvořák	"Als die alte Mutter", Op. 55, No. 4 •
		- Intermission -
(4)	Beethoven	*Leonore Overture*, No. 3, Op. 72b
(5)	Wagner	"Morgenlich leuchtend" from *Die Meistersinger von Nürnberg*, Act 3
(6)	Wagner	Prelude to Act 1 of *Die Meistersinger von Nürnberg*

SOLOIST (3 & 5) R. Martin.
SOURCE Program; see illustration on opposite page.

247. February 3, 1910, 8:15 p.m.
248. February 4, 1910, 2:30 p.m.
NEW YORK - Carnegie Hall [2,800 seats]

Sixth Regular Subscription Concert [1]

(1)	Schumann	Symphony No. 4, D minor, Op. 120
(2)	Beethoven	"Ah! perfido!" Scene and Aria, Op. 65
(3)	Strauss	*Don Juan*, Tone Poem, Op. 20
(4)	Three *Lieder* with Orchestra:	
	a) Strauss	"Hymnus," Op. 33, No. 3
	b) Wolf	"Er ist's"
	c) Fiedler	"Die Musikantin," Op. 5
(5)	Wagner	Overture to *Tannhäuser*

SOLOIST (2 & 4) T. Koenen.

CARNEGIE HALL

THE PHILHARMONIC SOCIETY
OF NEW YORK

1909—Sixty-eighth Season—1910

GUSTAV MAHLER - - Conductor

February 13, at 3 o'clock

**FOURTH
SUNDAY AFTERNOON CONCERT**

Soloist, PASQUALE AMATO, Baritone

In Memoriam

RICHARD WAGNER
Born in Leipzig, May 22nd, 1813.
Died in Venice, February 13th, 1883.

Program

Kaisermarsch

Eine Faust Overture

Program continued on second page following

PROGRAM—Continued.

Siegfried Idyll

Wotan's Abschied und Feuerzauber, "Die Walkure" (Pasquale Amato)

Vorspiel, "Die Meistersinger"

Monologue—Hans Sachs

Die Meistersinger, "Wahn, Wahn, Ueberall Wahn." (Pasquale Amato)

Overture, "Tannhauser"

Mr. Amato uses the Hartmann Piano

The Steinway is the Official Piano used by the Philharmonic Society.

For special announcements see second page following

250

CARNEGIE HALL

THE PHILHARMONIC SOCIETY
OF NEW YORK

1909—Sixty-eighth Season—1910

GUSTAV MAHLER - - Conductor

Thursday Evening, February 17, at 8.15
—AND—
Friday Afternoon, February 18, at 2.30

**SEVENTH CONCERTS
OF THE FIRST SERIES**

THE MACDOWELL CHORUS
MR. KURT SCHINDLER, Conductor

ASSISTING

Program

TSCHAIKOWSKY—Fantasy Overture, "Romeo and Juliet"

Program continued on second page following

PROGRAM—Continued.

DEBUSSY—Notturnes

    a. Clouds

    b. Fêtes

    c. Sirens

ORCHESTRA and the MacDOWELL CHORUS

WAGNER—"Eine Faust Overtüre"

WAGNER—"Siegfried Idyl"

BERLIOZ—Overture "Carneval Romaine"

The Steinway is the Official Piano used by the Philharmonic Society.

For special announcements see second page following

251 & 252

| New York–Brooklyn | 1910 | Concerts Nos. 247–252 |

SOURCE Program; see illustration on previous page.
NOTE [1] Mahler's original program draft includes Beethoven's Symphony No. 7, Bizet's *L'Arlésienne* Suite, Chabrier's *España,* plus various unspecified vocal solos with Koenen (ZR II, 271).
REVIEW HLG IV, 662-663; ZR II, 341.

249. **February 11, 1910, 8:15 p.m.**
BROOKLYN - The Academy of Music [2,086 seats]

- Above program repeated -

NOTE All items except for the *Tannhäuser* Overture appeared for the last time in Mahler's programs.

250. **February 13, 1910, 3 p.m.**
NEW YORK - Carnegie Hall [2,800 seats]

Fourth Sunday Afternoon Concert: In Memoriam Richard Wagner

All-Wagner Program

(1) *Kaisermarsch*
(2) *Eine Faust-Ouverture*
(3) Wotan's Farewell and Magic Fire Music from *Die Walküre* •
(4) *Siegfried Idyll*
(5) Prelude to Act 1 of *Die Meistersinger von Nürnberg*
(6) "Wahn! Wahn! Überall Wahn!" from *Die Meistersinger von Nürnberg*
(7) Overture to *Tannhäuser*

SOLOIST (3 & 6) P. Amato.
SOURCE Program; see illustration on opposite page.
REVIEW HLG IV, 664-665; ZR II, 342–343.

251. **February 17, 1910, 8:15 p.m.**
252. **February 18, 1910, 2:30 p.m.**
NEW YORK - Carnegie Hall [2,800 seats]

Seventh Regular Subscription Concert [1]

(1) Tchaikovsky — *Romeo and Juliet*, Fantasy-Overture
(2) Debussy — *Trois Nocturnes* •
(3) Wagner — *Eine Faust-Ouverture*
(4) Wagner — *Siegfried Idyll*
(5) Berlioz — *Le carnaval romain*, Overture, Op. 9 •

CHORUS (2) The MacDowell Choir, cond. Kurt Schindler.
SOURCE Program; see illustration on opposite page.
NOTE [1] Mahler's original program draft includes Tchaikovsky's *Romeo and Juliet,* his own Seventh Symphony and Weber's Overture to *Oberon* (ZR II, 271).
REVIEW HLG IV, 665-667; ZR II, 343–344.

253

YALE UNIVERSITY
WOOLSEY HALL
FEBRUARY 23RD, AT 8:15 P. M.

FIRST TIME
IN
NEW HAVEN

The
Philharmonic Society
of New York

FOUNDED 1842

Gustav Mahler, Conductor

SOLOIST - **Olga Samaroff** - PIANO
(HER FIRST APPEARANCE IN NEW HAVEN)
AND THE ENTIRE
PHILHARMONIC ORCHESTRA
ONE HUNDRED PERFORMERS

254

The Philharmonic Society
of New York

1909... SIXTY-EIGHTH SEASON ...1910

Gustav Mahler . . . Conductor

THURSDAY, FEBRUARY 24
AT 8:15 P. M.

First Concert at
The Court Square Theatre
SPRINGFIELD

255

The Philharmonic Society
of New York

1909... SIXTY-EIGHTH SEASON ...1910

Gustav Mahler . . . Conductor

FRIDAY, FEBRUARY 25
AT 8:15 P. M.

First Concert at
Infantry Hall
PROVIDENCE

256

The Philharmonic Society
of New York

1909... SIXTY-EIGHTH SEASON ...1910

Gustav Mahler . . . Conductor

SATURDAY, FEBRUARY 26
AT 8:00 P. M.

First Concert at
Symphony Hall
BOSTON

| New Haven–Springfield–Providence–Boston | 1910 | Concerts Nos. 253–256 |

253. February 23, 1910, 8:15 p.m.
NEW HAVEN - Woolsey Hall [2,695 seats]

    (1) Berlioz   *Symphonie fantastique*, Op. 14
    (2) Bach–Mahler   Suite for Orchestra
    (3) Grieg   Piano Concerto, A minor, Op. 16 •
    (4) Strauss   *Till Eulenspiegels lustige Streiche*, Op. 28

SOLOIST (3) O. Samaroff.
SOURCE Program; see illustration on opposite page.
REVIEW HLG IV, 669-671; ZR II, 344–345.

254. February 24, 1910, 8:15 p.m.
SPRINGFIELD - The Court Square Theater [1,860 seats]

    (1) Berlioz   *Symphonie fantastique*, Op. 14
    (2) Bach–Mahler   Suite for Orchestra
    (3) Handel   "Quanto dolci, quanto care," from *Flavio, Re di Longobardi* •
    (4) Mozart   "Voi, che sapete," from *Le nozze di Figaro* •
    (5) Strauss   *Till Eulenspiegels lustige Streiche*, Op. 28
    (6) Wagner   Prelude to Act 1 of *Die Meistersinger von Nürnberg*

SOLOIST (3 & 4) C. Rider-Kelsey.
SOURCE Program; see illustration on opposite page.
REVIEW HLG IV, 673-674; ZR II, 345–346.

255. February 25, 1910, 8:15 p.m.
PROVIDENCE - Infantry Hall [2,000 seats]

    (1) Berlioz   *Symphonie fantastique*, Op. 14
    (2) Vieuxtemps   Violin Concerto No. 5, A minor, Op. 37
    (3) Strauss   *Till Eulenspiegels lustige Streiche*, Op. 28
    (4) Wagner   Prelude to Act 1 of *Die Meistersinger von Nürnberg*

SOLOIST (2) T. Spiering.
SOURCE Program; see illustration on opposite page.
REVIEW HLG IV, 676; ZR II, 347.

256. February 26, 1910, 8 p.m.
BOSTON - Symphony Hall [2,631 seats]

    (1) Berlioz   *Symphonie fantastique*, Op. 14
    (2) Bach–Mahler   Suite for Orchestra
    (3) Beethoven   *Leonore* Overture No. 3, Op. 72b
    (4) Strauss   *Till Eulenspiegels lustige Streiche*, Op. 28

SOLOIST (2) A. S. Hyde, organ.

CARNEGIE HALL

THE PHILHARMONIC SOCIETY
OF NEW YORK

1909—Sixty-eighth Season—1910

GUSTAV MAHLER - - Conductor

Wednesday Evening, March 2, at 8.15

FIFTH HISTORICAL CONCERT

WAGNER-LISZT

Soloist: CARL JÖRN, Tenor

PROGRAM

WAGNER—

Overture, "The Flying Dutchman"

Prelude, "Lohengrin"

Vorspiel, "Parsifal"

a. Love Song, "Die Walküre"

b. Prize Song, "Die Meistersinger"

Funeral March, "Die Goetterdaemmerung"

Program continued on second page following

PROGRAM—Continued.

LISZT—

"Les Preludes"

"Mazeppa"

The Steinway is the Official Piano used by the Philharmonic Society.

For special announcements see second page following

CARNEGIE HALL

THE PHILHARMONIC SOCIETY
OF NEW YORK

1909—Sixty-eighth Season—1910

GUSTAV MAHLER - - Conductor

Friday Afternoon, March 4, 1910
At 2.30 o'clock

FOURTH BEETHOVEN CONCERT

Soloist: OLGA SAMAROFF, Piano

PROGRAM

Overture, "Zur Namensfeier"

Concerto for Piano in G major

Program continued on second page following

PROGRAM—Continued.

Symphony No. 7, in A major, Op. 93

   I. Introduction, Poco Sostenuto, A major 4-4; leading into Vivace, A major, 6-8

   II. Allegretto, A minor, 2-4

   III. Scherzo, Presto, F major, 3-4; with trio, Assai meno Presto, D major, 3-4

   IV. Finale, Allegro con brio, A major, 2-4

Mme. Samaroff uses the Steinway Piano

The Steinway is the Official Piano used by the Philharmonic Society.

For special announcements see second page following

SOURCE Program; see illustration on previous page.
NOTE Mahler's original program draft (with his estimated durations) includes Brahms's Third Symphony (40 min.), Beethoven's *Leonore* Overture No. 3, (13 min.) and Overture to *Coriolan* (7 min.), his own Bach Suite (20 min.), and Wagner's *Meistersinger* Prelude (9 min.).
REVIEW HLG IV, 677-683; ZR II, 347–348.

257. **March 2, 1910, 8:15 p.m.**
NEW YORK - Carnegie Hall [2,800 seats]

Fifth Historical Concert

	(1)	Wagner	Overture to *Der fliegende Holländer*
	(2)	Wagner	Prelude to Act 1 of *Lohengrin*
	(3)	Wagner	Prelude to Act 1 of *Parsifal* •
	(4)	Wagner	"Winterstürme wichen dem Wonnemond," from *Die Walküre*
	(5)	Wagner	"Morgenlich leuchtend" from *Die Meistersinger von Nürnberg*, Act 3
	(6)	Wagner	"Siegfried's Tod," Funeral March, from *Götterdämmerung*
	(7)	Liszt	*Les Préludes*, Symphonic Poem
	(8)	Liszt	*Mazeppa*, Symphonic Poem •

SOLOIST (3 & 4) C. Jörn.
SOURCE Program; see illustration on opposite page.
REVIEW HLG IV, 653-654, 683-684; ZR II, 350–351.

258. **March 4, 1910, 2:30 p.m.**
NEW YORK - Carnegie Hall [2,800 seats]

Fourth Beethoven Concert

(1) *Zur Namensfeier*, Overture, Op. 115 •
(2) Piano Concerto No. 3, C minor, Op. 37 •[1]
(3) Symphony No. 7, A major, Op. 92

SOLOIST (2) Y. Mero.[2]
SOURCE Program; see illustration on opposite page.
NOTE [1] The program announces Beethoven's Fourth Piano Concerto.
[2] Replaced the indisposed Olga Samaroff.
REVIEW HLG IV, 685.

CARNEGIE HALL

THE PHILHARMONIC SOCIETY
OF NEW YORK

1909—Sixty-eighth Season—1910

GUSTAV MAHLER - - Conductor

Sunday Afternoon, March 6, 1910
At 3 o'clock

Soloist: JOSEF LHEVINNE, Piano

Tschaikowsky Program

Overture, "Romeo and Juliet"

Symphony, No. 6, "Pathetic," B minor

   I. Introduction, Adagio, B minor, 4-4; Allegro non troppo, B minor, 4-4

   II. Allegro con grazia, D major, 5-4

   III. Allegro molto vivace, G major, 4-4 and 12-8

   IV. Finale, Adagio lamentoso, B minor, 3-4

Program continued on second page following

259

CARNEGIE HALL

THE PHILHARMONIC SOCIETY
OF NEW YORK

1909—Sixty-eighth Season—1910

GUSTAV MAHLER - - Conductor

Thursday Evening, March 10, at 8.15
—AND—
Friday Afternoon, March 11, at 2.30

EIGHTH CONCERTS OF THE FIRST SERIES

Soloist—FRITZ KREISLER—Violin

THE MACDOWELL CHORUS
Mr. KURT SCHINDLER, Conductor

PROGRAM

Suite Burlesque "Turandot" . BUSONI
(New, first time)

Concerto for Violin . . BRAHMS
FRITZ KREISLER

Program continued on second page following

260 & 261

The Philharmonic Society
of New York

1909... SIXTY-EIGHTH SEASON ...1910

Gustav Mahler ... Conductor

MONDAY, MARCH 14
AT 8:15 P. M.

Second Concert
AT THE
ACADEMY OF MUSIC
PHILADELPHIA

Programme

BERLIOZ. Symphony . . . . . . "Fantastique"

BEETHOVEN. . . . . Concerto for Violin
MR. FRITZ KREISLER

WAGNER. Overture . . . . . . "Tannhauser"

SOLOIST
FRITZ KREISLER
VIOLIN

PRINTED BY STYLES & CASH
NEW YORK

262

259. March 6, 1910, 3 p.m.
NEW YORK - Carnegie Hall [2,800 seats]

Fifth Sunday Afternoon Concert [1]

All-Tchaikovsky Program

- (1) *Romeo and Juliet*, Fantasy-Overture •
- (2) Symphony No. 6, B minor, Op. 74, "Pathétique"
- (3) Piano Concerto No. 1, B-flat minor, Op. 23 •
- (4) *1812 Overture*, Op. 49

SOLOIST (3) J. Lhévinne.
SOURCE Program; see illustration on opposite page.
NOTE [1] The preceding evening Mahler had conducted the American premiere of Tchaikovsky's *Pique Dame* at The Metropolitan Opera (repeated on March 9, 17, and 21).
REVIEW HLG IV, 694.

260. March 10, 1910, 8:15 p.m.
261. March 11, 1910, 2:30 p.m.
NEW YORK - Carnegie Hall [2,800 seats]

Eighth Regular Subscription Concert [1]

(1)	Busoni	Orchestral Suite from *Turandot*, Op. 41 • [2]
(2)	Brahms	Violin Concerto, D major, Op. 77 •
(3)	Debussy	*Prélude à l'après-midi d'un faune* •
(4)	Strauss	*Tod und Verklärung*, Tone Poem, Op. 24 •

SOLOIST (2) F. Kreisler.
CHORUS (1) The MacDowell Choir, cond. K. Schindler.
SOURCE Program; see illustration on opposite page.
NOTES [1] Mahler's original program draft includes Mendelssohn's *Scottish Symphony*, Beethoven's *Leonore* Overture No. 3, and the Strauss piece (ZR II, p. 271).
[2] First performance in New York. The Suite consists of 8 movements of which the 6th calls for a chorus.
REVIEW HLG IV, 695.

262. March 14, 1910, 8:15 p.m.
PHILADELPHIA - The Academy of Music [2,900 seats]

(1)	Berlioz	*Symphonie fantastique*, Op. 14 •
(2)	Beethoven	Violin Concerto, D major, Op. 61 •
(3)	Wagner	Overture to *Tannhäuser*

SOLOIST (2) F. Kreisler.
SOURCE Program; see illustration on opposite page.
REVIEW HLG IV, 698-700.

CARNEGIE HALL

THE PHILHARMONIC SOCIETY
OF NEW YORK

1909—Sixty-eighth Season—1910

GUSTAV MAHLER - - Conductor

Sunday Afternoon, March 27, at 3

Pension Fund Concert

Soloists:
CARL JORN
THEODORE SPIERING
EDNA SHOWALTER
JANET SPENCER
and the MACDOWELL CHORUS

PROGRAM

Overture, "The Flying Dutchman" *Wagner*

Prize Song, "Die Meistersinger" *Wagner*
CARL JÖRN

Program continued on second page following

PROGRAM—Continued.

a. "The Messengers of Peace" "Rienzi"
    Wagner
Solo. MISS EDNA SHOWALTER

b. Gesang Aus Singal . . *Brahms*

c. Serenade . . . *Schubert*
Solo. MISS JANET SPENCER

Concerto for Violin, No. 5, A minor
    Vieuxtemps
THEODORE SPIERING

Overture, "Leonore" No. 3, *Beethoven*

Aria from "The Bartered Bride" *Smetana*
CARL JÖRN

Symphonic Poem, "Les Preludes" *Liszt*

The Steinway is the Official Piano used by the Philharmonic Society.

For special announcements see second page following

263. March 18, 1910, 8:15 p.m.
BROOKLYN - The Academy of Music [2,086 seats]

All-Wagner Program

   (1) Overture to *Der fliegende Holländer*
   (2) *Eine Faust-Ouverture*
   (3) *Siegfried Idyll*
   (4) "Dich teure Halle," from *Tannhäuser*
   (5) Prelude to Act 1 of *Lohengrin*
   (6) Two songs from the *Wesendonck-Lieder*:
        a) "Schmerzen"
        b) "Im Treibhaus"
   (7) *Kaisermarsch* •

SOLOIST (4 & 6) C. Rider-Kelsey.
SOURCE Program; see illustration on page 250.

264. March 27, 1910, 3 p.m.
NEW YORK - Carnegie Hall [2,800 seats]

For the Pension Fund of the New York Philharmonic Orchestra

(1)	Wagner	Overture to *Der fliegende Holländer*
(2)	Wagner	"Morgenlich leuchtend," from *Die Meistersinger von Nürnberg* •
(3)	Wagner	"Ich sah' die Städte," from *Rienzi*, with Chorus •
(4)	Brahms	"Gesang aus Fingal," Op. 17, No. 4, for Women's Chorus, 2 Horns, and Harp •
(5)	Schubert	"Ständchen," D 921, for Contralto, Women's Chorus, and Orch. •
(6)	Vieuxtemps	Violin Concerto No. 5, A minor, Op. 37 •
(7)	Beethoven	*Leonore* Overture No. 3, Op. 72b
(8)	Smetana	"It must succeed ... How is it possible," from *The Bartered Bride* • [1]
(9)	Liszt	*Les Préludes*, Symphonic Poem

SOLOISTS (2 & 8) C. Jörn; (3) E. Showalter; (5) J. Spencer; (6) T. Spiering.
CHORUS (3–5) The MacDowell Women's Chorus, cond. K. Schindler.
SOURCE Program; see illustration on opposite page.
NOTE [1] Sung in German.

CARNEGIE HALL

THE PHILHARMONIC SOCIETY
OF NEW YORK

1909—Sixty-eighth Season—1910

GUSTAV MAHLER - - Conductor

Wednesday Evening, March 30, 1910
At 8.15 o'clock

LAST HISTORICAL CONCERT

Program

Overture, "Christelflein" . . *Pfitzner*

Symphony No. 4, E-flat major, "Romantic"
Bruckner
  I. Allegro molto moderato, E-flat major, 2-2;
  II. Andante, C minor, 4-4;
  III. Scherzo, B-flat major, 2-4 and Trio, G-flat major, 3-4; Finale, E-flat major, 2-2.

Program continued on second page following

PROGRAM—Continued

Two Preludes to "Guntram" (Acts I and II)
Richard Strauss

"Till Eulenspiegel" . *Richard Strauss*

The Steinway is the Official Piano used by the Philharmonic Society

For special announcements see second page following

CARNEGIE HALL

THE PHILHARMONIC SOCIETY
OF NEW YORK

1909—Sixty-eighth Season—1910

Friday Afternoon, April 1, at 2.30
LAST BEETHOVEN MATINEE

Saturday Evening, April 2, at 8.15
Farewell Concert
Of the Sixty-Eighth Season

GUSTAV MAHLER - - Conductor

Soloists:
Corinne Rider-Kelsey, Soprano
Viola Waterhouse, Soprano
Janet Spencer, Contralto
Dan Beddoe, Tenor
Paul Dufault, Tenor
Herbert Watrous, Bass
Ernest Hutcheson, Piano
The Bach Choir of Montclair
Mr. Clarence Dickinson, Conductor

BEETHOVEN PROGRAM

"Choral Fantasia" in C minor, for Pianoforte, Chorus and Orchestra, Op. 80

  I. Pianoforte Solo, Adagio, C minor, 4-4, leading into

Program continued on second page following

PROGRAM—Continued

  II. Finale, Pianoforte, Chorus and Orchestra
    (a) Allegro, C minor, 4-4;
    (b) Meno Allegro, C major, 2-4;
    (c) Allegro molto, C minor, alla breve;
    (d) Adagio ma non troppo, A major, 6-8;
    (e) Marcia assai vivace, F major, 2-4;
    (f) Allegro, C minor, 2-4;
    (g) Allegretto, ma non troppo (quasi Andante con moto) C major, 2-4 and Presto, the same.

Symphony No. 9, in D minor, Op. 125, Choral
  I. Allegro ma non troppo, D minor, 2-4;
  II. Scherzo, molto vivace, D minor, 3-4; Trio, Presto, D major, 4-4;
  III. Adagio molto e cantabile and Andante moderato, 3-4; B-flat, alternating with D and E-flat.
  IV. (a) Presto; (b) Recitatives for basses and recapitulation of themes from the preceding movement); (c) Presto; (d) Allegro assai, D major, 4-4.

The Steinway is the Official Piano used by the Philharmonic Society.

For special announcements see second page following

265. March 30, 1910, 8:15 p.m.
NEW YORK - Carnegie Hall [2,800 seats]

Sixth Historical Concert

(1)	Pfitzner	Overture to *Das Christ-Elflein*, Op. 20 • [1]
(3)	Bruckner	Symphony No. 4, E-flat major, "Romantic" •
(4)	Strauss	Preludes to Acts 1 and 2 of *Guntram*, Op. 25 •
(5)	Strauss	*Till Eulenspiegels lustige Streiche*, Op. 28

SOURCE Program; see illustration on opposite page.
NOTE [1] The originally announced program did not include Pfitzner's Overture.
REVIEW HLG IV, 701-703; ZR II, 359–361.

266. April 1, 1910, 2:30 p.m.
267. April 2, 1910, 8:15 p.m.
NEW YORK - Carnegie Hall [2,800 seats]

Fifth Beethoven Concert

(1) Fantasy, C minor, for Piano, Chorus, and Orchestra, Op. 80 •
(2) Symphony No. 9, D minor, Op. 125 •

SOLOISTS (1) E. Hutcheson; (2) C. Rider-Kelsey, V. Waterhouse, J. Spencer, D. Beddoe, P. Dufault, and H. Watrous.
CHORUS The Bach Choir of Montclair (200 voices, cond. C. Dickinson).
SOURCE Program; see illustration on opposite page.
REVIEW HLG IV, 703-707; ZR II, 363–365.

- End of Season -

ASSOCIATION ARTISTIQUE DES CONCERTS COLONNE

38ᵉ ANNÉE

Siège de la Société : 13, rue de Tocqueville (17ᵉ) Téléphone : 518-03

Dimanche 17 Avril, à 2 h. 1/2

24ᵉ Concert de l'Abonnement

Sous le Patronage de la

SOCIÉTÉ DES GRANDES AUDITIONS MUSICALES DE FRANCE

Mᵐᵉ la Comtesse Greffulhe, présidente

Le Roi d'Ys (Ouverture) . . . . ED. LALO
Violoncelle solo : M. JEAN BEDETTI.

Concerto en Ré pour Orgue et Orchestre (N° 10) . . . . HÆNDEL
Cadence de M. Alex. GUILMANT.
Adagio — Allegro — Aria — Allegro.
M. J. BONNET.

Sous la direction de M. GABRIEL PIERNÉ

DEUXIÈME SYMPHONIE
avec Soli, Chœurs et grand Orgue
DE
GUSTAV MAHLER
(1ʳᵉ Audition en France)

Allegro maestoso — Andante moderato — Scherzo-Urlicht — Finale

Soli : Mˡˡᵉ POVLA FRISCH,
Mˡˡᵉ HÉLÈNE DEMELLIER.

Soli, Chœurs et Orchestre : 300 Exécutants

Sous la direction de l'AUTEUR

GRAND ORGUE CAVAILLÉ-COLL

Ce Programme est distribué gratuitement. — Prière de ne pas entrer ni sortir pendant l'exécution des morceaux

7, Rue Drouot **PIANOS WEINGARTNER** 96, Boul. Saint-Germain

Prezzo Cent. 10

AUGUSTEO
Municipio di Roma
Regia Accademia di Santa Cecilia

XLI.

Giovedì 28 aprile alle ore 9 pom.

PRIMO CONCERTO ORCHESTRALE

diretto da

GUSTAV MAHLER

PROGRAMMA.

1. BACH (MAHLER) - *Suite.*
   a) *Ouverture.*
   b) *Rondeau.*
   c) *Air.*
   d) *Gavotte.*

2. STRAUSS - *Till Eulenspiegel.*

3. WAGNER - *Siegfried Idyll.*

4. Id. - *Tannhaüser.* Ouverture.

PREZZI

Platea: Poltrone distinte L. 4.50 - Poltrone L. 2 - Sedie L. 1.50
Anfiteatro L. 1 - Galleria L. 0.75 - Palchi L. 25
(tutto oltre l'ingresso)
Ingresso Cent. 50 - Loggione Cent. 50

Spinetta fabbricata dalla Casa Steinwey espressamente per il Maestro Mahler.

Domenica 1° maggio alle ore 5 pom. secondo concerto diretto da Gustav Mahler.

Roma - Cooperativa Tipografica Manuzio - Via di Porta Salaria, 23-A.

1909–1910 Season *cont.*
Epilogue

268. April 17, 1910, 2:30 p.m.
PARIS - Théâtre du Châtelet [2,500 seats]

Twenty-fourth Subscription Concert of the "Concerts Colonne"

(1)	Lalo	Overture to *Le Roi d'Ys*
(2)	Handel	Concerto No. 10, D major, for Organ and Orch.
		- Intermission -
(3)	Mahler	Symphony No. 2, C minor, "Resurrection" ● [1]

SOLOISTS (2) J. Bonnet [2]; (3) P. Frisch and H. Demellier [3].
CONDUCTORS (1 & 2) G. Pierné; (3) Mahler.
ORCHESTRA The Colonne Orchestra.
CHORUS An *ad hoc* chorus. (Orchestra, soloists and chorus numbered 300.)
SOURCE Handbill; see illustration on opposite page.
NOTES [1] First performance in France, given under the auspices of the "Societé des Grandes Auditions Musicales de France" presided by Comtesse Elizabeth Greffulhe. Two days earlier a performance of the symphony, for 2-pianos 4-hands (probably Hermann Behn's arrangement from 1895) was played by A. Casella and N. Salomon at a concert in the Bibliothèque Nationale.
[2] Joseph Bonnet probably also played the organ in Mahler's symphony.
[3] Replaced the originally announced Marcella Pregi.
REVIEW HLG IV, 731-756.

269. April 28, 1910, 9 p.m.
ROME - Augusteo [4,000 seats]

Primo Concerto Orchestrale

(1)	Bach–Mahler	Suite for Orchestra [1]
(2)	Strauss	*Till Eulenspiegels lustige Streiche*, Op. 28
(3)	Wagner	*Siegfried Idyll*
(4)	Wagner	Overture to *Tannhäuser*

ORCHESTRA Regia Accademia di Santa Cecilia.
SOURCE Handbill; see illustration on opposite page.
NOTE [1] First European performance. It appears that the specially prepared piano ("spinet," concert no. 223), which Steinway had constructed at Mahler's request, had been transported to Rome.
REVIEW HLG IV, 761-762.

Gustav Mahler:
Achte Symphonie

in zwei Teilen für Soli, Chöre, großes Orchester und Orgel

I. Teil: Hymnus: „Veni, creator spiritus"
II. Teil: Goethes Faust. II. (Schlußszene)

Uraufführung in der Neuen Musik-Festhalle der Ausstellung

12. September

Einzige Wiederholung: 13. September

Gustav Mahler's Eighth Symphony	Gustav Mahler: Huitième Symphonie
in two parts for solo-voices, choruses, grand orchestra and organ	en deux Parties pour Soli, Choeurs, grand Orchestre et Orgue
First performance in the New Music Festival Hall of the Exposition on September 12	Deux uniques auditions dans la Salle des Fêtes de Musique à l'Exposition première le 12 Septembre
The only repetition: September 13	seconde le 13 Septembre

Participants: AUSFÜHRENDE: Exécutants:

Dirigent:
Gustav Mahler

Soli:

Hofopernsängerin Gertrud Förstel (Wien)	I. Sopran und Magna peccatrix
Martha Winternitz-Dorda (Wien)	II. Sopran und Una poenitentium
Kammersängerin Irma Koboth (München)	Mater gloriosa
Ottilie Metzger (Hamburg)	I. Alt und Mulier Samaritana
Anna Erler-Schnaudt (München)	II. Alt und Maria Aegyptiaca
Kammersänger Felix Senius (Berlin)	Tenor und Doctor Marianus
Hofopernsänger Nicola Geisse-Winkel (Wiesbaden)	Bariton und Pater extaticus
K. u. k. Kammersänger Richard Mayr (Wien)	Baß und Pater profundus

Chöre:

Singverein der k. k. Gesellschaft der Musikfreunde Wien (250 Mitglieder)

Riedel-Verein Leipzig (250 Mitglieder)

Kinderchor der Zentral-Singschule München (350 Kinder)

Orchester:

Das verstärkte Orchester des Konzertvereins München

Besetzung: 24 erste Violinen, 20 zweite Violinen, 16 Bratschen, 12 Celli, 12 Kontrabässe, 4 Harfen, Celesta, Harmonium, Mandolinen, kleine Flöte, 4 große Flöten, 4 Oboen, Englisch-Horn, Es-Klarinette, 3 Klarinetten, Baßklarinette, 4 Fagotte, Kontrafagott, 8 Hörner, 4 Trompeten, 4 Posaunen, Baßtuba, Pauken, Schlagwerk. — Isoliert postiert: 4 Trompeten, 3 Posaunen.

Orgel:

Adolf Hempel (München)

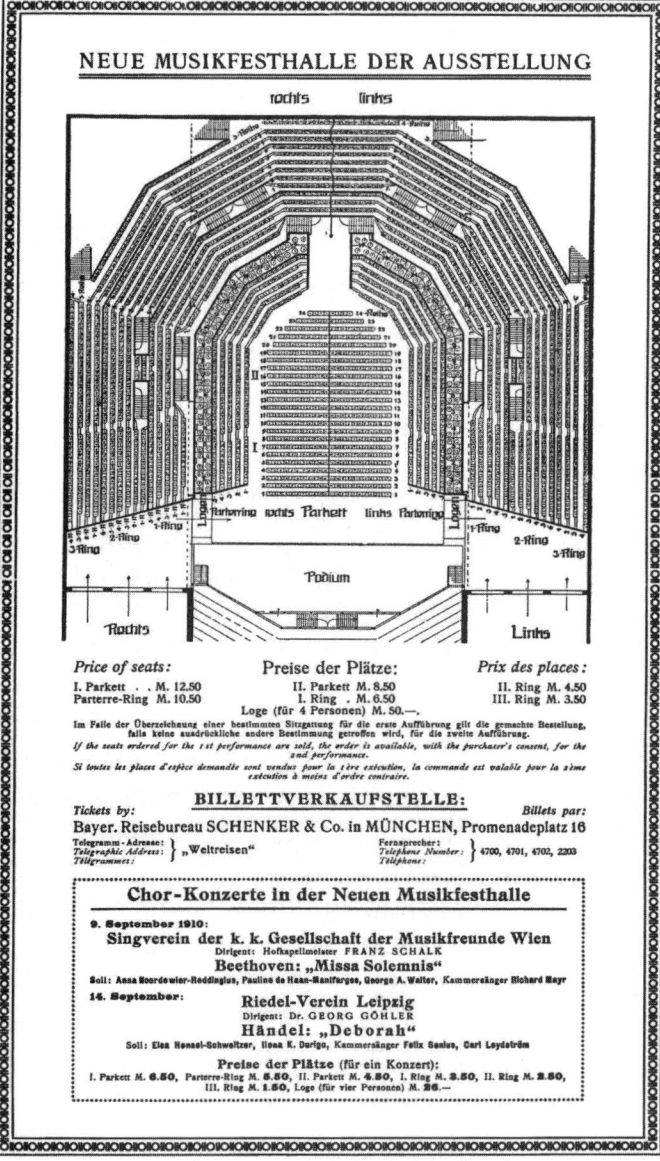

NEUE MUSIKFESTHALLE DER AUSSTELLUNG

Price of seats: Preise der Plätze: Prix des places:

I. Parkett . . M. 12.50   II. Parkett M. 8.50   II. Ring M. 4.50
Parterre-Ring M. 10.50   I. Ring . M. 6.50   III. Ring M. 3.50
Loge (für 4 Personen) M. 50.—

Im Falle der Überzeichnung einer bestimmten Sitzgattung gilt die erste Auffuhrung für die gemachte Bestellung, falls keine ausdrückliche andere Bestimmung getroffen wird, für die zweite Aufführung.

If the seats ordered for the 1st performance are sold, the order is available, with the purchaser's consent, for the 2nd performance.

Si toutes les places d'espèce demandée sont vendues pour la 1ère exécution, la commande est valable pour la 2ème exécution à moins d'ordre contraire.

BILLETTVERKAUFSTELLE:

Tickets by: Billets par:
Bayer. Reisebureau SCHENKER & Co. in MÜNCHEN, Promenadeplatz 16

Telegramm-Adresse: „Weltreisen"   Fernsprecher: 4700, 4701, 4702, 2203

Chor-Konzerte in der Neuen Musikfesthalle

9. September 1910:
Singverein der k. k. Gesellschaft der Musikfreunde Wien
Dirigent: Hofkapellmeister FRANZ SCHALK
Beethoven: „Missa Solemnis"
Soli: Anna Noordewier-Reddingius, Paulino de Haan-Manifarges, George A. Walter, Kammersänger Richard Mayr

14. September:
Riedel-Verein Leipzig
Dirigent: Dr. GEORG GÖHLER
Händel: „Deborah"
Soli: Elsa Hensel-Schweitzer, Ilona K. Durigo, Kammersänger Felix Senius, Carl Leydström

Preise der Plätze (für ein Konzert):
I. Parkett M. 6.50, Parterre-Ring M. 5.50, II. Parkett M. 4.50, I. Ring M. 3.50, II. Ring M. 2.50, III. Ring M. 1.50, Loge (für vier Personen) M. 26.—

Ausstellung München 1910 • Neue Musik-Festhalle.

Gustav Mahler VIII. Symphonie

Erste Aufführung

Montag, 12. September 1910, ~~abends 8~~

Beginn 7½ Uhr abends. Mk. 4.—

2. Ring links   **2. Reihe, Sitz 9**

Garderobe D links

Ohne Kontroll-Coupon ungültig.

270. **May 1, 1910, 5 p.m.**
ROME - Augusteo [4,000 seats]

Secondo Concerto Orchestrale [1]

(1)	Tchaikovsky	Symphony No. 6, B minor, Op. 74, "Pathétique"
		- Intermission -
(2)	Wagner	Prelude to Act 1 of *Die Meistersinger von Nürnberg*
(3)	Wagner	*Siegfried Idyll*
(4)	Beethoven	*Leonore* Overture No. 3, Op. 72b

ORCHESTRA Regia Accademia di Santa Cecilia.
SOURCE Program reconstructed from previews and reviews.
NOTE [1] Mahler was contractually bound to conduct *three* concerts in Rome, the two preceding, and a third on May 5. However, from various letters it appears that after the initial rehearsals he decided to cancel the last concert. This quite unprecedented, even unheard-of step was caused by his great dissatisfaction with the orchestra, which he found to be "undisciplined and indolent." Clearly, Mahler had not had the same experience with the orchestra during his first visit to Rome three years earlier (in 1907, concerts 196–197); otherwise he certainly would not have accepted the invitation. But this time many of the musicians had apparently taken up summer jobs elsewhere, and the substitutes engaged for Mahler's concerts proved to be not only incompetent but also unreliable.
An unpublished letter that Mahler wrote to his German impresario, Norbert Salter, gives the impression that Mahler was also irritated with some program changes, which it seems that Salter had not informed him about in due time. Among the works Mahler had considered for the cancelled concert were Alfredo Casella's not-yet-published Rhapsody for Orchestra, *Italia*, Op. 11, and Busoni's Suite from *Turandot*, Op. 41.
REVIEW HLG IV, 764-766.

Ausstellung
München·1910

neue musik·festhalle

Gustav Mahler
Uraufführung·d·
VIII·Symphonie

für 8 Soli·3 Chöre
gr·Orchester u·Orgel
unter Leitung·d·
Komponisten

1·Aufführung 12·September
einzige Wiederholung 13·Spt·

| Munich | 1910 | Concerts Nos. 271–272 |

Season 1910–1911
Prelude

271. September 12, 1910, 7:30 p.m. [1]
272. September 13, 1910, 7:30 p.m.
MUNICH - Neue Musik-Festhalle [3,000 seats] [2]

Ausstellung München (Munich Exhibition)

    Mahler   Symphony No. 8, E-flat major ● [3]

SOLOISTS	1st movement	2nd movement
Gertrude Förstel	Soprano I	*Una poenitentium*
Martha Winternitz-Dorda	Soprano II	*Magna peccatrix*
Emma Bellwidt [4]	Soprano III	*Mater gloriosa*
Ottilie Metzger	Contralto I	*Mulier Samaritana*
Anna Erler-Schnaudt	Contralto II	*Maria Aegyptiaca*
Felix Senius	Tenor	*Doctor Marianus*
Nicola Geisse-Winkel	Baritone	*Pater ecstaticus*
Richard Mayr	Bass	*Pater profundus*

ORCHESTRA The enlarged orchestra of the Munich "Konzertverein"; concertmaster E. Heyde [5]; a total of 170 players.
CHORUSES The "Singverein der k. k. Gesellschaft der Musikfreunde in Wien" (250 voices, cond. F. Schalk); The Leipzig "Riedel-Verein" (250 voices, cond. G. Göhler); the mixed children's choir from the Munich "Städtische Zentral-Singschule" (350 voices).
ORGAN A. Hempel.
SOURCE Program, handbill and concert ticket; see illustrations on previous and opposite pages.
NOTES [1] The general rehearsal took place at 2 p.m. on September 11.
[2] A huge exhibition hall (the first of six halls), on the large exhibition site close to "Bavaria Park," which, although completely reshaped, is still extant.
[3] World premiere.
[4] Originally Emma Bellwidt was scheduled to sing in both concerts. According to a notice in the *Münchener Neueste Nachrichten,* her child had suddenly fallen ill, which forced her to cancel the second concert. Her parts were given to Martha Winternitz-Dorda.
[5] In a letter from early September 1910 to the impresario Emil Gutmann (GMB 454/MSL 433) Mahler questioned, for the second time, the competence of Mr. Heyde and suggested that Arnold Rosé, his brother-in-law, replace him. Gutmann's response is not known, but apparently Mahler did, willfully, invite Rosé to one of the final rehearsals, but without warning the orchestra in advance; they naturally revolted. Mahler eventually had to be content with Mr. Heyde (AMM pp. 181–182).
REVIEW HLG IV, 964-1008.

CONCERT

for the Benefit of Widows and Orphans of Sailors.

Monday, October 24th 1910.

S. S. KAISER WILHELM II.
Captain O. Cüppers.

Chairman: Commodore ELBRIDGE T. GERRY.

Committee:

Mr. Harold F. Mc Cormick Hon. Nicholas Murray Butler

Mr. Edward R. Bacon Mr. William Guggenheim.

Concert-Direction: Mr. William Thorner.

Programme.

1. Ouverture — Orchestra
2. Piano Selections
   Miss Pilar Osorio
3. Les deux Grenadiers — Schumann
   Mr. L. Rothier
4. Violin solo — Mozart
   Professor F. Berber
5. Songs
   Miss Elizabeth Brickenstein

PART II.

— Address by the Chairman. —

6. Group by Chopin
   Master Pepito Arriola
7. Songs by Schumann
   Mr. G. Huberdeau
8. »Dich teuere Halle« — Wagner
   Miss Lenora Sparkes
9. Song
   Mr. John Mc Cormack
10. Liebestraum-Campanella   by Paganini and Liszt
    Master Pepito Arriola

At the Piano: Mr. Gustav Mahler.

273. **October 24, 1910, Soirée.**
S.S. Kaiser Wilhelm II (German Steamship)

For the Benefit of Widows and Orphans of the Seamen

(1)	Anon.	Overture (unspecified) for Orchestra
(2)	Anon.	Unspecified Piano Pieces
(3)	Schumann	"Les deux Grenadiers," *Lied*, Op. 49, No. 1 ● [1]
(4)	Mozart	Unspecified Work for Violin [probably with Piano acc.]
(5)	Anon.	Unspecified Songs

- Part II -
Address by the Chairman

(6)	Chopin	Unspecified Piano Pieces
(7)	Schumann	Unspecified *Lieder*
(8)	Wagner	"Dich teure Halle," from *Tannhäuser*
(9)	Anon.	Unspecified Song
(10a)	Liszt	*Liebesträume* [probably No. 3 in A-flat major] [2]
(10b)	Paganini–Liszt	*La Campanella*

SOLOISTS (2) P. Osorio; (3) L. Rothier; (4) F. Berber; (5) L. Brickenstein; (6 & 10a–b) P. Arriola; (7) G. Huberdeau; (8) L. Sparkes; (9) J. McCormack.

The piano accompanist of nos. 3–5 and 7–9 is not named. However, the handbill's bottom line, "At the Piano: Mr. Gustav Mahler," seems to indicate that he accompanied these items.

ORCHESTRA (1) Not identified, probably the steamer's dance band.

SOURCE Handbill; see illustration on opposite page.

NOTES [1] The original German title is "Die beiden Grenadiere." The French title suggests that it was sung in that language.

[2] Items 10a–b are confusingly listed as *one* composition, "*Liebestraum-Campanella*" by Paganini and Liszt. The latter composed three "Liebesträume," of which the third and most frequently played is a piano transcription of his *Lied* "O lieb, so lang du lieben kannst," to a poem by the German poet Ferdinand Freiligrath; "La Campanella" is a piano transcription of Paganini's *Rondo à la clochette* from his Violin Concerto No. 2 (3rd movement) in B minor, Op. 7, and published in Liszt's *Études d'exécution transcendente d'après Paganini* (No. 3 in A-flat minor).

PART XII
The New York Philharmonic Society's Sixty-Ninth Season
1910–1911
Management: Loudon Charlton

Easily the most important concert, not to mention the biggest, in Mahler's final phase as a conductor was the premiere of his heady, grandly affirmative Eighth Symphony – the so-called "Symphony of a Thousand" - in Munich in September 1910. The performance, given before an audience of about 3,000 that included such notables as Richard Strauss and Siegfried Wagner, Max Reinhardt and Thomas Mann, was easily Mahler's greatest lifetime success – and one of the last great premieres before the old Europe began to disintegrate four years later in the First World War.

It is worth recalling the circumstances surrounding this triumph. Mahler had been through a tortured summer, partly revealed in the anguished markings he had scribbled on the score of the Tenth Symphony that he had begun composing in his Toblach *Häuschen* but never lived to finish. He had discovered that Alma was having an affair with the young architect, Walter Gropius, and, fearing that he might be losing his own sense of balance for good, he went through an intense, albeit brief, session of psychoanalysis with Sigmund Freud. Alma promised to give up Gropius but in fact she continued to meet him, notably in Munich while her husband prepared for the premiere of the Eighth. Almost in passing, Mahler mentioned on the sidelines of rehearsals that he had had a sore throat but had largely sweated it out after a few hours in bed. His friends though were more worried about his health – and they were right to be.

Tougher challenges than ever faced him on his return to New York in October 1910. A few highlights apart, the public response during the 1909-1910 Philharmonic season had been disappointing and the financial deficit heavy. More money was raised, a business manager appointed and – somewhat surprisingly – the number of concerts increased. But part of the previous season's poor result was blamed on Mahler's ambitious, sometimes arcane programming, and as a result a body was set up by the orchestra's committee of guarantors to supervise the future choice of works. Naturally Mahler was riled, and it is a moot point whether the changes that emerged in the programming for his second season were really to the good. A new cycle of "National Programs with Great Soloists" (Italian, French, Norse etc.) looked attractive in theory but in practice its offerings were ill-balanced. Besides, Mahler was now drawing a stream of damning prose from one of New York's most influential critics, Henry Krehbiehl of the *Tribune*, who felt the conductor had slighted him during the previous season.

Despite all that, Mahler was often winning plaudits with the orchestra although his biggest triumphs were out of town. After a hectic start to the season in Manhattan and Brooklyn, he took the Philharmonic on a pre-Christmas (1910) tour to Pittsburgh, Cleveland and four towns in New York State. Audiences were enthusiastic and critical comment was almost embarrassingly exuberant (e.g. "Little Mahler whose gigantic power makes other conductors look like pygmies."). Back in New York in January, Mahler gave two performances of his (newly revised) Fourth Symphony, a piece that mystified American critics as much as it had their European counterparts. These were the last occasions on which he conducted one of his own works. At roughly the same time, he amazingly proposed that in the next season (i.e. 1911-1912) he should conduct up to 100 concerts, far more than hitherto and also demanded a higher salary for doing so.

The committee of guarantors balked at Mahler's salary demand and even began looking for another conductor, but – given time – the two sides would probably have reached a compromise. Time, though, was running out. In February, Mahler had a recurrence of the throat trouble that had afflicted him in Munich. His temperature soared but, insisting that he had often conducted himself back to health, he went off to give a concert at Carnegie Hall on February 21st. As it happened, his rival Toscanini was in the audience, presumably because the program was of music associated with Italy, not because of the conductor! It was Mahler's forty-eighth concert that season and turned out to be the last of his life. Soon afterwards he was found to have bacterial endocarditis – a serious ailment afflicting hearts that, like Mahler's, have suffered valvular damage. In those days, before antibiotics, almost no one survived it.

Philharmonic Society
of New York

NINETY-FIVE PLAYERS

GUSTAV MAHLER
Conductor

EIGHT SUNDAY AFTERNOON CONCERTS
..IN..
Carnegie Hall
Beginning Sunday Afternoon, November 13th
AT THREE O'CLOCK

Programme for November 13th

von WEBER - - - Overture, "Der Freischütz"

TSCHAIKOWSKY - - Symphony No. 5, E minor, opus 64
    I. Introduction: Andante - Allegro con anima
    II. Andante cantabile, con alcuna licenza
    III. Valse: Allegro moderato
    IV. Finale: Andante maestoso - Allegro vivace

INTERMISSION

BERLIOZ - - Excerpts from "The Damnation of Faust"
    (a) Minuet of the Will-o'-the-Wisps
    (b) Dance of the Sylphs
    (c) Rakoczy March

LISZT - - - - - - Mephisto Waltz

The Steinway Piano is the Official Piano of the Philharmonic Society

---

DATES and PRICES

| November 13 | January 15 | February 5 | February 26 |
| November 27 | January 22 | February 19 | March 12 |

SERIES TICKETS, $3.00, $5.00, $7.00 and $10.00
SINGLE TICKETS, 50 cents, 75 cents, $1.00 and $1.50
Seats now on sale at Box Office

MANAGEMENT - - - LOUDON CHARLTON

| New York–Brooklyn | 1910 | Concerts Nos. 274–277 |

274. November 1, 1910, 8:15 p.m.
275. November 4, 1910, 2:30 p.m.
NEW YORK - Carnegie Hall [2,800 seats]

First Regular Subscription Concert

(1) Bach–Mahler — Suite for Orchestra [1]
(2) Schubert — Symphony No. 9 (8), C major, D 944, "Great"
(3) Mozart — Ballet Music, from *Idomeneo*, K. 367 [2]
(4) Mozart — German Dances [3]
(5) Strauss — *Also sprach Zarathustra*, Symphonic Poem, Op. 30

SOURCE Program; see illustration on following page.
NOTES [1] Given "by request"; with "Mr. Mahler at the harpsichord," and "Mr. Arthur S. Hyde at the organ." Concert no. 223, note 2.
[2] Only the *Gavotte* and the *Passacaglia*.
[3] The number of "German Dances" and the Köchel number have not been established.
REVIEW HLG IV, 1042-1048; ZR II, 400–403.

276. November 6, 1910, 3 p.m.
BROOKLYN - The Academy of Music [2,086 seats]

Sunday Afternoon Concert

- Above program repeated -

SOURCE Handbill; see illustration on following page.
NOTE Nos. 2–5 appear for the last time in Mahler's programs.
REVIEW HLG IV, 1042-1048.

277. November 13, 1910, 3 p.m.
NEW YORK - Carnegie Hall [2,800 seats]

First Sunday Afternoon Concert

(1) Weber — Overture to *Der Freischütz* •
(2) Tchaikovsky — Symphony No. 5, E minor, Op. 64 •
   - Intermission -
(3) Berlioz — Three excerpts from *La Damnation de Faust*, Op. 24 •
   a) Menuet des follets
   b) Ballet des sylphes
   c) Marche hongroise
(4) Liszt — "Mephisto Waltz," for Orchestra •

SOURCE Program and handbill; see illustration on opposite page.
REVIEW HLG IV, 1049-1050.

THE PHILHARMONIC SOCIETY
OF NEW YORK
GUSTAV MAHLER - - Conductor

1910—Sixty-ninth Season—1911

Management, LOUDON CHARLTON

CARNEGIE HALL
Tuesday Evening, November 1, 1910
Friday Afternoon, November 4, 1910

PROGRAM

BACH—(by request)
    Suite, arranged by Mr. Mahler from the 2nd and 3rd Suites B minor, D major
    MR. MAHLER at the Harpsichord

SCHUBERT—
    Symphony, C major

Program continued on second page following

J. M. Gidding & Co.
WOMEN'S HIGH-CLASS OUTER APPAREL
Fifth Avenue, 46th and 47th Streets   New York

274 & 275

The Philharmonic Society
of New York

1910... SIXTY-NINTH SEASON ...1911

Gustav Mahler ... Conductor

MANAGEMENT LOUDON CHARLTON

Brooklyn Academy of Music
SUNDAY AFTERNOON, NOVEMBER SIXTH

... Programme ...

BACH (by request) Suite, arranged by Mr. Mahler from the 2nd and 3rd Suites B minor, D major
MR. MAHLER AT THE HARPSICHORD

SCHUBERT	-	Symphony, C major
MOZART	-	(a) Ballet Music from "Idomeneo" (b) Deutsche Tänze
R. STRAUSS	-	"Thus Spake Zarathustra"

Steinway Piano Used

276

THE PHILHARMONIC SOCIETY
OF NEW YORK
GUSTAV MAHLER - - Conductor

1910—Sixty-ninth Season—1911

Management, LOUDON CHARLTON

CARNEGIE HALL
Tuesday Evening, November 15, 1910
—AND—
Friday Afternoon, November 18, 1910

MR. JOSEF HOFMANN, Soloist

PROGRAM

SCHUMANN—Overture to "Manfred," Op. 115

DEBUSSY—Rondes de Printemps

Program continued on second page following

J. M. Gidding & Co.
WOMEN'S HIGH-CLASS OUTER APPAREL
Fifth Avenue, 46th and 47th Streets   New York

278 & 279

THE PHILHARMONIC SOCIETY
OF NEW YORK
GUSTAV MAHLER - - Conductor

1910—Sixty-ninth Season—1911

Management, LOUDON CHARLTON

CARNEGIE HALL
Tuesday Evening, November 22, 1910
At 8.15 o'clock

Friday Afternoon, November 25, 1910
At 2.30 o'clock

MME. ALMA GLUCK, Soloist

PROGRAM

1. CHERUBINI—Overture "Anakreon"

2. SCHUMANN—Symphony, C major, No. 2, op. 61
    I. Introduction: Sostenuto assai; Allegro, ma non troppo
    II. Scherzo: Allegro vivace
    III. Adagio espressivo
    IV. Finale: Allegro molto vivace

Program continued on second page following

J. M. Gidding & Co.
WOMEN'S HIGH-CLASS OUTER APPAREL
Fifth Avenue, 46th and 47th Streets   New York

281 & 282

| New York–Brooklyn | 1910 | Concerts Nos. 278–282 |

278. November 15, 1910, 8:15 p.m.
279. November 18, 1910, 2:30 p.m.
NEW YORK - Carnegie Hall [2,800 seats]

Second Regular Subscription Concert

- (1) Schumann — Overture to *Manfred*, Op. 115
- (2) Debussy — *Rondes de printemps*, from *Images* • [1]
- (3) Saint-Saëns — Piano Concerto No. 4, C minor, Op. 44 •
- - Intermission -
- (4) Brahms — Symphony No. 1, C minor, Op. 68

SOLOIST (3) J. Hofmann.
SOURCE Program; see illustration on opposite page.
NOTE [1] American premiere. The world premiere had taken place in Paris on March 2, 1910.
REVIEW HLG IV, 1051-1054; ZR II, 407–408.

280. November 20, 1910, 2:30 p.m.
BROOKLYN - The Academy of Music [2,086 seats]

- (1) Schumann — Overture to *Manfred*, Op. 115 •
- (2) Brahms — Symphony No. 1, C minor, Op. 68 •
- (3) Smetana — "Hajej muj andílku," from *The Kiss (Hubička)*
- (4) Mahler — "Ging heut' morgen übers Feld," from *Lieder eines fahrenden Gesellen* [1]
- (5) Mahler — One "Gesänge" (song) from *Des Knaben Wunderhorn* with Orch.: "Rheinlegendchen" [1]
- (6) Dvořák — *Carnaval*, Overture, Op. 92
- (7) Smetana — "Die Moldau," ("Vltava") from *Má vlast*, Symphonic Poem

SOLOIST (3–5) A. Gluck.
SOURCE Program.
NOTE [1] American premiere.
REVIEW HLG IV, 1054-1055; ZR II, 408.

281. November 22, 1910, 8:15 p.m.
282. November 25, 1910, 2:30 p.m.
NEW YORK - Carnegie Hall [2,800 seats]

Third Regular Subscription Concert

- (1) Cherubini — Overture to *Anacréon* • [1]
- (2) Schumann — Symphony No. 2, C major, Op. 61 •
- (3) Smetana — "Hajej muj andílku," from *The Kiss (Hubička)*
- (4) Mahler — "Ging heut' morgen übers Feld," from *Lieder eines fahrenden Gesellen* •

THE PHILHARMONIC SOCIETY
OF NEW YORK
GUSTAV MAHLER - - Conductor

1910—Sixty-ninth Season—1911

Management, LOUDON CHARLTON

CARNEGIE HALL
Sunday Afternoon, November 27, 1910
At 3 o'clock

MR. XAVER SCHARWENKA, Soloist

PROGRAM

1. RIMSKY-KORSAKOW—"Scheherezade"
   - I. "The Sea and Sinbad's Ship"
   - II. "The Story of the Kalendar Prince"
   - III. "The Young Prince and the Young Princess"
   - IV. "Festival at Bagdad"

Program continued on second page following

J. M. Gidding & Co.
WOMEN'S HIGH-CLASS OUTER APPAREL
Fifth Avenue, 46th and 47th Streets   New York

PROGRAM—Continued

2. XAVER SCHARWENKA—Concerto No. 4, F minor
   - Allegro patetico
   - Intermezzo: Allegretto molto tranquillo
   - Lento mesto—Allegro con fuoco

3. CHABRIER—"España"

Mr. Scharwenka uses the **Baldwin Piano**

The Steinway Piano is the official Piano of the Philharmonic Society

For special announcement see second page following

J. M. Gidding & Co.
WOMEN'S HIGH-CLASS OUTER APPAREL
Fifth Avenue, 46th and 47th Streets   New York

THE PHILHARMONIC SOCIETY
OF NEW YORK
GUSTAV MAHLER - - Conductor

1910—Sixty-ninth Season—1911

Management, LOUDON CHARLTON

CARNEGIE HALL
Tuesday Evening, November 29, 1910
At 8.15 o'clock

Friday Afternoon, December 2, 1910
At 2.30 o'clock

FRANCIS MACMILLEN, Soloist

PROGRAM

1. ELGAR—Variations on an Original Theme

2. GOLDMARK—Concerto in A minor, op. 28
   - I. Allegro moderato
   - II. Air: Andante
   - III. Moderato Allegretto

Program continued on second page following

J. M. Gidding & Co.
WOMEN'S HIGH-CLASS OUTER APPAREL
Fifth Avenue, 46th and 47th Streets   New York

PROGRAM—Continued

3. MOZART—Symphony in G minor
   - I. Allegro molto, alla breve
   - II. Andante
   - III. Menuet: Allegro
   - IV. Finale: Allegro assai, alla breve

4. MENDELSSOHN—Overture, "A Midsummer Night's Dream"

FRANK L. SEALY at the Organ

The Steinway Piano is the Official Piano of the Philharmonic Society.

For special announcement see second page following

J. M. Gidding & Co.
WOMEN'S HIGH-CLASS OUTER APPAREL
Fifth Avenue, 46th and 47th Streets   New York

	(5)	Mahler	One "Gesänge" (song) from *Des Knaben Wunderhorn* with Orch.: "Rheinlegendchen" •
	(6)	Dvořák	*Carnaval,* Overture, Op. 92
	(7)	Smetana	"Die Moldau," ("Vlatava") from *Má vlast,* Symphonic Poem

SOLOIST (3–5) A. Gluck
SOURCE Program; see illustration on previous page.
NOTE [1] Replaced the originally announced Overture to *Turandot* by Weber.
REVIEW HLG IV, 1055-1058; ZR II, 410–411.

283. **November 27, 1910, 3 p.m.**
NEW YORK - Carnegie Hall [2,800 seats]

Second Sunday Afternoon Concert

	(1)	Rimsky-Korsakov	*Scheherazade,* Symphonic Suite, Op. 35 •
			- Intermission -
	(2)	Scharwenka	Piano Concerto No. 4, F minor, Op. 82 • [1]
	(3)	Chabrier	*España,* Rhapsody for Orchestra

SOLOIST X. Scharwenka.
SOURCE Program; see illustration on opposite page.
NOTE [1] American premiere.
REVIEW HLG IV, 1058-1060; ZR II, 312–314.

284. **November 29, 1910, 8:15 p.m.**
285. **December 2, 1910, 2:30 p.m.**
NEW YORK - Carnegie Hall [2,800 seats]

Fourth Regular Subscription Concert

	(1)	Elgar	Variations on an Original Theme, Op. 36. "Enigma" •
	(2)	Goldmark	Violin Concerto, A minor, Op. 28 •
	(3)	Mozart	Symphony No. 40, G minor, K. 550 •
	(4)	Mendelssohn	Overture to *Ein Sommernachtstraum,* Op. 21 •

SOLOIST (2) F. MacMillan.
SOURCE Program; see illustration on opposite page.
REVIEW HLG IV, 1060-1061; ZR II, 415–416.

Soldiers Memorial Hall

Pittsburgh Orchestra Association

Presenting

New York Philharmonic Orchestra

Monday Evening, December 5, 1910

GUSTAV MAHLER, Conductor

Management
Mr. Loudon Charlton, New York

Resident Assistant
Miss May Beegle

Pittsburgh Orchestra Association Offices, 1516-1517 Farmers Bank Building
Telephone, 1897 Grant

| Tour from Pittsburgh to Utica | 1910 | Concerts Nos. 286–291 |

On December 4 the New York Philharmonic Orchestra left for a tour, performing the same program in six different cities (concerts 286–291).

286. December 5, 1910, 8:15 p.m.
   PITTSBURGH - Soldiers Memorial Hall [2,600 seats]

   (1) Bach–Mahler   Suite for Orchestra
   (2) Beethoven   Symphony No. 6, F major, Op. 68. "Pastoral"
   (3) Wagner   Prelude and "Liebestod," from *Tristan und Isolde*
   (4) Wagner   *Siegfried Idyll*
   (5) Wagner   Prelude to Act 1 of *Die Meistersinger von Nürnberg*

   SOURCE Program; see illustration on opposite page.
   REVIEW HLG IV, 1066-1067; ZR II, 416–418.

287. December 6, 1910, 8:15 p.m.
   CLEVELAND - Grays Armory [5,000 seats]

   SOURCE Program.
   REVIEW HLG IV, 1070-1071; ZR II, 418–419.

288. December 7, 1910, 8:15 p.m.
   BUFFALO - Convention Hall [5,000 seats]

   SOURCE Program.
   REVIEW HLG IV, 1074-1075; ZR II, 420.

289. December 8, 1910, 8:15 p.m.
   ROCHESTER - Convention Hall [3,000 seats]

   SOURCE Program.
   REVIEW HLG IV, 1077-1078; ZR II, 420–421.

290. December 9, 1910, 8:15 p.m.
   SYRACUSE - Wieting Opera House [2,150 seats]

   SOURCE Program.
   REVIEW HLG IV, 1079.

291. December 10, 1910, 8:15 p.m.
   UTICA - The Majestic Theater [1,420 seats]

   SOURCE Program.
   REVIEW HLG IV, 1080; ZR II, 422.

The Philharmonic Society
of New York

1910 ... SIXTY-NINTH SEASON ... 1911

Gustav Mahler ... Conductor

MANAGEMENT LOUDON CHARLTON

Carnegie Hall

TUESDAY NIGHT, DECEMBER 13
AT EIGHT-FIFTEEN

FRIDAY AFTERNOON, DECEMBER 16
AT TWO-THIRTY

Soloist
XAVER SCHARWENKA
Pianist

All-Beethoven Programme
Commemorating the birth of Beethoven, December 16, 1770

1. OVERTURE { "King Stephan"
              { "Coriolan"
2. SYMPHONY in F major, No. 8, opus 93
    - I Allegro vivace e con brio
    - II Allegretto Scherzando
    - III Tempo di Menuetto
    - IV Allegro vivace
3. CONCERTO for Pianoforte, in E-flat major, No. 5, opus 73
    - I Allegro
    - II Adagio un poco moto
    - III Allegro ma non troppo
4. OVERTURE "Leonore" No. 3

The Steinway Piano is the Official Piano of the Philharmonic Society

---

The Philharmonic Society
of New York

1910 ... SIXTY-NINTH SEASON ... 1911

Gustav Mahler ... Conductor

MANAGEMENT LOUDON CHARLTON

Brooklyn Academy of Music

SUNDAY AFTERNOON, DECEMBER EIGHTEENTH
AT THREE O'CLOCK

Soloist
EDOUARD DETHIER
VIOLINIST

All-Tschaikowsky Programme

1. SYMPHONY in C minor, No. 2, opus 17
    - I Introduction: Andante sostenuto; Allegro vivo
    - II Andantino marziale, quasi moderato
    - III Scherzo: Allegro molto vivace; Trio: L'istesso tempo
    - IV Finale: Moderato assai; Allegro vivo
2. CONCERTO in D major, opus 35
    - I Allegro moderato
    - II Canzonetta: Andante
    - III Finale: Allegro vivacissimo
3. SUITE No. 1, D minor, opus 43
    - I Introduction: Andante sostenuto; Fugue: Moderato con anima
    - II Divertimento: Allegro moderato
    - III Intermezzo: Andantino semplice
    - IV Marche miniature: Moderato con moto
    - V Scherzo: Allegro con moto
    - VI Gavotte: Allegro

The Steinway Piano is the Official Piano of the Philharmonic Society

292. December 13, 1910, 8:15 p.m.
293. December 16, 1910, 2:30 p.m.
NEW YORK - Carnegie Hall [2,800 seats]

Fifth Regular Subscription Concert: Commemorating the Birth of Beethoven on December 16, 1770.

All-Beethoven Program

    (1) Overture to *König Stephan*, Op. 117 •
    (2) Overture to *Coriolan*, Op. 62
    (3) Symphony No. 6, F major, Op. 68, "Pastoral" [1]
    - Intermission -
    (4) Piano Concerto No. 5, E-flat major, Op. 73, "Emperor" •
    (5) *Leonore* Overture No. 3, Op. 72b [2]

SOLOIST (4) X. Scharwenka.
SOURCE Program; see illustration on opposite page.
NOTES [1] A printed notice attached to the program booklet informs that "Instead of the Beethoven 8th Symphony announced for these programs, the "Pastoral" No. 6, in F major, Op. 68, will be performed."
[2] According to the December 14 review in *The New York Times*, the overture was third on the program. This is not confirmed by the other reviews.
REVIEW HLG IV, 1081-1083.

294. December 18, 1910, 3 p.m.
BROOKLYN - The Academy of Music [2,086 seats]

Sunday Afternoon Concert

All-Tchaikovsky Program

    (1) Orchestral Suite No. 1, D minor, Op. 43 [1]
    (2) Violin Concerto, D major, Op. 35
    (3) Symphony No. 2, C minor, Op. 17, "Little Russian" [1]

SOLOIST (2) É. Déthier.
SOURCE Program; see illustration on opposite page.
NOTE [1] The program booklet lists items 1 and 3 in reverse order, but a footnote on the front page (printed in red) informs: "It has been decided to reverse the order of the program, beginning with the Suite and closing with the Symphony."
REVIEW HLG IV, 1084; ZR II, 424–425.

The Philharmonic Society
of New York

1910 ... SIXTY-NINTH SEASON ... 1911

Gustav Mahler ... Conductor

MANAGEMENT LOUDON CHARLTON

Carnegie Hall

TUESDAY NIGHT, DECEMBER 27
AT EIGHT-FIFTEEN

FRIDAY AFTERNOON, DECEMBER 30
AT TWO-THIRTY

Soloist
EDOUARD DETHIER
VIOLINIST

All-Tschaikowsky Programme

1. SYMPHONY in C minor, No. 2, opus 17
   - I Introduction: Andante sostenuto; Allegro vivo
   - II Andantino marziale, quasi moderato
   - III Scherzo: Allegro molto vivace; Trio: L'istesso tempo
   - IV Finale: Moderato assai; Allegro vivo

2. CONCERTO in D major, opus 35
   - I Allegro moderato
   - II Canzonetta: Andante
   - III Finale: Allegro vivacissimo

3. SUITE No. 1, D minor, opus 43
   - I Introduction: Andante sostenuto; Fugue: Moderato con anima
   - II Divertimento: Allegro moderato
   - III Intermezzo: Andantino semplice
   - IV Marche miniature: Moderato con moto
   - V Scherzo: Allegro con moto
   - VI Gavotte: Allegro

The Steinway Piano is the Official Piano of the Philharmonic Society

295 & 296

The Philharmonic Society
of New York

1910 ... SIXTY-NINTH SEASON ... 1911

Gustav Mahler ... Conductor

MANAGEMENT LOUDON CHARLTON

Carnegie Hall

TUESDAY NIGHT, JANUARY 3
AT EIGHT-FIFTEEN

FRIDAY AFTERNOON, JANUARY 6
AT TWO-THIRTY

Soloist
EDMOND CLEMENT
TENOR

All-French Programme
(With MacDOWELL CHORUS—KURT SCHINDLER, Conductor)

1. SUITE (new) .... Enesco
2. SONGS
   - "Aubade du Roi d'Ys" ...... Lalo
   - "Le Mage" .... Massenet
   - "Rêve de Manon" .... Massenet
3. "IBERIA" (new) .... Debussy

INTERMISSION

4. L'ARLESIENNE SUITE No. 1 ..... Bizet
   (with Chorus)
5. "ODE À LA MUSIQUE" (new) ..... Chabrier
   (Solo and Chorus)
6. "ESPAÑA" (by request) .... Chabrier

The Steinway Piano is the Official Piano of the Philharmonic Society

This programme will be repeated at the Brooklyn Academy of Music, Sunday Afternoon, January 8th, at three o'clock.

298 & 299

| New York–Brooklyn | 1910–1911 | Concerts Nos. 295–299 |

295. December 27, 1910, 8:15 p.m.
296. December 30, 1910, 2:30 p.m.
NEW YORK - Carnegie Hall [2,800 seats]

Sixth Regular Subscription Concert

- Above program repeated -

SOLOIST (2) E. Déthier.
SOURCE Program; see illustration on opposite page.
NOTE Mahler's last performances of all three works.
REVIEW HLG IV, 1084-1085.

297. January 1, 1911, 3 p.m.
BROOKLYN - The Academy of Music [2,086 seats]

All-Wagner Program:

(1) Overture to *Rienzi*
(2) Prelude to Act 1 of *Lohengrin*
(3) "Einsam in trüben Tagen," from *Lohengrin*
(4) "Dich teure Halle," from *Tannhäuser*
(5) Funeral March, and Brünnhilde's Immolation Scene, from *Götterdämmerung*
(6) Overture to *Tannhäuser*

SOLOIST (3–5) J. Gadski.
SOURCE Program.
REVIEW HLG IV, 1120-1121.

298. January 3, 1911, 8:15 p.m.
299. January 6, 1911, 2:30 p.m.
NEW YORK - Carnegie Hall [2,800 seats]

Seventh Regular Subscription Concert. All-French Program

(1) Enescu — Suite No. 1, C major, Op. 9 [1]
(2) Lalo — "Puisqu'on ne peut fléchir ... Vainement, ma bien aimée" (Aubade), from *Le Roi d'Ys*
(3) Massenet — "Ah! parais! Astre de mon ciel ... Soulève l'ombre des ses voiles," from *Le mage*
(4) Massenet — "Instant charmant où la crainte ... En fermant les yeux," from *Manon*
(5) Debussy — *Iberia* from *Images* [1]

The Philharmonic Society
of New York

1910 ... SIXTY-NINTH SEASON ... 1911

Gustav Mahler ... Conductor

MANAGEMENT LOUDON CHARLTON

Brooklyn Academy of Music

SUNDAY AFTERNOON, JANUARY 8
AT THREE O'CLOCK

Soloist
EDMOND CLEMENT
TENOR

All-French Programme
(With MacDOWELL CHORUS—KURT SCHINDLER, Conductor)

1. SUITE (new) .... Enesco
2. SONGS
   "Aubade du Roi d'Ys" ...... Lalo
   "Le Mage" .... Massenet
   "Rêve de Manon" .... Massenet
3. "IBERIA" (new) .... Debussy

INTERMISSION

4. L'ARLESIENNE SUITE No. 1 .... Bizet
   (with Chorus)
5. "ODE À LA MUSIQUE" (new) ...... Chabrier
   (Solo and Chorus)
6. "ESPAÑA" (by request) .... Chabrier

The Steinway Piano is the Official Piano of the Philharmonic Society

---

THE PHILHARMONIC SOCIETY
OF NEW YORK

GUSTAV MAHLER - - Conductor

1910—Sixty-ninth Season—1911

Management, LOUDON CHARLTON

CARNEGIE HALL

Tuesday Evening, January 10, 1911
At 8.15 o'clock

Friday Afternoon, January 13, 1911
At 2.30 o'clock

Soloist: MME. JOHANNA GADSKI

All-Wagner Program

1. "A FAUST OVERTURE"
2. FOUR SONGS
   (a) "Schmerzen"
   (b) "Im Treibhaus"
   (c) "Stehe Still"
   (d) "Träume"

Program continued on second page following

J. M. Gidding & Co.
WOMEN'S HIGH-CLASS OUTER APPAREL
Fifth Avenue, 46th and 47th Streets New York

PROGRAM—Continued

3. OVERTURE, "The Flying Dutchman"

—Intermission—

4. PRELUDE and FINALE, "Tristan und Isolde"

5. "SIEGFRIED IDYL"

6. PRELUDE to "Die Meistersinger von Nürnberg"

The Steinway Piano is the Official Piano of the Philharmonic Society.

For special announcement see second page following

J. M. Gidding & Co.
WOMEN'S HIGH-CLASS OUTER APPAREL
Fifth Avenue, 46th and 47th Streets New York

(6)	Bizet	*L'Arlésienne* Suite [No. 1], with Chorus [2]
(7)	Chabrier	*Á la Musique*, for Solo Tenor, Women's Chorus & Orch. [1]
(8)	Chabrier	*España*, Rhapsody for Orchestra ["by request"]

SOLOIST (2–4, 7) E. Clément.
CHORUS (6 & 7) The MacDowell Chorus, cond. K. Schindler.
SOURCE Program; see illustration on previous page.
NOTES [1] First performance in New York.
[2] The program booklet explains: "To give a hearing to some of the vocal music composed by Bizet [...] Mr. Mahler has introduced three numbers between the Adagietto [No. 3] and the Carillon [No. 4]. The first of these is the Provençal Noël, the melody of which is the theme of the variations which make up the Prelude, or overture as Bizet called it. The second is another stanza of the same Christmas song, but in this instance without accompaniment. The middle number is a dance-song without text save a 'La, la, la,' which in the original play follows the instrumental introduction to the second act, and which is frequently used for ballet purposes in Bizet's opera *Carmen*. The text of the song is given as 'De bon matin j'ai recontré le train ...'" (H. E. Krehbiel). However, according to Krehbiel's review, only one of the three announced choral movements was played.
REVIEW HLG IV, 1117-1120; ZR II, 428.

300. January 8, 1911, 3 p.m.
BROOKLYN - The Academy of Music [2,086 seats]

Sunday Afternoon Concert

- Above program repeated -

SOLOIST (2–4, 7) E. Clément.
CHORUS (6 & 7) The MacDowell Chorus, cond. K. Schindler.
SOURCE Program; see illustration on opposite page.
NOTE Except for no. 4, none of the other works appear again in Mahler's programs.
REVIEW HLG IV, 1120.

301. January 10, 1911, 8:15 p.m.
302. January 13, 1911, 2:30 p.m.
NEW YORK - Carnegie Hall [2,800 seats]

Eighth Regular Subscription Concert

All-Wagner Program

    (1) *Eine Faust-Ouverture* •
    (2) From the *Wesendonck-Lieder*:
        a) "Schmerzen" •
        b) "Im Treibhaus" •
        c) "Stehe still" •
        d) "Träume"

THE PHILHARMONIC SOCIETY
OF NEW YORK

GUSTAV MAHLER - - Conductor

1910—Sixty-ninth Season—1911

Management, LOUDON CHARLTON

CARNEGIE HALL
Sunday Afternoon, January 15, 1911
At 3 o'clock

Soloist:
MME. JOHANNA GADSKI

All-Wagner Program

1. OVERTURE "Rienzi"
2. PRELUDE to "Lohengrin"

Program continued on second page following

PROGRAM—Continued

3. (a) "Lohengrin"—Elsa's Dream
   (b) "Tannhauser"—Elizabeth's Aria

—Intermission—

4. OVERTURE "Tannhauser"

5. FUNERAL MARCH
   "Gotterdammerung"

6. "Gotterdammerung"—
   Immolation Scene

The **Steinway Piano** is the Official Piano of the Philharmonic Society.

For special announcement see second page following

THE PHILHARMONIC SOCIETY
OF NEW YORK

GUSTAV MAHLER - - Conductor

1910—Sixty-ninth Season—1911

Management, LOUDON CHARLTON

CARNEGIE HALL
Tuesday Evening, January 17, 1911
At 8.15 o'clock
Friday Afternoon, January 20, 1911
At 2.30 o'clock

Soloist, MME. BELLA ALTEN
(Of the Metropolitan Opera House)

All-Modern Program

1. Overture "Das Kätchen von Heilbronn" .... *Pfitzner*
2. Symphony No. 4, in G major..... *Mahler*
   - I   Recht gemächlich
   - II In gemächlicher Bewegung
   - III Ruhevoll
   - IV Sehr behaglich
   - Solo Part: Mme. Alten

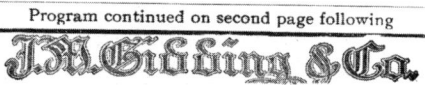

Program continued on second page following

PROGRAM—Continued

3. "Ein Heldenleben" Opus 40 ....
   .... *Richard Strauss*

The **Steinway Piano** is the Official Piano of the Philharmonic Society

For special announcement see second page following

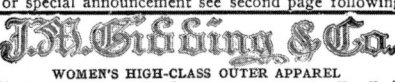

(3) Overture to *Der fliegende Holländer*
(4) Prelude and "Liebestod," from *Tristan und Isolde*
(5) *Siegfried Idyll*
(6) Prelude to Act 1 of *Die Meistersinger von Nürnberg*

SOLOIST (2 & 4) J. Gadski.
SOURCE Program; see illustration on previous page.
REVIEW HLG IV, 1121-1124; ZR II, 429.

303. **January 15, 1911, 3 p.m.**
NEW YORK - Carnegie Hall [2,800 seats]

Third Sunday Afternoon Concert

All-Wagner Program

(1) Overture to *Rienzi*
(2) Prelude to Act 1 of *Lohengrin*
(3) "Einsam in trüben Tagen," from *Lohengrin*
(4) "Dich teure Halle," from *Tannhäuser*
(5) Overture to *Tannhäuser*
(6) Funeral March, and Brünnhilde's Immolation Scene, from *Götterdämmerung*

SOLOIST (3 & 4, 6) J. Gadski.
SOURCE Program; see illustration on opposite page.
REVIEW HLG IV, 1124-1125.

304. **January 17, 1911, 8:15 p.m.**
305. **January 20, 1911, 2:30 p.m.**
NEW YORK - Carnegie Hall [2,800 seats]

Ninth Regular Subscription Concert. All-Modern Program

(1)	Pfitzner	Overture to *Das Käthchen von Heilbronn*, Op. 17a • [1]
(2)	Mahler	Symphony No. 4, G major • [2]
		- Intermission -
(3)	Strauss	*Ein Heldenleben*, Symphonic Poem, Op. 40 •

SOLOIST (2) B. Alten.
SOURCE Program; see illustration on opposite page.
NOTES [1] American premiere.
[2] The second U.S. performance, based on Mahler's final revision of the score from the preceding summer. The American premiere had already taken place in New York on November 6, 1904, with Walter Damrosch conducting the New York Symphony Orchestra.
REVIEW HLG IV, 1126-1132; ZR II, 435–441.

THE PHILHARMONIC SOCIETY
OF NEW YORK

GUSTAV MAHLER — Conductor

1910—Sixty-ninth Season—1911

Management, LOUDON CHARLTON

CARNEGIE HALL
Sunday Afternoon, January 22, 1911
At 2.30 o'clock

PROGRAM

1. Goldmark Overture—"In Springtime"

2. Tschaikowsky Symphony—"Pathetique"
   - I. Adagio; Allegro non troppo
   - II. Allegro con grazia
   - III. Allegro, molto vivace
   - IV. Finale: Adagio lamentoso

Program continued on second page following

J. M. Gidding & Co.
WOMEN'S HIGH-CLASS OUTER APPAREL
Fifth Avenue, 46th and 47th Streets — New York

PROGRAM—Continued

3. Weber-Weingartner—"Invitation to the Dance"

4. Liszt Symphonic Poem—"Tasso"

The Steinway Piano is the Official Piano of the Philharmonic Society.

For special announcement see second page following

J. M. Gidding & Co.
WOMEN'S HIGH-CLASS OUTER APPAREL
Fifth Avenue, 46th and 47th Streets — New York

The Philharmonic Society
of New York

1910... SIXTY-NINTH SEASON ...1911

Gustav Mahler ... Conductor

MANAGEMENT   LOUDON CHARLTON
LOCAL MANAGEMENT   T. ARTHUR SMITH

New National Theatre
TUESDAY AFTERNOON, JANUARY 24
AT 4.30 O'CLOCK

Soloist
MME. JOHANNA GADSKI

All-Wagner Programme
Overture to "Rienzi"
1. OVERTURE "The Flying Dutchman"
2. PRELUDE to "Lohengrin"
3. OVERTURE "Tannhäuser"
4. SOLOS
   - (a) "Tannhäuser"—Elizabeth's Aria
   - (b) "Lohengrin"—Elsa's Dream

   MME. GADSKI
5. SIEGFRIED IDYL
6. "TRISTAN und ISOLDE"—Prelude and Finale, Liebestod

   MME. GADSKI
7. PRELUDE to "Die Meistersinger"

The Steinway Piano is the Official Piano of the Philharmonic Society

306. January 22, 1911, 3 p.m.
NEW YORK - Carnegie Hall [2,800 seats]

Fourth Sunday Afternoon Concert

- (1) Goldmark — *Im Frühling*, Overture, Op. 36 •
- (2) Tchaikovsky — Symphony No. 6, B minor, Op. 74, "Pathétique"
- (3) Weber–Weingartner — *Aufforderung zum Tanze*, rondo brillant, Op. 65
- (4) Liszt — *Tasso, Lamento e Trionfo*, Symphonic Poem •

SOURCE Program; see illustration on opposite page.
REVIEW HLG IV, 1132-1135; ZR II, 446–447.

307. January 23, 1911, 3 p.m.
PHILADELPHIA - The Academy of Music [2,900 seats]

All-Wagner Program

- (1) Overture to *Der fliegende Holländer*
- (2) Prelude to Act 1 of *Lohengrin*
- (3) Overture to *Tannhäuser*
- (4) "Dich teure Halle," from *Tannhäuser*
- (5) "Einsam in trüben Tagen," from *Lohengrin*
- (6) *Siegfried Idyll*
- (7) Prelude and "Liebestod," from *Tristan und Isolde*
- (8) Prelude to Act 1 of *Die Meistersinger von Nürnberg*

SOLOIST (4–5, 7) J. Gadski.
SOURCE Program.
NOTE The Overture to *Rienzi* was originally announced but omitted at the last minute.
REVIEW HLG IV, 1135-1136; ZR II, 441–442.

308. January 24, 1911, 4:30 p.m.
WASHINGTON - New National Theater [1,900 seats]

- Above program repeated -

SOURCE Program; see illustration on opposite page.
NOTE This was the last performance of the *Siegfried Idyll*.
REVIEW HLG IV, 1136-1137; ZR II, 445.

THE PHILHARMONIC SOCIETY
OF NEW YORK

GUSTAV MAHLER - - Conductor

1910—Sixty-ninth Season—1911

Management, LOUDON CHARLTON

CARNEGIE HALL
Friday Afternoon, January 27, 1911
At 2.30 o'clock

Program

1. OVERTURE "Flying Dutchman"

2. TANNHÄUSER—Overture and Bacchanale

Program continued on second page following

J. M. Gidding & Co.
WOMEN'S HIGH-CLASS OUTER APPAREL
Fifth Avenue, 46th and 47th Streets   New York

The Philharmonic Society
of New York

1910... SIXTY-NINTH SEASON ...1911

Gustav Mahler ... Conductor

MANAGEMENT LOUDON CHARLTON

Brooklyn Academy of Music
SUNDAY AFTERNOON, JANUARY 29
AT THREE O'CLOCK

Soloist
MME. JOHANNA GADSKI

All-Wagner Programme

1. OVERTURE "Rienzi"
2. PRELUDE to "Lohengrin"
3. (a) "Lohengrin"—Elsa's Dream
   (b) "Tannhäuser"—Elizabeth's Aria
4. OVERTURE "Tannhäuser"
5. FUNERAL MARCH "Gotterdämmerung"
6. "Gotterdämmerung"—Immolation Scene

The Steinway Piano is the Official Piano of the Philharmonic Society

---

PROGRAM—Continued

3. (a) TANNHÄUSER—Introduction and Elizabeth's Aria

   (b) TANNHÄUSER—Elizabeth's Prayer

   (c) TRÄUME (by request)

4. PARSIFAL—Vorspiel and Glorification

5. TRISTAN UND ISOLDE— Vorspiel and Liebestod

6. WALKÜRE:
   (a) Ride of the Valkyries
   (b) Magic Fire Scene

The Steinway Piano is the Official Piano of the Philharmonic Society.

For special announcement see second page following

J. M. Gidding & Co.
WOMEN'S HIGH-CLASS OUTER APPAREL
Fifth Avenue, 46th and 47th Streets   New York

THE PHILHARMONIC SOCIETY
OF NEW YORK

GUSTAV MAHLER - - Conductor

1910—Sixty-ninth Season—1911

Management, LOUDON CHARLTON

CARNEGIE HALL
Tuesday Evening, January 31, 1911
At 8.15 o'clock

Friday Afternoon, February 3, 1911
At 2.30 o'clock

Program

1. MENDELSSOHN—Overture, "Melusine"

2. SCHUMANN—Symphony No. 3, in E flat (Rhenish), op. 97
   I. Lebhaft
   II. Scherzo: sehr massig
   III. Nicht schnell
   IV. Feierlich
   V. Lebhaft

Program continued on second page following

J. M. Gidding & Co.
WOMEN'S HIGH-CLASS OUTER APPAREL
Fifth Avenue, 46th and 47th Streets   New York

309. January 27, 1911, 2:30 p.m.
NEW YORK - Carnegie Hall [2,800 seats]

Extra Concert

All-Wagner Program

- (1) Overture to *Der fliegende Holländer*
- (2) Overture and Bacchanale from *Tannhäuser*
- (3) Introduction and "Dich teure Halle," from *Tannhäuser*
- (4) "Allmächt'ge Jungfrau" (Elisabeth's Prayer), from *Tannhäuser* •
- (5) "Träume," from the *Wesendonck-Lieder* [by request] •
- (6) Prelude & "Höchsten heiles Wunder," from *Parsifal* •
- (7) Prelude and "Liebestod," from *Tristan und Isolde* •
- (8) Walkürenritt, & Feuerzauber, from *Die Walküre* •

SOLOIST (3–5, 7) J. Gadski.
SOURCE Program; see illustration on opposite page.
REVIEW HLG IV, 1125-1126.

310. January 29, 1911, 3 p.m.
BROOKLYN - The Academy of Music [2,086 seats]

Sunday Afternoon Concert

All-Wagner Program

- (1) Overture to *Rienzi* •
- (2) Prelude to Act 1 of *Lohengrin*
- (3) "Einsam in trüben Tagen," from *Lohengrin* •
- (4) "Dich teure Halle," from *Tannhäuser* •
- (5) Overture to *Tannhäuser*
- (6) Funeral March, and Brünnhilde's Immolation Scene, from *Götterdämmerung*

SOLOIST (3–4, 6) J. Gadski.
SOURCE Program; see illustration on opposite page.

311. January 31, 1911, 8:15 p.m.
312. February 3, 1911, 2:30 p.m.
NEW YORK - Carnegie Hall [2,800 seats]

Tenth Regular Subscription Concert

(1)	Mendelssohn	*Das Märchen von der schönen Melusine*, Overture, Op. 32 •
(2)	Schumann	Symphony No. 3, E-flat major, Op. 97, "Rhenish" •
		- Intermission -
(3)	Wagner	Prelude to Act 1 of *Lohengrin* •
(4)	Bizet	*Roma*, Suite de Concert No. 3 • [1]

THE PHILHARMONIC SOCIETY
OF NEW YORK

GUSTAV MAHLER - - Conductor

1910—Sixty-ninth Season—1911

Management, LOUDON CHARLTON

CARNEGIE HALL
Sunday Afternoon, February 5, 1911
At 3 o'clock

Soloist:
MR. ERNEST HUTCHESON, Pianist

PROGRAM

1. LALO—Overture, "Le Roi d'Ys"

2. SCHUBERT—Symphony in B minor, (Unfinished)
   I. Allegro moderato
   II. Andante con moto

Program continued on second page following

J.M.Gidding & Co.
WOMEN'S HIGH-CLASS OUTER APPAREL
Fifth Avenue, 46th and 47th Streets   New York

PROGRAM—Continued

3. MAC DOWELL—Concerto in D minor, op. 23
   I. Larghetto calmato; Poco piu mosso e con passione
   II. Presto giocoso
   III. Largo; molto allegro

—INTERMISSION—

4. WAGNER—
   (a) Overture, "Flying Dutchman"
   (b) Waldweben, "Siegfried"
   (c) Prelude, "Die Meistersinger"

The Steinway Piano is the Official Piano of the Philharmonic Society

For special announcement see second page following

J.M.Gidding & Co.
WOMEN'S HIGH-CLASS OUTER APPAREL
Fifth Avenue, 46th and 47th Streets   New York

THE PHILHARMONIC SOCIETY
OF NEW YORK

GUSTAV MAHLER - - Conductor

1910—Sixty-ninth Season—1911

Management, LOUDON CHARLTON

CARNEGIE HALL
Tuesday Evening, February 7, 1911
At 8.15 o'clock
Friday Afternoon, February 10, 1911
At 2.30 o'clock

Soloist, DAVID BISPHAM, Baritone

PROGRAM

1. BERLIOZ Three movements from "Romeo and Juliet," op 17
   I. Romeo alone — Sadness — Concert and Ball. Grand Fête at Capulet's house
   Andante malinconico e sostenuto; Allegro; larghetto espressivo; allegro.
   II. Love Scene, Adagio. Capulet's Garden at Night; Juliet on the Balcony, Romeo in the Garden below.
   III. Scherzo; prestissimo. Queen Mab, or the Dream Fairy.

Program continued on second page following

J.M.Gidding & Co.
WOMEN'S HIGH-CLASS OUTER APPAREL
Fifth Avenue, 46th and 47th Streets   New York

PROGRAM—Continued

2. (a) WAGNER. Meistersinger, Introduction to Act 3 and Sachs's Monologue.
   (b) R. STRAUSS. Pilgrim's Morning Song.

—INTERMISSION—

3. BEETHOVEN. Symphony in A major, No. 7, op. 92.
   I. Introduction: Poco sostenuto; vivace. II. Allegretto. III. Scherzo; Presto. Trio: Assai meno presto. IV. Finale: Allegro con brio.

The Steinway Piano is the Official Piano of the Philharmonic Society.

For special announcement see second page following

J.M.Gidding & Co.
WOMEN'S HIGH-CLASS OUTER APPAREL
Fifth Avenue, 46th and 47th Streets   New York

SOURCE Program; see illustration on previous page.
NOTE [1] First performance in New York.
REVIEW HLG IV, 1137-1138.

313. February 5, 1911, 3 p.m.
NEW YORK - Carnegie Hall [2,800 seats]

Fifth Sunday Afternoon Concert

(1)	Lalo	Overture to *Le Roi d'Ys* •
(2)	Schubert	Symphony No. 8 (7), B minor, D 759, "Unfinished" •
(3)	MacDowell	Piano Concerto No. 2, D minor, Op. 23 •
		- Intermission -
(4)	Wagner	Overture to *Der fliegende Holländer* •
(5)	Wagner	Waldweben, from *Siegfried* •
(6)	Wagner	Prelude to Act 1 of *Die Meistersinger von Nürnberg* •

SOLOIST (3) E. Hutcheson.
SOURCE Program; see illustration on opposite page.
REVIEW HLG IV, 1139.

314. February 7, 1911, 8:15 p.m.
315. February 10, 1911, 2:30 p.m.
NEW YORK - Carnegie Hall [2,800 seats]

Eleventh Regular Subscription Concert

(1)	Berlioz	Three excerpts from *Roméo et Juliette*, Op. 17 •
		a) Grande fête chez Capulet
		b) Scène d'amour
		c) La Reine Mab, ou La Fête des songes (Scherzo)
(2)	Wagner	Prelude to Act 3 of *Die Meistersinger von Nürnberg*
(3)	Wagner	"Wahn! Wahn! Überall Wahn!" from
		Die Meistersinger von Nürnberg
(4)	Strauss	"Pilgers Morgenlied," *Lied*, Op. 33, No. 4, with Orch.
		- Intermission -
(5)	Beethoven	Symphony No. 7, A major, Op. 92

SOLOIST (3 & 4) D. Bispham.
SOURCE Program; see illustration on opposite page.
REVIEW HLG IV, 1140-1141.

The Philharmonic Society
of New York

1910 ... SIXTY-NINTH SEASON ... 1911

Gustav Mahler ... Conductor

MANAGEMENT   LOUDON CHARLTON

Brooklyn Academy of Music

SUNDAY AFTERNOON, FEBRUARY 12
AT THREE O'CLOCK

Soloist

MR. DAVID BISPHAM
Baritone

Programme

1. WEBER — Overture "Oberon"
2. TSCHAIKOWSKY — Symphony Pathetique, VI, B minor
   - I Introduction: adagio; allegro, non troppo
   - II Allegro con grazia
   - III Allegro molto vivace
   - IV Finale: adagio lamentoso

INTERMISSION

3. (a) WAGNER — Meistersinger, Introduction to Act III and Sachs' Monologue
   (b) R. STRAUSS — Pilgrim's Morning Song
4. LISZT — Symphonic Poem, "Les Preludes"

The Steinway Piano is the Official Piano of the Philharmonic Society

---

THE PHILHARMONIC SOCIETY
OF NEW YORK

GUSTAV MAHLER — Conductor

1910—Sixty-ninth Season—1911

Management, LOUDON CHARLTON

CARNEGIE HALL

Tuesday Evening, February 14, 1911
at 8.15 o'clock

Friday Afternoon, February 17, 1911
At 2.30 o'clock

Soloist, Mme. KIRKBY-LUNN, Contralto

PROGRAM

1. STANFORD ..... Symphony in F minor, (Irish) op. 28
   - I. Allegro moderato
   - II. Allegro molto vivace
   - III. Andante con moto
   - IV. Finale: Allegro moderato ma con fuoco

Program continued on second page following

J. M. Gidding & Co.
WOMEN'S HIGH-CLASS OUTER APPAREL
Fifth Avenue, 46th and 47th Streets   New York

PROGRAM—Continued

2. ELGAR .... Sea Pictures
   (a) "In Haven"
   (b) "Sabbath Morning at Sea"
   (c) "Where Corals Lie"

—INTERMISSION—

3. LOEFFLER .... La Villanelle du Diable
   (MR. FRANK L. SEALY at the Organ)

4. MacDOWELL ... (a) "The Saracens"
                  (b) "Die Schöne Alda"

5. HADLEY .... Culprit Fay

The Steinway Piano is the official Piano of the Philharmonic Society

For special announcement see second page following

J. M. Gidding & Co.
WOMEN'S HIGH-CLASS OUTER APPAREL
Fifth Avenue, 46th and 47th Streets   New York

316. **February 12, 1911, 3 p.m.**
BROOKLYN - The Academy of Music [2,086 seats]

Supplementary Sunday Afternoon Concert

(1) Weber — Overture to *Oberon*
(2) Tchaikovsky — Symphony No. 6, B minor, Op. 74, "Pathétique" •
- Intermission -
(3) Wagner — Prelude to Act 3 and "Was duftet doch die Flieder," from *Die Meistersinger von Nürnberg* •
(4) Strauss — "Pilgers Morgenlied," *Lied*, Op. 33, No. 4, with Orch. •
(5) Liszt — *Les Préludes*, Symphonic Poem

SOLOIST (3 & 4) D. Bispham.
SOURCE Program; see illustration on opposite page.
NOTE A preview of this concert, in the program booklet to concert 310, announces a complete performance of Berlioz's dramatic symphony *Roméo et Juliette*, followed by the Wagner and the Strauss compositions; Beethoven's Symphony No. 7 was to conclude the evening.
REVIEW HLG IV, 1148.

317. **February 14, 1911, 8:15 p.m.**
NEW YORK - Carnegie Hall [2,800 seats]

Twelfth Regular Subscription Concert. English-American Program

(1) Chadwick — *Melpomene*, Dramatic Overture [1]
(2) Stanford — Symphony No. 3, F minor, Op. 28, "Irish"
(3) Elgar — *Sea Pictures*, Op. 37, for Contralto and Orch.
   a) "Sea Slumber Song" [1]
   b) "In Haven"
   c) "Sabbath Morning at Sea"
   d) "Where Corals Lie"
(4) Loeffler — *La Villanelle du Diable*, Fantasie symphonique, Op. 9
(5) MacDowell — The Saracens & The Lovely Alda, from the Symphonic Poem *The Song of Roland*, Op. 30 [2]
(6) Hadley — *The Culprit Fay*, Rhapsody for Orchestra, Op. 62

SOLOIST (3) L. Kirkby-Lunn; (4) F. L. Sealy, organ.
SOURCE Program; see illustration on opposite page.
NOTES [1] Added to the original program: "In response to a general request."
[2] The originally announced program had only listed the "March of the Saracens."
REVIEW HLG IV, 1146-1148.

PARSONS' THEATER
HOME of HIGH CLASS PLAYS
TONIGHT at 8:15.

A GREAT MAN WITH A GREAT BIG ORCHESTRA

Symphonic Event Of The Season.
FIRST ANNUAL APPEARANCE

PHILHARMONIC SOCIETY OF NEW YORK.

World's Greatest Symphonic Conductor,
GUSTAV MAHLER.
100 Performers. Superb Novel Program.
Seats on Sale, $2.00, $1.50, $1.00, 75c.
Mr. Mahler will play the Harpsichord in the Bach Suite.

The Philharmonic Society
of New York

1910... SIXTY-NINTH SEASON ...1911

Gustav Mahler ... Conductor

MANAGEMENT   LOUDON CHARLTON
LOCAL MANAGEMENT   WM. F. A. ENGEL

Parsons Theatre

THURSDAY EVENING, FEBRUARY 16
AT 8.15 O'CLOCK

Programme

1. BACH-MAHLER — Suite for Orchestra
   (MR. MAHLER AT THE HARPSICHORD)
2. BEETHOVEN   Symphony VI, Pastoral, F major, op. 68
   I. JOYFUL IMPRESSIONS ON ARRIVING IN THE COUNTRY
      Allegro ma non troppo
   II. SCENE BY THE BROOK
      Andante molto moto
   III. MERRY-MAKING OF THE COUNTRY FOLK
      Allegro
   IV. THUNDER-STORM, TEMPEST
      Allegro
   V. SHEPHERD'S SONG; GLADNESS AFTER THE STORM
      Allegretto

   INTERMISSION

3. WEBER-WEINGARTNER — Invitation to the Dance
4. LISZT — Symphonic Poem "Les Preludes"

The Steinway Piano is the Official Piano of the Philharmonic Society

---

THE PHILHARMONIC SOCIETY
OF NEW YORK

GUSTAV MAHLER — Conductor

1910—Sixty-ninth Season—1911

Management, LOUDON CHARLTON

CARNEGIE HALL
Sunday Afternoon, February 19, 1911
At 3 o'clock

Soloist: **FREDERIC FRADKIN**, Violinist

PROGRAM

1. WEBER—Overture "Oberon"
2. BEETHOVEN—Symphony in A major, No. 7, Op. 92
   I. Introduction: Poco sostenuto; vivace
   II. Allegretto
   III. Scherzo: Presto.   Trio:—
      Assai meno presto
   IV. Finale: Allegro con brio

Program continued on second page following

J. M. Gidding & Co.
WOMEN'S HIGH-CLASS OUTER APPAREL
Fifth Avenue, 46th and 47th Streets   New York

PROGRAM—Continued

—Intermission—

3. MENDELSSOHN—
   Violin Concerto E minor, Op. 64

4. LISZT—Symphonic Poem, "Les Preludes"

The Steinway Piano is the official Piano of the Philharmonic Society

For special announcement see second page following

J. M. Gidding & Co.
WOMEN'S HIGH-CLASS OUTER APPAREL
Fifth Avenue, 46th and 47th Streets   New York

318. **February 15, 1911, 8:15 p.m.**
SPRINGFIELD - The Court Square Theater [1,860 seats]

- (1) Bach–Mahler — Suite for Orchestra
- (2) Beethoven — Symphony No. 6, F major, Op. 68, "Pastoral"

- Intermission -

- (3) Weber–Weingartner — *Aufforderung zum Tanze*, rondo brillant, Op. 65
- (4) Liszt — *Les Préludes*, Symphonic Poem

SOURCE Program.
REVIEW HLG IV, 1150-1151.

319. **February 16, 1911, 8:15 p.m.**
HARTFORD - Parsons Theater [1,700 seats]

- Above program repeated -

SOURCE Program and newspaper advertisement; see illustrations on opposite page.
NOTE Mahler's last performances of all these works.
REVIEW HLG IV, 1150, 1152-1153.

320. **February 17, 1911, 2:30 p.m.**
NEW YORK - Carnegie Hall [2,800 seats]

Twelfth Regular Subscription Concert. All-English-American Program

- (1) Chadwick — *Melpomene*, Dramatic Overture •
- (2) Stanford — Symphony No. 3, F minor, Op. 28, "Irish" •
- (3) Elgar — *Sea Pictures*, Op. 37, for Contralto and Orch. •
  - a) "Sea Slumber Song" [1]
  - b) "In Haven"
  - c) "Sabbath Morning at Sea"
  - d) "Where Corals Lie"
- (4) Loeffler — *La Villanelle du Diable*, Fantasie symphonique, Op. 9 •
- (5) MacDowell — The Saracens & The Lovely Alda, from the Symphonic Poem *The Song of Roland*, Op. 30 •
- (6) Hadley — *The Culprit Fay*, Rhapsody for Orchestra, Op. 62 •

SOLOIST (3) L. Kirkby-Lunn.
SOURCE Program; see illustration on previous page.
REVIEW HLG IV, 1146-1148.

The Philharmonic Society
of New York

1910 ... SIXTY-NINTH SEASON ... 1911

Gustav Mahler ... Conductor

MANAGEMENT   LOUDON CHARLTON

Carnegie Hall

TUESDAY NIGHT, FEBRUARY 21
AT EIGHT-FIFTEEN

FRIDAY AFTERNOON, FEBRUARY 24
AT TWO-THIRTY

Soloist
ERNESTO CONSOLO
Pianist

Programme

1. SINIGAGLIA - Overture, "Le baruffe Chiozzotte, op. 32
2. MENDELSSOHN - Symphony No. 4, "Italian", op. 90
   - I Allegro vivace
   - II Andante con moto
   - III Con moto moderato
   - IV Saltarello: Presto

   INTERMISSION

3. MARTUCCI - - Concerto in B-flat minor, op. 66
   - I Allegro giusto
   - II Larghetto
   - III Allegro con spirito

4. BUSONI - - - - - "Berceuse élégiaque"
5. BOSSI "Intermezzi Goldoniani", for string orchestra, op. 127
   - I Preludio e Minuetto: Preludio, Allegro con fuoco; Minuetto. Con grazia; with Trio, Poco piu mosso
   - II Gagliardo: Vivace
   - III Coprifuoco: Blandamente
   - IV Minuetto e Musetta: Minuetto, con moto; Musetta, alquanto meno mosso
   - V Serenatina: Allegretto tranquillo
   - VI Burlesca: Con molto brio

The Steinway Piano is the Official Piano of the Philharmonic Society

| New York | 1911 | Concerts Nos. 321–323 |

321. **February 19, 1911, 3 p.m.**
NEW YORK - Carnegie Hall [2,800 seats]

Sixth Sunday Afternoon Concert

(1) Weber — Overture to *Oberon* •
(2) Beethoven — Symphony No. 7, A major, Op. 92 • [1]
- Intermission -
(3) Mendelssohn — Violin Concerto, E minor, Op. 64 •
(4) Liszt — *Les Préludes*, Symphonic Poem •

SOLOIST (3) F. Fradkin.
SOURCE Program; see illustration on previous page.
NOTE [1] The preview in the program booklet to concert 317 announces Beethoven's Symphony No. 3, "Eroica."
REVIEW HLG IV, 1154.

322. **February 21, 1911, 8:15 p.m.**
323. **February 24, 1911, 2:30 p.m.** [1]
NEW YORK - Carnegie Hall [2,800 seats]

Thirteenth Regular Subscription Concert. All-Italian Program

(1) Sinigaglia — *Le Baruffe Chiozzotte*, Overture, Op. 32 • [2]
(2) Mendelssohn — Symphony No. 4, A major, Op. 90, "Italian" • [3]
- Intermission -
(3) Martucci — Piano Concerto No. 2, B-flat minor, Op. 66 • [2]
(4) Busoni — *Berceuse élégiaque. Des Mannes Wiegenlied am Sarge seiner Mutter* • [4]
(5) Bossi — *Intermezzi Goldoniani*, Op. 127, for String Orch. •

SOLOIST (3) E. Consolo.
SOURCE Program; see illustration on opposite page.
NOTES [1] Cancelled by Mahler who was replaced by Theodore Spiering. Concert 323 is concert A1 in Appendix I.
[2] First performance in New York.
[3] In his review, on February 22, in the New York *Daily Tribune*, H.E. Krehbiel reports that [Giovanni] Sgambati's D-major Symphony, Op. 16, [published 1883] had been originally scheduled, "but a panic fear seized upon somebody in authority and this fine symphony was stricken out and Mendelssohn's Symphony in A substituted for it." (This was Mahler's first performance of Mendelssohn's *Italian* Symphony.)
[4] World premiere. The review in *The New York Times* reports that Busoni attended the concert, sharing a box with Arturo Toscanini. This is confirmed by a letter from Busoni to his wife.
REVIEW HLG IV, 1178-1181; ZR II, 456–458.

Part XIII
Appendix I: The Season's Remaining Concerts

It appears that Mahler was not feeling well when he climbed the podium on February 21. His friend, Dr. Joseph Fraenkel, had advised against his appearance (AMM, p. 189). However, the ever conscientious Mahler, who had cancelled performances due to sickness only a few times over his long conducting career, disregarded his doctor's advice and conducted what sadly proved to be his last concert. The following morning Mahler cancelled the repeat performance on the 24th, which only emphasizes the gravity of his illness.

Theodore Spiering stepped in as Mahler's substitute at the first cancelled concert, and continued to replace Mahler during the season's remaining five weeks. However, Spiering's name never appeared in the printed programs, which all announce Mahler as conductor, even the improvised extra concerts that were not part of the Philharmonic's scheduled subscription concerts. This can only mean that Mahler constantly hoped that he would soon recover his health and resume work with the Philharmonic Orchestra.

It is not known whether or not Mahler took an active part in programming the concerts during his illness.

The Viennese newspapers did not take any notice of Mahler's illness before March 24, 1911, when the *Neue Freie Presse* announced that Anna Moll, Mahler's mother-in-law, had left Vienna for New York in order to support her daughter in looking after Mahler.

| New York – Princeton – Washington | 1911 | Appendix Nos. A 1–4 |

An asterisk * indicates compositions new to Mahler's repertoire.

A 1. **February 24, 1911, 2:30 p.m.**
NEW YORK - Carnegie Hall [2,800 seats]

- Concert no. 322 repeated -

CONDUCTOR Theodore Spiering, except for the Busoni, which was conducted by the composer.

A 2. **February 26, 1911, 3 p.m.**
NEW YORK - Carnegie Hall [2,800 seats]

(1)	Goldmark	*Sakuntala*, Concert Overture, Op. 13
(2)	Beethoven	Symphony No. 3, E-flat major, Op. 55, "Eroica"
		- Intermission -
(3)	Wagner	Siegfried's Rhine Journey, from *Götterdämmerung*
(4)	Wagner	Good Friday Spell, from *Parsifal*
(5)	Wagner	*Kaisermarsch*

CONDUCTOR Theodore Spiering.

A 3. **February 27, 1911, 3 p.m.**
PRINCETON - Alexander Hall [891 seats]

(1)	Wagner	Overture to *Der fliegende Holländer*
(2)	Beethoven	Symphony No. 7, A major, Op. 92
		- Intermission -
(3)	Weber–Weingartner	*Aufforderung zum Tanze,* rondo brillant, Op. 65
(4)	Bizet	*L'Arlésienne* Suite [No. 1] [1]
(5)	Liszt	*Les Préludes*, Symphonic Poem

CONDUCTOR Theodore Spiering.
NOTE [1] Chorus unknown.

A 4. **February 28, 1911, 4:30 p.m.**
WASHINGTON - New National Theater [1,900 seats]

(1)	MacDowell	Piano Concerto No. 2, D minor, Op. 23 [1]
(2)	Beethoven	Symphony No. 6, F major, Op. 68, "Pastoral"
		- Intermission -
(3)	Weber	Overture to "Oberon"
(4)	Weber–Weingartner	*Aufforderung zum Tanze,* rondo brillant, Op. 65
(5)	Liszt	*Les Préludes*, Symphonic Poem

SOLOIST (1) E. Hutcheson.
CONDUCTOR Theodore Spiering.
NOTE [1] Replaced the announced Bach–Mahler Suite for Orchestra.

| New York | 1911 | Appendix Nos. A 5–8 |

A 5. March 3, 1911, 8:15 p.m.
NEW YORK - Carnegie Hall [2,800 seats]

(1)	Mussorgsky	*Joshua*, Biblical cantata for Contralto, Bass, Chorus, and Orchestra
(2)	Borodin	Three excerpts from *Prince Igor,* for Soloists, Chorus, and Orchestra:
		a) Polovtsian Maidens' Chorus
		b) Villagers' Chorus
		c) Polovtsian Dances and Chorus
		– Intermission –
(3)	Chabrier	*España*, Rhapsody for Orchestra
(4)	Chabrier	*Briséis,* ou Les amants de Corinthe, Act I

SOLOISTS (1) C. Sapin & L. Rothier (2a) C. Sapin (2b) V. Waterhouse (4) A. Gluck, C. Bressler-Gianoli, E. Clément, D. Gilly, L. Rothier.
CONDUCTOR Kurt Schindler.
CHORUS The MacDowell Choir.

A 6. March 5, 1911, 3 p.m.
NEW YORK - Carnegie Hall [2,800 seats]

Eighth Sunday Afternoon Concert. Special Request Program

(1)	Mendelssohn	*Die Hebriden* (*Fingal's Cave*), Overture, Op. 26
(2)	Dvořák	*Symphony No. 9, E minor, Op. 95, "From the New World"
		– Intermission –
(3)	Grieg	*Peer Gynt* Suite No. 1, Op. 46
(4)	Wagner	Walkürenritt, from *Die Walküre*
(5)	Wagner	Prelude and "Liebestod," from *Tristan und Isolde*
(6)	Wagner	Overture to *Der fliegende Holländer*

CONDUCTOR Theodore Spiering.

A 7. March 7, 1911, 8:15 p.m.
A 8. March 10, 1911, 2:30 p.m.
NEW YORK - Carnegie Hall [2,800 seats]

Fourteenth Regular Subscription Concert [1]

(1)	Weber	Overture to *Der Freischütz*
(2)	Schillings	*Introduction to Act 3 of *Der Pfeifertag* [2]
(3)	Schubert	Symphony No. 8 (7), B minor, D 759, "Unfinished"
		– Intermission –
(4)	Strauss	*Lieder* with Orchestra:
		a) *"Verführung," Op. 33, No. 1
		b) *"Freundliche Vision," Op. 48, No. 1
		c) *"Heimliche Aufforderung," Op. 27, No. 3
(5)	Glazunov	*Le Printemps,* Tableau Musical, Op. 34
(6)	Strauss	*Tod und Verklärung*, Tone Poem, Op. 24

SOLOIST (4) G. Hamlin.
CONDUCTOR Theodore Spiering.
NOTES [1] Advertised in the January 17 program booklet as a "Living Composers Program."
[2] American premiere.

| New York – Brooklyn | 1911 | Appendix Nos. A 9–12 |

A 9. **March 12, 1911, 3 p.m.**
NEW YORK - Carnegie Hall [2,800 seats]

Ninth Sunday Afternoon Concert (Extra Concert)

- (1) Beethoven — Overture to *Egmont*, Op. 84
- (2) Schumann — Symphony No. 3, E-flat major, Op. 97, "Rhenish"
- - Intermission -
- (3) Saint-Saëns — *Two arias from *Samson et Delilah*:
  a) "Printemps qui commence"
  b) "Mon Cœur s'ouvre à ta voix"
- (4) Grieg — Triumphal March from *Sigurd Jorsalfar*, Op. 56
- (5) Grieg — *"At the Cloister Gate," from *Foran Sydens kloster*, Op. 20, for Soloists and Women's Chorus
- (6) Bizet — *L'Arlésienne* Suite, No. 1, with Chorus

SOLOISTS (3 & 5) L. Kirkby-Lunn; (5) E. Sands Dunham.
CONDUCTOR Theodore Spiering.
CHORUS (5 & 6) The MacDowell Chorus, cond. Kurt Schindler.

A 10. **March 14, 1911, 8:15 p.m.**
A 11. **March 17, 1911, 2:30 p.m.**
NEW YORK - Carnegie Hall [2,800 seats]

Fifteenth Regular Subscription Concert. Norse-Slavic Program

- (1) Svendsen — *Carnival in Paris*, Op. 9
- (2) Tchaikovsky — *Francesca da Rimini*, Op. 32
- - Intermission -
- (3) Sibelius — *Violin Concerto, D minor, Op. 47
- (4) Dvořák — *Symphony No. 9, E minor, Op. 95, "From the New World"

SOLOIST (3) M. Powell.
CONDUCTOR Theodore Spiering.
NOTE An early preview of concert A 10 had announced, apart from the Sibelius Concerto and the Svendsen piece, the Overture *In the South* by Elgar, and Gustave Charpentier's *Impressions d'Italie*.
Similarly, a preview of concert A 11 had announced Borodin's *Symphony No. 2, N.W.Gade's Overture *Nachklänge von Ossian*, Op. 1, Grieg's Incidental Music to *Sigurd Jorsalfar*, plus some unspecified songs, and finally Sibelius' *Pohjola's Daughter*, Op. 49.

A 12. **March 19, 1911, 3 p.m.**
BROOKLYN - The Academy of Music [2,086 seats]

Extraordinary Sunday Afternoon Concert: Special Request Program

- (1) Mendelssohn — *Die Hebriden (Fingal's Cave)*, Overture, Op. 26
- (2) Dvořák — Symphony No. 9, E minor, Op. 95, "From the New World"
- - Intermission -
- (3) Bruch — *Violin Concerto, No. 1, G minor, Op. 26
- (4) Wagner — Walkürenritt, from *Die Walküre*

(5)	Wagner	Prelude and "Liebestod," from *Tristan und Isolde*
(6)	Wagner	Overture to *Der fliegende Holländer*

SOLOIST (3) K. Parlow.
CONDUCTOR Theodore Spiering.

A 13. March 21, 1911, 8:15 p.m.
NEW YORK - Carnegie Hall [2,800 seats]

Sixteenth Regular Subscription Concert. All-German Program

(1)	Wagner	Overture and Bacchanale from *Tannhäuser*
(2)	Wagner	"Höre mit Sinn was ich sage," from *Götterdämmerung*
(3)	Strauss	*Till Eulenspiegels lustige Streiche*, Op. 28
(4)	Wagner	"Gerechter Gott ... In seiner Blüthe," from *Rienzi*
		- Intermission -
(5)	Beethoven	Symphony No. 5, C minor, Op. 67

SOLOIST (2 & 4) E. Schumann-Heink.
CONDUCTOR Theodore Spiering.
NOTE According to an early preview the program originally consisted of Gluck's Overture to *Iphigenie en Aulide*, Beethoven's Symphony No. 5, an unspecified Wagner overture, Schubert's Lied "Die Allmacht" (orch. by Liszt), and Strauss' *Till Eulenspiegel*.

A 14. March 22, 1911, 8:15 p.m.
NEWARK - The Krueger Auditorium [2,500 seats]

(1)	Wagner	Overture to *Der fliegende Holländer*
(2)	Tchaikovsky	Symphony No. 6, B minor, Op. 74, "Pathétique"
		- Intermission -
(3)	Wagner	Good Friday Spell, from *Parsifal*
(4)	Wagner	Walkürenritt, from *Die Walküre*
(5)	Wagner	Prelude and "Liebestod," from *Tristan und Isolde*
(6)	Wagner	Prelude to Act 1 of *Die Meistersinger von Nürnberg*

CONDUCTOR Theodore Spiering.

A 15. March 24, 1911, 2:30 p.m.
NEW YORK - Carnegie Hall [2,800 seats]

- Repeat of concert A 13 of March 21, 1911 -

CONDUCTOR Theodore Spiering.

A 16. March 27, 1911, 8:15 p.m.
PRINCETON - Alexander Hall [891 seats]

(1)	Beethoven	*Leonore* Overture No. 3, Op. 72b
(2)	Tchaikovsky	Symphony No. 6, B minor, Op. 74, "Pathétique"
		- Intermission -

(3)	Saint-Saëns	Two arias from *Samson et Delilah*: a) "Printemps qui commence" b) "Mon Cœur s'ouvre à ta voix"
(4)	Wagner	Walkürenritt, from *Die Walküre*
(5)	Wagner	Prelude and "Liebestod," from *Tristan und Isolde*

SOLOIST (3 & 5) L. Kirkby-Lunn.
CONDUCTOR Theodore Spiering.

A 17. March 28, 1911, 4:30 p.m.
WASHINGTON - New National Theater [1,900 seats]

(1)	Beethoven	*Leonore* Overture No. 3, Op. 72b
(2)	Tchaikovsky	Symphony No. 6, B minor, Op. 74, "Pathétique"
		- Intermission -
(3)	Saint-Saëns	Two arias from *Samson et Delilah*: a) "Printemps qui commence" b) "Mon Cœur s'ouvre à ta voix"
(4)	Wagner	Siegfried's Rhine Journey, from *Die Götterdämmerung*
(5)	Chabrier	*España*, Rhapsody for Orchestra

SOLOIST (3) L. Kirkby-Lunn.
CONDUCTOR Theodore Spiering.

A 18. April 2, 1911, 3 p.m.
NEW YORK - Carnegie Hall [2,800 seats]

Extraordinary Concert. In Aid of the "Wage Earners League"

(1)	Wagner	Overture to *Tannhäuser*
(2)	Tchaikovsky	Symphony No. 6, B minor, Op. 74, "Pathétique"
(3)	Wagner	Good Friday Spell, from *Parsifal*
(4)	Wagner	Feuerzauber, from *Die Walküre*
(5)	Rubinstein	Piano Concerto No. 4, D minor, Op. 70
(6)	Wagner	*Kaisermarsch*

SOLOIST (5) L. Ornstein.
CONDUCTOR Theodore Spiering.
SOURCE An advertisement in *The New York Times* from April 1, 1911.

Epilogue

On April 8, six days after the above concert took place, Mahler left New York and sailed for Europe, Paris being his first destination. He arrived there on April 17. Alas, the three weeks that Mahler spent in Paris—first in a hotel and soon afterwards a clinic in the suburb of Neuilly—did not bring any improvement to his health. He must have realized that his case was hopeless and, according to his own wishes, it was finally decided that he should travel to Vienna.

At noon on May 12, Mahler left the French capital by train, and the following evening arrived in Vienna, where he was brought straight to a sanatorium. Five days later, on the evening of May 18, 1911, he died, barely 51 years old. Four days later he was buried at the Grinzing cemetery.

Appendix II: COMPOSERS INDEX

The number listed refers to the *Concert Number*. Works in a concert not conducted by Mahler are marked with an asterisk *. Concert numbers with the prefix "A" indicate that Mahler was unable to perform due to illness (starting with concert 323 or A 1.)
Mahler's stage repertoire is listed in Appendix VI: *Mahler at the Opera*, p. 365.

ABT, Franz (1819–1885)
"Mir träumte von einem Königskind," for A-Cappella Chorus *132
"Sonntagsmorgen," Op. 192, No. 1, for Mixed Chorus *12

ADAM, Adolphe Charles (1803–1856)
La Poupée de Nuremberg: Aria (unspecified) 55

ALÁRD, Delphin (1815–1888)
Concerto for 2 Violins (unspecified), with Piano Acc. 8

d'ALBERT, Eugene (1864–1932)
"Das Mädchen und der Schmetterling," *Lied*, Op. 3 67
Scherzo, Op.16, No. 2, for Piano *182

ALYABYEV, Alexander (1787-1851)
"The Nightingale", *Lied* 31

ANONYMOUS
Braun Maidelein, arr. for Chorus by Hugo Jüngst *132
Lieder (unspecified) 273
Two Hungarian Folk Songs ("Lehullott a rezgö nyárfa levele" & "Ritka búza, ritka rozs")
    with Piano Acc. 37
Overtures (unspecified) *273
Quartets (unspecified) for Men's Chorus *7
"Schilflied," *Lied* 37
Swedish Folk Songs (unspecified, except for "Pehr svinaherde"
    ["Per, the Swineherd"] and "Ack, Wärmeland, du sköna") 29

ARDITI, Luigi (1822–1903)
Forosetta, Tarantella, for Soprano and Orchestra 37

BACH, Johann Sebastian (1685–1750)
Aria and Chorus, arr. C. Saint-Saëns for Piano *11
Matthäus-Passion, BWV 244
—"Wir setzen uns," No. 78, for Chorus and Orchestra 85
—"Wenn ich einmal soll scheiden," No. 72, for Chorus and Orchestra *60
Piano Concerto No. 1, D minor, BWV 1052, ed. F. Busoni 136
Prelude on Hassler's "Herzlich thut mich verlangen," A minor, BWV 727, for Organ *60
Singet dem Herrn ein neues Leid, Motet No. 1, BWV 225 .... *180
Prelude, Fugue and Chorale, arr. for Orchestra by J.J. Abert *36
Prelude and Fugue, No. 16, G minor, BWV 861, for Piano *31
Suite for Orchestra, arr. G. Mahler from the Orchestral Suites or Overtures Nos. 2 & 3,
    BWV 1067–1068 .... 223, 226, 227, 237, 239, 253, 254, 256,
    .... 269, 274, 275, 276, 286, 287, 288, 289, 290, 291, 318, 319
Toccata and Fugue, D minor, BWV 565, arr. C. Tausig for Piano *33
Violin Concerto No. 2, E major, BWV 1042, ed. F.A. Gevaërt 223
"Willst du dein Herz mir schenken," *Lied*, BWV 518 31

BECKER, Reinhold (1842–1924)
"Erwärtung," *Lied*, Op. 61, No. 4 .... *57
"Ganz leise," *Lied*, Op. 61, No. 5 .... *57

BEETHOVEN, Ludwig van (1770–1827)
"Ah perfido!" Scene and Aria, Op. 65, for Soprano and Orchestra 200, 247, 248, 249
An die ferne Geliebte, Op. 98, *Lied*-cycle with Piano Acc. *177
"An die Hoffnung," *Lied*, Op. 94 .... *98
Coriolan, Overture, Op. 62 .... *57, 67, 89, 99, *109, 137, 177, 179, 193, 199,
.... 201, 202, 207, 210, 211, 231, 232, 234, 245, 292, 293
Egmont, Incidental Music to Goethe's Play, Op. 84
— Overture .... 2, 13, 55, 80, 108, 115, 130, *142, 147, 217, 234, 244, A 9
— "Freudvoll und Leidvoll," *Lied*, with Orchestra 107
— "Die Trommel gerühret," *Lied*, with Orchestra 107
Fantasy, C minor, Op. 80, for Piano, Chorus, and Orchestra 266, 267
Fidelio
— Overture, Op. 72 .... 112, 224
— "Abscheulicher ... Komm Hoffnung" 95
— Introduction to Act 2, and "Gott! welch Dunkel hier ... In des Lebens
    Frühlingstagen" 45
Die Geschöpfe des Prometheus, Overture, Op. 43 .... *3, 135
König Stephan, Overture, Op. 117 .... *144, 292, 293
Leonore Overture No. 1, Op. 138 .... *141b, 224
Leonore Overture No. 2, Op. 72a 224
Leonore Overture No. 3, Op. 72b 38, 44, 45, 71, *98, 126, 128, 136, 151, *163,
    *165, *181,*194, 205, 206, 209, 214, 224, 228, 246, 256, 264, 270, 292, 293, A 16-17
Piano Concerto No. 3, C minor, Op. 37 258
Piano Concerto No. 4, G major, Op. 58 .... *141a, 178
Piano Concerto No. 5, E-flat major, Op. 73, "Emperor" 112, 235, 236, 237, 292, 293
Romance No.1, F major, Op. 50, for Violin and Orchestra 130
Rondo, G major, Op. 51, No. 2, for Piano *72
String Quartet No. 11, F minor, Op. 95, "Serioso," arr. G. Mahler for String Orchestra
    (ed. David Matthews, pub. London 1991) 103
Symphony No. 1, C major, Op. 21 .... 137, *218, *219
Symphony No. 2, D major, Op. 36 .... 118, 224
Symphony No. 3, E-flat major, Op. 55, "Eroica" 48, 60, 97, 99, 131, 134,
.... 146, 196, 221, 222, 225, A 2
Symphony No. 4, B-flat major, Op. 60 .... 137, 234
Symphony No. 5, C minor, Op. 67 .... 39, 51, 54, 93, 94, 95, 116, 117, 128,
.... 198, 199, 201, 213, 228, 229, 230, 238, 240, A 13, A 15
Symphony No. 6, F major, Op. 68, "Pastoral" 70, 74, 77, 78, 120, 238, 286, 287
.... 288, 289, 290, 291, 292, 293, 318, 319, A 4
Symphony No. 7, A major, Op. 92 .... 61, 65, 112, 153, 197, 200, 207,
.... 210, 216, 258, 314, 315, 321, A 3
— (2nd mvmt., Allegretto) 127
Symphony No. 8, F major, Op. 93 .... 102, *109, *141a, *175
Symphony No. 9, D minor, Op. 125 .... *27, 28, 76, 114, 123, 124,
.... 139, 177, 217, 266, 267
— excerpt, 4th mvmt.: "Seid umschlungen Millionen," arr. G. Mahler for 6 Trombones 149
Trio for Piano, Violin, and Cello (unspecified) 7
32 Variations, C minor, WoO. 80, for Piano *31
Violin Concerto, D major, Op. 61 .... 234, 262
Violin Sonata No. 7, C minor, Op. 30, No. 2 21
Violin Sonata No. 9, A major, Op. 47, "Kreutzer" 18

...BEETHOVEN continued
Die Weihe des Hauses, Overture, Op. 124 ...... 119, 123, 124, 221, 222
Zur Namensfeier, Overture, Op. 115 ...... 76, 258

BEHN, Hermann (1859–1927)
Lieder (unspecified) 79

BERLIOZ, Hector (1803–1869)
Le carnaval romain, Overture, Op. 9 ...... 66, 121, 151, 152, 200, 251, 252
La Damnation de Faust, Op. 24 (selections) *98, 277
Ráckóci March *42
Rob Roy, Overture *133, 134
Roméo et Juliette, Op. 17 (Grande fête chez Capulet,
    La reine Mab, Scène d'amour) 314, 315
Symphonie fantastique, Op. 14 ...... 72, 100, 130, 235, 236, 244, 245,
    ...... 253, 254, 255, 256, 262
— 2nd & 3rd mvmts 94

BISCHOFF, Hermann (1868–1936)
Lieder with Orchestra ("Das Trinklied," "Der Schlaf," "Bewegte See") *169

BIZET, Georges (1838–1875)
L'Arlésienne Suite No. 1 (with Additional Chorus) ...... 298, 299, 300, A 3, A 9
— Menuetto 67
La Jolie fille de Perth: "Quand la flamme de l'amour" 225
"Pastorale," Song 67
Roma, Suite de Concert No. 3 ...... 102, 311, 312

BOCCHERINI, Luigi (1743–1805)
String Quintet, E major, Op. 11, No. 5, arr. for String Orchestra (Minuet) *15, 29

BORODIN, Alexander (1834–1887)
Prince Igor, Three Excerpts ...... A 5

BOSSI, Marco Enrico (1861–1925)
Intermezzi Goldoniani, Op. 127, for String Orchestra ...... 322, A 1

BRAHMS, Johannes (1833–1897)
"Die Boten der Liebe," Duet, Op. 61, No. 4 ...... *26
"Da unten im Tale," Terzetto *73
Ein deutsches Requiem, Op. 45 ("Selig sind, die da Leid tragen" &
    "Denn alles Fleisch es ist wie Gras") *60
"Gesang aus Fingal," Op. 17, No. 4, for Women's Chorus, 2 Horns, & Harp 264
Three Hungarian Dances (unspecified), arr. J. Joachim for Violin and Piano 29
"Immer leiser wird mein Schlummer," *Lied*, Op. 105, No. 2 ...... *142
"Liebestreu," *Lied*, Op. 3, No. 1 ...... *10, 15, 21
Lied (unspecified) 94
"Die Mainacht," *Lied*, Op. 43, No. 2 ...... *86, *87
Piano Concerto No.1, D minor, Op.15 73
Rhapsody, Op. 53, for Contralto, Men's Chorus, and Orchestra *176
Symphony No.1, C minor, Op. 68 ...... 278, 279, 280
Symphony No. 2, D major, Op. 73 101
Symphony No. 3, F major, Op. 90 ...... 67, 119, 226, 227, 243
Variations on a Theme by Joseph Haydn, Op. 56a 126

...BRAHMS continued
Violin Concerto, D major, Op. 77 .... 120, 260, 261
Volkslieder, [9] Neue deutsche, with Piano Acc (pub. 1894):
—"Och Moder, ich well en Ding han" 65
—"Es reit ein Herr" 65
—"Feinsliebchen" 65
—"Jungfräulein, soll ich" 65
—"Mein Mädel hat einen Rosenmund" 65
—"Schwesterlein" 65
—"Soll sich der Mond" 65
—"So will ich frisch und frölich" 65
— "Wo gehst du hin, du Stolze" 65
"Wiegenlied," Lied, Op. 49, No. 4 .... 40, *129

BRUCH, Max (1838–1920)
Violin Concerto No.1, G minor, Op. 26 .... A 12

BRUCKNER, Anton (1824–1896)
Mass No. 1, D minor, for Soloists, Chorus, & Orchestra 53
Symphony No. 3, D minor (Scherzo - 3rd mvmt.) 29
Symphony No. 4, E-flat major, "Romantic" 73, 122, 265
— 3rd mvmt, Scherzo 131
Symphony No. 5, B-flat major 141
Symphony No. 6, A major 108
Te Deum, for Soloists, Chorus, & Orchestra 49, 53, 96

BÜLOW, Hans von (1830–1894)
Des Sängers Fluch, Symphonic Ballad, Op. 16 .... *64
Lacerta, Impromptu, Op. 27, for Piano *31

BUNGERT, August (1845–1915)
"Der Sandträger," Lied, Op. 49, No. 12 44

BUONONCINI, Giovanni Battista (1672–1747)
"Per la gloria d'adorarvi," from Griselda 67

BUSONI, Ferruccio (1866–1924)
Berceuse élégiaque. Des Mannes Wiegenlied am Sarge seiner Mutter, for
    Orchestra .... 322, A 1
Turandot, Orchestral Suite, Op. 41 .... 260, 261
    (see Bach Piano Concerto, and Liszt Spanische Rhapsodie)

CHABRIER, Alexis Emanuel (1841–1894)
Briséis, Opera (incomplete), Act 1 .... A 5
España, Rhapsody, for Orchestra .... 283, 298, 299, 300, A 5, A 17
Á la Musique, for Tenor, Women's Chorus, & Orchestra 298, 299, 300

CHADWICK, George Whitefield (1854–1937)
Melpomene, Dramatic Overture 317, 320

CHERUBINI, Luigi (1760–1842)
Anacréon, Overture 281, 282
Les Abencérages, Overture *36
String Quartet No. 3, D minor *31, *35

Composer's Index

CHOPIN, Frédéric (1810–1849)
Ballade, for Piano 8
Berceuse, Op. 57 .... *89
Étude, Op. 10, No. 2 .... *163
Étude, Op. 10, No. 4 .... *10
Impromptu (unspecified), for Piano 18
Nocturne, Op. 27, No. 2 .... *10, *163
Nocturne, Op. 48, No. 1 .... *75
Nocturne, Op. 62, No. 1 .... *182
Piano Concerto No. 1, E minor, Op. 11 .... *10, *146
Piano Concerto No. 2, F minor, Op. 21 .... *11
Polonaise No. 6, A-flat major, Op. 53 .... 15, 18, *146
Scherzo No. 1, Op. 20 .... *163
Piano Pieces (unspecified) *273
Waltz (unspecified), for Piano *147

CORNELIUS, Peter (1824–1874)
"Wiegenlied," Op. 1, No. 3, *Lied* *142

CUI, César (1835–1918)
Cavatine, Op. 25, for Violin & Piano *148

DEBUSSY, Claude (1862–1918)
From *Images*:
— No. 2: *Iberia* 298, 299, 300
— No. 3: *Rondes de printemps*: 278, 279
Trois Nocturnes, for Orchestra (Nuáges, Fêtes, Sirenes) 251, 252
Prélude à l'après-midi d'un faune 260, 261

DELIBES, Léo (1836–1891)
Lakmé: "Où va la jeune Hindoue," Act 2 .... *146

DONIZETTI, Gaetano (1797–1848)
Don Pasquale: Act 1 (complete) *215
La Favorita: "Oh, mio Fernando" 41
Linda di Chamounix: "O luce di quest' anima" 33
Lucia di Lammermoor, Potpourri for 2 Pianos *3

DORN, Alexander Julius (1833–1901)
"Schneeglöckchen," *Lied*, Op. 85 15

DUKAS, Paul (1865–1935)
L'Apprenti sorcier, Scherzo after Goethe's Ballad, for Orchestra 226, 227

DÜRRNER, Johannes (1810-1859)
"Sturmbeschwörung," for Boys' Choir 3

DVOŘÁK, Antonín (1841–1904)
"Als die alte Mutter," Op. 55, No. 4 246
Carnival, Overture, Op. 92 .... 280, 281, 282
Heldenlied, Symphonic Poem, Op. 111 101
In der Natur, Concert Overture, Op. 91 .... *141a, 243, 244
Scherzo capriccioso, Op. 66, for Orchestra 230
Serenade, D minor, Op. 44, for Wind Instruments 141

...DVOŘÁK continued
Symphony No. 9, E minor, Op. 95, "From the New World" .... A 6, A 10-12
Die Waldtaube, Symphonic Poem, Op. 110 119

ECKERT, Carl Anton (1820–1879)
"Schweizer Echo-Lied," *Lied,* Op. 21 .... *26
"Schifferlied," for Men's Chorus.. *4
"Überselig," *Lied*, Op. 29, No. 5 33

ELGAR, Edward (1857–1934)
Sea Pictures, Op. 37, for Contralto & Orchestra ("Sea Slumber Song," "In Haven,"
  "Sabbath Morning at Sea," "Where Corals Lie") 317, 320
Variations on an Original Theme, "Enigma," Op. 36 .... 284, 285

ENGELSBERG, E. S. *(pseudonym for Eduard Schön)* (1825-1879)
"So weit," for Boys' Choir 3

ENESCU, George (1881–1955)
Suite No. 1, C major, Op. 9, for Orchestra 298, 299, 300

ERKEL, Ferenc (1810–1893)
Festival Overture.. *42

ERNST, Heinrich Wilhelm (1814–1865)
Violin Concerto (unspecified), with Piano Acc. 7

ERTEL, Jean Paul (1865–1933)
Der Mensch, Symphonic Poem, Op. 9 .... *178

ESSER, Heinrich (1818–1872)
"Grüner Frühling*," Lied* *26

FABRICIUS, Jakob (1840–1900)
"Durch die stille Sommernacht," Terzetto *73
"Jetzt, o Frühling," Terzetto *73

FAURÉ, Gabriel (1845–1924)
Hymne à Apollon, Op. 63bis for Men's Chorus and instruments 69

FIBY, Heinrich (1834–1917)
"Österreich, mein Vaterland," Op. 3, for Men's Chorus *4

FIEDLER, Max (1859–1939)
"Die Musikantin," *Lied*, Op. 5, with Orchestra 200, 247, 248, 249

FIELITZ, Alexander von (1860–1930)
Lied (unspecified)... 94

FISCHER, Carl Ludwig (1816–1877)
"Frühlingsnacht," Op. 17, No. 3, for Men's Chorus *33

FLOTOW, Friedrich von (1812–1883)
Alessandro Stradella: "So war es denn erreicht...
Seid meiner Wonne stille Zeuge," Act 2 30

FOERSTER, Josef Bohuslav (1859–1951)
"Aubade," *Lied* *86, *87
Symphony No. 3, D major, Op. 36, "Das Leben" 86, 87

FRANCK, César (1822–1890)
Symphonic Variations, for Piano & Orchestra 136

FRANZ, Robert (1815–1892)
"Wenn der Frühling auf die Berge," *Lied*, Op. 42, No. 6 44

FUCHS, Johann Nepomuk (1842–1899)
Serenade No. 3, E minor, Op. 21, for String Orchestra *15

GALL, Jan (1856–1902)
"Mädchen mit dem rothen Mündchen," *Lied* 33

GIORDANI, Tomasso (1730–1806)
"Caro mio ben," *Lied*, with Orchestra 246

GLAZUNOV, Alexander (1865–1936)
Le Printemps, Tableau Musical, Op. 34, for Orchestra .... A 7-8

GLINKA, Mikhail (1804–1857)
Nocturne, for Cello and Piano 33

GODEFROID, Jules (1811–1840)
Danse des Sylphes, for Harp *11

GOETZ, Hermann (1840–1876)
Symphony, F major, Op. 9 105

GOLDMARK, Karl (1830–1915)
"Frühlingsnetz," Op. 15, for Men's Chorus, Acc. by Piano & Four French horns *132
Im Frühling, Overture, Op. 36 .... 125, 131, 306
Symphony No. 1, E-flat major, Op. 26, "Ländliche Hochzeit," *57
Sakuntala, Concert Overture, Op.13 .... 24, A 2
Violin Concerto, A minor, Op. 28 .... 284, 285

GOUNOD, Charles (1818–1893)
"Au Printemps" ("Frühlingslied"), *Lied* *26
Faust, Act 2, complete *205
Meditation on Bach's C-major Prelude (different arrangements) *10, *16
Romeo et Juliette: "Je veux vivre dans ce rêve" 93

GRÉTRY, André Ernst (1742–1813)
Céphale et Procris: "C'est ici le beau Céphale... Naissantes fleurs" 223

GRIEG, Edvard (1843–1907)
Foran Sydens kloster ("At the Cloister Gate"), Op. 20 .... A 9
"Ich liebe dich," *Lied*, Op. 5, No. 3 29
"Landkjennung" ("Land Sighting"), Op. 31, for Baritone, Men's Chorus & Orchestra ...*132
Peer Gynt Suite No.1, Op. 46 .... A 6
Piano Concerto, A minor, Op. 16 .... 72, 253
Sigurd Jorsalfar, Op. 56: Triumphal March .... 245, A 9

GRIMM, Julius Otto (1827–1903)
"Ich fahr' dahin," A-Cappella Terzetto (folk song arrangement)..*73
Suite in C major, Op. 10, for String Orchestra *15

HADLEY, Henry Kimball (1871–1937)
The Culprit Fay, Op. 62, Rhapsody, after a Poem by J.R. Drake 317, 320

HALÉVY, Jacques (1799–1862)
La Juive: "Rachel, quand du Seigneur" ("Gott erleuchte meinen Sinn") 41

HANDEL, George Frideric (1685–1759)
Concerto No. 10, D major, for Organ and Orch. *268
Flavio, Re di Longobardi: "Quanto dolci, quanto care" 223, 254
Messiah, Oratorio: "I know that my Redeemer liveth," Part 3 85
Samson, Oratorio: "O hör mein Flehen" 85
Xerxes, Oratorio: "Ombra mai fu" (Largo) 225
— arr. Josef Hellmesberger, Sr., for String Orchestra and Organ 96

HASLINGER, Carl (1816–1868)
"Ein schöner Tod," *Lied* 18

HAUER, Carl Heinrich (1828–1892)
"Einen Brief soll ich schreiben," *Lied*, Op. 32 33

HAUSEGGER, Siegmund von (1872–1948)
Dionysische Phantasie, Symphonic Poem for Orchestra *169

HAYDN, Josef (1732–1809)
Gott erhalte Franz der Kaiser (Austrian National Hymn) *12
Die Jahreszeiten, Oratorio 23
Die Schöpfung, Oratorio 59, 62, 68, 81, 82, 88
— "Auf starkem Fittiche" *109, 229
— "Und Gott sprach ... Gleich öffnet sich der Erde Schoß" 29
"Poco adagio, cantabile" (Theme and Variations on the Emperor's Hymn) from
    String Quartet in C major, Op. 76, No. 3, arr. for String Orchestra......................... 101
Symphony No. 88, G major *141b
Symphony No. 99, E-flat major 52
Symphony No.101, D major, "Clock" 45
Symphony No.103, E-flat major, "Drum Roll" 125, 148
Symphony No.104, D major, "London" 106, 223
Symphony in G major, arr. for Piano 4-Hands, (3rd mvmt.) 2

HEINEFETTER, Wilhelm (1835–1934)
"Im wunderschönen Monat Mai," *Lied*, Op. 18, No. 4 29

Composer's Index

HERBECK, Johann (1831–1877)
"Werners Gruß aus Welschland," *Lied*, Op. 8, No. 1, for Men's Chorus *129
"Zum Walde," for Men's Chorus *132

HERMANN, Hans G. (1870–1931)
"Drei Wanderer," *Lied*, Op. 5, No. 3 ...... *98

HINRICHS, Friedrich (1820–1892)
"Die Prinzessin," *Lied*, Op. 1, No. 3 ...... *26

HÖLZL, Franz (1808–1884)
"Hab' ich in der Brust ein Vöglein," *Lied* 16
"In den Augen liegt das Herz," *Lied* 16

HUBER, Károly (1828–1885)
Festival March, for Orchestra *42

HUMMEL, Johann Evangelist H. (1832–?)
"Festmarsch," (Festival March) *3

HUMMEL, Johann Nepomuk (1778–1837)
Piano Septet, D minor, Op. 74 (1st movement) *10

HUMPERDINCK, Engelbert (1854–1921)
Maurische Rhapsodie, Orchestral Suite *107

HUTTER, Hermann (1848–1926)
"Bergfahrt," *Lied* *57

JANSA, Leopold (1795–1875)
Double Rondo, Op. 33, for 2 Violins and Piano *4

JENSEN, Adolf (1837–1879)
"Frühlingslied", *Lied* 31
"Murmelndes Lüftchen," *Lied*, Op. 21, No. 4 ...... *151

JOMELLI, Niccolo (1714–1774)
"La calandrina," *Arietta* *151

KIENZL, Wilhelm (1857–1941)
Two Symphonic Entr'acts from *Don Quixote* *107

KIRCHNER, Friedrich (1840–1907)
"Es wäre so," *Lied* *10

KITTL, Johann Friedrich (1806–1868)
Concert Overture, D major, Op. 22 ...... *7

KOCH, Friedrich Ernst (1862–1927)
"Das Sonnenlied," Op. 26, for Soloists, Chorus, and Orchestra (excerpts) *155

KREBS, Carl (1804–1880)
Vater unser ("Lord's Prayer"), Op. 198, for Voice and Orchestra 85, 96

KREMSER, Eduard (1838–1914)
"Dankgebet," for Men's Chorus *132
"An die Madonna," Op. 134, for Tenor Solo & Men's Chorus *129
Two *Altniederländische Volkslieder*... ....*129

KREUTZER, Conradin (1780–1849)
"Schäfers Sonntagslied," Op. 23, for Men's Chorus *33

KRZYZANOWSKI, Rudolf (1862–1911)
Piano Quartet (or Quintet), C minor (1st mvmt.) 8
Sextet for Strings (Adagio) *11

KÜCKEN, Friedrich Wilhelm (1810–1882)
"Gut' Nacht, fahr' wohl," *Lied*, Op. 52, No. 1 12

KUNTZE, Karl (1817–1883)
"Ein Kaffeekränzchen," Op. 231, with Piano Acc. 18

KUNZE, Gustav (1810–1868)
Mein Österreich, March, Op. 117 ....*4

LACHNER, Franz (1803–1890)
Suite No. 6, Op. 150, for String Orchestra (Gavotte) *57

LALO, Éduard (1823–1892)
Le Roi d'Ys
 — Overture *268, 313
 — "Vainement, ma bien aimée" (Aubade) 298, 299, 300
Symphonie espagnole, D minor, Op. 21, for Violin & Orchestra 51, 66

LAUB, Ferdinand (1832–1875)
Polonaise, Op. 8, for Violin & Piano 12

LEONCAVALLO, Ruggero (1858–1919)
Pagliacci
 — Act 1, complete *205
 — "Si può?...Un nido di memorie" (Prologue)..*57

LISZT, Franz (1811–1886)
Fantasy on Donizetti's *Lucrezia Borgia*, for Piano *33
Festklänge, Symphonic Poem 42, 105
Gnomenreigen, for Piano 7, *31
Hungarian Rhapsody No. 6, D-flat major, for Piano *72, *75
Hungarian Rhapsody (unspecified), for Piano 12, *89
La Campanella (Paganini Étude No. 3, A-flat minor)..*273
Liebesträume, No. 3, for Piano *273
Les Préludes, Symphonic Poem.....................*143, 257, 264, 316, 318, 319, 321, A 3-4
Mazeppa, Symphonic Poem 221, 222, 257
"Mephisto Waltz" ("Der Tanz in der Dorfschenke"), from Two Episodes
 from Lenau's *Faust*, for Orchestra 125, 277
Paraphrase on the "Wedding March" from Mendelssohn's
 Ein Sommernachtstraum, for Piano 3

... LISZT continued
Piano Concerto No. 1, E-flat major 151, *187
Piano Concerto No. 2, A major. *104, 230
Piano Sonata, B minor *89
Rhapsodie espagnole, ed. F. Busoni, for Piano & Orchestra 65
Tasso, Lamento e trionfo, Symphonic Poem 306
Valse mélancolique *31
"Weimars Volkslied," for Men's Chorus and Winds *64
   (see Paganini *La Campanella,* Schubert *Wanderer Fantasy*,
   and Weber *Konzertstück*, Op. 79)

LITOLFF, Henry Charles (1818–1891)
Overture to *Maximilian Robespierre*, Op. 55.. *26

LOEFFLER, Charles Martin (1861–1935)
La Villanelle du Diable, Fantasie symphonique, Op. 9 .... 317, 320

LOEWE, Carl (1796–1869)
"Der Fischer," *Lied*, Op. 43, No. 1 35
"Des Goldschmieds Töchterlein," *Lied*, Op. 8, No.1 33
"Heinrich der Vogler," *Lied*, Op. 56, No. 1 33
"Hochzeitslied," *Lied*, Op. 20, No. 1 44
"Kleiner Haushalt," *Lied*, Op. 71 .... 30, 35
Lieder (unspecified) 79

MACDOWELL, Edward (1860–1908)
Piano Concerto No. 2, D minor, Op. 23 ....313, A 4
The Saracens & The Lovely Alda from *The Song of Roland*, Op. 30 .... 317, 320

MAHLER, Gustav (1860–1911)
"Gesänge" (songs) from *Des Knaben Wunderhorn*, with Orchestral or
   Piano Acc. (comp. 1892–1901; pub. 1900, except when noted):
— "Des Antonius von Padua Fischpredigt" (comp. 1893) 173, 174, 178, 186
— "Das himmlische Leben" (1892; pub. 1902, as part of Symphony No. 4) 55
— "Das irdische Leben" (1892) 121, 178, 186
— "Lied des Verfolgten im Turm" (1898) 173, 174, 178
— "Lob des hohen Verstandes" (1896) 174
— "Revelge" (1899; pub. 1905) 173, 174, 178
— "Rheinlegendchen" (1893) 55, 57, 173, 174, 280, 281, 282
— "Der Schildwache Nachtlied," (1892) 55, 57, 173, 174, 178, 186
— "Der Tamboursg'sell" (1901; pub. 1905) 173, 174, 178
— "Trost im Unglück" (1892) 55, 57, 173, 174
— "Verlor'ne Müh'" (1892) 55, 174
— "Wer hat dies Liedlein erdacht?" ["Dort oben am Berg"] (1892) 55, 121, 174
— "Wo die schönen Trompeten blasen" (1898).. 121
Kindertotenlieder (comp. 1901–1904; pub.1905) 173, 174, 178, 183, 195, 243, 244
Das klagende Lied, for Soloists, Chorus, & Orchestra (comp. 1878–1880;
   pub. 1901) 140, 145, 184
Lieder eines fahrenden Gesellen (comp. 1884–1885; pub. 1897), with
   Orchestra or Piano Acc. (complete).. 84, 195
— No. 2: "Ging heut' morgen übers Feld" 29, 121, 280, 281, 282
— No. 4: "Die zwei blauen Augen" 121
Lieder und Gesänge, with Piano Acc. (comp. ca. 1880–1890; pub. 1892):
— "Ablösung im Sommer".. 195
— "Aus! Aus!" *194

...MAHLER continued
— "Erinnerung" 35, *194
— "Frühlingsmorgen" 29, 35
— "Hans und Grethe" [formerly "Maitanz im grünen"] 29
— "Nicht Wiedersehen" 195
— "Scheiden und Meiden" 35
— "Selbstgefühl" 195
— "Starke Einbildungskraft" 195
— "Um schlimme Kinder artig zu machen" 195
Piano Quartet (or Quintet) (1876: lost) 8
Piano Quintet (Scherzo) (1878: lost) 11
[4] *Rückert-Lieder*, with Orch. or Piano Acc. (comp. 1901; pub. 1905):
— "Blicke mir nicht in die Lieder" 173, 174, 195
— "Ich atmet' einen linden Duft" 173, 174, 195
— "Ich bin der Welt abhanden gekommen" 173, 174, 178, 183, 186, 195
— "Um Mitternacht" 173, 174, 178, *194, 195
Sonata for Violin and Piano (1875–1906: lost) 7, 8
Symphony No. 1, D major (1888–1896/pub. 1899):
   (a) as Symphonic Poem (5 mvmts.) 36
   (b) as *Titan*, Symphonic Poem/Symphony (5 mvmts.) 55, 64
   (c) as Symphony No.1, D major (4 mvmts.) 84, 98, 109, 135, 152, 153,
   .... 158, 188, 194, 198, 206, 231, 232
Symphony No. 2, C minor, "Resurrection" (1888-1894; pub. 1897): 83, 104, 113, 133,
   .... 155, 167, 168, 203, 212, 268
— 1st mvmt. 75, 84, 89
— 2nd mvmt. 75, 89
— 3rd mvmt. 75
Symphony No. 3, D minor (1895–1896; pub. 1902) 150, 156, 157, 159, 160,
   .... 161, 162, 164, 170, 171, 172, 186, 189, 190, 192
— 2nd mvmt. ("Was mir die Blumen auf der Wiese erzählen") 95
Symphony No. 4, G major (1899–1901; pub. 1902) 142, 143, 144, 145,
   .... 151, 163, 166 (twice), 193, 304, 305
— 4th mvmt., "Das himmlische Leben" (as a solo song) 55
Symphony No. 5 (1901–1902; pub. 1904) 165, 175, 176, 179, 180,
   .... 181, 182, 183, 202
— 4th mvmt. (Adagietto) 197
Symphony No. 6, A minor, "Tragic" (1903–1904; pub.1906) 185, 187, 191
Symphony No. 7, B minor (1904–1905; pub. 1909) 208, 209, 218, 219, 220
Symphony No. 8, E-flat major (1906–1907; pub.1910–1912) 271, 272
   (see Bach Suite; Beethoven String Quartet, Op. 95, & Symphony No. 9;
   Schubert String Quartet)

MARSCHNER, Heinrich (1795–1861)
Hans Heiling: "An jenem Tag" 55

MARTUCCI, Giuseppe (1856–1909)
Piano Concerto No. 2, B-flat minor, Op. 66 .... 322, A1

MASSENET, Jules (1842–1912)
Hérodiade: Salomé's Aria (unspecified) 41
Le jongleur de Notre-Dame: "La viérge entand ... Fleurissait une sauge"
   (Légende) 225
Le mage: "Soulève l'ombre des ses voiles" 298, 299, 300

... MASSENET continued
Manon: "En ferment les yeux" (*Le Rêve de Manon*) 298, 299, 300
"Ouvre tes yeux bleus," Song 67
Le Roi de Lahore: Duet (unspecified) 37

MATTEI, Tito (1847–1914)
"Es ist nicht wahr" ("Non è ver'"), Op. 20, No. 1, *Romance* 16

MÉHUL, Etienne Henry (1763–1817)
"Gebet," (Prayer) for Boys' Choir 3

MENDELSSOHN, Felix (1809–1847)
"Auf Flügeln des Gesanges," *Lied*, Op. 34, No. 2 .... *163
Capriccio brillant, B minor, Op. 22, for Piano and Orchestra, arr. for Piano and
    String Quartet/Orchestra 15
Elijah, Oratorio, Op. 70
— "Lift thine eyes," ("Hebe deine Augen auf,") Terzetto *73, 85
— "O rest in the Lord," ("Sei stille dem Herrn") *59, *62, 68
— "If with all your hearts," ("So Ihr mich von ganzen Herzen suchet") 85
— "Hear ye, Israel," ("Höre Israel") *62
"Gruß," Duet, Op. 63, No. 3 .... *26
Die Hebriden (*Fingal's Cave*), Overture, Op. 26 .... 55, 71, *75, 105, 206,
    .... A 6, A 12
"Herbstlied," Duet, Op. 63, No. 4 .... *26
"Ich hör' ein Vöglein," *Lied* *10
Das Märchen von der schönen Melusine, Overture, Op. 32 .... 311, 312
Meeresstille und glückliche Fahrt, Overture, Op. 27 122
"Morgengebet," for Mixed Chorus *12
Paulus, Oratorio, Op. 36 (complete) 25
— "Gott sei mir gnädig" 21, *59, *62, 68
Ein Sommernachtstraum, Overture, Op. 21 .... 51, 101, 284, 285
Symphony No. 3, A minor, Op. 56, "Scottish" 138
Symphony No. 4, A major, Op. 90, "Italian" .... 322, A 1
"Venetianisches Gondellied: Wenn durch die Piazetta," Op. 57, No. 5 .... *10
Violin Concerto, E minor, Op. 64 .... 228, 233, 321
"Wenn sich zwei Herzen scheiden", *Lied*, Op. 99, No. 5 30

MEYER-HELMUND, Erik (1861–1932)
"Du fragst mich täglich," *Lied*, Op. 5, No. 5 33
"Der Schwur," *Lied*, Op. 8, No. 4 .... *26, 30

MEYERBEER, Giacomo (1791–1864)
Fantasy (unspecified), for Orchestra *3
Le Prophète
— "Ah! Mon fils!" 14, 16
— "Donnez, donnez, pour une pauvre âme" 29

MIHALOVICH, Ödön (1842–1929)
"Royal Hymn," for Chorus and Orchestra 42
Toldi's Liebe, Overture 42

MOJSISOVICS, Roderich von (1877–1953)
Romantische Fantasie, Op. 9, for Organ (3rd movement) *178

MOSZKOWSKI, Moritz (1854–1925)
"Serenata," *Lied*, Op. 15, No. 1 .... *151
Violin Concerto, C major, Op. 30 71

MUSSORGSKY, Modest (1839–1881)
Joshua, Biblical cantata .... A 5

MOZART, Wolfgang Amadeus (1756–1791)
Don Giovanni, K. 527:
— "Deh, vieni alla finestra" 14
— "La ci darem la mano," Duet 214
— Recitative and Aria (unspecified), for Soprano with Piano Acc. 16
— Aria (unspecified), arr. for Trombone *11
German Dances (unspecified), for Orchestra 274, 275, 276
Idomeneo, K. 367, Ballet Music: Gavotte & Passacaglia 274, 275, 276
Le nozze di Figaro, K. 492:
— "Deh vieni, non tardar" 45, 229
— "Non so più cosa son" 21
— "Voi, che sapete" *36, 254
— March, Act 4 215
— Aria (unspecified) *10
Maurerische Trauermusik, K. 477 .... 22, *185
Piano Concerto E-flat major, K. 271, K. 482 or K. 499 .... *202
Requiem, D minor, K. 626 .... 49, 81, 85, 96
Serenade, G major, "Eine kleine Nachtmusik," K. 525 .... *158
String Quartet No. 21, D major, K. 575 .... *35
Symphony No. 40, G minor, K. 550 .... 29, 43, 65, 99, 128, 146, 284, 285
Symphony No. 41, C major, K. 551, "Jupiter" 116, 117, 179, 229
Symphony in G major (unspecified) *142
Violin Concerto No. 4, G major, K. 216 .... *176
Unspecified Work for Violin (and Piano?) 273

MÜLLER, Adolf (1801–1886)
Das Mädchen von der Spule, Overture *16

NEDBAL, Oskar (1874-1930)
Der faule Hans, Ballet *154

NESSLER, Viktor (1841–1890)
"Fantasy on motives" from *Der Trompeter von Säckingen*, for Military Band *26

NICOLAI, Otto (1810–1849)
Die lustigen Weiber von Windsor, Overture 154

PAGANINI, Niccolò (1782–1840)
Violin Concerto No.1, D major, Op. 6 (1st mvmt.) 51
Violin Concerto No. 3, B minor, Op. 7 (3rd mvmt.), see Liszt *La Campanella*

PAISIELLO, Giovanni (1740–1816)
"Chi vuol la zingarella," *Canzone* 67

Composer's Index

PEROSI, Lorenzo (1872–1956)
La risurrezione di Lazzaro, Oratorio 110, 111

PETERS, Guido (1866–1937)
Symphony No. 2, E minor (1st & 4th mvmts.) *178

PFITZNER, Hans (1869–1949)
Das Christ-Elflein, Overture, Op. 20 265
Das Käthchen von Heilbronn, Overture to Kleist's play, Op. 17a 304, 305

PFOHL, Ferdinand (1863–1949)
"Satanella," Op. 6, No. 3, *Lied* *86, *87

PHILIPP, Rudolf (1858–1936)
"Herzallerliebster Schatz," *Lied* *86, *87
"O Welt, du bist so wunderschön," *Lied,* Op. 31 .... *86, *87

POPPER, David (1843–1913)
Warum, Op. 3, No. 2, for Cello and Piano 33

PUCCINI, Giacomo (1858–1924)
La Bohème, Act 3, complete *205
Madama Butterfly, Act 1, complete *205

RACHMANINOFF, Sergei (1873–1943)
Piano Concerto No. 2, C minor, Op. 18 .... *202
Piano Concerto No. 3, D minor, Op. 30 239

RAFF, Joseph Joachim (1822–1882)
Violin Concerto No. 2, A minor, Op. 206 29

RAMEAU, Jean-Philippe (1683–1764)
Gavotte, for Orchestra 246
Rigaudon, Ballet from the Opera *Dardanus*, ed. F.A. Gevaërt 105, 223

REINECKE, Carl (1824–1910)
König Manfred, Prelude to Act 5 .... *57
"Luftschloß," *Lied*, Op. 185 33
Lied (unspecified) 94

REISENAUER, Alfred (1863–1907)
"Der wunde Ritter," *Lied*, Op. 13, No. 3 .... *142

RENNES, Cathárina van (1858–1940)
"Belooning," Terzetto Op. 10 .... *73
"Kerstnacht," Terzetto, Op. 10 .... *73

RIMSKY-KORSAKOFF, Nikolai (1844–1908)
Scheherazade, Symphonic Suite, Op. 35 283

RÖSCH, Friedrich (1862–1925)
"Bekenntnis," *Lied* *143
"Lied vom Winde," *Lied* *143
"Wie wundersam," *Lied* *143

ROSSINI, Gioachino (1792–1868)
Il barbiere di Siviglia:
— "Una voce poco fa" *146
— Aria (unspecified) 12
— Act 2 (complete) *215
Stabat Mater, for Soloists, Chorus, and Orchestra 46, 47
Guillaume Tell: "Sombre fôret, désert triste " 14

RUBINSTEIN, Anton (1829–1894)
"Der Asra," *Lied*, Op. 32, No. 6 70
Cello Concerto, A minor, Op. 65 .... *64
The Demon, Ballet Music (Two Dances) 70
"Es blinkt der Tau," *Lied*, Op. 72, No. 1 .... *26, 70
"Gelb rollt mir zu Füßen," *Lied*, Op. 34, No. 9 29
"Neue Liebe," *Lied*, Op. 57, No. 3 70
Piano Concerto No. 4, D minor, Op. 70 .... 67, *163, A 18
Symphony No. 2, C major, Op. 42, "Ocean" (1st mvmt.) 70
"Der Traum," *Lied*, Op. 8, No. 1 70
"Wanderers Nachtlied," Duet, Op. 48 .... *26

SAINT-SAËNS, Camille (1835–1921)
Danse macabre, Op. 40 .... *104
Havanaise, Op. 83, for Violin & Piano *148
Piano Concerto No. 4, C minor, Op. 44 .... *75, 278, 279
Samson et Delilah, Two Arias .... A 9, A 16-17
   (see also Bach Aria and Chorus)

SARASATE, Pablo de (1844–1908)
Muñeira, Thème varié (Montagnarde), Op. 32, for Violin and Orchestra 66

SAUER, Émil (1862–1942)
Étude (unspecified) *147
Piano Concerto No. 1, E minor 147

SAURET, Émile (1852–1920)
Elegie and Rondo, Op. 38, for Violin and Orchestra 71

SCARLATTI, Alessandro (1660–1725)
Le violette, Canzonetta 67

SCARLATTI, Domenico (1685–1757)
Piano Sonata, D minor, "Pastorale" *67

SCHARWENKA, Franz Xaver (1854–1920)
Piano Concerto No.1, B-flat minor, Op. 32 (1st mvmt., Allegro patetico) 10
Piano Concerto No. 4, F minor, Op. 82 283

SCHILLING-ZIEMSSEN, Hans Eduard (1868–1950)
"Ew'ges Licht," Op. 7, for Tenor and Orchestra *155

Composer's Index

SCHILLINGS, Max (von) (1868–1933)
"Dem Verklärten," Op. 21 for Baritone, Chorus, and Orchestra *184
Der Pfeifertag, Introduction to Act 3 ....A 7-8

SCHUBERT, Franz (1797–1828)
Fantasy, "Wanderer," C major, Op. 15, D 760, for Piano 7, 8
— arr. F. Liszt for Piano and Orchestra 182
"Der Gondelfahrer," D 809, for Men's Chorus...*129
Impromptu, A-flat major, Op. 143, No. 2, D 935, for Piano..*72
Lieder for voice and piano:
— "Die Allmacht," D 852 .... *86, *87
— "Am Meer," D 957, No. 12 .... 90, 91
— "An die Musik," D 547 .... 90, 91
— "An Schwager Kronos," D 369... 29
— "Aufenthalt," D 957, No. 5 40
— "Bei Dir allein," D 866, No. 2 ....*165
— "Du bist die Ruh'," D 776 .... 90, 91
— "Das Echo," D 868 .... 90, 91
— "Der Neugierige" (from *Die schöne Müllerin*, D 795, No. 6) 31
— "Die Forelle," D 550 ....*163
— "Frühlingsglaube," D 686b... 44
— "Frühlingsgruß," (unspecified) *57
— "Gretchen am Spinnrade," Op. 2, D 118 .... 90, 91
— "Heidenröslein," D 257 67
— "Horch! Horch! die Lerch!" D 889 .... 90, 91
— "Das Lied im Grünen," D 917...*165
— "Liebesbotschaft," D 957, No. 1.. 21
— "Nacht und Träume," D 827 ....*165
— "Sei mir gegrüßt," D 305 ....*98
— "Suleika,"Op. 14, No. 1, D 720 .... 90, 91
— "Trockne Blumen," No. 18, D 795... 90, 91
— "Der Wanderer," D 649 .... 37, 90, 91
— "Wandrers Nachtlied," No. 2, D 768 .... 90, 91
— "Wohin" (from *Die schöne Müllerin*, D 795, No. 2) 94
Lieder (unspecified) 17, 79
Piano Sonata, A minor, (1st mvmt.) 6, 12
Rosamunde, Overture, see *Zauberharfe*
— Incidental Music, Op. 26, D 797 ....*26
— "Sehnsucht," D 656, for Five Part A-Cappella Chorus *132
— "Ständchen," D 921, for Contralto, Chorus, & Orch. *165, 264
"Death and the Maiden" String Quartet, No. 14, D minor, D 810,
    Andante con moto (2nd mvmt.) arr. for String Orchestra by G. Mahler
    [ed. D. Mitchell & D. Matthews, pub. London 1983]... 67
Symphony No. 8 (7), B minor, D 759, "Unfinished" 90, 91, 100, 131, 231, 232,
.... 233, 246, 313, A 7-8
Symphony No. 9 (8), C major, D 944, "Great" 66, 126, 274, 275, 276
Die Zauberharfe, D 644, Overture 90, 91, 108

SCHULHOFF, Julius (1825–1898)
Le Zephir, for Harp *10

SCHULZ-DELITZ, N.
"Ave Maria," for Women's Chorus...*21

333

SCHUMANN, Robert (1810–1856)
Die Braut von Messina, Overture, Op. 100 20
Humoreske, B-flat major, Op. 20, for Piano (excerpt)... 9, 12
Julius Caesar, Overture, Op. 128 19
Lieder, Duets, & Quartets for Voices and Piano:
— "Ballade vom Haideknaben," Op. 122, No. 1.. 30
— "Der Contrabandiste," Op. 74, No.10. 33
— "Die beiden Grenadiere," ("Les deux Grenadiers,") Op. 49, No.1...................... 17, 273
— "Er ist's," *Lied*, Op. 79, No. 24 ....*26
— "Es ist verrathen," Op. 74, No. 5 44
— "Frühlingsnacht," Op. 39, No. 12 .... 29, 40
— "Ich bin geliebt," Op. 74, No. 9.. 44
— "Ich wand're nicht," Op. 51, No. 3..*86, *87
— "Intermezzo," Op. 39, No. 2 ....*86, *87
— "Liebesgarten," Op. 34, No. 1 44
— "Die Lotusblume," Op. 25, No. 7 44
— "Mit Myrthen und Rosen," Op. 24, No. 9 .... 44, *98
— "Die Mondnacht," *Lied*, Op. 39, No. 5..*163
— "Spanisches Liederspiel," Op. 74 (excerpts) 26, 44
— "Waldesgespräch," *Lied*, Op. 39, No. 3..*142
— "Wanderlied," Op. 35, No. 3 .... 33, *86, *87
— "Widmung," *Lied*, Op. 25, No. 1 44
Lieder (unspecified)... 79, 94, 273
Manfred, Overture, Op. 115 .... 135, 216, 278, 279, 280
Piano Concerto, A minor, Op. 54 .... 89, 245
"Ritornelle," Op. 65, for Men's Chorus *129, *132
Symphony No. 1, B-flat major, Op. 38, "Spring" 71, 103, 193, 211
Symphony No. 2, C major, Op. 61 .... 280, 281
Symphony No. 3, E-flat major, Op. 97, "Rhenish" .... 311, 312, A 9
Symphony No. 4, D minor, Op. 120 .... 121, 233, 247, 248, 249
Waldszenen, No. 7 ("Vogel als Prophet") & 8 ("Jagdlied"), Op. 82, for Piano: 15

SCUDERI, Salvatore (1845–1927)
"Dormi pure," *Serenade*, with Orchestra 246

SIBELIUS, Jean (1865–1957)
Violin Concerto, D minor, Op. 47 ....A 10-11

SIMON, Antony Yulievich (1850–1916)
Piano Concerto, A-flat major, Op. 19 93

SINIGAGLIA, Leone (1868–1944)
Le Baruffe Chiozzotte, Overture, Op. 32 ....322, A 1

SMETANA, Bedřich (1824–1884)
The Bartered Bride (*Prodaná névesta*):
— Overture 207, 211, 239, 240, 241, 242, 243
— "It must succeed" ("Jak možná vèrit") 264
The Kiss (*Hubička*): "Hajej, muj andílku", ("Schlafe mein Engelein,")
  arr. Kurt Schindler for Chorus 280, 281, 282
Libuse, Overture 136
"Die Moldau," ("Vltava") from *Má vlast*, Symphonic Poem................... 136, 280, 281, 282

SOMMER, Hans (1837–1922)
"Wiegenlied," *Lied*, Op. 41, No. 1 94

SPOHR, Ludwig (1784–1859)
Jessonda, Overture, Op. 63 120
Violin Concerto No. 10, A minor, Op. 62, with Piano Acc. 21

STANFORD, Charles Villiers (1852–1924)
Symphony No. 3, F minor, Op. 28, "Irish" 317, 320

STAVENHAGEN, Bernhard (1862–1914)
Piano Concerto, B minor, Op. 4 ....*64

STOIBER, Ernst (1833–1889)
"Festhymne," for Men's Chorus and Piano 12

STORCH, Anton Maria (1813–1887)
"Nachtzauber," for Men's Chorus *132

STRAUß, Josef (1827–1870)
"Deutsche Grüsse," Waltz, Op. 101 ....*26

STRAUSS, Richard (1864–1949)
Also sprach Zarathustra, Symphonic Poem, Op. 30.....................................274, 275, 276
Aus Italien, Symphonic Fantasy, G major, Op. 16 118
Don Juan, Tone Poem, Op. 20 .... 247, 248, 249
Feuersnot, Op. 50: "Liebesszene" ["Love Scene"] *143
"Freundliche Vision," *Lied*, Op. 48, No. 1 ....A 7-8
Guntram, Op. 25 (excerpts):
— Prelude to Act 1 .... 72, 107, 265
— Prelude to Act 2 .... 107, 265
"Heimliche Aufforderung," *Lied*, Op. 27, No. 3 ....A 7-8
Ein Heldenleben, Symphonic Poem, Op. 40 .... 304, 305
"Hymnus," *Lied*, Op. 33, No. 3, with Orchestra *133, 187, 200, 247, 248, 249
"Pilgers Morgenlied," *Lied*, Op. 33, No. 4, with Orchestra 314, 315, 316
Symphonia Domestica, Op. 53 .... 169, *176
"Taillefer," Op. 52, for Soloists, Chorus, and Orchestra..*184
Till Eulenspiegels lustige Streiche, Op. 28 ....221, 222, 230, 237, 240,
....253, 254, 255, 256, 265, 269, A 13, A 15
Tod und Verklärung, Tone Poem, Op. 24 .... 260, 261, A 7-8
"Verführung," *Lied*, Op. 33, No. 1 ....A 7-8

SUCHER, Josef (1843–1908)
"Liebesglück" *Lied*.. 12a

SUPPÉ, Franz von (1820–1895)
"Das Vergißmeinnicht" *Lied* 16, 30
"Das letzte Lied," *Lied* *4
"O du mein Österreich," *Lied*, arr. for Brass Band & solo *Flügelhorn* *4

SVENDSEN, Johan Severin (1840–1911)
Carnival in Paris, Op. 9, for Orchestra ....A 10-11

SZABÓ, Ferenc Xavér (1846–1911)
Dramatic Symphony... *42

TAUBERT, Wilhelm (1811–1891)
"Der Vogel im Walde," *Lied*, Op.158 30
"Wiegenlied," *Lied*, Op. 27, No. 5.. 44

TAUSIG, Carl (1841–1871)
Fantaisie de Concert on Moniuszko's *Halka*, for Piano, Op. 2 .... *151

TCHAIKOVSKY, Pyotr Ilyich (1842–1893)
Eugene Onegin: Letter Scene 58
Francesca di Rimini, Op. 32, Symphonic Fantasia .... A 10-11
Manfred, Symphony in Four Pictures, Op. 58.. 138, 147
1812 Overture, Op. 49 .... 103, 259
Piano Concerto No.1, B-flat minor, Op. 23 259
Romeo and Juliet, Fantasy-Overture 58, 197, 210, 251, 252, 259
Orchestral Suite No.1, D major, Op. 43 .... 294, 295, 296
Symphony No. 2, C minor, Op. 17, "Little Russian" 294, 295, 296
Symphony No. 5, E minor, Op. 64 277
Symphony No. 6, B minor, Op. 74, "Pathétique" *141b, 241, 242, 259,
.... 270, 306, 316, A 14, A 16-18
Violin Concerto, D major, Op. 35 .... 148, 294, 295, 296

THALBERG, Sigismond (1812–1871)
Grand Fantasy and Variations on Bellini's *Norma*, Op. 12, for 2 Pianos,
  arr. for Piano Solo, or Fantasy on Themes from Bellini's opera
  Norma, Op. 57, No. 4, for Piano Solo 4, 5

THOMAS, Ambroise (1811–1896)
Mignon:
— "Je suis Titania" (Polonaise)... 43
— "Connais-tu le pays?" *36

TOSTI, Francesco Paolo (1846–1916)
"Chanson d'amour," *Lied*... *26

TRUHN, Friedrich Hieronymus (1811–1886)
"Herr Schmied, beschlagt mir mein Rößlein" *Lied*, Op. 66, No. 4 16

TSCHIRCH, Friedrich Wilhelm (1818–1892)
"Frühlingsglaube," for Men's Chorus... *33

UMLAUF, Ignaz (1746–1796)
Lied (unspecified)... 94

URBAN, Heinrich (1837–1901)
"Frühlingslied" for Women's Chorus *21

VERDI, Giuseppe (1813–1901)
Aida
— "Celeste Aida" 14
— Act 2 complete 154
La traviata: "È strano... Sempre libera"... 17
— Act 1 (complete)... *215
Il trovatore, Act 4, Scene 1.. *205
Un ballo in maschera: Aria (unspecified) *10

Composer's Index

VIEUXTEMPS, Henri (1820–1881)
Ballade et Polonaise de Concert, Op. 38, for Violin & Piano 16
Tarantella, Op. 22, No. 5, for Violin & Piano 7
Violin Concerto No. 4, D minor, Op. 31 (1st mvmt.) 8
Violin Concerto No. 5, A minor, Op. 37 .... 255, 264

VOGL, Frantisek Arnold (1821–1891)
"Rudolf von Habsburg," *Lied*, for Bass and Orchestra *12

VOLKMANN, Friedrich Robert (1815-1883)
"Die Bekehrte," Op. 54, *Lied* 31

WAGNER, Richard (1813–1883)
"Dors mon enfant" ["Schlummerlied"], *Lied* *34
Eine Faust-Ouverture *34, 70, 134, 140, 147, 213, 250, 251, 252,
.... 263, 301, 302
"Festmarsch," (Festival March) (unspecified) *4
Der fliegende Holländer, Overture 257, 263, 264, 301, 302, 307,
.... 308, 309, 313, A 3, A 6, A 12, A 14
Götterdämmerung
— "Schweigt eures Jammer" (Brünnhilde's Immolation Scene) 297, 303, 310
— Siegfried's Rhine Journey .... A 2, A 17
— "Siegfried's Tod," Funeral March 63, 92, 148, 225, 257, 297, 303, 310
— "Starke Scheite schichtet" *64
— "Zu neuen Thaten," Duet *27, *28
— "Höre mit Sinn was ich sage" .... A 13, A 15
Huldigungsmarsch, E-flat major 32
Kaisermarsch, B-flat major .... 29, *64, 122, 250, 263, A 2, A 18
"Das Liebesmahl der Apostel," for Men's Chorus and Orchestra *129
Lohengrin
— Prelude to Act 1 .... 257, 263, 297, 303, 307, 308, 310, 311, 312
— "Einsam in trüben Tagen" 297, 303, 307, 308, 310
— "In fernem Land," Act 3, with Orchestral Acc. *129
— Duet (unspecified) for Elsa & Ortrud 50
— Finale I (unspecified), arr. for Military Band *16
Die Meistersinger von Nürnberg
— Act 3, complete *205
— Prelude to Act 1 .... 43, 45, 73, 94, 128, 148, 153, 187, 196, 198, 199, 200, 201,
.... 202, 207, 210, 211, 220, 225, 228, 235, 236, 240, 246, 250, 254, 255,
.... 270, 286, 287, 288, 289, 290, 291, 301, 302, 307, 308, 313, A 14
— Prelude to Act 3 .... 314, 315, 316
— "Was duftet doch die Flieder" 316
— "Wahn! Wahn! Überall Wahn!" 250, 314, 315
— "Morgenlich leuchtend," Act 3 .... 246, 257, 264
"Mignonne" ["Die Rose"], *Lied* *34
Parsifal
— Prelude to Act 1 .... *114, 257
— Prelude & "Höchsten heiles Wunder," arr. for Orchestra 309
— Transformation Music, Act 1 .... 27, 28, *114
— "Zum letzten Liebesmahle" (Grail Scene) 27, 28
— Act 1 & Act 3 Finales 34, *114
— Good Friday Spell .... *114, A 2, A 14, A 18

...WAGNER continued
Rienzi
— Overture 93, 95, 297, 303, 310
— "Gerechter Gott" .... A 13, A 15
— "Ich sah' die Städte" 264
Siegfried: Waldweben, for Orchestra 313
Siegfried Idyll 51, 66, 93, 102, 216, 250, 251, 252, 263, 269, 270,
.... 286, 287, 288, 289, 290, 291, 301, 302, 307, 308
Symphony, C major *34
Tannhäuser
— Overture 45, 131, 152, *158, 216, 247, 248, 249, 250, 262, 269,
.... 297, 303, 307, 308, 310, A 18
— Overture and Bacchanale .... 309, A 13, A 15
— "Dich teure Halle" 95, 263, 273, 297, 303, 307, 308, 309, 310
— "Allmächt'ge Jungfrau" 309
— "Pilgrims' Chorus" *132
Tristan und Isolde:
— Prelude to Act 1 .... 72, 153
— Prelude to Act 1 & Isolde's Liebestod (voice and orchestra) 301, 302, 307, 308, 309
— Prelude & "Liebestod," Act 3 (arr. for Orchestra) 50, 130, 132, 146, 196, 199, 201,
.... 202, 207, 209, 237, 239, 241, 242, 286,
.... 287, 288, 289, 290, 291, A 6, A 12, A 14, A 16
Waldweben, see *Siegfried*
Die Walküre:
— "Winterstürme wichen dem Wonnemond" 257
— "Winterstürme wichen dem Wonnemond" & Final Duet, Act 1 45
— Walkürenritt, Original 50
— Walkürenritt, arr. for Orchestra .... 309, 310, A 6, A 12, A 14, A 16
— Feuerzauber, arr. for Orchestra .... 309, A 18
— Wotan's Farewell & Magic Fire Music 250
Wesendonck-Lieder (5) with Piano or Orchestra Acc.
— "Im Treibhaus" *64, 263, 301, 302
— "Schmerzen" *64, 263, 301, 302
— "Stehe still" *64, 301, 302
— "Träume" *34, 50, *64, 301, 302, 309
— "Der Engel" *34, *64

WAGNER, Siegfried (1869–1930)
Der Bärenhäuter, Overture *107

WALLNÖFER, Adolf (1854–1946)
"Dort unter'm Lindenbaum," *Lied*, Op. 3, No. 1 .... *26
"Woher die Liebe," *Lied*, Op. 24, No. 2 .... *26

WEBER, Carl-Maria von (1786–1826)
Aufforderung zum Tanze, rondo brillant, Op. 65, orch. F. Weingartner (1896) 95, 306,
.... 318, 319, A 3-4
Euryanthe:
— Overture *12, 116, 117, *188
— "So weih' ich mich" 41
Der Freischütz, Overture .... 129, 148, 182, 197, 277, A 7-8
Jubel–Overture, Op. 59 56
Konzertstück, F minor, Op. 79, for Piano & Orchestra, ed. F. Liszt 65, *104, 125,
.... 226, 227

... WEBER continued
Oberon, Overture .... 43, *75, 100, 128, *158, 213, 316, 321, A 4
Polonaise, E major, Op. 21, arr. F. Liszt for Piano *11
Rondo (unspecified) for Clarinet and Piano..*11
Turandot, Overture, Op. 37. 141

WEINGARTNER, Felix von (1863–1942)
"Erdriese," *Lied*, Op. 39, No. 3, with Orchestra... 243, 244
"Frühlingsgespenster," *Lied*, Op. 19, No. 4, with Orchestra 187
"Letzter Tanz," *Lied*, Op. 36, No. 2, with Orchestra 243, 244
"Die Wallfahrt nach Kevlar," Op. 12, Ballad, for Contralto and Orchestra *142
   (see Weber *Aufforderung zum Tanz,* orch. Weingartner)

WESTMEYER, Wilhelm (1829–1880)
Das Engellied, arr. for Military Band... *26
Kaiser-Ouverture *4

WIENIAWSKI, Henri (1835–1880)
Fantaisie brillant on motifs from Gounod's opera *Faust*, Op. 20, for
   Violin and Piano 18

WILHELM II, German Emperor (1859–1941)
"Sang an Aegir," for Chorus & Orchestra, orch. Albert Becker .... 69 (twice)

WINTER, Peter von (1754–1825)
"Allmächtige Sonne," from *Das unterbrochene Opferfest*, for Soprano 29

WOLF, Hugo (1860–1903)
Italienische Serenade, arr. for small Orchestra by Max Reger *188
"Anakreons Grab," *Lied*, with Orchestra 243, 244
"Er ist's," *Lied*, with Orchestra 187, 200, 247, 248, 249
"Der Freund," *Lied*..*89
"Der Genesene an die Hoffnung," *Lied* *89
"Heimweh," *Lied* *89
"Der Rattenfänger," *Lied*, with Orchestra 243, 244
"Das Ständchen," *Lied* *89
"Der Tambour," *Lied* *89
"Verborgenheit," *Lied* *89

ZAMARA, Antonio (1829–1901)
Variations on Gounod's "Au Printemps," for Harp *10

Appendix III: Mahler's Repertoire

> I: Symphonies; II: Symphonic Poems; III: Overtures; IV: Miscellaneous Orchestral Works;
> V: Instrumental Concertos; VI: Choral Works; VII: Lieder & Arias;
> VIII: Chamber Music and Piano Works; IX: 2 Tables

I: Symphonies
233 complete performances of 44 titles
16 performances of 13 separate movements, including an excerpt from one movement

Beethoven, Ludwig van
- No. 1, C major, Op. 21 1
- No. 2, D major, Op. 36 2
- No. 3, E flat major, Op. 55 11
- No. 4, B flat major, Op. 60 2
- No. 5, C minor, Op. 67 18
- No. 6, F major, Op. 68 16
- No. 7, A major, Op. 92 13
  - -- 2nd movement 1
- No. 8, F major, Op. 93 1
- No. 9, D minor, Op. 125 10
  - -- 4th movement (excerpt) 1
- Total 2   74

Berlioz, Hector
- *Symphonie fantastique* 12
  - -- 2nd & 3rd movements .... each 1

Brahms, Johannes
- No. 1, C minor, Op. 68 3
- No. 2, D major, Op. 73 1
- No. 3, F major, Op. 90 5

Bruckner, Anton
- No. 3, D minor: Scherzo movement   1
- No. 4, E flat major 3
  - -- Scherzo movement 1
- No. 5, B flat major 1
- No. 6, A minor 1

Foerster, Josef Bohuslav
- No. 3, D major 2

Goetz, Hermann
- F major, Op. 9 1

Haydn, Josef
- No. 99, E flat major 1
- No. 101, D major 1
- No. 103, E flat major 2
- No. 104, D major 2
- Symphony in G major (excerpt) 1

Mahler, Gustav
- No. 1, D major 16
- No. 2, C minor 10
  - -- 1st movement 3
  - -- 2nd movement. 2
  - -- 3rd movement. 1
- No. 3, D minor 15
  - -- 2nd movement 1
- No. 4, G major 11
  - -- 4th movement 1
- No. 5 9
  - -- 4th movement 1
- No. 6, A minor 3
- No. 7 5
- No. 8, E flat major 2
- Total 9   71

Mendelssohn, Felix
- No. 3, A minor, Op. 56 1
- No. 4, A major, Op. 90 1

Mozart, Wolfgang Amadeus
- No. 40, G minor 8
- No. 41, C major 4

Schubert, Franz
- No. 8 (7), B minor 9
- No. 9 (8), C major 5

Schumann, Robert
- No. 1, B flat major, Op. 38 4
- No. 2, C major, Op. 61 2
- No. 3, E flat major, Op. 97 2
- No. 4, D minor, Op. 120 5

Stanford, Charles Villiers
- No. 3, F minor, Op. 28 2

Tchaikovsky, Pyotr
- No. 2, C minor, Op. 17 3
- No. 5, E minor, Op. 64 1
- No. 6, B minor, Op. 74 6

II: Symphonic Poems
67 performances of 26 titles

Berlioz, Hector
    Faust (3 excerpts) 1
    Roméo et Juliette (3 excerpts) 2
Chabrier, Alexis Emmanuel
    España 4
Debussy, Claude
    Prélude à l'après-midi d'un faune 2
    Iberia 3
    Trois Nocturnes 2
    Rondes des printemps 2
Dukas, Paul
    L'Apprenti sorcier 2
Dvořák, Antonin
    Heldenlied (Hero's Song) 1
    Die Waldtaube (The Wild Dove) 1
Liszt, Franz
    Festklänge 2
    Les Préludes 7
    Mazeppa 3
    Tasso 1

Loeffler, Charles
    La Villanelle du Diable 2
MacDowell, Edward
    The Song of Roland 2
Rimsky-Korsakoff, Nikolai
    Scheherazade 1
Smetana, Bedřich
    Moldau 4
Strauss, Richard
    Also sprach Zarathustra 3
    Aus Italien 1
    Don Juan 3
    Ein Heldenleben 2
    Symphonia domestica 1
    Till Eulenspiegels 11
    Tod und Verklärung 2
    Total *23*
Tchaikovsky, Pyotr
    Manfred 2

III: Opera and Concert Overtures, Vorspiel, etc.
267 performances of 52 titles

Beethoven, Ludwig van
    Coriolan 19
    Egmont 11
    Fidelio 2
    König Stephan 2
    Leonore I 1
    Leonore II 1
    Leonore III 20
    Prometheus 1
    Die Weihe des Hauses 5
    Zur Namensfeier 2
    Total *64*
Berlioz, Hector
    Rob Roy 1
    Carnaval romain 7
Chadwick, George
    Melpomene 2
Cherubini, Luigi
    Anacréon 2
Dvořák, Antonin
    Carnival 3
    In Nature's Realm 2
Goldmark, Karl
    Im Frühling 3
    Sakuntala 1
Lalo, Eduard
    Le Roi d'Ys 1

Mendelssohn, Felix
    Die Hebriden (Fingal's Cave) 4
    Märchen von der schönen Melusine 2
    Meeresstille und glückliche Fahrt 1
Mihalovich, Ödön
    Toldi's Liebe 1
Nicolai, Otto
    Die lustigen Weiber von Windsor 1
Pfitzner, Hans
    Das Christ-Elflein 1
    Das Käthchen von Heilbronn 2
Schubert, Franz
    Die Zauberharfe (Rosamunde) 3
Schumann, Robert
    Die Braut von Messina 1
    Julius Caesar 1
    Manfred 5
Sinigaglia, Leone
    La Baruffe Chiozzotte 1
Smetana, Bedřich
    The Bartered Bride 7
    Libuse 1
Spohr, Ludwig
    Jessonda 1
Strauss, Richard
    Guntram, Act I 3
    -- Act II 2

Tchaikovsky, Pyotr
- *1812 Overture* 2
- *Romeo and Juliet* 6

Wagner, Richard
- *Eine Faust-Ouverture* 11
- *Der fliegende Holländer* 9
- *Lohengrin*, Act I 9
- *Die Meistersinger*, Act I 39
- -- Act III 3
- *Parsifal*, Act I 2
- *Rienzi* 5

Tannhäuser 16
Tristan und Isolde 27
Total *121*

Weber, Carl-Maria von
- *Euryanthe* 2
- *Der Freischütz* 5
- *Jubel* Overture 1
- *Oberon* 6
- *Turandot* 1
- Total *15*

IV: Miscellaneous Orchestral Works (including arrangements)
131 performances of 35 titles

Bach, J. S. (arr. by G. Mahler)
- Suite for Orchestra 20

Beethoven, Ludwig van - G. Mahler
- String Quartet, Op. 95 1
- Excerpt from Symphony No. 9 1

Bizet, Georges
- Suite from *L'Arlésienne* 3
- *Roma*, Suite 3

Boccherini, Luigi
- Minuet from String Quintet 1

Bossi, Marco Enrico
- *Intermezzi Goldoniani* 1

Brahmnnes, Johannnes
- Variations on a Theme by Haydn 1

Busoni, Ferruccio
- *Berceuse élégiaque* 1
- *Turandot*, Orchestral Suite 2

Dvořák, Antonin
- Scherzo capriccioso 1
- Serenade, Op. 44 1

Elgar, Edward
- "Enigma"-Variations 2

Enescu, George
- Orchestral Suite, Op. 9 3

Grieg, Edvard
- Triumphal March 1

Hadley, Henry
- *The Culprit Fay* 2

Handel, George Frideric
- Largo from *Xerxes* 1

Haydn, Josef
- String Quartet movement 1

Liszt, Franz
- "Mephisto Waltz" 2

Mozart, Wolfgang Amadeus
- German Dances 3
- Ballet music from *Idomeneo* 3

Rameau, Jean-Philippe
- *Rigaudon* 2

Rubinstein, Anton
- Ballet Music from *The Demon* 1

Schubert, Franz (orch. by G. Mahler)
- "Death and the Maiden" String Quartet, 2nd movement 1

Tchaikovsky, Pyotr
- Suite No. 1, Op. 43 3

Wagner, Richard
- Feuerzauber from *Die Walküre* 1
- *Huldigungsmarsch* 1
- *Kaisermarsch* 4
- "Liebestod" from *Tristan* 25
- *Siegfried Idyll* 21
- "Siegfried's Tod"/*Götterdämmerung* 8
- "Zum letzten Liebesmahle"/*Parsifal* 2
- Waldweben from *Siegfried* 1
- Walkürenritt from *Die Walküre* 3

Weber, Carl-Maria von (orch. by F. Weingartner)
- *Aufforderung zum Tanze* 4

V: Instrumental Concertos

61 complete performances of 39 titles
3 performances of 3 separate movements

Alárd, Delphin
    Concerto for 2 Violins 1
Bach, Johann Sebastian
    Piano Concerto No. 1, D minor 1
    Violin Concerto No. 2, E major 1
Beethoven, Ludwig van
    Piano Concerto No. 3, C minor 1
    Piano Concerto No. 4, G major 1
    Piano Concerto No. 5, E flat major........ 6
    Romance No. 1, F major for Violin 1
    Violin Concerto D major, Op. 61 2
Brahms, Johannes
    Piano Concerto No. 1, D minor 1
    Violin Concerto, D major 3
Ernst, Heinrich Wilhelm
    Violin Concerto (unspecified) 1
Franck, César
    Symphonic Variations for Piano 1
Goldmark, Karl
    Violin Concerto 2
Grieg, Edvard
    Piano Concerto 2
Lalo, Éduard
    Symphonie espagnole for Violin 2
Liszt, Franz
    Piano Concerto No. 1, E flat major 1
    Piano Concerto No. 2, A major 1
    Rhapsodie espagnole for Piano 1
MacDowell, Edward
    Piano Concerto No. 2, D minor 1
Martucci, Giuseppe
    Piano Concerto No. 2, B-flat minor 1
Mendelssohn, Felix
    Capriccio brillant, Op. 22 1
    Violin Concerto, E minor 3

Moszkowski, Moritz
    Violin Concerto, C major, Op. 30.......... 1
Paganini, Niccolò
    Violin Concerto, Op. 6, 1st mov. 1
Rachmaninoff, Sergei
    Piano Concerto No. 3, D minor 1
Raff, Joseph Joachim
    Violin Concerto No. 2, A minor 1
Rubinstein, Anton
    Piano Concerto No. 4, D minor 1
Saint-Saëns, Camille
    Piano Concerto No. 4, C minor............. 2
Sarasate, Pablo de
    Muñeira, Op. 32 for Violin 1
Sauer, Émil
    Piano Concerto, E minor 1
Sauret, Émile
    Elegie and Rondo for Violin 1
Scharwenka, Franz Xaver
    Piano Concerto No. 1, 1st mov. 1
    Piano Concerto No. 4, F minor 1
Schubert, Franz (arr. by F. Liszt)
    Fantasy, "Wanderer" for Piano 1
Schumann, Robert
    Piano Concerto, Op. 54 2
Simon, Antony Yulievich
    Piano Concerto, Op. 19 1
Spohr, Louis
    Violin Concerto No. 10, A minor 1
Tchaikovsky, Pyotr
    Piano Concerto No. 1, B-flat minor 1
    Violin Concerto, Op. 35 4
Vieuxtemps, Henri
    Violin Concerto No. 4, 1st mov. 1
    Violin Concerto No. 5, A minor 2
Weber, Carl-Maria von
    Konzertstück for Piano, Op. 79 4

VI: Choral Works

34 complete performances of 16 titles
2 excerpts of 2 titles

Bach, Johann Sebastian
    Matthäus-Passion (excerpt) 1
Beethoven, Ludwig van
    Fantasy, Op. 80 for Piano...................... 2
Brahms, Johannes
    "Gesang aus Fingal," Op. 17 (excerpt) ... 1
Bruckner, Anton
    Mass, D minor 1
    Te Deum 3

Chabrier, Alexis Emanuel
    Á la Musique 3
Fauré, Gabriel
    Hymne á Apollon 1
Haydn, Josef
    Die Jahreszeiten 1
    Die Schöpfung 6
Mahler, Gustav
    Das klagende Lied 3

Mendelssohn, Felix
Paulus 1
Mihalovich, Ödön
"Royal Hymn" 1
Mozart, Wolfgang Amadeus
Requiem 4
Perosi, Lorenzo
La risurrezione di Lazzaro 2

Rossini, Gioachino
Stabat Mater 2
Schubert, Franz
Ständchen (D 921) 1
Stoiber, Ernst
"Festhymne" 1
Wilhelm II
"Sang an Aegir" 2

VII: Lieder and Arias
235 performances of 144 songs
94 performances of 58 opera excerpts

Adam, Adolphe Charles
Aria, *La Poupée de Nuremberg* 1
d'Albert, Eugene
Das Mädchen und das Schmetterling... 1
Anonymous
"Schilflied" 1
Unspecified (2 songs) 2
Arditi, Luigi
Forosetta 1
Beethoven, Ludwig van
"Ah perfido!" 4
2 Arias from *Fidelio* 2
"Freudvoll und Leidvoll" from *Egmont* .. 1
"Die Trommel gerührt" from *Egmont*... 1
Behn, Hermann
Lieder (unspecified) 1
Bizet, Georges
Aria, *La Jolie fille de Perth* 1
"Pastorale" 1
Brahms, Johannes
"Liebestreu" 2
9 *Neue deutsche Volkslieder*................ 1
"Wiegenlied" 1
Bungert, August
"Der Sandträger" 1
Buononcini, Giovanni Battista
"Per la gloria d'adorar" 1
Donizetti, Gaetano
Aria from *La Favorita* 1
Aria from *Linda di Chamounix* 1
Dorn, Alexander Julius
"Schneeglöckchen" 1
Elgar, Edward
"In Haven" 2
"Sabbath Morning at Sea" 2
"Sea Slumber Song" 2
"Where Corals Lie" 2

Fiedler, Max
"Die Musikantin" 4
Flotow, Friedrich von
Aria from *Alessandro Stradella* 1
Franz, Robert
"Wenn der Frühling auf die Berge" 1
Gall, Jan
"Mädchen mit dem rothen Mündchen" . 1
Gounod, Charles
Aria from *Romeo et Juliette* 1
Grétry, André Ernst
Aria from *Céphale et Procris* 1
Grieg, Edvard
"Ich liebe dich" 1
Halévy, Jacques
Aria from *La Juive* 1
Handel, George Frideric
Aria from *Flavio* 2
Aria from *Messiah* 1
Aria from *Samson* 1
Aria from *Xerxes* 2
Haslinger, Carl
"Ein schöner Tod" 1
Hauer, Carl Heinrich
"Einen Brief soll ich schreiben" 1
Haydn, Josef
2 Arias from *Die Schöpfung* 2
Heinefetter, Wilhelm
"Im wunderschönen Monat Mai" 1
Hölzl, Franz
"Hab' ich in der Brust ein Vöglein" 1
"In den Augen liegt das Herz" 1
Hungarian Folk Songs (2) 1
Krebs, Carl
Vater Unser 2
Kücken, Friedrich Wilhelm
"Gut' Nacht, fahr' wohl" 1

Lalo, Éduard
- Aria from *Le Roi d'Ys* ... 3

Loewe, Carl
- "Der Fischer" ... 1
- "Des Goldschmieds Töchterlein" ... 1
- "Heinrich der Vogler" ... 1
- "Hochzeitslied" ... 1
- "Kleiner Haushalt" ... 2
- Lieder (unspecified) ... 1

Mahler, Gustav
- "Ablösung im Sommer" ... 1
- "Des Antonius von Padua" ... 4
- "Blicke mir nicht in die Lieder" ... 3
- "Erinnerung" ... 1
- "Frühlingsmorgen" ... 2
- "Gieng heut' morgen übers Feld" ... 5
- "Hans und Grethe" ... 1
- "Das himmlische Leben" ... 1
- "Ich atmet' einen linden Duft" ... 3
- "Ich bin der Welt abhanden" ... 6
- "Das irdische Leben" ... 3
- *Kindertotenlieder* (5) ... 7
- "Lied des Verfolgten im Turm" ... 3
- *Lieder eines fahrenden Gesellen* (4) ... 2
- "Lob des hohen Verstandes" ... 1
- "Nicht Wiedersehen" ... 1
- "Revelge" ... 3
- "Rheinlegendchen" ... 7
- "Scheiden und Meiden" ... 1
- "Der Schildwache Nachtlied" ... 6
- "Selbstgefühl" ... 1
- "Starke Einbildungskraft" ... 1
- "Der Tamboursg'sell" ... 3
- "Trost im Unglück" ... 4
- "Um Mitternacht" ... 4
- "Um schlimme Kinder artig" ... 1
- "Verlor'ne Müh'" ... 2
- "Wer hat dies Liedlein erdacht" ... 3
- "Wo die schönen Trompeten" ... 1
- "Die zwei blauen Augen" ... 1
- Total ... 82

Marschner, Heinrich
- Aria from *Hans Heiling* ... 1

Massenet, Jules
- Aria from *Hérodiade* ... 1
- Aria from *Le jongleur de Notre-Dame* ... 1
- Aria from *Le mage* ... 3
- Aria from *Manon* ... 3
- "Ouvre tes yeux bleus" ... 1
- Duet from *Le Roi de Lahore* ... 1

Mattei, Tito
- "Es ist nicht wahr" ... 1

Mendelssohn, Felix
- 2 Arias from *Elijah* ... 2
- Terzetto from *Elijah* ... 1
- "Wenn sich zwei Herzen scheiden" ... 1

Meyer-Helmund, Erik
- "Du fragst mich täglich" ... 1
- "Der Schwur" ... 1

Meyerbeer, Giacomo
- 2 Arias from *Le Prophète* ... 3

Mozart, Wolfgang Amadeus
- 3 Arias from *Don Giovanni* ... 3
- 3 Arias from *Le nozze di Figaro* ... 4

Paisiello, Giovanni
- "Chi vuol la zingarella" ... 1

Reinecke, Carl
- "Luftschloß" ... 1

Rossini, Gioachino
- Aria from *Guillaume Tell* ... 1

Rubinstein, Anton
- "Der Asra" ... 1
- "Es blinkt der Tau" ... 1
- "Gelb rollt mir zu Füßen" ... 1
- "Neue Liebe" ... 1
- "Der Traum" ... 1

Scarlatti, Alessandro
- *Le violette* ... 1

Schubert, Franz
- "Am Meer" ... 2
- "An die Musik" ... 2
- "An Schwager Kronos" ... 1
- "Aufenthalt" ... 1
- "Du bist die Ruh'" ... 2
- "Das Echo" ... 2
- "Der Neugierige" ... 1
- "Frühlingsglaube" ... 1
- "Gretchen am Spinnrade" ... 2
- "Heidenröslein" ... 1
- "Horch! Horch! die Lerch!" ... 2
- "Liebesbotschaft" ... 1
- "Suleika" ... 2
- "Trockne Blumen" ... 2
- "Der Wanderer" ... 3
- "Wandrers Nachtlied" ... 2
- Lieder (unspecified) ... 2

Schumann, Robert
- "Ballade vom Haidenknaben" ... 1
- "Der Contrabandiste" ... 1
- "Die beiden Grenadiere" ... 2
- "Es ist verrathen" ... 1
- "Frühlingsnacht" ... 2
- "Ich bin geliebt" ... 1
- "Liebesgarten" ... 1
- "Die Lotusblume" ... 1
- "Mit Myrthen und Rosen" ... 1
- "Spanisches Liederspiel" ... 2
- "Wanderlied" ... 1
- "Widmung" ... 1
- Lieder (unspecified) ... 3

Smetana, Bedřich
- Aria from *The Bartered Bride* ... 1

Strauss, Richard
    "Hymnus" 5
    "Pilgers Morgenlied" 3
Suppé, Franz von
    "Das Vergißmeinnicht" 2
Swedish Folk Songs (3) 1
Taubert, Wilhelm
    "Der Vogel im Walde" 1
    "Wiegenlied" 1
Tchaikovsky, Pyotr
    Aria from *Eugene Onegin* 1
Thomas, Ambroise
    Aria from *Mignon* 1
Truhn, Friedrich Hieronymus
    "Herr Schmied" 1
Verdi, Giuseppe
    Aria from *Aida* 1
    Aria from *La traviata* 1

Wagner, Richard
    Aria from *Götterdämmerung* 3
    Aria from *Lohengrin* 5
    Duet from *Lohengrin* 1
    3 Arias from *Die Meistersinger* 7
    Aria from *Rienzi* 1
    2 Arias from *Tannhäuser* 10
    Aria from *Tristan* ("Liebestod") 5
    4 excerpts from *Die Walküre* 4
    Wesendonck-Lieder (5) 12
Weber, Carl Maria von
    Aria from *Euryanthe* 1
Weingartner, Felix von
    "Erdriese" 2
    "Frühlingsgespenster" 1
    "Letzter Tanz" 2
Wolf, Hugo
    "Anakreons Grab" 2
    "Er ist's" 5
    "Der Rattenfänger" 2

VIII: Chamber Music and Piano Works
29 performances of 26 titles

Beethoven, Ludwig van
    Piano Trio (unspecified) 1
    Violin Sonata, No. 7, C minor, Op. 30, 2   1
    Violin Sonata, No. 9, A major, Op. 47 ... 1
Brahms, Johannes
    3 Hungarian Dances, Violin & Piano 1
Chopin, Frédéric
    Ballade, for Piano (unspecified) 1
    Impromptu, for Piano (unspecified) 1
    Polonaise No. 6, A flat major, Op. 53 ... 2
Laub, Ferdinand
    Polonaise, Op. 8, for Violin & Piano 1
Liszt, Franz
    Gnomenreigen, for Piano 1
    Hungarian Rhapsody (unspecified) 1
    Paraphrase on Mendelssohn's
    "Wedding March," for Piano 1

Mahler, Gustav
    Piano Quartet (or Quintet) 1
    Piano Quintet, Scherzo 1
    Sonata for Violin & Piano 2
Mozart, Wolfgang Amadeus
    Unspecified work for Violin & Piano 1
Schubert, Franz
    Fantasy, "Wanderer" for Piano 2
    Piano Sonata, A minor, 1st movement . 2
Schumann, Robert
    Humoreske, Op. 20 (excerpt) 2
    Waldszenen, Op. 82 (two excerpts) 1
Thalberg, Sigismond
    Fantasy on *Norma* for Piano 2
Vieuxtemps, Henri
    Ballade et Polonaise for Violin & Piano   1
    Tarantella for Violin & Piano 1
Wieniawski, Henri
    Fantaisie on *Faust* for Violin & Piano .. 1

IX: Summary of Mahler's Performances

	Number of		Performances of own works *	
Categories	Works	Performances	Works	Performances
I: Symphonies (complete)	44	233	8	71
Ia: separate movements	13	16	6	9
II: Symphonic Poems	26	67		
III: Overtures	52	267		
IV: Misc. Orchestral Works	35	131		
V: Instrumental Concertos	39	61		
VI: Choral Works	16	34	1	3
VII: Lieder and Arias	144	235	30	82
VIII: Chamber Music	26	29	3	4
Totals	**395**	**1,073**	**48**	**169**

* Mahler's performances of his own works are included in the previous columns.

Summary of Performances by Composer

Composer	Number of Works	Number of Performances	Composer	Number of Works	Number of Performances
Wagner	36	235	Goldmark	3	6
Mahler	55	169	Lalo	3	6
Beethoven	36	166	Vieuxtemps	4	5
Schubert	25	53	Weingartner	3	5
Schumann	23	43	Chopin	3	4
Strauss	10	36	Grieg	3	4
Mozart	12	30	Fiedler	1	4
Tchaikovsky	10	29	Busoni	2	3
Berlioz	7	25	MacDowell	2	3
Weber	8	24	Pfitzner	2	3
Bach	4	23	Rossini	2	3
Brahms	13	22	Enescu	1	3
Liszt	11	21	Meyerbeer	1	3
Mendelssohn	11	18	Mihalovich	2	2
Haydn	9	17	Scharwenka	2	2
Smetana	4	13	Donizetti	2	2
Bruckner	7	11	Hölzl	2	2
Dvořák	7	10	Meyer-Helmund	2	2
Massenet	6	10	Reinecke	2	2
Elgar	5	10	Spohr	2	2
Debussy	4	9	Taubert	2	2
Wolf	3	9	Verdi	2	2
Bizet	4	8	Chadwick	1	2
Rubinstein	7	7	Cherubini	1	2
Loewe	6	7	Dukas	1	2
Handel	5	7	Foerster	1	2
Chabrier	2	7	Hadley	1	2

Composer	Number of Works	Number of Performances	Composer	Number of Works	Number of Performances
Krebs	1	2	Grétry	1	1
Loeffler	1	2	Halévy	1	1
Perosi	1	2	Haslinger	1	1
Rameau	1	2	Hauer	1	1
Saint-Saëns	1	2	Heinefetter	1	1
Stanford	1	2	Kücken	1	1
Suppé	1	2	Laub	1	1
Thalberg	1	2	Marschner	1	1
Wilhelm II	1	2	Martucci	1	1
Adam	1	1	Mattei	1	1
Alárd	1	1	Moszkowski	1	1
d'Albert	1	1	Nicolai	1	1
Arditi	1	1	Paganini	1	1
Behn	1	1	Paisiello	1	1
Boccherini	1	1	Rachmaninoff	1	1
Bossi	1	1	Raff	1	1
Bungert	1	1	Rimsky-Korsakoff	1	1
Buononcini	1	1	Sarasate	1	1
Dorn	1	1	Sauer	1	1
Ernst	1	1	Sauret	1	1
Fauré	1	1	Scarlatti	1	1
Flotow	1	1	Simon	1	1
Franck	1	1	Sinigaglia	1	1
Franz	1	1	Stoiber	1	1
Gall	1	1	Thomas	1	1
Goetz	1	1	Truhn	1	1
Gounod	1	1	Wieniawski	1	1

Appendix IV: Mahler's Concert Itinerary
Alphabetical according to city

Date	Venue	Capacity	Program	Concert No.

ALTONA (Germany)

1893
Nov. 22 — Stadttheater — conductor — Haydn — 59

1894
Nov. 21 — Stadttheater — conductor — Haydn — 68

1895
Nov. 20 — Stadttheater — conductor — Haydn — 82

1896
Nov. 18 — Stadttheater — conductor — Haydn — 88

AMSTERDAM (Holland)

1903
Oct. 22 — The Concertgebouw — composer-conductor — Mahler Sym. No. 3 — 156
Oct. 23 — The Concertgebouw — composer-conductor — Mahler Sym. No. 3 — 157
Oct. 25 — The Concertgebouw — composer-conductor — Mahler Sym. No. 1 — 158

1904
Oct. 23 — The Concertgebouw — composer-conductor — Mahler Sym. No. 4 (twice) — 166
Oct. 26 — The Concertgebouw — composer-conductor — Mahler Sym. No. 2 — 167
Oct. 27 — The Concertgebouw — composer-conductor — Mahler Sym. No. 2 — 168

1906
Mar. 8 — The Concertgebouw — composer-conductor — All Mahler program — 183
Mar. 10 — The Concertgebouw — composer-conductor — Mahler *Das klagende Lied* — 184

1909
Oct. 3 — The Concertgebouw — composer-conductor — Mahler Sym. No. 7 — 219
Oct. 7 — The Concertgebouw — composer-conductor — Mahler Sym. No. 7, mixed — 220

ANTWERP (Anvers, Belgium)

1906
Mar. 5 — Théatre Royal — composer-conductor — Mahler Sym. No. 5, mixed — 182

BASEL (Switzerland)

1903
June 15 — Das Münster — composer-conductor — Mahler Sym. No. 2 — 155

BERLIN (Germany)

1895
Mar. 4 — Philharmonie — composer-conductor — Mahler Sym. No. 2 (sel.) — 75
Dec. 13 — Philharmonie — composer-conductor — Mahler Sym. No. 2 (premiere) — 83

1896
Mar. 16 — Philharmonie — composer-conductor — All Mahler program — 84

1901
Dec. 16 — Kroll Oper — composer-conductor — Mahler Sym. No. 4 — 143

1907
Jan. 14 — Philharmonie — composer-conductor — Mahler Sym. No. 3 — 192
Feb. 14 — Künstlerhaus — composer-piano acc. — Mahler *Lieder* recital — 195

BOSTON (Massachusetts, USA)

1910
Feb. 26 — Symphony Hall — conductor — mixed program — 256

BRESLAU (Germany/Wroclaw, Poland)

1905
Dec. 20 — Konzerthaus — composer-conductor — Mahler Sym. No. 5 — 181

1906
Oct. 24 — Konzerthaus — composer-conductor — All Mahler program — 186

BROOKLYN (New York, USA)

1909
Dec. 3	Academy of Music	conductor	mixed program	228

1910
Jan. 8	Academy of Music	conductor	mixed program	237
Jan. 28	Academy of Music	composer-conductor	Mahler *Kindertotenlieder*, mixed.	244
Feb. 11	Academy of Music	conductor	mixed program	249
Mar. 18	Academy of Music	conductor	All Wagner program	263
Nov. 6	Academy of Music	conductor	mixed program	276
Nov. 20	Academy of Music	composer-conductor	Mahler *Lieder*, mixed	280
Dec. 18	Academy of Music	conductor	All Tchaikovsky program	294

1911
Jan. 1	Academy of Music	conductor	All Wagner program	297
Jan. 8	Academy of Music	conductor	mixed program	300
Jan. 29	Academy of Music	conductor	All Wagner program	310
Feb. 12	Academy of Music	conductor	mixed program	316

BRÜNN (Austria/Brno, Czech Republic)

1906
Nov. 11	Deutsches Haus	composer-conductor	Mahler Sym. No. 1	188

BUDAPEST (Hungary)

1889
Nov. 13	Vigadó, small hall	composer-piano acc.	Mahler *Lieder*, mixed	35
Nov. 20	Vigadó, large hall	composer-conductor	Mahler Sym. No. 1	36
Dec. 11	Folk Theater	conductor	mixed program	37

1890
Jan. 3	Royal Opera House	conductor	mixed program	38
Feb. 24	Royal Opera House	conductor	mixed program	39
Mar. 12	The Kasino	piano acc.	mixed program	40
April 16	Royal Opera House	conductor	mixed program	41
Oct. 29	Royal Opera House	conductor	mixed program	42
Dec. 5	Royal Opera House	conductor	mixed program	43

1897
Mar. 31	Vigadó, large hall	composer-conductor	Mahler Sym. No. 3, mixed	95

BUFFALO (New York, USA)

1910
Dec. 7	Convention Hall	conductor	mixed program	288

CLEVELAND (Ohio, USA)

1910
Dec. 6	Gray's Armory	conductor	mixed program	287

COLOGNE (Köln, Germany)

1904
Mar. 27	Gürzenich	composer-conductor	Mahler Sym. No. 3	164
Oct. 18	Gürzenich	composer-conductor	Mahler Sym. No. 5 (premiere)	165

DEN HAAG ('s-Gravenhage [The Hague], Holland)

1909
Oct. 2	Gebouw van Kunst	composer-conductor	Mahler Sym. No. 7	218

ESSEN (Germany)

1906
May 27	Städtischer Saalbau	composer-conductor	Mahler Sym. No.6 (premiere)	185

FRANKFURT am MAIN (Germany)

1899
Mar. 8   Das Neue Opernhaus   composer-conductor   Mahler Sym. No. 1 109

1903
Dec. 2   Das Neue Opernhaus   composer-conductor   Mahler Sym. No. 3 159

1907
Jan. 18   Saalbau   composer-conductor   Mahler Sym. No. 4, mixed 193

GRAZ (Austria)

1905
June 1   Stephanie-Saal   composer-conductor   Mahler *Lieder* recital 178

1906
Dec. 3   Stadttheater   composer-conductor   Mahler Sym. No. 3 189
Dec. 23   Stadttheater   composer-conductor   Mahler Sym. No. 3 190

HAMBURG (Germany)

1891
May 27   Stadttheater   piano acc.   mixed program 44

1892
Feb. 29   Stadttheater   conductor   Rossini 46
Mar. 3   Stadttheater   conductor   Rossini 47
Mar. 14   Stadttheater   conductor   All Beethoven program 48
April 15   Stadttheater   conductor   mixed program 49
Dec. 12   Convent Garten   conductor   mixed program 51

1893
Mar. 19   Stadttheater   conductor   mixed program 52
Mar. 31   Stadttheater   conductor   All Bruckner program 53
Apr. 15   Stadttheater   conductor   All Beethoven program 54
Oct. 27   Concerthaus Hmbg.   composer-conductor   Mahler Sym. No.1 & *Lieder*, mix 55
Nov. 10   Stadttheater   conductor   mixed program 56
Nov. 18   Stadttheater   conductor   mixed program 58

1894
Feb. 26   Convent Garten   conductor   mixed program 60
Mar. 3   Stadttheater   conductor   All Beethoven program 61
Mar. 23   Stadttheater   conductor   mixed program 62
Mar. 29   Stadttheater   conductor   Wagner 63
Oct. 22   Convent Garten   conductor, piano acc.   mixed program 65
Nov. 5   Convent Garten   conductor   mixed program 66
Nov. 19   Convent Garten   conductor, piano acc.   mixed program 67
Nov. 24   Stadttheater   conductor   mixed program 69
Dec. 3   Convent Garten   conductor, piano acc.   mixed program 70

1895
Jan. 21   Convent Garten   conductor   mixed program 71
Feb. 4   Convent Garten   conductor   mixed program 72
Feb. 18   Convent Garten   conductor   mixed program 73
Mar. 1   Stadttheater   conductor   All Beethoven program 74
Mar. 11   Convent Garten   conductor   All Beethoven program 76
Mar. 17   Stadttheater   conductor   All Beethoven program 77
Mar. 26   Stadttheater   conductor   above concert repeated 78
Mar. 31   Stadttheater   conductor, piano acc.   mixed program 79
April 2   Stadttheater   conductor   All Beethoven program 80
April 12   Stadttheater   conductor   mixed program 81

1896
April 2   Stadttheater   conductor   mixed program 85
April 13   Stadttheater   conductor   mixed program 86
April 25   Stadttheater   conductor   above concert repeated 87

...*Hamburg, continued* (1897)

1897
Jan. 30	Stadttheater	conductor, piano acc.	All Schubert program	90
Feb. 1	Stadttheater	conductor, piano acc.	above concert repeated	91
Feb. 12	Foyer, Stadttheater	conductor	Wagner	92
April 16	Stadttheater	conductor	mixed program	96
April 24	Stadttheater	conductor	All Beethoven program	97

1905
Mar. 13	Convent Garten	composer-conductor	Mahler Sym. No. 5	175

1908
Nov. 9	Musikhalle	conductor	mixed program	210

HARTFORD (Connecticut, USA)

1911
Feb. 16	Parsons Theater	conductor	mixed program	319

HEIDELBERG (Germany)

1904
Feb. 1	Stadthalle	composer-conductor	Mahler Sym. No. 3	160

HELSINKI (Finland/Helsingfors, Russia)

1907
Nov. 1	University Hall	conductor	mixed program	201

IGLAU (Austria/Jihlava, Czech Republic)

1870
Oct. 13	Stadttheater	solo pianist	program unknown	1

1871
Jan. 15	Gymnasium	pianist	mixed program	2

1872
Nov. 11	Gymnasium	solo pianist	mixed program	3

1873
April 20	Stadttheater	solo pianist	mixed program	4
May 17	Hotel Czap	solo pianist	mixed program	5

1876
July 31	Hotel Czap	solo pianist & acc.	Mahler, Violin Sonata, mixed	7
Sep. 12	Hotel Czap	solo pianist & acc.	Mahler, Piano Quintet, mixed	8

1879
April 24	Stadttheater	solo pianist & acc.	mixed program	12

1883
Aug. 11	Stadttheater	solo pianist & acc.	mixed program	18

KAISER WILHELM II (German Steamship)

1910
Oct. 24		piano acc.	mixed program	273

KAISERIN AUGUSTE VICTORIA (German Steamship)

1907
Dec. 18		piano acc.	program unknown	204

KASSEL (Germany)

1884
Jan. 19	Royal Theater	conductor	Schumann	19
Mar. 11	Royal Theater	conductor	Schumann	20
Mar. 23	Hanusch Saal	piano acc.	mixed program	21
Oct. 18	Royal Theater	conductor	Mozart	22

1885
Feb. 19	Royal Theater	conductor	Goldmark	24
June 29	Festival Hall	conductor	Mendelssohn	2

KREFELD (Germany)

1902
June 9   Stadthalle   composer-conductor   Mahler Sym. No. 3 (premiere) .   150

LAIBACH (Austria/Ljubljana, Slovenia)

1881
Sep. 24   Theatre   conductor   Beethoven   13
1882
Feb. 4   Theatre   conductor   mixed program   14
Mar. 5   Redoutensaal   solo pianist   mixed program   15
April 2   Theatre   piano acc.   mixed program   16

LEIPZIG (Germany)

1887
Mar. 19   Altes Gewandhaus   piano acc.   mixed program   31
Mar. 22   Statdttheater   conductor   All Wagner program   32
April 30   Altes Gewandhaus   piano acc.   mixed program   33
Nov. 30   Stadttheater   conductor   All Wagner program   34
1896
Dec. 14   Albert Halle   composer-conductor   Mahler Sym. No. 2, mixed   89
1904
Nov. 28   Zoo Garden Hall   composer-conductor   Mahler Sym. No. 3   170

LEMBERG (Austria/Lviv, Ukraine)

1903
April 2   Philharmonie   composer-conductor   Mahler No. 1, mixed program ...   152
April 4   Philharmonie   composer-conductor   Mahler No. 1, mixed program ...   153

LIÈGE (Belgium)

1899
Jan. 22   Royal Theater   composer-conductor   Mahler Sym. No. 2   104

LINZ (Austria)

1907
Jan. 20   Stadttheater   composer-conductor   Mahler Sym. No. 1   194

LONDON (England)

1892
June 29   St. James's Hall   conductor   All Wagner program   50

LÜBECK (Germany)

1891
Nov. 27   Colosseum   conductor   mixed program   45

MAINZ (Germany)

1904
Mar. 23   Liedertafel   composer-conductor   Mahler Sym. No. 4   163

MANNHEIM (Germany)

1904
Feb. 2   Rosengarten   composer-conductor   Mahler Sym. No. 3   161

MOSCOW (Russia)

1897
Mar. 15   Hall of the Nobles   conductor   mixed program   93

MUNICH (München, Germany)

1897
Mar. 24	Kaim-Saal	conductor	mixed program	94

1900
Oct. 20	Kaim-Saal	composer-conductor	Mahler Sym. No. 2	133

1901
Nov. 25	Kaim-Saal	composer-conductor	Mahler Sym. No. 4 (premiere)	142

1906
Nov. 8	Tonhalle	composer-conductor	Mahler Sym. No. 6	187

1908
Oct. 27	Königliches Odeon	composer-conductor	Mahler Sym. No. 7, mixed	209

1910
Sep. 12	Musik-Festhalle	composer-conductor	Mahler Sym. No. 8 (premiere)	271
Sep. 13	Musik-Festhalle	composer-conductor	Mahler Sym. No. 8	272

MÜNDEN (Germany)

1885
Feb. 13	Hotel Nickel	conductor	Haydn	23

NEW HAVEN (Connecticut, USA)

1910
Feb. 23	Woolsey Hall	conductor	mixed program	253

NEW YORK (New York, USA)

1908
Mar. 24	Metropolitan	conductor	Beethoven	205
Nov. 29	Carnegie Hall	conductor	mixed program	211
Dec. 8	Carnegie Hall	composer-conductor	Mahler Sym. No. 2	212
Dec. 13	Carnegie Hall	conductor	mixed program	213

1909
Jan. 10	Metropolitan	conductor	mixed program	214
Feb. 6	Metropolitan	conductor	Mozart	215
Mar. 31	Carnegie Hall	conductor	mixed program	216
April 6	Carnegie Hall	conductor	All Beethoven program	217
Nov. 4	Carnegie Hall	conductor	mixed program	221
Nov. 5	Carnegie Hall	conductor	above concert repeated	222
Nov. 10	Carnegie Hall	conductor	mixed program	223
Nov. 19	Carnegie Hall	conductor	All Beethoven program	224
Nov. 21	Carnegie Hall	conductor	mixed program	225
Nov. 25	Carnegie Hall	conductor	mixed program	226
Nov. 26	Carnegie Hall	conductor	above concert repeated	227
Dec. 8	Carnegie Hall	conductor	mixed program	229
Dec. 12	Carnegie Hall	conductor	mixed program	230
Dec. 16	Carnegie Hall	composer-conductor	Mahler Sym. No. 1, mixed	231
Dec. 17	Carnegie Hall	composer-conductor	above concert repeated	232
Dec. 29	Carnegie Hall	conductor	mixed program	233
Dec. 31	Carnegie Hall	conductor	All Beethoven program	234

1910
Jan. 6	Carnegie Hall	conductor	mixed program	235
Jan. 7	Carnegie Hall	conductor	above concert repeated	236
Jan. 14	Carnegie Hall	conductor	All Beethoven program	238
Jan. 16	Carnegie Hall	conductor	mixed program	239
Jan. 20	Carnegie Hall	conductor	mixed program	241
Jan. 21	Carnegie Hall	conductor	above concert repeated	242
Jan. 26	Carnegie Hall	composer-conductor	Mahler *Kindertotenlieder*, mixed	243
Jan. 30	Carnegie Hall	conductor	mixed program	245
Feb. 1	The New Theater	conductor	mixed program	246
Feb. 3	Carnegie Hall	conductor	mixed program	247
Feb. 4	Carnegie Hall	conductor	above concert repeated	248

...New York, continued (1910)

Feb. 13	Carnegie Hall	conductor	All Wagner program	250
Feb. 17	Carnegie Hall	conductor	mixed program	251
Feb. 18	Carnegie Hall	conductor	above concert repeated	252
Mar. 2	Carnegie Hall	conductor	mixed program	257
Mar. 4	Carnegie Hall	conductor	All Beethoven program	258
Mar. 6	Carnegie Hall	conductor	All Tchaikovsky program	259
Mar. 10	Carnegie Hall	conductor	mixed program	260
Mar. 11	Carnegie Hall	conductor	above concert repeated	261
Mar. 27	Carnegie Hall	conductor	mixed program	264
Mar. 30	Carnegie Hall	conductor	mixed program	265
April 1	Carnegie Hall	conductor	All Beethoven program	266
April 2	Carnegie Hall	conductor	above concert repeated	267
Nov. 1	Carnegie Hall	conductor	mixed program	274
Nov. 4	Carnegie Hall	conductor	above concert repeated	275
Nov. 13	Carnegie Hall	conductor	mixed program	277
Nov. 15	Carnegie Hall	conductor	mixed program	278
Nov. 18	Carnegie Hall	conductor	above concert repeated	279
Nov. 22	Carnegie Hall	composer-conductor	Mahler *Lieder*, mixed	281
Nov. 25	Carnegie Hall	composer-conductor	above concert repeated	282
Nov. 27	Carnegie Hall	conductor	mixed program	283
Nov. 29	Carnegie Hall	conductor	mixed program	284
Dec. 2	Carnegie Hall	conductor	above concert repeated	285
Dec. 13	Carnegie Hall	conductor	All Beethoven program	292
Dec. 16	Carnegie Hall	conductor	above concert repeated	293
Dec. 27	Carnegie Hall	conductor	All Tchaikovsky program	295
Dec. 30	Carnegie Hall	conductor	above concert repeated	296

1911

Jan. 3	Carnegie Hall	conductor	mixed program	298
Jan. 6	Carnegie Hall	conductor	above concert repeated	299
Jan. 10	Carnegie Hall	conductor	All Wagner program	301
Jan. 13	Carnegie Hall	conductor	above concert repeated	302
Jan. 15	Carnegie Hall	conductor	All Wagner program	303
Jan. 17	Carnegie Hall	composer-conductor	Mahler Sym. No. 4, mixed	304
Jan. 20	Carnegie Hall	composer-conductor	above concert repeated	305
Jan. 22	Carnegie Hall	conductor	mixed program	306
Jan. 27	Carnegie Hall	conductor	All Wagner program	309
Jan. 31	Carnegie Hall	conductor	mixed program	311
Feb. 3	Carnegie Hall	conductor	above concert repeated	312
Feb. 5	Carnegie Hall	conductor	mixed program	313
Feb. 7	Carnegie Hall	conductor	mixed program	314
Feb. 10	Carnegie Hall	conductor	above concert repeated	315
Feb. 14	Carnegie Hall	conductor	mixed program	317
Feb. 17	Carnegie Hall	conductor	mixed program	320
Feb. 19	Carnegie Hall	conductor	mixed program	321
Feb. 21	Carnegie Hall	conductor	mixed program	322

OLMÜTZ (Austria/Olomouc, Czech Republic)

1883

Feb. 24	Deutsches Casino	piano acc.	mixed program	17

PARIS (France)

1900

June 18	Châtelet	conductor	mixed program	128
June 19	Châtelet	conductor	mixed program	129
June 20	Trocadero	conductor	mixed program	130
June 21	Trocadero	conductor	mixed program	131
June 22	Trocadero	conductor	mixed program	132

1910

April 17	Châtelet	composer-conductor	Mahler Sym. No. 2, mixed	268

PHILADELPHIA (Pennsylvania, USA)

1910
Jan. 17	Academy of Music	conductor	mixed program	240
Mar. 14	Academy of Music	conductor	mixed program	262

1911
Jan. 23	Academy of Music	conductor	All Wagner program	307

PITTSBURGH (Pennsylvania, USA)

1910
Dec. 5	Soldiers Memorial Hall	conductor	mixed program	286

PRAGUE (Czech Republic)

1885
Oct. 10	Grand Hotel	piano acc.	mixed program	26

1886
Feb. 13	Royal Theater	conductor	mixed program	27
Feb. 21	Royal Theater	conductor	above concert repeated	28
April 18	Grand Hotel	conductor & piano acc.	Mahler *Lieder*, mixed	29
May 7	Interim Theater	piano acc.	mixed program	30

1898
Mar. 3	Landestheater	composer-conductor	Mahler Sym. No. 1, mixed	98

1899
June 4	Landestheater	conductor	mixed program	114

1904
Feb. 25	Landestheater	composer-conductor	Mahler Sym. No. 3	162

1908
May 23	Exhib. Concert Hall	conductor	mixed program	207
Sep. 19	Exhib. Concert Hall	composer-conductor	Mahler Sym. No. 7 (premiere)	208

PROVIDENCE (Rhode Island, USA)

1910
Feb. 25	Infantry Hall	conductor	mixed program	255

ROCHESTER (New York, USA)

1910
Dec. 8	Convention Hall	conductor	mixed program	289

ROME (Italy)

1907
Mar. 25	Augusteo	conductor	mixed program	196
April 1	Augusteo	composer-conductor	Mahler Sym. No. 5/4, mixed	197

1910
April 28	Augusteo	conductor	mixed program	269
May 1	Augusteo	conductor	mixed program	270

ST. PETERSBURG (Russia)

1902
Mar. 18	Hall of the Nobles	conductor	mixed program	146
Mar. 22	Hall of the Nobles	conductor	mixed program	147
Mar. 27	Hall of the Nobles	conductor	mixed program	148

1907
Oct. 26	Music Conservatory	conductor	mixed program	200
Nov. 9	Music Conservatory	composer-conductor	Mahler Sym. No. 5	202

SPRINGFIELD (Massachusetts, USA)

1910
Feb. 24	Court Sq. Theater	conductor	mixed program	254

1911
Feb. 15	Court Sq. Theater	conductor	mixed program	318

STRASSBURG (Germany/Strasbourg, France)

1905
May 21	Sängerhaus	composer-conductor	Mahler Sym. No. 5, mixed.........	176
May 22	Sängerhaus	conductor	All Beethoven program	177

SYRACUSE (New York, USA)

1910
Dec. 9	Wieting Opera Hs.	conductor	mixed program.........................	290

TRIEST (Austria/Trieste, Italy)

1905
Dec. 1	Politeama Rossetti	composer-conductor	Mahler Sym. No. 5, mixed.........	179

1907
April 4	Teatro Communale	composer-conductor	Mahler Sym. No. 1, mixed.........	198

UTICA (New York, USA)

1910
Dec. 10	The Majestic Theater	conductor	mixed program.........................	291

VIENNA (Wien, Austria)

1876
June 23	Conservatory	pianist	mixed program.........................	6

1877
June 21	Conservatory	pianist	mixed program.........................	9
Oct. 20	Conservatory	pianist	mixed program.........................	10

1878
July 11	Conservatory	composer-pianist	Mahler Piano Quintet, mixed	11

1879
Nov. 22	Cottage-Verein	pianist	mixed program.........................	12a

1898
Nov. 6	Musikverein	conductor	mixed program.........................	99
Nov. 20	Musikverein	conductor	mixed program.........................	100
Dec. 4	Musikverein	conductor	mixed program.........................	101
Dec. 18	Musikverein	conductor	mixed program.........................	102

1899
Jan. 15	Musikverein	conductor	mixed program.........................	103
Jan. 29	Musikverein	conductor	mixed program.........................	105
Feb. 10	Court Opera	conductor	Haydn	106
Feb. 19	Musikverein	conductor	mixed program.........................	107
Feb. 26	Musikverein	conductor	mixed program.........................	108
Mar. 13	Musikverein	conductor	Perosi......................................	110
Mar. 14	Musikverein	conductor	above concert repeated	111
Mar. 19	Musikverein	conductor	All Beethoven program	112
April 9	Musikverein	composer-conductor	Mahler Sym. No. 2	113
Aug. 27	Court Opera	conductor	mixed program.........................	115
Nov. 5	Musikverein	conductor	mixed program.........................	116
Nov. 8	Musikverein	conductor	above concert repeated	117
Nov. 19	Musikverein	conductor	mixed program.........................	118
Dec. 3	Musikverein	conductor	mixed program.........................	119
Dec. 17	Musikverein	conductor	mixed program.........................	120

1900
Jan. 14	Musikverein	composer-conductor	Mahler *Lieder*, mixed	121
Jan. 28	Musikverein	conductor	mixed program.........................	122
Feb. 18	Musikverein	conductor	All Beethoven program	123
Feb. 22	Musikverein	conductor	above concert repeated	124
Mar. 18	Musikverein	conductor	mixed program.........................	125
April 1	Musikverein	conductor	mixed program.........................	126
April 23	Augustinerkirche	conductor	All Beethoven program	127
Nov. 4	Musikverein	conductor	mixed program.........................	134

...*Vienna, continued* (1900)

Nov. 18	Musikverein	composer-conductor	Mahler Sym. No. 1, mixed	135
Dec. 2	Musikverein	conductor	mixed program	136
Dec. 16	Musikverein	conductor	All Beethoven program	137
1901				
Jan. 13	Musikverein	conductor	mixed program	138
Jan. 27	Musikverein	conductor	All Beethoven program	139
Feb. 17	Musikverein	composer-conductor	Mahler *Das klagende Lied*, mix	140
Feb. 24	Musikverein	conductor	mixed program	141
1902				
Jan. 12	Musikverein	composer-conductor	Mahler Sym. No. 4, mixed	144
Jan. 20	Musikverein	composer-conductor	Mahler No. 4, *Das klagende Lied*	145
April 14	Secession	conductor	All Beethoven program	149
1903				
April 28	Court Opera	conductor	mixed program	154
1904				
Nov. 23	Musikverein	conductor	mixed program	169
Dec. 14	Musikverein	composer-conductor	Mahler Sym. No. 3	171
Dec. 22	Musikverein	composer-conductor	above concert repeated	172
1905				
Jan. 29	Musikverein	composer-conductor	Mahler *Lieder* (premieres)	173
Feb. 3	Musikverein	composer-conductor	Mahler *Lieder*	174
Dec. 7	Musikverein	composer-conductor	Mahler Sym. No. 5, mixed	180
1907				
Jan. 4	Musikverein	composer-conductor	Mahler Sym. No. 6	191
Nov. 24	Musikverein	composer-conductor	Mahler Sym. No. 2	203

WASHINGTON (D.C., USA)

1911

Jan. 24	National Theater	conductor	All Wagner program	308

WEIMAR (Germany)

1894

June 3	Theater	composer-conductor	Mahler Sym. No. 1 ("Titan"), mixed	64

WIESBADEN (Germany)

1893

Nov. 17	Kurhaus	composer-conductor	Mahler *Lieder*, mixed	57
1903				
Jan. 23	Kurhaus	composer-conductor	Mahler Sym. No. 4, mixed	151
1907				
Oct. 9	Neues Kurhaus	conductor	mixed program	199
1908				
May 8	Neues Kurhaus	composer-conductor	Mahler Sym. No. 1, mixed	206

WLASCHIM (Austria/Vlašim, Czech Republic)

1881

Aug. 18	"Karl IV" Restaurant	pianist	program unknown	12b

Appendix V: Mahler's Soloists

(A) Singers, (B) Pianists, (C) Violinists, (D) Cellists

The following soloists performed with Mahler. The number listed refers to the *Concert Number*.

(A) Singers

Alten, Bella	229, 304, 305	Erler-Schnaudt, Anna	271, 272
Alvary, Max	44		
Amato, Pasquale	250	Farrar, Geraldine	214
Amenth, Arthur	16	Feinhals, Elise	133
Andes, Ottilie	33	Felden, Hedi	58, 81, 83
Andriessen, Pelagie	33, 50	Fellwock, Ottilie	162
Antonova, Maria	93	Fischer, Caroline	14, 16
Artner, Josephine von	59, 62, 68, 76, 79, 81–83, 85, 88, 96	Fischer, Ms. *N.*	18
		Fobes, Grace	151
		Förstel, Gertrude	203, 271, 272
Barensfeld, Lotte von	110, 111, 113	Frank, Betty	29, 30
Beck, Josef	30	Frauscher, Moritz	139
Becker, Stefanie	163	Frisch, Povla	268
Beddoe, Daniel	217, 266, 267	Fröhlich, Mathilde	50
Bělohlávek, Mrs. *N.*	18	Fuchs, Hans	17
Bellwidt, Emma	271	Fusco, Amelia	110, 111
Bettaque, Katharina	49, 53, 58		
Bianchi, Bianca	35, 37	Gadski, Johanna	297, 301-303, 307-310
Birrenkoven, Wilhelm	68, 79, 82, 85, 90, 91, 96	Gassebner, Ida	12a
Bispham, David	314-316	Gausche, Hermann	76
Bognar, Friederike	30	Geisse-Winkel, Nicola	271, 272
Brickenstein, Elisabeth	273	Geller-Wolter, Louise	150
Broulik, Franz	37	Gentner-Fischer, Else	193
Bruck, Leontine	14, 16	Gießwein, Max	85, 96
Bünz, Anna	76	Gilibert, Charles	225
Bulß, Paul	25, 55, 57	Giordani, Luiga	12
Burgstaller, Alois	204	Gluck, Alma	280-282
		Greeff, Paul	23
Carobbi, Silla	110, 111	Grosser, Julius	81
Caro-Lucas, Mrs. *N.*	104	Grüning, Wilhelm	81, 88
Charles-Hirsch, Caroline	31, 33	Gudehus, Heinrich	25
Claus, Mathilde Fränkel	114	Guszalewicz, Eugen	114
Clément, Edmond	298-300	Gutheil-Schoder, Marie	174
Coenen, Lucie	184		
Combs, Laura	212	Hertzer-Deppe, Marie	164, 170
Cronberger, Wilhelm	46, 47, 49	Hesch, Wilhelm	81, 123, 124
		Hess, Ludwig	177
Daeglau, Toni	186	Hilgermann, Laura	26, 30, 40, 41
Dawison, Max	114	Hoffmann, Baptist	79, 81, 85
Demellier, Hélène	268	Holtzmann-Weymouth, Minnie	204
Demuth, Leopold	90, 91, 96	Huberdeau, Gustave	273
Denis-Stavenhagen, Agnes	133		
Dietz, Johanna Margarethe	177	Joachim, Amalie	65
Doerter, Nicola	76	Jörn, Carl	257, 264
Dufault, Paul	266, 267	Jungblut, Albert	184
Eames, Emma	50	Katzmayr, Marie	123, 124
Ehrl, Felix	14, 26	Kirkby-Lunn, Louise	317, 320
Elizza, Elise	139, 140, 145, 203	Kittel, Hermine	145, 155-157, 171, 172, 203
Elmblad, Johannes	29		
Erl, Freidrich	16	Klafsky, Katharina	46, 47

361

Knüpfer-Egli, Maria	155
Koenen, Tilly	187, 200, 247, 248
Kofler, Betty	160, 161
Kollár, Sophie	50
Kornfeld, Sonja	81
Kraus, Felix von	177
Kraus-Osborne, Adrienne von	177
Kurz, Selma	121
Kußmitsch, Karoline	139
Landau, Leopold	49, 53, 59, 62
Lehmann, Lilli	43
Lignière, Marthe	104
Lißmann, Friedrich	44, 49, 53, 59
Lißmann, Marie	44, 49, 53
Lorent, Mathieu	88
Luzzatto, Alessandro	14, 16
Mahlendorf, Dina	184
Martin, Riccardo	246
Mayer, Mathilde	17
Mayr, Richard	271, 272
McCormack, John	273
Meisslinger, Louise	50
Messchaert, Johannes	195
Metzger, Ottilie	271, 272
Michalek, Margarethe	142, 144, 145
Mikon, Leopold	18
Mildenburg, Anna von	85, 90, 91, 96, 140, 145
Milles, Ledwina	17
Moser, Anton	173, 174, 178
Neumann, Gertrude	81
Ney, David	37, 41
Oldenboom-Lütkemann, Alida	166-168
Ott, Camilla/Mila von	18
Paalen, Bella	189, 190, 203
Pacal, Franz	123, 124, 139
Palloni, Marie Antoinetta	67
Papier-Paumgartner, Rosa	25
Petzer-Löscher, Mrs. N.	p. 25
Philippi, Maria	184
Plaichinger, Thila	143
Polna, Olga	44
Polscher, Klara	94
Pregi, Marcella	108, 113
Prévost, Henri	41
Ralph, Paula	50
Rellée, Leonore	123, 124
Rénard, Marie	29
Richter, Johanne Emma	23
Rider-Kelsey, Corinne	217, 223, 254, 263, 266, 267
Rochelle, Marie	26
Rodemund, Carl	81
Rossini, Paolini	37
Rothier, Léon	273
Ruzek, Marie	114
Saak, Theresa Marie	81
Schelper, Otto	33
Schmedes, Erik	145, 178
Schrödter, Fritz	140, 173, 174, 178
Schuch-Prosska, Clementine	55
Schumann-Heink, Ernestine	44, 46, 47, 49, 50, 53, 68, 79, 81, 85, 90, 91, 96
Schütte-Harmsen, Georg	12a
Schwarz, Mrs. N.	18
Scotti, Antonio	214
Sedlmair, Sophie	95
Seidel, Gustav	45, 53
Senius, Felix	271, 272
Seret, Maria	192
Sharn, Katherina M.	204
Showalter, Edna	264
Sieber, Josephine	21
Simon, Hugo	23
Simon, Lina	50
Sistermans, Anton	84
Sparkes, Leonore	273
Spencer, Janet	217, 264, 266, 267
Stapelfeldt, Martha	167, 168
Stein-Bailey, Gertrude	212
Trampisch, Mrs. N.	18
Traubmann, Sophie	50, 81
Unger, Ernst	16
Uplegger, Emma	50
Vaccari, Guido	110, 111
Vasquez-Molina, Italia	41
Vaupél, Emil	110, 111
Vilmar, Wilhelm	62, 68, 81, 82, 88
Wagner, Theodor	21
Waldmann, Ignaz	62, 68, 81, 82
Walker, Edyth	140, 145
Wallnöfer, Adolf	26
Warhanek, Mrs. N.	18
Waterhouse, Viola	266, 267
Watrous, Herbert	217, 266, 267
Weber, Clara	159
Weidemann, Friedrich	173, 174, 178, 186
Weidmann, Fritz	81
Wiegand, Heinrich	46, 47, 49, 53
Winternitz-Dorda, Martha	271, 272
Witschl, Caroline	15
Wittekopf, Rudolf	96
Wolff-Kauer, Marie	45
Wüllner, Ludwig	243, 244
Zalsman, Gerard	183

Zur Mühlen, Raimund von   70

(B) Pianists

d'Albert, Eugen	151, 182	Hutcheson, Ernest	266, 267, 313
Bloomfield-Zeisler, Fannie	67	Lhévinne, Josef	259
Busoni, Ferruccio	65, 112, 125, 177, 235-237	Mero, Yolanda	230, 258
		Rachmaninoff, Sergei	239
Carreño, Maria Teresa	72, 226, 227	Samaroff, Olga	253
Consolo, Ernesto	322	Sapelnikov, Vasily	89
Freund, Robert	73	Sauer, Emil von	147
Friedberg, Carl	136	Scharwenka, Franz Xaver	283, 292, 293
Gallico, Paolo	245	Staub, Victor	93
Hofmann, Josef	278, 279		

(C) Violinists

Berber, Felix	273	Petchnikov, Alexander	148
Déthier, Édouard	294-296	Powell, Maud	228, 233, 234
Dilcher, Hugo	21	Rosé, Arnold	130
Fradkin, Fredric	321	Sarasate, Pablo de	66
Gerstner, Hans	16	Sauret, Emile	71
Grünberg, Eugen	8	Schraml, Richard	7
Halir, Carl	29, 51	Siebert, August	8
Heyde, Erhard M.	271, 272	Skallitzky, Friedrich	11
Kreisler, Fritz	260-262	Soldat-Roeger, Marie	120
Kreuzinger, Johann	11	Spiering, Theodore	223, 255, 264
Krzyzanowski, Rudolf (vla.)	8	Wahl, Stefan	11
MacMillan, Francis	284, 285	Žižka, J.	12
Ott, Camilla/Mila von	18		

(D) Cellists

Eichler, *N.*	7	Rosenblum/Rosé, Eduard	11

Appendix VI: *Mahler at the Opera*
1880-1910

Mahler's main source of income from 1880 to 1909 was as Kapellmeister at various municipal theatres and opera houses in Austria, Germany and the USA. In addition, he held the post of Artistic Director, first in Budapest (1888-1891) and later in Vienna (1897-1907). Discounting very few periods of unemployment, holidays and illness, Mahler worked approximately 252 months, or almost 21 full calendar years.

The repertoire Mahler conducted was extensive, diverse and of a very wide range. In addition to operas, it included operettas, incidental music for plays, farces and other light music. The only theatrical category he never touched was a full-scale *Ballet*. He did however conduct ballet interludes in various operas. Ironically, after his death, many choreographers created dance set to Mahler's music.

The following survey of Mahler's stage repertoire is comprised of 157 titles, and is arranged alphabetically by composers/authors and horizontally in chronological order according to the cities in which he worked. The number of performances he conducted is specified with a summed total. Please note that only *complete* operas are registered, amounting to a total of 2,025 performances, by 79 composers (123 different operas). In addition, he conducted 9 performances of single acts from various operas by different composers.

Unfortunately the present survey is incomplete. Most significant is the omission of Mahler's first engagement at the small spa theater in *Bad Hall*, Austria, in the summer of 1880. All we know about this brief period in Mahler's life (May 15 to September 30, 1880) is that the theater presented approximately four afternoon performances per week (at 4:30 or 5 p.m.), and that the repertoire consisted of "the best and most recent operettas, comedies etc." Only seven theater posters have survived: six between June 10 and 26, and one from August 1. They give a fairly good picture of the range and scope of the repertoire.

Mahler's repertoire during his two seasons at the Royal Theater in *Kassel* (1883-1885) cannot be established precisely, because the surviving documents do not record the conductor of incidental music to comedies, farces and plays etc., which Mahler - in his capacity as "Chor- und Musikdirektor" - was contractually bound to conduct.

This survey is based upon personal research in the relevant cities and elsewhere, and is mainly reconstructed from newspaper advertisements and reviews. The only exceptions are Mahler's years in Vienna and New York, where detailed records are preserved.

Abbreviations

Lai: Laibach, 1881-1882, includes 3 operettas in Bad Hall in 1880 and one guest appearance in Iglau, Sept. 1882
O: Olmütz, 1883
Ka: Kassel, 1883-1885
Pr: Prague, 1885-1886, includes five guest appearances in August 1888
Lpz: Leipzig, 1886-1888
Bu: Budapest, 1888-1891
Ha: Hamburg, 1891-1897, includes guest appearances in London, June-July 1892
V: Vienna, 1897-1907
NY: New York (Metropolitan Opera), 1908-1909, plus five guest appearances in March 1910

An asterisk * indicates a world premiere

Mahler at the Opera
The Repertoire, 1880-1910
(All titles are in the original language)

	Lai	O	Ka	Pr	Lpz	Bu	Ha	V	NY	Total
ADAM, Adolphe										
- Le Brasseur de Preston			2							2
- La Poupée de Nuremberg			3							3
- Le Postillon de Lonjumeau			1							1
d'ALBERT, Eugen										
- Die Abreise								6		6
AUBER, Daniel François										
- Fra Diavolo								8		8
- Le Maçon			4		2					6
- La Muette de Portici		1								1
- La Part du diable			2							2
BEETHOVEN, Ludwig van										
- Egmont (Goethe's play)	1		2				1			4
- Fidelio				1	4	1	43	19	4	72
BELLINI, Vincenzo										
- Norma				2			10			12
BIZET, Georges										
- Carmen		3			3		18	6		30
- Djamileh							12	19		31
BLECH, Leo										
- Das war ich								3		3
BLODEK, Vilém										
- V studni (Im Brunnen)							6			6
BOIELDIEU, François Adrien										
- La Dame blanche			1					13		14
- Jean de Paris					4					4
BRUCH, Max										
- Die Loreley					9					9
BRÜLL, Ignaz										
- Gloria*								1		1
BRUNEAU, Alfred										
- L'Attaque du moulin							2			2
- Le Rêve							2			2
CHARPENTIER, Gustave										
- Louise								8		8
CHERUBINI, Luigi										
- Les deux journées				2			6			8
CORNELIUS, Peter										
- Der Barbier von Bagdad					3					3
DELIBES, Léo										
- Le Roi l'a dit			4							4
DONIZETTI, Gaetano										
- La Fille du régiment			2							2
- Lucrezia Borgia	4									4

	Lai	O	Ka	Pr	Lpz	Bu	Ha	V	NY	Total
FLOTOW, Friedrich										
- Alessandro Stradella	2		2							4
- Martha	4				1					5
- Ein Wintermärchen			3							3
FORSTER, Josef										
- Der dot Mon*								3		3
FRANCHETTI, Alberto										
- Asrael						4	5			9
- Cristoforo Colombo							3			3
GENÉE, Richard										
- Der Seekadett	2									2
GIORDANO, Umberto										
- Andrea Chénier							8			8
GLUCK, Christoph Willibald										
- Armide					2					2
- Iphigénie en Aulide				2				5		7
GOETHE, Johann Wolfgang										
- Faust I & II (play) [1]			4		8					12
GOETZ, Hermann										
- Widerspenstigen Zähmung					2		2	8		12
GOLDMARK, Karl										
- Das Heimchen am Herd							21			21
- Die Königin von Saba							1	3		4
- Die Kriegsgefangene*								4		4
GOUNOD, Charles										
- Faust (Marguerite)	3		1		1	1	3	4		13
HALÉVY, Jacques										
- La Juive					1	1		2		4
HARTMANN, Emil										
- Ragnhild (Runenzauber)*							2			2
HAYDN, Josef										
- Lo speziale (Der Apotheker)							10	7		17
HOCHBERG, Bolko von										
- Der Wärwolf							2			2
HUMPERDINCK, Engelbert										
- Hänsel und Gretel							50			50
KASKEL, Karl von										
- Hochzeitsmorgen*							7			7
- Sjula							3			3

NOTES [1] Goethe's *Faust I & II* is a play with music by various composers, mostly by Peter Josef Lindpaintner (1791-1856).

	Lai	O	Ka	Pr	Lpz	Bu	Ha	V	NY	Total
KIENZL, Wilhelm										
- *Der Evangelimann*							7			7
KRETSCHMER, Edmund										
- *Heinrich der Löwe*					2					2
KREUTZER, Conradin										
- *Das Nachtlager in Granada*					6					6
- *Der Verschwender* (play)		1	3							4
LECOCQ, Charles										
- *Giroflé-Girofla*	2									2
- *La Fille de Madame Angot*	1									1
LEONCAVALLO, Ruggero										
- *La bohème*								6		6
LINDNER, Eugen										
- *Ramiro*					4					4
LORTZING, Albert										
- *Die Opernprobe*								9		9
- *Undine*				2						2
- *Der Waffenschmied*					5	4		4		13
- *Zar und Zimmermann*								13		13
MAHLER, Gustav										
- *Trompeter von Säkkingen**		1								1
- *Das Volkslied**		2								2
MAILLART, Aimé										
- *Les Dragons de Villars*		2			9					11
MARSCHNER, Heinrich										
- *Hans Heiling*		2	1		6			2		11
- *Der Templer und die Jüdin*		2			7	6				15
- *Der Vampyr*							1			1
MASCAGNI, Pietro										
- *Cavalleria rusticana*						13	7			20
- *L'amico Fritz*						15				15
MASSENET, Jules										
- *Werther*							11			11
MÉHUL, Étienne										
- *Joseph [en Égypte]*		2					11			13
MENDELSSOHN, Felix										
- *Loreley*		6			2					8
- *A Midsummer Night's Dream*	1	3		2						6
MEYERBEER, Giacomo										
- *L'Africaine*		1			3					4
- *Les Huguenots*		1			7			8		16
- *Le Prophète*				2	3		2	1		8
- *Robert le diable*		1	4		5					10

Mahler at the Opera

	Lai	O	Ka	Pr	Lpz	Bu	Ha	V	NY	Total
MILLÖCKER, Karl										
- *Der Bettelstudent*							10			10
- *Drei Paar Schuhe*	1									1
- *Die durchgegangene Weiber*	2									2
- *Hasemann's Tochter* (play)			5							5
MOZART, Wolfgang Amadeus										
- *Bastien und Bastienne*							3			3
- *Così fan tutte*				2	3			13		18
- *Don Giovanni*				3	2	6	26	16	6	59
- *Die Entführung a. d. Serail*			1	1				16		18
- *Le nozze di Figaro*					6	4	15	50	8	83
- *Die Zauberflöte*	5				2		29	38		74
Mozart performances, totals:	5	1	6	13	10	73	133	14		255
NESSLER, Viktor										
- *Der Rattenfänger von Hameln*			3							3
- *Der Trompeter von Säkkingen*				27	4					31
NICOLAI, Otto										
- *Die lustigen Weiber v. Windsor*					1	11	2	10		24
OFFENBACH, Jacques										
- *Barbe-bleue*	1									1
- *La belle Hélène*	1									1
- *Les Contes d'Hoffmann*					7			8		15
- *Französische Schwaben*			1							1
- *Jeanne qui pleure et Jean qui rit*			1							1
- *Le Mariage aux lanternes*	2		4							6
- *Orphée aux enfers*			2							2
- *La vie parisienne*	2									2
PFITZNER, Hans										
- *Die Rose vom Liebesgarten*								7		7
PILLWITZ, Ferdinand										
- *Rataplan, der kleine Tambour*			5							5
PLANQUETTE, Robert										
- *Les cloches de Corneville*	3									3
PUCCINI, Giacomo										
- *Le Villi*								1		1
RAIMUND, Ferdinand										
- *Bauer als Millionär* (play) [2]			2							2
REITER, Josef										
- *Der Bundschuh**								4		4
REZNICEK, Emil von										
- *Donna Diana*								7		7

NOTES [2] The music was composed by Joseph Drechsler (1782-1852).

369

	Lai	O	Ka	Pr	Lpz	Bu	Ha	V	NY	Total
ROSSINI, Gioachino										
- Il barbiere di Siviglia	5		1		5		2	2		15
- Guillaume Tell					1		2			3
RUBINSTEIN, Anton										
- The Demon							1	5		6
SCHUBERT, Franz										
- Der häusliche Krieg			2		1					3
SMETANA, Bedřich										
- Dalibor							4	21		25
- The Bartered Bride							37	11	5	53
- The Kiss							6			6
- The Two Widows							3			3
SPOHR, Louis										
- Jessonda					2					2
SPONTINI, Gaspare										
- Fernand Cortez					2					2
STRAUSS, Johann										
- Cagliostro in Wien	2									2
- Die Fledermaus	2						20	1		23
- Der lustige Krieg	12									12
STRAUSS, Richard										
- Feuersnot								4		4
SUPPÉ, Franz von										
- Boccaccio	6									6
- Donna Juanita	5									5
- Fatinitza	3									3
- Flotte Burschen	1									1
TASCA, Pierantonio										
- A Santa Lucia							2			2
THOMAS, Ambroise										
- Mignon							3	5		8
TCHAIKOVSKY, Pyotr										
- Eugene Onegin							3	20		23
- Pique Dame								13	4	17
- Iolanta							7	8		15
URICH, Jean										
- Le Pilote							3			3

	Lai	O	Ka	Pr	Lpz	Bu	Ha	V	NY	Total
VERDI, Giuseppe										
- *Aida*					2			14		16
- *Ernani*	3									3
- *Falstaff*								16	6	22
- *Rigoletto*		1	1							2
- *La traviata*							3			3
- *Il trovatore*	7	1	1	1			1	1		12
- *Un ballo in maschera*		2	5							7
WAGNER, Richard										
- *Der fliegende Holländer*					11		7	11		29
- *Götterdämmerung*							18	10		28
- *Lohengrin*					11	7	7	19		44
- *Die Meistersinger*				5	1		30	10		46
- *Das Rheingold*				6	5	8	8	20		47
- *Rienzi*					8		3	2		13
- *Siegfried*					6		34	12	5	57
- *Tannhäuser*				5	11		68	8		92
- *Tristan und Isolde*							23	37	11	71
- *Die Walküre*				6	9	17	34	16	5	87
Wagner performances, totals:				22	62	32	232	145	21	514
WAGNER, Siegfried										
- *Der Bärenhäuter*								14		14
WEBER, Carl-Maria von										
- *Abu Hassan*			3							3
- *Die drei Pintos* (cplt.by Mahler)				5	13					18
- *Euryanthe*							2	9		11
- *Der Freischütz*	3		4	1	10		34	14		66
- *Oberon*					5		4			9
- *Preciosa* (play)	1				1					2
WOLF, Hugo										
- *Der Corregidor*								5		5
WOLF-FERRARI, Ermanno										
- *Le donne curiose*								10		10
ZEMLINSKY, Alexander von										
- *Es war einmal*								11		11
Total performances	87	14	97	73	219	95	745	647	48	2025

Updated from the original article: *Mahler im Opernhaus. Eine Bilanz seiner Bühnentätigkeit (1880-1910)*, pp. 163-173 from "*Neue Mahleriana*. Essays in Honour of Henry-Louis de La Grange on his Seventieth Birthday" (Peter Lang Verlag, Bern, 1997).

Appendix VII: GENERAL INDEX

Works performed by Mahler are not included in this index but can be found in Appendix II: *Composers Index*, p. 317. Mahler's stage repertoire is listed in Appendix VI: *Mahler at the Opera*, p. 365.

Capitalized NAMES indicate artists who performed with Mahler.

Numbers refer to concert numbers. Numbers indicated with "p" are page numbers.

Abbazia (Austria/Opatija, Croatia): 141
Abert, Johann Joseph (1832–1915) German composer: 36
Academy of Music, see Brooklyn and Philadelphia
Accademia di Santa Cecilia, Regia (Rome): 269–270
Adler, Guido (1855–1941) Austrian musicologist and professor: p. 25
Akademischer Gesang Verein, see Marburg
d'ALBERT, Eugen (1864–1932) German pianist and composer: 151, 182
Albert-Halle, see Leipzig
Alexander Hall, see Princeton
"Alland", *Sanatorium* (Vienna): 110–111
Allgemeiner Deutscher Musikverein: 64, 150, 155, 178, 185
ALTEN, Bella (1877–1962) Polish soprano: 229, 304, 305
Altona (Germany), *Stadttheater*: 59, 77, 82, 88
ALVARY, Max (1858–1898) German tenor: 44, 50
AMATO, Pasquale (1878–1942) Italian baritone: 250
AMENTH, Arthur; Austrian tenor: 16
Amsterdam (Holland)
— *Bevordering der Toonkunst* (Choral Society to promote music): 156, 157, 167, 168
— *Concertgebouw*: 156–158, 166–168, 183, 184, 219, 220
— *Verbetering van den Volkszang* (Choral Society to promote folk songs): 156, 157, 167, 168
ANDES, Ottilie (1860–1909) German soprano: 33
Andrássy, Countess Emmanuel: 43
ANDRIESSEN, Pelagie (1860–1937) Austrian soprano: 33, 50
Anna-Schultzen-Asten Chor (Berlin chorus): 192
ANTONOVA, Maria; Russian soprano: 93
Antwerp/Anvers (Belgium): Royal Theater: 182
Armbrust, Carl (1849–96) German organist: 60
Arnhem (Holland): 183
Arriolo, Pepito/José Rodriguez (1886–1954) Spanish pianist: 273
ARTNER, Josephine von (1867–1932) Czech-German soprano: 59, 62, 68, 76, 79, 81, 82, 83, 85, 86, 87, 88, 96
Auguste Victoria (1858–1921) German Empress: 21; also German Steamship: 204
Augusteo, see Rome
Augustine, Saint, Church of, see Wien

Bach, Johann Sebastian (1685–1750)
— *Brandenburg* Concerto No. 1, BWV 1046: 141b
— Suite for Orchestra No. 2, B minor, BWV 1067: 223
— Suite for Orchestra No. 3, D major, BWV 1068: 223
— Sinfonia, F major, BWV 1071: 141b
— Suite for Orchestra (arr. by Mahler, 1909): 230
Bach Choir of Montclair, New Jersey: 217, 266, 267
Bach-Gesellschaft, see Hamburg
Bach-Verein, see Heidelberg
BARENSFELD, Lotte von; Austrian mezzo-soprano: 110, 111, 113
Basel (Switzerland)
— *Allgemeine Musikalische Gesellschaft* (General Musical Society of Basel): 155
— *Basler Gesangverein* (The Basel Choral Society): 155
— *Liedertafel* (choral society): 155
— *Münster* (the Cathedral): 155
Bauernfeld, Eduard (1802–1890) Austrian writer
— *Bürgerlich und Romantisch* (play): 13
Baumbach, Rudolf (1840–1905) German poet
— *Das begrabene Lied* (poem): 18
BECK, Josef (1850–1903) Austrian baritone: 30
Becker, Albert (1834–1899) German composer: 69
BECKER, Stephanie; German soprano: 163
BEDDOE, Daniel (1863–1937) English tenor: 217, 266, 267
Beethoven, Ludwig van (1770–1827)
— *Coriolan*, Overture, Op. 62: 94, 146, 256
— *Fidelio*, Opera: 48, 54, 56, 61, 74, 77, 78, 97
— *Leonore* Overture No. 3, Op. 72b: 260
— Piano Concerto No. 3, C minor, Op. 37: 104
— Piano Concerto No. 4, G major, Op. 54: 256
— Symphony No. 3, E-flat major, Op. 55, "Eroica": 201, 321
— Symphony No. 7, A major, Op. 92: 213, 247, 316
— Symphony No. 8, F major, Op. 93: 292–293
— Symphony No. 9, D minor, Op. 125: 25, 149
— "Turkish March" from "Die Ruinen von Athen", Op. 113: 104
BĚLOHLÁVEK, Mrs. *N.;* amateur singer/actress: 18
Behn, Hermann (1859–1927) German composer and lawyer: 83, 92, 268

General Index

Behr, Therese (1876–1959) German contralto: 142
Behrkan, Wilhelm; German businessman: 83
Bellini, Vincenzo (1801–1835):
— *Norma;* "Casta diva", p. 25
BELLWIDT, Emma (1879–1937) German soprano: 271
Beniczky, Ferenc (1833–1905) Hungarian Secretary of State, Intendant of the Budapest Opera: p. 73
Benkö, Heinrich (1858–193?) Hungarian violinist and conductor: 10
BERBER, Felix (1871–1930) German violinist: 273
Berlin (Germany):
— *Anna-Schultzen-Asten* (children's chorus): 192
— *Kroll Opera House:* 143
— *Künstlerhaus* (House of Artists): 195
— *Nikolai-Marien-Kirche Chor* (church choir): 192
— *Philharmonie* (and Phil. Orch.): 55, 75–78, 83, 84
— *Sängerbund des Lehrervereins* (The Schoolteachers Choral Society): 83
— *Stern'scher Gesangverein* (The Chorus of the Stern Music Conservatory): 83
— *Tonkünstler* Orchestra: 143
— *Verein für Kunst* (Society of Arts): 195
Berlioz, Hector (1803–1869): 159
— Dramatic Symphony, *Romeo et Juliet,* Op. 17: 316
— *Symphonie fantastique,* Op. 14: 94, 241
BETTAQUE, Katharina (1862–1921?) German Soprano: 49, 53, 58, 62
BIANCHI, Bianca (1858–1947) German Soprano: 35, 37
Biart, Victor (1876–?) German pianist: 151
BIRRENKOVEN, Wilhelm (1865–1955) German Tenor: 68, 79, 82, 85, 90, 91, 96
Bischoff, Hermann (1868–1936) German composer and conductor: 169
Bismarck, Otto, Fürst von (1815–1898) German politician: 80
BISPHAM, David (1857–1921) American bass-baritone: 314–316
Bizet, Georges (1838–1875)
— *Carmen:* 299
— *L'Arlésienne* Suite [No. 1]: 247, 248
Blech, Leo (1871–1958) German conductor and composer: 162
BLOOMFIELD-ZEISLER, Fannie (1866–1927) Austrian pianist: 67
Boepple, Paul (1867–1917) Swiss baritone: 155
BOGNAR, Friederike (1840–1914) German actress: 30
Bohemia (German Prague newspaper) 26, 29, 30
BONNET, Joseph (1884–1944) French organist: 268
Borodin, Alexander (1834–1887)
— Symphony No. 2, B minor: A 10–11
Boronat, Olympia (1867–1934) Italian soprano: 146
Boston (Massachusetts), *Symphony Hall:* 256
Bovy, Samuel; French conductor: 205
Braga, Hermine (1859–19?): Austrian soprano 36
Brahms, Johannes (1832–1897)
— Symphony No. 3, F major, Op. 90: 256
Braunschweig (Brunswick, Germany): 25
BREDE, Albrecht (1834–1920) German chorus master: 25
Bremen (Germany): *Stadttheater* (Germany): p. 49
Breslau/Wroclaw (Germany/Poland)
— *Konzerthaus* (Concert Hall): 181, 186
— *Magdalenen Gymnasium* (Chorus): 186
— *Orchesterverein* (Orchestral Society): 181, 186
— *Singakademie* (Choral Society): 186
Bressler-Gianoli, Clotilde (1874–1912) Swiss contralto: A 5
BRICKENSTEIN, Elisabeth; German soprano: 273
Brooklyn (New York), *Academy of Music*: 228, 237, 244, 249, 263, 276, 280, 294, 297, 300, 310, 316, A 12
Brosch, Carl (1863–?) Austrian flutist: 10
BROULIK, Franz (1854–1931) Austrian tenor: 37
BRUCK, Leontine; Austrian contralto: 14, 16
Bruch, Max (1838–1920) German composer: p. 57
Bruckmüller, Ernst; hotel owner in Iglau: 18
— Hans (1862–193?) Austrian pianist, lawyer, son of Ernst: 18
Bruckner, Anton (1824–1896): 18
— Symphony No. 3, D minor, arr. by Mahler: 29
— Symphony No. 4, E-flat major: 148
Brünn (Austria/Brno, Czech Republic): 18
— *Deutsches Haus* (German House, concert hall): 188
— Philharmonic Orchestra: 188
Bryson Day Nursery (New York): 246, p. 241
Budapest: 35–43, 95
— *Deutsches Theater* (The German Theater): 38
— *Kasino-Saal* (Casino Hall): 40
— *Kinderfreund* (Children's Friend, a charitable society): 40, 43
— National Theater: 43
— *Népszinház* (The Hungarian Folk Theater): 37
— Philharmonic Society: 36
— *Polyclinic* (hospital): 39
— Royal Hungarian Opera House: 38, 39, 41–43
— *Vigadó* (concert hall): 35, 36, 95
Bülow, Hans Guido, Freiherr von (1830–1894) German pianist, conductor and composer: 51, 54, 60, 63, 71–73, 76, 92; p. 39, 75, 77
BÜNZ, Anna; German contralto: 76

Buffalo (New York): *Convention Hall*: 288
BULß, Paul (1847–1902) German baritone: 25, 55, 57
Burchard, Gustav (1859–?) German actor and writer, *Franz Schubert* (play): 90, 91
BURGSTALLER, Alois (1871–1945) German tenor: 204
Burkert, Otto (1880–19?) German organist: 178
BUSONI, Ferruccio (1866–1924) Italian-German pianist and composer: 33, 65, 112, 125, 177, 235, 236, 237, A 1
— Suite from *Turandot,* Op. 41: 270

Cäcilien-Verein, see Hamburg
Cairo (Egypt) : 60
Calm, *N.*; German poet, *Des Seemann's Braut* (poem): 21
CAROBBI, Silla; Italian baritone: 110, 111
CARO-LUCAS, Mrs. *N.*; Belgian contralto: 104
CARREÑO, Maria Teresa (1853–1917) Venezuelan pianist: 72, 226, 227
Casella, Alfredo (1883–1947) Italian composer and pianist: 268
— *Italia,* Rhapsody, Op. 11, for Orchestra: 270
Casino (Kasino), see Budapest and Wiesbaden
Casseler Allgemeine Zeitung (Kassel): 24
Casseler Oratorien Verein (Oratorio Society, chorus, Kassel): 25
Chabrier, Alexis Emmanuel (1841–1894), España, for Orchestra: 247, 248
CHARLES-HIRSCH, Caroline (1853–1931) Austrian soprano: 31, 33
Charlton, Loudon (1869–1931) American impresario, manager of the New York Philharmonic: p. 279
Charpentier, Gustave (1860–1956), *Impression d'Italie,* for Orchestra: A 10, A 11
Châtelet, see Paris
Cherubini, Luigi (1760–1842), *Les deux journée* (Der Wasserträger): 44
Chopin, Frédéric (1810–1849)
— Ballade for piano: 18
— Piano pieces (unspecified): 104
CLAUS, Mathilde Fränkel (1868–193?) Austrian mezzo-soprano: 114
CLÉMENT, Edmond (1867–1928) French tenor: 298–300, A 5
Cleveland (Ohio): *Grays's Armory*: 287
COENEN, Lucie; Dutch soprano: 184
Cologne (Köln, Germany): 164, 165
— Gürzenich Chorus: 164, 165
— Gürzenich Orchestra: 150, 164, 165
Colosseum, see Lübeck
COMBS, Laura; American contralto: 212
Concertgebouw, see Amsterdam
Concerthaus Hamburg, see Hamburg
Concordia Verein, see Prague

Conried, Heinrich (1855–1909) director of the New York Metropolitan Opera: 205
CONSOLO, Ernesto (1864–1931) Italian pianist: 322, A 1
Convent Garten, see Hamburg
Convention Hall, see Buffalo and Rochester
Corver, Anna; Dutch mezzo-soprano: 73
Court Square Theater, see Springfield
Covent Garden, see London
CRONBERGER, Wilhelm (1858–1926) German tenor: 46, 47, 49
Czap, Franz (hotel owner, Iglau): 4, 5, 7, 8
Czech National Theater (Prague): 12b, 98
Czerny, Mr. *N.*; Austrian army conductor: 16

DAEGLAU, Toni/Antonia; German contralto: 186
Damrosch, Frank (1859–1937) American conductor: 212
Damrosch, Walter (1862–1950) American conductor: 239, 304, 305
Darmstadt (Germany): 142
DAWISON [Davidsohn], Max (1869–1953) German bass: 114
Delphi (Greece): 69
DEMELLIER, Hélène (1877–1961) French mezzo-soprano: 268
DEMUTH, Leopold (1861–1910) Czech baritone: 90, 91, 96
Denemy, Gottfried, Theater Director (Iglau): 1
DENIS-STAVENHAGEN, Agnes (1860–1945) German soprano: 133
Destinn, Emmy (1878–1930) Czech soprano: 143
DÉTHIER, Édouard (1886–1962) Belgian violinist: 294–296
Deutsches Haus, see Brünn
DICKINSON, Clarence (1873–1969) American organist and chorus master: 217, 266, 267
DIETZ, Johanna Margarethe (1867–1960) German soprano: 177
DILCHER, Hugo (1840–1908) German violinist: 21
DITTRICH, Rudolf (1861–1919) Austrian organist: 203
DOERTER, Nicola; German tenor: 76
Dohnányi, Ernö/Ernest von (1877–1960) Hungarian pianist and composer: 187
Dohrn, Georg (1867–1942) German conductor: 181, 186
Donizetti, Gaetano (1797–1848), *Don Pasquale*: 215
Droste-Hülshoff, Annette von (1797–1848) German poetess, *Die junge Mutter* (poem): 21
Dubrovnik (Croatia/Ragusa, Austria): 18
Düsseldorf (Germany): 25

DUFAULT, Paul (1872-1930) Canadian tenor: 266, 267
Dulov, Georgy (1875–1940) Russian pianist: 148
Duncan, Isadora (1877–1927) English dancer: 213
Dunham, Edna Sands (1885–?) English soprano: A 9
Dupuis, Sylvain (1856–1931) Belgian conductor: 104
Dvořák, Antonín (1841–1904), Serenade, E major, Op. 22, for Strings: 15
Dworzak, N.; Czech pianist: 4

EAMES, Emma (1865–1952) American soprano: 50
Eibenschütz, Ilona (1872–1967) Hungarian pianist: 141a
EHRL, Felix (1855–?) Austrian bass: 14, 26
EICHLER, Mr. N.; Austrian cellist: 7
Elgar, Edward (1857–1937), *In the South (Alassio)*, Concert Overture, Op. 50: A 10–11
Elisabeth (1837–1898) Austrian Empress: 12
ELIZZA, Elise (1870–1926) Austrian soprano: 139, 140, 145, 203
ELMBLAD, Johannes Wilhelm (1853–1910) Swedish bass: 27, 29
Elsner, Wilhelm (1869–1903) Austrian tenor: 114
Ende-Andriessen, Pelagie (1860–1937) See Andriessen
Epstein, Julius (1832–1926) Austrian pianist and piano professor: 25
Erben, Robert (1862–1925) Austrian conductor: 52
Erkel, Sándor (Alexander) (1846–1900) Hungarian conductor: 36, 42
ERL, Friedrich (1856–1913) German tenor: 16
ERLER-SCHNAUDT, Anna (1878–1963) German contralto: 271, 272
Essen (Germany): *Städtischer Saalbau:* 185
Eulenburg, Count Philipp (1847–1921): 69

FARRAR, Geraldine (1882–1967) American soprano: 214
FEINHALS, Elise (1869–1924) German contralto: 133
FELDEN, Hedi/Hedwig (1874–1922) Czech contralto: 58, 81, 83
FELLWOCK, Ottilie (1877–?) American–Austrian contralto:162
Ferrari, Rodolfo (1865–1919) Italian conductor: 205
Fiedler, August Max (1859–1939) German conductor: 175
Fimpel, Alexander (1861–?) Austrian cellist: 10, 11
FISCHER, Caroline; Austrian soprano: 14, 16
Fischer, Heinrich (1828–1917) Austrian conductor: 3, 4, 7, 12
FISCHER, Ms. N.; amateur singer/actress: 18
Fischer, Richard; Swiss tenor: 155
Fischer, Theodor (1859–1934) Austrian lawyer, *Recollections on Mahler:* p. x
Fischhof, Robert (1856–1918) Austrian pianist and composer: 11
FOBES, Grace; English soprano: 151
FÖRSTEL, Gertrude (1880–1950) Austrian soprano: 203, 271, 272
Foerster, Josef Bohuslav (1859–1951) Czech composer and music critic: 86, 87
Foerster-Lauterer, Bertha (1869–1936) Czech soprano: 86, 87
FRADKIN, Fredric (1892–1962) American violinist: 321
Fränkel-Claus, Mathilde, see Claus
Franck, César (1822–1890) Symphonic Variations, for Piano and Orch.: 230
Frank, Gustav (1859–1923) Mahler's cousin: 12b
FRANK, Betty (1860/64–192?) Austrian soprano: 26, 27, 28, 29, 30, p. 185
Frankfurt am Main (Germany): 142, 194
— *Museums-Gesellschaft* (Music Society): 193
— *Neues Opernhaus* (New Opera House): 109, 159
— *Saalbau* (concert hall): 193
Franz Joseph I (1830–1916) Austrian emperor: 12, 207
FRAUSCHER, Moritz (1859–1916) Austrian: bass 139
Freiberg, Otto (1846–1926) German chorus master: 25
Fremdenblatt (Hamburg newspaper): 73
FREUND, Robert (1852–1936) Hungarian-Swiss Pianist: 73
Fried, Oskar (1871–1941) German conductor: 191
FRIEDBERG, Carl (1872–1955) German pianist: 136
FRISCH [Frijsh], Povla (1881–1960) Danish soprano: 268
FRÖHLICH, Mathilde (1867–19?) Austrian soprano: 50
Früh, Adolf; German chorus master: 25
Früh'scher Gesang-Verein (Choir, Nordhausen): 25
FUCHS, Hans; Austrian bass: 17
FUSCO, Amelia; Italian soprano: 110, 111

Gade, Niels Wilhelm (1817–1890) Danish Composer, *Nachklänge von Ossian*, Overture, Op. 1: A 10–11
GADSKI, Johanna Emilia Agnes (1872–1932) German soprano: 297, 301–303, 307–310
GALLICO, Paolo (1868–1955) Austrian-American pianist: 245

Gärtner, Heinrich (1865–1929) German bass: 114
GASSEBNER, Ida (1849–?) Austrian soprano: 12a
GAUSCHE, Hermann; German bass: 76
GEISSE-WINKEL, Nicola (1872–1932) German baritone: 271, 272
GELLER-WOLTER, Louise (1863–1935) German contralto: 150
GENTNER-FISCHER, Else (1883–1943) German soprano: 193
Georg I, King of Saxony (1832–1904): 154
Gernsheim, Friedrich (1839–1916) German chorus master and composer: 83
GERSTNER, Hans (1851–1939) Bohemian violinist: 16
Gewandhaus Hall and Orchestra, see Leipzig
GIEßWEIN, Max (1864 –1932) German tenor: 85–87, 96
GILIBERT, Charles (1866–1910) French baritone: 225
Gilly, Dinh (1877–1940), Algerian baritone: A 5
Gilsa, Adolf von und zu (1838–1910), German theater intendant (Kassel): 25; p. 35, 39, 45
Giltsch, Colonel; Army conductor: 170
GIORDANI, Luiga; Singer: 12
Gisela (1856–1932) Austrian Archduchess: 4
GLAUS, Albrecht (1853–1919) Swiss organist: 155
GLUCK, Alma (1884–1938) Romanian-American soprano: 280–282, A 5
Gluck, Christopf Willibald (1714–1787)
— *Iphigénie en Aulide*, Overture : 223, A 13
— *Orfeo ed Euridice* : 52
Goethe, Johann Wolfgang (1749–1832) German poet and dramatist: 115
Göhler, Georg (1874–1954) German conductor: 271, 272
Göstl, Angelica (1861–?) Austrian harpist: 11
Götze, Marie Ritter (1865–1922) German contralto: 83
Goldberg, Albert (1847–1905) German baritone and stage director (Leipzig): p. 33
Goldmark, Karl (1830–1915) Austrian composer, *Sakuntala,* Concert Overture, Op. 13: 19, 226, A 2
Gosche, Richard (1824–1889) German professor of literature: 33
Gray's Armory, see Cleveland
Graz (Austria): 27
— *Franz-Josef Bürgerschule* (children's choir): 189–190
— *Singverein* (Choral Society): 189–190
— *Stadttheater* (Municipal Theater): 189–190
— *Stephanien-Saal* (concert hall): 178
GREEFF, Paul (1854–1923) German bass: 23
Greffulhe, Elisabeth (1860–1952) Comtesse de Caraman-Chimay: 268

Grieg, Edvard (1843–1907)
— *Peer Gynt* Suite No. 1, Op. 46: 245, A 6
— *Sigurd Jorsalfar,* Incidental Music, Op. 56: A 10–11
Grillparzer, Franz (1791–1872) Austrian playwright: 2
— *Der Traum, ein Leben* (play): 24
Grinzing Cemetery (Vienna): p. 316
Grosscurth, Emma; German pianist: 31
Großmann, Josef (1876–1898) Austrian conductor: 150, 159
GROSSER, Julius; German bass: 81
Grün, Jacob Moritz (1837–1916) Austrian violinist, concertmaster of the Vienna Philharmonic until 1897: 12a
GRÜNBERG, Eugen (1854–1929) Austrian violinist: 8
GRÜNING, Wilhelm (1858–1942) German tenor: 81, 88
GUDEHUS, Heinrich (1854–1909) German tenor: 25
Gunz, Paula (1860–?) Austrian harpist: 10
Gürzenich Hall and Orchestra, see Cologne
GUSZALEWICZ, Eugen (1867–1907) Czech tenor: 114
GUTHEIL-SCHODER, Marie (1874–1935) German-Austrian soprano: 174
Gutmann, Emil (1877–1920) Austrian impresario (Munich): p. 275

Haag, Den (The Hague, Holland): 183
— Gebouw van Kunst en Wetenschappen (Building for the Art and Science, concert hall): 218
Haan-Manifarges, Pauline de (1872–1954): Dutch contralto: 156, 157
Haarlem (Holland): 183
Haase, Hermann (1862–1934) German sculptor: 92
HALIR, Carl (1859–1909) Czech violinist: 29, 51
Hall of Nobles, see St. Petersburg
Hamburg (Germany): 44–97, 175, 210
— *Bach-Gesellschaft* (The Bach Choral Society): 76
— *Cäcilien-Verein* (Cecelia Choral Society): 60
— *Concerthaus Hamburg* (Concert Hall): 55
— *Convent Garten* (concert hall): 51, 60, 65–67, 70–73, 76, 175
— *Fremdenblatt* (newspaper): 73
— Große Michaeliskirche (Great Church of St. Michael): 63
— *Musikhalle* (The Music Hall): 210
— *Stadttheater* (Municipal Theater): 44–49, 52–54, 56–58, 61–63, 69, 74, 77–97
— Verein für Kunst und Wissenschaft (Society of Art and Science): 80

General Index

Hamerling, Robert (1830–1889) Austrian poet, *Liebe im Schnee* (poem): 21
Hamlin, George John (1868–1932) American tenor: A 7–8
Handel, George Frideric (1685–1759)
— Concerto Grosso No. 12, B minor, Op. 6: 223
Hanusch-Saal, see Kassel
Harmsen, Georg Schütte (1853–?) Austrian tenor: 10
Hartford (Connecticut), *Parsons Theater:* 319
Hausegger, Siegmund von (1872–1948) German conductor: 133
Haydn, Josef (1732–1809)
— *Lo speziale* ("Der Apotheker"): 106
— Symphony in D minor: 229
Haydter, Alexander (1872–1919) Austrian bass: 114
Hegar, Frieda; Swiss mezzo-soprano: 155
Heidelberg (Germany)
— *Bach-Verein* (The Bach Choral Society): 160–161
— *Großherzogl. Gymnasium* (Choir of the Grand Ducal Gymnasium): 160–161
— *Stadthalle* (Municipal Hall): 160
HEINK, see Schumann-Heink
HELLMESBERGER Sr., Josef (1828–1893) Austrian violinist and conductor: 10; p. 33
Hellmesberger Jr., Josef (1855–1907) Austrian conductor and composer: 141, 141a, 144
Helsinki (Russia/Finland), *Universitetets Solennitetssal* (University Assembly Hall): 201
HEMPEL, Adolf Ferdinand (1868–1946) German organist: 271, 272
Hermann, Margarete; German chorus master: 192
Hertz, Alfred (1872–1942) German-American Conductor: 205
HERTZER-DEPPE, Marie (1868–?) German contralto: 164, 170
HESCH (Hes), Wilhelm/Willy (1860–1908) Czech bass: 81,123, 124, 139
HESS, Ludwig (1877–1944) German tenor: 177
Hessische Morgenzeitung (newspaper, Kassel): 23
HESSLER, Friedrich (1838–?) Austrian chorus master: 27, 28, 114
HEUKEROTH, Martin S. (1853–1936) Dutch conductor: 184
Heuckeshoven, Fritz (1854–?) German tenor: 23
Heusner, Amélie (1862–1938) Belgian–German actress and singer, wife of Arthur Nikisch: p. 47
HEYDE, Erhard M. (1883–19?) German violinist: 271, 272
HILGERMANN, Laura (1859–1947) Austrian soprano: 26, 30, 40, 41, 139, 140
Hindermann, Anna (1872–1955) Swiss contralto: 155
HOFFMANN, Baptist (1864–1937) German bass: 79, 81, 85–87
HOFMANN, Josef (1876–1957) Polish pianist: 75, 163, 278, 279
Hofmann, Ms. *N.*; German pianist: 21
Holzbauer, Ignaz Jakob (1711–1783), *Günther von Schwarzburg* (opera): 52
HOLTZMANN-WEYMOUTH, Minnie (1879–1950) American soprano: 204
HUBERDEAU, Gustave (1874–1945) French bass: 273
Huhn, Charlotte (1865–1925) German soprano: 94
Hummel, Johann E. (1832–?) Austrian composer
— *Erzherzog Leopold Salvator,* March, Op. 530: 3
— *Für unser Vaterland,* March, Op. 334: 3
— *Kronprinz Rudolf-Marsch,* Op. 300: 3
Humperdinck, Engelbert (1854–1921): 107
— *Hänsel und Gretel:* 69, 79
Hunold, Erich (1869–1923) German baritone: 114
HUTCHESON, Ernest (1871–1951) Australian-American pianist: 266, 267, 313, A 4
HYDE, Arthur Sewall (1875–1920) American organist: 223, 226, 227, 253, 254, 256

Iglau (Jihlava, Austria/Czech Republic): p. 1, 9, 35, 65
— Czap, Hotel: 4–8
— *Gymnasium* (secondary school): 2, 3, 8; p. 9
— Johannesplatz: 5
— *Männergesang-Verein* (Men's Choral Society): 7, 12
— *Stadtkapelle* (Municipal Orchestra): 3, 7, 12
— *Stadttheater* (Municipal Theater): 1, 12, 18
— *Vermittler, Der* (newspaper): 1, 3
Infantry Hall, see Providence, Rhode Island
Interim Theater, German, see Prague
Ischia (Italian island): 18

Jahn, Wilhelm (1834–1900) Austrian conductor and Director of the Vienna Court Opera: 108,127
James's Hall, St., see London
JOACHIM, Amalie (1839–1899) German soprano: 55, 65
JÖRN, Carl (1873–1947) German tenor: 257, 264
Jong, Jeanette de (1872–?) Dutch soprano: 73
JUNGBLUT, Albert (1874–?) Swiss tenor: 184

Kaim Orchestra & Saal, see Munich
Kaiser Wilhelm II (German Steamship): 273
Kaiserin Auguste Victoria (German Steamship): 204
Kaitan (Stelzer), Gustav (1871–19?) Austrian Tenor: 194
Kappeller, Carl (1859–?) Austrian clarinettist: 11

Karlsruhe (Germany): 142
Kassel (Germany): 19–25
— *Allgemeine Zeitung* (newspaper): 24
— *Hanusch-Saal* (Hanusch Hall): 21
— *Musik Festhalle* (Music Festival Hall): 25
— *Oratorien-Verein* (Oratorio Society): 25
Kassel (Germany):
— Royal Theater: 19, 20, 22, 24
KATZMAYR, Marie (1869–19?) Austrian soprano: 123, 124
Kienzl, Wilhelm (1857–1941) German-Austrian composer and conductor: 107; p. 73, p. 127
KIRKBY-LUNN, Louise (1873–1930) English mezzo-soprano: 317, 320, A 9, A 16–17
KITTEL, Hermine (1879–1948) Austrian contralto: 145, 155–157, 171, 172, 203
KLAFSKY, Katharina (1855–1896) Hungarian soprano: 46, 47
Kleist, Heinrich (1777–1811) German writer, *Friedrich, Prinz von Homburg* (play): 22
Klengel, Julius (1859–1933) German cellist: 64
Klimt, Gustav (1860–1918) Austrian artist: 149
Klinger, Max (1857–1920) German artist; Statue of Beethoven: 149
Knoch, Ernst; German pianist: 177
KNÜPFER-EGLI, Maria (1872–1924) German soprano: 155
KOENEN, Tilly (1873–1941) Dutch contralto: 187, 200, 247–249
Kofler, Alois; Austrian organist: 178
KOFLER, Betty (1874–1933) German contralto: 160, 161
Kohn, Elsa; Austrian singer: 10
KOLLÁR, Sophie (1862–1912) Bohemian soprano: 50
KORNFELD, Sonja; German soprano: 81
Koziol, Marie (b. 1865) Austrian pianist: p. 9
Krancsevics, Dragomir (1847–1929) Hungarian violinist and leader of a string quartet: 35
KRAUS, Felix von (1870–1937) Austrian bass: 177
KRAUS-OSBORNE, Adrienne von (1873–1951) American-German contralto: 156, 157, 176, 177
Krause, Emil (1840–1916) German music critic: 73
Krause, Theodor (1836–1910) German chorus master: 192
Krefeld (or Crefeld, Germany): 150
— *Oratorien-Verein* (Oratorio Choral Society): 150
— *Saint Anna* Church's Choir: 150
— *Stadthalle* (Municipal Hall): 150
Krehbiel, Henry Edward (1854–1923)   American music critic: 298, 299, 322
KREISLER, Fritz (1875–1962) Austrian violinist: 260–262
Kremser, Eduard (1838–1914) Austrian conductor: 132

Krenn, Franz (1816–1897) Austrian composer and professor: p. 9
KREUZINGER, Johann (1857–1917) Austrian violinist: 11
Kroichevsky, Nicolai; Russian conductor: 146
Kroll Opera House, see Berlin
Krueger Auditorium, see Newark
Krone, Hotel, see München
KRZYZANOWSKI, Rudolf (1862–1911) Austrian violinist, composer, and conductor: 8, 90, 91
Kunze, Gustav (1810–1868) Austrian composer, *Mein Österreich*, March, Op. 117: 4
KURZ, Selma (1874–1933) Austrian soprano: 121
KUßMITSCH, Karoline (1873–19?) Austrian mezzo-soprano: 139, 140

Laibach (Austria/Ljubljana, Slovenia): p. 23, 25
— *Landestheater* (Regional Theater): 13, 14, 16
— Philharmonic Society: 15
— *Redoutensaal* (concert hall): 15
— *26th Regimentscapelle* (Band of the 26th Regiment): 16
Laibacher Zeitung (newspaper): 13–16
Lamm, Emma (1860–?) Austrian soprano: 10
LANDAU, Leopold (1841–1894) Hungarian-German tenor: 49, 53, 59, 62
Lang, Caroline; German soprano: 89
Langsdorf, Marie; German soprano: 25
Lassen, Eduard (1830–1904) Danish-German composer and conductor: 64
Laube'sche Capelle (symphony orchestra, Hamburg): 55
Lausanne (Switzerland): 155
Lehár, Sr., Franz (1838–1898) Austrian conductor: 26
LEHMANN, Lilli (1848–1929) German soprano: 43
Lehrergesangverein, see Leipzig and Munich
Leifels, Felix F. (?–1934) American double-bass player and manager of the New York Philharmonic: (1909–1910) p. 246
Leipzig (Germany): 191; pp. 25, 29–32
— *Albert-Halle* (concert hall): 89
— *Altes Gewandhaus* (The Old Gewandhaus, concert hall): 31, 33
— Band of the 107th Military Regiment: 170
— *Gewandhaus Concerts*: p. 33
— *Kristallpalast* (Crystal Palace, concert hall): 89
— *Lehrergesangverein* (The Schoolteachers' Choir): 34
— *Liszt-Verein* (Liszt Society): 89
— *Neues Stadttheater* (New Municipal Theater): 28, 32, 34
— *Phönix, Gesangverein* (Choral Society Phönix): 33
— *Riedel-Verein* (Riedel Choral Society): 34, 273
— *Singakademie* (Choral Society): 170
— *Zoologischer Garden* (concert hall): 170

General Index

Lemberg (Austria/Lviv, Ukraine) *Philharmonie:* 152, 153
Leoncavallo, Ruggero (1858–1919) Italian composer, *Pagliacci* ("Bajazzo"): 58
Leopold (1846–1930) Bavarian Prince: 4
Leschetizky, Theodor (1830–1915) Polish pianist: 12a
Leuckart, F.E.C., music publisher (Leipzig): 18
Lewinsky-Precheisen, Olga (1853–1935) Austrian actress: 21, 33
Lewy, Gustav (1824–1901) Austrian impresario: pp. 25, 33, 35
LHÉVINNE, Josef (1874–1944) Russian pianist: 259
Liebetrau, Asta (1858–?) Austrian pianist: 11
Liedertafel, see Mainz and Basel
Liège (in German: Lüttich; Belgium)
— Royal Music Conservatory: 104
— *Societe Royale La Légia* (chorus): 104
LIGNIÈRE, Marthe; Belgian soprano: 104
Linz (Austria): 53
— *Landschaftliches Theater* (Regional Theater): 194
LIßMANN, Heinrich Friedrich (1847–1894) German bass: 44, 49, 53, 59
LIßMANN, Marie (1847–1928) German soprano: 44, 49, 53
Liszt, Franz (1811–1886) Hungarian composer and pianist.
— *Mazeppa,* Symphonic Poem: 95
Liszt-Verein (Liszt Society of Leipzig): 89
Litolff, Henry Charles (1818–1891) English composer, Overture, *Robespierre,* Op. 55: 26
Löhr, Fritz (1859–1924) Austrian archeologist: p. 73
— Uda (Ludovica), wife of above: p. 73
Löwe, Ferdinand (1863–1925) Austrian conductor: 113, 178
Löwe, Gustav (1865–?) Austrian actor: 28
Löwenfeld, Max (1848–?) Austrian actor: 30
Lohse, Otto (1859–1925) German conductor: 59, 62
London:
— *Covent Garden Royal Theater:* 50
— *Drury Lane Royal Theater:* 50
— *St. James's Hall:* 50
LORENT, Mathieu (1857–1925) German bass: 88
Lübeck (Germany):
— *Colosseum* (concert hall): 45
— *Brahms-Institut:* p. 87
Lüstner, Louis (1840–1918) German pianist: 151
Luitpold (1821–1912), Bavarian Prince-Regent: 4
LUZZATTO, Alessandro (1856–?) Bass: 14, 16

MACDOWELL CHORUS (New York): 251, 252, 260, 261, 263, 299, 300, A 5, A 9
MACMILLAN, Francis (1885–1973) American violinist: 284, 285
Mährischer Grenzbote (newspaper, Iglau): 5, 8, 18
Mährischer Tageblatt (newspaper, Olmütz): 17
MAHLENDORF, Dina; Dutch soprano: 184
MAHLER and his Family:
— Alma Maria (1879–1964) wife: 37, 113, 135, 149, 166, 171, 185, 188, 191, 245; p. 129, 167, 225, 279
— Alois/Hans (1868–1931) brother: p. 73
— Anna Justine, "Gucki" (1904–1988) daughter: p. 94
— Bernhard (1827–1889) father: p. 1
— Emma (1875–1933) sister: 11; p. 21, 73
— Ernst (1862–1875) brother: p. 1
— **Gustav** (1860–1911)
  — *Blumine* (1st symphony, 2nd mvmt.): 84
  — *Die drei Pintos,* see Weber: p. 61, 63
  — *Kindertotenlieder:* p. 327
  — *Des Knaben Wunderhorn,* Songs from: 140, 145, 178
  — *Lieder eines fahrenden Gesellen:* p. 39
  — Piano Quartet or Quintet: p. 15
  — Symphonic Poem/Symphony No. 1: 113, 145; pp. 61–65
  — Symphony No. 2, 1st mvmt.: p. 113
  — Symphony No. 3: 4, 94, 140
  — Symphony No. 4: 113, 153
  — Symphony No. 7: 251
  — *Der Trompeter von Säkkingen:* p. 61
— Justine Ernestine (1868–1938) sister: 94; p. 99
— Leopoldine (1863–1889) sister: p. 1
— Maria (1837–1889) mother: p. 1, 73
— Maria Anna, "Putzi" (1902–1907) daughter: pp. 167, 225
— Otto (1873–1895) brother: p. 73
Maiernigg am Wörthersee (Austria): p. 167, 225
Mainz (Germany): 84
— *Liedertafel* (chorus): 163
Majestic Theater, see Utica
Manas, Josef; Czech conductor: 114
Mannheim (Germany), *Musensaal des Rosengarten* (concert hall): 161
Marburg (Germany), *Akademischer Gesang-Verein* (Academic Choral Society): 25
Margulies, Adele (1863–1949) Austrian-American pianist: 10
Mariinsky Theater, see St. Petersburg
Markus, Desider (1870–?) Hungarian conductor: 114
Marteau, Henri (1874–1934) French-Swedish violinist: 176

General Index

MARTIN, Riccardo (1874–1952) American tenor: 246
Maszkowsky, Rafael (1838–1901) German conductor: 55
Materna, Leopold (1871–1948) Austrian conductor: 194
MAYER, Mathilde; Austrian contralto: 17
MAYR, Richard (1877–1935) Austrian bass: 271, 272
McCORMACK, John (1884–1945) English tenor: 273
Mehrkens, Friedrich Adolf (1840–1899) German chorus master: 76
Meiningen (Germany): 155
— The Court Opera Orchestra: 25, 64; p. 39
MEISSLINGER, Louise (1858–?) Austrian contralto: 50
Mendelssohn-Bartholdy, Felix (1807–1847)
— Symphony No. 3, A minor, "Scottish": 260
Mengelberg, Willem (1871–1951) Dutch conductor: 158, 166, 183, 184, 191, 218, 219
MERO, Yolanda (1887–1963) Hungarian pianist: 230, 245, 258
MESSCHAERT, Johannes (1857–1922) Dutch baritone: 195
Messina (Sicily, Italy): 214
Metropolitan Opera, see New York
METZGER, Ottilie (1878–1943) German contralto: 271, 272
Michaeliskirche, see Hamburg
MICHALEK, Margarethe (Rita) (1878–1944) Austrian soprano: 121, 142, 144, 145
MIKON, Leopold; amateur bass: 4, 12, 18
MILDENBURG, Anna von (1872–1947) Austrian soprano: 85, 90, 91, 96, 140, 145
MILLES, Ledwina; Austrian soprano: 17
Mitchell, Donald (b.1925) musicologist: 188, 191
Montags-Zeitung (German paper in New York): 204
Moran-Olden, Fanny (1856–1905) German soprano: 33, 34
Moscow (Russia), *Assembly Hall of the Nobles:* 93
MOSER, Anton (1872–1909) Austrian baritone: 173, 174, 178
Mozart, Wolfgang Amadeus (1756–1791)
— *Bastien und Bastienne:* 69
— *Don Giovanni:* p. 73
— Serenade "Notturno": 229
— Symphony No. 40, G minor: 241
— *Die Zauberflöte:* 115, 141
Muck, Karl (1859–1940) German conductor: 27, 28; p. 63
MÜLLER, Albin; German chorus master: 25
Münch, Ernest (1859–1928) French conductor: 176
Munich (Germany): p. 63
— *Hugo Wolf-Verein* (HW Society): 133

— *Kaim* Orchestra: 94, 113, 133, 142, 199
— *Kaim-Saal* (Kaim Concert Hall): 94, 133, 142
— *Königliche Odeon* (Royal Odeon, concert hall): 209
— *Königliche Kapelle* (Royal Orchestra): 133
— *Lehrergesangverein* (The Schoolteachers' Choral Society): 133
— *Musik Fest-Halle* (Music Festival Hall): 271, 272
— *Porge'scher Chor-Verein* (Choral Society): 133
— *Tonhalle* (concert hall): 187
— *Tonkünstler* Orchestra: 209
— *Zentral-Singschule, Städtische* (Municipal
— Central School of Singing, a children's choir): 271, 272
Münden (or Hannoversch-Münden, Germany): 23, 25; p. 39
— *Chorverein* (Choral Society): 23, 25
— Hotel *Krone* (The Crown Hotel): 23
Musch, Carl; Austrian baritone: 132
Musical America (music magazine, New York): 237
Musik, Die (music magazine, Berlin): 152
Musik Festhalle, see Kassel, Munich
Musikhalle, see Hamburg
Mysz-Gmeiner, Lula (1876–1948) German contralto: 165

Nedbal, Oscar (1874–1930) Czech composer and conductor, *Der faule Hans* (ballet): 154
NEDVED, Anton (1829–1896) Austrian conductor: 15
Népszinház (Folk Theater), see Budapest
Nessler, Viktor (1841–1890) Alsatian composer: 26
Neue Freie Presse (newspaper, Vienna): 127, 153
Neues Wiener Tagblatt (newspaper, Vienna): 145
Neuilly (Paris, France): p. 316
Neumann, Angelo (1838–1908) Theater Director in Prague: 27; pp. 47, 49, 63
NEUMANN, Gertrude; German soprano: 81
Neuss, Amalia (1860–?) Austrian pianist: 11
Newark (New Jersey): *The Krueger Auditorium:* A 14
New Haven (Connecticut): *Woolsey Hall:* 253
New National Theater, see Washington
New York City
— *Bryson Day Nursery:* 246; p. 241
— *Carnegie Hall:* passim
— *Metropolitan Opera House:* 205, 214, 215
— *New Theater:* 246
— *New York Symphony:* 211–213, 239
— *New York Times:* 292, 293, 322
— *New York Tribune:* 213, 321
NEY, David (1842–1905) Hungarian bass: 37, 41
Nicklas-Kempner, Selma (1849–1928) German soprano: 70

General Index

Niederrheinische Musikfest (Düsseldorf): 25
Nikisch, Arthur (1855–1922) Hungarian-German conductor: 34, 89, 150, 170, 192; p. 47, 57, 61
Nordhausen (Germany): 25
Nowak, Franz (1856–19?) Czech conductor: 57
Nuremberg (Germany): 142

Odeon, Königliche, see Munich
OLDENBOOM-LÜTKEMANN, Alida (1869–1942) Dutch soprano: 166–168
Olmütz (Austria/Olomuoc, Czech Republic)
— *Damen-Verein* (Women's Society): 17
— *Deutsches Kasino* (German Casino): 17
Oratorio Society, see Krefeld, New York
Ornstein, Leo (1892–2002) Ukrainian-American pianist and composer: A 18
Osorio, Pilar; Italian pianist: 273
OTT/Edle von Ottenfeld, Camilla Ottilie/Mila von (1858–1938) Austrian violinist: 18

PAALEN, Bella (1881–1964) Hungarian contralto: 189, 190, 203
PACAL, Franz (1865–1938) Austrian tenor: 123, 124, 139
PALLONI, Marie Antoinetta, Italian soprano: 67
PAPIER-PAUMGARTNER, Rosa (1858–1932) Austrian mezzo-soprano: 25
Paris (France)
— *Bibliothèque Nationale:* 268
— *Concerts Colonne:* 268
— *Palais du Trocadero* (concert hall): 130–132
— *Théâtre Municipal du Châtelet* (concert hall): 128, 129, 268
Parlow, Kathleen (1890–1963) Canadian violinist: A 12
Parsons Theater, see Hartford, Connecticut
Perger, Richard von (1854–1911) Austrian chorus master: 129, 132
Pester Lloyd, German newspaper, Budapest: 35–37, 40, 42
Petri, Henri Wilhelm (1856–1914) String Quartet: 31
PETCHNIKOV, Alexander (1873–1948) Russian violinist: 148
Petzer-Löscher, Mrs. *N.*; Czech soprano: p. 25
Philadelphia (Pennsylvania): 205
— *Academy of Music:* 240, 262, 307
Philharmonie, see Berlin and Lemberg
Philippi, Maria (1875–1944) German contralto: 184
Phönix (Choral Society, Leipzig): 33
Pierné, Gabriel (1863–1937) French composer and conductor: 268
Pirk, Sarolta Le (1865–1948) Austrian soprano: 26
Pittsburgh (Pennsylvania), *Soldiers Memorial Hall:* 286
PLAICHINGER, Thila/Mathilde (1868–1939) Austrian soprano: 143
Pohlig, Carl (1864–1928) Bohemian-German conductor: 82, 86, 87
Politeama Rosetti, see Trieste
Pollini, Bernhard (1838–1897) German Theater Director in Hamburg: pp. 73, 75, 99
POLNA, Olga (1869–1936) German soprano: 44
POLSCHER, Klara; German mezzo-soprano: 94
Porges'cher Chorverein, see Munich
POWELL, Maud (1868–1920) American violinist: 228, 233, 234, A 10–11
Prague (Prag, Austria/Praha, Czech Rep.)
— *Abendblatt, Prager* (German newspaper): 28
— *Baumgarten* (Stromovka Park): 207
— Czech National Theater: 98
— *Concordia-Verein* (journalist society): 26
— Czech Philharmonic Orchestra: 207, 208
— *Deutscher Männergesangverein* (German Men's Choral Society): 27, 28, 114
— *Deutscher Singverein* (German Choral Society): 114
— Deutsches Interim Theater (German Interim Theater): 30
— *Grand-Hotel, Wintergarten* of: 26, 29
— Königlich Deutsches Landestheater (Royal German Regional Theater): 27, 28
— Královská Obora (The Royal Game, a park): 207, 208
— *Neues Deutsches Theater* (New German Theater): 98, 114, 162
— *Prager Tagblatt* (newspaper): 26, 30
— *Schulpfenning-Verein* (charitable society): 28
— *Sct. Veit Gesangverein* (choral society): 27
— *Sängerverein Tauwitz* (choral society): 114
— *Zwischenactszeitung* (German weekly theater and music magazine): 29
PREGI (née Corradi), Marcella (1866–1958) Swiss contralto: 108, 113, 268
Presse, Die, see Vienna
Preuss, Arthur (1878–1944) Austrian tenor: 140
PRÉVOST, Henri (1858–?) French tenor: 41
Prill, Carl (1864–1931) Austrian violinist: 132
Princeton (New Jersey): *Alexander Hall:* A 3, A 16
Prohaska, Leopold: 12
Providence (Rhode Island), *Infantry Hall:* 255
Pugno, Raoul (1852–1914) French pianist: 202

RACHMANINOFF, Sergei (1873–1943) Russian composer and pianist: 239
Radó-Hilgermann, see Hilgermann
Raimann, Rezsö/Rudolf (1861–1913) Hungarian composer, pianist and conductor: *Sinan basa* (operetta): 43
Raimund, Ferdinand (1790–1836) Austrian Playwright, *Der Verschwender* (play with

music): 14
RALPH, Paula (1860–1922) Austrian contralto: 50
Ratz, Erwin (1898–1973) Austrian musicologist and professor: 191
Red Cross, The, see *Rote Kreuz*
Redouten Saal, see Budapest (Vigadó) and Laibach
Rehbock, Friedrich (1861–1940) German pianist and conductor: 26
Reinecke, Carl (1824–1910) German composer and conductor: p. 57
RELLÉE, Leonore; Italian mezzo-soprano: 123,124
RÉNARD, Marie (1863–1939) Austrian soprano: 29
RICHTER, Johanne Emma (1859–1944?) German soprano: 23; p. 39
RIDER-KELSEY, Corinne (1877–1947) American soprano: 217, 223, 254, 263, 266, 267
Riggenbach-Hegar, Valerie; Swiss soprano: 155
Ritter, Hertha (18?–1913) German mezzo-soprano: 133
ROCHELLE, Marie; Austrian soprano: 26, 27, 28
Rochester (New York): *Convention Hall:* 289
RODEMUND, Carl (1856–1919) Austrian tenor: 81
Rome (Italy), *Augusteo* (concert hall): 196, 197, 269, 270
ROSÉ, Arnold Josef (1863–1946) Austrian violinist: 130, 271, 272
Rosen, Katherina (1860–?) Austrian soprano: 26, 29
ROSENBLUM/Rosé, Eduard (1859–1943) Austrian cellist: 11
Rosengarten (Rose Garden), see Mannheim
Rossini, Gioacchino (1792–1868)
— *Il barbiere di Siviglia:* 215
— *Guillaume Tell* (William Tell): 46, 47
ROSSINI, Paolini, Hungarian soprano: 37
Rote Kreuz, Das (The Red Cross): 18
ROTHIER, Léon (1874–1951) French bass: 273, A 5
Rottenberg, Ludwig (1864–1932) Austrian-German conductor: 109
Rotterdam (Holland): 183
Rozhdestvensky, Gennadi (b. 1931) Russian conductor: 122
Rubinstein, Anton (1829–1894) Russian composer and pianist: 70; p. 57
RUZEK, Marie (1864–1914) Czech soprano: 114
Rychetsky, Jiri, Czech professor: 2

SAAK, Theresa Marie (1868–19?) Czech soprano: 81
Saalbau, see Essen and Frankfurt, Germany
St. Petersburg (Russia)
— *Assembly Hall of the Nobles:* 146–148
— The Imperial Music Conservatory: 200, 202
— Mariinsky Theater Orchestra: 146–148, 200, 202
— Philharmonic Society: 146–148
Salomon, *N.*; French pianist: 268
Salter, Norbert (1869–?) Austrian cellist and impresario: 270
SAMAROFF, Olga (1882–1948) American pianist: 253, 258
Sapin, Cara; contralto: A 5
SAPELNIKOV, Vasily (1868–1941) Russian pianist: 89
SARASATE, Pablo de (1844–1908) Spanish violinist and composer: 66
SAUER, Emil von (1862–1942) German pianist and composer: 147
SAURET, Emile (1852–1920) French violinist and composer: 71
Schacko, Hedwig (1868–1932) German soprano: 109
Schalk, Franz (1863–1931) Austrian conductor: 98, 141, 141b, 180, 271, 272
SCHARWENKA, Franz Xaver (1850–1924) Polish-German pianist and composer: 283, 292, 293
Schaumann, Franz (1863–1915) Austrian tenor: p. 25
Scheffel, Johann Viktor von (1826–1886) German poet and author, *Der Trompeter von Säckingen*: p. 61
Scheidemantel, Karl (1859–1923) German baritone: 98
Schelling, Ernest Henry (1876–1939) American pianist, composer and conductor: 146
SCHELPER, Otto (1844–1906) German baritone: 33
Schiller, Friedrich (1759–1805) German poet: 3
— *Die Braut von Messina* (play): 20
Schindler-Mahler, Alma Maria (1879–1964): 37, 113, 135; p. 129, 167
SCHINDLER, Kurt (1882–1935) German-American pianist and conductor: 251, 252, 260, 261, 264, 298–300, A 5, A 9
Schlesinger, Bruno, see Walter, Bruno
SCHMEDES, Erik (1868–1931) Danish-Austrian tenor: 145, 178
Schönberg, Arnold (1874–1951) Austrian composer: 113, 169, 171
Schönberger, Benno (1865–?) Austrian pianist: 10
Scholz, Auguste (1865–?) Austrian actress: 30
Schott's Söhne, B. (German music publisher): 84
SCHRAML, Richard (1857–?) Austrian violinist: 4, 7
SCHRAML, *N.*; Austrian violinist, brother of Richard Schraml: 4

General Index

— *Parsifal*: p. 35
— *Das Rheingold:* p. 65, 73
— *Rienzi,* Overture: 307
— *Siegfried:* 205
— *Die Walküre:* p. 65, 73
Wagner, Siegfried (1869–1930) German composer and conductor: 107
WAGNER, Theodor; German baritone: 21
WAHL, Stefan (1859–1911) Austrian violinist: 11
WALDMANN, Ignaz; Hungarian bass: 62, 68, 81, 82
WALKER, Edyth (1870–1950) American contralto: 140, 145
WALLNÖFER, Adolf (1854–1946) Austrian tenor and composer: 26–28
Walter, Bruno (nee Schlesinger, 1876–1962) German conductor: 69
WARHANEK, Mrs. *N.;* amateur singer/actress 18
Washington, D.C., *New National Theater:* 308, A 17
WATERHOUSE, Viola; American soprano: 266, 267, A 5
WATROUS, Herbert (1868–1947) American bass: 217, 266, 267
Weber, Alexander Carl Maria von (1849–1897) grandson of the following, army captain: p. 61
Weber, Carl Maria von (1786–1826)
— *Die drei Pintos* ("completed" by Mahler): p. 61, 63
— *Euryanthe,* Overture: 235
— *Oberon,* Overture: 251
— *Polacca brillante,* Op. 72: 11
— *Turandot,* Overture, Op. 37: 138, 281
WEBER, Clara (1865–1919) German contralto: 159
Weber, Franz (1858–?) Austrian organist: 10
Weber, Marion Mathilde von (1856–1931) wife of A. Carl von Weber: p. 61
Weber, Wilhelm (1860–?) Austrian double-bass player: 10
WEIDEMANN, Friedrich (1871–1919) Austrian bass: 169, 173, 174, 178, 183, 186
WEIDMANN, Fritz (1857–1910) Czech-German tenor: 81
Weimar (Germany): 25, 84
— *Chorverein* (choral society): 64
— *Großherzogliches Theater* (Grand Ducal Theater): 64
— *Hofkapelle* (Royal Orchestra): 25, 64
— *Singakademie* (choral society): 64
Weinberger, Josef (1855–1928) Austrian music publisher: 107
Weingartner, Felix von (1863–1942) Austrian conductor and composer: 142, 150, 192
Weiss, Joseph (1864–1945) Hungarian pianist: 245
Weltlinger, Simon (1854–?) Austrian tenor: 10

Wessely, Hans (1862–1926) Austrian violinist: 10
Westmeyer, Wilhelm (1829–1880) German composer and pianist: 26
WIEGAND, Joseph Anton Heinrich (1842–1899) German bass: 46, 47, 49, 53
Wien, see Vienna
Wiesbaden (Germany)
— *Kasino-Saal* (Casino, concert hall): 57, 151
— *Kurhaus-Orchester* (Casino Orchestra): 199
— *Neuer Kasino-Saal* (New Casino Hall): 199, 206
Wieting Opera House, see Syracuse
Wildenbruch, Ernst von (1845–1909) German poet and dramatist: 21
— *Der Fürst von Verona* (play): 33
Wilhelm I (1797–1888) German Emperor: 32
Wilhelm II, Kaiser (German Steamship): 273
Winderstein, Hans (1856–1925) German conductor: 89, 191
Winderstein Symphony Orchestra (Leipzig): 170
Winkelmann, Hermann (1849–1912) German-Austrian tenor: 129, 132, 139
Winter, Hans (1858–?) Austrian violist: 11
WINTERNITZ-DORDA, Martha (1885–1958) Austrian soprano: 271, 272
WITSCHL, Caroline; Austrian soprano: 15
WITTEKOPF, Rudolf (1863–1942) German bass: 96
Wlaschim (Vlašim, Austria/Czech Republic): p. 23
— Karl IV, Restaurant: 12b; p. 23
Wolf-Verein, Hugo, see Munich
Wolff, Hermann (1845–1902) German impresario (Berlin): 71, 76; p. 99
WOLFF-KAUER, Marie; German soprano: 45
Wolfsohn, Henry (1842–1909) German-American impresario: 216, 217
Woolsey Hall, see New Haven, Connecticut
Wüllner, Franz (1832–1902) German conductor: 164
WÜLLNER, Ludwig (1858–1938) German baritone, son of Franz: 243, 244

Yale University (New Haven, Connecticut): 64

ZALSMAN, Gerard (1871–1949) Dutch baritone: 183
Zamara, Therese (1859–?) Austrian harpist: 12a
Zemlinsky, Alexander (1871–1942) Austrian composer and conductor: 169
Zentral-Singschule, Städtische, see Munich
Zichy, Count Géza (1849–1924) Hungarian pianist and composer: p. 73
ŽIŽKA, Johann (1859–1913) Czech violinist: 12
Zoologischer Garten (concert hall), see Leipzig
Zottmann, Franz (1859–1909) Austrian pianist: 10

Zottmann, Nina (1836–1903) German singing teacher: 21
ZUR MÜHLEN, Raimund von (1854–1931) German tenor: 70
Zwischenactszeitung (Prague weekly theater and music magazine): 29

About the Author

Knud Martner receiving the gold medal from
the Internationale Gustav Mahler Gesellschaft in Vienna

Knud Martner was born in Dalum, Denmark, near Odense, on July 8, 1940, exactly 80 years and 1 day after Mahler. He has worked in music publishing in Denmark and Switzerland. His first encounter with Mahler's music was in 1965 at a concert in Copehagen, and Mahler has remained his favorite composer and second occupation ever since. In 2007, he was honored by the Internationale Gustav Mahler Gesellschaft in Vienna with the Society's Golden Mahler Medal for his dedication to research and publications on Mahler. He lives in Copenhagen.

He is the author or editor of several books, including *Gustav Mahler: Selected Letters*; *Gustav Mahler im Konzertsaal, 1870-1911*; Ferdinand Pfohl's *Gustav Mahler: Eindrücke und Erinnerungen aus den Hamburger Jahren*; Alma Mahler's *Gustav Mahler: Memories and Letters*, with Donald Mitchell and *Ein Glück ohne Ruh'. Die Briefe Gustav Mahlers an Alma*, together with Henry-Louis de La Grange and Günther Weiß.

He is currently working on two new titles: *Gustav Mahler-Chronik, 1860-1911* (in German); a detailed chronicle of Mahler's life documenting his theater repertoires, all contemporary performances of his works (ca. 480 concerts), and includes a comprehensive catalog of his works; and *Verwelkte Blütenträume. Die Werke von Alma Maria Maria Schindler-Mahler. Ein rekonstruiertes Werkverzeichnis* which includes biographical notes on her early years.

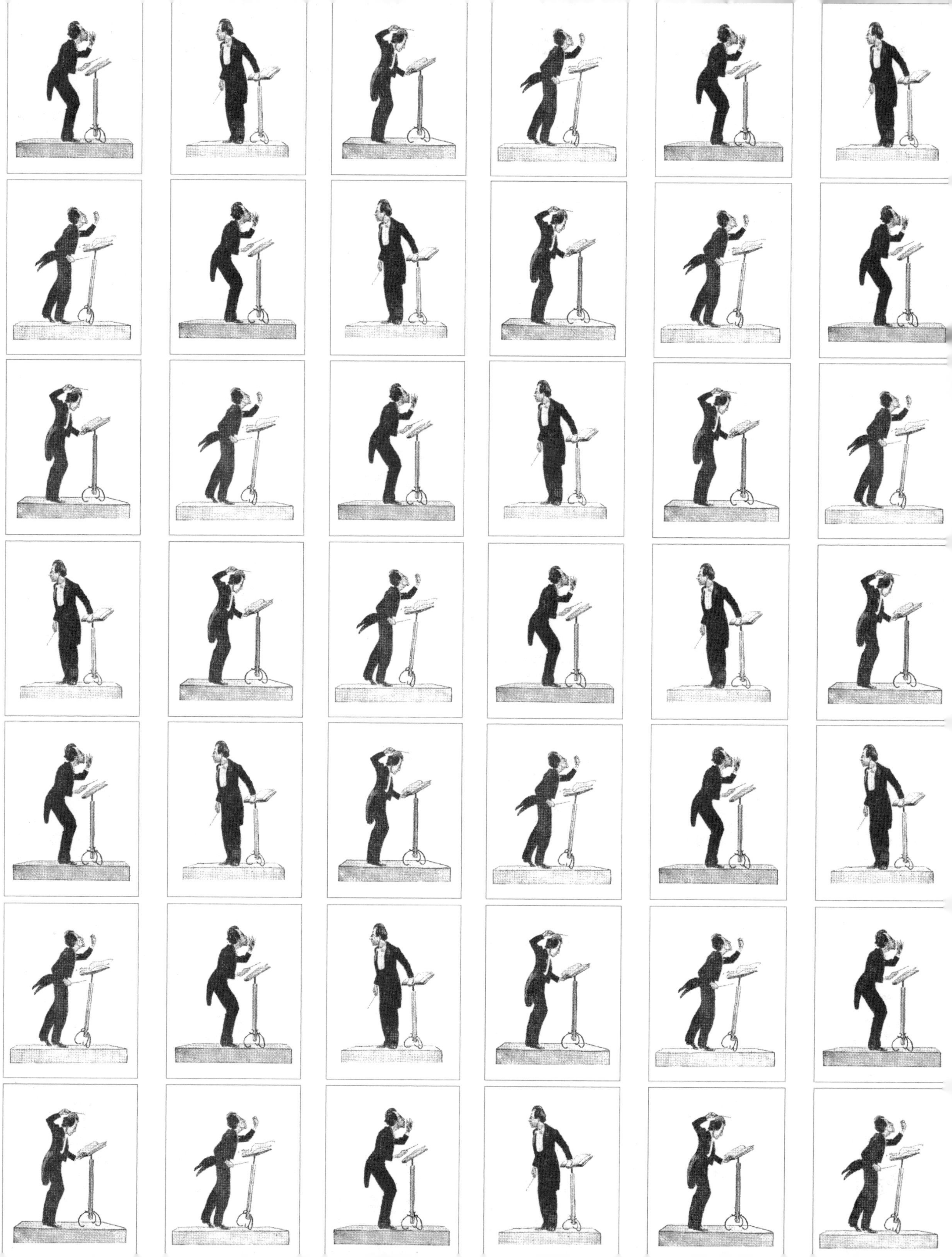